# GEORGE YEO

on Bonsai, Banyan and the Tao

# GEORGE YEO

## on Bonsai, Banyan and the Tao

edited by

**Asad-ul Iqbal Latif** and **Lee Huay Leng**

Your Eminence, Cardinal DiNardo,

Thank you for being our Pastor in our journey through Houston.

With warmest regards,

George Yeo

Jun 15, 2018

World Scientific

NEW JERSEY • LONDON • SINGAPORE • BEIJING • SHANGHAI • HONG KONG • TAIPEI • CHENNAI

*Published by*

World Scientific Publishing Co. Pte. Ltd.
5 Toh Tuck Link, Singapore 596224
*USA office:* 27 Warren Street, Suite 401-402, Hackensack, NJ 07601
*UK office:* 57 Shelton Street, Covent Garden, London WC2H 9HE

**Library of Congress Cataloging-in-Publication Data**
Yeo, George Yong-Boon, author.
[Speeches. Selections.]
George Yeo on bonsai, banyan and the tao / edited by Asad-ul Iqbal Latif and Lee Huay Leng.
pages cm
ISBN 978-9814518697 (hardcover : alk. paper)
1. Singapore--Politics and government--1990– 2. Singapore--Foreign relations. 3. Singapore--Civilization. 4. Southeast Asia--Strategic aspects. I. Asad Latif, editor. II. Li, Huiling, 1971– editor. III. Title.
DS610.73.Y46A5 2014
082--dc23

2014018387

**British Library Cataloguing-in-Publication Data**
A catalogue record for this book is available from the British Library.

Front cover photo by Ray Chua

First published 2015
Reprinted 2015



Printed in Singapore

*to my wife*

*Jennifer*

# CONTENTS

## CULTURE AND VALUES

## APPENDIX

# FOREWORD

## by Amartya Sen

This is a wonderful book by one of the foremost statesmen and social thinkers of our time. Though the themes covered display a huge variety in this wide-ranging collection of essays and speeches by George Yeo, there is a foundational interest that motivates his illuminating and powerful reflections. This relates to a unifying concern about the exceptionally large possibilities of Asia's place in global relations. Some of Asia's rich possibilities have been realised, but others remain to be fully grasped yet, and Yeo is particularly interested in analysing how the potentials can be more comprehensively harvested.

One reason why the city-state of Singapore often seems to be punching well above its weight in world affairs, aside from its remarkable material and economic success, is the presence of cerebral and articulate leaders who are able to speak with clarity and focus. Going beyond their understanding of the limitations and possibilities of their own country in the relentlessly changing world scenario, leaders like George Yeo invite us to join them in the global dialogue about Asia. This book gives plentiful examples of how pertinent and enlightening Yeo's intellectual investigations have been.

George Yeo distinguished himself as a scholar at Cambridge, as an officer who rose swiftly through the ranks of the military, and as a politician whose ministerial portfolios ranged from Arts and Health to Foreign Affairs and Trade and Industry. In each of those roles, he sought to combine the calling of the intellectual, whose primary and central contribution tends to lie in unearthing the truth, and in clarifying how it influences what we have reason to do. One of Yeo's basic commitments is to draw attention consistently to the need to act with a sense of purpose, drawing on scrutinised knowledge, amidst continuous change in the world around us. Yeo's essays on culture, in particular, deserve close reading because he discerns in that realm of human agency both continuities and disruptions that transcend the day-to-day demands of our economic lives — forceful as they are.

Speaking more personally, I have had the great pleasure of working with George Yeo during the long drawn-out but ultimately fruitful Nalanda project. His belief in the recreation of an ancient university — more than six hundred years older than the first European university (in Bologna) — which embodied the region's intellectual interaction and cross-border collaboration brought out to me Yeo's strong faith in a future that can draw on Asia's pre-colonial past and produce something new and outstanding from which the contemporary world — in Asia as well as elsewhere — can greatly benefit. Yeo has made an exceptional contribution in giving shape to the vision behind the new Nalanda University, combining ancient understanding and wisdom with modern knowledge and science. I feel very fortunate in having developed a strong friendship with a person whose remarkable qualities I greatly admire, and whose far-reaching reflections I have enormous pleasure in presenting to the reading public across the world.

Amartya Sen *is Thomas W. Lamont University Professor, and Professor of Economics and Philosophy, at Harvard University and was until 2004 the Master of Trinity College, Cambridge. Earlier on he was Professor of Economics at Jadavpur University Calcutta, the Delhi School of*

*Economics, and the London School of Economics, and Drummond Professor of Political Economy at Oxford University.*

*Amartya Sen's awards include Bharat Ratna (India); Commandeur de la Légion d'Honneur (France); the National Humanities Medal (USA); and the Sveriges Riksbank Prize in Economic Sciences in memory of Alfred Nobel (Sweden).*

# FOREWORD

## by Wang Gungwu

When I came to Singapore in January 1996, I was involved with three agencies that, for me, marked a new era for the city-state. I learnt that all three were initiated by George Yeo who had become Minister for Information and the Arts in 1991 at the age of 36, one of the youngest ministers in the Singapore Cabinet. The three agencies were the National Arts Council, the National Library Board and the National Heritage Board. The first was established in 1991, the second came out of a Library Review in 1992 and the third followed in 1993. In three successive years, he started Singapore on a path that has now enlivened the cultural life of its people beyond recognition.

That was only a beginning. Yeo was the moving force behind several other major projects all aimed at helping Singapore to reach out and connect with a fast-changing world. One of his messages was particularly clear: to meet the challenges of its future, its people must take heed of its rich past. When he went on to be Minister for Trade and Industry and then for Foreign Affairs, that message became broader and deeper. He brought it with him to enlarge Singapore's influence in the region and elsewhere at a time when major economic and political changes were taking place, notably the financial crisis of 1998 and the remarkable rise of China into the 21st century.

George Yeo was a brilliant student and a successful soldier before becoming a popular and effective politician. Since 2011, he has embarked on yet another career as a top business executive. His admirers, who have followed his public career, know how much he has achieved but I doubt if many were aware of the full range of his interests and the way he has thought about so many areas of life. This collection of his speeches shows us what led him to the life of public service and what he wanted to bring to that commitment.

Every reader will take away something from the collection. For me, I found that two words capture some of the recurring themes in his thinking: balance and trust. With the idea of balance, it reminds me of the Chinese word *quanheng* (权衡), a concept that guides his understanding of the past in the present. The notion of trust, on the other hand, permeates his thinking about what binds a state and its people and knits the cohesion that open global societies need more than ever.

George Yeo's determination to see Nalanda University revived symbolises the practice of balance best. In that ancient institution, he saw a deep faith linked with a universal openness. Rebuilding it in the 21st century marks a marriage of the traditional with the modern global that, at the same time, can bring Asia and Europe, China and India and the eastern and western halves of Asia together. The politician in him also saw a role for Nalanda to imagine a new sense of region that could lift Asia to a higher realm of consciousness.

As for trust, this fundamental quality challenges our future at many levels. Yeo sees it not only as the principle that enables inter-state and inter-corporation transactions to occur seamlessly, but also as the key relationship between generations, between teacher and student, the governing and the governed, the sceptical scientist and the faithful believer. His appeal to us to focus on trust ties many of his speeches together. Again, the practical man that he is does not stop there. He does not hesitate to remind us of the leading concern in our region today, the deficit of trust behind the tensions that has led the American hegemon to see a rising China as a potential threat.

The editors are both media professionals and understandably noted the part that George Yeo played in that area for Singapore. But I think they have emphasised his most distinctive contributions to modernising Singapore life and thought in the three main sections of the volume that bring together much of his best writings on politics and values. The editors have selected well and I congratulate them for so successfully portraying George Yeo in public action. I thought I knew what made me personally appreciate him as a political figure. The fuller picture revealed in his speeches shows us someone who is searching deeply and widely for answers to the human condition. This is someone we should all want to know better.

**Wang Gungwu** *is a Commander of the British Empire (CBE); Fellow, and former President, of the Australian Academy of the Humanities; Foreign Honorary Member of the American Academy of Arts and Science; Member of Academia Sinica; Honorary Member of the Chinese Academy of Social Science. He was conferred the International Academic Prize, Fukuoka Asian Culture Prizes. In Singapore, he is Chairman of the Institute of Southeast Asian Studies. At the National University of Singapore, he is Chairman of the Lee Kuan Yew School of Public Policy and of the East Asian Institute. He was the Vice-Chairman of the Chinese Heritage Centre and Board Member of the S. Rajaratnam School of International Studies at the Nanyang Technological University, Singapore.*

# FOREWORD

## by Nicolas Berggruen

If Singapore punches well above its weight in global affairs, it has been due to the superior quality of its governing class over the short decades of that city-state's rise from colonial poverty to the first rank of nations. Lee Kuan Yew set the standard. George Yeo carried it forward for his generation as one of Asia's leading scholars/practitioners.

More than a leader in Singapore, though, George has been a genuine bridge between East and West. I don't mean this only in the traditional diplomatic sense of relations between states. George has also been an envoy among civilisations and a translator between cultures. In our 21st Century Council meetings with other leaders and intellectuals from around the world, everyone listens attentively when George speaks because they know he dwells in that rarified space which borders East and West and fathoms both.

His involvement with Amartya Sen in Nalanda University is bringing about a renaissance of ancient Asian knowledge and connections. I can't think of another statesman, no less a devout Catholic from a Confucian-influenced culture, who can discuss the dialectics of Hegel and Taoism in casual conversation. Above all, whoever is privileged to meet George goes away impressed by a man in balance, possessed of a certain serenity of mind and evident wisdom that one always associates with the great sages.

George is also, lest we forget, a pragmatic political mind and a practical administrator who, along with his colleagues in the Singapore government over the years, has shown the world that good governance — highly competent and uncorrupted — is indeed possible.

As can easily be seen in this splendid collection of speeches and essays, George Yeo's knowledge is wide-ranging as well. He can speak informatively about everything from the arrival and impact of the internet in traditional societies to the role of city-regions in a globalised world to the woes and wonders of multi-ethnic and multi-religious polities.

The reader will be well-rewarded by delving into this rich depository of insights and ideas. We are fortunate to be able to learn from one of Asia's enduring figures whose reflections on the experiences and challenges of our tumultuous era are now ours to share.

Nicolas Berggruen *is the Chairman of the Berggruen Institute, which is engaged in issues of political governance, philosophy and culture. He is also the Chairman of Berggruen Holdings, a private company, the direct investment vehicle of The Nicolas Berggruen Charitable Foundation. He is a founder of the Institute's 21st Century Council; a member of the Think Long Committee for California; and a member of the Council for the Future of Europe.*

# ACKNOWLEDGEMENTS

I thank Dr Phua Kok Khoo for encouraging me to get this book done. He has been a dear friend for many years. After my mother passed away in 1991, Dr Phua often accompanied my father on his annual visit to relatives in China till he passed away in 1996.

I am very grateful to Asad Latif and Lee Huay Leng for patiently going through my past speeches, writings and interviews and making the selection. They did it out of friendship and, I think, also out of shared belief. They worked on both the English and Chinese versions together. I would like also to acknowledge Chow Wan Ee for doing the Chinese translation and Tan Hong Khoon for sponsoring it.

I thank the wonderful men and women of World Scientific for their professional work, especially He Hua, Juliet Lee and Kim Tan. They patiently nudged me on to meet the publication deadline.

I owe a special debt of gratitude to Lilian Lee, my personal assistant in government for 23 years. She was meticulous in the way she kept my records even as my responsibilities changed. Without her, retrieving and compiling old speeches and writings would have been considerably more difficult. She was also able to decipher my bad handwriting, some dating back 30 years. She remains the link to my past for the four secretaries who now assist me in Singapore and Hong Kong — Cynthia Lin at the Lee Kuan Yew School of Public Policy, Christine Voon at Kuok Singapore, Florence Yu at Kerry Group HQ and Merlim Ho at Kerry Logistics HQ.

I would like to take this opportunity to thank the many people who have helped me over the years:

— teachers and schoolmates who taught and inspired me, some no longer with us;
— old colleagues in the SAF with many of whom I still stay in close touch;
— colleagues in various government ministries including but not confined to MINDEF, MITA, Finance, Health, MTI and MFA;
— comrades in the PAP. It was a privilege to serve under Lee Kuan Yew, Goh Chok Tong, Lee Hsien Loong and others;
— many lifelong friends and supporters in grassroots organisations including the fine men and women of the People's Association;
— residents of Aljunied GRC whom I had the privilege of serving for 23 years;
— those responsible for my security especially Anthony Tan who was my personal security officer from 1990 to 2011;
— Robert Kuok and Kuok/Kerry Group colleagues who settled me into the private sector and taught me much;
— many overseas colleagues and friends who helped me in and out of government;
— My Taijigong master Sim Pooh Ho and his son Sim Pern Yiau who opened a window in my mind to a universe I did not know existed;
— young Singaporeans who introduced me to the social media and made it a part of my life.

I would also like to record my deep thanks to Amartya Sen, Wang Gungwu and Nicolas Berggruen for their kind and thoughtful Forewords. I am fortunate to have them as dear friends and soulmates.

My wife and children, my wife's parents, my wife's sister and her family, my late parents, my siblings and their families have been steadfast in their support of my work in public life. In my first parliamentary term, my wife delivered our first three children (Edwina, Edward and William) in quick succession. Frederick arrived a little later. Frederick was diagnosed to have leukaemia at the age of 3. He went through two and half years of chemotherapy but had a relapse two years later. Despite a second round of chemotherapy, the leukaemia came back. In August 2004, just after I became Foreign Minister, the rest of the family including my mother-in-law accompanied Freddy to St. Jude Children Research Hospital in Memphis, Tennessee where he received a bone marrow transplant. By the grace of God, he survived. Freddy's battle with leukemia over many years was stressful for everyone but kept the family tightly knit. I sometimes wonder how life would have been different for different members of my family had I not entered politics. The night I lost the elections in May 2011, my two older children were in Peking University watching proceedings live on television with other Singapore students. It must have been hard on them.

There are many others — friends, relatives and strangers — whose support, goodwill and prayers have sustained me over the years. Some still engage me on Facebook. To all of you, thanks!

Above all, I acknowledge our Creator who wishes us to live our lives abundantly.

George Yeo

# COMMENTARY

## by Asad-ul Iqbal Latif

### The Intellectual as Politician

The British historian Edward Hallett Carr's tart observation that no one has ever lived in Plato's republic is a warning against romanticising utopias. Whether it is authoritarian Platonism; the communistic humanism of More's *Utopia*; the classless and stateless absolutism of Marxism-Leninism; or the hierarchic familial harmony of the Confucian order, the truth is that no one has lived in any of them — and never will. Utopias by definition do not and cannot exist: The moment someone tries to realise the principles of a utopia in actual political practice and institutions, reality kills the elusive charm of the idea of perfection.

Yet, no state is worth having if its founding and motivating ideas do not derive from a possibility of human perfection. This irony — that utopias are necessary to guide behaviour precisely because they cannot be realised — is one that political thinkers face. It taunts the political practitioner and the philosophical statesman because, unlike pure thinkers, they are in charge of running a state and running it to some purpose.

George Yong-Boon Yeo — scholar, philosopher, soldier, statesman, Catholic, *taichi* practitioner, consummate family man, and man with the million-dollar smile (without GST) — grapples with this fundamental *praxis* in this book. Born on September 13, 1954, he excelled academically. He went on to become a President's Scholar and Singapore Armed Forces Scholar at

Christ's College, Cambridge, where he graduated with a Double First in Engineering. He later attended Harvard Business School and graduated as a Baker Scholar.

Yeo rose to be a Brigadier-General in the Republic of Singapore Air Force (RSAF). He served as the Chief of Staff of the RSAF and as the Director of Joint Operations and Planning at the Ministry of Defence. He was inducted into politics as a People's Action Party (PAP) candidate in the 1988 General Election. He served in the Cabinet in the ministries of Information and the Arts, Health, Trade and Industry, and Foreign Affairs. He lost his parliamentary seat in the 2011 General Election.

During his political career, Yeo belied the stereotype — which is no more than that — of engineers as technocratic drivers of the Singapore system. As the selection of essays in this book shows, ideas permeate his calling as a political leader deeply. This is true of many leaders, but Yeo's ideas possess an astringent agency drawn from the intellectual frontlines where the key definitions and directions of the good life of politics have been sought, if not found: the dialectical jousting between the individual and society, freedom and responsibility, market forces and social equity, nationalism and internationalism, and so on. Running through these dyads is a single thread that ties them together morally: the tension between ends and means in political action.

It was quickly clear that Yeo was not formed in the more traditional mode of some leaders. His 1991 speech on pruning the banyan tree of the Singapore state, a political canopy under which nothing could grow, heralded an era of activism by civil society, which had hitherto been seen as a threat to the dominance of the PAP state. The speech might not seem startling today, but it generated strong interest at a time when the transition from Prime Minister Lee Kuan Yew's first-generation leadership to Prime Minister Goh Chok Tong's second-generation leadership was creating new political possibilities and expectations. Yeo, a third-generation leader, was already looking far ahead although the second generation had just taken over.

Yeo may be called a liberal conservative. An iconic product of Singapore's meritocratic but authoritarian system, he was a political conservative, believing in the need for discipline and stability above all in a city-state whose paucity of natural resources left it without a margin for error. Nevertheless, he was far-sighted enough to recognise that order and stability could survive only if the system were liberalised judiciously from within so as to attract and retain the idealism and energy of a younger and liberal citizenry.

## Culture

Culture features heavily on Yeo's intellectual map. From his speeches on the subject, it is clear that he sees it as an immutable source of human action. This is not to say, of course, that culture itself is immutable: Instead, culture exists precisely because it is open to change, expands to incorporate foreignness, and restores disturbed balances by seeking a new equilibrium in alteration and acceleration. But culture, in this living sense, is intrinsic to the human understanding of reality and the human need for action to change reality.

Yeo's "culturalist" reading of democracy in Singapore might disappoint those who believe in the autonomous necessity and agency of democracy in the maturing of any political society anywhere. But as he notes, while the transition to democracy is an empirically-observable historical trend, what form the transition takes, when and how it occurs, and what its consequences are, emerge from the cultural make-up of a nation. In any case, the institutions of equally legitimate democratic systems can and do differ considerably. The most obvious example is the democratic legitimacy of the American presidential system, which differs not only from European parliamentary systems but also from the French presidential system. Also, the first-past-the-post electoral system is widely considered legitimate, although the proportional representation system arguably is more democratic because it is more representative, this being the key goal of democracy. Just as these systems exist, the idea of democracy with Singapore characteristics should not be a difficult one to argue for. Yeo does this admirably, with intellectual honesty and argumentative credibility. The culture of a people does have important consequences for both the shape and the effectiveness of its political system.

Yeo's sensitivity to culture informs his understanding of China. China is a multiple-track civilisation where Confucianism, Legalism, communism and capitalism coexist in real time. One of the virtues of Yeo's unfolding assessment of the country is his intellectual alertness to this multi-dimensionality of contemporary Chinese culture. Readers will find neither of the two dominant narratives about China here: one, that China is a wronged civilisation which therefore is entitled to do whatever it deems right in order to settle scores with history; and the other, that China is the exemplar of Oriental despotism which the "free" world can never trust sufficiently to leave to its own devices. Yeo's nuanced reading of China's complex modernity goes beyond easy historical dichotomies to provide a sophisticated account of its place in the world.

China's coming of age in the contemporary world casts other major players — the United States, Japan and India — in comparative relief. Yeo assesses these international actors impartially, with the same eye on culture that he directs at China. As the leader of the Singapore team which negotiated free-trade agreements with the United States, Japan, Australia and other countries, Yeo is acutely aware of the primacy of self-interest in international politics. But he keeps seeking the deeper underpinnings of that self-interest in the cultural self-images of nations which decide how they determine what their long-term economic and political interests are. Countries are pragmatic in their relations with others. How, in the first place, they decide what is pragmatic derives ultimately from their cultural universe of possibilities.

This book is a compilation of speeches selected from the entire range of what Yeo penned and delivered before and throughout his political life. It covers domestic issues, which have not lost their resonance today; and international realities in Southeast Asia, Northeast Asia, and the United States within which Singapore will have to survive and thrive.

## Politics and Media

Apart from the metaphor of pruning the banyan tree of authoritarianism, around which so much of George Yeo's political legacy is structured, democracy features prominently among the themes covered in this section. Yeo is forthright that democracy is not a matter of choice but of necessity. More than the mechanism of one-person-one-vote, what is central to democracy is "a value system which recognises the good in every individual". Indeed, he says that modern civilisation would be impossible without "the free, cooperative effort of a large number of thinking individuals."

Some would question his assertion that traditional Asian values need to balance the "individualising effects of the free market", as they might his emphasis on the usefulness of centralised decision-making, but there is no doubt that he accepts and indeed celebrates the enabling role of democracy in achieving the good life of politics. However, he is emphatic that there are different kinds of democracy. As he puts it inimitably, democracy "is not a species of political organisation but a genus containing within it many competing species" — from America to Europe and Japan.

Naturally for a democrat, Yeo is a keen believer in the importance of institutions. "Good institutions last longer than individuals," he argues. "Nations with good institutions survive bad luck and bad leaders." Given the centrality of charismatic leadership in the early politics of independent Singapore, these are bold statements to make. In fact, he says bluntly that "what we should be looking for are not new Lee Kuan Yews but strong institutions." Yeo's perceptive comments on cultural DNA and free will illuminate his understanding of both the agency and the limitations of human instincts in the formation and preservation of political institutions.

Yeo's thoughts on the overriding importance of able leadership and political consensus in good governance must be read in this context. His remarks on the role of the civil service display the insights of a politician who, although a first-rate thinker, is also aware that bureaucratic institutions are essential to translate ideals into ideas and politics into policies.

Long before these issues became politicised in partisan ways, Yeo shows his concern with growth with equity and makes an abiding case for democratic socialism in upholding fairness in the political economy of a globalising Singapore. He is concerned as well with the creation of a human rights framework that is both deeply responsive and sustainable.

Yeo's comments on the media combine a philosopher's understanding of one of the most powerful cultural phenomena in the world, and a scientist's curiosity in the technology which is changing the media landscape.

# Commentary

## by Lee Huay Leng

Mr George Yeo entered politics in 1988 when he joined the People's Action Party to run for parliament. When *Lianhe Zaobao* reported about the introduction of this PAP's 33-year-old candidate, it quoted Mr Yeo's words, saying: "I want to remain like a young man." The report's opening paragraph summed up the aspirations that Mr Yeo expressed at the press conference: "George Yeo's ideal is to be a member of parliament who expresses his true self and who identifies with the young people."

As a debutant to the political scene, Mr Yeo spoke to the press about the government's style and its detachment from the younger people. He said that some younger Singaporeans, especially the better educated, were cynical of the government, and that the challenge that he and his younger colleagues faced was how they could "reattach these younger ones, to get these people back to the Government."

*The Straits Times* highlighted Mr Yeo's emphasis on building the Singaporean sense of belonging and their sense of national honour and national identity, but which should not be reduced to "narrow and small-minded nationalism."

That was the year 1988. Today, 27 years later, as we take stock of the state of affairs in Singapore and look back at what Mr Yeo had spoken in the press interviews — whatever the Chinese or English press have chosen to highlight — his observations and views then are still of great reference value today. As a nation-state, a quarter-century in the history of Singapore is not a long time. All these years, this young nation has continued to excogitate over the same concerns: national survival and the people's sense of identity. Understandably, this is a natural process in any country's development trajectory. But a quarter-century experience for any individual is certainly not a short encounter. Mr Yeo's cogitations did not start with his political career. As early as his student days, during the 1970s, when the environment in Southeast Asia was capricious and the Vietnam War still going on, he was already observing the political situation and ideological trend with great assiduity. During his Cambridge University days, he was the President of the Malaysia-Singapore Association, and what is documented in his student-day journal, which he has kept till now, leaves written footprints of his thoughts and insights of world affairs as a young intellectual.

During his 23-year political career, Mr Yeo's personality profile as a thinker-politician has set him apart from the Cabinet comprising mainly second- and third-generation PAP political leaders. As a Cabinet minister, he was in a position to follow through his ideas, and to influence the nation's policies and course. Just reading Mr Yeo's views and discourse today would not have come across as anything unusual, given the openness and rapid flow of information these days; at times, they may even seem slightly conservative. Some of the ideas that he has advocated have, over these years, become a part of Singapore's operation strategy, therefore nothing too refreshing or arresting. But if we look at the dates of those speeches, and compare what he said against the historical context, we will realise how far he was ahead of his time. We will see how Singapore's environment and culture — between the late 1980s till 2011 — had enabled a thinker with political astuteness and foresight to stage his ideas; and when his ideas are transformed into policies, how these policies have become so closely linked to life in Singapore.

In 1990, Mr Yeo was appointed by Mr Goh Chok Tong, who just took over as Prime Minister, as Acting Minister for Information and the Arts. That was the beginning of a second generation's era after Mr Lee Kuan Yew's 31 years in office. Shortly after he took office, he gave a monumental speech at the National University of Singapore when he introduced in his political discourse the word "civic society." Civic society was not new to Singapore, but little about the concept was discussed during the 1990s; if at all, only within the academia. But what George Yeo presented was not a cursory mention, but a catholic elaboration of the entire concept of civic society. I believe he must have given it some lengthy thinking. When he talked about the importance of space for the civic society, he said:

> This leads me to make a general point about community self-help and the Singapore soul. For our civic institutions to grow, the state must withdraw a little and provide more space for local initiative. If the state is overpowering and intrudes into every sphere of community life, the result will be disastrous. All of us are then reduced to guests in a hotel. By arrogating to itself all powers, Communism, especially Soviet Communism, created an immoral system. By making everyone dependent on the state, the system destroyed the soul of the community.

When referring to the relationship between the state and the civic society, he compared Singapore to a banyan tree:

> The problem now is that under a banyan tree very little else can grow. When state institutions are too pervasive, civic institutions cannot thrive. Therefore it is necessary to prune the banyan tree so that other plants can also grow. You know what our friends in Hong Kong say of us: we take care of our people so well, our people have become soft.
>
> In other words, it is civic life which creates 'public affections' and the soul in our society. It is civic life which holds a democracy together. We have to make the effort ourselves. The Government can help but the Government cannot build up civic life from top down.
>
> ... Let me add that there has to be a proper balance between centralization and de-centralization. We have

> to prune the banyan tree, but we cannot do without the banyan tree. Singapore will always need a strong centre to react quickly to a changing competitive environment. We need some pluralism but not too much because too much will also destroy us. In other words, we prune judiciously.

Who should prune the banyan tree? It seemed that it had to be the banyan tree itself: Mr Yeo's proposition was well-received by the English-speaking civic society, and this speech has become a classic piece which one inevitably cites when referring to him.

To Singapore, Mr Yeo proffered the aspiration of transcending territorial limits. When he entered parliament after winning the elections, he mentioned many times the need for internal revamping and the possibility of external development. In his mind, Singapore is inextricably linked to the world. What he referred to was not the geopolitical reasons that older generation PAP leaders gave, or that we should leapfrog other economies in the region and connect directly with the western world. Mr Yeo believed that we should use the world as Singapore's oyster to broaden our frontiers. To him, not only is Singapore inseparable from the world, but the economy and technology are inseparable from culture, and the present is inseparable from the past. Whether he was speaking to students or the general public in Singapore, he was sure to put Singapore within the context of the world: being cosmopolitan, the second pair of wings, refusal to be inward-looking or parochial. He believes that Singapore should look outward to develop its economy, that Singaporeans have a distinct sense of identity when they travel the world, and that we should stay united internally and make friends in different parts of the world. He also thinks that we should cherish and make use of Singapore's cultural links with other regions, and maintain our cultural origins in China, Malaysia, Indonesia and India.

As to the tensions between different ethnic groups which arise now and then when Singapore searches for its sense of identity,

Mr Yeo accepted it with equanimity. He does not focus on their antagonism, but took a positive view in the value their differences can give Singapore. As Minister for Trade and Industry, he addressed Singapore General Hospital Forum in 2001, saying:

> It is important to understand why we are what we are because, if we do not understand how we got here, we will not know how to move forward ... Without these tensions, we cannot maintain our broadband capability and our links to the world.

He also discussed the importance of having a Big Singapore mentality: "The Singaporean can be Chinese, Malay, Indian or Eurasian, but he must have a big mind and a big heart, and he should think of Singapore not only in terms of our island geography, but also against the backdrop of our Asian and Anglo-Saxon history and connections ... ."

He further shares: "We must educate all our children with that larger mental compass. That is the difference between the mentality of a Small Singapore and that of a Big Singapore. A Small Singapore mentality finds the region with all its problems uncomfortable and our diversity a constant source of friction and irritation. A Big Singapore mentality engages the region, celebrates our diversity and uses it to access economic and cultural spaces all over the world. And by bringing our children up in this way, the entire world becomes their oyster, and others in the world will then want to join them and be like them. "

When so many Singaporeans today are more concerned with their personal and domestic matters, what are the merits and our illumination of those words spoken more than a decade ago?

Mr Yeo spoke quite substantially about culture. In 1990, he discussed the importance of Malay language being international and Singaporean at the same time, and that Malay literature should be translated to bring the different races in Singapore closer. When he talked about the Chinese culture in Singapore, it was expounded within the framework of the global trend of cultural identity of overseas Chinese. Shortly after he joined politics, the attention he gave to topics such as the preservation of *Wanqingyuan* (Sun Yat Sen Nanyang Memorial Hall), or the status of the Chinese-educated or Nanyang University graduates, or the Chinese language standard in Singapore, was rare among the new generation leaders. And although Mr Yeo spoke mainly in English, his depth of knowledge and unique perspectives helped him build a special relationship with the Chinese-speaking community.

Selecting and compiling this collection of speeches and essays is no small task. There are nearly a thousand scripts and several rounds of screening and deciding. I had a hard time, as many were excellently written. From the reader's perspective, apart from the more heavy-going ones, some speeches that he delivered at neighbourhood schools whose audience were "non-elites" were on refreshing topics and with invigorating candour:

> ... we have to treat one another as individuals who are different yet equal. Put in another way, we must value human relationships. Friendships should not be made and broken like things. We must feel deeply for each other, for our parents, for our brothers and sisters, for our friends. If we do what is right and refrain from doing what is wrong, it should not be because someone is watching but because it makes us feel good inside. Every one of us must have his own dignity and self-esteem. Yes, we compete very hard in Singapore. We compete to do well in school, to get a place in the poly or JC, for jobs, for status, for money. Competition helps to bring out the best in us. But competition can also bring out the worst in us. There must be limits to competition. Our sense of competition must be tempered by a sense of co-operation and compassion. We must have human feelings. We are not machines. Everyone has a right to be here and to do his own thing. But everyone also has a duty to others. We have one life to live. We must live it well.

When he graced the opening of Takashimaya Department Store in 1993, he talked about the interdependence of commerce and culture, and elaborated the importance of culture to the society:

> Our real concern is not with objects but with the mentality of our people. In the new world we are entering, it is important to be good at science and mathematics but it is not enough to be only good in science and mathematics. We must also have artistic sense. With science and mathematics, we can produce accurately and efficiently. But to create high value, we must also produce artistically. Consider Teenage Mutant Ninja Turtle toys. Yes, they must be well-made to meet first world standards of quality and safety. But for such work, workers in China can do under proper supervision. The value of Teenage Mutant Ninja Turtles is not in the physical production but in the concept, in the design and in the marketing.

Excelling in Math and Science does not suffice, for it must be balanced to include the humanities and the arts. This was the inspiration he drew from Ninja Turtles.

> Our intellectual development and our artistic development are like the *yin* and *yang* in Chinese thinking. Balance is very important. The scholar-mandarin is a Confucianist in public life but a Taoist in his private life. In the Japanese mind, the philosophy of *zen* cannot be separated from the drive to excel. The more *yang* we want, the more *yin* we must have. Thus, to reach higher levels of economic development, we need higher levels of cultural development.

Perhaps the above means little in present-day 2014. But 20 years ago, a newcomer who beheld such breadth and depth was a valuable asset, and the general public looked forward to a different — possibly social and cultural, if not political — environment. For George Yeo had the political stage on which he decided the props and the plot. During the days when he was at the helm of the

Ministry of Information and the Arts, he created a different and far-reaching cultural landscape for Singapore.

In 1996, Mr Yeo led a delegation as chairman of Young PAP, PAP's youth wing, to the United States on a study tour. The delegation was to study the US presidential primary elections. During the tour, he intentionally selected Utah as one of the stops to remind the PAP members that they should not look only at Los Angeles and New York, as that would only be a skewed understanding of the United States. At that time, I had been a journalist for two years, and was sent to follow the delegation to observe and report on their tour. There were three incidents about Mr Yeo which till now I cannot forget.

The first occurred when we were at Salt Lake City in Utah State. The mayor was hoping that we could interview her to help promote Salt Lake City in Singapore. To us, Salt Lake City was a distant city, and we had no idea how many of our *Lianhe Zaobao*'s readers were interested in investing in and touring Salt Lake City. I remembered Mr Yeo coming to remind us, the accompanying journalists, that we should promise only if we could deliver, and that we were to tell the mayor frankly if it was inappropriate, and to do away with perfunctory courtesy.

The second concerned the tension between China and the US when Lee Teng Hui visited the US. Mr Yeo spoke *ad lib*, at Salt Lake City, for 40 minutes at the dinner banquet hosted by the mayor. The script was in his head. He articulated the history and conflicts between the China and the US with unfailing ease and the erudition of an avid reader and a deep thinker.

The third incident happened when we were in Washington. Apart from visiting the Thomas Jefferson Memorial which commemorates the third American President Thomas Jefferson responsible for drafting the 1776 *Declaration of Independence*, Mr Yeo specifically requested to visit Monticello, where Jefferson used to live. How Jefferson's home looked like was immaterial. What mattered most was the experience to revisit history.

This selection of speeches may be read as current affairs commentaries with a strong academic flavour. But Mr Yeo started as a political freshman to becoming an important Cabinet member, and has held ministerial posts in the Ministry of Information and the Arts, Ministry of Health, Ministry of Trade and Industry and Ministry of Foreign Affairs. Indeed, when we compare what he said to the changes that Singapore underwent during the past two decades or so, including Singapore's status in the world, one could read beyond the philosophical bent and perhaps delight in the other pleasures that this book brings.

Without George Yeo, perhaps only the senior Cabinet members would know what an ideal, multi-talented Cabinet truly misses. But as the world is reshaped by forces of change, Singapore will yet again be transformed; and when the powers of the civil society must forge ahead in these times of change, I cannot help but wonder: If Mr Yeo had not exited from the stage, if he were still right in the middle of the act, what would he be thinking? How would the banyan tree look like?

# INTRODUCTION

This book is a collection of my past speeches and writings. They are jointly selected by Asad Latif and Lee Huay Leng for the English and Chinese versions of the book in consultation with me. Dr Phua Kok Khoo, Founder and Chairman of World Scientific had repeatedly persuaded me to write a book about my views on politics and culture since my time in the Foreign Ministry. I replied, repeatedly, that I was not in a frame of mind to do so. While in government, there were too many issues to grapple with. After I left government in 2011, my life entered a new phase and there were too many new challenges to face. I am not an academic and feel no inclination to discourse on society and government in an abstract way. As for writing the memoirs of my years in government, that would involve combing through records in various ministries, the PAP, Parliament and the constituency I served, over 23 years. Much material would still be classified. It is also easy for my recounting to be misunderstood as self-serving. In all the roles I played, I worked as a member of a team and claiming specific responsibility for particular acts of commission or omission could be invidious. Hence, when Dr Phua suggested that my speeches be compiled instead, I thought it a good idea. They are all already in the public domain. When I left the Ministry of Trade and Industry (MTI) in 2004, my colleagues took the trouble of compiling the key speeches I made into a souvenir book with the somewhat flattering title: *George Yeo — A Curious and Lively Mind*. Only a few dozen copies were published, beautifully bound Chinese-style, paid for by the Chairmen of MTI statutory boards and senior staff. In fact, the collection of speeches in that book covered quite well the key events and decisions during my seven years in the Ministry. I passed that book to Dr Phua who thought that it could be a model for this book.

Just before campaigning began for the May 2011 General Election, a friend of mine who is a professional pollster told me confidentially that his analysis of the trends indicated that my team would garner 43 to 47% of the votes. I kept this piece of information to myself, not wanting to demoralise my team mates. As it turned out, his forecast range precisely bracketed the 45% we received. Despite being mentally prepared for a loss, the loss when it came was painful. The Workers' Party had fielded its first team against my colleagues and me in Aljunied Group Representation Constituency (GRC) in a high-stakes bid to break the PAP's dominance of the Singapore Parliament. Over three electoral terms, the boundaries of Aljunied GRC had shifted to envelop the sole Opposition constituency in Singapore at Hougang. It was not surprising that the Workers' Party should attempt the breakout through Aljunied GRC although this could not have been the only reason. In my speech congratulating the Workers' Party candidates, I expressed the hope that they would look after the constituents whom I had the privilege of serving over two decades. A day or two later, Workers' Party leader Low Thia Khiang remarked that the PAP team lost not because it had performed badly but because the people wanted more Opposition members in Parliament. At a media conference the following week, I announced my retirement from parliamentary politics. In the subsequent weeks, pressure built up within and outside the PAP for me to run for the elected Presidency in August. This was despite my having indicated earlier that I thought myself temperamentally unsuited for the responsibility. Initially, Prime Minister Lee Hsien Loong supported my candidacy but when Dr Tony Tan, former Deputy PM and PAP Chairman, indicated his willingness to run with the PAP's support, I bowed out. I would only have contested out of duty, not ambition. It should not be an exercise in self-justification. Two individuals I respected discouraged me from standing for the Presidency. My *taijigong* master, Sim Pooh Ho, who lives in Kunming, took a Taoist view. He took me on as a disciple only after I left government. He said that the times were changing and it was better for me to be free, not to do less, but perhaps to do more. His words then sounded a bit mysterious to me. Robert Kuok whom I had known for over 20 years, and looked up to as a wise man, also advised me not to stand for the Presidency. Through two separate channels, he passed word that the Presidency was not for me and invited me to join him instead which I did after a decent interval. Two years later, I was appointed by Pope Francis as member of an eight-person commission charged to recommend changes to the administrative and financial structure of the Vatican. Before flying to Rome for the first meeting, I called on Archbishop William Goh for his blessing and advice. Archbishop Goh began by observing that I could not serve the Holy Father if I had not lost the elections. At that moment, I recalled the words of Master Sim.

I describe myself as a Taoist to close friends — in a philosophical not religious sense. I have been fascinated by the *Tao Te Ching* since undergraduate days and, in recent years, by the *I Ching* as well. Before joining the PAP in August 1988, I was required to write a short essay about my core values. Although I do not have a copy of it despite repeated searches, I remember clearly that what I wrote is more or less this: "My core values are Chinese and Christian. As a Chinese, I am both Confucianist and Taoist. The Confucianist side of me believes that civilisation is only possible with effort and organisation. For society to enjoy peace and to progress, there must be good government and human beings must have a sense of *li* (propriety and respect in human relationships). The Taoist side of me accepts that whatever we do, there are larger currents at play which are beyond our control and to which we are subject. My mother, who was born in Chaozhou and only came to Singapore after marrying my father at the age of 18, had a great influence on my sense of being a Chinese. And, as a Christian, I believe in love as the highest virtue in life and the sanctity of the individual." When Goh Chok Tong became Prime Minister in November 1990, he appointed me to head the new Ministry of Information and the Arts. I designed the logo as a stylized yin-yang in green and red — green representing nature of which we are a part and, red, the life force of civilisation. My Senior Parliamentary Secretary Ho Kah Leong drew the logo in Chinese brush and left me to dot the red eye in the old Taoist tradition.

Human society is going through profound change, perhaps as dramatic as the shift from nomadic existence to settled agricultural life or from feudal to industrial society. The motive force is of course the digital revolution. Old structures are crumbling everywhere. Information technology and the social media are undermining hierarchical relationships. Many countries are experiencing institutional crisis. The relationships between parents and children, between teachers and students, between priests and laity, between doctors and patients, between government leaders and the citizenry, are all changing. In developed countries, the incomes of middle classes are stagnating or in decline. The work many do is progressively taken over by machines, algorithms and foreigners. For large numbers, the best is past. Lacking hope, mass unhappiness among middle classes has become a growing phenomenon. A small minority grows wealthier either because they are already rich or because they are smart, well-connected or lucky. Perhaps the situation has to get worse before it gets better. The new technologies unleashed by the digital revolution enable better and higher forms of human organisation to emerge but not before old ones are brought down. The search for new pathways to that future is the story of today. Throughout history, in times of great change, the future is first to be discerned in the freer cities where conditions favour social experimentation. In some ways, the future evolution of Asia can already be seen in the struggles of cities like Singapore and Hong Kong.

It is natural that the young should play a major role in this great transformation. As hierarchies give way to networks, it is younger members of society who adapt the most readily. As Chairman of the Young PAP in the 90s, I encouraged a group of young men and women to start a Young PAP website. After telling them not to get me into trouble with party bosses and government regulators, I left them to their own devices. It was skunk work but showed promise. When blogs became popular, I asked a young friend to let me blog on his website. I also had another friend start a new site for me to blog on with a different reach. Learning the new social media was interesting and helped me keep in touch with a younger generation. As Facebook took off in Singapore, I was encouraged to start an account by another group of young supporters. They held my hand initially. After a few weeks, I was happy to be on my own. Within a year, after my Facebook account reached the limit of 5,000 friends, I started a public page. Working with young Singaporeans changed me. I learn much from them and many in turn feel responsible for me. Towards the end of the 2011 election campaign, I posted a short video message to young Singaporeans which quickly went viral in Singapore and abroad. In network society, communication is only effective if it is viral. After leaving party politics, I considered winding down my Facebook accounts but was discouraged by many people. In any case, posting on Facebook is now commonplace. It is nice that the children of some friends became my Facebook friends. In an unexpected way, my early adoption of the social media also brought me closer to my four children who became my critics and consultants. If we fail to engage and involve the young, if we only want to change them without allowing them to change us, the transition from a hierarchical to a network society will be a troubled one. It is for this reason that I support activities which encourage young Singaporeans to see Singapore's future in positive terms. Bringing down an old order without a clear sense of what should replace it can lead to unnecessary tragedy. Successful social transformation requires the young to be included as internal agents of change. This challenge, we also see in Hong Kong today. Recalling my own involvement in undergraduate student politics in Cambridge, I feel a certain empathy with Hong Kong students in their desire to improve social and political conditions despite the limitations of one-country-two-systems. If youth has no passion, society has no future.

Under Lee Kuan Yew, Singapore was unabashedly a hierarchical society. When asked if Singapore was a nanny state, he replied that, if it were one, he was proud to have fostered it. But he also knew that Singapore society was entering a new phase. In November 1990, Lee Kuan Yew stepped aside to let Goh Chok Tong take over as Prime Minister. The state retreated a little; controls were carefully loosened; greater diversity was tolerated if not selectively encouraged. As Minister for Information and the Arts, I was happy to push some boundaries — censorship, use of dialects and Singlish, greater emphasis of pre-PAP history and promotion of our diverse ancestral heritage. These were all sensitive issues and I had to manage senior Cabinet colleagues artfully. A speech I made about the need to prune the banyan tree in order that civic participation could flourish resonated with many Singaporeans. Pruning the banyan tree means cutting down hierarchy. Letting more sunlight through enables the social network to be better energised.

Diversity causes tension. In hierarchical societies, diversity is frowned upon because it makes top-down organisation more difficult. Standardization improves efficiency but it also leads to oppression. There is a trade-off which Kuo Pao Kun poked fun at in his popular play "The Coffin Is Too Big for the Hole". Many years ago, the late Cardinal Jan Schotte told me this story about Pope John Paul II whom he served as the secretary of the Synod of Bishops in the Vatican. Drafting a speech for the Holy Father, Cardinal Schotte inserted a sentence for the Pope to say that "despite our differences, we are one". John Paul II gently chided him and replaced "despite" with "because of". "Because of our differences, we are one." The particularity of the individual is sacrosanct. Each of us is unique; each is ultimately responsible for his own life. The correction by the Pope was not of style but of deep principle. Diversity is not to be merely tolerated; it is to be celebrated. For those who believe in God, every human being carries a divine imprint which unites us. For Confucianists and atheists, every human being has a moral core which also makes us one. We may disagree over man's spiritual nature but there is something deep in all of us, probably encoded in our DNA, which bows before the ideal of human fraternity and which is moved by the cries of a child. This of course has not stopped slaughter over religious beliefs. Unity in diversity is easy to say. Living it requires a daily examination of conscience. I recounted Cardinal Schotte's story to a group of young supporters who were helping me raise funds for a public sculpture by a lake in my old political constituency. They were inspired and designed a badge with

the Pope's amended formulation. In their enthused response, I draw hope for Singapore's future. Singapore is what it is only because it is diverse. As a member of Parliament, I regularly officiated at ceremonies to welcome new citizens. Invariably, my speech made the same point. Although Singapore does not recognise multiple citizenships, we encourage new citizens to maintain old links and cherish their ethnic and religious heritage. Singapore is enriched by their addition and our international network enhanced. However, there is one requirement to being Singaporean which is this: a new citizen has to enlarge his heart and broaden his mind to embrace those who are different from him. In other words, becoming Singaporean means becoming a bigger person even though Singapore is a small country. Needless to say, those of us who are already citizens should also manifest this same largeness of mind and spirit.

As a small country, we should always have a modest view of ourselves. Foreigners may compliment us for our achievements but sometimes these are just words of courtesy. In the 90s, a Singapore businessman was told that a Shanghai leader, who was a member of the Politburo of the Central Committee of the Chinese Communist Party, described Singapore as a bonsai to a visiting US Cabinet Secretary. My businessman friend was most offended by the remark. Did he think that Singaporeans were incapable of doing big things? I understood my friend's reaction but did not feel quite the same way. After all, it is not easy to grow and maintain a bonsai. Some bonsais last a long time and they can be very valuable. With the spirit of Ah Q, I also told myself that if a Chinese leader considered the Singapore bonsai though small to be of the same stock as the Chinese people, that is a great compliment to us since China is a great country. From then on, when talking about Singapore's relations with China, I would describe Singapore as a bonsai which is of occasional interest to China because of genetic similarities. Singapore also shares genes with Malaysia, Indonesia and India. When President Habibie in a moment of anger dismissed Singapore as a little red dot, Singaporeans started wearing that little dot as a badge of pride. This, strangely, has endeared us to many Indonesians. But it is an Indian friend who sized us up (or down) most accurately. During his first term as Chief Minister of the southern Indian state of Andhra Pradesh, N. Chandrababu Naidu compared the workings of Singapore to nanotechnology. Yes, we are small but we pack a lot into a tiny space and are able to network Singapore to the entire world. Singapore is of interest to many people because, though small, it has all the attributes of a country unlike Hong Kong. Nobel laureate Sydney Brenner encouraged Singapore to study the genome of the fugu fish some years ago because it has the shortest genome among vertebrates. This made it easier to relate gene to function. Singapore is like the fugu fish. I have had long conversations with Nicolas Berggruen of the Berggruen Institute of Governance about the positive and negative aspects of the Singapore system. He is fascinated by Singapore society because it is small enough to be studied as a complete social, economic and political model.

Singapore is not intelligible in itself. Its economy, culture and politics can only be understood in the context of the region it serves. Singapore is only one node in a dense network of many nodes. Whether the Singapore node grows or shrinks depends on the health of the network and our ability to link up with other nodes and add value. Our diversity is therefore a great strength. Joel Kotkin describes Singapore as a home for many tribes. This enables us to arbitrage across cultural domains. Indeed this arbitrage is at the heart of our economy and foreign policy. As Minister for Information and the Arts, Trade and Industry, and Foreign Affairs, I devoted considerable time to the development of our cultural connections because they underlay our economic, political and social life. These efforts also brought me closer to the many minority communities living in Singapore. I was very touched when Buddhist, Muslim and Jewish friends congratulated me on my Vatican appointment. Diversity is, however, also our vulnerability. Every channel which connects us to the world outside also brings infection. Maintaining Singapore's integrity and security is therefore a continuing challenge. Two conditions have to be met for a city-state to stay independent. First, its foreign policy has to be nimble and adjust to a shifting external balance of power. Second, the citizenry must be united in its common defence against external subversion and aggression. The external and internal equations have to be solved simultaneously. Only when Singaporeans feel secure about their own place at home can they turn outwards and do big things together. I spent 16 years as a soldier, first in the Army, then the Air Force and, finally, in the Joint Staff. The Singapore Armed Forces is a well-equipped and well-trained militia. Its fighting ability is completely dependent on the unity of diverse Singaporeans and their commitment to a common, righteous cause. By being prepared for war, we are more likely to have peace. It is better not to be put to the test.

If we can maintain peace in Asia for another ten to twenty years, the region will be transformed beyond recognition and become a powerhouse of the global economy. While trials of strength are inevitable, Sino-US relations are unlikely to deteriorate too badly. Even when China's economy overtakes that of the US in size, the US will remain the dominant military and political power in the world for decades to come. American popular culture has already taken over the world. Unlike the US, China is not a missionary power. So long as it is able to maintain its own political and cultural universe within, China has no ambition to compete with the US for global supremacy without. If China is also a missionary power, like the former Soviet Union, another hot or cold war is inevitable. Happily, China is not and a titanic clash between the US and China is not inevitable. Between China and India, they are more likely to cooperate than to fight. Except for a minor border war in 1962, which has been largely forgotten in China, the long history of contact between them has been peaceful. Each recognises the other as an ancient people. I have the privilege of joining Amartya Sen, Wang Gungwu and others in reviving an ancient Indian university in the state of Bihar. For centuries, Nalanda was a great university attracting students from different parts of Asia, the most famous being the two great Buddhist monks from Tang China — Xuanzang and Yijing. It was from the records of these two monks that India recovered a large chunk of its own history. Nalanda was a light to the world and, hopefully, will be again, promoting the philosophy of man living in harmony with man, man living in harmony with nature, and man living as part of nature. This ideal is not only desirable today, it is a necessity. The greatest danger in the age we live is technological development racing too far ahead of man's moral development. We need men of goodwill coming together from all directions to reflect on the moral challenges of our times and help point the way forward. Nalanda can provide one such meeting place. I hope, Singapore, another.

George Yeo

# SINGAPORE AND POLITICS

# Defending Singapore

*...civilisation is conceived, not in ease, but in hardship.*

Fellow Soldiers of the Singapore Armed Forces

After 16 years I leave the SAF with a heavy heart. I leave the SAF grateful for what it has taught me and for the friends I have made — superiors, peers and subordinates — in the Army, the Navy and Air Force. I will always treasure the memories. But I shall still be a reservist and, in that sense, will remain a part of the SAF. And the SAF will always be a part of me. As indeed it must be a part of every Singaporean. For ours is a citizen armed force and we may all be called to arms in an emergency.

Without a strong SAF, there is no independent Singapore. Even with a strong SAF, there is no guarantee that Singapore will always be independent. Our circumstances are difficult. We are geographically very small. The Swiss think they are small. But those who come to Singapore realise how big Switzerland really is by comparison.

I had to grapple with this problem of Singapore's size for much of my career in the SAF, first in the Army, then the Air Force, and finally in the Joint Staff. The problem is always the same. We have very little land. We don't have the air space. Even the seas are claimed by others. We are forced to plan very tightly, organise very carefully.

---

In August 1988, George Yeo resigned from the SAF to enter politics. This speech was made at a parade organised to send him off at Khatib camp.

Life in Singapore is not easy. The truth is we have to work much harder than others to survive.

But will hardship make us or break us? Are we strengthened or weakened in the process? Arnold J. Toynbee, the English historian, in his massive book *A Study of History* tells us that civilisation is conceived, not in ease, but in hardship. The greater the stimulus, the greater is the response. It was the trauma of the Sahara drying up that drove the ancient Egyptians into the insalubrious marshes of the Nile Valley, to drain it, cultivate the land and in the end to create a civilisation that endured thousands of years. They did not choose to go into the marshes. They went in because they had no choice. Chinese civilisation also began, not in the comfortable basin of the Yangtze, but under the harsh, severe conditions of the Yellow River Valley. The Empire of Sri Vijaya was the same. A coastal people who inhabited the banks of the great river estuaries of southern Sumatra, surrounded on the landward side by impenetrable malarial swamps, fanned out into the archipelagic waters of Southeast Asia, and created a trading empire founded on control of the sea. They have bequeathed to us Bahasa Melayu, now the national language of Indonesia, Malaysia and Singapore.

Singapore did not become independent by choice. The sensible course of action in 1963 was federation into a much larger Malaysia. But federation did not work out and we were forced to face the world alone in 1965. We could have been driven to despair. We were not. Instead, with even greater determination, we went on to organise ourselves, to build up the economy and to evolve institutions which are uniquely Singaporean.

But will we continue to succeed? Twenty-three years is after all not a long time in the life of a nation. An Australian Embassy official I met recently told me that the most common reason given by Singaporeans wanting to emigrate is the wish of a better life for their children. Not for themselves, but for their children! They fear not the nearer term but the longer term future. Now these are able people who prefer to flee rather than to fight. Why do they worry? They worry because they are not sure whether Southeast Asia will continue to be stable. They doubt whether Singapore can long remain prosperous and free.

And they may be right! They will be right if we are not internally strong and externally nimble. We will fail if we are a house divided, if our leadership is weak, if we do not have a clear sense of what our essential interests are, and if we do not have the resolve to be the master of our own destiny. We may be too small to really compare ourselves to Egypt or China or Sri Vijaya. But is there any example in history then of a small nation-state surviving any reasonable length of time? An example for us to take comfort in? A model to follow?

There is a brilliant example. And it too had the lion as a symbol, the winged lion of the evangelist Saint Mark. Venice, or the Most Serene Republic as she called herself, lasted over a thousand years. For much of this period she flourished as the mistress of the Mediterranean, her merchants well known throughout Europe and Asia for their business acumen, their industry and their sense of honour. The exploits of Marco Polo are familiar to us. Shakespeare in two plays, *Othello* and *The Merchant of Venice*, provides a picture of the heights Venice reached in the development of law, of government, of art and culture. Until Napoleon came, Venice was never successfully invaded. She was never occupied, never ravaged.

How did a collection of small islands much smaller in total land area than Singapore, in a shallow lagoon itself only about 200 square miles — the size of Singapore — with a population never exceeding a few hundreds of thousands, come to make such a mark on history? Why did sane men from the European mainland decide, in the first place, to cross the water to settle on these swampy, inhospitable, unpromising islands?

Like our forefathers from China and India, like today's Vietnamese boat people, the first Venetians left the mainland because conditions there were intolerable. Those were dark days in Europe, when the Western Roman Empire was disintegrating, when successive waves of barbarians swept across the mainland, raping and pillaging, wreaking death and destruction wherever they went. Better the safety of these islands separated from the mainland by at least two to three miles of water than face the wrath of Alaric the Goth or Attila the Hun.

Under the pressure of hardship, Venice built up her defences, her economy and her institutions. The similarities to Singapore are remarkable and we do well to draw lessons from her experience.

The defence of Venice was founded on naval power. She had a mighty complex of naval dockyards and workshops which gave the Arabic word "arsenal" to the English language. At its peak, that arsenal had a workforce of over 16,000 with the capability to launch fully equipped warships at the rate of one every few hours.

That military power was used, first, in the defence of the Republic and, second, in opening up sea lanes, trading routes and markets for her merchants. Venetian participation in the Crusades were never borne of romance, but always motivated by economic advantage. Hers was a wise foreign policy: never to be involved unnecessarily in the politics and strife of her neighbours on the mainland. Genoa, a keen competitor to Venice, lacked that wisdom. Genoa entangled herself with the wars of northern Italy and lost her independence as a result.

Venice instead turned her insularity to advantage. Always sensitive to the requirements of trade, which was her lifeblood, she evolved a system of administration founded on constitutional principles, the rule of law and the collective interests of her merchants. Slowly but steadily with each invasion successfully repelled, with each crisis successfully overcome, she developed in her people that famous Venetian spirit which bonded Venetians everywhere together. A tradition of public service supplied the men of ability needed for her effective governance.

But Venice never felt invulnerable. She never took her success for granted. It was this sense of insecurity which spurred her on, which kept her guards up, her citizens united and her institutions vital.

The achievement of Venice is an inspiration to us in Singapore, of how a tiny Republic can overcome the limitations of its size and build up an economic empire based, not on territorial aggrandisement, but on defence, diplomacy and free trade. Though our country may be small, our minds must never be. Like the merchants of Venice, we have to be both nationalistic and cosmopolitan at the same time. Our spirit, too, must be that of the lion.

The job of the SAF, like that of the Venetian Navy, is to keep the island safe from predators and the lines of communication open to trade and travel. Without her navy, there would have been no Venice. Without the SAF, there can be no Singapore. The challenge to us is how to keep the SAF strong, relevant and effective.

# Political Challenges Facing Singapore

*Our security will be jeopardised if we are, internally, a nation divided. Others will exploit our weakness.*

## Three Legs

In my talk this afternoon, I want to make the point that there are three legs supporting our society today and all three legs must be strong if we are to progress into the next decade and the next century. These three legs are: first, the Chinese-speaking population; second, the minority groups; and, third, the yuppies.

## Chinese-Speaking Population

The Chinese-speaking population make up the first leg. I am not referring only to the Chinese-educated. I include those, who even though they were educated mainly in English, are still more comfortable in Mandarin. They are by far the largest segment of Singapore. They watch Channel 8 rather than Channel 5. The viewership of Channel 8 is two to three times that of Channel 5. Despite this, the advertising rates in Channel 5 are higher. That is because those who watch Channel 5 have more money to spend, so advertisers pay more to catch their attention. But, politically, the Channel 8 viewers are more important. The Chinese *Radio and TV Times*, a weekly, has a readership of about 150,000. The English edition has a readership of less than 50,000.

---

Talk delivered at NAYTI (National Youth Leadership Training Institute), 27 November 1988.

This group now provides the core support to the PAP. It was not so in the past when the Barisan was active. It was this group the PAP had to win over, and which it did by setting up grassroot organisations, building up a base of support and solving the problem of inadequate housing and unemployment. The Barisan was discredited and the PAP coasted from election victory to election victory. In the last GE, this group was still the PAP's most important supporters. In my GRC, Aljunied, the opposition SDP was unable to reach out to this group. Ashley Seow, Jufrie, Morris Neo — none of them could speak Mandarin. We made an issue of this and Chin Harn Tong regaled the voters in Mandarin and Hokkien.

Although the Chinese-speaking electorate will gradually become smaller, it will never disappear and it will always be significant. Our Chinese students may all study EL1 and CL2 in school but a large proportion will continue to prefer Channel 8, the Chinese *Radio and TV Times* and the Chinese newspapers.

**Minority Groups**

The second leg consists of the minority groups. Minorities make up a quarter of Singapore's population. Being minorities, they feel insecure, and being insecure, they are naturally more sensitive. Chinese Singaporeans who travel overseas often complain that they are discriminated against by white waiters or waitresses. That is part of the minority syndrome.

Although the PAP can probably still win without the support of the minority groups, it would be foolish for the PAP to alienate the Malays and the Indians. We will be a poorer and an uglier society if that happens. In marginal constituencies we may lose. Eunos GRC, for example, would have gone to the Workers' Party if a more credible Malay candidate had been fielded. The sight of Khalid Baboo enthusiastically applauding and garlanding Francis Seow offended many Malay voters. All that was needed for the WP to win was a switch by some 700 Malay voters.

Our relationship with Malaysia and Indonesia will also be more complicated if the PAP is not a multiracial party. Our security will be jeopardised if we are, internally, a nation divided. Others will exploit our weakness.

So let us never ignore the importance of this second leg, the support of the minority groups in Singapore.

**Yuppies**

The yuppies make up the third leg. I use the term yuppies loosely to include those who are better educated, more comfortable in the English language, more Westernised and more likely to be reading *The Straits Times* and watching Channel 5. They are economically more well-off and better represented in our 5-room and executive HDB flats.

Many in this group are cynical about the PAP and the PAP government. They resent the control. They want more freedom. They see in Francis Seow a symbol of a liberal, Westernised Singapore. I don't think they approve of Francis Seow's character, but they are prepared to overlook his faults.

This is the group created by the very success of the PAP government. They are perhaps the most creative segment in Singapore society. And, for as long as Singapore continues to progress, they are a growing group. Being more articulate, their views matter even more than their numbers.

Unlike the minority groups, there is no fundamental reason why the yuppies should feel alienated. I am not talking about the rebellious phase young people go through. Our yuppies include professionals in their 30s, holding important jobs, and are married. In most societies, such people form the establishment. They are defenders and apologists of the system.

The problem is partly a historical one. The PAP today and its influence in the grassroot organisations is a direct result of the struggle against the Communists. The thinking, the assumptions, the organisational methods developed in a certain period of our history. There was no yuppy phenomenon then. Our organisation has not quite evolved to win over the yuppies. Our grassroots hold out little appeal to them.

The yuppies pose a political challenge to us: how to adapt to a changing political ground, how to take Singapore into the next decade and the next century. They are still a thin leg now but that leg will become more important and we must make sure it is strong. They do not lack patriotism. They may not be interested in (Citizens'

Consultative Committee) CCC-organised activities but they will volunteer for the Community Chest. And it is this social conscience we must harness for Singapore's development.

## The Future

All three legs are needed. We cannot take for granted the Chinese-speaking ground. We must not be insensitive to the aspirations of the Malays and the Indians. And we dismiss the yuppies at our own peril.

To put it positively, we need the social strength of the Chinese-speaking core of our population. Being largely Confucianist, they give stability to our social framework. We need the minority groups to help connect us to the rest of Southeast Asia. They add diversity, colour and strength to our society. And we need the dynamism and the creativity of the yuppies to secure our future. They are increasingly our links with the rest of the world.

The 21st century will be the century of the Pacific. We are part of a renaissance the scale of which is unprecedented in human history. We may be a small nation but the world is our oyster. We are already capital exporters. Singaporeans are following Singaporean money overseas in growing numbers. We can be a great nation if we manage our internal affairs well. Our heterogeneous, cosmopolitan nature will be a weakness if we are divided. But if we stay united, all three legs strong and in mutual support, we will be a great nation. In a sense we show the way for others to follow. Nations are becoming more and more alike. Cultural differences are still important but they are far less pronounced than ever before. Imagine what it was like when Admiral Cheng Ho first reached Madagascar or when Albuquerque occupied Malacca or, only in the last century, when the Europeans knocked on the doors of Japan and Korea. Today, you can fly to Nairobi or Santiago or Xi'an, and, with relatively little effort, fit in to local conditions. Today, any foreigner will feel at home in Singapore, in Orchard Road, because we are an open society and we are a hub of a transportation, information and communication network that makes this world more and more, one global village. It may be our destiny to help bring about such a happy outcome.

# A Flexible Civil Service

*Leadership must also be moral. That is the second condition for a successful civil service.*

## The Civil Service as an Institution

To many people, a flexible civil service is a contradiction of ideas. The word "bureaucracy" in the dictionary has two meanings: the first, a clinical one, describing a body of nonelective government officials; the second, a pejorative one, characterising an administration marked by rigidity and narrow adherence to rules. At Harvard's Commencement Ceremony, business school graduates wave dollar bills while public administration graduates scatter rolls of red tape.

The self-mocking humour of these public administration graduates has a basis in reality. The civil service makes rules and polices them. Civil servants can never operate with the flexibility and licence enjoyed by those in the private sector.

In many societies, it is the civil service which provides institutional stability. Anyone who flies into India will be impressed or frustrated — depending on your frame of mind — by the care and thoroughness with which Indian immigration officers check your travel documents. Every form is carefully inspected, gone over with green or red ink, then stamped and double-stamped. Rush the officer at your peril because he takes his job very seriously.

---

Opening address delivered at MSD (Management Services Department) Seminar on "Business Management Practices for a Better Public Service", Singapore, 2 December 1988.

These are minor expressions of a vast, proud administration — the Indian Civil Service. We may complain about the bureaucratism but without the two great institutions left behind by the British Raj, the Indian Civil Service and the Indian Army, the sub-continent would have come apart a long time ago. Interestingly, till today, you cannot become an officer in the Indian Administrative Service or the Indian Army without first learning to ride a horse. The Congress Party was a great institution too when it fought the Raj but is now fragmented because of the divisive politics of India. In many countries where the civil service is weak, it is normally the Army which moves in as the most organised force, with politically disastrous consequences.

The continuity of Chinese civilisation would also not have been possible without the mandarinate. The first Emperor, Qin Shi Huang, succeeded in conquering an empire over two thousand years ago but the Qin Dynasty could not hold it together. It fell to the first Han emperor, Liu Bang, to create a civil service founded on the Classics and the Imperial Examination System. Successive dynasties were able to reconstitute the empire because that civil service supplied able administrators and moral legitimacy for the governance of a large number of people over a vast geographical area.

This continuity in Chinese civilisation was an amazing feat in human history. A comparable achievement in Europe would have been as if the Roman Empire re-gathered itself again and again from the Atlantic to the Urals. Rome succeeded in developing a professional civil service only in the third century AD — the members of the Equestrian Order drawn from the commercial class — by which time it was too late. The principal beneficiary of professional civil service development in the Roman Empire was, in the end, not the empire itself which declined and fell but the Roman Catholic Church. Indeed, the continuity of the Church matches that of Chinese civilisation, one sustained by a civil service of priests, the other by a civil service of mandarins.

## Conditions for a Successful Civil Service

The role of the civil service in Singapore is, fundamentally, no different. It is to provide stability and continuity. The test is how long we succeed in keeping Singapore free, independent and prosperous.

Three conditions must be met. First, the civil service must bring in the best and the brightest. The civil service is *de facto* the corporate staff of Singapore Inc, and you should not be running the country if you are second-rate. I am not saying that all of the best and the brightest must be inducted. Neither am I suggesting that all who join must submit to perpetual vows. The point is that those who eventually make it into the higher civil service must be from among the most able in Singapore. Only then can there be a claim to national leadership.

That leadership is not only intellectual; it must also be moral. That is the second condition for a successful civil service. The moral basis of the civil service of the Roman Church is the Christian Bible. The moral basis of the Chinese mandarinate was and may well again be Confucianism. In Singapore, the moral basis of the civil service is gradually taking shape. Some aspects are clear, like intolerance of corruption and commitment to national independence, but others are not. Our national values, when they are settled, must eventually be reflected in the way the civil service carries itself.

### The Need for Flexibility

I discuss the nature of the civil service and its role in society in order to establish the context for our seminar today. The seminar topic is "Business Management Practices for a Better Public Service". The objective is greater flexibility.

We need greater flexibility because technology has made this a volatile world in the economic and commercial sense. To prosper, even to survive, Singapore and Singaporeans must constantly adapt and adjust to changes in the external environment, an external environment over which we have no control. Leisurely response is simply not on. For most products, you measure your competitive advantage in short years. For some products in the computer field and in fashion, you measure your advantage in months. Others are always catching up and you have to move on. The effect of the revolution in information technology is relentless. Labour may not be completely mobile. But capital and information are. The result is a high premium placed on speed of response and the ability to combine the efforts of large numbers of human beings in a common, concerted effort.

A lethargic civil service will hold back everyone and everything. Yet flexibility sometimes goes against the grain of the civil service because of the traditional emphasis on stability and continuity. The problem is one of balance. Today's seminar will help us achieve a balance that is more in keeping with the times. What need not be a part of the public sector should not be. That is the reason for divestment and privatisation. What parts can be run like private corporations should be. That is the reason for re-structuring the hospitals and introducing management accounting and transfer pricing. Personnel management practice in the public sector must be responsive to changing conditions and market forces.

## Conclusion

A flexible civil service need not be a self-contradiction. That is the challenge before us. If the service is slow to change, it will be depleted of talent, public policies will bear little resemblance to reality and all will be lost. If the service is too much like the private sector, it will lose its essential institutional character and Singapore with it also. We want the best of both worlds. We can have the best of both worlds if we continue to succeed in recruiting able men and women of character into the ranks of a professional and self-confident civil service. Like the priests of the Roman Church and the mandarins of Imperial China we have a mission before us and it is worthy of us all.

# NATIONAL IDENTITIES IN A CHANGING WORLD

*We cannot change the world but the more we understand global trends the more will we be able to change ourselves to benefit from those trends.*

## 1. Introduction

### *The Tides of Change*

The Chinese historical novel *Romance of the Three Kingdoms* began with these famous lines:

> *Tian xia da shi* (天下大势)
> *Fen jiu bi he* (分久必合)
> *He jiu bi fen* (合久必分)
> (Empires wax and wane. Long disunity leads to unity; long unity leads to disunity.)

After 400 years of unity, the Han empire in the 3rd century was disintegrating into three kingdoms. The Chinese world was in utter disarray. There was nothing mortal men could do to prevent the decline. We had to wait till the 6th century before China was once again re-unified under the Sui and Tang dynasties.

There is a tide in the lives of nations which ebbs and flows. The political map is never static. Historical atlases illustrate this graphically in coloured maps and arrows.

Because the lifespans of human beings are much shorter than the lifespans of nations, it is easy to forget that there is always an

---

Speech given at the Pre-University Seminar, National University of Singapore on 19 June 1989, shortly after the Tiananmen Incident in China.

underlying historical process at work, constantly changing the political correlation of forces. For those who live in big countries, it may not matter very much to the historical outcome whether or not individuals are conscious of national trends. Except under very special circumstances, there is often not very much an individual could do to change these trends anyway.

In the period of the Three Kingdoms, the great strategist Zhuge Liang was at first reluctant to get involved in the civil war because he knew the situation was hopeless. But the Han Prince Liu Bei importuned him. Brilliant as he was, and tried as he did, Zhuge Liang was unable to save the empire. Look at the US today; look at the Soviet Union; look at China. They have able men in abundance, many who know what is wrong and what ought to be done. Yet there is little they can do as individuals to affect the general flow of development. Big countries are like supertankers. They cannot change direction quickly.

But small countries like small boats can. And that is both our strength and our weakness.

### *Small Nations*

The advantage of living in a small country is that, as individuals, we are much better able to influence our national destiny. We can do very little to change the courses of the big powers but we can align our course in relation to theirs so that we are not in collision with them and our passage is smooth.

We cannot change the world but the more we understand global trends the more will we be able to change ourselves to benefit from those trends.

Unfortunately, this is easier said than done. The Nepalis describe their country as a soft yam, a soft yam wedged between the two large boulders of India and China. It is not a comfortable place, and there is hardly anything they can do to shift position.

Our position is not as precarious. I wish to make two points today on how we can improve our position. First, the necessity to constantly look out at the world around us — when big boulders are rolling and knocking into one another we must be very alert to avoid being crushed or damaged. Second, understanding the global trends at work — what we must do to maximise our chances of success in a changing world environment. We must not be a helpless yam. I therefore prefer the metaphor of a small, high-powered speedboat to that of a sad potato.

## 2. The World Around Us

### *A Different World*

First: the world around us. These are exciting times. Never before in human history has there been such a widespread sentiment that we are one interconnected world, whatever the national flag we fly.

Hiroshima and Nagasaki have brought home the realisation that a Third World War will be the last for all of civilised mankind. The fear of a nuclear holocaust has put limits to the national ambitions of big powers. To push national ambitions unilaterally beyond such limits must lead to national self-destruction. In a paradoxical way, it is the atomic bomb which has given to Europe a period of peace which the continent had never experienced before in its history. In other parts of the world, the same nuclear threat has kept conflicts within regional bounds.

We cannot put the nuclear genie back into the bottle, which is just as well. It civilises us even as it haunts us.

The threat of environmental disaster is another factor drawing the nations of the world closer together. Environmental issues were the concern of fringe groups in the past. But no longer. Gorbachev raised the subject in the UN General Assembly last year. Thatcher voiced her concern recently. And Bush is also weighing in. It is not a joke. Chernobyl, the warming of the earth because of greenhouse gases in the atmosphere, holes in the ozone layer which let in harmful ultra-violet radiation, the mass destruction of tropical rain forests in the Amazon and elsewhere which will deprive the world of a huge reservoir of biological raw material — all this is now common knowledge. Disaster will befall all of mankind if nations do not act in concert to preserve the fragile environment in which we live. It is not as urgent a threat as that of nuclear warfare, but it is no less dangerous and certainly more insidious. The "greens" are right to remind us that we live in the same ark, like the ark of Noah in the Old Testament.

The instinct of nations is to be selfish. Nations have no permanent relations, only permanent interests. Be that as it may, in environmental matters, the interests of nations are inexorably coinciding. If an asteroid were streaking towards the planet Earth on a collision course, it must be in the interest of all nations to work together.

In the economic field, the nations of the world are already working together. The interdependence of markets was painfully obvious in October 1987 when stockmarkets around the world took a nosedive. No national economy is closed. No national economy can afford to be closed. Governments which ignore market forces will be defeated by the market.

This is the age of easy travel and instant communication. At the touch of a button, you can transfer any amount of money from one country to another, or take a position in the Singapore International Monetary Exchange (SIMEX) and close it in the Chicago Mercantile Exchange. The value of a product is increasingly in the information needed to produce it, not in the raw material from which it is made. Because capital and knowledge are mobile, the pressure is on governments to accommodate markets, and not the other way around.

For this reason, the Four Modernisations in China and *perestroika* in the Soviet Union are matters of necessity, not choice. In a less dramatic way, India and Indonesia are also de-regulating and opening up their economies. Even very closed societies like Burma and Albania are irresistibly drawn to the same conclusion.

These three factors — the nuclear threat, the environmental threat and the interdependence of national economies — usher in a new phase in the history of mankind. Looked at from a different angle, human beings are being forced to live together by the revolution in science and technology.

What is the result of all this? We cannot know for sure but some trends are discernible.

### *From Military to Economic Competition*

Some amount of cultural convergence is inevitable. The Americans, the Europeans, the Soviets, the Chinese, the Japanese, will become more, not less alike. Underlying the world's revulsion at the brutal crackdown in Tiananmen is a growing consciousness that we belong to a common humanity. Compared to a hundred, fifty, even ten years ago, the capital cities of the world have become more similar.

But the competition among nations will continue. It is in the nature of man to compete. Large-scale conventional warfare may no longer be possible, but regional conflicts will not cease. Competition will increasingly shift from the military to the economic arena. Multinational corporations will become even more important in this new era of global business competition. Much of international politics is already preoccupied with problems of trade and finance.

### *World Organisations*

International organisations will play a bigger role. In New York last year, Soviet General Secretary Gorbachev told UN Secretary General Perez de Cuellar that "history is on your side". From a Marxist, that is quite a compliment. The inescapable fact is that although nations will continue to compete, that competition must take place within a framework that does not lead to nuclear war, environmental disaster or global financial collapse.

Whether there will ever be a single world government to hold the ring no one can say. There will certainly not be one for many years to come. Nations guard jealously their sovereign rights and surrender them only when they have to. But by a gradual process, international organisations evolve to tackle specific problems. The Single European Market in 1992 which removes national barriers to trade is one such example. Even within that framework of a single market, there will be differences of national views over the speed and degree of integration. France and West Germany are in favour of monetary union. Britain is not. Whatever the problems, the Single European Market is a historic achievement. Not since Rome has Western and Southern Europe been so united politically and economically. These changes will have a profound impact on the future of Eastern Europe as the Russian empire loosens its grip.

### *The Decline of Russia and the Rise of East Asia*

The restructuring of the Russian Empire and the rise of East Asia dominate events in the world today.

The expansionism of imperial Russia in the 19th century was only briefly interrupted by the First World War and the Bolshevik Revolution. It continued past the Second World War and had possibly its last hurrah in Afghanistan. The last of the old-style empires is now so out of sync with the demands of a modern economy, it must reform or perish. Communism was supposed to unleash the productive forces of the peoples of the Soviet Union. It led instead to the opposite. Karl Marx would have approved of *glasnost* and *perestroika*. The transformation will, however, not be smooth. A second revolution is necessary and success is uncertain. In this traumatic period, the Soviet Union, as it twists and turns in its efforts to modernise, can remain very dangerous and the free world will be mad to lower its guard.

Coupled to the restructuring of the Soviet Union is the rise of East Asia, which is already shifting the world's centre of gravity to the Pacific. The phenomenal progress of Japan and the newly industrialised economies is well documented. But it is developments in China which will have the most important long-term consequences for East, Northeast and Southeast Asia. The drama unfolding on a continental scale in China may well herald an epoch of dynastic resurgence. Despite the enormous difficulties of economic and political adjustment, a major transformation is underway. Everytime the dynasty was strong in China, its influence reached out into Central, Northeast and Southeast Asia, whether it was China under Qin, Han, Sui, Tang, Sung, Yuan, Ming or Qing. Such is the cycle of Chinese history. In applying to host the Olympics in the year 2000, a resurgent China is re-asserting its role on the world stage. Although the recent tragedy at Tiananmen has set China back many years, the process of modernisation is ultimately irreversible. In studying China, one must always take a long view.

In 1991, for the first time, a railway line will connect Alma Ata in Soviet Kazakhstan to Urumqi in Chinese Xinjiang, financed by the Soviet Union and made possible by the general relaxation of tension between the two countries. The old silk route linking Europe to East

Asia will then be re-opened, and with it, symbolically, a new chapter in world history.

Southeast Asia will be greatly affected by all these developments. The war in Cambodia, which became Vietnam's Vietnam, will end sooner or later. For Vietnam, having been taught that aggression does not pay, the main reason for ASEAN unity will no longer apply. This presents a new challenge to the six member-states. A new basis must be found for continued friendship and cooperation. The alternative is a divided Southeast Asia and renewed big power interference in our affairs.

## 3. Maximising Our Chances

### *Challenge and Response*

My purpose in discussing at some length the breathtaking changes in the world around us is to set the backdrop for the next part of my talk to you today, which is how we should maximise our chances for survival and prosperity in the next century. You are now about 16–17 years old, and likely to live another 60 years, which takes us to the year 2050. That is a good target to work to. There is no certainty at all there will still be a Republic of Singapore in the year 2050. Singapore island as a geographical fact, there will always be; but a politically independent Singapore, a home for all of us and for our children and grandchildren — that we cannot take for granted.

Being a small country, we must be very alert to the changes taking place in the environment in which we exist. Supertankers and medium-size ships are turning and switching lanes. We ignore them at our peril. There are political dangers if the Americans leave a power vacuum and ASEAN fragments. There are economic dangers if political antagonisms lead to disruptions in trade flows. Our trade is three times our GNP. Our economic vulnerability is therefore extreme.

To prosper, indeed just to survive, we must respond quickly to threats and opportunities. Not only do we have to run a tight ship, we need good radars, powerful engines and plentiful reserves of fuel and other supplies. Above all we must be a good crew.

### *Size and Diversity*

We cannot decide our national identity autonomously. To begin with, we are to a large extent the prisoners of our history and our institutional inheritance. That is the starting point. Then we must determine what are the qualities we need to survive in a changing world. I explained in some detail the sea changes taking place in the world and in Southeast Asia because we do not exist in a vacuum. We survive because we possess certain competitive advantages. Why, despite our size and our heterogeneous make-up, are we successful?

Being small can be an advantage because we are able to react and adjust more quickly. For example, we do not have traditional, rural constituencies to worry about. The cities subsidise the countryside in most countries. We do not, because we have no countryside. SIA and Telecoms enjoy a head-start because they do not have to operate unprofitable connections. Because we are small, communication is easy. The operational capability of the Singapore Armed Forces (SAF) is founded on our ability to contact reservists in a flash and get them back to camp in a hurry. So being compact has its advantages.

Our heterogenous make-up can also be a plus. Yes, problems of race, language, culture and religion preoccupy us. Wrongly managed, such diversity becomes explosive. Properly managed, they reinforce the network of trading links which makes us a great city-state.

Multiracialism enhances our national strength. Those of you who study material science will understand how dissimilar atoms in the crystal lattice improve the overall performance of the crystal. It is the same with our society. Indeed, in addition to Chinese, Malays, Indians and Eurasians, we accommodate at any time a large expatriate population of Americans, Japanese and Europeans. We are comfortable with diversity because our unity is based on diversity. We are fundamentally a trading nation. It has always been so from the time of Raffles, and it will always be so. We are an international switchboard, not just for goods and people, but also for money and information. Hence we are a port, an airport, a financial centre and a communications centre. Even in manufacturing, our strength is in swing production, in our quickness to exploit transient opportunities. We succeed because we are open and cosmopolitan. It is therefore our multi-racial character that has enabled us to become a centre of commerce in Asia.

We did not choose to be small and diverse. We inherited those characteristics from British rule, and we have turned them to advantage. The more integrated the world economy becomes, the more global the division of labour, the more trade will grow, the better we can be. We are well poised to capitalise on the changes taking place around us because we are compact, open and swift in our response. The trends on the whole favour us. Whether it is China, India or Burma opening up, we are ready.

But success is never pre-ordained. We are what we are only because our forefathers have dared to overcome all kinds of difficulties. We will be able to take our place in the world only if we in turn are prepared to struggle together to secure our future.

### *Three Contradictions*

You will be discussing the subject of "Shared Values for all Singaporeans" over the next few days. It is a very important subject. The strength of a nation is in its people, in the efforts of individuals and in the way their separate efforts are combined, in the kind of crew we are. National characteristics are very hard to change, but because we are a small nation, we have a measure of control over the values which bind our society together. This is the advantage a small boat has over a supertanker. The question is what kind of a society we want to be in this brave, new world. There are three contradictions in our society we must reconcile — three contradictions I offer for your consideration.

The first contradiction is that between being cosmopolitan and being nationalistic. Our outlook must always be cosmopolitan. We will be irrelevant if we are narrow and small-minded. After all, trade is our life and with better communication and easier travel, we will become even more internationalised. The number of foreigners coming to Singapore increases every year. Look how multi-national Orchard Road and the CBD have become. The more we succeed, the more open we will become. The more open we are, the more we will prosper.

But internationalisation has its risks because we are still a young nation and our sense of being a nation is not strong. It is because we do not have a strong national identity that we need this seminar on shared values. Our forefathers came here to make a living; they never imagined that the city would become a nation. But it did, maybe by a fluke of history, and we must make it work. Without a sense of nationhood, the SAF is nothing even if we can afford the most advanced weapons. The SAF is no more than a militia of free citizens who believe that this nation is worth defending. It took many years to establish National Service in Singapore. There is another reason why we must develop a strong nationalism. If the lines of trade which brought our forefathers to Singapore also lead our children to leave Singapore, all will be lost. No nation can endure, deprived of its best talent. We must create a deep sense of home in Singapore so that when Singaporeans travel abroad to work, study, or play, their instinct is to return.

We must balance this contradiction between being cosmopolitan and being nationalistic. We cannot be a trading nation if we are not cosmopolitan. We cannot be a nation if we are not nationalistic. We must be both at the same time.

The second contradiction is that between being democratic and being centralised. Democracy is not a matter of choice but of necessity. I am not just talking about one-person-one-vote which is only one aspect of democracy. I am referring to a value system which recognises the good in every individual. The whole society benefits when the full potential of every individual is realised. We live in an information-intensive age. Modern civilisation is not possible without the free, cooperative effort of a large number of thinking individuals.

We should however be careful not to be simplistic in our understanding of democracy. In Britain, democracy took centuries to evolve, and universal franchise or one-person-one-vote was only introduced in 1928. In Japan, women were given the vote only after the Second World War, in Switzerland only in 1971. The general principle was to give the vote progressively to those who had an interest in making the system work, namely, the propertied classes.

One-person-one-vote is stable only when there is a large middle class all sharing a common interest in the survival of the state. The democratisation process taking place in Taiwan and South Korea reflects the aspiration of growing middle classes, in effect, a demand for an extension of democratic participation from the few to the many. In many countries without middle classes, communist parties took over, styling themselves people's democracies. The theory was that power had to be wrested from the bourgeois classes and held in trust by the party for the proletariat. The result was instead the bureaucratisation of the party and stagnation in the economy.

Democracy in Singapore will grow deeper roots as we become a more middle-class society. The democratic institutions we build up must however strengthen, not weaken, us nationally. The fact is we are small and we must be internally flexible. We are price takers in the world market. We adjust to the world, not the other way around. Our institutions cannot be too rigid. A strong sense of collective survival must undergird our institutions. Group interests must never be forgotten. For example, Parliament has vested in our Government great powers to compulsorily acquire land, powers which ride roughshod over individual property rights. In the early days, it was a system of rough justice. But without such powers, Singapore would not have been able to develop the infrastructure needed for trade and economic development. Municipal issues are important and must be debated, but they should never crowd out larger national considerations. In other words, democracy in Singapore must always be practised within a framework of centralised decision-making.

Here again, the choice is not between being democratic and being centralised. We must be both. We need democracy to achieve political consensus. And, as a small country, we need centralised decision-making to survive in an uncertain world environment. We can be both if our instincts are communitarian. Either we hang together or we hang separately. For this reason, we need traditional Asian values to balance the individualising effects of the free market.

The third contradiction is that between being efficient and being humane. Our national finances are healthy because government policies are based on sound, economic principles. The Government's approach to problems is practical and utilitarian. The test of policy is: Does it work? Does it produce the desired effect? Few deny that we have a government that is effective and efficient.

Efficiency often means competition in a free market. By harnessing the desire of every person to better himself, Adam Smith's market economy creates the most wealth for society as a whole. But in any competition, there are winners and losers. The losers are also our citizens. For the system as a whole to survive, the losers must be looked after, and their dignity preserved. Efficiency and competition must therefore be tempered by compassion and humanity.

Unfortunately, there is a sense that the Government is more concerned with ends than with means, that we are not immoral but we are amoral, that we have become a society without a soul. This is a fair concern especially among younger Singaporeans. The solution does not lie in comprehensive state welfare. That way leads to calamity, as we see all too well in other countries. The better solution is private initiatives by individuals and groups of individuals to help those who are less well-off. The Government should also help, but the principal effort should be non-government. Let the Government concentrate on being efficient but let us, as members of the community, be compassionate in the way we treat our fellow human beings. We should build upon the philanthropic tradition of our local business and religious communities in health, education and welfare. The activities of the Community Chest and other such organisations deserve our full support. Even in school, our desire to do well in examinations should not make us selfish and unfeeling. It is in our nature to be competitive. But it is also in our nature to be cooperative and altruistic.

Thus there is a balance to be struck between being generous and exhausting the source of that generosity. To be completely ungenerous will demean us as a people and undermine the moral basis of our society. To be overly generous will lead us to economic collapse and therefore the loss of the very means which enable us to be generous in the first place.

***Excellence***

These are three contradictions we must reconcile: to be cosmopolitan and nationalistic at the same time, to be democratic and centralised at the same time, and to be efficient and humane at the same time. How do we harmonise these three contradictions? It is not easy, yet it must be done if we are to be a great people. Formula One engines are not easy to maintain. They have to be fine-tuned all the time. Our speedboat is the same. I don't think we can remain free and independent if we lose our determination to reconcile the contradictions in our society.

I am always heartened by the example of the Swiss people. For Germans, French and Italians to be so united, for Catholics and Protestants to co-exist so harmoniously, now seems so natural. It was not salubrious Alpine air or clanging cow bells which brought about such amity, but centuries of strife and warfare. They decided, in their mountain fastness, that they will be different from the other contending Europeans. The Swiss Confederation which began in 1291 is a marvel of unity in diversity; of a people doggedly nationalistic and neutral, yet internationalist in their outlook; of a nation so democratic that major issues are settled by public referenda; a practical yet humane people who even as they refuse to join the UN are always represented in humanitarian organisations. In recent years, the countries around Switzerland are at peace but still the Swiss take no chances. They take defence most seriously and new tunnels are dug every year into their mountain redoubt.

Like the Swiss people, it may be our destiny to be forever insecure, and for that insecurity to drive us obsessively to excel. On a modest scale, we too show others the way to the future. We are multi-racial in a way which most nations are not. We are internationalist and that is the way the world is moving. We combine the best of East and West even as the East and the West are struggling to understand and learn from each other.

## 4. Conclusion

We live in stirring times. All around the world, there is a broad current of political change. Where it will all lead to we cannot be sure. But no country is unaffected. Not even the mighty Chinese Communist Party can hold back very long the tidal flow. Great challenges lie before us, both dangers and opportunities. Our Darwinian duty is to survive and prosper as an independent nation, to the year 2050, at least when most of you will still be around. The values we share must be the values which enable us to survive and prosper in this new age. You are a privileged group in our society. God has endowed you with intellectual and other gifts. The State and your parents provide you the wherewithal to succeed. You too have a duty to excel, a duty to contribute.

# EXCELLENCE

*Excellence is not a natural state ...*

Below the water's surface on which the swan glides with such apparent effortlessness, webbed feet paddle furiously. That which seems graceful and elegant is often the result of practice and hard work. Excellence is not a natural state: it comes from effort, arduous effort. In historian Arnold Toynbee's survey of human civilisations, the "arduousness of excellence" is a recurring theme. In the Mayan ruins of Central America, in the manner in which the jungle so completely reclaimed those ancient cities, we witness what effort was made to maintain the excellence of civilisation. Without that effort, the land quickly reverted to its natural state — the jungle.

Excellence is a continuing struggle. Its essence is not in the physical objects, like buildings and gardens, but in the spirit of that struggle. A city can be destroyed but, as long as the culture is intact, it can be rebuilt, sometimes with greater splendour. Germany and Japan, physically devastated during the Second World War, were rebuilt phoenix-like in less than a generation. Wherever Germans and Japanese are found, they display efficiency and excellence, the sources of which run deep in their culture and history.

---

This essay was written for a book *Singapore: island, city, state* published in 1990 to mark the 25th anniversary of Singapore's independence. The author remembers with gratitude the care with which S.R. Nathan, at that time Singapore High Commissioner in Kuala Lumpur, later President of Singapore, went through the draft.

Excellence for Singapore requires a similar examination of national spirit. The island became a city, the city became a state, and the state endures only as long as it continues to excel. Can it? To answer the question, we must turn to the culture and history of its people.

By an accident of imperial rivalry between the British and the Dutch, the island became a city. The island is one of many in the Johor-Riau archipelago which the British East India Company could have chosen. But Raffles decided on Singapore and made it the centre of British trade between India and China. Although the Dutch opposed this encroachment in their East Indies at first, they soon settled with the British in the Treaty of 1824 a division of Southeast Asia between themselves, with Singapore on the British side.

The city would have been stillborn had Singapore ended up on the other side of the line. Dutch interests were concentrated in Java. When the Dutch wrested Malacca from the Portuguese in 1641, they squeezed that city to feed Batavia (Jakarta) which was their trading centre. Although the Dutch held Malacca longer than the Portuguese, they left behind much less. Portuguese Malacca (1511–1641) is well remembered — not Dutch Malacca (1641–1824), for such was the policy of deliberate neglect. Singapore would have suffered a similar fate in Dutch hands.

In British hands, the city grew and became the headquarters of Empire in the Far East. From the days of Raffles it was multi-racial, but with an increasing Chinese population. Qing China was in decline, and revolution and famine were widespread in the Chinese heartland. In contrast, economic opportunities were abundant in the Nanyang where the European powers kept law and order. So by the boatloads the Chinese poured in from southern China, and Singapore became a major destination in Southeast Asia.

There was no serious racial problem in the colonial period when the European empires held sway. The problem came to the fore only after the end of the Second World War, in the nationalist phase of Southeast Asian history. The problem in British Malaya, including Singapore, was particularly acute because no one race was in the majority. There was, in addition to the clash of cultures, a clash of nationalisms.

Against Chinese nationalism in Malaya, which was tied to the Kuomintang (KMT) and the Chinese Communist Party (CCP), and Indian, which was tied to the Indian Independence struggle, Malay nationalism insisted on the Malays remaining dominant in Malaya. In 1957, when Malaya became independent, Singapore was not included in the Federation partly because the British still needed the crown colony as a military base and partly because Malaya and Singapore together had more non-Malays. That would have held back Malayan independence.

But the logic of federation was compelling, and the absurdity of an independent Singapore obvious. By also drawing in the Bornean territories, the indigenous races in Malaysia became dominant within a larger Malaysia. That ought to have done the trick. Alas, it did not. The strain of accommodating competing racial demands became intolerable. Singapore, which Tunku Abdul Rahman had wanted to make the New York of Malaysia, was forced to go it alone. Thus, while it was an accident of Empire that made the island a city, it was the legacy of that Empire that made the city a nation-state.

The psyche of Singapore was deeply affected by the trauma of that unwanted independence. A profound sense of insecurity took over. It was not just the insecurity of being small. It was also the insecurity of being largely Chinese in a largely non-Chinese Southeast Asia.

Singapore's struggle to survive and prosper has always been linked to the drama of the Nanyang Chinese. From Song times, the Chinese had migrated into Southeast Asia. It was, however, only in European times that the large-scale migration of Chinese into Southeast Asia took place. As shopkeepers, traders, labourers, miners, craftsmen and financiers, they were vital for the health of the colonial economy. In 1947, there were an estimated 9 million Chinese in Southeast Asia and in 1960 some 12 million. There are probably 20 million today.

Because the Nanyang Chinese commanded an economic position out of proportion to their numbers, they were often resented by the indigenous people, especially in the post-colonial nationalist period. In his pamphlet "The Jews of the East," Thai King Rama VI wrote: "No matter where they live, what nationality they assume, Chinese remain essentially Chinese. But theirs is race loyalty, not love of country and, for the sake of convenience, they will register themselves as nationals of foreign countries, even when they are living in China itself. But such registration does not mean that they cease to act like Chinese. They will be loyal to their adopted country only as long as it suits their interests. What makes them undesirable is their racial consciousness; they regard their residence in the country as temporary and are unwilling to become its citizens. The purpose of every Chinese immigrant is to amass as much money as possible and then to depart — the fact that not all of them manage to do this does not alter their common motive." Justified or not, this was the common perception in the region.

In every Southeast Asian country, at one time or another, there has been this so-called "Chinese problem". The PAP's campaign for a "Malaysian Malaysia" was seen as another attempt by the Nanyang Chinese to gain acceptance and by the indigenous people to refuse it, when it was in reality a clash of political philosophy. Nationalist Malay opposition was predictably strong. Economic power was already in non-Malay hands. If political power was also conceded, the Malays feared they might be forever reduced to a subject people in their own land.

When Singapore became independent, the tables were suddenly turned. The Chinese became the majority in Singapore. Many expected the new organising principle to be Chinese racial domination, but that did not happen, because it would have led Singapore, externally, into collision with its neighbours and, internally, into racial strife. The solution lay instead in transcending the destructive politics of race by the establishment of a political system founded on multi-racial principles and equal opportunity, which was in fact the PAP's political philosophy since its founding in 1954.

It is said that the Singapore flag is a combination of the Indonesian and Malayan flags, whatever may be the official explanation for the red and white, the crescent and the five stars. The geographical fact of being lodged deep in the Malay world cannot be changed, and must therefore be accommodated. Although Chineseness as an inherited civilisation can never be forgotten, as Rama VI observed, Chinese chauvinism as the basis of state policy would have immediately brought Singapore into conflict with Indonesia and Malaysia. The consequence would have been economic disaster, at the very least. Perhaps the story of the flag is true.

A cornerstone of the state's foreign policy, which was never to be a "third China" or a Nanyang Chinese outpost of the KMT or CCP, was thus laid from the beginning. To reinforce the point, Singapore declared very early that it would establish diplomatic relations with the People's Republic of China only after Malaysia and Indonesia had done so.

Domestically, the commitment to multi-racialism assumed religious proportions. From 1959, the national language was Malay but the languages of all four main racial groups were made official with English to continue as the language of administration. Theology is here of greater importance than efficiency. Every public ceremony must include elements of all four main cultures. The form became inseparable from the substance. It was and remains a necessary obsession, and a clue to the complex which drives the people on. The situation has improved and will continue to improve, but there will never be an end to the domestic debate of what multi-racialism is or should be. Every aspect of civic life is affected, from education to religion to national security.

This multi-racial ideal is the product of an attempt to reconcile deep-seated racial tensions which will not go away. Like the oyster which cannot get rid of the grit in its side, this attempt has, however, produced several valuable pearls. Bilingualism is one. The ancestral pull, which is essentially one of sentiment, is at least as strong as the national pull. Both are accommodated through the use of the mother tongue and the English language. The Group Representation Constituency (GRC) is another. Voting along racial lines remains a natural tendency in parliamentary elections and politically easy to exploit in an open society. In a one-man-one-vote democracy, the temptation would be for all parties to field Chinese candidates. The result must eventually be disastrous. By forcing all political parties which aspire to govern to field a minimum number of candidates from the minority races, the GRC helps protect the delicate multi-racial balance. But the problem is never solved. New antagonisms will surface, and fresh solutions will always have to be found.

In its determination to preserve the multi-racial character of Singapore, the nation takes on a cosmopolitan personality which is wonderfully suited to its economic livelihood, that of international trade. An easy acceptance of foreigners characterises the people. The economic success of Singapore is partly to be explained by the fact that it is a favourite city of Americans. Europeans and Japanese. The multi-racial obsession is thus an essential element in the nation's drive to excel.

The other obsession is that of smallness. By becoming a nation, the city was cut off from its historical hinterland. Even worse than Vienna after the First World War, Singapore became a capital city without an empire, without even a countryside.

The island may be sufficient for a city but it lacks space for a country. One of the first acts of nationhood was the creation of the Singapore Armed Forces (SAF). But where was the space to train? So from its conception, the SAF looked overseas for training facilities. Enormous logistical difficulties had to be overcome to establish a network of training bases in a number of countries. The SAF transcended the problem of size through globalisation — a theme repeated again and again in the story of independent Singapore.

There was, for example, no protected domestic routes for Singapore Airlines (SIA) to ply when Malaysia-Singapore Airways divided into its two national components. Like the SAF, there was no alternative but to look outwards. Here again, necessity was the mother of invention. The spirit of SIA has its source in Singapore's smallness. Because the disadvantages are acute, the airline has always to innovate and excel.

This preoccupation with smallness has engendered a transcending spirit in the people. To overcome the absurdity of size, they have to look beyond their immediate confines, reach out to the world and make Singapore a global city. In a different age, such an amount of human energy bottled up in a city-state would have led its armies to fan out and conquer, or perish in the adventure. This is unthinkable today. And happily so. Instead, the battles are to be fought in the economic arena, in the international marketplace.

But the dynamism of a city can only be sustained if it receives a constant replenishment of talented and hungry people from the countryside. Singapore no longer enjoys this natural supply because fences separate the city from its traditional hinterland. No city can long remain vigorous if it is only able to tap its own resource of people for talent and enterprise. Wall Street is nothing if only native New Yorkers are available. Therefore, in order not to decline, Singapore must also look outwards for men and women of ability to join its ranks, if not as citizens, then at least as friends and fellow travellers.

This aspect of Singapore's globalisation has yet to be fully played out. Because the population problem is so fundamental, it will preoccupy Singaporeans for a long time to come. The nation's long-term survival is at stake. Again, a way to break out of the integument of size must be found.

In Hong Kong and 1997 there may be an opportunity. Singapore's population decline must be reversed, and in a way which does not disrupt the present multiracial mix. No other policy is politically tenable, nor indeed desirable, as the existing composition has served the nation well. To drain Singapore's neighbours of talented individuals is not the answer. Their economic development will be affected which cannot be to Singapore's own advantage. A beggar-thy-neighbour policy would be both unwise and unneighbourly.

Hong Kong is one potential source because many of its inhabitants will want to leave before and after 1997. It is of course not in Singapore's interest to undermine Hong Kong or China. Indeed, Singapore's continued success is inextricably linked to the prosperity of all Asia. But if people and money are leaving Hong Kong anyway, it is better that they flow to Southeast Asia than out of the region to North America and Australia.

In Singapore they can continue to contribute to the progress of the whole region. The time it takes to fly from Singapore to Hong Kong is, after all, only a few minutes longer than the flight from Hong Kong to Beijing. There is also no danger that Hong Kong will ever be depleted of people. It has an entire continent to draw upon. Both Hong Kong and China must therefore find Singapore a useful backstop to the outflow of talent and capital.

Because of this, Hong Kong and Singapore may well become twin cities in the next century of the Pacific, one serving the Chinese mainland, the other Southeast Asia. Whatever the assurances from Beijing, and however sincere these assurances may be, the management of investment risk calls for a certain diversification of Hong Kong capital outside Hong Kong. The growth areas of Southeast Asia are attractive. It is likely that the links between Hong Kong and the region will grow, especially in business and finance.

Thus, by a twist of history, the two cities may come to share much more in common in the future. There are precedents in the past. Before the Second World War, many businesses and families straddled Singapore and Guangzhou, Shantou or Xiamen. Singapore's link to South India is of a similar kind, a link which is bound to become more important as the Indian economy expands. And of course Singapore's economic and familial links to the cities and towns of Malaysia have never been severed despite political separation.

A trading city survives in a complex and changing world environment by continuously reconfiguring its network of international links. The competition is relentless and no advantage endures forever. Because the future is full of surprises, success for Singapore is never secure. It is precisely this insecurity which keeps Singaporeans alert to dangers and opportunities, which drives the people to create and excel. Twinning Hong Kong and Singapore is perhaps one such creative response to the challenges of a new age.

We live in historic times. Unable to revitalise its economy, the Soviet Union must restructure its foreign and domestic policies or perish and be consigned to the rubbish heap of history. We are at the end of the Cold War and at the beginning of a new era in world politics. The United States is also in relative decline. Whether it has enough domestic political resolve to reverse this decline, no one can be sure. It is still the world's largest economy and a nation richly endowed with natural resources and talented individuals. America may yet recover. But the manichean East-West division of the world after the Second World War is past, and in its place is a more complex, multi-polar community of nations.

Asia is on the ascent. Japan is followed by the Four Little Dragons and behind them are the countries of ASEAN, China and India. Traditional societies are at long last adjusting to the impact of modernisation from the West. Singapore is a part of this remarkable Asian phenomenon.

Europe is rediscovering itself. The Single European Market of 1992 and the loosening grip of the Soviet Union on Eastern Europe is giving to all Europeans a new sense of common destiny, one in which even the Russians are keen to partake. Not since the days of Rome have Europeans thought of themselves in such terms.

Indeed, all of humanity is caught up in a growing consciousness of one world. It started with the threat of a global nuclear holocaust which could end human civilisation. It has been fueled by fears of environmental disaster. National economies have become so interdependent, there is, in fact, a single world financial system. The cultures of the world are converging at a pace unknown in world history. Travel is easy and communication instant. And still the revolution in technology which made all this possible continues unabated. What will the future bring?

For Singapore, global trends are on the whole favourable. In an age where competition has shifted from the military sphere to the economic, and the meaning of nationhood has become less absolute, Singapore's diversity and smallness may not be such crippling disadvantages after all. Indeed, they are also sources of strength. The city-state has always been open to the world because there was no alternative. Now that the world itself is opening up in an unprecedented way, Singapore is well poised to benefit from these historic changes.

One of the paradoxes of Singapore is the cosmopolitan character of its nationalism. The city was cosmopolitan before it became a slate. And the city-state must become even more cosmopolitan if it is to prosper in the next decade and the next century. What then is the essence of its nationalism?

Even Singaporeans are hard put to provide an answer because the idea of Singapore is perhaps better defined by what it is not than by what it is. Its historical memory as a nation is only 25 years — short compared to the life of the city, and shorter still compared to the history of the civilisations to which the different races belong. There was nothing inevitable about the establishment of an independent republic. Indeed, the opposite was true. In 1961, Lee Kuan Yew said: "Everybody knows that merger is inevitable. The Tunku has said merger is inevitable. The PAP have also said that merger is inevitable. The Communists also admit that merger is inevitable. The inevitable is now happening. Some people can try to postpone the inevitable. But no one can stop it."

When Singapore separated in 1965, its nationhood began as a reaction against the bitterness of its experience in Malaysia. The arguments in favour of merger were still valid but there were now, borne of experience, more powerful arguments for a separate existence. Undaunted, the leaders soldiered on. They were an extraordinary group of determined men thrown up by the anti-colonial struggle. The people responded. Singaporean nationalism had to be cooked in a hurry without the fire of war or revolution. Although a certain artificiality characterised the forced nationalism of the first 25 years, it worked and a sense of nationhood has taken root. Singaporeans are proud to be Singaporeans, especially when they are overseas.

But the roots are not deep. Every year a disturbing number of Singaporeans emigrate to Canada, Australia and the United States. In a way, this is to be expected, given the wide use of the English language, the ease of travel, the speed of communications, the openness of the economy, and the opportunities available. Most Singaporeans who reach the higher echelons in the public and private sectors would have lived many months or years overseas either to study, work or play. The worry is that the more cosmopolitan Singapore becomes, the greater will be the number of Singaporeans who desire to leave. Singapore will not be able to maintain the same level of excellence if it loses too many of its citizens to other countries.

This tension between being nationalistic and being cosmopolitan cannot be wished away. It has to be gingerly managed. If the sense of being Singaporean is strong, fewer will renounce their citizenship and the Singaporean diaspora overseas will remain self-consciously Singaporean and a source of national strength. Everything must, therefore, be done to cultivate this sense of being Singaporean. It cannot be a narrow, dogmatic nationalism which will stifle initiative, inhibit trade and drive intelligent people away. It has to be broad-minded, practical, idealistic, attractive enough so that even others will want to join — and also distinctively Singaporean.

This is the major challenge in the next phase of Singapore's history. Ancient trading peoples, like the Jews and the Parsees, build their identify on race and religion. Singapore's ideal cannot be racial or religious. It has to be political, like that of the Venetians and the Swiss.

That political ideal manifests itself in the civic life of the Republic and its spirit. Civic life encompasses the way the citizens manage their own affairs, the democratic life of the people, their rituals and ceremonies, and their artistic pursuits. In all this Singapore has made great progress. The political institutions are maturing. Mass celebrations are becoming more common. Art and culture are beginning to flourish. And overseas, too, Singaporeans are organising themselves, and linking up with each other and with the home island.

The Singapore spirit is also more identifiable today. Already in international business the Singapore label has acquired a certain reputation for quality and efficiency. The nation is well known for its multiracialism, its comfort with foreigners and its orderliness. Traditional Asian values are leavened by Western science and democracy. Corruption is anathema. There is a practical approach to problems and a determination to succeed. Upon such values are the national institutions founded.

Singapore's physical beauty matches its civic life. Over the last three decades, the entire city has been virtually reconstructed, with a good deal of the past preserved. The architecture of the buildings, the open spaces, the waterfront, the equatorial lushness, the mix of East and West and old and new, all make it one of the most splendid cities in the world.

In the next phase of Singapore's history, the emphasis will shift from basic nation-building to the internationalisation of its political and economic structure. This shift is brought about by the need to transcend the limitation of size and made possible by the success of the last 25 years. Globalisation is not a matter of choice. It is the only way for the economy to continue growing and for the nation to continue thriving. The alternative is decline and stagnation. In so developing, Singapore becomes a dynamo drawing on and contributing to the economic growth of all Southeast Asia.

The idea of Singapore has always to be larger than the island itself. In a single world economy, the ambition is to become like a giant MNC with headquarters in Singapore and operations worldwide. Like IBM and Nestle, Singapore International welcomes whoever can make a contribution, whatever his race or religion, as long as he can fit into the corporate culture. But much more than an MNC, Singapore International represents an ideal of human organisation, of a free people who are both a city and a nation, of a cosmopolis in the world community of nations.

This, then, is the state at 25. The nation's achievements are only partially explained by the ancestral cultures of its people. The drive to excel can only be understood in relation to the twin obsessions of the people and their leaders — the first, that of maintaining unity in diversity; and the second, that of continually overcoming the constraint of size. These are iron necessities which, together with the cultural inheritance of the people, give to the Singapore spirit its distinctive inimitable character.

In an unfavourable environment, such a combination can come unstuck. But by good fortune, the signs are propitious. Military force as a method of competition is receding in importance. Increasingly, what matters is a people's ability to compete and cooperate in the global marketplace. In an age where capital, information and people are all mobile, Singapore's diversity and smallness make it uniquely well adapted to changing threats and opportunities.

The adaptation is not entirely fortuitous. Because the city had always lived on trade, its economy foreshadowed the global division of labour that modern technology is forcing on all nations. The trading instincts of Singapore are those which all nations must now have to survive and prosper. The cultures of the world are tending towards where Singapore already is. In that sense, Singapore has always been Singapore International. From an international city of Empire. Singapore has now become an international nation-city of the world. And one distinguished by its indomitable spirit of excellence.

# THE NEXT 25 YEARS

*It is in our nature to be both selfish and altruistic. A society succeeds when its culture harnesses in a balanced way this conflicting pull.*

**Luck, Leaders and Institutions**

Looking ahead to the next 25 years, the biggest concern of most Singaporeans, and the concern too of many foreigners, is how to replace PM Lee Kuan Yew and the other remarkable men in his generation. It is this problem I want to discuss with you today.

After 25 years of independence, our country is in good shape. There is every chance that we will make it to developed country status by the year 2000. The economy is doing well. Our finances are sound. Global trends are on the whole favourable to Singapore's continuing prosperity. ASEAN is booming. The prospects for regional economic cooperation have never been better.

We got here by a combination of good luck and good leadership. Without good luck, by which I refer to external factors not within our control, there would not have been the favourable conditions which made possible the rapid development of the last 25 years. Without good leaders, we would not have been able to capitalise on our good luck and turn independence in 1965 from disaster to opportunity.

The problem for us is how to continue the success for decades to come. We cannot always presume on good luck. Although the auspices look favourable for the next 5 to 10 years, we can never be sure. Beyond that, no one knows. As for good leaders, we can never be sure either because politics is full of surprises.

---

Speech given at the Pre-University Seminar, Kallang Theatre, 18 June 1990.

To really endure as a nation, what we need are good institutions. Good institutions last longer than individuals. Nations with good institutions survive bad luck and bad leaders. In the nature of things, bad luck does not last forever. As for bad leaders, good institutions will eventually throw them out. We need only to look at countries like the US, Great Britain and Japan for examples of bad leaders. Good institutions will also increase the chances of good leaders emerging.

In other words, what we should be looking for are not new Lee Kuan Yews but strong institutions. How then do we develop strong institutions? Many people say the Army runs on Standard Operating Procedures or SOPs, and the Civil Service on Instruction Manuals or IMs. If that were the case, we need only to get the right procedures or manuals and we will build great institutions. Unfortunately it is not so simple. Institutions are built not top-down but bottom-up. They are animated not by instructions but by instincts — human instincts.

**The Cultural DNA and Free Will**

Our instincts are in part biologically determined, like the love of a mother for her child. The social behaviour of ants, birds and many other animals is largely determined by their biological DNA. In the case of human beings, however, our instincts are determined not just by our biological DNA but also by our cultural DNA. It is the cultural DNA which sets us apart from the other social animals and which makes civilisation possible.

There are many similarities between the biological DNA and the cultural DNA. Both are subject to the Darwinian process of mutation, competition and selection. In the same way as the biological DNA creates the organs and physiological systems which make biological life possible, the cultural DNA creates the institutions and social systems which make social life possible. Like the biological DNA, the cultural DNA is slow to change.

The cultural DNA carries the historical memory of a community, its values and attitudes, its worldview of life and religion, and its knowledge of science and technology. It is transmitted through myths and rituals, in parables and holy books, from kindergartens to universities, and reinforced daily by institutional practice. If you take members of a community from one place and transport them to another place, they will recreate in that new place similar practices and institutions. In this way, the early Greeks colonised the shores of the Mediterranean, and the Polynesian seafarers the islands of the Pacific. When Malacca fell to the Portuguese in 1511, the refugees who scattered helped establish little Malaccas all over the Malay archipelago, all with remarkably similar social structures, with *sultans, bendaharas, laksamanas, shahbandars* and *temenggongs*.

Over time, the cultural DNA does mutate and diverge. The good mutations, like Ninja turtles, will succeed and propagate themselves. The bad ones will fail and become extinct. It took a long time for us to reach here. Homo sapiens appeared some millions of years ago, but civilised homo sapiens appeared only some 10,000 years ago. It took millions of years for the cultural DNA to evolve to a point which made possible the early civilisations.

While the responsibility to transmit the biological DNA falls principally on the younger members of a community, the responsibility to transmit the cultural DNA falls principally on the older members. Age is the repository of experience, and experience confers wisdom. A community that ignores the experience of its older members puts itself at a severe disadvantage. It is not therefore by chance that all the great philosophies and all the great religions teach us to revere those who are our senior.

It is important for us to understand the nature of the cultural DNA. If we want to build strong institutions, we must ask what instincts we must cultivate as individual members of a Singaporean community, what Tocqueville in his study *Democracy in America* called "habits of the heart". We must first know what we are, what we have inherited from our history. We cannot deny our past. Rousseau emphasised that we must take into account the history, character, habits, religion, economic base and education of a people. Only then can we discuss "the social contract". Only then can we exercise our free will. Engels argued that "freedom is the recognition of necessity". We are only as free as when we do not ignore our biological and cultural inheritance. Using the concept of calculus, each generation can only make a small change of $\Delta x$ to its cultural DNA, except in extreme revolutionary situations. To change *x* in a major way, we must wait many generations and integrate over many years.

## Selfishness and Altruism

At the most fundamental level, we are in our biological nature both selfish and altruistic. This duality exists in many species of animals. Self-sacrifice for the sake of the group is not at all uncommon in nature. For animals like ants, birds and apes, there is a competitive advantage in operating as a group. Individual members may perish, but the group survives, and it is the group as a whole rather than the individual which becomes responsible for passing on the genetic material. In such cases, Darwinian selection takes place at the level of the group; in other words, not the survival of the fittest individual, but the survival of the fittest group. Altruism can therefore be an advantage in natural selection.

As social animals, we cannot deny this altruism, this gregariousness in our biological make-up. Unlike ants or birds, our social behaviour is not wholly pre-determined by our biologicial DNA. The cultural DNA is also at work. And depending on the level of science and technology, some forms of group organisation and group behaviour are superior to others.

For example, when a society is heavily dependent on the careful regulation of water for agriculture, highly centralised social structures develop to impose order. This we can discern in the civilisations of Egypt, Mesopotamia, China and Java. When it relies on the domestication and grazing of animals, nomadic culture develops. And so on. The competition is relentless. When communities come into contact, the strong will absorb the weak and spread its cultural DNA.

## Failure of Communism

The failure of Communism in the evolution of human society is instructive. There are two main causes. First, in its romantic desire to make man completely altruistic, it denies what we are biologically. There is a selfishness in all of us which cannot be wished away. The idea, from each according to his ability, to each according to his needs, goes against the grain of human nature. Because the communist countries could not reconcile reality to the ideal, hypocrisy and corruption became widespread. A pretense was created that everyone was equal and equally rewarded, when in fact they were not equal and not at all equally rewarded. What started as a moral crusade became an immoral system.

The second reason for the failure of Communism is the march of technology. Technology has made the division of labour so complex, any totalitarian system, any system of centralised economic planning, must fail. In a simpler world, autocratic structures can work to regulate the flow of water and the supply of grain, or even to develop heavy industries like in the Soviet Union in the 1930s. But no longer.

It is this explosion in technology which makes the market economy and democratic government so necessary at this period in human history. Only the invisible hand of the market can regulate economic production in all its complexity and direct supply to demand. Because people, ideas and capital are all mobile, no government can long govern in a way which opposes the popular will. Whether it is Romania, Burma or North Korea, the democractic change must come. The democratic wave is unstoppable.

## Democracy and Socialism

Democracy is a broad movement. British democracy is different from the American, although both are essentially Anglo-Saxon. Swiss democracy is founded on a pluralistic society of independent cantons. In a fascinating article in Petir recently, the Swiss ambassador wrote that because the Swiss are "divided by language, ethnicity, religion or race", the Westminster model of democracy as simple majority rule has "little relevance to the problem of how to secure democracy for a country like Switzerland". And if you study Japanese democracy, it is altogether another species. In the evolution of the cultural DNA, I would describe democratic government more as a genus than as a species. The competition in the future will mainly be between different species of democratic systems. The competition has not ceased and we are certainly not at "the end of history (as put forth by Francis Fukuyama)".

Socialism is not dead. This may sound surprising but I go back to the biological DNA. As I argued earlier, we are not only selfish, we are also altruistic. To deny that we are selfish must lead to failure, which was the failure of Communism. To deny that we are altruistic must also lead to grief, more about which later. Both capitalism and socialism have roots in our very genetic structure.

When we probe into the corporate systems of Japanese companies, we discover that there is a strong sense of internal socialism. Managers are encouraged to be close to workers. They share the same toilets, the same canteens. No special car parks for executives. It works. Because of this internal socialism, Japanese companies do much better than American companies which are rent by internal divisions, between shareholders and management, between management and unions, and among workers.

Individualism in America has reached a point where it makes America weak. It is not only in American companies. It is also in the legal system. And in the mass media which treat elected officials with contempt. I cannot believe that the American system of government today is the system envisioned by the founding fathers and encapsulated so beautifully in the original Constitution. Indeed, there has been a reaction. The Reagan years signalled a change of course. But it will take time. The cultural DNA is slow to change. The challenge of competition from Asia and from Europe will accelerate the process of change. For America to stay in the race, it must find a way to prevail over the formidable group instincts of Japanese and Germans.

## World Competition

There is one great strength in the American cultural DNA. Because they are a nation of immigrants, there is a largeness in their behaviour which facilitates cooperation with others. There is a tolerance of diversity you will not find in equal measure among Germans, and much less so, among Japanese. In a world economy, where companies must globalise to be competitive, this American strength will matter much more. It enables them to tap talent from around the world. Take the example of American companies in Singapore. Compared to other foreign companies, American companies generally offer better career prospects for talented Singaporeans. It is common for

Singaporeans to hold the top positions in Singapore. Because of this, American companies attract a greater share of Singaporean talent. This is also true elsewhere in the world. It gives American companies a considerable advantage. Many able Japanese executives, frustrated in Japanese companies because they are not from Tokyo University or because they have lived too many years overseas or because they are women, end up working for American companies. No other country draws every year to its shores and to its corporations so many enterprising and energetic foreigners.

**Singaporean Instincts**

There is a lesson for us here. We must be conscious of the nature of world competition because whether we get to celebrate our 50th or 100th anniversary depends on whether our social instincts are relevant to the challenges of a new age. That is the Darwinian test.

Let me suggest what some of our social instincts should be.

First, we must feel for others. If each Singaporean thinks only for himself, our society will break up. It will be impossible to build institutions. We are a very competitive society which is good because competition is a spur to excellence. But this competitiveness must be tempered by loyalty to other members of the group. Many of you will enter National Service after your A-level exams. You will learn what a chore it is to carry stretchers. You will also learn why you have to carry stretchers. If you do not carry stretchers in combat, if there are no medics and doctors, no ambulances and helicopters for casualty evacuation, no one will fight. It must be clear to everyone that those who are injured will be looked after. For the group to win, the stronger members must help carry the weaker members. And those who are strong today may be weak tomorrow. You may be at the top of the world now but remember that life has a way of confounding us. The Greeks call it *hubris*. We are not gods. Our attitude should always be to help others in the way we want others to help us when we are in their position. It is a basic principle. If we want our family to be united, our school to excel, our nation to be strong, there must be a sense of concern for others. We must not only think deeply, we must feel deeply. This is the socialist ideal, and a necessary counter-weight to the excesses of competition.

Second, our sense of humanity cannot stop at the borders of Singapore. It is untenable. Charity begins at home but it cannot end at home. As the world shrinks, our sense of a common humanity must grow. For example, how could we not rejoice with the Germans when the Berlin Wall came down? How can we shut our eyes to the starving in Africa? No, our values must have a universal content, like religious values. Only then are they worthy of us. It is wrong to say that this is a problem of government. The government's principal responsibility, the government's fiduciary responsibility, is to its Singaporean voters, not to non-Singaporeans. It is not for the government to be generous with our money when we ourselves are not so inclined. In a democracy, the government can only be as generous to non-Singaporeans as Singaporeans want the government to be with taxpayers' money. Instead, as private individuals and organisations, let our conscience stir us to action.

Third, we should cultivate a regional instinct. The ASEAN spirit is very important. The Europeans are teaching the world how human beings can transcend the divisions of nationality. For centuries, the nations of Europe have been fighting and killing each other in horrible wars, French against Germans, Spanish against French, English against Germans, Austrians against Italians, Poles against Russians, and so on. It is all pointless. Now they are learning to work together in a European Community. A political union of Europe is on the cards, not a unitary state, but more likely a loose federation. Europeans like Helmut Schmidt are convinced that political union is a matter of time. It is interesting to see the convergence of Western and Eastern Europe from two opposite ends: in the West, free nations coming closer together, and in the East, nations breaking loose from the Soviet empire. Let me suggest to you that the democratic system for a federation of Europe will be closer to that of the Swiss than that of London or Paris.

We in ASEAN should learn from Europe. It will take many years, but we too must learn that we will all be better off by sacrificing some of our national prerogatives. It is the way the world is moving, as markets globalise and as the world economy becomes more integrated.

In 1928, young people from all over the Dutch East Indies gathered in Java to swear an oath to the ideal of a single Indonesian nation. They proclaimed the Sumpah Pemuda — *satu tanah air, satu bangsa, satu bahasa* or, *one country, one nation, one language*. It would not be till 1945 before the Indonesians declared independence, and 1949 before they achieved it, but as early as 1928, the youths had committed themselves to the idea, despite the fact that they were drawn from so many different islands, spoke so many different languages and practised such different religions. We need a similar commitment to the idea of ASEAN. Already the economics are nudging us in that direction. Of course, there will be many obstacles to overcome and much cynicism to be brushed aside. But let us, the young people of Southeast Asia, make the commitment now for we will be the leaders of tomorrow, and it will then be a better tomorrow.

## Conclusion

We got here because fortune smiled on us. We had good luck and we had good leaders like PM Lee. But to endure as a nation, we need strong institutions. Strong institutions are the reflection of the social instincts of the people. If the instincts are wrong, the institutions will be weak. Our instincts are not only biological, they are also cultural. What distinguishes homo sapiens from the other social animals is our cultural DNA.

It is in our nature to be both selfish and altruistic. A society succeeds when its culture harnesses in a balanced way this conflicting pull. As technology changes, the balance between competition and cooperation changes. Communism failed because it tried to ignore the selfish side of human nature and because central planning could not cope with the complexity of the modern economy. Democracy has become the new wave. But democracy is a broad movement. In the future, the principal competition will not be between democracy and authoritarianism but between different forms of democracy. The American model, the Japanese model, the Swiss model, are all in competition. The Soviet Union will gradually evolve its own model.

And in China, socialism with Chinese characteristics will eventually be replaced by democracy with Chinese characteristics, which is of course the case in Taiwan today. Socialism is, however, not dead because it expresses a part of our altruistic instinct. It is the level and manner in which socialism should be applied that has changed.

What then should our social instincts be in Singapore? What social instincts will best meet the needs of the times? To the extent that, by an exercise of our free will, we can shape our cultural DNA, I make three suggestions:

1. First, cultivate not just the mind, but also the heart and the spirit. We will not hold together if all our instincts are selfish.
2. Second, hold values which are universal because we belong to a common humanity. It is absurd for our sense of humanity to end at our water's edge.
3. Third, be fully a part of the region. We in ASEAN should learn from the Europeans and recognise that, in this brave new world, we are all better off by being part of a larger community of nations. Of course it will take time and much effort. But while we prepare for the worst in Southeast Asia, we should also work for the best.

As young people, we have a special responsibility because we are the future. Conventional wisdom is often too conservative, too cautious and too cynical. We should not wait for the government to instruct us because, in the end, it is what we are as a people that determines the kind of government we have. May I end by repeating what Paul told Timothy: *Let no man despise thy youth.*

# Importance of Democratic Values in Our National Value System

*Our institutions, like our values, are still evolving.*

## Democracy Is Not Individualism

Mr Speaker, Sir, our desire to preserve traditional Asian values should not lead to a de-emphasis of democratic values in Singapore. Being more communitarian should not mean we become less democratic. It means we should be less individualistic. It would be wrong to equate democracy with individualism. That was not the meaning of democracy as the ancient Greeks understood it. That was not the democracy idealised in the West in the age of Enlightenment.

In his famous Gettysburg Address, Abraham Lincoln summarised democracy as 'government of the people, by the people, and for the people'. The democracy Lincoln described so succinctly is as much concerned with the duties of individuals to the community as it is with the rights of individuals.

## Lack of Democracy in Traditional Asian Societies

The relative backwardness of Asian societies for a long time was partly the result of a lack of democracy. Feudal thinking prevented the modernisation of these societies. Societal values are hard to change. Japan took one generation to make the leap. Even so the Meiji Restoration was not enough. It took the Second World War, two atomic bombs and the American occupation which followed to make Japan the industrial democracy it is today. For China, a country with

---

Maiden speech in Parliament on 19 January 1989 during the debate on the President's Address.

a much larger population spread over a much larger geographical area, modernisation takes much longer.

From the loss of Hong Kong in the Opium War of 1842 to the eventual return of Hong Kong in 1997, China would have taken some 150 years to achieve this great transformation. Even today, there is a raging controversy in China over the exhibition of nude paintings. The Culture Minister himself had to declare recently that the exhibition should be seen as an attack on feudal thinking. And you can be sure we have not heard the last of this fascinating subject.

### The Importance of Democracy Values in Our National Value System

Mr Speaker, Sir, there could have been no progress in traditional Asian societies without democracy. For this reason, democratic values should be an integral part of our national value system. We are a democratic nation, yes, but we do not have a long tradition of democracy. It is not in our ancestral cultures unlike, for example, the Anglo-Saxon peoples.

For centuries, since Magna Carta in the days of King John and Robin Hood, the Anglo-Saxon peoples have evolved a tradition of democratic representation so tenacious that wherever they may be transplanted on this earth, they re-create, basically, the same political system. In the end the institutions we fashion must reflect the values that are in us. Therefore, if we want Singapore to endure as a strong democracy, we must ensure that the democratic values which sustain our national institutions are deeply held by our people, and from their childhood.

Legally, the Constitution is supreme. But, politically, the Constitution is only as durable as the community wants it to be. Many Third World countries are democratic in the constitutional sense when they first become independent. But for as long as the people themselves are not imbued with the ideas and the ideals of democracy, such constitutional experiments often do not endure.

It is very difficult to have a democratic government without democratic values and democratic traditions. We are still building up such traditions in Singapore. Dr Lee Siew Choh's agreement to take up his NCMP seat in Parliament is a milestone in the development of our democracy.* He is of my father's generation and already a historical personage in Singapore whether or not we agree with his political views. By coming back to this House after so many years, he affirms to all Singaporeans the Constitutional principle that this is the way we state and settle our political differences — an important democratic principle that we do well to confirm, not only for ourselves but also for our children and for our children's children.

**Syncretism**

Mr Speaker, Sir, we are right to worry that we may become too Westernised, too individualistic in the American sense. For us that will be disastrous. We are particularly vulnerable because of our size and our exposure through the English language. But our problem, though more acute, is not unique. In much the same way, the other NICs face the same challenge. Look at political developments in South Korea, in Taiwan, in Hong Kong. China too. Even Gorbachev's Russia.

We are not choosing between East and West. We are deciding what synthesis of East and West will best carry us as a society into the 21st century. Dr Sun Yat Sen, the founder of Republican China in 1911, propounded the "Three Principles of the People" (*San Min Zhu Yi*) as the basis for a democratic, industrial nation-state. The three principles were nationalism (*Minzu*), democracy (*Minquan*) and the people's welfare (*Minsheng*). Dr Sun was himself the product of Western missionary education and a convert to Christianity. The Chinese Government he formed was divided into five branches (Yuans), three derived from the US Constitution, the Executive Yuan, the Legislative Yuan and the Judiciary Yuan, and two from Imperial China, the Examination Yuan and the Control or Censorial Yuan. This is still the structure of government in Taipei today. The structure is an interesting, syncretic blend of democratic Western institutions and traditional Chinese ones.

---

*Dr Lee became Singapore's first-ever Non-Constituency Member of Parliament in 1988.

Our approach must be the same in Singapore. We remain as committed to the ideals of democracy but in a way relevant to our history and our circumstances. Our institutions, like our values, are still evolving. The British left us valuable assets in the legal system, the Civil Service, and Parliament. We build on these assets; we modify them; we improve. Like the introduction of GRCs and NCMPs. And, eventually, an elected Presidency or some such safeguard on the exercise of executive power.

Singaporeans want a livelier democracy, particularly younger Singaporeans. This is in accord with the times. We live in an age where because of the minute division of labour even minor tasks require the cooperative effort of a large number of free individuals. You cannot force people to create works of art, to write good software or even just to provide efficient service over the counter if they are not willing. That is why QC circles have become so important in industry. QC circles are a part of the democratisation process in work organisation. A diversity of views is an insurance against the unexpected and the unforeseen. Singapore cannot become a great nation in this information age without a lively democracy. Even the Russians now agree that without democracy no further economic progress is possible. History, it seems, is now on the side of democracy.

Our fear is a democracy perverted by an elevation of the self over all societal considerations, signs of which we see in the West. Here it may be the turn of the West to learn from the East. To misquote Kipling, East is East and West is West, and indeed the twain shall meet. All over America and Europe, business schools and management experts are trying hard to discover the secret of success of Japanese companies. There is really no secret.

As the CEO of Sony, Akio Morita, put it in a recent interview with *Newsweek*, the problem in the West is one of excessive individualism. But, alas, national characteristics are not easy to change. It will take time for Western societies to correct this growing imbalance in their value system. They too must adjust.

We are trying to avoid having such an imbalance in Singapore. So we must stress communitarian values. For the Chinese, communitarian values are mainly Confucianist values. Those Confucianist values which are harmful to progress, we must reject, as Dr Sun Yat Sen and the makers of modern Republican China did. We should preserve only those which are relevant and, emphasise, at the same time, the importance of democratic values without which a modern industrial society cannot be built. In short, our shared values must be both democratic and communitarian. We should therefore not leave out democratic values in our national value system. There will otherwise be a lack of balance in presentation.

**Our Future in the Pacific**

Mr Speaker, Sir, the next century will be the century of the Pacific, of the Western Pacific where Western values have successfully leavened traditional Eastern societies, and of the Eastern Pacific where Eastern ideas will in turn re-invigorate Western societies. Singapore's success to date is a part of the larger success story of the string of islands and peninsulas which skirt the Chinese mainland. Singapore's success in the future will be a part of the larger Pacific drama now unfolding before our very eyes. It must be against such a backdrop of cultural and intellectual ferment in the Pacific that we debate what set of shared values will best enable us to take our rightful place on that stage.

# PAP VALUES FOR THE NEXT LAP

*As young Singaporeans we have to take a long view. If we are too pedestrian and dare not dream, then we may only have ourselves to blame. In the end, we are the ones who will inherit the future.*

## What Are We?

At its core, the Youth Wing must be founded on a set of shared political beliefs. Social activities, though important, are secondary to political work.

Because of changes in the world and in Singapore, our old beliefs must be updated and modified to incorporate the challenges of a new age. Although we still call ourselves a democratic-socialist party, some doubt if we are still committed to either. Against the democracy practised in the West, we appear imperfect and defensive. Against the socialism which has demonstrably failed in so many parts of the world, we are proudly heretical. So what are we? It is necessary to clarify this in our own minds because we are a political party.

The PAP in the 1950s and 1960s had no doubts what its beliefs were when it fought against colonialism, communism and communalism. Indeed, democratic-socialism was defined in terms of those great struggles. The success of that period carried the Party and Singapore through the 1970s and 1980s. The 1990s are a different matter. Now is the right time for re-examination and re-definition.

---

Published in September 1991 in the PAP Youth Wing 5th anniversary commemorative book, *Youth in Action*. In April 1993, the Youth Wing was renamed Young PAP.

## A Great Turning Point

We are at a great turning point in post-war world history. The old certitudes are gone. The Cold War has ended. Communism is in crisis. New poles have appeared in Western Europe and in Japan. But what the shape of the new world will be no one can be sure. The problem of the Soviet Union is now not one of strength but of weakness. A Soviet Union in decay will spread infections around the world. That the United States would win militarily in the Gulf War was never in serious doubt. That it can win the post-war peace in the years ahead is less certain. From the Maghreb to Central Asia, Islam is still making its historic response to the challenge of modernisation. Underlying all this are powerful forces integrating the world economy and forcing human communities into ever-closer contact with each other.

Here in Singapore, we are also at a turning point. Mr Goh Chok Tong has just taken over the reins of leadership from Mr Lee Kuan Yew. A younger generation of leaders must now prove to a younger generation of Singaporeans that they are worthy of their support. Our political beliefs for the 1990s and the next century must enable the PAP to win the support of the great majority of Singaporeans. They must reflect the profound changes taking place in the world. Singaporeans want the PAP to remain the mainstream party because they know this will provide the stability needed for Singapore's continuing economic success. Political continuity enables us to plan long-term and adjust quickly to changed circumstances. It is an important part of our national competitive advantage.

## Five Main Ideas

I would cluster the political beliefs we need in the next lap around five main ideas:

- The Market Economy
- Socialism
- Democracy
- Multiracialism
- International Cooperation

### The Market Economy

The logic of the market is irresistible. With the revolution in information and communication technology, no society can be closed. Governments which resist the market will be defeated by it. It is the market which has subverted the control of central authorities in the Soviet Union and China.

Operating as efficient a market economy as possible in Singapore is therefore central to everything else. This means the rule of law, impartial and corruption-free administration, the safeguard of property rights and a market-based reward system.

We live in a world where capital and labour are both mobile. If we want investment and talent to flow into Singapore, we have to be competitive. If we are not competitive, even our own capital and labour will flow out. There is no escaping the market and this is the reason for our pragmatism.

### Socialism

Carried to its extreme, however, the market undermines itself. This is so because in any competition there are winners and losers. If the losers lose time and again and feel they have little to gain from the system, despair will set in. The losers and those who empathise with them will then work to subvert the system. Whether it is competition within a society or competition between societies, the rules of such "unfair" competition will be disputed. When that happens, the result is revolt or trade war. The elegance and logic of the market becomes irrelevant. Thus, to enable the market to function efficiently, competition must be tempered by cooperation and compassion.

Socialism is not dead. It is being transformed by failure. Socialist parties are in power in many European countries. Of course, what socialism means has changed and many latter-day socialists are unable to state their beliefs precisely. The fact is socialism is an ideal which will never go away because it springs from the altruism that is in the very nature of man. Altruism prompts re-distribution and re-distribution is necessary to hold a group together.

The great mistake of socialism was to try to use state power to effect massive re-distribution, in democratic societies through majority vote, and in communist societies by dictatorship. Instead of binding a community closer together, state socialism divides. It weakens the work ethic. It takes the sense of altruism out of the re-distributive process.

The PAP can either drop the term "socialism" or re-interpret it. We should not drop socialism, because we are still committed to the altruism and compassion which helped give birth to the Party. What socialism should mean for us is not state welfarism, which has failed in so many countries, but community support for one another and selective state intervention to help equalise opportunities.

State welfarism must fail because it goes against the market. Capital and talent will migrate to escape its clutches. Community support, in contrast, is voluntary. It soothes the hurt of competition, reducing the resentment competition causes. To create a comprehensive structure of community support we need a range of civic organisations. Our Party should express its ideal of socialism through such civic organisations. As for equality of opportunities, our Party should continue to support selective state intervention, especially in the areas of education, housing and health.

Communitarianism is really a particular form of socialism. Both flow from the social instinct of man. American scholars prefer "communitarianism" because it does not have the negative connotation of socialism. In reality the ideas overlap. What is clear is that the utopian extreme of "from each according to his ability, to each according to his need" cannot work. Because human beings are both altruistic and selfish, both instincts must be accommodated. The problem is therefore not one of choosing between extremes but one of balance. Socialism or communitarianism is a necessary counterweight to the individualism competition engenders. Crutches are bad but helping hands are necessary. It does not matter whether we use "socialism" or "communitarianism" so long as we are clear what we intend and what the pitfalls are. For political impact, I would prefer to subsume communitarianism under socialism. We should not appear to be changing religions.

To be sustainable, our practice of socialism has to conform to the market. This is the way the National Trades Union Congress

(NTUC) works. This is the way Japanese corporations look after their staff. This is the way the Government has committed itself to making education, housing and basic healthcare available to all, not only through subsidies but also through schemes like the Central Provident Fund (CPF), Medisave, and now Edusave. The objective is always to harness market forces to produce better results for all. We cooperate to compete more effectively. Ours is the socialism that works.

## Democracy

As with socialism, we are evolving our own variant of democracy. We do not know if democracy is an eternal ideal, or the highest form of political organisation mankind is capable of. Against the sweep of history, it has become widespread only in recent years. It was invoked in the fight against colonialism and communism. It is the current today because of the way technology is transforming the world economy. By democracy, I do not. mean, simplistically, Westminster-style parliamentary government or the American Bill of Rights. I am referring to a historical process which forces governments to engage the enthusiasm of increasing numbers in order to govern effectively. Without a widening circle of popular representation and participation, no national economy can advance very far. Some countries may initially go through a Pinochet-phase which helps to get the market economy going, but once a middle-class emerges and property ownership is dispersed, democracy becomes essential.

In tomorrow's world, property will be even more dispersed because it will increasingly be based on knowledge and expertise. No national authority will be able to prevent by force the migration of such properly. You can nationalise steel mills and impound gold bars, but you cannot stop the flow of information. Like Chile, China and the Soviet Union have to go through an authoritarian phase before they too become democratic but it will be in ways unique to themselves and fitted to their history and tradition. That was the path South Korea and Taiwan took. Singapore was fortunate because we inherited democratic institutions from the start.

How long the present democratic tide will flow no one knows. We must also not forget that what is appropriate for one period of human history may not be for another. Human genetic engineering, for example, will confront mankind with the most profound moral challenge and change the way human societies are organised.

In the evolution of human societies, democracy as a broad movement is not all of the same species. It is better described as a genus with many species in competition with each other. From an Asian perspective, the American species is an extreme development, well adapted for opening up a richly endowed continent largely empty but one not likely to be suited for the transformation of an ancient civilisation like China. The Japanese hybrid has been obviously successful but for how long more no one can say. All are imperfect and all are subject to the Darwinian test of competition and selection. Some are evolutionary dead-ends. Many experiments in democracy have failed, and many more are destined to fail.

Against such a historical perspective, it is natural and necessary for Singapore to practise a form of democracy which is distinctively our own, broadly similar to practices elsewhere, but adapted to our society and environment. The Internal Security Act, for example, was needed to protect the development of our democracy. It is still needed but, as a safeguard against its abuse, presidential review is now provided for. Communism may no longer be a serious threat but communalism will long remain one, for which the normal judicial process will remain ineffective.

Our democracy has served us well. It would have failed had we not made changes to the institutions the British bequeathed us. We must continue to adapt. We need not be defensive just because we are different from the Americans or Europeans. We should learn from them, yes, but we are neither American nor European, and I am not at all sure that we want to be completely like them even if it were possible. In 50 to 100 years' time, some of the Asian models of democracy may well be judged superior to other varieties.

## Multiracialism

As with socialism and democracy, our Party's belief in multiracialism must also be updated and refreshed. Those who say that we should leave well enough alone are wrong. That we are able to maintain racial and religious harmony is because we act early to defuse problems that can loom very large very quickly. If untended, race relations in Singapore can still easily deteriorate. We are greatly influenced by the world outside. When the Golden Temple was stormed, Sikh Singaporeans recoiled. When tanks rolled into Tiananmen, Chinese Singaporeans were outraged. When the Americans bombed Iraq, Malay Singaporeans felt pain. It is better that we recognise our society for what it is, warts and all, than to pretend that we have no weakness. Only then can our multiracialism succeed.

The Party must never waver in its commitment to the multiracial ideal. We stood firm even when Singapore was in Malaysia. We introduced Group Representation Constituencies (GRCs) to ensure that all political parties which aspire to power are multiracial. The Party's multiracial policies, and its commitment to fielding a multiracial slate of MPs and Ministers, are fundamental reasons for the absence of racial politics in Singapore.

In a sense, multiracialism is a challenge to all nations. No nation is homogeneous. The world is not. Yet we all have to live together on this planet. The multiracial ideal is therefore a universal ideal. Successfully managed, multiracialism can be very beautiful. Mismanaged, it can turn very ugly. We have to work at it.

For example, Article 152 in our Constitution recognises the special challenges facing the Malay community. While the PAP's commitment to Article 152 should not change, our implementation of it cannot be frozen. As the Malay community progresses, so too must the measures we take to help it move forward.

All ethnic communities must strike a balance between preserving our separate pasts and securing our common future. We need deep roots to weather the changes sweeping the world but these roots should all be supporting the same tree.

I doubt if we can ever stop worrying about race and religion. We are like the juggler who cannot rest because he has so many balls in the air.

## International Cooperation

All states confront the twin problems of economic production and security. First, we must eat. Then, we must prevent others from eating us up. Everything else follows from these two basic requirements. Small states like Singapore are obviously more vulnerable and survive better by cooperating with other states. It is no wonder that small states are often the most internationalist. They have the most to gain from international cooperation.

Our first response to this challenge was to merge into Malaysia. Although that failed, the logic of cooperating with others and being of use to others still applies. Indeed that was Raffles' vision and it has not changed. What has changed is the configuration of links we need to maximise our economic and survival chances.

The Growth Triangle is of historic importance. It is developing under the pressure of international competition. By cooperating, Singapore, Johore and the Riaus compete more effectively with the rest of the world than if each were to act singly. The economics and the politics are linked together. Good political relations have made possible this economic cooperation, but this economic cooperation will in turn bind us more closely together politically. The triangle will eventually transform the politics and the economics of ASEAN and Southeast Asia. In Europe, Belgium, the Netherlands and Luxembourg were the first countries to get together, not long after the War, to establish the Benelux customs union. That led to the Treaty of Rome in 1958 and we have now the prospect of a Single European Market in 1992.

As young Singaporeans we have to take a long view. If we are too pedestrian and dare not dream, then we may only have ourselves to blame. In the end, we are the ones who will inherit the future. It is therefore necessary for the Youth Wing to look outwards and make contact with other young people, in the region and beyond.

Our basic approach should be to work for more international cooperation because that is good for everyone. We must also be flexible because there are many practical problems to overcome. We should be like the water that flows downhill, never expecting the course to be straight, meandering around hard places, but inexorably moving towards our objective.

No nation is an island, least of all Singapore. For this reason, the PAP has always been internationalist. It must remain so. But the specific content has to change with the changes technology is forcing on us all. We can never turn inwards, for that will be the end of us.

In a larger sense, nothing has changed. From the beginning, the PAP believed in the market, in socialism, in democracy, in multiracialism and in international cooperation. But, like a renewal of faith, these beliefs must now be brought up to date and given new life. Our thinking has to reflect the times we live in.

At the national level, we have formulated a set of values for all Singaporeans to share, whatever our party affiliations. Our Party beliefs should be consistent with these values.

Settling our Party beliefs is an important task. If the Youth Wing is to play a role, it must know what it believes in, not just abstractly, but also in concrete terms. Only then can we enthuse ourselves and others with us.

# Civic Society — Between the Family and the State

*Without struggle, the soul will never grow. It is because of struggle that fierce loyalties develop.*

## Not Just a Hotel

In the years to come, one of the major issues we have to confront is how to manage the phenomenon of multiple loyalties. We live in a world shrinking by the day. As our economy develops, more Singaporeans will travel overseas for work, study and leisure. Many Singaporeans will live overseas for months if not years. It is natural that some of these Singaporeans should feel attached to more than one community.

This situation is of course not unique to Singapore. Other countries also face this problem. Human talent has never been more mobile in the world. To compete for this pool of human talent, a number of countries now accept the idea of dual citizenship. The British and the Americans allow it; they adopt a practical approach. The Irish give passports to those who are only a quarter Irish to win over millions of Irish Americans and Australians. The French and the Taiwanese are liberal with those who are of French and Taiwanese descent. Despite the importance of national service, both the Israelis and the Turks have also made adjustments to changed patterns of migration. For them, half a loaf is better than no bread. Even the Swiss accept dual nationality but they are more relaxed with those who are Swiss-born. It is much harder for a foreigner to take up Swiss citizenship.

---

National University of Singapore Society (NUSS) Inaugural Lecture, World Trade Centre, 20 June 1991.

For all these countries, the rules allowing multiple citizenships are never fully publicised. Invariably, approval is on a case-by-case basis. But the way the game is being played is clear: it is to attract and to co-opt human talent. Ultimately, it is human capital which determines how strong and how competitive a society is.

Here in Singapore we do not allow dual citizenship as a rule but we are quite liberal with permanent residents (PRs). Recently, the suggestion has been made in Parliament and elsewhere that we should review our policy. Many Singaporeans are uncomfortable because we are still a young nation and allowing dual citizenship will dilute our sense of nationhood. This is a legitimate concern. The issues are, however, complex. We are not talking about choosing between black and white. Today, a Singapore PR enjoys almost all the privileges of citizenship so we do in fact have a situation that approximates dual citizenship. In the same way, many Singaporeans take up PR in Canada, Australia or the US, without any intention of giving up their Singapore citizenship.

The problem is not simply one of rules and regulations. It is really one of emotional attachment. If a Singaporean loves Singapore, he will always be Singaporean whatever passport he carries. Conversely, if a Singaporean treats Singapore merely as a hotel, restricting the travel documents he carries will not help very much. When it does not benefit him, he will be off. The problem is how to make Singapore more than just a nice hotel to stay in, how to make it a home worth living and caring for.

## Creating the Soul

It is therefore not enough just to improve the standard of living or the quality of life. Yes, it is pleasant to live in a city that is clean, green and safe, that has good facilities, where traffic jams are few and far between, where the phones work and where the golf greens are well watered. But all this we can get at any five-star hotel resort. They are not enough.

What we must have is a soul — and that money cannot buy. Yet, without it, Singapore is only a hotel however well run the country may be. And we cannot make a hotel a home by preventing the guests from leaving.

How then do we create this Singapore soul? The soul of a people is an interesting subject in the study of human communities. The great mythologies offer a clue. They tell us that the soul of a people is created when they are struggling to overcome great odds. In overcoming these odds together, they develop their identity as a group, and this identity is carried from generation to generation in the form of myths. These myths may be based on actual historical experiences, but they are exaggerated to make the heroes larger than life and their exertions superhuman. For example, the Ramayana and the Mahabharata mythologised the great encounters of the Aryan people when they entered the Indian sub-continent. In the same way, the Iliad and the Odyssey described in epic form the Greek colonisation of the shores and islands of the Mediterranean and the Black Sea. Xuan Zang's Journey to the West traced not only the route taken by Buddhism from India to China but also the attempts by the Han people to pacify the Western borders. In the Niebelung, we discern the rise of the German spirit as the Teutonic knights moved down the Danube.

What the myths tell us is that the multi-faceted soul of a people is forged in struggle. I am referring not only to epic struggles, but also the struggles of daily life, the totality of a people's response to a set of challenges. It is not the destination which is important but getting there. It is during the Long March that the soul in all its complexity is created and not after the arrival at Yan'an.

## Between the Family and the State

When we examine our soul in Singapore, we discover elements which are fully formed and elements which are still crystallising. The ethnic and religious components have been forged hundreds if not thousands of years ago. They will survive even if there were no Singapore. The Singaporean component of our soul is, however, still being formed.

There are two major parts to this Singaporean component. At the national level, we have created institutions which will serve us for generations to come, institutions like the Civil Service, National Service, Central Provident Fund (CPF), Medisave, the Housing Development Board (HDB), bilingual education, multi-racial group representation, the National Trades Union Congress (NTUC) and so on. These are institutions unique to Singapore, institutions created in response to the huge problems of the 1960s and the 1970s. At the national level, the act of creation has been largely accomplished and this is now largely internalised in the Singapore soul.

But below the level of the state, at the level of civic life, the Singapore soul is still evolving. Yes, the state is strong. The family, is also strong. But civic society, which is the stratum of social life between the state and the family, is still weak. Without a strong civic society, the Singapore soul will be incomplete. If the creation of a strong state was a major task of the last lap, the creation of a strong civic society must be a major task of the next lap.

To go back to the hotel room metaphor, it is not enough to have a good hotel or a well-run state. There are other well-run hotels. It is also not enough to have strong families because families can move from hotel to hotel and still remain intact. What we need lies in between. What we need are individuals and families who feel a responsibility to help build and to help run the hotel. When that happens, the hotel becomes a home.

What we need therefore is a whole array of civic organisations which anchor Singaporeans, as individuals and as families, to the country. I am not saying that direct emotional attachment to the state is not important. It is important. But human emotions soar to such abstract levels only occasionally, and usually only during times of great crisis. Even in times of war, soldiers relate more to their peers and to their section, platoon and company commanders than they do to their brigade or division. Human beings have a strong need to belong to small groups, to little platoons, where the human links are direct and personal. These civic groups give individuals and families their sense of place and involvement in the larger community.

## Religion, Education, Local Government, Total Defence and Culture

What are these civic institutions? I would group them broadly around five major activities: religion, education, local government, Total Defence and culture.

Every place of religious worship is also a place for people to meet and to do good work. Mosques, temples, churches and synagogues are important focal points in any society. Human energies are mobilised to garner resources, to organise activities, to help the needy. In making the effort, a certain spirit develops which gives life to the particular centre and secure for it the emotional commitment of its members. Even when members live overseas, the links remain. To help Christian Singaporeans who live in Australia and Canada, for example, some churches send pastors from Singapore to minister to them. We must of course not forget that religious activities can also divide us as a people, as is indeed the case in so many countries. I would say that so long as we avoid extreme positions, civic activities organised around religious worship is a positive, not a negative, force.

Schools, polytechnics, colleges and universities should also be important centres for civic life. Now that we have good systems and curriculums in place, more attention should be given to building up the social life around each education establishment — Old Boy's Associations (OBAs), Parent-Teacher Associations (PTAs) and associations like Council for Development of Singapore Malay/Muslim Community (MENDAKI) and the National University of Singapore Society (NUSS). It is not what the Education Ministry does that brings life to a school. It is what students, parents, old boys and old girls do for themselves. In fact, the more they strive for themselves, the stronger the school spirit or the community spirit becomes. For this reason, it is important that our schools, especially our independent schools, our polytechnics and our universities undertake to raise a part of the funds they need.

The example of Harvard is instructive. Loyalties to Harvard are not to the University direct because the University is too big and impersonal. Instead, these loyalties are channelled through the schools — through Harvard College, the Law School, the Kennedy School, the Business School and others. I graduated from the Business School and, believe me, till I die the School will not let me forget. Every graduating section of about 90 students in every graduating class of 700–800 appoints a section secretary and a fund-raising secretary before the students disperse. Class notes are compiled regularly and old boys are updated on each other's activities every three months through the alumni bulletin. We are tracked — from graduation to obituary. It is interesting scanning these class notes from time to time. The new graduates talk about jobs, getting married, and having children. The older ones talk about their careers, about class reunions, about children getting married, about health problems and so on. Then when they get really old, the class notes get shorter as the alumni die off. What is the objective? It is to maintain a powerful social network and to raise funds for the School. We are constantly reminded of the need to chip in. For good measure, a note goes out every year to everyone in the class listing those who have contributed and the amounts. It is quite a formidable operation. Professor Tommy Koh told me that his law class at its 25th Reunion raised US$1 million for the Law School.

I have talked about civic institutions formed around religious worship and education. Let me now cover the other three briefly — local government, Total Defence and culture.

Local government should be progressively extended. This has been difficult in the past because of the physical redevelopment of our island over the last 25 years and the need for central direction. Constituency boundaries had to be redrawn every few years to keep up with the relocation of population centres. But this process will slow down. As the population becomes more settled, residential areas will mature and towns will become more important. Each town will then have its local character, the kind of character which can be found today in places like Serangoon Gardens and Katong. The older housing estates like Toa Payoh are also becoming more interesting. Town councils will help us create a network of local government which Singaporeans can relate to more intimately. By local government, I refer to both political and non-political civic agencies — mayors, town councillors, justices of the peace, Citizens' Consultative Committees (CCCs), Residents' Committtees (RCs), community centres, management associations, rotary clubs, charity organisations, trade union cooperatives and so on. A country like Luxembourg, which is much smaller than Singapore in population size, has a more developed structure of local government. When local residents do things for themselves, they feel a greater sense of ownership, responsibility and control.

Like local government, we need also to create civic organisations around Total Defence. In the last lap, Total Defence concentrated on the build-up of the Singapore Armed Forces (SAF) and Civil Defence, particularly the establishment of operational units and training systems — on the hard parts as it were. Now we must also give emphasis to the soft parts, and get regulars, national servicemen, reservists and volunteers to organise more social activities for themselves and their families. When there is a crisis, like the Hotel New World disaster or the hijack of SQ 117, deep emotions are aroused which bond Singaporeans to Total Defence. I remember attending a meeting in the Ministry of Defence (MINDEF) chaired by Dr Yeo Ning Hong the morning of the successful storming of SQ 117. I felt like shaking hands with everyone wearing a uniform. But crises are rare and thankfully so. We cannot depend on crises to forge all our emotional links to the state. Here again, we need local organisations. The Singapore Armed Forces Reservists' Association (SAFRA), for example, will try to work at a more local level and facilitate the organisation of family-based activities. The Police and Civil Defence are also organising their own reservist associations. Look at the Swiss. This year they are celebrating their 700th anniversary. Even when they are overseas, they feel a strong affiliation to their operational units. We are only 25 years old but we should know where we are heading.

The last group of civic organisations I want to talk about are the organisations concerned with culture and the arts. Some, like the Nanyang Academy of Fine Arts, have a long history. Others, like the Sub-Station, are comparatively new. Over the last few years, there has been a general blossoming of the arts which augurs well for the future. The great majority of our art organisations are, however, still struggling to be viable. All are competing for support, for state, corporate and individual support. At the risk of being misunderstood, let me say that this struggle is a good thing, not a bad thing. Without struggle, the soul will never grow. It is because of struggle that fierce loyalties develop. Of course the government must offer a helping hand if the arts are to flourish at all but this helping hand must not create dependency.

## Pruning the Banyan Tree

This leads me to make a general point about community self-help and the Singapore soul. For our civic institutions to grow, the state must withdraw a little and provide more space for local initiatives. If the state is overpowering and intrudes into every sphere of community life, the result will be disastrous. All of us are then reduced to guests in a hotel. By arrogating to itself all powers, Communism, especially Soviet Communism, created an immoral system. By making everyone dependent on the state, the system destroyed the soul of the community.

In the case of Singapore, we went through a centralising phase because we had to build a nation. Under the British, there were independent schools, community hospitals, clan associations, and so on, but they pulled our society in different directions. The British were not interested in creating a nation. As was the case elsewhere in the Empire, British policy was to divide and rule. When Singapore became independent, the creation of strong national institutions was therefore of overriding importance. To provide the basics quickly, we built state systems for education, health, housing and so on. Schools and hospitals were virtually nationalised. Because racial and religious harmony was paramount, chauvinism of all kinds had to be restrained. To defend ourselves, National Service (NS) was introduced. To house the population, the Government built up the Housing Development Board (HDB) and the Central Provident Fund (CPF). These centralised programmes made possible the remarkable achievements of Singapore in the first phase of our national development.

The problem now is that under a banyan tree very little else can grow. When state institutions are too pervasive, civic institutions cannot thrive. Therefore it is necessary to prune the banyan tree so that other plants can also grow. You know what our friends in Hong Kong say of us: We take care of our people so well, our people have become soft.

If we want the state to be less intrusive, we must do more for ourselves. This means taking the initiative, running around, raising money (which is never pleasant), and suffering all manner of inefficiencies to get a job done. We all know that the politics in civic organisations can sometimes be very petty and very complicated. But when the job is finally done, the satisfaction is sweet precisely because everyone contributed to the final product.

In a book called *In Pursuit of Happiness and Good Government*, Charles Murray made the point repeatedly that good government leaves plenty of room for local loyalties to develop. Edmund Burke said that "... to love the little platoon we belong to in society is the first principle (the germ as it were) of public affections. It is the first link in the series by which we proceed towards a love to our country, and to mankind." Mencius stressed a long time ago that governing a state is like frying small fish; it must be lightly done. De Tocqueville wrote in *Democracy in America* that "the township is the only association so well rooted in nature that wherever men assemble it forms itself. Communal society therefore exists among all peoples, whatever be their customs and laws. Man creates kingdoms and republics, but townships seem to spring directly from the hand of God." De Tocqueville added that "it is in the township, the centre of the ordinary business of life, that the desire for esteem [and] the pursuit of substantial interests ... are concentrated; these passions ... take on a different character when exercised so close to home and, in a sense, within the family circle .... Daily duties performed or rights exercised keep municipal life constantly alive. There is a continual gentle political activity which keeps society on the move without turmoil."

In other words, it is civic life which creates "public affections" and the soul in our society. It is civic life which holds a democracy together. We have to make the effort ourselves. The government can help but the government cannot build up civic life from top down. For example, I understand that the NUSS will be organising a lyric theatre company which, as Minister for the Arts, is a project I support and applaud. The initiative comes from the NUSS and its success will depend on the exertions of the NUSS. The Ministry of Information and the Arts (MITA) will help here and there, the way we help others, but that's all. I am sure you will succeed and the NUSS will be the better for it. In the same way, the Government can spend money to build more halls of residence in the University but whether they develop strong traditions will depend on students and faculty. We need strong halls because they underpin the civic life of a university. It is through the halls that students develop lifelong loyalties towards the University.

Let me add that there has to be a proper balance between centralisation and decentralisation. We have to prune the banyan tree, but we cannot do without the banyan tree. Singapore will always need a strong centre to react quickly to a changing competitive environment. We need some pluralism but not too much because too much will also destroy us. In other words, we prune judiciously.

## A New Pattern of Competition

The livelier our civic society, the more varied our civic organisations, the more points of emotional attachment there will be to Singapore. Then it will not matter whether Singaporeans are in Singapore or overseas. However attractive other cities may be, this will always be home because this is where the heart is. The fact that Singaporeans overseas are becoming more keen to organise themselves is a very good sign. We should encourage them and help them to help themselves.

The international competition for human capital is really a competition for hearts and minds. All along the Pacific Rim, vigorous Asian communities are forming. Because of high population densities in Asia and low population densities in North America and Australasia, the flow of Asians to cities like Los Angeles, San Francisco, Vancouver, Perth, Sydney, Auckland and Wellington will continue well into the next century. These Asian communities will never be fully absorbed into the American, Canadian or Australian society. They will remain partially Asian at least and retain economic, cultural and family ties with cities in East and Southeast Asia. All along the Pacific Rim, Asian communities will be in communication, cooperation and competition with one another. This pattern is not unlike that of the Greek colonisation of the islands and coastal areas of the Mediterranean and the Black Sea over 2,500 years ago. Because of over-population on the Greek peninsula, many Greeks left their city-states to found colonies which then became independent. They traded with each other and met for the Olympic

Games. We are witnessing an analogous phenomenon on the Pacific Rim. In the next century, we in Singapore will be one of many dynamic Asian communities on the Pacific Rim. We will have to compete for our share of human capital, especially for Asian hearts and Asian minds. And if we are only a hotel, we will fail. The simple fact is that to win minds, we have to win hearts.

### The 21st Century

I therefore come back to the starting point of my argument. If we are not to be only a hotel, we must have a soul. To develop that soul, we need a lively civic society. The State must pull back some so that the circle of public participation can grow. When Singaporeans in their little platoons struggle to make life better for themselves and for their fellow countrymen, they develop the affections and traditions which make our hotel a home. Then it will not matter so much whether they live in Singapore or overseas. We will then be able to take our place as one of the more remarkable communities on the Pacific Rim in the next century.

# Lessons of History

*We should forgive, but we must never forget ... because those who ignore the lessons of history are condemned to become victims a second time.*

We are gathered here this morning to commemorate the 50th Anniversary of the start of the Second World War in the Pacific. At 4 a.m. on 8 December 1941, 7 December on the other side of the Pacific, the first wave of aircraft from the Japanese Imperial Army in Indo-China bombed Singapore. Japanese troops landed at Singora, Pattani and Kota Bahru early that same morning, and moved quickly southwards. Penang fell on 16 December 1941, Kuala Lumpur on 11 January 1941. On 31 January 1942, Japanese troops reached the Johore shore opposite Singapore and began an artillery bombardment of our island. The troops crossed the Straits on 7 February 1942. On 15 February 1942, the first day of the Chinese New Year, Percival surrendered unconditionally to Yamashita.

Then began a reign of terror, the *sook ching*, when thousands of Singaporeans were killed and many more tortured. Brutalised by the long war in China and seeing Singapore as the centre of the Nanyang Chinese resistance against Japan, the Imperial Army was determined to terrorise the local population into submission. The bitter memories of the Japanese occupation will long remain in the collective consciousness of all Singaporeans.

But our objective is not just to commemorate what happened half a century ago. It is also to learn from the past in order to better

---

Speech delivered at the launch of the commemoration of the 50th Anniversary of the Fall of Singapore, National Museum, 8 December 1991.

secure the future for ourselves and for our children. There are two important lessons for us to remember.

The first lesson is the need to construct a structure of peace in the region which enables conflicts among nations to be settled in a peaceful manner without recourse to violence. The message must be driven home that violence does not pay, whether the aggressor was Japan in the Second World War, Vietnam in Cambodia or Iraq in Kuwait.

We need a structure of peace at two levels. On one level, we need an Asian-Pacific architecture which balances and brings together in peaceful cooperation the United States, Japan, China, Russia and India. Over the next 10 years, the existing equilibrium in the Asia-Pacific will come under great stress. The relative decline of the United States, the growing economic power of Japan, the break-up of the Soviet Union and the leadership transition in China mean that a new equilibrium must be established. We need political and economic institutions which keep disputes among the major powers within bounds. It was precisely the lack of such institutions which brought about the war in the Pacific. Imperial powers were then in furious contention. The United States retaliated against the Japanese invasion of China and the occupation of French Indo-China with an embargo on strategic materials, principally oil. The result was a war which led to the deaths of tens of millions in Asia. We have the opportunity now to build a different kind of co-prosperity sphere in the Asia-Pacific region. We must seize it.

But it is not enough just to have the big powers in balance. We also need a structure of peace in the immediate region around us. This is why ASEAN is so important to Singapore. Before the Japanese could invade Malaya, it had to first occupy Indo-China and then obtain the agreement of Thailand for the passage of its forces. Malaya fell before Singapore did. And it was from Singapore that Japanese forces invaded Sumatra and other parts of the Dutch East Indies. Thus, the security of Indonesia, Singapore and Malaysia is indivisible; the security of Malaysia and Thailand is indivisible; and the security of Thailand and Indo-China is also indivisible. The more we cooperate politically in ASEAN, the more our economies are integrated, the safer our future will be. United we stand, divided we fall. Divided, our own interests are likely to be traded off in the larger game played by the big powers.

In other words, to have peace in Singapore, we need peace in Southeast Asia and peace in the Asia-Pacific region. Singapore's foreign policy is therefore directed towards the creation of a structure of peace which balances the major powers and which facilitates political and economic cooperation in Southeast Asia and in the Asia-Pacific region.

But it is in the nature of man to be violent and we must never assume that there will never be war again. Peace is the result of the balance of power, not its absence. Political power abhors a power vacuum. When that balance breaks down, as it does again and again in human history, we must be prepared. There is no guarantee that we will be able to find peaceful answers to the destabilisation factors I mentioned earlier. Regional conflicts can break out again. When that happens, we can ask others for help but we must be able to look after ourselves.

This is the second lesson we should learn from the Second World War. Singapore was a bastion of the British Empire, its most important East of Suez, and grandly proclaimed to be so. Japan eyed Singapore for the same strategic reason. But when the chips were down, Britain's priorities were in Europe, not in Asia. London had no choice. Britain herself was under severe air attack from Nazi Germany. But this gave no consolation to those who bore the brunt of Japanese barbarity in Singapore.

On the larger chessboard of international politics, a minor piece like Singapore is never indispensible. While we should always make ourselves useful to others, we must never be under the illusion that we are indispensible to anyone. We must always be prepared to stand up for ourselves. This is what independence means and there is no greater expression of our independence than the SAF. Hong Kong is similar to Singapore in many ways, but on this point we are completely different. Hong Kong is now a British colony and will revert to China as a Special Administrative Region in 1997. It does not need an army. We have the SAF. The price we pay for our independence is 6% of our annual GDP and the effort of our entire citizenry in Total Defence, as national servicemen, as reservists and volunteers and as supporting wives and mothers. We need not be as helpless as we were 50 years ago.

The Japanese Diet had earlier indicated its wish to pass a resolution apologising for the Pacific War but changed its mind a few days ago for lack of a parliamentary consensus. It is a pity. If we are asked to forgive, we should forgive, but we must never forget. We must never forget, not because we are unable to forgive fully, not because we still harbour bitterness in our hearts, but because those who ignore the lessons of history are condemned to become victims a second time. We remember in order that we do not have to forgive again.

The multimedia package on the Second World War, jointly produced by the National Computer Board, the National Museum and other organisations, will help us remember the painful events that took place. I thank Apple Singapore for its generous support.

# Democracy

*The test of democracy is not how we measure up against someone else's theoretical construct but what works for us given our history and circumstances.*

There is no agreed definition of what democracy is. Democracy is as difficult to define as socialism. I rather see democracy as a broad movement which seeks to progressively widen the circle of participation in the governance of a society. In that sense, democracy is a rejection of feudalism, a rejection of absolutist monarchy, a rejection of class or caste rule. It is never simply a matter of one-man-one-vote. At the core of the democratic ideal is the belief that while we are not equal physically or intellectually, we are equal spiritually.

As the first speaker, let me set our discussion on Asian democracy against a wider perspective of how democracy has evolved over time and space. The historical experiences of democracy have been very varied. We all look back to Athenian democracy but Athens had many slaves with no voting rights at all.

Anglo-Saxon democracy developed over many centuries before the franchise became universal. It was only after the Second World War that democracy in the UK meant one-man-one-vote. But many in Scotland today consider this English oppression and want their own Parliament. In Canada, Quebec may one day secede. In the US, the Blacks were only fully enfranchised in 1965 a century after the Civil War but whether this has led to their upliftment is arguable.

---

Remarks at the Forum on "The Pro-Democracy Crisis in Asia: Are There Lessons to Learn for Singapore?", 22 October 1992.

The Swiss had to confront the problem of minorities from the beginning. From the time of the Confederation 700 years ago, the Swiss accommodated ethnic, language and religious diversity in their midst. It was not always peaceful. The religious wars which engulfed Europe during the Reformation and Counter-Reformation affected Switzerland as well. But Swiss democracy took a very different path from Anglo-Saxon democracy from the outset, with the cantons retaining a great deal of autonomy and self-government.

It can be said that the Swiss pioneered the idea of "subsidiarity" which is probably the best way forward for the European Community and the whole world today. Political power should be devolved to the lowest level possible. In other words, one-man-one-vote should apply only at the homogeneous group level while one-group-one-vote should be the general principle at the federal level.

Thus, democracy in the UN means one-nation-one-vote which gives one vote to China with 1.2 billion people and also one vote to San Marino with only 24,000 people. But of course China is in the UN Security Council while San Marino is not.

In Japan, what matters is not so much the formal voting process but the ceaseless bargaining and consensus-building within the body politic. In countries like Japan and Thailand, money politics is deeply entrenched. In Japan recently, an army officer shocked everyone by calling for *a coup d'état to* cleanse the system. In Thailand, corruption has led to coups and counter-coups. In Singapore, you do not have to be rich to become an MP and you do not become rich after becoming one.

We must not equate democracy with one-man-one-vote in a simplistic manner, without taking into account the economic reality and the interests of sub-groups. Take, for example, the UN and world government. The OECD countries, who are constantly preaching democracy to Third World countries, would be absolutely horrified if one-man-one-vote were to apply to the whole world. They will be dispossessed by the teeming millions in Asia, Africa and Latin America. The problem of democracy is not one-man-one-vote *per se*, but how one-man-one-vote is translated into an institutional structure of power and government which is considered legitimate, accepted by most people to be fair and just, and which produces stability and growth.

Our concern is not with democracy as an abstract ideal but the kind of democracy that is evolving. Does it throw up good governments? Does it lead to social and economic development? Are minorities looked after? Are the rich obscenely rich? Or the poor miserably poor? Do people feel safe? I ofter wonder what Filipino democracy means to the many Filipinas who are forced by poverty to leave home to work as domestic maids around the world.

When Stan Sasser of *The New Yorker* described Singapore as a city of fear, we are justified to ask which is the city of fear — Singapore or New York? I would jog at the East Coast Park even when it is dark but there are places in New York I would not go to in bright daylight.

The test of democracy is not how we measure up against someone else's theoretical construct but what works for us given our history and circumstances. It is a Darwinian test. What succeeds will endure.

In other words, democracy is not an end-point in human history. It is not a species of political organisation but a genus containing within it many competing species. America is one species. Switzerland, a second. The European Community, a third. Japan, a fourth, and so on. Global competition will decide which species are stronger and which are weaker. To a greater or lesser extent, all are in turmoil because of the end of the Cold War, the globalisation of the world economy and the revolution in technology. Like Europe, Canada and the US, Asian societies are also in a state of flux. Singaporean democracy is relatively stable because we inherited solid institutions from the British and we have made adjustments to them as we progressed. We are also a city-state without a countryside to worry about. The upheavals we have seen in South Korea, Taiwan and Thailand were largely the result of power shifting from the countryside to the cities. China is going through such a transformation now. We don't face this problem.

National development is like walking on two legs. If the economic leg keeps moving while the political leg is immobile, the nation will falter. If both legs try to move together, the nation will collapse in disorder. Or like Myanmar, both legs stand still and the world passes it by. We must never stand still in Singapore. However, I do not think we want to walk the path of Western societies where extreme individualism and the breakdown of the family are giving rise to all kinds of social problems. The lesson for us is: We find our own way to the future.

Democracy in Singapore must take into account three big considerations:

a. First, our multiracial make-up. If one-man-one-vote leads to the tyranny of the Chinese over the minority groups, there will be strife. I do not think we will ever want books like Salman Rushdie's *The Satanic Verses* to be freely available in Singapore, whatever our American or European friends may tell us.
b. Second, our security. Our multiracial composition complicates the problem of our security. For example, while our relationship with China and Taiwan may be excellent and built upon a certain cultural affinity, we must never become a Chinese outpost in Southeast Asia. Democracy in Singapore must respect the sensitivities of our neighbours. No government can allow the press in Singapore to be irresponsible in the way it reports on our relationship with Malaysia, Indonesia, China or Taiwan.
c. Third, our economic development. The bottomline is our international competitiveness. Our democratic processes must strike a balance between centralising enough power to allow us to respond quickly to changing external conditions and decentralising enough to allow room for creativity and individual expression. In our recent public discussions on censorship and on language and values, it is clear that many Singaporeans want clear limits put on the right of expression.

There is no such thing as absolute freedom. Kissinger once said that absolute security for one side must mean absolute insecurity for the other. It is the same with freedom. Absolute freedom for some must mean absolute non-freedom for others. As in our approach to censorship, we have to find our own balance between individual freedom and social order.

Let me end by saying that whatever the democratic system, there must be a moral purpose. Laws alone can never solve all the problems of human society. Many of the problems in Western democracy today stem from a moral breakdown. Sooner or later, there will be a backlash but it may be decades before the balance is restored. In the meantime, East Asian societies will throw up models for others to follow, including some of the models of democracy and business organisation now evolving in our part of the world.

# Young PAP — Recasting the Net

*It is now the turn of another generation to run the race and to prepare yet another generation for their turn.*

## PM's Call

After winning the Marine Parade by-election in December last year, Prime Minister (PM) Goh Chok Tong asked young Singaporeans to come forward and serve the country. The Prime Minister made this call because of his concern for the future of Singapore, not so much for the next five or ten years, but for the next century. He was looking far ahead.

Looking far ahead has become part of our reputation in the world. Others envy our ability to plan ahead. The reason we are able to is not because we are cleverer but because we are more united and we have good leaders.

In fact, preoccupation with the short term is the biggest problem of most democracies in the world today. With one man, one vote, it is not easy to fight off pressure to do popular things. No politician likes to raise prices. No politician likes to introduce the Goods and Services Tax (GST), however good this may be for the country in the long run. This is why so many countries are in trouble. It is easier to spend more than to raise fees. When there is not enough money, it is easier to borrow than to increase taxes. This is what has happened to the United States and Australia. Or, when others refuse to lend, the government can simply print more money to cover the deficit.

---

PAP Current Affairs talk, given on 25 April 1993.

This of course leads to inflation and devaluation, which is the problem of countries like Brazil and Russia.

In a democracy, if everyone votes according to how his wallet is immediately affected, the country will quickly go downhill. All political parties will then be competing to give the shop away and nothing will be left for the next generation. For a democracy to work, the voter must not only worry for himself, he must also worry for his children and grandchildren. While we must be concerned for ourselves, we must also be concerned for the well-being of society as a whole. This is a question of morality and social values. Without strong moral underpinnings, democracy cannot work. For democracy in Singapore to work, we need good leaders and a keen sense of nationhood.

## Favourable External Factors

Singapore is in a good position today. Internally, the Marine Parade by-election has shown that when the issues are clearly put to voters, they respond in a rational way. I was surprised by what Bertha Henson and Sumiko Tan wrote in *The Straits Times* recently about our party branches being hollowed out. How could we have achieved such a great victory at Marine Parade if our branches were as weak as they described? But it does not matter. Sometimes it is better that our opponents underestimate us.

Externally, our international position has never been better. Surprisingly, Singapore is now being held up by big countries like China and India as a model and an inspiration. This is partly because of SM Lee and partly because Singapore is too small to threaten anyone. In a small way, Singapore gives China confidence that it is possible to achieve complete modernisation without the loss of traditional values, and without crime, prostitution and drugs proliferating. Singapore provides some proof to India that a democracy with institutions inherited from the British can be secular and dynamic, provided racial, religious and language issues are kept under control.

Many countries now want to do business with us. They are interested to study how we solve our problems. They welcome our investors. We have a good reputation. Just the other day, I was talking to two businessmen who do business in China. One said that being

Singaporean was like having a gold card. The other said, no, no, it is like having a platinum card. Whatever it is, we have a reputation for integrity and for high standards. We must safeguard this reputation, and not let one or two bad apples spoil the whole barrel.

We are now working hard to create an external economy, the way the Dutch, the Swiss and the people of Hong Kong have done. It will take many years but the process has begun in earnest. All over Singapore, people are talking about opportunities in China, Vietnam and other countries. Even students in the junior colleges, polytechnics and universities are thinking along similar lines. It is a good sign. In one generation, the nature of our society will change. The nature of our domestic politics will also change.

Putting it in perspective, the first lap in the history of Singapore was internal development — forging national unity, building the Singapore Armed Forces, reducing unemployment, educating the young, housing the population, and so on. To achieve all this, the People's Action Party (PAP) had to fight first, the colonialists, then, the communists and finally, the communalists. Now the challenges are of a different kind. In this next lap, we must create an external economy. We must think in international terms and stay united as Singaporeans even as we romp all over the world. We must have good relations with as many countries as possible. We should put to good use our cultural links with the rest of Asia. If we were de-cultured Chinese, our links to China would not be as important. If we were de-cultured Malays, our links to Malaysia and Indonesia would be weak. If we were de-cultured Indians, we would not be as effective a partner in India's progress.

Because of rapid growth in Asia, our political and cultural assets are of great economic value. This growth in Asia is likely to continue for many more years to come. In less than 20 years, the centre of the world economy will shift from North America to East Asia. If India and Australia also succeed in reforming their economies, the whole Asian region, with over half the world's population, will prosper in a way never seen before in human history.

We are at the centre of this region, as well connected to China and Japan as we are to India and Australia. A whole continent is being re-opened. If we play our cards right, we can be a New York or a London in the role we play as a city. The cards are political, economic and cultural.

### *Internationalism*

Politically, we must be internationalist in our outlook. This is why ASEAN, APEC and the UN are so important to us. We are never a passenger at these forums. We play our part and many countries do value our participation.

### *Market Economy*

Economically, we support an open trading system and the free flow of capital and knowledge. The greater the international division of labour, the greater the wealth produced in the world, the greater the benefits to us in Singapore.

### *Multi-culturalism*

Culturally, our diversity is a precious asset provided we keep extremism in check. Culturally, we are a part of China, a part of Indonesia and Malaysia, a part of India and a part of the West. This makes foreigners feel at home in Singapore. Among many Japanese, Indians, Americans and Europeans, Singapore is their favourite foreign city in Asia. Conversely, Singaporeans are comfortable whether we are in China, India, Thailand, Australia or America. But we must always be watchful of extreme tendencies in our society in matters of race, language and religion. This is why we will always need the Internal Security Act (ISA), whatever our Western friends may tell us.

If we play our cards right — our political, economic and cultural cards — our world will be much bigger and all kinds of opportunities will open up for our children and grandchildren. However, to achieve this, we must have the right internal factors.

## Critical Internal Factors

If we do not have good leaders, if we lose our solidarity, all our good cards will be wasted. To play the game well, we need close rapport between ourselves and our leaders. This is easier said than done. In many countries, the leaders are corrupt and care more for themselves than for the country. In many democracies, the voters themselves expect to be bribed, as a result of which it is no wonder that their leaders are corrupt.

### *Democracy*

We need democracy to help prevent the corruption of absolute power, the kind we see in North Korea and Iraq, but democracy is no guarantee that there will then be no corruption. Look at Japan and Italy. The scandals seem never to end. When a Member of Parliament (MP) is expected to give gifts at every wedding and funeral, he must find money. The corruption then becomes part of the system itself, which makes it very hard to clean up. Every Japanese MP needs at least $2–3 million a year to get re-elected.

Every democracy faces its own set of problems. In Japan, corrupt politics has not affected long-range planning because long-range planning is carried out by an elite corps of civil servants. In many Western countries, politics is very short-term, which results in growing budget deficits and foreign debt. In the former Soviet Union and in India, democracy has led to ethnic strife. In the case of India, one could reasonably argue that without the suspension of democracy and the imposition of direct Presidential rule at critical junctures, India would have broken up a long time ago. Every society must find its own solutions. Democracy is not a panacea. Democracy in Singapore has to take into account our need to plan for the long-term, our small size, our social divisions and the importance of human resource development. Some Westerners describe our democracy as "soft authoritarianism". I call theirs "hard liberalism". It does not matter. What is important is that our democracy works for us.

### *Socialism*

In the same way, our socialism must also work for us. Our Party is a democratic-socialist party. A society that preaches only competition and capitalism, where individuals care only for themselves, cannot stay united for very long. When individuals who do poorly rebel against the system and try to bring it down, the result is social strife. When they actually succeed in removing competition, the result is even worse. In the Soviet Union and China, the replacement of the market economy by state socialism was a disaster. State socialism has been shown to be a dead-end. But socialism itself is not dead because it springs from the hearts of men. It is part of our social instinct to help the handicapped and the less fortunate. We must always be socialist in preventing extreme poverty. We must always be socialist in helping everyone rise to the limit of his potential regardless of parentage, race, language or religion. Our policy to subsidise health, education and housing is a form of socialism. The way our unions look after the welfare of workers is a form of socialism. Group effort and communitarianism are all forms of socialism. So too the bonds which hold the family together. Ours is a supply-side socialism which concentrates on human resource development, not a demand-side socialism which tries to pull everyone down to the same level. Ours is a socialism based on rights and duties, and not on rights alone. In this way, we overcome the side-effects of competition, while avoiding the pitfalls of state socialism.

Competition and socialism must always be kept in balance. Too much socialism will blunt our ability to compete in the world. This is why the Singapore Democratic Party's policy of creating envy and social division is very dangerous. To exploit the opportunities knocking on our doors, we need domestic consensus, not conflict.

### Importance of a Broad Consensus

We need a broad consensus, a common understanding of the strengths and weaknesses of Singapore, and a common response towards external opportunities and threats. Then we will succeed. If we turn inwards and spend all our time arguing about how the furniture should be arranged and re-arranged, we will be left behind, the way the Philippines has been left behind.

Creating that broad consensus is the job of the PAP. Without the PAP, we would not have been able to complete the last lap. Without the PAP, we will not be able to run the next lap. The challenges are different but they are just as real. We have good cards but the competition is very stiff and the stakes are very high.

It *is* the job of the PAP. But who is the PAP? It is us — ordinary men and women who feel strongly for Singapore and want to get involved. An earlier generation who felt strongly got involved, and got us to where we are today. It is now the turn of another generation to run the race and to prepare yet another generation for their turn.

**Young PAP**

The PAP Youth Wing was formed in September 1986 under BG Lee Hsien Loong to help hand over the baton from one generation to another. Much has happened since then. We had a General Election in September 1988. In November 1990, Mr Goh took over as Prime Minister. In August 1991, another General Election was called. In November 1992, PM Goh took over the Secretary-Generalship of our Party and went on to win the Marine Parade by-election in a convincing way.

This transition in Singapore coincided with the end of the Cold War and the emergence of a very different world. In June 1989, the Tiananmen demonstrations in Beijing were ruthlessly put down. In November 1989, the Berlin Wall crumbled. On 2 August 1990, Saddam Hussein invaded Kuwait but was thrown out by US-led forces in early 1991. In August that year, when the coup in Moscow failed, Yeltsin forced Gorbachev to dissolve the Communist Party. By the end of the year, the Soviet Union was finished. All countries, big and small, are now adjusting their positions in response to these dramatic changes. With ideology as less important, international politics is increasingly dominated by economic considerations.

To take into account the changes that have taken place in Singapore and in the world, a major review of the Youth Wing was undertaken last year. The Central Executive Committee (CEC) recently approved the recommendations made.

The Youth Wing has been renamed Young PAP and its membership age limit is now raised from 35 to 40 years. The Chinese, Malay and Tamil translations remain unchanged.

To press on with the renewal of our Party, a major recruitment drive will be launched by Young PAP Vice-Chairman, Mr Lim Hng Kiang. It will have two prongs. One prong is directed at the Party branches. We need to bring in more younger members. To increase their sense of involvement, elections will be held to elect branch and district YP representatives. Details of election procedures will be worked out over the next few months.

The other prong is directed at graduates from the universities and polytechnics. It is partly to signal our interest in this group that we have renamed the Youth Wing to Young PAP (YP). Just as a big corporation like Shell or DBS would take care to recruit from every graduating class, so too should the Young PAP. We will reach out to all professions so that all segments of our society are represented. In sharpening our appeal to graduates and professionals, we should never lose touch with Chinese, Malay and Indian-speaking young Singaporeans who may not be proficient in English. We must never forget the multi-racial basis of our Party.

A greater range of activities will be organised. A Policy Studies Group (PSG) has been formed under Mr Sin Boon Ann to analyse policy alternatives and make recommendations to the main Party. The PSG will be free to take its own position on policy matters. It should study both domestic issues and external affairs. The two are not separate. Our domestic policies must always take into account the external challenges which confront us. As party activists, we should be aware of the connections and help explain them to the man in the street.

To increase our own awareness of external affairs and to facilitate contact with young political leaders in other countries, an International Relations Section will be formed. Although we are not part of an international network of fraternal political parties — not since the PAP left the Socialist International — we do receive visitors from political parties of other countries and keep up friendly ties with them. We expect such exchanges to increase. On our side, we will organise visits to countries like Malaysia, Indonesia, China and Vietnam. In this post-Cold War world, politics and business must go together.

Last year, the Young PAP established a Headquarters (HQ) Branch under Mr Christopher Goh, for new members who have not yet decided which constituency they would like to work in. The HQ Branch organises regular luncheon talks on a wide range of political and non-political subjects for all YP members and for invited guests. The format of these luncheon talks is similar to those organised by associations like the Rotary Club. We have to adopt a marketing approach and create different products for different market segments. Expectations have changed. Compare our community centres today with those of yesteryear. In the past, *ping pong* tables and TV sets were a draw. Today, they are not worth a second look. We have to adjust to changes in the market.

There are many young Singaporeans who are keen to participate in YP activities but who are not prepared for the time being to become card-carrying members of our Party. The CEC has agreed to the YP creating an affiliate membership for them. Affiliate members of the YP are not PAP members. They are our friends. They occupy a different market segment.

We must reach out to both young men and young women. To coordinate and combine the activities of the YP and the Women's Wing, a representative from the Women's Wing now sits on the HQ Committee of the YP. The present Women's Wing's representative is Ms Ying Wai Lin.

To market the Young PAP more effectively to members of the public, a Public Affairs Section was established last year under Ms Peggy Chua. We will use *Petir* to communicate to our members in all the four official languages. If necessary, we will have our own circular as well. We have crafted a mission statement for the YP and a new logo to be used in conjunction with the Party logo.

The mission of the YP is to help the PAP maintain its position as the mainstream political party of Singapore, by expressing the aspirations of young Singaporeans and by recruiting supporters, members and leaders for the Party from among young Singaporeans.

Because every generation is different, the mainstream position of the Party must change with the times. By bringing in each new generation, we keep the PAP well-centred in the political life of Singapore.

The logo has both formal and informal elements. The colours are our Party colours. The capital letters YP are in red while the base is a calligraphic YP in blue. From another perspective, the YP is riding on waves of support. The YP logo should be used in conjunction with our Party logo. Having a separate logo for the YP reflects our identity as a distinct group within the PAP. As the mainstream party, the PAP covers a broad range. Within that range, it is natural that the YP should occasionally take positions which do not coincide with the central tendency. And if the YP correctly expresses the aspirations of younger Singaporeans, its position may well help to determine the future direction of that central tendency.

**National Service**

To secure the long-term future of Singapore, we need a broad consensus gathered around the PAP as the mainstream party. For the next one or two General Elections, the Young PAP may not be critical to the Party, but as we enter the next century, a new generation must be in place to shoulder the burden. Planning long-term for the Party is as important as planning long-term for defence and economic development. The SAF and the Civil Service plan for succession very carefully. Big corporations like Shell and Nestle plan for succession very carefully. We must do the same as a political party. At all levels, succession should not be something improvised at the eleventh hour or, worse, left to chance. Of course, politics is full of surprises and no amount of planning can anticipate the unforeseen and the unforeseeable. But that must not become a reason for us to do nothing. We must still plan for the future, not rigidly but in a flexible way.

Political continuity is very important. Political continuity under the Liberal Democratic Party (LDP) has been a critical factor in the post-war development of Japan. Now all that is threatened by corruption. In the case of Taiwan and South Korea, there was no democracy under martial law. Martial law provided policy continuity but political pressure built up and when the lid was removed, the pot boiled over. The South Korean economy is now in serious trouble. In Taiwan, rapid democratisation has stoked native Taiwanese sentiments. This may complicate Taiwan's future relationship with the Mainland. In both South Korea and Taiwan, political corruption is a big problem. In the case of Hong Kong, the problem of political continuity is even more acute with the reversion to Chinese rule in 1997.

We have been fortunate in Singapore. We are independent and we have kept the PAP clean. We have been able to maintain our position as the mainstream political party General Election after General Election. A certain bond of trust exists between the PAP and the people of Singapore. Our policies may not always be popular but no one believes that we are pursuing them on our own behalf. To keep the Party vital and in touch, we need a constant infusion of new blood. We need good leaders at all levels. Without Mr Lee Kuan Yew and his generation, we would not be here today. Good leadership is crucial. This is why PM Goh has asked a new generation of young Singaporeans to come forward.

We need to get young Singaporeans involved and as many as possible. I know we are all very busy in Singapore. We are busy with our careers, busy getting married and busy raising families. But many of us still find time to do social work in one way or another. There may be a lack of time but there is no lack of ideas or ideals. We must be fired by the same sense of duty in political work as we are in social work. In many countries, politics is debased because politicians are driven more by ambition than by duty. In many countries, good men are found more in the private sector than in the public sector. In Singapore, that will be a disaster.

In Singapore, politics should be a part of national service. Like national service in the SAF, we need fresh recruits to replace those who have reached their Operationally Ready Date (ORD). We need younger reservists to replace older ones. There is a world out there to conquer. That should be our greatest motivation. If we succeed, Singapore will become much more than a small nation. We will be a city-state like the Venetian Republic, with interests and influence radiating into large parts of the world. Then, not only will Singaporeans be proud to remain Singaporean, others will line up to join our ranks. The PAP is the vanguard. Our own ranks must be kept fighting fit. This is why the Party has to recast the net again and again to bring in new combatants. That net is the Young PAP. I hope the fish will oblige.

# ASIAN SOCIALISM

*Asian forms of democracy are evolving in ways more suited to our histories and cultures, and may meet our specific needs better.*

One free evening in Chengdu last year, I dropped by a local pub for a glass of beer with some friends. The pub affected a German atmosphere. A local group belted out Hong Kong and Taiwanese pop songs. When they rested, the TV set pumped out MTV rap. Chinese and foreigners mingled freely as if Chengdu was Singapore. I mused to myself how much the world has changed. It was not so very long ago when Sichuan, deep in the west of China, was the last refuge of the Kuomintang (KMT). While Japanese aircraft bombed Chongqing and Chengdu, the Japanese Imperial Army itself could not, or dared not, advance so far up the Yangtze.

Of course, what has really changed is the technology in communication and transportation. In an earlier period of industrialisation, the scale economies of mass production led to highly centralised modes of organisation. Empires were needed to secure sources of raw material and captive markets for surplus production. The same technology gave birth to the horrible military machines which devastated large parts of the world in two world wars. Then the nuclear genie appeared and gave the world some stability during the Cold War. In the meantime, governments became monstrosities, both in the capitalist world, in the form of the welfare state, and in

---

Opening speech at the Conference on 'The Rise of Industrial Asia', Regent Hotel, 16 June 1994.

the socialist world, in the form of the Stalinist planned economy. All this is changing once again as a result of the technological revolution.

Once again, the pendulum of history is swinging back. Size is no longer as important as it was in the past. Indeed, size can become a serious handicap in the organisation of businesses, armed forces and governments. Being big like dinosaurs might once have been an advantage. No longer. It is like the response of the biological world to major climatic change. To thrive in the new age, the intelligence and sprightliness of mammals are required. Empires have become too unwieldy. The last imploded — bringing an end to the Cold War. Big nation-states face major crises of re-organisation. If they are unable to, they will break up as some in Africa will. The political systems of countries like China, India, Indonesia and Brazil are coming under increasing stress as a result of the same changes in technology and production. Institutional structures more suited to agricultural and early industrial societies are being challenged as never before. Even in advanced countries, new institutional arrangements are needed to allow for a greater devolution of power to provinces and city-regions. Weak governments in North America, Europe and Japan are manifestations of such institutional crises.

Economically, the world is breaking up from empires and big nation-states to smaller states, provinces and city-regions. Already small states, each with a population of less than 10 million, make up two-thirds of UN members. Increasingly, it is at the level of city-regions that competition for human talent and investments takes place. This is not to say that the nation-state is no longer important or that it will disappear. It will not, but its power to tax and redistribute wealth is weakening by the day. Never before in history have the factors of economic production been so mobile.

However, for trade to take place, and for human talent and investments to cross borders, there must be reasonable stability. Regional and international arrangements have thus become very important for the establishment of rules of exchange and conflict resolution. We still need a balance of power among nation-states. But the technology which is changing economic production is also changing the role military power plays in the balance of power.

First, mutual assured destruction makes nuclear warfare difficult to contemplate. This is a factor for stability. At the regional level, military technology favours the defender. This, the Americans learnt at great cost in Vietnam and the Soviet Union in Afghanistan. Modern weapons may have pin-point accuracy but they do not make the subjugation of a foreign people any easier. Indeed, in the hands of the defender, hand-held missiles can inflict great damage against a technologically-superior invading force. For the Soviet Union, the game changed once the *mujahiddeen* was supplied Stinger missiles. Unless technology changes again, there can be no military solutions to the problems of Northern Ireland, Sri Lanka and Bosnia. For example, if the Bosnian Serbs press too hard, they will get no peace because the Muslims will never give up. This is the new reality in the world.

Wars will become more limited in scale and scope, but there will be more of them. Empires are not going to be recreated in the forseeable future, not even in the former Soviet Union. Instead, terrorism will plague the world, including nuclear terrorism. It will become more and more difficult to prevent nuclear proliferation.

The threat of terrorism, whether by rogue governments or by fanatical groups, greatly complicates national security calculations. External defence will no longer be sufficient. A society, to protect itself, will need immune systems like those of a living organism — in other words, defence in depth and defence at the local level. Walled defences no longer work. Instead, cellular constructions, with cells separated by semi-permeable membranes, and complex internal systems will be needed.

For example, the free movement of peoples will have to be controlled. Already, security checks at airports have become more and more cumbersome. Pressures to tighten border controls in the European Union are bound to increase as the problem of illegal migration from the East and the South grows. Even within national borders, control over the free movement of foreigners will become a political issue in many countries. Many of the controls will have to be subtle like those which keep Beverly Hills less crime-ridden than other parts of Los Angeles and, even there, it is a daily battle to keep it that way. Human migration in a crowded world with all its accompanying problems and the responses to such migration will be one of the great political themes of the next century.

I have sketched these trend changes in the world as a backdrop to our discussion on the relevance of the Singapore model to other developing countries. In an age of empires, Singapore cannot be independent. In an age of nation-states, Singapore is too small to be of much interest except as an oddity. In an age of city-regions, however, Singapore's experience as a city-state becomes useful to others. Indeed, we are somewhat embarrassed by the quite-sudden interest in the Singapore experience in the last few years, not just by countries in the region, but also by big countries like China and India, and by distant countries like South Africa, Kazakhstan and the new Palestinian state. The reason is not because Singapore has changed in recent years but because the world is breaking up into city-regions, each of a size and scale comparable to that of Singapore. China, for example, is now divided administratively into city-regions of about 2 to 10 million people each. Each enjoys considerable autonomy. Each must solve problems of urban planning, housing, transportation, road-congestion, attracting investments, job-creation, education, policing, terrorism and so on. Singapore has become a ready-made model for them to study, not only our successes but also our mistakes.

As an independent city-state, Singapore enjoys certain advantages over city-regions which are parts of nation-states. In the past, we saw only disadvantages — loss of traditional hinterlands, limited domestic market for our factories and profound security vulnerabilities. Thus, an earlier generation of Singaporean leaders sought independence from the British through merger with Malaysia. Now, the rules have changed in our favour. Now, we are glad not to have an agricultural constituency to worry about. This greatly simplifies our domestic politics. Our lack of an assured hinterland and the smallness of our domestic market have forced us to be internationally competitive from the start. We have had to work much harder to keep our port and airport busy and our aeroplanes filled more so than others which enjoyed protected monopoly positions. This has made us stronger. Singaporeans know instinctively that there is no free lunch. We cannot afford to play games with monetary policy or the tax system. We contribute no revenues to a central government. Neither do we collect subsidies. Out of what we earn, we have to provide for the economic, security, cultural and social needs of three million people.

The greatest advantage we have is our ability to control the movement of people into Singapore. Without this, Singapore would be like many other fast-growing cities in the Third World, with high crime rates, traffic congestion, slums, prostitution, drug addiction and severe environmental pollution. Instead of indiscriminate urban drift, we selectively in-migrate people into Singapore based on talent, income and other criteria. In the last two years, for every two babies we produce in Singapore, we import one migrant.

Over the next few decades, urbanisation on an unprecedented scale will take place all over Asia, a process involving over two billion people. The ability of local governments to cope with this surge of population from the countryside to the cities will decide which city-regions will succeed more than others. Many will wish that they can regulate this inflow of human beings the way we are able to in Singapore. For them, the central government far away in Beijing or New Delhi is unable to solve many of their local problems.

All over the world, institutions which evolved in response to the needs of an earlier period of industrialisation are no longer adequate for the challenges of the next century. Smaller, more responsive units of organisation are needed. A new pattern of competition and cooperation among city-regions will appear, not unlike the pattern in Europe before the age of nation-states, with international organisations like the old Hanseatic League providing loose coordination.

In this new world, a new balance between rights and duties, between independence and interdependence, and between competition and cooperation will have to be found. Indeed, the ideas of democracy and socialism, which are as old as man, will have to be reinterpreted afresh.

East Asia will make a major contribution to this reinterpretation, not because East Asians are wiser, but because it is in East Asia where old institutions have been the most completely destroyed over the last few hundred years. It started with the colonisation of Southeast Asia and the foreign encroachment into China. In the middle part of the 19th century, the Taiping Revolution ravaged large parts of China and led to the death of 20 million Chinese. The Meiji Restoration of 1868 and the Republican Revolution of 1911 swept aside ancient institutions, not only physically, but, more importantly, in the minds of hundreds of millions of people. These upheavals were followed by the horrors of the Pacific War, by decolonisation and by Communism in China and, with it, the tragic events of the Great Leap Forward and the Cultural Revolution. There were also the Korean War, the wars in Indo-China, the Malayan Emergency and the 1965 Coup and Counter-coup in Indonesia.

It has been almost 150 years of war and revolution bringing untold suffering to countless millions. But precisely because the destruction has been so complete, reconstruction — both physically and in our memory — has been made much easier. The ground has been well-cleared for new plants to take root. With the exception of Japan which modernised first, the countries of East Asia are in a relatively youthful phase of their development. Institutions are still plastic. A certain can-do spirit, sometimes bordering on foolhardiness, fills the air. The disorder and confusion we see in East Asia today are those of organic growth, reminiscent of the disorder and confusion in the US in the 19th century.

South Asia, in contrast, did not experience as much destruction. Much more of the past lives on. Caste and religious divisions remain deep-seated. The bureaucratic stranglehold of the Indian Civil Service will need a revolution to uproot. While there has been dramatic reform of the Indian economy in the last three years, the ground has not been as well-cleared for reconstruction. Thus, South Asia's growth rates are not likely to match those of East Asia. It is in East Asia where radically new institutional arrangements are being tried and where new forms of democracy and socialism are evolving.

It is common for Western liberals to sneer when East Asians talk about Asian forms of democracy. They forget that Western democracy itself evolved over many centuries and took many different forms, and not always for the better. Indeed, Western democracy today faces serious problems. Once property and education criteria are removed, and the vote becomes universal, democracy without group solidarity can become a game where wealth is redistributed from the rich to the poor and from the disorganised many to the organised few. The temptation to borrow from future generations who have no votes is always strong. No democracy can function well without strong moral underpinnings supported by the entire community. Democracies which see only rights without obligations eventually destroy themselves.

Let me make the same point in a different way. If a simple system of one-man-one-vote is so fundamental, why not spread it throughout the world and let the whole world elect a government which then decides how best to allocate global revenues? Well, the rich of the world will immediately secede because the teeming masses of the Third World will stand to inherit the earth. Clearly, democracy only works within a community whose members feel morally for one another and for their offsprings. Even in the European Union, a simple system of one-man-one-vote will not be acceptable, hence the principle of subsidiarity.

Indeed, as the world breaks up economically into city-regions, democratic institutions need to adapt to this new economic reality. For democracy to work well, it should get smaller, not bigger. In fact, this is the way democracy is gradually evolving in China. Over the last 15 years, power has been steadily devolved to provinces and city-regions. Limited election of local governments have become well-established. This important development is often missed by Western observers. They forget that for a country of 1.2 billion people, one-man-one-vote for all of China is as absurd a notion as one-man-one-vote for the whole world or one-man-one-vote for the whole of Europe.

For Singapore, one-man-one-vote works reasonably well because we are small and there is a strong sense of solidarity, of everyone being in the same small boat. For example, we go out of our way to accommodate minority concerns. When we were part of Malaysia, one-man-one-vote did not work as well because of racial polarisation, which was why we separated. In advanced countries, big democracy is preventing system reform. Take, for example, the conflicting interests of Los Angeles and the Bay Area in California, or Tokyo and the Kansai Area in Japan. A certain disaggregation will make the overall system work better but this is practically impossible to carry out because existing political institutions are too entrenched. In the US, the Constitution cannot be changed. In China, the Constitution changes all the time.

Other aspects of an evolving East Asian democracy also bear watching. Consider the treatment of minorities. In a winner-takes-all, one-man-one-vote situation, minorities must revolt against a dominant majority. Other ways must be found to ensure fair minority representation. In Singapore, we created Group Representation Constituencies which forced all major political parties to field a multi-racial slate of candidates in parliamentary elections. In Indonesia, *pancasila* democracy consciously plays down Javanese dominance. In ASEAN, considerable importance is given to consensus-building. Simple vote-counts are rarely taken. The ASEAN method of consensus-building has become an integral part of the APEC process. Even Vietnam, once the common enemy, now wants to join ASEAN and APEC.

I am not saying that Asian forms of democracy are superior to Western forms, only that they are evolving in ways more suited to our histories and cultures, and may meet our specific needs better. Of course, the modern idea of democracy itself came from the West. We will continue to learn from Western ideas of democracy, adapting what is good and rejecting what is bad, but the result will be something quintessentially our own. What will remain the same between East and West is the ideal of representative government reflecting, directly or indirectly, the wishes of the people.

Socialism, too, is evolving in an interesting way in Asia. Consider the case of Singapore. Are we socialist? In many ways, yes, especially in our massive subsidy of housing, health and education. Official visitors from communist China have remarked to us that Singapore is more socialist than China. But Singapore's socialism is consciously supply-side, and structured to increase production rather than consumption.

Partly because we were able to learn from the mistakes made in the West, and partly because the traditions are different, welfare policies in Japan and the NIEs do not result in the same wastage and cynicism. The poor and the sick are still helped but in ways which require from them a sense of gratitude and a commitment to help themselves.

Just as democracy must get smaller, socialism must also get smaller. Socialism will never die, of course, because it springs from the very nature of man as a social animal. At the least, the family will always stay socialist. For many East Asian societies, it is not only the family which is socialist, it is the entire extended family and sometimes the entire clan. Japanese *zaibatsus* and Korean *chaebols* have always practised socialism within the corporation. Socialism works when it strengthens group responsibility. It is dysfunctional when it leads to individual irresponsibility. In Singapore, we deliberately work our welfare policies through the family. Our objective is to strengthen the family net, not weaken it.

We have consciously avoided Western social security systems which are not unlike the unbreakable communal iron rice bowls in Maoist China. They encourage the buffet syndrome, i.e., pay your dues and take all you can. If these social security systems were to be redesigned from scratch, they are more likely to follow Singapore's Central Provident Fund with each individual having his own individual retirement account (IRA). Singapore's Central Provident Fund system is now being copied in parts of China and elsewhere.

Another aspect of Asian socialism worth noting is land tenure. Because of the evils of land concentration in the past, the political instinct in many Asian countries is to lease land out for fixed terms instead of alienating land on freehold. In Singapore, it is 30 years for industrial land and for golf courses and 99 years for new houses, apartment blocks and office buildings. In China, leases vary from 50 to 70 years. Vietnam is still experimenting. Not being freehold, the land reverts to the whole community when the lease runs out. This prevents the growth of a *rentier* class and enables the comprehensive redevelopment of large tracts of land at periodic intervals.

In advanced countries, it is no longer possible to make major changes to the basic structures of democracy and socialism. They are mature societies with established ways. Governments which are too radical get voted out. In Asia today, particularly in East Asia, institutions are still plastic. Major experiments in democracy and socialism are still being conducted. Some will succeed; others will fail. A few may one day be of interest to the West.

The Singapore model is of some relevance because technology is breaking the world up into city-regions and we have a headstart in operating at that level. I hope I have not been presumptuous in highlighting some aspects of the Singapore experience. When Harry Rowen and Gail Neale wrote to me, their letter referred to the Rise *and Fall* of Industrial Asia. It was a typo but I took to heart the unintended warning that the pendulum of history swings both ways, and that all success is ephemeral. I was therefore very concerned to set the Singapore experience in historical perspective. If Western influence had not affected every facet of life in Asia, this enormous transformation would not have been possible. In the same way, the rise of Industrial Asia will eventually have far-reaching effects on the rest of the world, including the Western world.

# The Public Health System

*Good medical services are not provided by individuals alone.*

Tonight we are here to celebrate the 10th Anniversary of NUH. Conceived as a district hospital in the 1970s, the Kent Ridge hospital has now become the principal teaching hospital of the Medical Faculty. It has done well. In the public mind, the National University Hospital (NUH) is a premier hospital and a centre of medical excellence. The fact that members of the public are prepared to pay slightly higher rates at NUH attests to this high standing. The consistently high occupancy of NUH wards is another clear indicator.

This year, we also celebrate the 90th Anniversary of the Medical Faculty. For many decades, Singapore has been a regional medical centre serving a region much larger than itself. Indeed, Singapore was the capital city of the British empire in Southeast Asia and played a key role in attracting medical talent from different parts, training them to serve the entire hinterland. Despite the end of the empire, Singapore today continues to play the same role as a regional medical centre, and we should work hard to be of continuing service to the entire region. A few years ago, I met a Cabinet Minister from India at a social function. He told me that his dental crown was done at NUH. Getting a crown done requires many visits to the dentist and he had come down from India many times for this purpose. He was full of

---

Speech delivered at the National University Hospital (NUH) 10th Anniversary Dinner & Dance, Westin Hotel, 24 June 1995.

praise for his NUH dentist. He told me that he had suggested to his dentist that he should open a practice in Bombay which would make him a millionaire in no time. But the dentist, a professor, declined politely, saying that he preferred to work in Singapore. At that time I was not the Health Minister, but I was very impressed by his high regard for NUH services.

Good medical services are not provided by individuals alone. Good medical services are the products of a complex system which accumulates knowledge, does research, attracts talented individuals, trains them, inspires them, and maintains a high level of professionalism and integrity generation after generation. When we appreciate the good work done by our dentist or surgeon, we must not forget that this good work is the product of an entire health system evolving over the years to nurture such talents.

Before I entered politics, I worked in the Air Force for many years. In the early 1980s, we invited the Israeli Air Force commander to Singapore to advise us on the development of our own Air Force. At that time, we did not have many fighter pilots. To free them of administrative work, many senior positions in the Air Force were held by non-pilots, including army officers like myself. The Israeli Air Force commander, a thoughtful man, said that a good Air Force not only trained fighter pilots. A good Air Force was an entire system which threw up able commanders down the line. I heard him at that time but I did not really grasp the meaning of his words. It was only years later, after encountering and overcoming all kinds of difficulties, that I appreciated the profundity of his comments. To train good fighter pilots, we need good commanders; to have good commanders, we need good training. It is a system which feeds back on itself in a positive way and is kept together by a strong *esprit de corps* and a desire by the more senior members to train successors and be happy when their juniors do better than they themselves.

Our health system, like the Air Force, is a complex system with many parts. Members of the public see only the products of this complex system. Most do not know that good medical services are possible only because all the parts perform excellently and work in harmony. Our public hospitals and national centres all play dual roles.

On one hand, they provide immediate and excellent service; on the other, they train successors better than themselves. This second mission to train successors is a long drawn out process. A patient can be operated on in a few minutes or a few hours. A cancer patient may receive treatment for a few years. But to train a full-fledged consultant to do good work, we need 15 to 20 years. In other words, our public health system is not only providing medical services, it is at the same time keeping the pipeline of consultants and specialists filled and flowing.

This is the difference between NUH and Mount Elizabeth Hospital (Mount E). For some high quality services, Mount E may be as good as NUH. But Mount E cannot reproduce itself while NUH reproduces itself continuously. Singapore's health system can survive quite adequately without Mount E but Singapore's health system will eventually grind to a halt if NUH stops training undergraduate and postgraduate medical students.

The relationship between private hospitals and public hospitals is like that between commercial airlines and the Republic of Singapore Air Force (RSAF). Fighter pilots, who are past their prime or want a change of environment, leave the RSAF to become commercial pilots with SIA and other airlines. It is an easier life, often materially more rewarding, usually less stressful, but a different kind of life. Flying a Boeing 747 is quite different from flying an F16 in a combat situation. The RSAF encourages many of its pilots to seek second careers in commercial airlines eventually because it is too small to hold everyone back. It is important for the RSAF to have a flow-through of officers and to keep the average age relatively young. Furthermore, Singaporean pilots working in commercial airlines still go back to the Air Force for national service.

In the same way, doctors who leave our public hospitals for private practice are also called back to do national service, and many are happy to do so. Sad though we are to lose some of our more able doctors to the private sector, our long-term strategic objective is in fact to promote the growth of the private sector and increase their share of hospital beds, from 20% to 30%. They are still a part of the total health system and play an important role in helping Singapore maintain its position as a regional medical centre.

However, it is not private hospitals but public hospitals which are at the heart of the total health system and NUH plays a key role. In public hospitals, the task of imparting knowledge to juniors is critical. There must be a desire to teach. We must not be like the *kung fu* masters of old who pass only nine-tenths of what they know to their disciples who in turn pass only nine-tenths of what they know down the line. Then, instead of growth, we will have exponential decay. In our system, seniors must have the sense of responsibility and the generosity of spirit to help juniors blossom. Medical technology is advancing rapidly. Sometimes younger doctors sent for training in America come back with more knowledge of new techniques than their own superiors in Singapore. This is to be rejoiced at, not a reason to feel insecure. Furthermore, technical knowledge is no substitute for wisdom, which sometimes only age and experience can confer. What we want is an institutional culture which brings seniors and juniors together in partnership, in joint responsibility for services provided to members of the public and for the future of the public health system.

Teaching is key. NUH's role in teaching is key. Unless NUH helps the Medical Faculty train good, upright doctors, Singapore's health system will decline and Singapore's position as a regional medical centre will diminish. Like what the Israeli Air Force commander once said, we must have a system to throw up future leaders. It is not the intention of the public hospitals to monopolise all talents for themselves. In the same way as the RSAF is happy to lose pilots to Singapore Airlines so long as it is able to retain some of the very best for itself, so, too, should our public hospitals be prepared to see many good doctors leave for the private sector, so long as we are able to retain a fair share of the best, the brightest and the good-hearted for ourselves. Therefore, we must ensure that those whom we wish to retain as leaders in the various fields are paid adequately in relation to the market. Of course, while pay is important, it is never the only factor. What we must have is an overall work environment which makes institutional work rewarding and fulfilling in every sense, including the satisfaction of public service, doing research and teaching.

To improve the student-bed ratio in NUS, the Health Ministry has recently agreed to affiliate the whole of Alexandra Hospital (AH) to the Medical Faculty. This was done on 1 April this year. AH is now a secondary-care hospital, backed by the expertise of NUS professors. Professor Aw Tar Choon from NUS is the new Medical Director of AH. We took half a step in 1993 — when half of the wards at AH were affiliated — but the arrangement proved unwieldy, creating administrative problems for the hospital. This new arrangement should work better and enable NUS professors to be rotated to AH together with students who are sent there for training.

AH will, however, remain a government hospital and will continue to be the cheapest public hospital in Singapore, providing very good value for money. It will continue to specialise in geriatrics and work closely with the Singapore Armed Forces Medical Corps to develop military medicine. With the affiliation of AH to NUS, the student-bed ratio stands at 1:2.7, and this will improve to 3.2 when NUH Phase 3 is completed at the middle of next year. This will give the Medical Faculty a student-bed ratio comparable to those in leading medical schools like UCSF with a ratio of 3.2, Stanford with a ratio of 4.0 and Tokyo University also with a ratio of 4.0.

I must emphasise that while NUH and AH have a primary teaching role, all our other public hospitals will remain teaching hospitals. Singapore General Hospital (SGH), in particular, must remain a major teaching hospital of the Medical Faculty. It is unnecessary for departments in NUH to fear that the development of other public hospitals and the establishment of national centres will erode their position. For this reason, I asked Dr Aline Wong, at the recent topping-up ceremony of the new KK Women's and Children's Hospital, to underline the point that the new KK will be a major teaching hospital for NUS and that the Obstetrics and Gynaecology (O&G) and Paediatric departments in NUH will have access to facilities there. Indeed, it should be the objective of NUH departments to make use of all public health facilities to build up expertise, do research and pursue medical excellence.

Of course, there will always be a sense of competition among public hospitals. This can be healthy and in the public interest. However, we have to strike a balance between competition and cooperation. Where we can play it loose, some degree of competition is good and will result in better service to the public, like in cardiology and medical oncology. But where heavy investment in resources is required — like the new gamma knife facility, or where there are overriding reasons to centralise, like in heart and liver transplant surgery — the Ministry of Health (MOH) will encourage and even insist on cooperation. Leaders in the public health system must have the helicopter vision to understand when competition is good and when cooperation is essential. MOH's position is clear: In selecting and promoting leaders in the public health system, in addition to professional knowledge and competence, we must also consider the leadership ability of senior doctors to see beyond their own departmental interests. We must encourage more cross-posting of able senior doctors among our public hospitals, national centres and MOH. It was partly to overcome some of the problems over turf that NUH was brought back to MOH last year, with the Board answering directly to the Minister. We now have a much better working relationship and I took the opportunity at the Budget Debate in Parliament to clarify the position. The important thing is for all of us to see the entire health system in Singapore as an organic whole and for each of us to play our part in that totality.

I am very pleased to see many younger doctors who are able, well-trained and enthusiastic gradually moving into positions of leadership. So long as we keep the pipeline of talent filled and flowing and maintain a culture which puts a premium on leadership, professionalism and integrity, our public health system will continue to do well. Then when we meet again 10 years from now for the 20th anniversary of NUH and the 100th anniversary of the Medical Faculty, there will be even more reasons to celebrate.

# HEALTHCARE IN EAST ASIA

*Like biological life, human societies go through life cycles. Good healthcare systems extend that life cycle.*

Mr President, on behalf of the people and government of Singapore, I extend to you, the Vice-Presidents and other officers of the 49th World Health Assembly our heartiest congratulations on your election. I would also like to congratulate the DIrector-General and his staff on the good work of the World Health Organisation (WHO).

East Asia is going through an economic and social transformation on a scale never seen before in human history. Overall poverty levels have come down dramatically and should continue to decline in the coming decades. In the 21st century, large parts of East Asia will be middle-class. The rapid growth that started in Japan and spread to the newly industrialised economies (NIEs) is now gradually encompassing all of Southeast Asia and China. All this development is causing a fundamental change in the structure of the healthcare sector in various countries. While the problems of communicable diseases and malnutrition will still be with us for many more years to come, they will increasingly give way to new problems of providing for the more complex healthcare needs of middle-class societies.

Thus, we see a rapidly growing healthcare industry in East Asia serving these new middle-classes. The process is still in the initial phases and will continue well into the next century. New hospitals are sprouting up all over East Asia to meet the growing demand. Public healthcare systems set up to meet the basic healthcare needs

---

Address at the 49th World Health Assembly, Geneva, Switzerland, 21 May 1996.

of primarily rural societies are no longer adequate. Many national systems are being reformed and restructured to meet new needs and to provide a better balance between the public and private sectors. The healthcare industry in East Asia will be one of the fastest growing industries in the world. While governments are responding in the best way they can, there are limits to the public financing of middle-class healthcare services in any country. Private capital will become more important. The result will be a growing difference in the quality and range of healthcare facilities available to the rich and the not-so-rich, which will in turn create political tensions.

Contrasting the rapid growth of the healthcare industry in East Asia is the mature state of the healthcare industry in North America and Western Europe. In the United States, the healthcare industry has ballooned out of control, soaking up 14% of the GNP and growing. No society can bear such a burden for long. In any society across time and space, there must be a proper balance between resources invested in productive sectors and resources set aside for the aged, the sick and the needy. The healthcare crisis in the United States is a huge political problem which will take many years to resolve. All analysts see an over-supply situation in the United States for the next 10 to 20 years.

But it is in the United States and the other developed countries that medical science is the most advanced and where the knowledge exists to meet the growing healthcare needs of East Asia. Globally, what we are seeing is an excess of healthcare resources in North America and Western Europe, both in trained personnel and technology, and an under-supply situation in East Asia. There is thus a great opportunity for transfer across the oceans which will be of mutual benefit. Healthcare entrepreneurs will play a key role in directing excess supply to meet excess demand.

However, developing countries in East Asia would do well to learn from the mistakes made in the design of national healthcare systems in the developed countries and avoid the moral hazards of extensive third-party payment, whether by insurance companies or through public financing. Healthcare institutions in East Asia outside Japan are still in an embryonic phase of their development. Mistakes made now in the design of these institutions will have profound consequences for the future. In the same way, pitfalls avoided now will ensure that future generations will enjoy good healthcare at prices they can afford, and with minimal wastage of public and private resources.

In designing or reforming their national healthcare systems, East Asian countries should be mindful of the following considerations.

1. **Keep It Small**

   It is always easy to spend too much on healthcare if someone else shoulders the burden. Community healthcare systems should therefore insist on individual responsibility. Healthcare risks should be pooled at the lowest level possible where costs and benefits are quickly felt, and common sense less uncommon. Singapore has a population of three million. We are like a large Health Maintenance Organisaton (HMO), comparable in size to Kaiser Permanente. There is little advantage for Singapore to pool the healthcare risks of its three million people with another city or country. Indeed, three million may already be too big.

2. **Beyond Basic Healthcare, Let the Market Decide**

   In all societies, healthcare demands are often variegated and subjective. Plastic surgeries and orthodontics may be important for some individuals but not to others. No government can make such judgements in a satisfactory way for individuals. It is best to let the market meet these demands and price them accurately. But at the same time, no government can abdicate all responsibility to the market. In all societies, a minimum level of basic healthcare universally available is needed for political consensus. No society can hold together if the rich are gorging themselves while the poor starve. But beyond that basic level, the market should be allowed to work its magic.

3. **Re-Discover Holistic Medicine**

   East Asia has a tradition of holistic healthcare going back hundreds, if not thousands, of years. In the early period of modernisation, the importance of traditional medicine was downplayed because of the apparent superiority of Western medicine. But Western medicine has its limitations. In reforming their national healthcare systems, East Asian societies will draw upon their long traditions of holistic medicine. This will provide a more comprehensive range of healthcare facilities, especially for the elderly. It is also one way of tempering some of the excesses of technology and reducing healthcare costs.

4. **Avoid Excessive Politicisation**

   The more politicised a country's healthcare system is, the less likely it is to work well because long-term considerations will give way to short-term political needs. Of course, no society can avoid healthcare being an important political issue. Like taxation systems, the key is good design in the early stages of development. Institutional arrangements, once settled, are hard to change. If co-payments are not introduced at the beginning, they are hard to introduce later on. Compounding this problem in East Asia are two factors. One is rapid urbanisation and the growth of many new cities every year for which all kinds of healthcare facilities must be provided. Without clear-sighted long-range national policies, small problems can become very big. National authorities will be hard put to provide adequate healthcare facilities if they are fully subsidised from the national purse. The other big factor is the aging of the population in East Asia, starting with Japan at the turn of the century, the NIEs 10 to 20 years later and the rest of Southeast Asia and China after that. Healthcare systems designed for young populations may not be suitable for elderly populations. But we must age as surely as winter follows autumn. Unless these long-term problems are anticipated and planned for, entire societies can break down because of crushing public healthcare burdens.

Like biological life, human societies go through life cycles. Good healthcare systems extend that life cycle. Defective systems shorten it. Whether or not East Asian societies are able to evolve good healthcare systems will influence the course of the next century. The challenge of meeting the healthcare needs of growing middle-classes in East Asia in the coming decades will be enormous. We must ensure that whatever role the State plays, the responsibility for healthcare and healthy living should remain firmly anchored in individuals and their families. Government at both the municipal and national levels should bear part of the burden but must never bear most or all of it. To anticipate the growing problems of urbanisation and aging, governments should avoid excessive subsidisation when populations are young because it is never easy to reduce the level of subsidy in any society. There must always be a circumspect view of third-party payment, because of the moral hazards involved. Holistic medicine which is an important part of our heritage should be harnessed. If the systems are well designed, they will be politically sustainable over long periods and will enable the economic growth of East Asia to continue well into the next century. This growth will in turn create enormous opportunities for healthcare industries in North America and Western Europe.

Singapore exists at the crossroads of East and West. We have a healthcare system that tries to strike a balance between individual responsibility, family responsibility and group responsibility. We require every individual to build up his own medical savings for himself and his family. His employer shares some of the burden. The government carries the rest. This is the long-term position we take. Our population is still young. While healthcare constitutes only 3% of the GNP today, we expect this proportion to grow to 6–8% as our population ages. We are also facilitating the scientific development of Traditional Chinese Medicine which still enjoys wide popularity among many Singaporeans. We are encouraging the private sector in Singapore to expand, both to meet the needs of Singaporeans and to service the region. We are also working with WHO agencies to cooperate and exchange experiences with other countries.

# A Big Singapore

*If Singapore is reserved for Singaporeans alone, we would have a very small Singapore. What we must strive for is a Big Singapore mentality.*

A few weeks ago, I went to a neighbourhood coffeeshop with some of my grassroots leaders after a meet-the-people session, a political clinic which all PAP MPs hold weekly. It was a pleasant tropical evening. We were sitting around a table outside the coffeeshop beneath the stars at Kampong Kembangan. At the next table were two French couples who, like us, were also enjoying their coffee and the conversation. They were behaving as Singaporeans would. Part of the charm of the Singapore landscape is our neighbourhood coffeeshop, which is what the neighbourhood pub is to the Englishman. Today, all over Singapore, foreigners live in our Housing Development Board (HDB) estates, including many who are working as professionals here. They shop in our markets. They eat in our hawker centres, wearing shorts and slippers as many locals do. They are a welcome addition to our lives in Singapore. They make a big contribution to the Singapore economy.

This is the kind of world we are moving into in the next century. Human talent from all four corners of the world work and live here in Singapore. In the reverse direction, more and more Singaporeans are fanning out to other countries and continents in search of fame and

---

Speech at the launch of 'Contact Singapore', 30 July 1997. *Note*: Contact Singapore is an agency of the Singapore government whose primary function is to draw people from around the world to work, invest and live in Singapore, with the ultimate aim of boosting economic development.

fortune. Indeed, this is part of our regionalisation drive. In a shrinking world, human talent has become very mobile. Everyone recognises that a good person in a key position can make a decisive difference to the well-being of an organisation. A top surgeon in a leading role can alter the reputation of a hospital. A gifted conductor can transform the performance of a symphony orchestra. A dedicated principal can lift the spirit of an entire school. In a competitive world, the most important thing is to have the right person in the right job. Thus, the competition for human talent in the world is becoming more and more intense.

We have seen many such periods in human history. During the period of the Chinese warring states and the Greek city-states, scholars wandered around seeking the patronage of wise lords. Able princes went out of their way to attract the services of talented individuals. The city-states which gathered the most talents become the most successful. So it was too during the European Renaissance when cities and princes competed for the best and the brightest in all fields of human endeavour, from shipbuilding and navigation to the arts and music.

Singapore needs talent from all over the world. To attract talent from all over the world into Singapore, we must welcome them into our community and treat them well. If we do not welcome young Frenchmen into our coffeeshops, if they do not feel at ease in Singapore. If we do not make them feel at home, then we do not deserve to have them. And Singapore as a whole will be much the poorer. If Singapore can be a second or third home for them, many more will come and our side will be much strengthened.

What we need, therefore, is a culture which is outwardly-oriented. What we need is a Singapore mentality that is global and cosmopolitan. This requires Singaporeans to feel secure about themselves. If we are big-hearted, we will welcome foreign talent into our midst. If we are small-hearted, we will always find reasons to be unhappy with them. At all levels, from the top to the bottom, we need a Singapore culture that is outwardly-oriented without fearing that this would somehow threaten our own positions.

This is easier said than done. There will always be insecurities felt by some of us. We must manage these insecurities well. For example, we go out of our way to recruit bright students into our schools, polytechnics and universities from ASEAN countries, China, India and elsewhere. Many of these foreign students do well, very often better than our own students. We can react in one or two ways. We can rejoice in the fact that we have been successful in attracting talent here, thereby raising our overall standards. Or, we can react in an insecure way, and complain that foreign students are not loyal to Singapore, crowd us out and make use of Singapore as a stepping stone to other places.

Our proper response is, firstly, to help all Singaporeans to develop to their full potential and to be the best that they can be. Having done that, we must bring in foreigners who can help us do more than what we can do by ourselves. Of course, all other things being equal, we must favour Singaporeans over foreigners. That is the right thing to do. Indeed, the government has systematically ensured that, in all our policies, Singaporeans enjoy the privileges of citizenship. But we must also not discriminate against foreigners just because they are foreigners. That would be very short-sighted indeed. If Singapore is reserved for Singaporeans alone, we would have a very small Singapore. In a Small Singapore, Singaporeans who are talented would emigrate to greener pastures. If, instead, we promote the idea of a Big Singapore, then even the Singaporeans who live many years overseas would not want to give up their citizenships. The opposite would happen. Others would clamour to join our ranks. What we must strive for is a Big Singapore mentality. What we must avoid strenuously is a Small Singapore mentality.

The Contact Singapore programme we are launching today is part of Big Singapore. This is a project to encourage foreign talent from all over the world to come to Singapore — to work, live and play here. We welcome them here not only as tourists but also as partners and co-workers. It does not matter whether they are here as professionals, managers, artists, artisans or students — so long as they have a contribution to make to Singapore and to Singaporeans, we welcome them. They help to make Singapore richer and more beautiful.

Under the Contact Singapore programme, we will establish centres all over the world to encourage this inflow of talent into Singapore. Because of the particularly close relationship that we have with Australia, our first centre is being launched in Sydney today. The next centre will be in Perth. After that, we will launch Contact Singapore in overseas centres in Vancouver, Boston, Los Angeles and London in the coming months. They will now play a larger role in our overall efforts to create a Big Singapore.

In order to succeed, the benefits of Contact Singapore must be two-way. For example, the greater the number of Australians working in Singapore, the better this must be for both Singapore and Australia. In the end, what we are trying to achieve is to make Singapore a part of the consciousness of Australia, and to make Australia a part of the consciousness of Singapore. In the same way, we should try to make Singapore a part of Japan, of America, of China, of Europe and of India. We also want them to become a part of us. As we say in Chinese, *wo xin zhong you ni, ni xin zhong you wo* (我心中有你，你心中有我): "We have you in our hearts and we hope that you have us in your hearts." If we succeed in doing this, Singapore will truly become "Singapore Unlimited", a Big Singapore for our children and grandchildren.

# Worldwide Web: Strengthening the Singapore Network

*... the state is not completely above society. They exist together, drawing strength from each other.*

## From a Hierarchical World to a Web World

In discussing the role of civil society in Singapore, we need first to look at the way the world is going, for we do not exist in isolation. We are not an island. The world is going through a major transformation brought about by the revolution in information technology. The current Asian crisis, which is both economic and political, is part of it. Old structures are being undermined, while new structures have yet to crystallise. The transition is an exciting one, full of hopes, but also full of dangers. It may well extend many decades and will certainly define the first half of the next century.

We are moving from a hierarchical world to a web world. The dissolution of old hierarchies is taking place not only internationally but also domestically within each country. International trade and the global economy are important aspects of this web world.

The power of the state is weakening, especially the power of large states. Take an area like telecommunications. In the old days, local telephony and international telephony were provided by monopolies and cartels. Today, there is increasingly free competition. With satellite handphones, no government will be able to maintain its monopoly position. Even hotels which exploit their local monopoly position to levy hefty charges on telephone calls will be bypassed. The implications

Speech at the Institute of Policy Studies Conference on "Civil Society: Harnessing State-Society Synergies", Orchard Hotel, 6 May 1998.

are far-reaching. One day, even the Chinese government will not be able to control the evolution of the Chinese Internet.

Or take the growth of electronic commerce. Many of us are familiar with the cyber-bookshop Amazon.com. We are now able to bypass local book distributors by buying books on the Internet. On Amazon.com, one can buy books weeks before they appear in our local bookshops. But it is not only bookshops and book distributors who are bypassed; tax authorities are also bypassed because it is difficult to collect GST on small items which are brought in by parcel post. As electronic commerce grows, the ability of national authorities to levy taxes will be severely weakened. Capital and human talent are mobile as never before. Thus, governments are forced to compete with each other in the level of direct and indirect taxes they levy because individuals and corporations will have more ways to bypass national authorities. Government authorities which try to tax their citizens worldwide, like the US Government, run the risk of wealthy individuals giving up their citizenships for other citizenships which impose lower levies. For all multinational corporations, international tax planning is a key corporate function.

In the financial industry, the bypassing of old hierarchies is called disintermediation. Disintermediation now applies not only to financial institutions but also to other economic structures, and to social and political structures as well. Monopoly positions are harder and harder to maintain. The ultimate monopoly being weakened is the state. It is said that the essence of the state is its monopoly of legitimate violence against those who live within its jurisdiction. This applies not only to criminals. It applies also to those who do not pay their taxes and to those who want their children educated in a different way. With the global market creeping into more and more areas of society, this monopoly power of the state becomes weaker. Either the state conforms to the market or the market will find ways to defeat the state. However, the state will not disappear. It will remain important but will be forced to compete internationally for financial and human resources.

An obvious example is the current financial crisis in Asia. Governments which were able for a long time to redirect investment and redistribute income have lost much of their power. To use jargon which has recently become fashionable, the market exposes and punishes crony capitalism. Of course, this is a process which has been ongoing for some time now. The welfare state is in crisis throughout the world, whether it is the Fabian-Keynesian model or the communist-socialist one. It was market disintermediation which led to the collapse of the Soviet Union and which forced China to integrate into the world economy. Affirmative action all over the world is called into question because of the distortion it causes to the market.

The collapse of the Soviet Union and its aftermath give us an idea of what happens when the hierarchical world becomes a web world. The Russian government today collects far less revenue than its predecessor. Some say it is less than 10% of GNP. No one is quite sure. Local authorities have become much more powerful in Russia. Legally possessing weapons, the army, the KGB and the police have become semi-autonomous power centres. Mafia groups have become rampant, behaving like small governments. Life goes on. Moscow and St Petersburg today have become much livelier compared to the old days, but Russia has become a messier world.

Disintermediation will cause the whole world to become messier. The weakening of the state has not been fully counterbalanced by a strengthening of regional and international institutions, most of which, like the IMF, were created in response to the challenges of an earlier age. Below the level of the state, city-regions and cities have become more powerful. MNCs today are, in some ways, jurisdictions unto themselves. If they are domiciled in a particular country or listed in a particular stock market, it is not by force but by choice.

In the same way, civic organisations in each country will become stronger as the state loses some of its monopoly power. It becomes easier for them to find alternative sources of finance and forge their own international connections. Their members are freer to travel and to meet their counterparts in international conferences. Thus, in all countries, including China and India, non-government organisations have proliferated. However, there is also a darker side to this phenomenon. Criminals, terrorists and paedophilies are also able to network in the same way.

## Civil Society and Singapore

What is the implication of all this on Singapore and on state-society relations in Singapore? In the coming decades, Singapore's status as a city-state will probably be a great advantage to us. Compared to cities in big countries, we have greater powers of self-determination. This enables us to have our own laws and to keep out the slums. Without this ability, we will be hard put to solve urban problems like housing, traffic congestion, crime, education, healthcare and so on. The politics of a city-state are also much simpler. We do not have farmers and agricultural lobbies to worry about. Singaporeans know instinctively that the business of Singapore is business. If we do not work, we do not eat. If we are not competitive in the global market, we will die. Thus, Singaporeans know we cannot take too many liberties with ourselves. Without this common focus, the PAP government could not have remained dominant for so long.

Last week, I met a group of senior journalists from India. They were full of praise for us. When I replied that Singapore is easier to manage because we are a small country, their reply was that being a small country is a great advantage. Their remark is worth pondering over. In the old days, Indians were proud that India was a big country. Today, they face the frustration of not being able to break out from India's multiple hierarchies. This makes it difficult for India to adjust to new opportunities. Singapore, in contrast, can turn on a five-cent coin.

Singapore would certainly be poorer off if it were a part of India, as we were from 1819–1867 under the British East India Company. Equally, Singapore today would not be better off if we were part of Malaysia, Indonesia or China. There was a time when an earlier generation of leaders believed passionately that Singapore could not survive on its own, which was why the PAP then fought for merger with Malaysia. The world has completely changed. Technology has changed in our favour and we are lucky to be in the position that we are in. To be sure, the pendulum of history may well swing the other way a hundred years from now, but that would be a different story. In the meantime, we have become a web cluster in the worldwide web.

As for state-society relations in Singapore, it is also going through a major transformation. In the old paradigm, the state was hard while society was soft. In the web world, the state and society exist in parallel. The organisation of Singapore is becoming less hierarchical. In the public sector, we have reduced the core, giving more flexibility to the rest. Government departments have been corporatised. Statutory boards have been privatised. Government-linked corporations have become more market-driven, increasingly operating outside the country. Even government ministries have become autonomous agencies, each managing and optimising its own budget.

This decentralisation, which is a response to new necessities, extends across all of Singapore. In Parliament, the introduction of Nominated MPs has brought new life to the House and a greater diversity in political debates. Local governments have assumed greater responsibilities. Town Councils now play an important role in our lives. The nine Community Development Councils are working as government-sponsored civic organisations. We have progressively widened the circle of participation in local government.

Many government committees have become civic committees, like those involved in keeping Singapore clean and green, discouraging smoking, and promoting a healthy lifestyle and the speaking of Mandarin. This trend will continue. Singaporeans with the ability and desire to contribute are called to serve in one way or another. In some cases, the problem is of the same individuals being called to serve in too many areas, but that is not a bad sign. On the whole, we now have a diverse range of Singaporeans volunteering and they have steered many of these committees in new directions. I hope even more will come forward to lead.

Civil society is also flourishing in other sectors. The number of civic organisations based on religious beliefs have increased. Many are involved in running community hospitals, hospices, halfway houses and other welfare facilities. Those which receive direct or indirect government assistance are required to serve all Singaporeans, regardless of race, language or religion. Most are happy to do so.

Civic organisations based on ethnic affiliation and particular social causes have become more active. Clan associations are rejuvenating themselves with varying success. MENDAKI, the

Singapore Indian Development Association (SINDA), the Chinese Development Assistance Council (CDAC), the Eurasian Association and the Association of Muslim Professionals (AMP) have become important self-help groups. The Association of Women for Action and Research (AWARE), the Roundtable and Sintercom encourage us to be more socially conscious. In the past, such organisations tended to be politically motivated, sometimes causing them to clash with the state. In fact, some of them directed Singaporeans to their ancestral homelands and had to be restrained. Today, they operate within the bounds of the state and increasingly with a common Singapore starting point. This does not make us monolithic. Singapore is a heterogeneous society and differences of opinion are natural. As our common consciousness grows, the bounds of debate will be relaxed but, realistically, we will always need an outer perimeter to hold our society together.

For example, our universities, polytechnics and schools have become livelier and more diverse. Alumni networks have strengthened considerably. Fund-raising has become a part of our lives. Every so often, we are asked to sing, dance or eat for a good cause.

In the cultural field, we have also achieved some success. We now have a good range of art and heritage groups. They make a big contribution to our social and cultural life. Take, for example, the recent Singapore International Film Festival. It was the most successful ever and we are well on our way to becoming the Asian Film Festival centre. The Film Festival was not started by any government agency. It was conceived by a group of private individuals. It was only after the Festival showed promise that government agencies like the Economic Development Board (EDB), the National Arts Council (NAC) and the Singapore Tourism Board (STB) gave their support. Recently, we established a Film Commission, consisting of members from the private sector, to promote the film industry, both Singapore as a movie hub and also the production of local films. Singaporeans are the world's greatest moviegoers. I thought that as a result of the economic downturn, our cinemas would also suffer a drop in attendance. But the contrary happened. Cinema attendance went up, probably because it is a cheap form of entertainment. One other aspect of the Film

Festival is also worth remembering. If we did not relax censorship and introduce film classification, the Film Festival would not have taken off. By a judicious pruning of the banyan tree, we have enabled a new plant to grow.

National Service has also become a part of our civil society. Most of the Singapore Armed Forces Reservists Association (SAFRA) activities are now organised by national servicemen themselves. Singaporeans have become quite good at organising big events because of the training they receive in National Service. A point here is worth remembering. National Service can only work if Singaporeans themselves believe in it and are possessed of a voluntary spirit. Without that spirit of sacrifice, National Service will break down, however draconian our laws are. If Singaporeans do not wish to fight for Singapore, they will be absent without official leave (AWOL) in a crisis and there is little the SAF can do about it. National Service is perhaps the most important expression of state-society relations. A state lacking self-confidence will never arm its own citizenry.

## State and Society

What we are now seeing is a new mutually reinforcing relationship between the state and society. While the Singapore state supports the growth of civic organisations, the state has not got total control over them. In fact, the state increasingly relies on them to do the things which the government by itself is not good at doing. If the government asks a smoker to give up smoking, he may resent it. If his peers discourage him, it is a different matter. However, we do need more bottom-up initiatives to achieve a better balance between state and society.

Of course, old instincts sometimes die hard. Without a top-down direction, many civic organisations are plagued by internal disputes. There are deep cultural reasons for this. The separation of powers is not a tradition in Asian society. Without central leadership, many Asian societies do not hold together naturally. The Singapore society is half-Asian and half-Western. We have to strike our own balance. Some civic organisations have experienced difficulty getting the requisite governmental approvals to do things. This is partly because united front activities in the past politicised many civic organisations, causing them to come under security scrutiny. This problem is much less now but we have to be watchful nonetheless. The more we share a common Singapore consciousness, the more civic society can flourish in a way which strengthens the state.

In the coming years, it is good state-society relations which will enable Singapore to compete and survive in the web world. In a messier world, with multiple and overlapping jurisdictions, trust will become a very important quality. When larger systems break down, it is internal networks of trust which will enable trade to carry on and economic life to continue. In the web world, trust networks enjoy a high premium. The Singapore label today enjoys a high premium because others trust us. In a crisis, there is a flight to quality and a flight to trusted networks and jurisdictions. Our strength as a financial centre rests completely upon this intangible quality of trust, trust in the impartiality of our courts, trust in the fairness of our regulations and trust in the professionalism of our officers. This trust is reposed not only in the Singapore government but also in Singapore banks and companies. Indeed, this trust extends to Singaporeans as individuals. And also to foreign companies which are based in Singapore. For example, a listing on the Singapore Stock Exchange is highly desirable for many mainland Chinese companies because it is a stamp of good housekeeping, thereby enabling such companies to raise capital at a lower cost in the international financial market.

State-society relations in Singapore must achieve two things. First, it must reinforce the reputation of the Singapore label. The label is not something superficial. The label reflects the positive elements which Singapore represents. If our passport or banknotes were worthless, others would not try to fake them.

Second, our state-society relations should expand and extend the Singapore network into the region and beyond. Every civic organisation has its own international connections. Each maintains its own network of friends in the world. Collectively, the networks maintained by our private sector organisations, both economic and non-economic, are much larger than the formal networks maintained by the government through its various agencies. In every city around the world, we should promote state-society relations among Singaporeans and extend this network to our friends in that city.

Two weeks ago, when I was in Beijing to attend a conference, I caught a bad flu and thought I should see a doctor. But I did not know whom to consult. It chanced that the manager of the Shangri-La Beijing Hotel was a Singaporean and a good friend of our ambassador. He recommended a doctor in the hotel. The doctor prescribed me both Western and Chinese medicines, none of which I was familiar with. The Singaporean manager assured me that he and other Singaporeans working in the hotel have taken the same medicines before, without ill effects. So assured, I took the prescription and felt much better the following day. It is such networks, small and big, which augment our strengths overseas.

The Singapore International Foundation, which is a government-supported civic organisation, has done a lot to network Singaporeans around the world. In many cities in Asia, North America, Europe and Australia, we have Singapore clubs and student organisations helping us to maintain this international network.

We must, however, not confine our network to Singaporeans alone. We are too small to be of consequence otherwise. We need friends and, from among them, we should welcome new members into our community. Into Singapore now, we welcome 20,000–30,000 new migrants every year. This is a large percentage compared to the average of 50,000 babies that we produce. In addition, hundreds of thousands of foreigners work in Singapore on employment passes and work permits. In the opposite direction, we have more and more Singaporeans working overseas, working side by side with the locals in other countries. This is the way to multiply our strength and influence. Good state-society relations worldwide help to extend the Singaporean network of trust.

## The Singapore Idea

We are bound together by the Singapore idea. It is not easy to define what exactly constitute the Singapore idea. It involves both the heart and the mind, and probably includes aspects like good governance, civic responsibility, honesty, strong families, hard work, a spirit of voluntarism, the use of many languages and a deep respect for racial and religious diversity. Each aspect by itself is neither remarkable nor exclusive to Singapore, but collectively they are powerful. When Singaporeans travel, they sense acutely the aspects which they miss. When Singaporeans board a SIA plane to fly home, they feel halfway home even though they may still be hundreds or thousands of miles away.

In your conference today on civic society in Singapore, I hope you will be able to define more precisely the Singapore idea and find new and better ways to bind state and society together. For it is in working together that we optimise our position in the world. In the web world, the state is not completely above society. They exist together, drawing strength from each other. If one unfortunate day the state is destroyed, it should be for society to recreate it. This was how the German and Japanese states rose again from the ashes of the Second World War. Our challenge is to create such a society. Although Singapore society was largely created by the state, it has to be Singapore society which ensures the state's long-term existence.

# The Military and the Nation State

*A nation like ours cannot be properly forged in prosperity.*

The phenomenon of the nation state — as the highest, the most stable and effective political expression of human beings organised into groups — continues to confound those who decry the barbarity of old-fashioned nationalism, and who wish for its supersession by a form of social organisation dedicated to higher principles. Should we be surprised that Communism in theory preaches proletarian internationalism but in practice practises a nationalism no less cynical?

So long as the nation state is necessary in this period of human history, it must preserve itself. Hence, it is ultimately founded on military power, or to be more precise, the balance of such powers, which by limiting the competition between states makes possible their peaceful relationship with each other. In this contest, nationalism and patriotism are but the group instinct for collective survival. They are virtues because they are vital to the existence of the nation state and to the military preservation of its interests.

The small state is able to assert its independence only to the extent that it can find room in the interstices in between the contending interests of the larger states around it. Unless such a state is internally united, it cannot be strong enough externally to avoid being crushed or absorbed by others. And its conduct of foreign policy is only as effective as it is able,

---

This short essay was published in 1981 for *POINTER*, an SAF journal, when George Yeo was a Major in the SAF. It first appeared in *POINTER*, Vol. 6, No. 3, January 1981 and was republished in Vol. 25, No. 4, October–December 1999. Reprinted with permission from *POINTER*.

if need be by military force, to prevent the balance of power from being tilted against it. If on the international chessboard the small state cannot be queen, it should at least strive to be a bishop and not be contented to remain a helpless pawn.

The case of Singapore begs many questions. Her institutions are young if not fragile, her diverse cultural heritage a recurrent source of conflict, her people still largely possessed of the mentality of the trading post, flushed in the general economic prosperity but myopic in its perception of the future. Indeed the history of the Republic thus far has been the history of the forging of disparate elements into one nation. As a people, we do not have the fanatical discipline of the Japanese. We are not, unlike the Jews, fired by an all-consuming sense of destiny. We have only ourselves. And National Service becomes both a strength and a weakness. It is a strength because it establishes the independence of the state; a weakness because those upon whom falls the burden of providing that confidence to the citizenry are themselves in need of the same confidence. For they too are a part of that citizenry. And they must first be convinced that the resources invested in the military, that the attention given to its development, that the priority placed on its effectiveness are final proof of the determination of this nation to survive as an independent nation.

The questions are easily asked; they cannot be answered in the abstract. A nation like ours cannot be properly forged in prosperity. The prosperity only affords the time and buys the means with which to make preparations. For it may have to be in white heat when we truly melt into a nation, and when that day comes, the melting pot — which itself must not melt — will be the military.

# STRENGTHENING THE SME SECTOR

*The most important message to register is that no one can stand still. If we don't change, we'll be changed.*

**Strengthening the SME Sector**

There are about 100,000 SMEs in Singapore today. They represent over 90% of business establishments. Although SMEs employ more than half the workforce in Singapore, they generate only one-third of the total value-added. This is to be expected because, being small, SMEs tend to be less efficient.

On the whole, Singapore's SME sector is not as dynamic as Taiwan's or Hong Kong's. After the communist takeover on the Chinese mainland, both Taiwan and Hong Kong received large numbers of refugees, a number of whom were businessmen. In Taiwan, local Taiwanese were excluded from governmental positions, causing many of the more able ones to go into business. In Singapore, we depended much more on MNCs to generate economic development. This was a correct policy because our population base was and still is small, being only half that of Hong Kong's and a fraction of Taiwan's. Furthermore, because we had to build up a whole range of governmental institutions, including the SAF and other critical services, the public sector absorbed a large share of the available talent in the last 35 years. We must therefore take a realistic approach to what our SME sector is able to achieve.

However, despite these limitations, there is much more we can do to strengthen the SME sector in Singapore. There are a few

Speech at the opening of SME 21 Conference, 5 January 2000.

trends which are favourable. For example, our educational profile will continue to see dramatic improvements in the coming years. Among Singaporeans above the age of 40, less than 1 in 2 have more than 6 years of education which is very much a Third World profile. Below the age of 30, the profile is that of a First World country. The point of inflection is between the ages of 30 and 40. These better-educated younger Singaporeans are helping to create a new economy. They provide a solid foundation for the growth of strong SMEs in the future. Furthermore, as the public sector is no longer sucking in a disproportionate share of our young talent, more will be available to the private sector. The globalisation of the Singapore economy, our widespread use of English and the attraction of foreign talent onto our shores will also be helpful.

## Challenge of Globalisation

Traditionally in many countries, SMEs dominate the areas where the forces of globalisation are least able to penetrate. So-called mom-and-pop shops survive because their local environments are protected. Not surprisingly, it is the tradeable sector which enjoys the highest productivity, and the non-tradeable sector which lags behind. Globalisation is increasingly making all sectors tradeable to a greater or lesser degree. Instead of fighting globalisation, we should work with it to make our economy more efficient.

Take our local provision shop as an example. Nowadays, it is not only competing with NTUC Fairprice, it must also reckon with foreign supermarkets like Carrefour. Unless the local provision shop upgrades itself — supply management, inventory control, accounting, marketing, the whole value chain — it will come under severe competitive pressure. Very often, unless better-educated younger family members enter the business, such SMEs have no future. In the same way, the chicken rice stall is being forced to compete with fast-food outlets like KFC and McDonald's. One solution is to become a franchisee but even that requires a certain knowledge of computer systems, modern accounting methods and marketing.

With the Internet explosion and e-commerce, the forces of globalisation will become stronger in the future. It is therefore crucial for us to anticipate the trends early and make adjustments to them. No sector will be spared.

## SME 21 — by Sector

The objective of SME 21 is to facilitate this process of adjustment so that many of our SMEs will emerge as winners in this global game. The key is information and education. To be forewarned is to be forearmed. For example, the Productivity and Standards Board (PSB) of Singapore has done a good job promoting franchising in Singapore. This has enabled many of our SMEs to take shortcuts to the future. Some of our own local companies have in turn franchised their products to others in the region, like Bee Cheng Hiang, the sweetmeat manufacturer. I am surprised that our world-famous chicken rice has still not been franchised overseas.

SME 21 is a plan developed by PSB in broad consultation with industry representatives to help the development of successful SMEs in Singapore. As SMEs cover a broad range, PSB will give particular attention to key sectors like construction and retailing. For construction, we have already announced the Construction 21 plan which is jointly led by the Ministry of National Development and the Ministry of Manpower. PSB plays a critical role in setting standards and promoting standardisation for the construction industry.

For the retail sector, PSB's objective is to double the productivity from $28,000 per worker today to $56,000 in 10 years' time. This is not overly ambitious a target because the present productivity of the retail sector is only one-third that of the manufacturing sector. Singaporeans love shopping. We should make it cheaper and more pleasant for them to do so. Our retail density is one of the highest in Asia. In 1997, there were 18,000 retail establishments in Singapore employing about 75,000 workers. Some consolidation is necessary.

In addition to the construction and retail sectors, PSB is identifying other non-tradeable domestic service sectors to target. These are likely to include the hotel, food and cleaning sectors. We hope also to double their productivity in 10 years.

## SME 21 — Individual Firms

While PSB can offer all kinds of courses and schemes, individual firms must take on the challenge of globalisation themselves. The most important message to register is that no one can stand still. If we don't change, we'll be changed. And those who are able to change early will enjoy an advantage over those who are slow.

The first thing we must change is the way we look at the world. Whether we like it or not, the competition will increasingly be global. To respond to such global competition, we must learn from others and make use of foreign ideas and foreign expertise. Take our most successful local "pao" (dumpling) manufacturer Kong Guan. It grew from a little coffeeshop stall into its present 1,000-outlet business. Kong Guan has 50% of the local "pao" market. The company makes use of modern manufacturing technology and engages foreign consultants to improve its management methods. It is now expanding rapidly into the region.

PSB's intention is to increase the number of SMEs like Kong Guan. Under SME 21, PSB hopes to triple the number of SMEs with annual sales turnover of $10 million or more in 10 years, from 2,000 now to 6,000 in 2010. PSB has also set a target to quadruple the number of SMEs transacting on the Internet from about 8,000 now to 32,000 before the year 2010.

## SME 21 — Strategic Orientation

To help our SMEs plug into the global network quickly, PSB will develop Singapore into an SME hub. We already have a German SME centre and a French SME centre in Singapore. A Nordic centre is being planned for. We will encourage other countries to establish similar SME centres in Singapore. This will provide good information to our local SMEs and enable them to source more cheaply and sell more dearly. Hopefully, good local-foreign partnerships will also be forged to exploit opportunities in other countries.

The presence of foreign SMEs in Singapore will encourage the cross-fertilisation of best practices, expertise and ideas, and help our own local SMEs to upgrade themselves and find new markets. What we want to develop in Singapore is a lively entrepreneurial culture with links to all four corners of the world.

We should build on the good progress made in recent years. Between 1988 and 1997, the value-added per worker increased substantially by 73% from $30,000 to $52,000, though this is still significantly lower than the non-SME sector. The improvement is partly the result of systematic deregulation in Singapore. For example, our sale of HDB shops has transformed the SME sector in our housing estates and put resources to much better use. Our coffeeshops are visibly more productive, enjoying much higher turnovers. We are now seeing interesting new business configurations all over the island. We should continue to free up the SME sector so that our smaller businessmen will have more room to explore new possibilities. I have asked PSB to work with HDB, JTC and other economic agencies to see what else we can do.

**Local Entrepreneurship**

During the recent economic crisis, Singapore weathered the storm much better than many other countries in the region. This is principally because of good government and the strength of our institutions. We have emerged stronger as a result of the crisis. But we are entering a new period with global competition becoming more intense. As a city-state, Singapore's strategy is to link up with other global players, big and small, in order to strengthen our overall competitive position. MNCs will always play an important role here. In fact, we must make Singapore their command and control base for the entire region. At the same time, however, we must build up local entrepreneurship so that we are also their partners, not just their employees. This is an important challenge for Singapore in the next phase of our economic development. We need more local entrepreneurship in all sectors, not just in traditional areas like trading, real estate and banking, but also in new areas like high-tech manufacturing, creative services, the Internet and e-commerce.

The SME sector is our nursery to produce world-class local entrepreneurs for the 21st century. Some will fail but others will succeed. The recent changes to our bankruptcy laws make it easier for those who fail to try again. This is important. We must also encourage our students in the polytechnics and universities to be interested in business. As part of SME 21, PSB will do more to promote the student enterprise clubs in our tertiary institutions. We should continue publicising the success stories of young Singaporean entrepreneurs so that they become models for others to follow. Sim Wong Hoo's recent book *Chaotic Thoughts from the Old Millennium* is an inspiring book to read. The Government can play its role, PSB can assist particular sectors but, in the end, we need individuals to take up the challenge, and I hope many will.

# Beyond Economic Growth

*Instead of fragmenting and scattering, we must try to build up an international network that unites around a set of ideas and ideals, and tie us back emotionally to geographical Singapore.*

Today, the Department of Statistics (DOS) is releasing its ninth Advance Data Release, which summarises the progress that Singapore has made in the past decade. Together with the first paper on Singapore's demographic profile released in August 2000, DOS has released a total of 10 papers based on Census 2000 data. The media have given extensive coverage on these releases.

This latest release on "A Decade of Progress" is a good report card on how we have developed as a people and as a country. If we look at the indicators over the past two decades from 1980 to 2000, we can see enormous progress in how we live and work, in our education and in our quality of life. The data show what we knew all along: that Singapore has changed for the better year after year, decade after decade, since Independence. The Census generated many quantitative indicators on our progress. DOS has prepared a table summarising these changes which will be circulated to you.

The progress of a country does not come about as a matter of course. Data from the World Bank show that there are countries in the developing world with declining standards of living and life expectancies. We need good government, hard work and favourable conditions to make progress. Good government is obviously crucial. Without good government, we would not have gotten here and,

Speech at the media briefing on the release of Census 2000 publication 'A Decade of Progress', 20 February 2001.

without good government, we will not be able to overcome severe challenges in the future. Good government enabled us to exploit favourable historical conditions. Let me now touch on three trends which favoured us in the past and how changes in these trends will affect us in the future.

## Favourable Demographics

First, favourable demographics were a great help. The bulk of the baby boomers who were born after the war came of age when Singapore started taking off. The baby boomers provided the necessary entry-level manpower for our industries in the 1970s and 1980s, and now they form the bulk of our managerial class.

Because of the fall in birth rate in the early 1970s and 1980s, we have benefited tremendously from a declining dependency ratio. In 1970, the median age of Singapore was only 20 years, and the young dependency ratio was 68, which meant that for every hundred working-age persons there were 68 young dependents. Since then, the ratio has fallen by half to 30 in 2000.

Lower dependency ratio means that as the economy expands, we would have much more resources to spend on fewer dependents. There are fewer children to feed and educate. This enables us to look after our young better.

However, these favourable demographic conditions would start to turn against us in 10 years' time. The baby boomers are fast moving into the pre-retirement ages. In 2000, there were about 27,000 sixty-year olds. In another 10 years, this would almost double to 48,000. Their replacement in the labour market will have to come from younger age groups that are much smaller in size. The declining young dependency ratio is an early warning indicator for us. Given the present birth trends, the young dependency ratio will drop further to about 26. This means that the future supply of workers from our own sources will be limited.

At the same time, the old dependency ratio will increase rapidly as the baby boomers move into the elderly age groups. The old dependency ratio is expected to rise to over 30 by 2030 from a low 10 in 2000. The median age of the population has gone up from

29 years in 1990 to 34 years in 2000, and will reach 41 in 2030. Not only will we have an older workforce, we will also have to take care of a much larger elderly population.

**Better Education and Healthcare**

The second trend of better education and healthcare reinforced the positive demographic changes in our population. The late baby boomers and post-baby boomers have benefited greatly from expanded and improved education and healthcare systems. They are much better taken care of than the older generations. Because we are starting from a lower base, we are able to make much faster progress. But, human capital investment will work its way through the age structure, and the incremental returns will become less and less, as we become a First World country. Take the proportion of young adults with upper secondary or higher education as an example. In 1990, the proportion was 18%. In 2000, the proportion jumped to 49%, an increase of 31 percentage points. But among the future adults, the increase will be much smaller.

In the future, the progress of our country will have to be measured by new yardsticks, as the conventional indicators would have leveled off. The easy gains have been made. Scaling the heights will be much more difficult. Literacy rate for example is now 93%. Among the young it is already at 100%. Future gains will be far less dramatic.

How then should we measure the progress of our people? The number of patents filed by Singaporeans? The number of new companies created? The numbers of international awards won? Our positions in international rankings? This is something we need to think about and a challenge for the Department of Statistics.

**Favourable Geopolitics**

The third trend which favoured us was geopolitics. During the Cold War, Singapore benefited from the support of the Western powers and Japan. After 1965, we were able to make Singapore attractive to MNCs. In the 1970s and 1980s, many of our people made their living working in consumer electronic factories. When the Plaza Accord of

1985 revalued the Japanese Yen, it brought about a boom in non-Communist Southeast Asia as investments poured into the region. This continued until the Asian Financial Crisis in 1997.

We are entering a new phase in global politics. The end of the Cold War has reduced the strategic importance of Southeast Asia to the big players. For example, it is difficult to get the Western powers to focus on Indonesia and help it through this difficult period. China, on the other hand, has gained prominence politically and economically. It will be a serious competitor for foreign investment in the coming years.

Will the region provide us with a supporting environment to progress further? There will be opportunities, but the going will be much harder.

**The Next 10 Years**

Casting our eyes 10 years ahead, what will the 2010 Census tell us? We will probably do better than the 2000 snapshot because of sheer momentum. The systems we have put in will continue to produce results. Our economic fundamentals are good, our education system will continue to improve, our social infrastructure will become more sophisticated and, in many aspects, we will probably have the economic, educational and cultural profile of a First World country.

But some trends will change adversely, and the future will be more complicated. Let me highlight three responses to some of the future challenges that we will face:

(a) First, the importance of foreign talent. The government encourages the immigration of talent, both to alleviate adverse demographic trends and in response to the fact that further gains in educational attainments will become more difficult as we achieve First World standards. Quantitatively, we need numbers to grow our economy. Qualitatively, as innate abilities become more important, we must compete for our share of global talent.

(b) Second, with globalisation, we must diversify our links and think in terms of a wider region. The immediate region has supported our growth in the past few decades. ASEAN's importance will remain, as this is our immediate neighbourhood. But the stimulus for future growth will have to come from a wider region and beyond. The world has become smaller. Overseas opportunities are no longer as distant as they were perceived to be in the past. For many years to come, like Switzerland and the Netherlands, we will become a significant capital exporter to a wider region which will include China, India and Australia. The free trade agreements (FTAs) we are negotiating will create more opportunities for our economy and better secure our links to North America, Japan, Europe and Australasia.

(c) Third, we must strengthen the Singapore Spirit. Globalisation can weaken our sense of being Singaporean as more migrants come in, and as Singaporeans travel the world to work, live, study and play. We must therefore strengthen our bonds as Singaporeans so that, despite the changes, Singaporeans remain self-consciously Singaporean with a sense of our own destiny. Instead of fragmenting and scattering, we must try to build up an international network that unites around a set of ideas and ideals, and tie us back emotionally to geographical Singapore. These ideas and ideals must of course be much larger than our geographical reality so that those who join our ranks, far from feeling confined, are liberated and better able to fulfil their potential regardless of race or religion. At home, the institutions that bind us together must evolve to meet these future challenges: the family, community organisations and civil society all have a role to play in strengthening the Singapore spirit. Overseas voting becomes a necessity. So too the safeguarding of our collective financial reserves. If we do all these things well, and provided we continue to have good government, the 2010 Census will show us to be still healthy and growing. Otherwise, the snapshot then will be worrying.

# Valuing Talent

*"People are our most important asset" is not a cliché anymore. It has taken on a new meaning in the Knowledge Economy.*

Distinguished Guests, Friends and Colleagues

We are here today to launch the new Firefly initiative which is a collaborative programme to develop talent in the Ministry of Trade and Industry (MTI) and six of its statutory boards. I am also taking this opportunity to announce the establishment of a new Public Sector Economist Service.

## Employees as Voluntary Investors

A few months ago, my old professor from the Harvard Business School, Christopher Bartlett, visited Singapore and proposed a different way of looking at the employer-employee relationship. He said that we should view employees as "voluntary investors" of their own intellectual capital. Just as traditional investors are free to move their capital around, employees are also free to invest their talent in the areas where it brings them the highest return. Just as investors would evaluate the risks and returns of their investments, employees too would weigh the opportunity costs and benefits of joining a particular organisation before committing to one, and never permanently. The old Japanese system of life-time employment no longer works. It is hard to maximise returns on your capital if you are stuck in certain stocks.

---

Speech at the launch of Firefly, 6 April 2001.

Professor Bartlett's idea reflects the quiet revolution in talent management. Organisations have come to accept that talent, rather than financial capital, is their most important asset. "People are our most important asset" is not a cliché anymore. It has taken on a new meaning in the Knowledge Economy.

**Generation Y Demographics**

Because talent is increasingly a form of capital, it has become more difficult to manage. The balance between employers and employees has shifted in favour of employees. Educated employees enjoy greater choices and naturally become more demanding. 30 years ago, when a young man or woman secured a job upon graduation, there was a sense of relief and gratitude. The scholarship bond meant guaranteed employment. Today, the bright graduate is bombarded with multiple job offers. The current global economic slowdown may dampen the employment market temporarily but the world demand for top talent will not slacken.

A study conducted in the US last year, at the height of the dot-com boom, found that 25% of students expected to make their first million before 30, and two-thirds expected to be more successful than their parents. Only 20% expected to stay with their first employer for more than three years. Although the collapse of NASDAQ has restored a sense of reality, the long-term trend, which is propelled by technological developments, remains unchanged.

We are similarly affected in Singapore. Because our economy is completely open and English is in widespread use, young Singaporeans enjoy much the same options as young Americans. The competition for talent is global whether we like it or not.

For parents and employers, these trends are unsettling. The war for talent will force companies to organise themselves better, and to be more responsive to the market. Companies have to market themselves to employees as "voluntary investors" the way they market themselves to financial investors.

The challenge is especially great for the public sector as an employer. We have no choice but to compete in the same arena for talent. How do we create schemes that are attractive enough so that individuals will want to invest their talent in the public service and grow with it? We are not just talking about risks and rewards, but also the quality of the work environment, opportunities for personal development and psychological and spiritual satisfaction.

A career in the public service should not only be financially rewarding, it should also be a challenge to do good, to make a difference to the lives of ordinary Singaporeans. There are many ways to make a difference. In the MTI family, we help to build infrastructure, create capabilities and improve conditions for sustained economic growth. What we do affects the lives of many people. What we do can improve or diminish the life prospects of the next generation of Singaporeans. This is the larger purpose we work for beyond our individual job assignments. Unlike the private sector, the public service is also a calling. It can provide a special job satisfaction not found in the private sector.

## Firefly

The Firefly idea will enhance our overall investment yield as individual investors in the public service. Through Firefly, MTI and its six economic promotion agencies, namely EDB, JTC, NSTB, PSB, TDB and STB, will be better able to compete for talent. By pooling our resources and increasing career choices, we will enhance our ability to recruit, nurture and retain good officers.

In our headhunt for Firefly talent, we will market the six statutory boards as a group. This offers the individual greater opportunities for personal development including overseas postings if that is the preference.

Talented Fireflies will have the opportunity to try different kinds of jobs, both within their parent agency and across agencies. This will help young Fireflies to broaden their perspective before specialising. This is especially important when the global economy is going through rapid change.

The Firefly idea will also enable experienced officers to acquire new expertise. Our goal is to make life-long learning a way of life, a part of our survival instinct. We hope that Fireflies will continue to "re-invest" in the MTI family and find their work rewarding and fulfilling.

This Firefly idea came about as a result of the recent leadership changes in our statutory boards. There was a strong feeling that we were not optimising our human resources by not cross-posting them at a young age. Mr Philip Yeo, in particular, believes passionately that the nurturing of young talent is the key to our long-term success.

## Economist Service

In a similar way, we have to cross-post talent across government ministries. This should not apply only to Administrative Officers. We are therefore starting a new Economist Service for the public sector. It will be an umbrella service for all economists working in government ministries and statutory boards, in the same way that the Legal and Accountancy Services are the umbrella services for lawyers and accountants in the public sector. MTI will drive the Economist Service.

As a specialist service, the Economist Service offers Public Sector Economists a challenging professional career with wide prospects. Like Fireflies, Public Sector Economists will have the opportunity to serve in different ministries and statutory boards in the course of their career. They can choose from a range of economic sub-specialties. With a single service, we will be better able to offer them better management and professional training. Remuneration in the Economist Service will be benchmarked against the salaries of economists in the private sector to ensure that we attract our share of the brightest economic brains in the country.

With the Economist Service, we hope to build up a core group of economic experts in various parts of the public sector. As our economy becomes more complex and globalised, we need more sophisticated economic analysis of policy alternatives.

## Continued Economic Growth for Singapore

The Firefly idea and the Economist Service will help the public sector compete for the talent we need. While our economy has done well in the last four decades, the international competition is relentless. We have to work hard and work smart to stay ahead in the global game. Our ability to attract top talent will be decisive.

Having sound macroeconomic policies alone is not sufficient. We must also create conducive microeconomic environments for innovation, enterprise development and wealth creation. We have to harness the power of competition in specific domains. Every industry domain has its particular characteristics. Information and Communication Technology (ICT) regulation, for example, is different from energy market management in important ways.

## Going Forward

Looking ahead, there are three key challenges for the public sector in talent recruitment and management.

First, we have to attract a diversity of talent into our fold. Diversity is important because the future is often unpredictable.

Second, we have to develop officers with both breadth and depth. Not all officers are capable of both.

Third, we need to build a strong network of Fireflies and Public Sector Economists so that the whole is much greater than the sum of the parts. We will encourage not only professional interaction, but also social and intellectual networking. We are considering setting up a Firefly Academy to help our Fireflies and Economists interact, brainstorm ideas and learn from each other.

I congratulate the inter-agency team that has germinated and developed the Firefly idea. To implement it well, we have to learn from practical experience and make adjustments along the way. Firefly and the new Economist Service will make a difference to the quality of economic management in Singapore.

# GOVERNING FOR THE COMMON GOOD

*In a sense, the struggle for good governance is the story of mankind.*

Mr Chairman, The Honorable Prime Minister Kevin Rudd
His Excellency Bapak President Susilo Bambang Yudhoyono
His Majesty Sultan Haji Hassanal Bolkiah
His Excellency Prime Minister Xanana Gusmao
His Excellency Bapak Hassan Wirajuda
Excellencies
Ladies and Gentlemen

**Democracy as a Means Towards Good Governance**

We need good governance at all levels. To overcome the current global financial crisis which is threatening to become a global economic crisis, we need good global governance. The institutions established at Bretton Woods after the end of the Second World War are not well suited to the realities of a 21st century multi-polar reality. At the national level, many governments in the world are not functioning properly. Large numbers of their citizens are forced by economic hardship to migrate to other countries in search of a better livelihood. In countless villages around the world, far away from the influence of central authorities, there is oppression and injustice.

In a sense, the struggle for good governance is the story of mankind. Unlike animals like apes and chimpanzees, our social structures are only partly hard-wired in our DNA. We are a species that can organise ourselves in almost limitless ways depending on our

Speech at the Bali Democracy Forum, Bali, 10 December 2008.

history and the challenges we face. We do this through culture and institutions. The human beings living today are not much different genetically from the human beings living, let us say, 2,000 years ago. But our social organisations have become much more complex. In 2,000 years' time, provided we have not destroyed ourselves, we would have developed vastly different social systems to colonise space.

Against the sweep of history, democracy represented a major advance in human organisation. It has never been the only way to organise human society. Even in Greece where it first flowered, it was a fragile innovation which did not last. Conditions only became ripe many centuries later in Western Europe for democracy to strike deep roots and spread. In some ways, we can see the First World War, the Second World War and the Cold War as contests between the democratic idea and autocracy of one kind or another. It was principally a struggle within Western society but its effects quickly influenced the rest of the world. In China, Sun Yat Sen established the Xingzhonghui ("Revive China Society"). In Indonesia, the Budi Utomo organisation was formed. It eventually led to the end of empires and the establishment of new nation-states.

Democracy is therefore a broad current in human history. It takes different forms, often in competition with one another. It is a means to achieve better governance, never an end in itself. What is important is to put human beings living in communities at the heart of everything we try to do. The word "demos" referring to people has as its specific context people living in community. We associate counting votes with democracy but there are so many ways to structure a voting system which can lead to very different outcomes. The key is good governance. Democracy should always be structured to facilitate good governance, never to make it harder. Here, I am making a case for a pragmatic view of democracy instead of an ideological view.

## Democracy with Singapore Characteristics

Singapore's democracy is a work in progress. We inherited laws and institutions from the British which we have adapted to our own circumstances. Being a small city-state with no natural resources except people and a good geographical location, we have to be pragmatic. We can only make a decent living if we provide a service to others and if the neighbourhood where we live in is in peace. We are not dealing with abstractions. Broadly speaking, Singapore democracy serves three objectives.

First, the rule of law. Good governance requires the rule of law. Without proper laws defining the limits of freedom, there can be no freedom. Without good laws protecting property rights, investments will not be made and long-term development will be affected. Having good laws on the statute books is not enough. Laws must be implemented and enforced fairly and consistently in a transparent way or they risk becoming dead letters or, worse, instruments of oppression. There must therefore be some separation of powers and an independent judiciary. Corruption is always a problem that has to be combated.

Second, a balance must be struck between the short term and the long term, and between the interest of the individual and the interest of the community. Electoral politics put pressure on governments to respond quickly to the needs of voters. Nobel Laureate Dr Amartya Sen pointed out that famines in India have become a phenomenon of the colonial past because Indian politicians today know they would be thrown out of office if they did not respond quickly to food shortages. All this is good but the problem with electoral politics is that the time horizon of political leaders shortens and pandering to the demands of special interest groups may be unavoidable. Larger and longer term considerations are often set aside as politicians concentrate on winning the next elections. It is worth remembering that the word "demagoguery" has the same root word as the word "democracy". There is always a strong temptation to be populist, to borrow from the future, because the future has no votes, instead of investing in it. The mass media can either moderate or accentuate this dynamic. Without clear rules, newspapers and TV stations can be forced by competitive pressure to outdo each other in sensationalism. The result is more heat than light. In Singapore, we require newspapers and TV stations to report accurately. As opinion multipliers, it is important that what they multiply is accurate and not distorted. There is also the New Media which became a major factor in the election of Barack Obama. All over the world, countries are grappling with how this New Media should be managed as it is two-edged. When all is said and done, democratic systems which create a good balance between the short term and the long term, and between the individual and the community, will be better able to achieve economic growth and security.

Third, we must protect the rights of minority groups. No country on earth is homogeneous. Unless special provisions are made, majority rule can lead to the systematic marginalisation of ethnic, religious and other groups. Without well-constructed rules, one-man-one-vote can be oppressive to them. Singapore being a multi-ethnic and multi-religious society, we are very sensitive to the protection of minority rights. For example, Muslim Singaporeans can resort to Shariah laws for family matters. Although the Constitution guarantees freedom of religious practice, we put curbs on proselytisation. It is an endless balancing act — Punjabi Sikhs riding motorcycles in Singapore are allowed to wear turbans instead of crash helmets but Muslim girls in secular schools are not allowed to wear headscarves which are not part of the school uniform. In order to ensure full representation of ethnic minorities in our Parliament, multi-member constituencies have been created which require political parties contesting them to field slates of candidates with a minimum number of minority candidates.

By taking a pragmatic approach, Singapore's democratic system tries to meet these three objectives of ensuring the rule of law; striking a balance between the short term and the long term, and between the individual and the community; and protecting the rights of minority groups. However, as the global environment changes, as technology changes, our system has to evolve in tandem. For example, with the growing number of Singaporeans living overseas, we have had to find ways to enfranchise some of them. Maintaining a sense of belonging to a larger Singapore community is essential. Without voters feeling a sense of commitment to one another, a democratic system cannot work well. Democracy breaks down when rights are not balanced by obligations.

## Global Democracy

In the community of nations, we subscribe to the general principle of democracy but with important variations. Nations are considered equal even though we know they are not. In the United Nations and the WTO, every member has one vote, and small countries with populations of less than 10 million are in the majority, which is good for small countries like Singapore. But size and power do matter. The five Permanent Members of the UN Security Council were the victorious powers after the Second World War and the proposal to increase the number of Permanent Members is the subject of endless dispute. When President Bush recently called a meeting to discuss a new global financial architecture, only leaders of the G20 countries were invited. This is the reality of the world.

As with democracy within each country, it is better that we take a pragmatic approach to democracy among the community of nations. We cannot act on the basis of abstract principles. Imagine the whole world voting for the UN Secretary General on the basis of one human being, one vote. Even if it could be practically done, such a procedure would never be accepted by many countries.

We are more likely to improve global governance by making adjustments which are realistic and incremental. Reforming the UN is doable if we don't try to be too ambitious. Creating a new global financial architecture in the world is best done by renovating existing institutions in a way which acknowledges the new multi-polar reality. Making progress on the Doha Development Agenda is possible if the key protagonists make compromises which respect each other's political needs. Putting together a post-Kyoto agreement on climate change requires the US, China, India and others to buy in, but not at too high a political price. None of this is easily accomplished but the alternative of failing will have disastrous consequences for all of us.

## ASEAN's Role

Here in Southeast Asia, we should do all we can to stabilise our own environment regardless of what we are able or not able to achieve globally. After 40 years, ASEAN has done remarkably well preserving the peace and in creating a common economic space despite the diversity of cultures, political systems and per capita incomes. We are improving regional governance through the adoption of the ASEAN Charter which will begin its implementation next week when the Foreign Ministers meet in Jakarta. Although there is still no agreement on details, we have agreed that ASEAN should establish a human rights body. Procedures for dispute settlement are being progressed, with those for trade disputes already in place. We are systematically enlarging our circle of friends to include countries around both the Pacific and Indian Oceans. We work with them to create a larger architecture of peace in the Asia-Pacific. Whether the agenda is UN reform, international finance, WTO or climate change, we in ASEAN will play our part.

Indonesia's leadership is indispensable in ASEAN. By respecting the equality of nations in Southeast Asia, President Soeharto greatly enhanced our regional resilience. At critical moments, Indonesia's leadership has proved decisive in advancing the ASEAN agenda. When I visited Pak Ali Alatas in hospital last week, we recalled how President Soeharto's decision made possible the launch of APEC in 1989. It was under his leadership that APEC established the Bogor Goals in 1994. In October 2003, the goal of an ASEAN community was agreed to under Indonesia's chairmanship here in Bali. It is right and fitting that President Susilo Bambang Yudhoyono has convened this international forum on democracy in Bali, which is a subject of abiding interest to all of us in ASEAN. Ten years ago, no objective observer of Indonesia could reasonably expect the country to make so much progress in establishing democratic constitutional rule with a high degree of devolution, giving independence to Timor Leste and negotiating a peace agreement with the Free Aceh Movement (GAM) in Aceh.

We are realistic enough in ASEAN to know that we cannot do much to change the world. But we can play a positive role in improving global governance by improving governance in our own region. To do this, we have to draw on the democratic idea, always putting human beings at the centre of our concerns.

Thank you.

# LEADERSHIP

*... never put ourselves to be a leader in anything.*

**Moderator Warren Fernandez***: I told you there'd be lots of history and philosophical references and Minister has not disappointed. I'm sure you have lots of questions for him but let me warm things up by taking up this jawbreaker that you mentioned, this "intermediation", and the need for leaders to build trust and respect. Can you tell us, in your view, how do you think political leaders are going to do that in this new age? What stays the same and what changes?

**Minister George Yeo**: First, there must be recognition that this transformation is a profound one. It's not going to go away. It's a little like climate change. If the climate is changing and you are unwilling or unable to change, I think you're in deep trouble. The first requirement is to be prepared to take the leap into a new position. You may take the wrong leap, and many will take wrong leaps, but that is part of the sifting process. In this new world, trust enjoys a special premium. In an agricultural society, without television, without broadcast facilities, you awe large numbers through drums, through music, through regalia. Chinese dynasties gave a lot of attention to ritual. Without ritual, you cannot govern a vast empire. Today you have telephoto lens, you can be a Pope, you can be an

---

Edited transcript of the Q&A session at the inaugural Fullerton-SJI Leadership Lecture, The Fullerton Hotel, 22 January 2010.

*Global Manager, Shell Eastern Petroleum. Currently *The Straits Times* editor.

emperor, you can be an Obama; it doesn't matter, people watch your every grimace, your every emotion, and if a picture looks too touched up, it is disbelieved. So you notice, on Facebook and the Internet, pictures which enjoy a high credibility are those which are not touched up, which look a little grainy and spontaneous. If in the old days combing your hair and looking spiffy are *de rigueur*, today, a certain informality helps because it makes you look more authentic. It's frightening, so even if you're the Pope, you have got to accept that people are going to take close-up pictures of you, people are going to take pictures of you behind the altar and what you do inside because everyone has a camera-phone. And if you are not what you put yourself out to be, I think you'll be quickly discovered and before you know it, you're out there on the Net. I've been blogging and posting on Facebook the last three years and I've had many such experiences. After a while, if you are not consistent and honest you'll be found out.

Singaporeans love postings about food. One day I had *char kway teow* and posted: "It is very good, my favourite stall." Immediately the question came: "Where is it?" I said: "Well, it is at Bedok Reservoir." "Which block?" I gave the block number. Within two days, there were postings, comments and reviews about the *char kway teow* stall. Some agreed with me, some disagreed with me. So you have to accept that, and if you are unable to be comfortable with yourself and be truthful in the presentation of yourself, I think you'll be discovered very quickly. Perhaps in the past that was not as important but going ahead into the future, I think it is very important. Be what you are and be accepted for what you are.

**Moderator**: Could you tell us a bit more about your blogging? I'm sure many people are interested in how you do it, how you find the time to do it, why you do it and what do you hope to achieve out of it.

**Minister**: I went into it not quite sure what the experience would be like. I was quite prepared to experiment and to call it off if it didn't work out well or consumed too much of my time. Then I found out that if I unfreeze and just move with the flow and take advice from my young friends, it became quite fun and I felt younger as a result [Laughter] and energised, because you get spontaneous responses which are sometimes quite touching. You know how important morale is. When your morale is up, you can read a book quickly and remember everything, you can write, you can compose poetry. When your spirits are down, your mind is a blank and everything looks gloomy and grey. In a group, we can lift each other's morale or we can help depress one another. Part of the essentials of leadership is the ability to get group spirits up — not leaders suppressing their own emotions and putting on a false front because that is brittle and cannot be sustained — but individuals cheering one another on, comforting each other when they have problems. Sometimes on Facebook in the most unexpected quarters you find people say: "Thank you" or "Hey, you're doing a good job." That brightens the day, lightens life's burdens. So I'm enjoying it and because of that it doesn't seem to consume too much time or energy. In fact, while waiting for my emails to decrypt, because in the Foreign Ministry everything is classified [Laughter], and it takes some time for the emails to encrypt or decrypt, I look at my Facebook — I have two computer screens — I give a reply, make new friends.

**Moderator:** Shall we take some questions from the floor? Yes, please. Ah, an SJI boy. Go ahead.

**Question**: I would just like to know how did your experience in SJI make a difference in you being a leader in society?

**Minister**: Well, I don't think of it in a conscious way. When you're in SJI, as Warren said, it's baked into you. "*Ora et labora.*" [Pray and work.] I can't remember who said it originally, whether it was Augustine or whether it was Ignatius, "Work as if everything depended on you and pray as if everything depended on God," [Laughter], which I think is a good philosophy of life. Do everything within your powers to make things better, but at the same time realise that there is a higher order, a higher flow, which you have no control over and which may in the end decide your fate and the outcome of what you do. So accept what life gives out and at the same time do not be fatalistic or inert. It's kind of a *yin-yang* thing, it's a bit contradictory but it is very well expressed in our school motto. If you ask me, the spirit of SJI comes to this. Don't just work, also pray and I'm referring to prayer not just in terms of saying the 'Our Father' and 'Hail Mary' but an attitude towards life, towards existence, towards why we are here. Just yesterday or the day before, someone asked a sarcastic question on my blogsite, I think an opposition supporter [Laughter]. There are quite a few of them appearing on my Facebook site. He said: "Oh, you as a higher mortal, what you think of us as lesser mortals?" I knew that I was being baited. I said I don't see myself as a higher mortal, I said we all come and go in the same way. What distinguishes us is how we spend our time in between. I said thank you for your kind words anyway. Sometimes people bait you but if your underlying disposition is a kind one, not a vindictive one, then I think the answer will come out right and it will calm things down. But if your deep nature is vindictive or aggressive, it will come out one way or another when you are provoked.

**Moderator**: Just to follow up on the young man's question…

**Minister**: Joe Conceicao, who used to be a teacher at St. Patrick's [School] likes to say this: "Know your centre, find your centre, be well-centred." And centering is simplicity. If you have a clear core position, then you can handle complexity with a certain calmness. But if you do not have a centre, and you are chasing all kinds of things, very quickly you will lose your balance. You can be practising *taiji* or *karate* or whatever; always have a centre, always go back to the centre.

**Moderator**: If I could follow up, you mentioned Brother McNally as being a source of inspiration. Were there others like him that inspired you to take up public service?

**Minister**: To take up public service?

**Moderator**: Or to play a leadership role or step up in leading when called upon?

**Minister**: In the course of your school life, there will always be a few teachers and a few individuals who have a disproportionate impact upon you and the way you look at yourself and the world. Brother [McNally] didn't influence me when I was a student; he inspired me much later after I entered politics. But there were teachers, and there were not many, in school or in the schools I went to — St. Stephen's, St. Patrick's, and SJI — who somehow touched me deeply and changed me.

**Moderator**: How did they change you?

**Minister**: Sometimes it could be a word of compliment. I remember in Secondary One, my History teacher — because I did very well for the exam — he said: "Oh, you must have memorised everything." I thought, "No, I didn't, I didn't memorise everything." But I felt it was a great compliment, and, you know, as a little kid, that motivates you, that gives you confidence. And sometimes, you get told off, and that also puts you right. I was making a bit too much noise in class one day and one of my teachers said: "Shut up!" in front of everybody. That knocked some sense into me. So it's like that. I think in life, you have a trajectory, and then you get propelled one way, you get knocked back and then you find your own balanced course. But not many, I think in the course of one's journey, can affect you like that, which is why good teachers are real treasures. And invariably the teachers who touched you the most are those who understand you the best, who reach into you and in that contact, in the chemistry, a transformation takes place. And you can't do that if teachers see teaching as only a job. It must be much more than that.

**Question**: Thank you, Minister for the speech. My name is Li Yu, I come from the Lee Kuan Yew School of Public Policy. My question is regarding Internet censorship, because, you know, a few days ago, Google actually sent a signal to the Chinese government regarding censorship. So what's your view towards censorship in China's context? And in what way do you think the network structure based on Internet technology will affect the leadership of the next generation? Thank you.

**Minister**: There's much more to the Google saga than what has come up in the public domain. I'm quite sure Chinese intelligence, US intelligence know much more than they're letting out. The problem is a fundamental one. Cyberspace is a new reality which will create all kinds of new problems and, in fact, all the challenges of law and order of governance, of market operations in the real world, have their reflections in cyberspace. Freedom, crime, privacy, intellectual property, standards, enforcement, harassment, recourse to justice and so on. The UN has got certain standards, I think under UNCITRAL or something. That sets a basic framework, but there are many challenges to the global governance of the Internet, of cyberspace which have not yet been overcome, and this will be a subject of great importance in the coming years. You can't homogenise values and regulatory systems in the Internet, as you can't homogenise and rationalise regulatory systems in the real world. In the real world, you accept that there's diversity, but there are layers and levels which people can meet and exchange. So too in cyberspace: There must be the principle of subsidiarity, you must be able to be yourself, to have your privacy, to have your separate existence and culture in cyberspace, while at the same time having enough portals for you to interact with others, so that you will benefit from all the advantages of connection and globalisation. So I see this tension between China and the US over Google as a necessary one. If it's not Google, it will be something else, or somewhere else. And it surfaces real problems, which have got to be addressed. You say this is a crime in your country but this is not a crime in my country, so you cannot expect me to enforce your laws in my country. But hacking must be against the law in both countries, in which case all national jurisdictions should oppose hacking or theft of intellectual property or destructive behaviour. But at the same time, when it comes to censorship in Europe, Holocaust denial is not allowed. In most countries, incest laws have got to be adhered to in cyberspace, but to varying degrees. Pornography, hate sites, different countries have different regulatory standards and we cannot deny countries their right to attempt to censor according to their own social norms — knowing at the same time that whatever you try to do, there will be bypasses. But you can always add friction to these bypasses.

**Moderator**: Minister, if I can just take that a little bit further with the issue of Internet censorship which was one of those that I flagged earlier on when I made my remarks. There is also the issue of censorship and at the moment there is a new review committee which is taking another look at that. And I wonder if you could say, having gone through the experience, what advice you would give to those who are leading the charge on the issue now? And the third point is the pruning of the Banyan Tree. It is still a work in progress: What's your assessment on whether there's still a need for more pruning in this new disintermediated world?

**Minister**: Censorship is not an easy subject to handle because of its very nature. But no one can accept a free-for-all because in any society, the young must be raised. And of all the species, human beings take the longest to achieve full maturity as adults. And the reason is not just physical. The reason is because there is a lot of social programming needed to make that individual a part of society. Many lines of software code have got to be input. From the time the child is born, he learns accents, tastes in food, languages, social norms, what is right, what is wrong and he becomes an adult. But in the first twenty years of his life, more or less, you have got to have a nursery and that nursery requires censorship. So no society, however much it proclaims freedom to be a higher ideal, will give up censorship because it has got to raise the next generation according to certain values and norms. Take the US, in fact there are many aspects of political correctness in the US, which from the perspective of other countries comes across as very much looking like censorship. You know, when you prepare your resume in America you can't have a photograph because otherwise people will judge you on the basis of your skin colour or whether you look one way or another. You can't give your age, you can't give your race. Ok, fair, that is the American system but other countries have other values, other starting points and end points and therefore they have other norms which they require people to adhere to. And it is not whether these regulations are water tight, hermetically sealed, which matter. I came to that conclusion very early when I was in the Ministry [of Information and the Arts]. What matters is the signal you are sending, what is approved, what is disapproved. Children observe adult behaviour, they get scolded, they get told off, they get praised and gradually they are channelled and their form is set, and that is important. And censorship is important for setting certain norms. So I don't see us — we will probably make adjustments because of the Internet, we will probably liberalise a bit more because there is no choice — I don't see us giving up the idea of censorship because it is so important for inter-generational continuity.

Now on the Banyan tree, whether we like it or not, instead of a Banyan tree we are beginning to see all kinds of growth. It is not just Singapore but all societies. The climate has changed, the ground has changed, the vegetation changes and that is inevitable. In some ways we should facilitate it and direct the tendencies so that we optimise the outcome. In other words, if you look at the world as a dense World Wide Web and nodes are competing with one another, our economic well-being requires us to be an important node with many synaptic connections to other nodes — economic links, cultural links, Free Trade Agreements, standardised access, free movement of money, of people, of ideas — then all the nutrients, all the energies will follow through Singapore and then we will light up. That is what we want to be. And because of our own history and the way we are organised we have to move in that direction. Being diverse, being connected, maintaining order amidst the diversity, treating diversity not as an inconvenience or as something to tolerate, but as something to be celebrated and as a strength. It does not mean that we give up all controls. If we do not swat flies, we will not be able to open our windows wide and we will then be short of oxygen. We have to take some risks and be prepared for occasional discomforts.

**Question**: Thank you, Minister, I am Ashok Riza. I have a thick Indian accent, I'm sorry. I am an Indian and I was a student of the Lee Kuan Yew School of Public Policy. I heard the Minister for Education speak at our school and I ask the same question that I am putting to you.

As you mentioned, education was a very important trait and the role of the teacher was also very important for creating and nurturing leadership. I am also a school teacher. I have been a school teacher for the last four years. Being in Singapore, I really appreciate the kind of structure that the education system has. My question is: For the Army and the Air Force and the Navy there are many scholarships for higher studies so that people are lured to pursuing those careers, so that they can achieve a scholarship that would allow them to further their careers. But on the other hand school teachers do not have any such scholarship. Do you think, in the general sense of speaking, should there be more incentive for teachers, for more intelligent people, to become teachers? I am not just talking about scholarships but other incentives to attack the problems of high rates of attrition and other problems that school teachers face.

**Minister**: I am not familiar with the scholarships that are available to teachers or would-be teachers in Singapore, but you know that we give a very high importance to education in Singapore and that we are very concerned about the quality of recruits in the teaching profession. We ensure that teachers are paid competitively and bright students have a range of scholarships available to them. From first principles, I do not see how we can afford not to give competitive scholarships to those who are interested in teaching but I am not familiar with teaching. I am not familiar with the details but maybe someone here can answer you specifically. But if it is what you say to me, then I think we have a problem. Can someone answer that question? I do not know. Is it true that there are no scholarships available for the teaching profession?

**Comment**: Minister, perhaps I can answer that question. We provide actually a whole range of scholarships including both overseas and local scholarships. In fact, the focus on educating talent is quite furious because we recognise that the education system has a need for that kind of talent.

**Minister**: That is what I thought.

**Question**: How do you feel about the present generation? The capacity that they have for leadership and do you have any advice to give them that would further develop their talent?

**Minister**: Those in your generation?

**Question**: Yes. [Laughter]

**Minister**: I think you are an improvement over an earlier generation — the kind of exposure that you have, the kind of knowledge in your head. I don't see any slackening. In fact, watching my own children — they seem to get less sleep than I get. I do not know what they do [Laughter] but the system does not allow them to be slack. The intensity is there, the opportunities are there, the facilities are infinitely better than what we had in the past. That must be the wish for any society, that each generation is an improvement over an earlier generation. If the next generation is an attenuation, an inferior replication of their forefathers, then something is wrong. And you must hope that your children will be better than you are. It is only when that is the case that the Singapore story is worth telling.

**Moderator**: From what you were saying earlier, you were saying that this new generation requires a different style of leadership.

**Minister**: Oh, absolutely. In the old days, our founder Saint John Baptist de La Salle was a revolutionary. He pioneered mass education, including education of poor children and he did that by classroom discipline, sometimes by physical punishment, by having teachers who were dedicated. The result was mass education which made possible the Industrial Revolution. Saint John Baptist de La Salle made a huge contribution to education in the world.

But we need now a new revolution because in a classroom of thirty or forty, everyone is different and it is only in recent years that we begin to understand what it means to be autistic or dyslexic or to have Attention Deficit [Hyperactivity] Disorder. In the old days, we would often describe these students as being naughty or lazy. Today we say: "Oh, maybe he has a problem and maybe we can treat the problem." Of course, sometimes it becomes an excuse! [Laughter] And beyond a certain point we say: "No, no, no, you're just being lazy or difficult and you must be put in your place." But knowing that we are all different changes the way we teach individual students. Some have better memories than others; some are more talented in languages; some are hyperactive. The tools are more available now and our teachers are becoming more cognizant about these subtleties and differences. I think that is all very good.

There is a "diversifying" of the education system in Singapore. What got us here was mostly mass education, top grade high quality mass education. Now we are beginning to have more pathways, so that depending on what your strengths and weaknesses are, you can still achieve your full potential. And I like in particular the slogan they have for ITE [Institute of Technical Education]. You know in Jack Neo's movie they said ITE — "It's The End". [Laughter] ITE has a very nice slogan: "Thinking Hands". Some students are not good in book work, some are not able to regurgitate but many are smart and know how to do things and get things done. And, if well-educated, provided with the right opportunities, right training, they can make a big contribution in the marketplace and to society.

Now that we have more resources and better-trained teachers, we are creating more pathways so that everybody can find his own place under the sun. It is all part of the pruning of the banyan tree. Some are shade plants, some need more sunlight, some need more water.

**Moderator**: Sir, if I could press this point a bit here. This new scenario you're painting is quite different from the traditional idea that we have of leaders being authority figure showing the way and having to lead. If I can borrow the dialect phrase, "*bor tua bor suay*" (没大没小), that sense of hierarchy, how are we going to make this transition from where we have been to where you say we need to go? What in your mind should be done — can you give us that?

**Minister**: I think we are all experimenting, we don't quite know what is the optimal balance point and it may vary from situation to situation. "*Bor tua bor suay*" expresses something very basic in our nature. All social animals have a pecking order. They may have to fight to establish that pecking order, but they have a pecking order. Without the pecking order, however defined, however policed, you can't create social organisation. If it is too rigid it is probably ineffective. But if there is no pecking order, group effort may not be possible. So philosophically there will always be a high and a low, big and small. But as to the operationalisation of that principle, I think it is contextual and it depends on the situation.

Take the armed forces — Army, Navy, Air Force. In the Army, hierarchy has always been more important, less in the Navy, least in the Air Force. Pilots, especially the fighter pilots, have always been individualistic. It is a job requirement, it is a technological requirement, it is a domain requirement, and our ability to tune for different situations is very important. And it requires from those in leadership positions a certain flexibility. And sometimes it is important for those who are in leading positions to become students in certain situations.

When I moved into Facebook, into blogging, I decided I knew much less than the young people around me. If I had wanted to put on airs and tried to pretend I knew when I did not, I would have learnt nothing. So I put myself into the position of a student again and they knew they were teaching me and they felt a sense of responsibility (to ensure) that I was well-educated. [Laughter] And that was fine because if they did not feel responsible for me, I would have made mistakes. And they still feel responsible for me. They help me to avoid mistakes. I would say a certain programmability is a requirement. If you think you know everything, you can't lead. You must accept that there are certain areas you do not know and be prepared to learn from others and take advice.

**Moderator**: The gentlemen who has been waiting very patiently.

**Question**: Thank you very much, Minister. My name is Hareen Narula. We've had some discussions on Facebook but what I'd like to ask you is to...

**Minister**: Which institution are you from?

**Question**: Sorry, I'm an entrepreneur. I'm here today under the umbrella of the Junior Pyramid. I have a legal background and I practised for a few years before going into business. Minister, I'd like you to turn inward and share, if you would, your thoughts on your personal life goals as a leader and what your expectations are for yourself as a leader, now that you are in a very conspicuous position of leadership and have broken new ground with your approach to the Internet and engaging the citizens. What would you like to have achieved as a leader in your own various positions of leadership, your expectations of yourself and what would you have considered a life of leadership well spent?

**Minister**: Warren asked me similar questions in the office as we discussed preparation for today's event. And I told him that I was not comfortable with the direction he was coming from — you know, you're a leader, what is expected of you and so on. Somehow I don't see myself in that way. I mean yes, you are in a leading position in the foreign ministry, you interact with staff, you interact with other people, you take advice, and you take decisions. Sometimes, [it is] for others to take decisions. It's less stressful that way. For myself, I take a more relaxed approach and if I have to lead, I lead; if I have to follow, I follow. If I need to be neither, that is wonderful. [Laughter]

**Quesion:** Thank you.

**Minister:** Thank you.

**Moderator**: But if I could just take up his question. How do you stay motivated, how do you stay grounded being a leader? Without letting it get to you, or as you said to that person on the Net that you're not a higher mortal, you come and go in the same way and what you do in between is what counts. How do you stay grounded in that?

**Minister**: That is a difficult question. You're asking about deep motive forces in a person — whether you are an optimist, whether you are a pessimist, what you consider to be a life well-lived. And I think it was Prophet Mohammed who said — I'm paraphrasing — that a person's life is judged by his offsprings, by the wealth, the physical things he has left behind, and by the ideas he has imparted. I think having offsprings is an important part of life, although some choose otherwise. The things that you bequeath to your children give you some comfort, but beyond a point you will harm them. As [Michael] Bloomberg said once, about his intention to donate most of his wealth to foundations: "I do not want to deprive my children the pleasure of making their own fortunes."

**Moderator**: I'm sure they wouldn't have minded. [Laughter]

**Minister**: I have always taken this position that we are a collection of atoms. We come together to be what we are, we grow, we age, and we die. Then, we return back to that atomic state. But in between, we have changed the world around us — some in a dramatic way, some in a small way. But big or small, do good, don't do harm. It should not be that the world, that society was better if you had not been born, if people wished you had not lived. And that's what I tell my children, whatever it is, do good. And depending on your destiny, your karma, you may do more good than others, but do what you can. And as they say in the *Opus Dei* — I'm not in *Opus Dei* [Laughter] — they have this slogan: "*vale la pena*" — it's all worthwhile. I was inspired by the kindness movement. You don't have to be heroic. If we can do a little good, do a little good, and the day is well-spent. But do not let the day pass without doing something. That's my thinking.

**Moderator:** Do we have time for one or two more questions?

**Minister:** Sure.

**Question:** Minister, thank you for your talk. I'd like to ask you one question...

**Minister:** Where are you from?

**Question**: I'm from China. I'm a student from the Lee Kuan Yew School of Public Policy. I'd like to ask you one question regarding our leadership. Out of all the great leaders of this world, one of my most admired ones is Minister Mentor Lee Kuan Yew. In many ways, he is very similar to our great leaders in China, like Chairman Mao and Deng Xiaoping — the one you mentioned just now. These are the people who have enough audacity to break rules, and also have great vision to establish long-lasting rules. But there comes the paradox of great leadership — the great leaders break rules, they establish new ones, and then they expect others to respect their rules. So like Mr Lee Kuan Yew once said, if there is anybody who would dare challenge what he has established for Singapore he may come up from his grave [Laughter] and help his people. So I'd like to ask about your views on leadership. Is it true that leadership is a product of time? In Mr Lee Kuan Yew's time, leadership requires his style, and now Singapore is already very established, enjoying an amazing level of success. Does that mean that Singapore leaders now need only respect the rules instead of break the rules? Does that mean that Singapore leaders need to stay in the comfort zone and enjoy his success?

**Minister**: [For] The general question, yes, I believe leadership is contextual and certain periods call for certain kinds of decisions. Certain periods call for heroic leadership. You cannot exercise leadership if you want to remain in your comfort zone. Change is always difficult and in life, you can't do anything worthwhile that is easy. Anything worthwhile is difficult. Because if it were easy, then it would already have been done. Those who are only interested to wallow in their comfort zone, they cannot be leaders because they will be unable to face criticism or challenges. Leadership means moving into new areas, it means causing discomfort to others and to yourself and persuading them that it is all worthwhile. This is effort; it is not leisure.

Yes, please.

**Question**: Thank you Minister Yeo. I'm from Hwa Chong Institution, I want to ask, how can we cultivate leaders of tomorrow, specifically in the business industry to have an ethical mind and not be driven by just economic interest or interest in other areas? So, I will like to ask that question, thank you.

**Minister**: A large part of leadership is inborn. If there is a strong figure in that group, the person less strong is less likely to be the leader. But if that person who is less strong becomes the strongest in the group, then he becomes the leader. So in that sense, leadership is relative and a large part of it is inborn. That's my view. Good mentors can see quite clearly in a child the kind of adult that the child will mature to become. And very often you can see aspects of leadership in young people. Of course they may flower in different ways and some bloom later than others.

**Question:** Hi, good afternoon Minister Yeo. I actually graduated from SJI International last year. I wanted to say that my respect for you has ballooned, simply because...

**Minister:** Ballooned?

**Audience**: Yes, ballooned — it has grown so much more, simply because you shared with us how you are willing to listen to young people as well. And I was thinking about this awareness about mutual respect with regards to leadership, and I find that yes, it is increasing but not fast enough. And there is this constant tension between the leaders and those being led — teachers and students, employers and employees. And as a young person who is traditionally viewed as inferior, I would like to say that perhaps we do realise and know that we are growing more in knowledge, and we do desire that mutual respect. So having experienced being in the position of a leader and also being led, I'm puzzled and sometimes frustrated as to how people sometimes ignore the upcoming transformation of leadership that we've talked about so far. So I'm just wondering, I don't think it can be answered right now in this seminar, but is there anyway we can increase this awareness in schools, this Darwinian process of changing leadership? In our society, perhaps talking about it on BlogTV [.sg], in schools and organisations — isn't sharing and discussing this change in leadership in a matured way better than ignoring it sometimes? Sometimes, that happens in schools, as far as students are concerned. Thank you.

**Minister**: We are quite conscious of this in Singapore, and there is almost a desire to help speed up this evolutionary process by exhortation, by structural reorganisation, and by just facilitating the spread of technology. We have always pushed for connectivity, pushed for broadband, introduced it into schools, encouraged students to go overseas to link up and try different things. All this is the result of policy. It's partly economically-driven, but partly it's the recognition that the world is changing and we've got to change ahead of others in order to secure our position. You may feel that we're not moving fast enough and there will always be some tension between generations — that's inevitable — but I would say on the whole, compared to other countries, we are more conscious of what's happening and pushing it in a deliberate way much more than others.

**Moderator**: I would like to ask you a question about your own portfolio at Foreign Affairs. Singapore is a small place, a small country, but we're often described as "punching beyond our weight". So, how does Singapore exercise leadership? Could you give us some examples of challenges we face, in trying to sort of lead?

**Minister**: The first thing we remind ourselves is never put ourselves to be a leader in anything. [Laughter] That's what we always remind ourselves, that's what we always remind our officers: Never ever claim a position of leadership. Be helpful to others, work with others, don't be too worried about who gets the credit. We have objectives. An ASEAN which is integrated, secures around us a zone of stability, which makes possible our continuing development. Have good relations with our neighbours, particularly with Indonesia and Malaysia, and — so long as it is not mistaken as weakness — be accommodating, be humble. So to answer your question (as to) whether there is a style of leadership in Foreign Affairs, it is the suppression of leadership. [Laughter]

**Moderator**: So is there any last question? If not I'll wrap it up. May be Minister, I have a burning question. I would like to ask you about Copenhagen and climate change. Was that a failure of leadership and how do you see it going forward?

**Minister**: I was not very hopeful that a grand bargain could be struck because the stakes were huge. When I was Trade Minister, I was involved in WTO negotiations and they were very tough. I used to coordinate agriculture and every time I went for meetings, I knew I would get no sleep, or hardly any sleep, the expectation of which was itself a source of stress. And in trade we have a positive sum because if you bring down tariffs, if you have more trade, the pie grows and then you can always share out the pieces and within each country you can help make up to those who are disadvantaged by opening up. The benefits of open trade are immediate. In the case of climate change, we're talking about billions, hundreds of billions, even trillions of dollars for benefits which may not be obvious in this generation. So you pay now in order that future generations will benefit, and how much they will benefit we're not sure. We know that the Earth is warming, we know that we are pumping a lot of carbon dioxide into the atmosphere. We're not quite sure how much of it is anthropogenic, caused by human beings. In the last few months, the science itself is being questioned a bit more. I'm presently reading a book which gives a sceptical view. So in this milieu, you're getting countries to take decisions which cost them a lot of resources. The instinct is to pass the cost on to somebody else. It is not easy. I had a discussion with the Mexican Ambassador this morning, because they [Mexico] are hosting the next meeting, a mini meeting in Mexico City. I said: "Don't set expectations so high that failure is guaranteed." Do what we can in modules and in pieces, and then little by little move us in that direction. A little progress gives confidence. People become more likely to cooperate. Go for the big bang [and you might] fail. Fail again, [and] people will be disheartened, everybody moves into Plan B and agreement becomes that much more difficult. This is going to be a protracted process. Better to be realistic, one step at a time, know the direction in which you want to move, and then as we gain experience, as we grow in trust, as science improves, as data comes in, we make adjustments along the way. And do the easy things first.

**Moderator**: Thank you, Minister. I'm sure you will all agree with me that this has been a fascinating discussion, from disintermediation to the Darwinian causes, and if you want to be energised and feel younger: start blogging [Laughter]. Please join me in thanking the Minister.

# The Mind of a Civil Servant

*The real relationship between ministers and civil servants is not a static relationship.*

I am honoured to be asked by Mr Ngiam Tong Dow for the launch of his book. I first knew him as a young Minister of Information and the Arts, and responsible for the launch of *The Next Lap* in 1990. I had always viewed him as a wise permanent secretary. In his book, he talked about the change that he and other senior civil servants felt when they worked under young ministers after having served pioneer leaders like Goh Keng Swee and Hon Sui Sen.

It is an interesting and very readable collection of speeches, articles and interviews on the Singapore Story through the eyes of a senior civil servant. In his long career, there was no aspect of the Singapore Story that he was not directly or indirectly connected with.

The Singapore Success Story complements the memoirs and speeches of MM Lee Kuan Yew, Goh Keng Swee and other Singapore political leaders. In the popular mind, the relationship between ministers and civil servants is often simplified in one of two extreme ways. In one, civil servants implement what their political masters want. That is the impression which good civil servants try to project, and maybe ministers too, when there is credit to be gained. The opposite simplification is the one caricatured in the British satire "Yes Minister", where the title belies the truth, which is that civil servants manipulate their ministers and are the real masters.

---

Speech at the launch of Ngiam Tong Dow's book *Dynamics of the Singapore Success Story*, The Fullerton Hotel, 19 November 2010.

The real relationship between ministers and civil servants falls somewhere in between. It is not a static relationship. A new minister should take good counsel from his permanent secretary (PS) to avoid making unnecessary mistakes. A more experienced minister may know more about his portfolio than a new PS and so should give closer guidance to his civil servants. Depending on the ministry, the issues of the day, the relative experience levels, and the personalities and capablilities of the minister and the PS, that relationship can be at different points on the continuum between the two extremes. I believe the Constitutional position is that while it is the PM who appoints permanent secretaries, the minister to whom a PS is appointed to serve must agree to the appointment.

Our formal system is inherited from the British. It makes a clear distinction between political appointments and the permanent civil service. In practice, however, principally because the PAP has been the governing party since internal self-government in 1959 and independence in 1965, many aspects of Singapore's governance resemble the Chinese bureaucratic state which Fairbanks, Needham and other scholars of Chinese history have written about, in particular, the practice of meritocracy in both the political and administrative elites. The induction of administrative talent into the PAP has become a Singapore hallmark, and is likely to persist. In the Singapore reality, the formal British system is built upon what is essentially a Chinese political and cultural substrate.

One illustration of this is the word "scholar" which is used to describe a civil servant, SAF officer or police officer, who is chosen on the basis of high academic achievement and given a scholarship at the point of recruitment. It is an English word which in a British, American or Indian context would be incomprehensible. For them, a scholar is a scholar doing academic research. In Singapore, the scholar is often an administrator not doing academic work at all. In fact, this is a Chinese idea expressed in English which has become a part of our vocabulary in Singapore. Singapore of course is only three-quarter Chinese and has to be multi-ethnic in her deep structure. However, the dominant political culture remains recognisably Chinese.

Seen against this common cultural background, it is perhaps not surprising that a China intent on reforming its public administration should take so much interest in the grooming of Singapore's adminstrative and political elites. In a curious way, the counterpart of our PSC (Public Service Commission) and PSD (Public Service Division) in China is the COD, the Central Organisation Department of the Chinese Communist Party. But only up to a point. The Chinese government is increasingly concerned with its own relationship with ordinary people, more and more of whom now live in cities. They are therefore experimenting with democracy at the lower levels, seeing it as an important feedback loop against corrupt, despotic or unresponsive local authority. Study visits to the PAP's meet-the-people sessions have now become almost compulsory for visiting Chinese delegations. Chinese leaders are convinced that Western or Indian democracy can never work in China. However, the hybrid that they see in the Singapore bonsai fascinates them.

All this is by way of background to Mr Ngiam's book. He speaks and writes like a Mandarin. When he was in the Civil Service, his views were expressed within government walls. In retirement outside those walls, he speaks and writes publicly, which sometimes raises eyebrows. But, and I can personally vouch for this, it is the same self-confident, high-minded individual whose starting and end point is what is good for Singapore and Singaporeans. When I was in MITA, Mr Ngiam was the Perm Sec in the Finance Ministry. He almost killed the Esplanade project about which he paid me a high compliment years later. On the revolutionary transformation of our National Library system, he gave his fullest support. The acquisiton of knowledge has always been his passion.

It is obvious reading Mr Ngiam that he has been following China's development since Deng Xiaoping's reform with the greatest interest. Part of this no doubt stems from the cultural similarity I talked about earlier. Though he regretted his own lack of mastery of the Chinese language, Mr Ngiam has a strong sense of his Hainanese roots. In fact, there was a Hainanese lunch group which included Tan Jee Say and Lim Hang Hing, to which I also belonged as an honorary Hainanese.

Could he like Hon Sui Sen and Howe Yoon Chong have joined politics? I don't know. But what I do know is that he is well aware of the pressures and constraints which political leaders face and which civil servants have to factor into their recommendations and in their implementation of Cabinet decisions.

When he asked if I could launch his book, I accepted immediately because it is an opportunity for me to thank him, to pay tribute to his many contributions and to recommend it as a valuable source of insights into the Singapore Story.

# A Struggle for the Soul of Singapore

*Our destiny is in our own hands.*

Dear voters of Aljunied, fellow Singaporeans,

A few weeks ago, I was walking through Hougang Mall and greeting the shoppers and the sales people. At the counter, I shook hands with an elderly lady. I could tell that she wanted to say something. I paused and looked at her, and she asked me (in Teochew), "杨部长，你可有时间吗？我要跟你说几句话." [Minister Yeo, do you have time? I need to speak with you.] I told her, "Auntie, 你说出来 [go ahead and speak]." She said, "政府需要照顾我们. [The government should take care of us.] 现在外地工人给我们老人家的压力很大. " And then she started to sob. She was telling me the pressure felt by older workers because of foreign workers. She said, "我们哪里可以和他们竞争? [How can we compete with them?]" I looked at her and said, "We will re-do our policies, and I'll make sure that what you've said, we will take up."

Then yesterday, outside my party branch at Blk 415 Hougang, I was there until 8pm plus, as I walked out, there was an old man, Mr. Wong, waiting for me. He said, "Can I speak to you?" I said, "Of course." Then he showed me his IC (identity card) and his party membership card, and he said he used to serve Yatiman Yusof and Mansor Sukaimi in Kembangan. I was from Kembangan before. He poured his heart out. He said, "I'm so worried. Every time people come to see MPs (Members of Parliament) at MPS (Meet-the-People Session), so many

---

Final rally speech delivered on 5 May 2011 for GE 2011 (before "cooling day" on 6 May 2011).

cases get rejected and they get angry with the government. Week by week, multiply by 5 because there are 5 divisions in the GRC." "Over many years," he said, "you'll have many people angry with the government." He said, "Don't laugh at me." I said, "No, I will not laugh at you. What you've said is very serious. Please continue to speak." He said, "Reconsider some of their requests. Don't just brush them off. I have got my own problems but I'm not here to talk about them. I'm here to talk about the PAP because I worry for the PAP."

In these 9 days, as we — the 5 candidates — go around, there has been an outpouring of emotion, pent-up emotion. So many people have cried, talking to us. They cover many things — housing, foreign workers, transportation, cost of living, CPF, healthcare. These are the sorrows of a people, of individuals who are unable to catch up. And I think now many of you know in this election, throughout Singapore, there is a cry from the heart, a cry that wants to be heard. Every time I'm approached by such an individual, psychologically, I tell myself it doesn't matter if I have to spend 20 minutes talking to that person. Because in talking to that person, I will understand more deeply what are the concerns. The reason why the Workers' Party has been able to draw huge crowds to their rallies is because they harp on these concerns. And people go there; when they listen, they feel a certain emotion, but it's a negative emotion, a negative agenda. The Workers' Party has come here to Aljunied GRC. They have no agenda for Aljunied GRC. It's very strange. We asked Mr. Low Thia Kiang and the others repeatedly, "Where are your plans for the voters?" Because before the voters decide on 7 May, they must know the details of the 2 teams. This is called due diligence. They said, "Vote us in first, then we'll tell you, then we will have the information." But the information is available publicly. Finally under pressure from many residents, last night they suddenly come out with a plan. But it is only the outline of a plan and that plan means nothing. Some of the candidates — when they go on their walkabouts — are very cheeky. When asked "where is your plan?", they said, "We will take the Aljunied PAP plan and make it our own." They will use our Aljunied plan, our "kway teow hot and nice" plan and make it their own.

This is of course a compliment to us but it is an insult to the people living in Aljunied. Because they should not be playing with people's lives. We know their ambitions, from Hougang to Aljunied, beating the drum on national issues, to Parliament, wrestle the driver, push him out, and take over. That is what they want. Pritam Singh said Sylvia Lim can be the Prime Minister. Then Low Thia Kiang can also be Prime Minister, maybe President. You know, they have nothing against our team. They have nothing against what we have done because they know what we have done and they dare not criticize us. They don't criticize me as Foreign Minister. Instead they compliment me, very strange. They said, "George can be President." We know the game they are playing and it's very cunning. They set up a website sponsored by members of the Workers' Party saying, "George Yeo for president." It is a joke but I don't think it's funny because it is a way to distract people from the election. I am not going anywhere. I have served the people of Aljunied for 23 years.

And over the years, there are bonds of friendship. When Kaki Bukit came under Aljunied, I went to the 538 market and I met a lady at the flower shop. She remembered me. Then she said, "I've grown old." I told her with a smile, that "we grow old together".

Over 23 years, I've gotten to know many people. I can't remember all their names. Usually I can remember their faces and they remind me of the things we've done in the past. And it is these friendships, these relationships, which make it so fulfilling to be an MP in Aljunied GRC.

There was a young man who is autistic and was accused of molesting a girl. But he did not know what he was doing, so his parents came to see me. They were very worried. I took up the case. The charges were dropped. The parents love him. Because he is autistic, he is very good in music and he plays the organ. When I visited him, he was so excited; he said, "Come, come," and he brought me to his bedroom. I took off my shoes and went into his bedroom. He wanted me to hear what he had composed being played by him. After a few years, I met him just the other night at a *getai*. He said, "Minister Yeo, Minister Yeo, come, come. I want to play again for you. I want to play at the getai but they wouldn't allow me."

This is what we do as MPs, in the grassroots. How can we just desert the people who elected us who have served and just go next door and say, "Ok, I will use these people now for other objectives." I am not going anywhere, I am staying in Aljunied GRC. The issue for the people of Aljunied is not the Workers' Party, which has limited capabilities, and I think people know, and they know that, in terms of looking after the people here, we have a track record. We've carried out our promises; we have our plans. There is a trust in what we do. They know that when we talk about Aljunied's plans, we will carry out those plans. And by the next election, we'll be judged by those plans. However, many people do want the Workers' Party, do want Mr Low Thia Kiang to remain in Parliament. He knows this, and his strategy is to force a choice by coming here, and this has caused a lot of discomfort among many people. In Zao Bao this morning, there was a letter. Someone said, "谁赢谁输，我们都是历史的罪人." The letter writer said, "Whoever wins, whoever loses, we are sinners in history." This is a dilemma which Low Thia Kiang has deliberately created for the people of Aljunied, and he does this by exploiting the resentment of the people. And because of this, I am not allowed to criticize the Workers' Party. I find it a little strange. One day, my son came back from camp; he is in NS, and he said, "Daddy, don't criticise the Workers' Party." I said, "How can I not criticise the Workers' Party — they are my opponents?" He said, "If you criticise the Workers' Party, people will be angry with you."

I pondered. What is the meaning of this? No, it's not the Workers' Party. The Workers' Party is merely being used as a loudspeaker for many Singaporeans who feel pain, who think that the government is high-handed and arrogant and they want to speak up. And the Workers' Party is there and they are using the Workers' Party. That is the real reason and that is why I say the real issue is not the Workers' Party but how we address the feelings, the heartfelt feelings of many people in Singapore which in this election have all come up. And in which all of us in our own way have heard. As a result of this in Aljunied, the election campaign is being fought on 2 levels. At the local level, frankly there is no contest. In terms of looking after you, your daily needs, the environment, safety, predictability, a good living environment — even the Workers' Party would concede that we will do better. When Low Thia Kiang was asked, he said, "Hougang is not a slum!" Well, we have much more higher standards than this. But there is another level at which the campaign is being fought, and that is this resentment against the government and I want to tell the people of Aljunied this, that my team mates and I will be your voice in government.

They know we will listen, listen hard and feed up, and help shape policies in parliament, in government and in the Cabinet. But we must not make light of the feelings. The feelings are still there and they are raw among old people, married people but especially young people. You know, when people are angry, sometimes they get very emotional; they lose their temper, we lose our temper. We say things, we do things, which we regret later. When we are angry, and someone tries to reason with us, we reject it. So when MM said, "You will have to repent," this created greater anger, greater resentment in many people.

Last night, I was having my *kway chap* supper in Blk 401,opposite Punggol Park. I went round shaking hands. And one Chinese man in his 40s said, "I am voting for the Workers' Party because of what MM Lee said." I looked at him with a certain sadness and I said," I respect your feeling." We must recognise that there is widespread unhappiness about the government. It is not only about specific policies. It is more than that and we must not allow the emotions to be all bottled up. Some of it is because of globalisation and technology. There is so much change in the world. Many of us feel that the world is turning too fast and we want the world to slow down because we can't catch up. Technology, iPhone, iPad, this, that — sometimes we feel that the older we are, the more obsolete we become, and this has created a sense of dislocation and stress. Older people who feel that, while in the past, the older you are the more you know, the more wisdom you have, the more you are respected, many now are feeling lonely. Their children are overseas doing this and that, and sometimes don't have time for them. And when they face more pressure from the government, it all comes out.

Singaporeans work very hard, long hours. When I go door-to-door visiting, from 7 to 9 pm, more than half of the households are empty.

Young couples, they want housing, they want to get married to form a family and they have issues. I am not saying that the government has necessarily done wrong. But we must exercise flexibility, because no two cases are the same. We are flesh and blood, we are not robots. We are not things and we have to be treated as human beings; this is very important.

Let me talk about the feelings of young people. I see many of my young friends in the audience today. In the last few years, they have taught me many things. They taught me how to blog, get onto Facebook, create a 2nd Facebook account, how to communicate, how not to communicate, how to speak, how to listen and I am very grateful to them. And because of them, I am running this campaign in a very different way from all my previous campaigns. But this is just the group which is helping me. There are other groups which I am not in touch with which also feel the same way, elsewhere in Singapore and some outside Singapore.

When I was in SMU, at a dialogue session, a girl asked me a question without emotion. She said, "We feel helpless." I said, "What do you mean?" She said, "We feel helpless. You decide on the casino; you build the casino," and she talked about other things. I explained to her that we spent years debating the casino. Somehow, she didn't feel engaged and many people feel that way. Two days ago, I was very busy and it was a long day. My young friends said, "Do a video recording and talk to them." So I went down to Queen Street, did a recording, and used a tele-prompter, but it did not come out right because I was reading. My eyes showed that I was reading. The producer said, "Speak from your heart," and after a few takes, I said I have got to rush off for a getai; it should be good enough. I looked at it. I look a bit tired, but I said, "Never mind. Just put it out." It went viral. To my shock, it went viral. I felt a little sad that it went viral. For it to go viral was of course very good for me politically but I felt sad about it because it was a simple message, 2 minutes and many people were moved by it. If they could be moved by such a short clip, it showed that they craved communication and they feel that somehow that we are talking at them and not talking to them. Unless we engage young people and allow them to teach us, I don't think we can communicate with them. Once there is communication, the influence becomes 2-way. They have influenced me and I have influenced those who helped me too, and the result is they are better and I am better, and this is what our country should be.

Because of globalization and technology, old structures, old hierarchies, and old relationships have broken down and new patterns, still unclear, are forming, in families, in schools, in churches, in temples and mosques, in the workplaces and in NGOs. And all kind of groups are mushrooming which are viable because they can link up with people in other countries. I get lobbied by the Cat Welfare Society, by the Guide Dogs Association of the Blind, by those who fly kites, by those who race quarter-scale cars, and many others. In our system, unless it comes under the People's Association, getting approval is often not easy. This problem, which causes a lot of pent-up frustration, I think is a deep problem, not a simple problem and it's not a problem just of the government, because at the core of the government is the PAP. This problem is also in the PAP. Because like everybody else in the world, we have to adjust to the new technology, to the new social forces at work which are breaking people into small groups, and find a way to create a new unity. And we can only create a new unity if we talk, if we talk to one another, if we listen, if we listen to one another, which means respect, which means trust. Respect and trust take a long time to build up. It can be easily destroyed but it is something we have to do, something which if we do well can create a new unity, similar to the unity we had which created Singapore, which an earlier generation had, to create Singapore with Lee Kuan Yew. In your hearts, you know that Singapore needs the PAP, that without the PAP, there'll be no Singapore. But we need a transformed PAP. It doesn't mean that all the problems will be solved but it means that there will be better communication and a greater feeling for people.

Years ago, when I first became an MP, when I conducted MPS, I remembered what a doctor told me, that you can rarely cure a serious illness. You can only sometimes cure a serious illness, but you can often ameliorate, which means make it less painful, and he said you can always comfort. I took that to heart. At MPSs, as MPs, this must be our approach. We cannot solve all problems. Sometimes we can make it easier for people by giving them vouchers, by financial help, by giving them something, to support them. But we can always comfort and we comfort by a listening ear. Let people complete their sentences before interrupting them; that is very important. Because it is only when they feel they've communicated, that they are prepared to receive. That's why they attend the Workers' Party rallies, because they want the loudspeaker to blare so loud that we have to hear it and still they are not sure. What we need is to hear these things ourselves. In the last 9 days, the 5 of us candidates have had intense discussions. It has been the most intense election campaign I ever had. It is my 6th. We talked about many things, we talked about the things that are right, we talked about the things that are wrong. We talked about the things that we have to do after the elections. We have all come to the conclusion that the PAP itself must be transformed. But before I made this speech, as I was drafting this speech, I spoke to PM because I knew he was coming to support us this evening. I said, "PM, this is what I am going to say." He said, "George, you and your team mates say what is in your hearts," and reflect the hearts of ordinary people. He said he will listen; he will listen hard. This is what we must do and I need your help because for us to have a voice in parliament, in government, in the PAP, we need a strong mandate. The stronger, the better. The stronger the mandate, the more influence we will be able to wield.

You know we live in an exciting part of the world. The American economy is not very good, the European economies are in trouble, deep problems. Young Americans, young Europeans are coming here looking for opportunities. China is changing beyond belief.

When I first went to my ancestral town in Ang Po [Anbu], near Teochew [Chaozhou], where my mother came from, it was such a poor place. I had to learn how to draw water from the well and how to do my "business" outdoor. In the evening, at 8 pm the light became dim, there were no refrigerators and so what leftover food we had, they boiled to kill the germs to keep till tomorrow. Today, when I visit my cousins, because the old ones have passed away, they drive me around in their BMWs, they treat me to banquets, they show me their bungalow houses. And this is all over China. And on the other side, there is India, also growing in a different way, but growing. I've been to many parts of India. You know I am involved in the Nalanda project, and I thank Mr Lee Bock Guan for coming here this evening to show us support. I am very grateful to him. Even a poor state like Bihar is making growth of over 10% a year. There is Vietnam, there is Indonesia. The whole region around us — 2 billion people, 3 billion people, half the world's population — is on the move and we are right in the middle. How can our future not be bright?

If we are united, and we have very good relationships with all our major trading partners — and I was involved in forging these relations as Trade Minister and as Foreign Minister — there are so many things that we can do, so many opportunities for Singaporeans. The sky is the limit, the world is our oyster, provided we are united. If we are divided, there will be problems, big problems. This destiny, our destiny in this century, is in our own hands. And this election in Aljunied is important not only for the people who live here but for the whole of Singapore.

Give us a strong mandate! We will work for a government and a PAP that will be able to create a new unity in Singapore, and understand and overcome many of the frustrations that are prevalent. We may not be able to solve all of them but we can alleviate some of them and we can be comforting to everybody. If we do that, it will be a different Singapore. Remember the Aljunied election is of decisive importance. On nomination day, I described it as a "决战 (jue zan)", a decisive battle. It is a decisive battle. It was a decisive battle deliberately provoked by Mr. Low Thia Kiang. We have to win it and we have to win it decisively, and we must fight for the transformation of the PAP and achieve this new unity. This is really a struggle for the soul of Singapore, and in this struggle we are all on the same side, all political parties are on the same side, all of us are on the same side. Let us work together, and we have to work together and renew hope in the Singapore with love. Live or die, we who are here will work with you and make it happen.

Thank you.

# CULTURE AND VALUES

# Language: Going Global But Remaining National

*Through translations, the different language groups in Singapore will better understand each other, and better share each other's cultural inheritance.*

Mr Chairman, Ladies and Gentlemen

It is not by accident that the Malay language is today the national language of Singapore, Malaysia, Indonesia and Brunei Darussalam. From the days of Sri Vijaya, the language spoken by the people living alongside the Straits of Malacca, the Straits of Singapore and the great rivers of Sumatra has been the major language of trade all over the archipelago. Because it is a language of trade, the Malay language has always shown great adaptability to changing conditions. It remains so today.

Although the English language is now the international language of trade, the Malay language will always remain an important language of trade in the region, especially in communication with our Malaysian, Indonesian and Bruneian neighbours. In this respect, the historical role of the Malay language in Southeast Asia has not changed.

The role has not changed but the language itself must change to meet the challenges of modernisation and the requirements of science and technology. While we treasure the past, we should also look to the future.

We have to strike a balance between two critical requirements. On the one hand, we want the Malay language in Singapore to be

Speech at the launching ceremony of the Malay Language Month, DBS Auditorium, 2 March 1990.

international. On the other, we want the Malay language to help us develop our Singaporean identity.

First: The international requirement. There are close to two hundred million Malay speakers in the world, which is a very large group compared to many other language groups in the world. Malay language development in Singapore must therefore keep in close touch with Malay language development in Malaysia, Indonesia and Brunei Darussalam. We must be broad-minded and learn from our ASEAN neighbours. It is the same with all the other language groups in Singapore. Singaporean English, Singaporean Chinese and Singaporean Tamil must not develop too differently from the way English, Chinese and Tamil are spoken and written elsewhere. We are after all a trading people. Our ability to communicate effectively with our trading partners is very important. This is the first requirement: to make sure that the Malay language in Singapore is international and an asset to our economic development.

The second requirement is to develop the Malay language in a way which also helps us build our national identity. After 25 years of independence, it is natural that the Malay language in Singapore should have its own distinctive character, and be a little different from Bahasa Malaysia, in the same way that Bahasa Malaysia and Bahasa Indonesia are distinguishable from each other. There is also a unique quality to Singaporean English, Singaporean Chinese and Singaporean Tamil. We are gradually becoming one people and one nation. The different language groups share much more in common today. This common experience is naturally reflected in the way the different language groups express themselves. In newspapers and TV journalism, the Singaporean element is very marked because the same events are simultaneously reported in four different languages every day. The same ideas are presented to the four language groups. This promotes mutual understanding and nation-building.

In literature and poetry, however, the style is as important, or even more important, than the substance. The translation can never capture the full flavour of the original. But even so, a poor translation is better than no translation. And, in some cases, like the translation of holy books like the Bible and the Quran, the translation can come very close in beauty and inspiration. We should make this effort to increase the supply of translation of each other's important works. We need not do everything ourselves. Most of the translations can be imported from other countries. But they should be made widely available. In the literature and the poetry, we find clues to the soul of a people, the unspoken assumptions, the basic values. For example, it is very useful for Chinese and Indian Singaporeans to know some of the stories from *Sejarah Melayu*, in English translation or in Malay, and for Malay Singaporeans to know some of the stories from *San Guo Yan Yi* (三国演义) or the *Romance of the Three Kingdoms*, which is also available in translation. I have met Javanese who are familiar with the characters of Guan Gong and Liu Bei. Shakespeare has been translated into so many languages. Julius Nyerere translated Shakespeare into Swahili. The Japanese perform Shakespeare in their Noh plays. Translations bring cultures closer together. Every culture has its good points. Through translations, the different language groups in Singapore will better understand each other, and better share each other's cultural inheritance. The whole society will thereby be enriched.

In short, we want the Malay language in Singapore to be international and Singaporean at the same time.

To achieve this, we must promote scholarship in the Malay language. Of course competence in ELI is very important because we have to compete internationally, but we must not neglect ML2 because that is needed for the preservation of Malay culture and Malay self-esteem. For those who are very talented, we should consider teaching [them] ML1. We must, however, be realistic. Most students are average. Most students can only cope with ELI and ML2. To pressure them all to do ML1 is unfair and unwise. But we must try to find some with the ability and the interest. They will make a big contribution to the community. It is vital for the morale of the whole community. In Malay, we say *bahasa jiwa bangsa*.

I am optimistic about the development of the Malay language in Singapore because it has a long-term economic basis. The economies of Singapore, Malaysia, Indonesia and Brunei Darussalam are becoming more integrated. To be able to speak Malay is an economic advantage, and an advantage that will grow with time.

First Deputy Prime Minister talked about the triangle of growth recently. Increasingly, Singapore, Johore and Batam constitute a single economic entity. In the past, Singapore, Johore and Batam were all part of the old Johore-Riau Empire, speaking the most standard form of the Malay language in the heart of archipelagic Southeast Asia. As we shared a common past, so we share a common future. The Malay language is an inseparable part of this common past and this common future.

I congratulate the Malay Language Committee for the good work it has done and wish it every success in the future.

# THE WANDERING SCHOLARS OF THE WORLD

*For Harvard men and for Singaporeans, the world is our oyster.*

## The Secret of Harvard

It is said that once you are a Harvard man, you always remain a Harvard man. For such is the prestige of the university, such is the imprint of its influence, you can never forget. You are not allowed to forget. Harvard is a remarkable institution. Where lies its magic? It cannot be the buildings. Yes, the buildings are special but they are not that old or that remarkable. It cannot be the professors. True, some are very good, but they come and go. It cannot be the richer or the more famous among the alumni either. Although Harvard produces more than its fair share of Nobel Prize winners and world leaders, the great majority of Harvard men do not make the headlines. The magic lies not in the physical reality or in particular individuals, but in the spirit of the institution. In 1903, William James said that "the true Harvard is the invisible Harvard in the souls of her more truth-seeking and independent and often very solitary sons". It is a universal spirit celebrated around the world.

This evening, I would like to make the argument that for Singapore to endure and to prosper, it must have a little of the Harvard spirit.

To endure and to prosper, we do not need physical size. How big is Harvard University? For Harvard men and for Singaporeans, the world is our oyster. Size is not the issue. Wealth is not the issue either. If only wealth were needed, we can replicate Harvards in the

Keynote address at the Harvard Club dinner, Pan Pacific Hotel, 25 November 1990.

oddest places, which obviously is not the case. Of course Harvard is a wealthy institution, and we in Singapore also aspire to wealth, but wealth is not the cause of success but its result.

The secret of Harvard is its ability to attract and to inspire able men and women from all over the world. If we in Singapore want to endure and to prosper, we too must attract and inspire able men and women from all over the world. Indeed, this is the main constraint to our long-term national development.

## The Mobility of World Talent

Talent has always been mobile. In the Zhan Guo (战国) period of China, the period of the Warring States, rival princes competed with each other for the services of wandering scholars. The wise princes who knew how to attract such scholars and how to keep them happy succeeded the most.

Because of the tremendous advances in communications and transportation, the scholars of the world have never been more mobile. I use the word "scholar" loosely to refer to anyone with talent and ability that can be applied internationally. Because of this international flow of human talent, the great cities of the world are all cosmopolitan in character. These cities vie with each other for international talent. They are today's analogue of the old warring states.

We in Singapore have to compete for our share. The problem must not be narrowly defined in terms of immigration or emigration policy alone. Let me use the example of sand on a beach. A beach is not static. At any one time, grains of sand are either being washed on or washed off. If the rocks which break the water are in the wrong places, a beach can quickly disappear because the grains of sand washed off are not replaced. If, however, the rocks are well-positioned, the beach grows. It is the same with international talent. If our total environment is unconducive, we will lose people through net emigration. Not only will foreigners not want to come, our home-grown talent will want to leave. But if our environment is favourable, not only will Singaporeans stay Singaporean, others will also want to become Singaporean. It is like Harvard. Harvard men stay Harvard men and non-Harvard men would like to be Harvard men.

In the historical novel, *Shui Hu Zhuan* (水浒传) or the *Water Margin*, the rebel stronghold Liang Shan Po (梁山泊) succeeded in attracting heroes from all over the land. It was not always the case. The original leader Wang Lun was an insecure man. He kept out men of talent because he feared their ability. Under him, Liang Shan Po did not amount to much. There were always too many tigers on his mountain. When he was replaced by Chao Gai, and later Song Jiang, Liang Shan Po blossomed. Not only were heroes welcome, they were actively sought after. There were never enough tigers on their mountain. Of course the heroes of Liang Shan Po were really bandits and fugitives, but that is not the point I am making. The point is the attitude towards talent and ability. In the other historical novel, the *Romance of the Three Kingdoms*, we see the same difference in attitude between Liu Bei and Cao Cao. Because of Liu Bei, the State of Shu was able to overcome its lack of size and resources by attracting able men like Zhuge Liang, Guan Yu and Zhang Fei. Cao Cao, in contrast, was a suspicious man who trusted no one. Like Liang Shan Po, there was always room in Shu for a new man to make his mark. Once again, it is not the physical reality which is important, but the spirit of the place.

## The Spirit of Singapore

We can create a similar spirit in Singapore. I am not talking about an act of will alone. That will be a pointless exercise in idealism. I would like to argue that historical circumstances have created the conditions which enable such a spirit to flourish in Singapore.

Zainul Abidin, formerly Chief Editor of *Berita Harian*, now CEO of MENDAKI, told me once that Singapore is a nation of minorities. Very strange, I thought. How could the Chinese be in the minority? He is right of course. Although the Chinese are in the majority in Singapore, they are a minority in the Nanyang. The minority psyche which pervades the minority Chinese communities elsewhere in Southeast Asia is also the psyche of the Chinese in Singapore. The historical experiences of the Nanyang Chinese have a profound effect on the way Chinese Singaporeans view their own destiny in Southeast Asia. Multiracialism in Singapore is therefore not just the expression of a political ideal, it is of practical political necessity; it is what we must be to live in peace in Southeast Asia.

The result is a political culture which is uniquely sensitive to ethnic and religious diversity. Here in Singapore, everyone is allowed his own temple. I use the word "temple" in a broad sense to mean culture and not religion alone. The temple is where a group preserves and propagates its distinctiveness. You can be Muslim or Jew, Chinese or Parsee, Sikh or Sinhalese, you will never have to renounce your ancestry or your heritage. In the madrasahs and synagogues, in the SAP schools and the khalsa, we affirm the diversity in our unity. That which is Singaporean is not a replacement but an overlay. In our political culture, we express a universal ideal. Indeed, the heterogeneity in our society reflects the heterogeneity of the world. We live in a world composed of minorities. No race, no religion, no language group commands a majority in the world. We are a microcosm of the world, a reflection of its paradoxes and contradictions.

The ideal does not maintain itself. It requires effort. When so many cultures and religions are in close contact, continuous effort is needed to maintain order and harmony. We will never stop debating about race, religion, culture and language in Singapore. The problems can never be fully resolved. We can curb extremism, we can enforce GRC representation, we can legislate to prevent religious disharmony, and so on, but there will always be new problems which require new solutions. The French ambassador, Mr Bernard de Montferrand, told me once that our situation is like that of a beautiful garden which stays beautiful only because the gardeners are always at work, now watering the plants, now weeding the beds, now fertilising, now spraying pesticides. Of course we must not overdo this. Then we become a bonsai. But we cannot do nothing either. Left to itself, the garden reverts to the jungle. The fact is civilisation requires continuous effort to maintain.

In making the effort, we sharpen our ability to compete for international talent, especially Asian talent. Consider the vast pool of "wandering scholars" from China and the sub-continent. For lack of opportunities in their own homelands, many sail forth to other lands in search of fame and fortune. In the West, there is sometimes a limit to what they can hope to achieve. They bump against a glass ceiling of subtle discrimination. For their children, there is the ever-present danger of de-culturalisation. Here in Singapore, we offer an alternative, an environment where they and their children can remain Chinese or Malay or Indian or whatever, and still continue to enjoy the amenities of the West. Here in Singapore, our advantage is that we are a curious mix of East and West.

This is our competitive advantage: the fact that we are both East and West. The challenge before us is how to make use of this advantage to create a total environment that is conducive to local and overseas talent, an oasis for the wandering scholars of the world.

We must pay attention to the physical setting. This is being done and we are fast becoming a very beautiful city in the tropics. We have been systematically investing in our public parks and buildings. A great city requires a strong physical reference.

A great city also requires a strong artistic reference. Therefore, we must pay more attention to the arts for the nourishment it provides and to maintain our competitive position in the world.

But above all, a great city needs a largeness of spirit which extends beyond its physical confines. I come back to the spirit of Harvard and Liang Shan Po. In physical terms, the place is always too small. For very able individuals, Singapore is too small. Any city is too small. For example, our top musicians need to live overseas before they can be recognised as top musicians. A Placido Domingo, a Yang Chen-Ning, a Lester Thurow, a Lee Kuan Yew needs the world to fulfil himself. This is true in all the professions and in business. In a shrinking world, talent cannot be monopolised by any particular university or city or country. If we can have 50% of a world talent, we gladly accept 50%. If we can have only 10%, we are grateful for that 10%. This has always been Harvard's philosophy. You are never exclusively a Harvard man. You are never monopolised by the institution. It is this largeness of spirit which enables such an amount of talent to be associated with

Harvard without there being a corresponding sense of crowding or insecurity.

To co-opt the talents of the world, we need the same largeness of spirit, so that the achievement of any one redounds to the glory of all. When an Ethiopian minister pays tribute to Tommy Koh's contribution to the Law of the Sea, it is a tribute to all Singaporeans. When the Mayor of Xiamen praises Liu Thai Ker for his contribution to the master-plan of the city, it is a compliment to all of us. In this way, we are all part of a winning team which others will also want to join.

This is the spirit behind Harvard's greatness. This is the spirit we too must cultivate to attract and inspire talent from all over the world. Then only can we also aspire to greatness.

# A ZOO WITH A VIEW OF LIFE

*... all mankind needs to tackle the problems of the environment, with an understanding that, by complex feedback loops, our actions can destroy us if we are not careful.*

We have a remarkable zoo. It is probably the finest in Asia and certainly among the best in the world. Last year, the Zoo had over 1.3 million visitors, including over half a million foreign tourists.

Like animals in the jungle, the Zoo has to compete very hard, competing not only with other tourist attractions in and outside Singapore, but also with other zoos in the world. There is no rest. The moment we become complacent and stop upgrading, we will slide behind. This new underwater viewing sealion and penguin exhibit will help us stay ahead.

Our Zoo has always been sensitive to the way it treats animals and presents them to visitors. In the barbaric past, which was not very long ago, animals were caught and caged like prisoners for the amusement of human beings. Now we know better, that on this living planet, all life forms are inter-related and inter-dependent. In his seminal work *The Origin of Species*, Charles Darwin wrote:

> When I view all beings ... as the lineal descendants of some few beings which lived long before, ... they seem to me to become ennobled.

---

Speech at the opening of "Underwater Viewing: Sea Lion and Penguin Exhibit" at the Singapore Zoological Gardens, 9 March 1991.

> ... [F]rom the war of nature, from famine to death, the most exalted object which we are capable of conceiving, namely, the production of the higher animals, directly follows. There is grandeur in this view of life ....

It is a view of life we should promote in the Zoo. It is a view of life all mankind needs to tackle the problems of the environment, with an understanding that, by complex feedback loops, our actions can destroy us if we are not careful.

We have to be more conscious of environmental issues. The Zoo has a duty to educate. I am glad that the Zoo has always given emphasis to such issues in all its programmes. We should continue to do so. Such a forward-looking approach will in turn help the Zoo to maintain its high ranking in the world. We must be pro-environment and seen to be.

I congratulate the management and staff for a job well done and wish the zoo continuing sucsess.

# Arts and Economics

*We should see the arts not as luxury or mere consumption but as investment in people and the environment.*

Every year we meet to honour artists and benefactors who have contributed significantly to the development of the arts in Singapore. We do this publicly to help make participation in the arts a way of life.

As our economy becomes more advanced, the arts become more important. We should see the arts not as luxury or mere consumption but as investment in people and the environment. We need a strong development of the arts to help make Singapore one of the major hub cities of the world.

To begin with, we need the arts to help us attract talented individuals to come, work and live here, and maybe to settle here. Why do 5-star hotels spend so much money on beautiful gardens, sculptures and art objects? It is to enable them to compete for 5-star guests. We have to compete for talent in the same way.

We also need the arts to help us produce goods and services which are competitive in the world market. We need an artistic culture. It is not enough just to have expensive works of art. That will be vulgar. We also need taste. We only need money to buy objects. We need much more than money to have taste. We need training, sometimes of a lifetime, and a supportive social environment. Without the taste, the objects, however expensive, will be in the wrong places and will somehow look wrong. With taste, even objects of modest

Speech at the 1990 Cultural Awards Presentation Ceremony, Marina Mandarin Hotel, 25 March 1991.

value can be made to look very attractive. With taste, we will be able to produce goods and services of far greater value.

I am not talking about the taste of a few individuals. That will be of little interest. I am talking about the taste of large numbers of Singaporeans and of foreigners living in Singapore. Without large numbers, the creative services cannot flourish. In Italy, music, design and fashion are highly developed. Why is this so? Yes, we know of Pavarotti and Versace, but the big names are only the tips of icebergs. Italy excels in these fields because large numbers of Italians enjoy music, appreciate good designs and fuss over the clothes they wear, both women and men, and from very early in life. It is a pattern of behaviour rooted in the culture of Italians and coded in their cultural DNA.

When we dine at a high-quality Japanese or French restaurant, the service is exquisite. From the welcome at the door, to the decor, to the food, to the music, to the toilet, there is punctilious attention to detail, and this is possible only because the entire staff of the restaurant is highly trained and motivated to please the customer and sensitive to his every need. Of course we have to pay but that's the point. The artistry pays for itself.

And that's the way Singapore Airlines (SIA) stays profitable despite the competition. A large part of the value added is in the service, the design and the ambience. The quality is obvious to the customer. What is not obvious is the way this quality is kept up. Many airlines imitate specific aspects of SIA — the logo, the cutlery, the advertisement — but the overall effect is just not there. There is not the same consistency. The secret is in the culture of SIA and the way it is organised, and that is infinitely more difficult to copy.

Corporations have their cultures but they are themselves part of larger national cultures. In fact, the culture of the larger community often pre-determines the areas in which its corporations can excel. The Germans may make better machines but because they don't enjoy their food as much as the French, their restaurants are never as good. Japanese restaurants are not the same when they are run by non-Japanese. In the arts, as in all other fields of human endeavour, no one, no people can be good in everything.

In other words, we have to choose. While we want to develop the arts in general in Singapore, we will also have to specialise in order to excel. We cannot spread our efforts in all directions. Our resources are finite. Who then should choose? The government? I don't think any department in government has a vastly superior insight on this matter. A committee of wise men? Can they be sure? In the end, we need some kind of a market mechanism, so that success is rewarded with more resources which in turn makes further success possible.

This relationship between the arts and economics is inescapable in the long term for any society. We come back to the Darwinian imperative. If the arts develop in a direction which strengthens the whole society, it will flourish. If instead the arts weaken society, then it must in the end eviscerate itself. I am not saying that every project in the arts must be commercialised. That's not only crass, it will not work. But taken as a whole, the arts must over time benefit the society which supports its activities.

For this reason, public funding of the arts should always incorporate a market test. We need a partnership of government and the private sector. Without the help of government, progress will be very difficult. But without the participation of the private sector, of corporations and individuals, the result will likely be perverse and distorted.

Let me summarise the argument: To be competitive in the next phase of our national development, we need to promote the arts. This involves not just a few individuals but large numbers of Singaporeans and foreigners living in Singapore as producers, consumers and benefactors of the arts. But the arts span a wide field. Which segments should we promote? Which will succeed? No one knows for sure. Because no one knows for sure, we have to build in a market test. Where it is necessary for government to help, it should always be in partnership with the private sector. What we want in the end is to make participation in the arts a way of life in Singapore, in a way which helps us remain competitive in a very competitive world.

It is thus quite appropriate that as we congratulate this year's Cultural Medallion winners, we also recognise the corporate and individual benefactors who help make their work possible.

# A Different Kind of Race

*Although we no longer live in an age of empires and territorial conquests, the competition among human societies continues … to the economic and cultural spheres.*

## Tides

When the Dutch PM was here recently, he told us that every year, the Dutch economy enjoys a 4% to 5% surplus on its current account, and this gets invested overseas. As a result, the Dutch economy worldwide is much larger than the Dutch economy in the Netherlands. Five to six hundred thousand Dutchmen live overseas out of a total population of 15 million, which is over 3%. Cumulatively, they are the third largest foreign investor in the US. Britain is first and Japan second.

This is quite an achievement. It is not a recent achievement but one which goes back to the end of the 16th century at the time of the Dutch war against Spain. The Dutch displayed their greatest genius on the waters. It was in those years that they penetrated into the most remote and desolate parts of the world with remarkable courage, exploring the Amazon, bringing tea into Europe from Formosa, founding in Batavia the capital of an empire in the East Indies and moving on to chart Australia and New Zealand. The war against Spain was fought not just on land but around the world. The result was not only independence for the Netherlands but also a far-flung Dutch empire, and the steady accumulation of overseas assets. The Dutch East India Company, the VOC, was formed in 1601, and has in the ABN bank today a direct descendant.

---

Speech at the Press Club Annual Dinner, Marina Mandarin Hotel, 26 April 1991.

There is a tide in the affairs of nations. When the tide flows, it has a certain irrepressible momentum. You cannot freeze the development of a nation at a particular point any more than you can stop the tide at a particular level or the life of a person at a particular age. In the struggle against Spain, the Dutch people developed strengths which carried them beyond their shores. Indeed, the power of Spain itself gestated in the long struggle to reconquer the peninsula from Islam, which once accomplished, led the Spaniards to fan out into the four corners of the world in search of the 3 G's — gold, glory and the Gospel.

While it is important for us to discern the tides that flow, we must beware of trying to predict the future. That is not possible. In relative terms, the Japanese tide today is flowing while the American is ebbing, for sure in the short term, but for how long more we cannot be sure because flows create counter-flows.

In the case of Singapore, the tide is flowing and gaining strength. Of course we cannot be absolutely certain that it will continue but if we wait till we are absolutely certain we will be too late. Only history is absolutely certain. Not to recognise the trend is to miss an opportunity which may not come our way again. Like the Netherlands, we are now accumulating year by year about a 5% surplus on our current account. We are steadily increasing our overseas assets, not by pumping oil out of the ground, but by hard work and thrift. To make the most use of these assets, we need more Singaporeans to live and work overseas. Although we no longer live in an age of empires and territorial conquests, the competition among human societies continues, only this competition has now shifted to the economic and cultural spheres. Managing this internationalisation of Singapore is a crucial task in the next lap of our national development. If we do it well, we can be like the Dutch economy. If we mismanage it, we can dampen the momentum of growth, cause the tide to ebb, and become no more than a backwater of little interest to the rest of the world.

### Remaining Different

It may sound contradictory, but we can internationalise successfully only if we succeed in remaining different. If we lose our distinctiveness, if we become like everyone else, so-called citizens of the world, we will fail.

A few years ago, a visitor from another small country gave a talk to Singapore Armed Forces (SAF) officers, members of the Temasek Society. To highlight the difficulties faced by small states, he used the metaphor of a bottle of whisky. If you uncork a bottle of whisky and throw it into the swimming pool, the whisky will mix with the water in the pool after a while and what is inside will be no different from what is outside. When that happens, he said, what is inside the bottle loses its value. His argument is that for a small country to survive it must remain different.

In our case, how can we keep the whisky bottle closed? Our economy is founded on trade and connected by a myriad thread to the rest of the world. Every year, over a million Singaporeans travel overseas. Over five million foreigners come in through Changi Airport, plus millions more via the Causeway. As a society, we are completely exposed and ventilated. We get TV programmes, films, books, magazines from all over the world. Our financial and other institutions are electronically linked to New York, London, Zurich and Tokyo. In other words, we are the bottle of whisky, fully uncorked, in the swimming pool.

How then do we maintain the concentration? We need distilleries in the bottle itself, so that even as whisky is seeping out, new whisky is produced. These distilleries are the institutions in our society which transmit culture and values, the family incubators, schools, temples, mosques and churches, National Service, Parliament, the statutory boards, big and small Singapore companies, coffeeshops, clan associations, museums, the local mass media, and so on. At every moment, they secrete the essence which keeps us Singaporean.

Within Singapore, there is no great problem because our national institutions are much stronger now in the next lap than in the last. The problem is outside Singapore. When Singaporeans live many years overseas, as increasingly many have to, they and their children risk losing their sense of being Singaporean. That will be a great loss to Singapore.

Of course, even if they lose their Singaporean-ness, they will not lose their Chinese-ness or Indian-ness or Malay-ness. That is because the Chinese, the Indians and the Malays are drawn from ancient cultures. The Chinese and the Indians have particularly strong diaspora cultures like Jews and Parsees. They may be completely cut off from home, but in their own tenacious ways, from mother to child and through ritual observances, they transmit the cultural genes. So, at the ethnic level, remaining different overseas is not so difficult. But remaining different as Singaporeans overseas is not so easy. This is because we are a young nation. We have to put in more effort and organise more consciously.

Spontaneously and by official encouragement, Singaporeans overseas have been organising themselves into clubs and associations. Often it is over "makan" which is natural. Sometimes it is to celebrate National Day. At other times, it is to meet visiting ministers or officials. For our 25th anniversary celebrations last year, quite a few came back for the festivities. Singapore Airlines (SIA) helped by providing special packages. What was most touching was the effort made by a few clubs to raise money for the 25th Anniversary Charity Fund. They raised over $25,000. We should have given it more publicity. Maybe the press will write about it.

The big problem is education for the children. Once an adult, the Singaporean overseas can never fully shed off his Singaporean-ness. Till he dies, he remains identifiably Singaporean in character, even if he has taken up some other citizenship. But the children are a separate matter. When they are educated overseas, it becomes much more difficult for the parents to keep them Singaporean, often not for lack of trying.

We have to ponder this over very carefully. Right now, we are experimenting, with boarding schools in Singapore, and with our first overseas school in HK. When the British ran an empire, the children were left behind in boarding schools. For the British ruling class, the next generation was raised in public schools like Eton and Harrow. Most big countries now establish overseas schools instead so that parents need not be separated from their children. In Singapore, the Americans, the Japanese, the Indonesians, the British, all have their own schools. Even small communities here like the French, the Germans, the Swiss and the Dutch have their own schools. For the Dutch, there are only 350 families in Singapore, yet they think it absolutely necessary to have a primary school and educate their young in their own way. We have to find our own solution so that Singaporean children overseas learn English and the mother tongue and grow up feeling Singaporean.

Besides education, there are other problems which we will face as we internationalise. The Singapore International Foundation will help provide the organisational framework to solve them but it will not be enough. All our flag-bearers will have to chip in — our overseas missions, SIA, Singapore MNCs, the big banks, government agencies like EDB and TDB, even cultural and religious organisations. The Dutch do this as a matter of course. All over the world they organise business associations, social clubs and charity organisations in addition to schools, and these are invariably supported by Dutch MNCs and Dutch foreign missions. KLM and Dutch shipping lines contribute in their own special way by distributing characteristic Dutch products like tulips, herring and Christmas trees.

Like the Dutch, we need multiple links to each other. Singaporean families overseas should receive regularly all kinds of information from home and about home, not just *The Straits Times* and the *Mirror*, but also magazines and newsletters from schools, golf clubs, churches, SAFRA, clan associations and so on. We must develop the instinct to keep fellow Singaporeans informed even when they are abroad. In this way we spin an international web and create valuable networks for business and other activities.

Singaporeans who arrive at a foreign location should be received and assisted by fellow Singaporeans already there. The Americans and Japanese do this very well. Everywhere in the world, they are organised. Handbooks are prepared and updated so that those from home can settle in quickly, know what the local customs and taboos are, where they can get good bargains, how they can get help — a whole catalogue of useful information. We must develop similar methods.

## Co-Opting Others

But however much we internationalise, there are only so many of us. We cannot rely only on ourselves. The Dutch and the Swiss face the same constraint. They get around the problem of numbers by recruiting others, which means accepting them as equals, as partners and making them feel they belong. Dutch MNCs like Shell, Philips and Unilever operate in this manner. So too Swiss MNCs like Nestlé. Wherever they are, they localise themselves. It is a different pattern from American and Japanese MNCs.

Many of us are familiar with Shell. When they recruit executives, it is with the intention to retain them for a lifetime, which means cultivating in them a strong loyalty to Shell worldwide. You know the maxim: Think globally, but act locally. It makes a lot of sense but it can only be achieved when there are overarching values which hold the entire organisation together. Shell's human resource appraisal system is designed to support this organisational strategy. American oil companies do not and cannot operate like Shell.

In the case of Philips, less than 7% of sales are in the Netherlands. Three-quarters of the staff and three-quarters of the assets are applied overseas. Management is totally internationalised right up to the highest levels. On the Supervisory Board at the top, 7 out of 13 members are non-Dutch. 2 out of 9 on the Group Management Committee are non-Dutch. 4 out of 9 product divisions are headed by non-Dutch CEOs. Close to half of all expatriates are non-Dutch. At its headquarters in Eindhoven, Philips sponsors an international school and an international club to help integrate the families of foreign staff.

Nestlé is another good example. Nestlé's executives worldwide, whatever their nationality, have a deep emotional attachment to the company. Nestlé brings them regularly to its headquarters in Vevey, to train them in computerisation and other areas and to update them. When these executives meet, a certain bonding takes place. Such training might have been cheaper in their various countries, but the purpose is not just training but acculturation so that at the top strata the executives feel responsibility for one another. They develop a deep commitment to the corporation.

We have to operate like the Dutch and the Swiss but in a way which maximises the advantage of our Asian-ness. We can overcome our lack of human resource by co-opting Asian talent, in particular, the large floating pool of Chinese and Indian talent in the world. By Indian talent, I refer to talent from the whole Indian sub-continent, not just India alone. As for Malay talent, the diaspora is still small. The reason why the Chinese and Indian diasporas are so big is because China and the countries of the sub-continent are still going through a difficult period of political, economic and social transformation. Because of the size of these countries, this transformation will take a long time to achieve. We can safely assume that for decades to come the Chinese and Indian diasporas, far from shrinking, will continue to grow. We should work together with as many of their members as possible.

It is relatively easy for Singaporeans to get along with them. When Chinese from the PRC, Taiwan, Hong Kong, America or Australia come to Singapore, they feel comfortable here because of our Chinese heritage, which we consciously keep alive. A few weeks ago, an American Chinese professor from Harvard visited us during the International Film Festival. I met him a couple of times. He told me he was struck by the ease with which he could engage us in conversation. Although his parents were from China, he was born and raised a thoroughbred American. Yet the cultural affinity was unmistakable. I'm sure many of us can cite any number of such cases. The experience is the same with Indians and Malays in America or Australia. And I'm not talking only about Indian Singaporeans meeting Indians or Malay Singaporeans meeting Malays. Chinese Singaporeans too feel a certain closeness when they meet non-Singaporean Indians and Malays. When I was in university, in both England and America, I felt very much at ease with Indian students from India. We could understand each other very well in a way which Hong Kongers or Taiwanese could not with them. And the reason is obvious. Here in Singapore, from very early in life, everyday, Chinese, Indians and Malays interact with one another. This multi-cultural facility is encoded in all Singaporeans.

Because of this Singaporean characteristic, around every Singapore Club overseas we find a penumbra of non-Singaporeans who take part in the activities, mostly Asians. And it is not just the food which draws them. It is something much deeper.

We should build Singapore International on this much larger base of human talent. The core is Singaporean but around the core, we should extend our network into the Chinese, Indian and Malay diasporas. Singaporean companies which expand overseas should depend not only on Singaporeans but also talent from this larger group. I'm not saying we should be exclusively Asian — that would be absurd — but we must know where we enjoy a leg up. If food is an advantage we enjoy, exploit it. If the Dutch can make use of herring, we can make much better use of the wonderful cuisines available in Singapore. To succeed, the Singapore label must be appealing to foreigners. Indeed the process of co-opting foreigners has already begun. SIA and Neptune Orient Lines (NOL) are good examples. Both bring together regularly foreign staff and agents either in Singapore or elsewhere. It may be costly but it helps. By treating foreigners who work with us or for us well and fairly, they will be more prepared to go the extra mile for us.

Let me caution that we should not look at these foreigners solely as potential migrants. Some may eventually take up Singapore PR or citizenship but many will not. There is no need for them to. You don't have to be Dutch to work for Philips or Swiss to work for Nestle. The world has shrunk so much, we cannot expect those who are very able to spend their entire lives in one city or one country. Our approach should be to welcome them as fellow travellers, to interest them to visit our little oasis, and to consider this oasis as a second or a third home. And if they wish to make Singapore their first home, we will of course be very happy.

This is a great challenge for the next lap. If we succeed, we can be like Switzerland and the Netherlands, and achieve their economic and cultural standards. If we don't, we will not become a developed country. It is not just a matter of extrapolating GNP trend lines and marking where the lines meet. Internationalisation for us is a matter of necessity, not choice.

## Information and the Arts

There are many dimensions to internationalisation. We talked about the economic dimension and how we must exploit our cultural position to achieve success. We must also build up the information infrastructure. This is where the media comes in, both the domestic and the foreign. We need the domestic media to feed the Singaporean core, not just in Singapore, but worldwide. What we now call the domestic media should really be called the Singaporean media, and as Singapore internationalises so too should the Singaporean media. We cannot proliferate the way the American, Japanese and European media have, but we cannot confine ourselves to Singapore. *The Straits Times* has made a start with the overseas edition. *Zaobao* now produces the newsletter we regularly circulate to Hong Kong AIP holders. We must do more.

We should also co-opt the foreign press. It is not realistic to expect from them the same commitment to Singapore but many are friendly and helpful. We should encourage them and make their work easier — help them help us.

The arts also play an important role. The arts can make the idea of Singapore much more attractive and give it a certain cachet. Man can't live by bread alone. Here again, we should build on our multi-cultural character. There are facets of us which are Chinese, facets which are Malay, facets which are Indian and also facets which are Western. To sparkle like a diamond, we need to polish the many facets which make us inimitably Singapore. We can neither be distinguished nor distinctive if our achievement is only economic. We will not be able to inspire others if we do not also shine in the arts. For this reason, the National Arts Council and the Singapore International Foundation will have to work very closely together.

## Conclusion

The next lap is a different kind of race requiring different skills. We must still run together but we have to organise ourselves differently. It is certainly not more of the same.

We have to look outwards to the world beyond, the way the Dutch and the Swiss have done for generations. We must seize opportunities open to us to internationalise. Indeed, we have no choice if we want to go forward. But there are dangers. If in internationalising we lose our distinctiveness as Singaporeans, we will fail. We must remain different, yet be different in a way which makes us attractive to others, especially Asians in the diaspora. Then we will be able to co-opt them as partners in our enterprise.

All this requires effort, conscious and deliberate effort, not least the effort of those in your profession, for which I thank you in advance.

# MALAY-MUSLIM COMMUNITY IN THE NEXT LAP

*On this shrinking planet, no race, no language, no religion is in the majority.*

The Malay-Muslim community in Singapore is going through a period of social and economic change. Such change is never easy. With good leadership and organisation, however, the result can be a stronger and a more dynamic Malay-Muslim community in Singapore. The Association of Muslim Professionals (AMP) can help bring about the transformation.

**Three Major Tensions**

There are three major tensions or three major opposing pulls which affect this transformation. These three tensions can have positive or negative effects depending on the way we respond to them. They are not avoidable. We cannot wish them away.

The first major tension is the one between being Malay and being Muslim. Hyphenating the two words does not remove the tension. Both MENDAKI and AMP have wrestled with this issue and will continue to do so. The idea of being Malay can be traced back to the early Malacca Sultanate and its encounter with the Portuguese. Malay nationalism became very strong after the Second World War over Britain's proposal to form the Malayan Union. Malayness became important as a political category.

---

Speech at the Association of Muslim Professionals Inauguration Dinner, Westin Hotel, 31 October 1991.

To be Malay is to be Muslim and Malay *adat* has always taken this into account. For this reason, Indian and Arab Muslims have always found a special place in the Malay society. Perak *adat*, for example, has formal provisions for the recognition of Arab Muslims as Malays.

But to be Muslim is to be part of a larger community of believers, the *ummah*. Some Muslims believe that being Muslim is all that should matter. Being Malay is of secondary importance. Indeed, they decry some of the traditional practices of the Malay community as being un-Islamic. For them, the religious idea of being Muslim is of far greater significance than the political and cultural idea of being Malay.

This tension between being Malay and being Muslim can be creative and positive if well managed. A broader definition of the community can bring in more people to join in the common cause of uplifting those in need. Too strict a definition of Malayness will disqualify many who are now leaders and supporters. But it will also not do to move to the other extreme and drop the term "Malay" altogether because that is an inalienable part of the community. Malays are proud to be Malay and rightly so.

The second major tension which affects the Malay-Muslim community is that between the *kampong* and the city. Of all the ethnic groups in Singapore, the Malays are the least urbanised. Yet there is no choice but to participate in the economic life of the city, and by extension, of the world.

Mosque on Friday and *bersanding* on Sunday are occasions when Malays return back to the environment of the *kampong* and when they are physically together again. It is at such times that the emotional batteries are re-charged and news of the community exchanged.

The pressures of the city are, however, insistent. For many Malays, urbanisation puts great strains on family and other social relationships. The alienation of young people becomes common. In some ways, rapid urbanisation has contributed to the problem of drug addiction and the high divorce rate. For Indian and Arab Muslims, the problem is less severe because they have been urbanised much longer and so are better able to cope with the stresses of city life.

While we cannot go back to the *kampong*, we can build a social support network like those in a *kampong*, to help those who are less able to adjust to a city environment. Managing the tension between the *kampong* and city is not easy but it must be done. Malay-Muslim leaders face this tension all the time. On the one hand, they are expected to give special attention to members of the community. On the other, they are required to be national and multi-racial in their approach. Malay MPs face this problem most acutely. AMP leaders will too.

The third major tension is that between cultural ties to Malaysia and cultural ties to Indonesia. Just as Chinese Singaporeans have cultural ties to China and Indian Singaporeans have cultural ties to the Indian sub-continent, so Malay Singaporeans have cultural ties to Malaysia and Indonesia. We cannot pretend that these ties do not exist. Before the Treaty of London in 1824, that is, before the British and the Dutch divided up our part of the world, Singapore's links were to all parts of the archipelago. Sang Nila Utama and Parameswara came from Sumatra. At different times, Singapore was part of Sri Vijaya, Majapahit and the Johore-Riau Empire.

Under British rule, our links were naturally much stronger with Malaya despite the fact that many Malays migrated to Singapore from Indonesia. From 1963 to 1965, we were part of Malaysia and had to fight off Sukarno's *konfrontasi*. It was only in the early 1970s that Singapore's relations with Indonesia warmed up.

With the growth triangle and the prospect of an ASEAN Free Trade Area in 15 years, Singapore's economic ties with Indonesia will grow dramatically. This will affect the way the Malay-Muslim community in Singapore sees itself. For one thing, new economic opportunities will be opened up. In many fields, there will be new points for comparison. Malaysia has a monarchy; Indonesia is republican. Islam is Malaysia's state religion; Indonesia has *pancasila*. And so on. I am not suggesting that the Malay-Muslim community should subordinate itself psychologically either to Malaysia or to Indonesia. Far from it. What I am saying is that in discovering or re-discovering Indonesia, Malay-Muslims in Singapore will be stimulated by new ways of seeing themselves and the world. Indonesia will present an additional model to Malaysia for cultural comparison. In the process of learning from others, we will be better able to see ourselves and to develop our own uniquely Singaporean model.

I have described three major tensions which affect the development of the Malay-Muslim community. Let me now discuss how we can make them work in our favour. I would like to touch on three areas for action.

## Three Areas for Action

The first is social infrastructure. The basic building block is the family which we must strengthen. We must never allow urbanisation to break up the family and alienate the young.

Beyond the family, we need a social support network of relatives, friends and civic organisations to replace the physical *kampong*. We cannot go back to the *kampong* but we can maintain the *kampong* spirit of *gotong-royong*. The fact that there are relatively few Malay-Muslims in old-age homes is an indication that such a network already exists. We need all kinds of organisations and we need leaders at all levels. Those who are more successful should help those who are less successful. The formation of AMP is therefore a very good sign.

Let me repeat that it is better to have a broader rather than a narrower definition of Malay-Muslim to enrich the pool of leaders available to the community. And as I have mentioned earlier, Indian and Arab Muslims are already more urbanised and can help the others to urbanise more successfully.

The second area for attention is education. In the world we live, knowledge is the key to everything else. Malay-Muslim parents are becoming very anxious about the education of their children. This is extremely important because without the commitment of the parents, no progress is possible. We need a whole range of education programmes, from kindergarten classes to postgraduate scholarships, to help educate every member of the community to his full potential. Science and mathematics must be emphasised because they are very important in a modern economy. For those without the aptitude, we should find other fields in which they can do well and make a contribution to society. This has been MENDAKI's approach, which is why the government backs it fully.

We should aim high but we must not be unrealistic in our expectations. We need to put in a lot of hard work over many years. It will not be easy and there will be all manner of disagreement within the community over what to do. But it is an effort worth making. The government will help. Non-Malay Muslims will also help. But no amount of outside help will be of use if the community does not help itself.

We will have to strike a good balance between quantity and quality. We cannot just concentrate on those who are already doing well. We must also look after those at the bottom who are struggling. At the same time, we also need a few shining stars to inspire the rest. *Berita Harian* has done a good job building up role models for the Malay-Muslim community. It is right to give full publicity to those who do well in examinations, business and public life.

But we must fight the temptation to always measure ourselves in relative terms against the other races. We cannot avoid comparison but we should concentrate on making steady progress year by year. Whether it is AMP or other Malay-Muslim organisations, our targets must be set realistically. In this way, we will not be disappointed. We must stay united and avoid pettiness. What is at stake is not our ego but our ability to raise the standard of living for as many members of the Malay-Muslim community as possible.

The third area for action is a continued commitment to multiracialism. We use the term "multiracialism" so often that we sometimes forget what it means. It does not mean that in becoming Singaporean we deny our heritage. A Malay-Muslim must not be forced to choose between being Malay-Muslim and being Singaporean. That is not acceptable. Part of the essence of being Singaporean is the right to retain our separate ethnic character. But that right carries a corresponding duty to accept that others of other races also have the same right.

The experiences of other countries show that ethnic differences can never be fully submerged. Look at the example of Yugoslavia or the Soviet Union or Canada today. The more ethnic differences are denied, the more they assert themselves, often with a vengeance. It is because we never try to remove ethnic differences that we have racial harmony in Singapore. It is only by acknowledging potential conflicts that we minimise them. We will never be able to stop worrying about problems of race, language and religion.

In reality, all countries face problems of race, language and religion, even countries like Britain and France. On this shrinking planet, no race, no language, no religion is in the majority. Chinese are a minority in the world. Muslims are a minority. Christians are a minority. We are all members of minority groups in the world and we have to live with one another. In other words, we are not unique in having to worry about such problems in Singapore. These are problems of all mankind.

But because we have always worried about such problems, we do in fact enjoy a certain advantage in the world. In Singapore, the races are mixed in our schools and housing estates, and in both the private and public sectors. From kindergarten all the way to university, from resident committees all the way up to the Cabinet, we are mixed. The Singaporean learns to be sensitive to others from a young age. We may be Chinese, Indian or Malay-Muslim but we learn very early not to take others for granted. This is why our national discussions on race, language and religion can be very beneficial. These discussions help us to find the optimal balance in our society. Sometimes we take; sometimes we give. We have to compromise; we cannot have everything our way. The desire to maintain overall peace and harmony is becoming ingrained in every Singaporean. To some extent, we have succeeded. Singaporeans are culturally sensitive in a way other people are not. We have a multi-channel facility and we know when to switch from one channel to another. This facility gives us a competitive advantage. Depending on whether we are dealing with Chinese, Javanese or Australians, we know how and when to adjust. It is our multiracialism which enables us to operate as a hub city and as an interphase for others. Dr Kenichi Ohmae made the same point to Singaporeans two weeks ago when he reminded us that Singapore's multiracialism helps us to be competitive in the borderless world of the future.

In other words, while we worry about our diversity, we also rejoice in it. From a sociological perspective, multiracialism is a psychological complex which helps define our personality as Singaporeans. It is this complex which makes Chinese Singaporeans different from Chinese in China. It is this complex which makes Malay-Muslim Singaporeans different from Malay-Muslims elsewhere. I therefore welcome the AMP's proposal to establish an award for Singaporeans who make a special contribution to multiracialism. I hope other ethnic groups will also join in. The proposal expresses the desire of Malay-Muslims to make the transition from the *kampong* to the multi-racial city and from the multiracial city to the multiracial world. I also support the AMP's launch of a book prize for the best academic exercise by an Honours Year student on an area of study of relevance to the Malay-Muslim community.

**Conclusion**

Let me conclude. I started by saying that Singapore's Malay-Muslim community is going through a period of tremendous change. The community is challenged by three major tensions — between being Malay and being Muslim, the opposing pulls of the *kampong* and the city, and a shift from close cultural ties primarily with Malaysia to close cultural ties with both Malaysia and Indonesia. These tensions are in fact challenges which the community has to respond to. I mentioned three areas which deserve our special attention — building up a social infrastructure to support the urbanisation process, education and a continued commitment to the multiracial ideal.

It is in responding to the challenge of change that the Malay-Muslim community makes its transformation into a community that is uniquely Singaporean and into one that is urbanised, self-confident and tolerant of others. The process cannot take place overnight. We must be patient but persistent. Malay-Muslim leaders must expect to go through all kinds of difficulties. That a group like the AMP should spontaneously organise itself without government prompting augurs well for the future. That you have been able to attract the support of both Malay-Muslims and non-Malay-Muslims speaks well of your approach. That your publicly declared standpoint is national and not narrowly Malay-Muslim makes your Association truly Singaporean. I wish you every success.

**[Ph1]** At a three-hour ceremony to honour the Yeo ancestors in Anbu in 2009. Being a Minister in the Singapore Government, I was asked to lead the ceremony which meant that I was led throughout on what to do.

**[Ph2]** My paternal grandfather, Yeo Teck Kuay (杨德科). He was born in Chaozhou and came to Malaya. After becoming wealthy from planting rubber along the Johor River, he built a big house in his home village and was addressed Teck Kuay Yah (德科爷). In 1949, the family properties were expropriated.
*Right*: My paternal grandmother, 彭富菜, was the third wife.

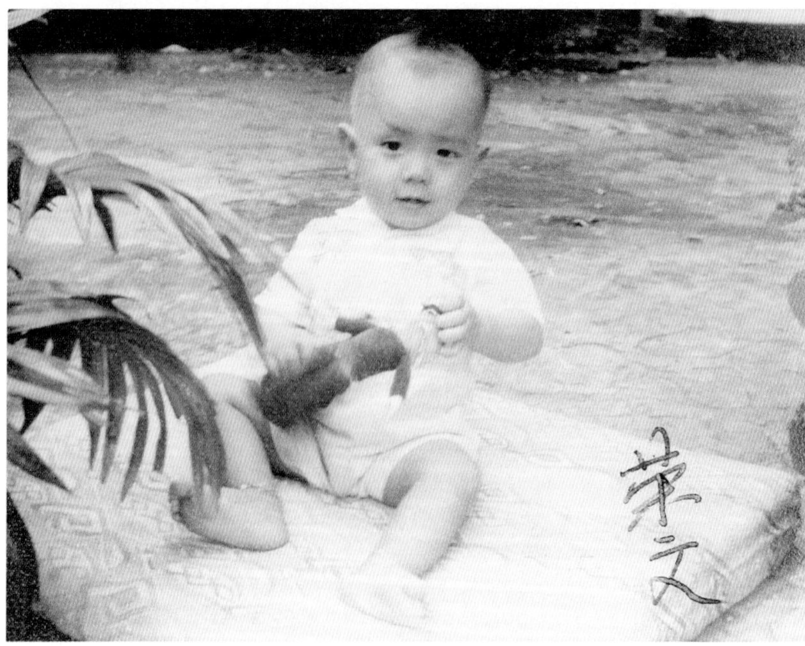

**[Ph3]** Picture of me as a toddler with my mother's handwriting.

**[Ph4]** My mother carrying me in Nara. During the war, my father worked in Daimaru which took over Robinsons' premises at Raffles Place. In 1954, they went to Japan for a holiday and visited old colleagues.

**[Ph5]** Family portrait with me in my father's arms. I had two more brothers who died during and after the war. My father was baptised a Catholic when he was a boarder in St. Joseph's Institution but stopped practising when he was an adult. He married my mother in Chaozhou in 1937 in a traditional wedding. When my third brother was dying in his arms, my father baptised him and the entire family became Catholic after that.

**[Ph6]** Primary 5 in St. Stephen's School after winning a prize in a pantun competition organised by 4PM, a Malay cultural organisation.

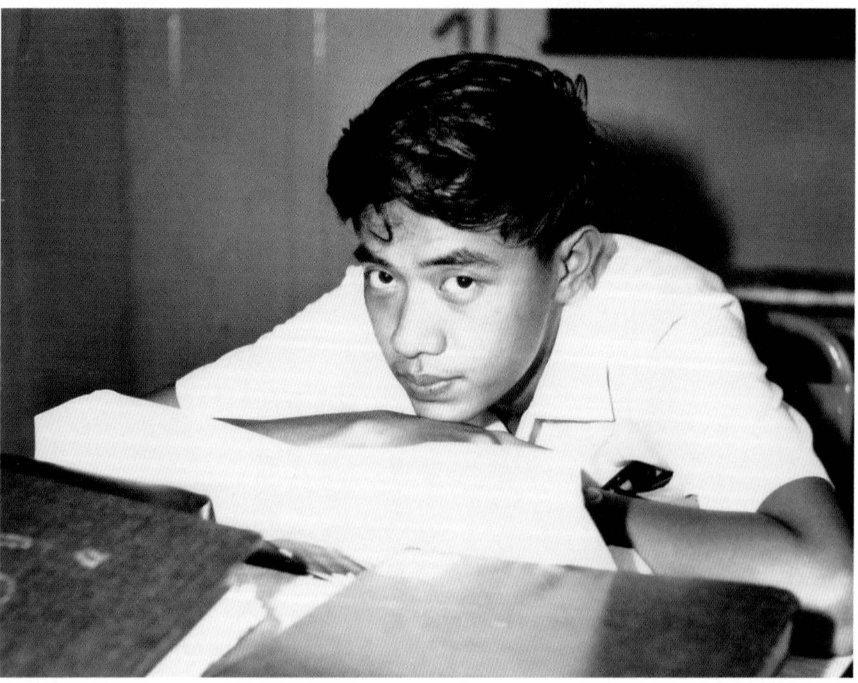

**[Ph7]** Caught napping in St. Joseph's Institution. I inherited from my father this irresistible urge to doze off after lunch for which I was punished in school and in the Army.

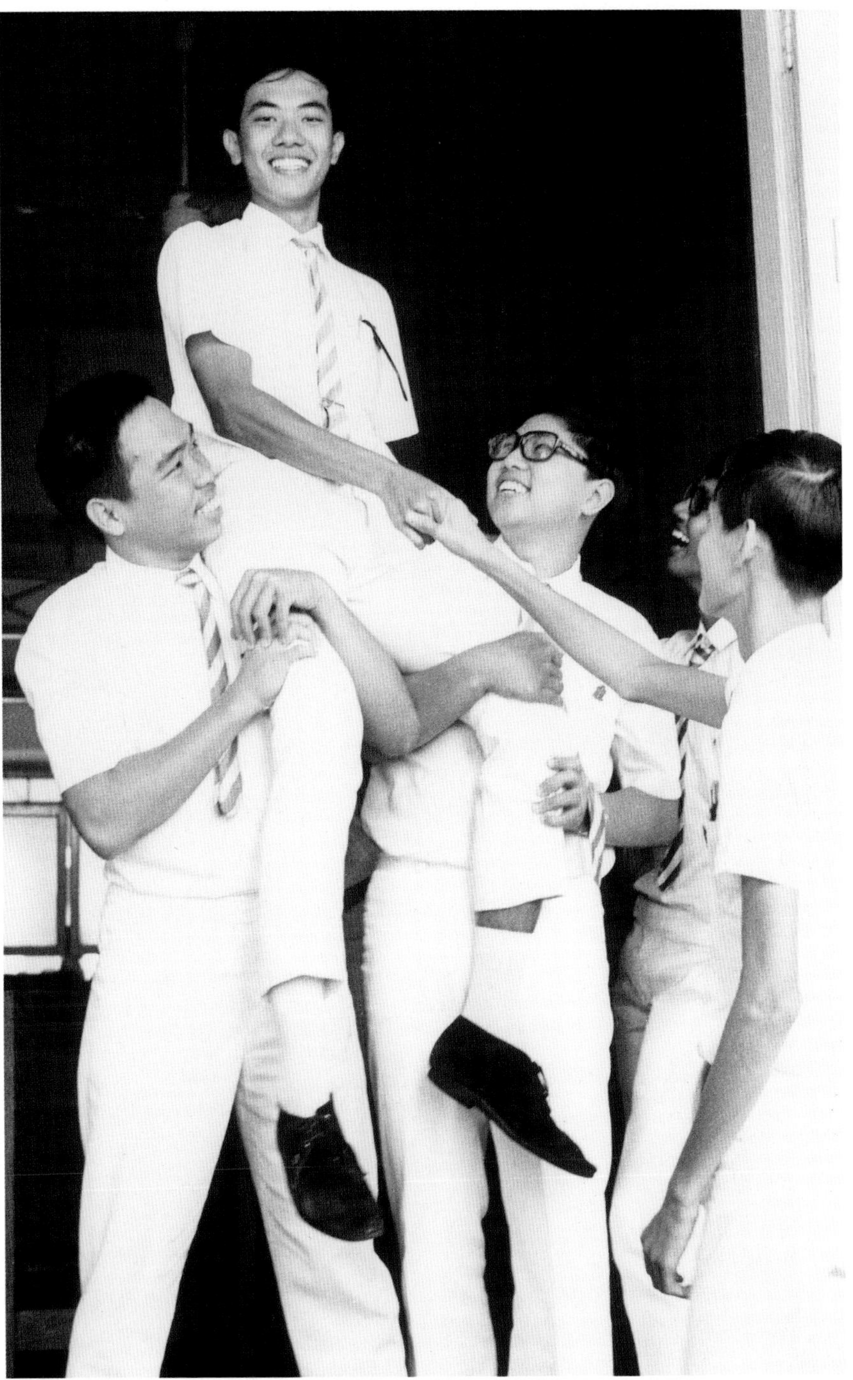

**[Ph8]** Picture taken by *The New Nation*, an old newspaper, after the 1972 GCE O-level examinations results were released.

**[Ph9]** As an officer cadet in SAFTI in 1973.

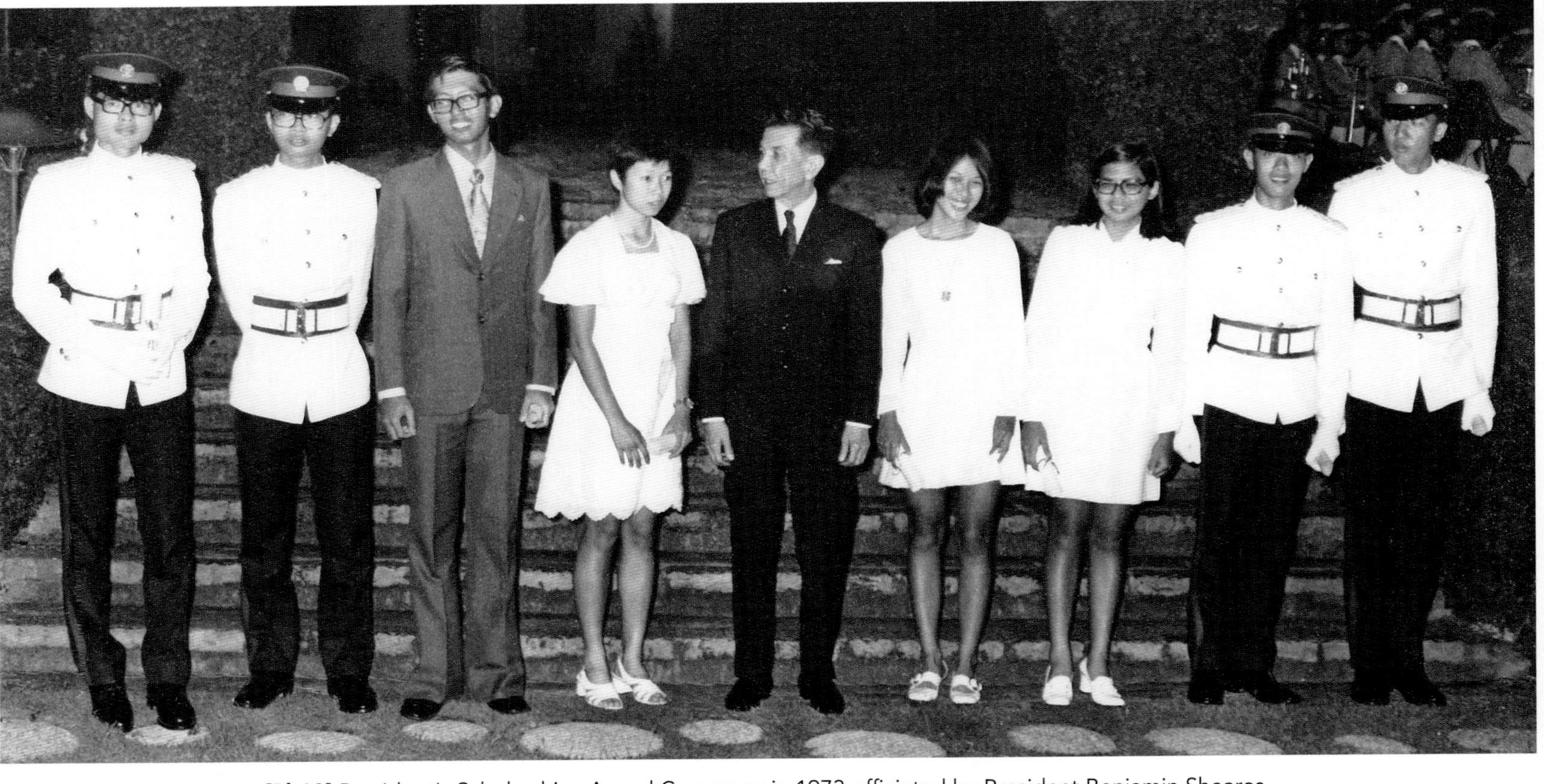

**[Ph10]** President's Scholarships Award Ceremony in 1973 officiated by President Benjamin Sheares. On extreme left, Lim Hng Kiang. On extreme right, Teo Chee Hean.

**[Ph11]** With Lee Hsien Loong, Lim Hng Kiang and others in 1973 at the Lake District in England.

**[Ph12]** At the top of Mount Snowdon in Wales in 1974. A group of us were told it was an easy climb even for grandmothers. Unfortunately, we took a wrong turning and had to clamber on all fours part of the way.

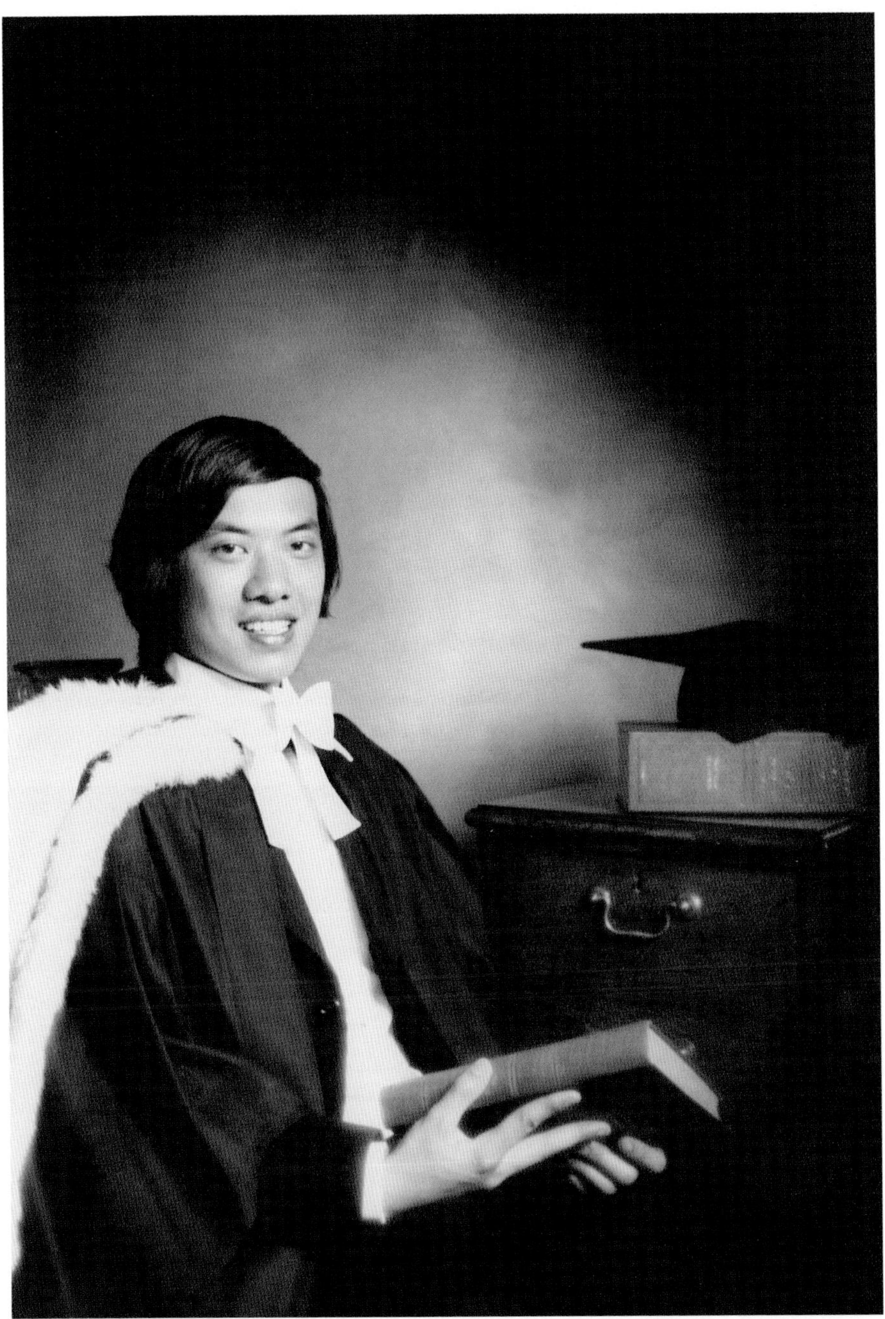

**[Ph13]** Graduation picture in Cambridge, UK, 1976.

**[Ph14]** Graduation day at the Senate House in Cambridge with Lim Hng Kiang and his parents (first three from left), my parents and my brother Peter (extreme right).

**[Ph15]** On my first visit to China in 1983 when I met my maternal grandparents for the first time. Picture of relatives from my mother's side in my mother's ancestral house in Anbu. My mother's family house was not expropriated in 1949 because my maternal grandfather was judged a good man in a public meeting.

**[Ph16]** My mother and I posing with my maternal grandparents, who were then in their 90s. My maternal grandmother, 林婵真 was not well and in pain unlike my maternal grandfather, 鄞纯煜 who was still in good humour. When she complained, he pinched her lightly on the nose to comfort her. My mother left the house as a young bride of 18. As the eldest daughter, she always felt responsible for them and remitted money regularly. When she first went back in 1978 with my father, as a grandmother, she knelt before them to ask forgiveness for her long absence.

**[Ph17]** I took this picture of my parents in their bridal chamber in the Yeo ancestral house.

**[Ph18]** Bowing before Yeo ancestors in Anbu in 2009.

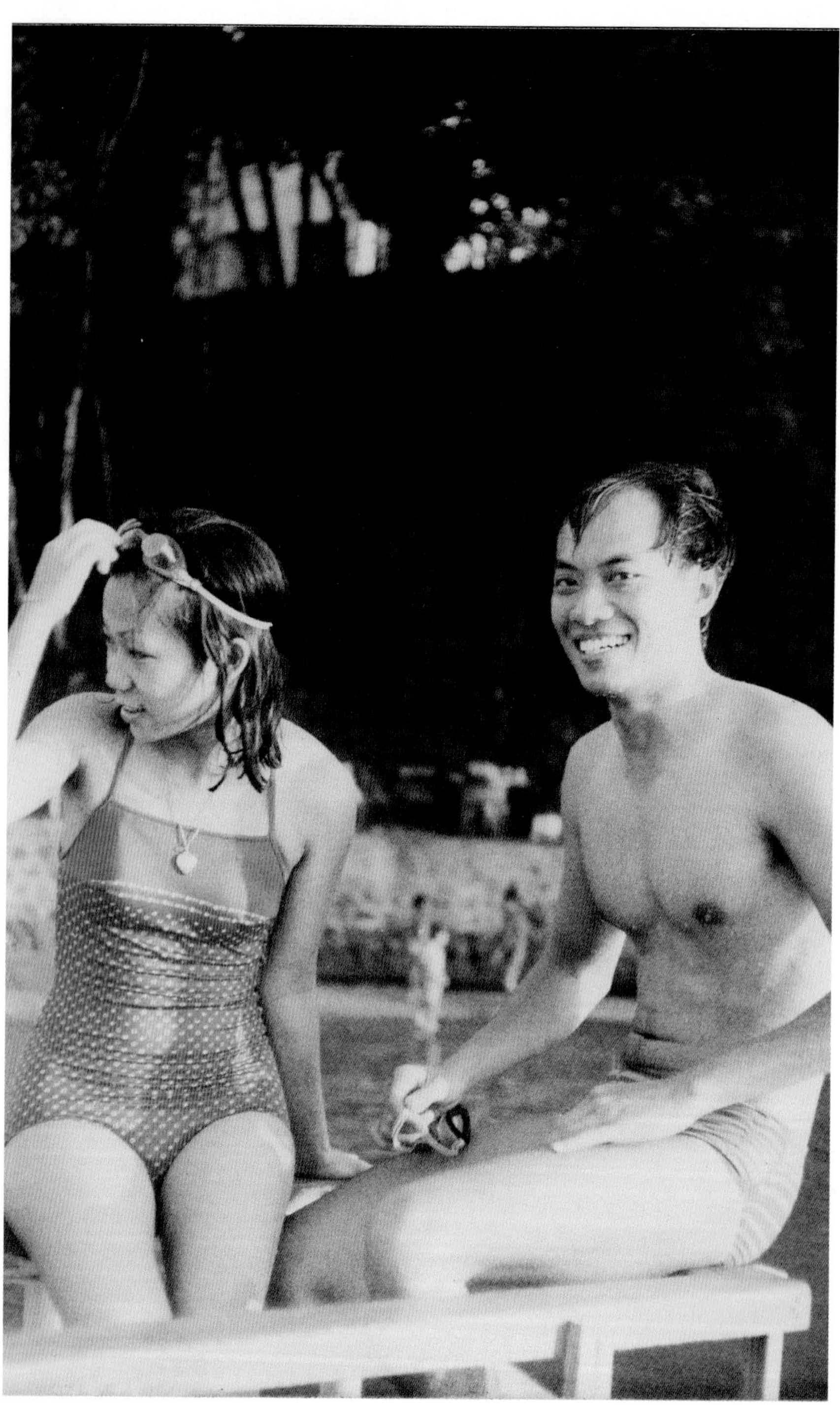

**[Ph19]** At Changi Beach Club in 1982 with my future wife.

**[Ph20]** Harvard Business School Section E, MBA Class of 1985, on the steps of Baker Library.

**[Ph21]** Our wedding at St. Paul Church, Cambridge, Massachusetts in 1984. It was attended by family members and close friends from the Harvard Business School. Sanjay Pradhan (third from left), a Hindu, and Leigh Walzer (fifth from left), an Orthodox Jew, were the ushers.

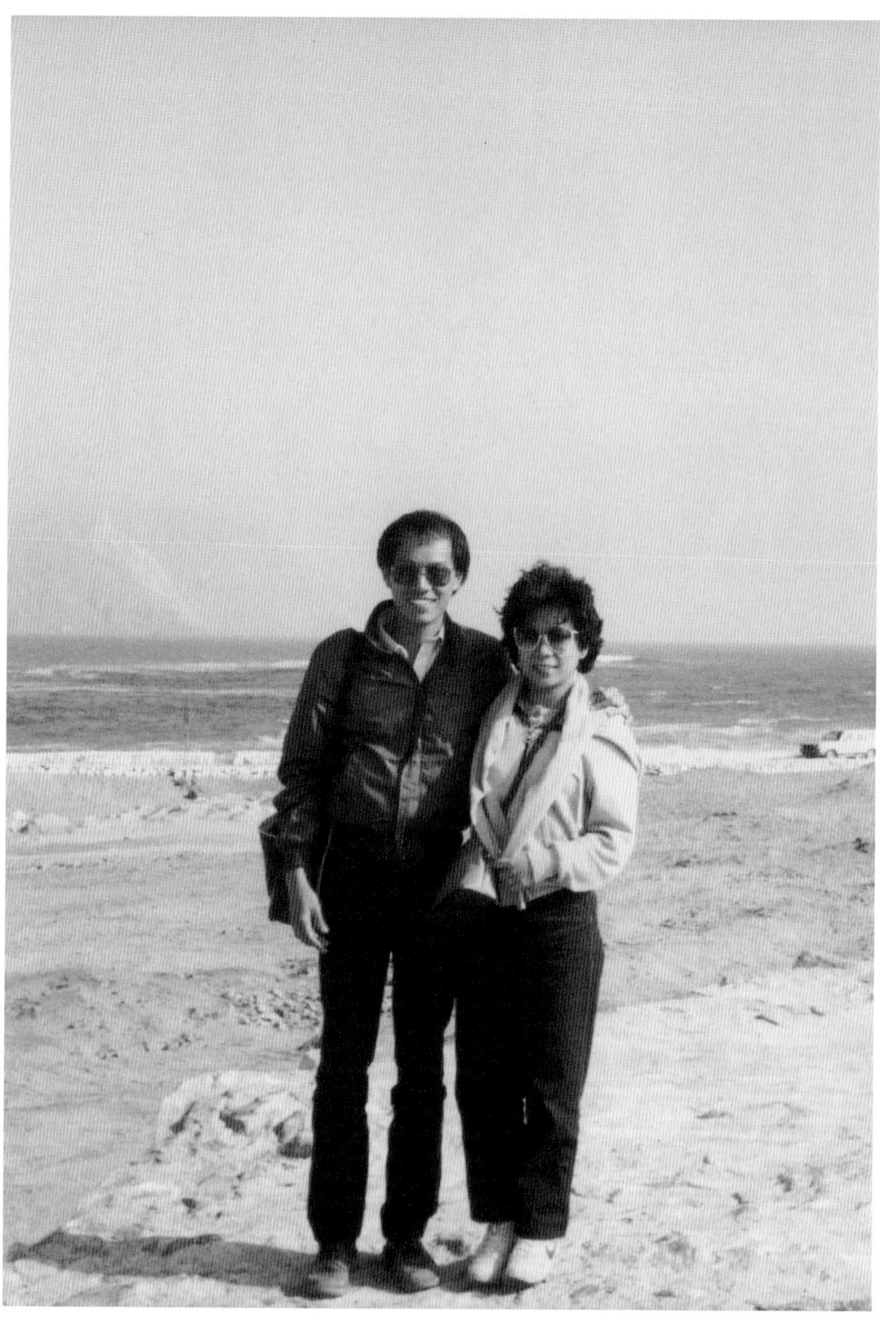

**[Ph22]** My wife and I on the Pacific coast in Arica, Chile, in the summer of 1984. Studying geography in secondary school, South America was always my favourite continent but it was too expensive to go on a tour there from Singapore. As it was much cheaper from Boston where both of us were studying, we decided on a two-week honeymoon in Brazil, Argentina, Chile, Bolivia and Peru. I found, to my pleasant surprise, that if we travelled to Machu Picchu via Arica and La Paz, we did not have to pay extra. There is no other reason to visit the little port of Arica in the Atacama Desert, one of the driest spots on earth.

**[Ph23]** Col Tan Jer Meng, old colleague from the SAF who saw action during Indonesian Confrontation, is like an uncle to my children. He often drove me during GE campaigning. In my early years of politics, he chaired the Management Committee of my Community Club. Picture taken in 1995 after a fishing trip when we caught a sea bass off Pulau Ubin as big as my youngest son who was then less than two years old.

**[Ph24]** I brought my wife and children to see my old tutor, Dr Vis Navaratnam, at Christ's College, Cambridge, in the late 90s. Years later, I found out that he and Prof S. S. Ratnam, the famous obstetrician who delivered two of my children, were classmates at medical school in Colombo.

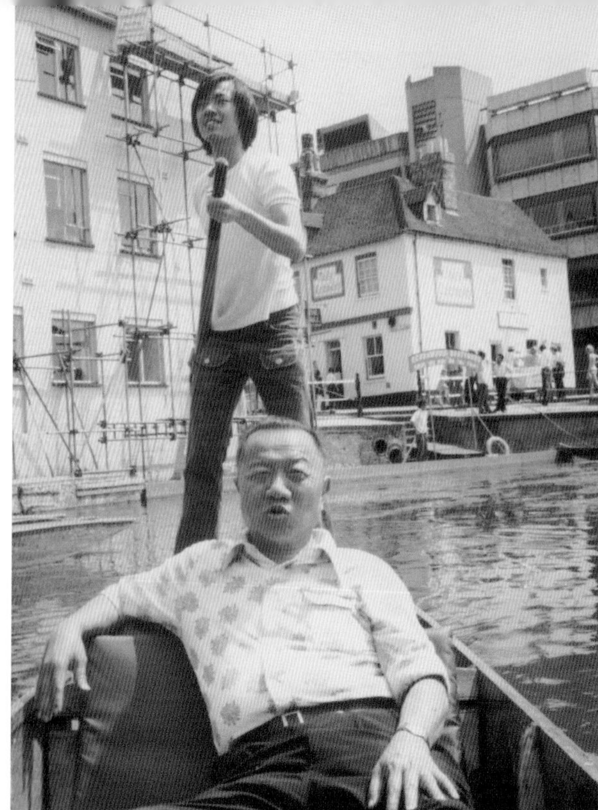

**[Ph25]** Punting my father on the River Cam in 1976.

**[Ph26]** Punting two of my sons on the River Cam in 2012.

**[Ph27]** Celebrating US Ambassador Jon Huntsman's 50th birthday in my house in Changi in 2010. My family felt greatly honoured by Minister Mentor Lee Kuan Yew's presence.

**[Ph28]** Increasingly difficult to get entire family together. Vacation in the Maldives with Grandma Mary who gets many more hits in the social media than me.

**[Ph29]** Christmas lunch with Auntie Polly in 2011 who helped to raise me as a child. She was my father's younger sister by the same mother.

**[Ph30]** Dinner in 2011 with Auntie Ah Hua who helped my mother look after us when we were young.

**[Ph31]** My family ate at Mong Hing Teochew Restaurant for over 40 years until it closed in 2013. Picture with the late founder Koh Khiang Siah and his family. On his right is my father-in-law Mark Leong who drove me to the Istana before the 1988 GE.

**[Ph32]** Commanding a Guard-of-Honour Contingent at a Signals Day Parade in 1977. I was OC of 3 Signals Battalion Signals Support Company.

**[Ph33]** With the men of Signals Support Company, 3 Signals Battalion in 1977.

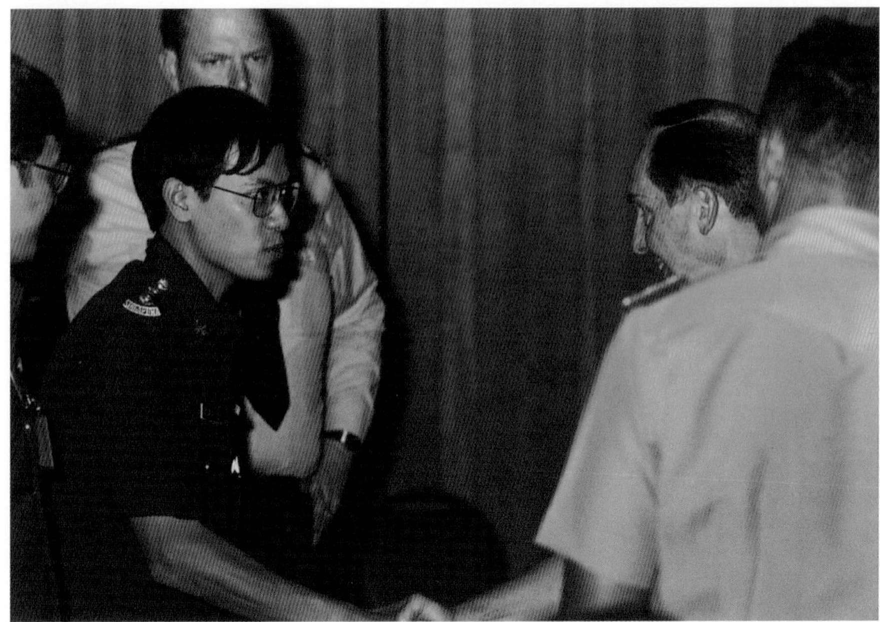

**[Ph34]** Greeting Commander-in-Chief, US Pacific Command, Adm Robert Long, at a conference in Honolulu in 1979.

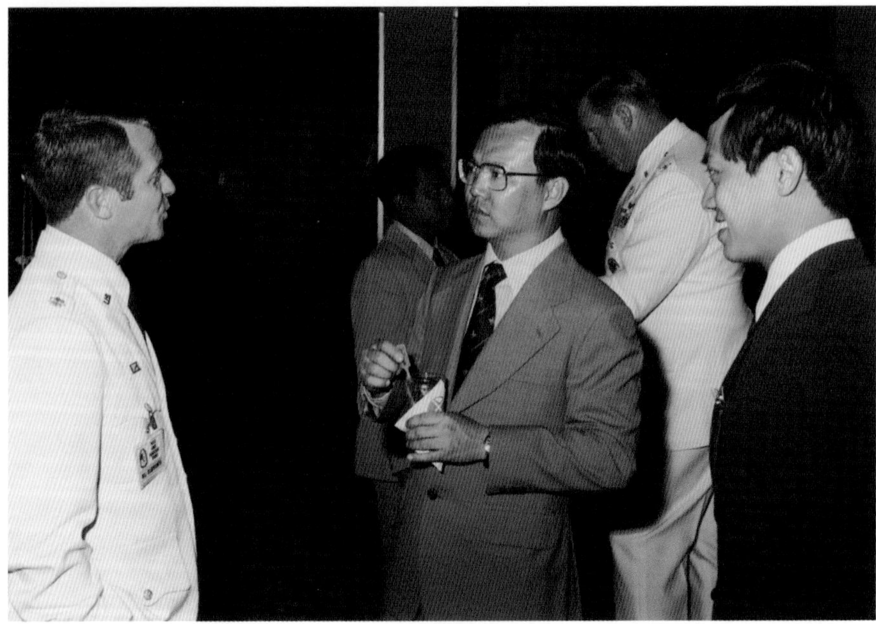

**[Ph35]** With Deputy Chief of General Staff, BG Tan Chin Tiong at the Pacific Armies Conference in Honolulu in 1979. BG Tan later became my Permanent Secretary in the Ministry of Information and the Arts. When I became Foreign Minister, he was Singapore's Ambassador to Japan.

**[Ph36]** Defence Minister Howe Yoon Chong officiating at the graduation ceremony of the 9th Batch of Singapore Command and Staff College in 1980. I was posted to the Air Force after that and got to know Minister Howe well.

**[Ph37]** Newly-minted Brigadier General in Air Force uniform in 1988. Moving from the Army to the Air Force in 1979 was a difficult transition. I continued wearing my Army uniform until I was directed to change to blue. While all Air Force uniforms at that time carried an aeroplane insignia on the collar, I wore the cross flags of the Signals Corp instead which was non-regulation. Later, the Air Force got rid of the collar insignia. It was only at that point that I started wearing regulation Air Force uniform.

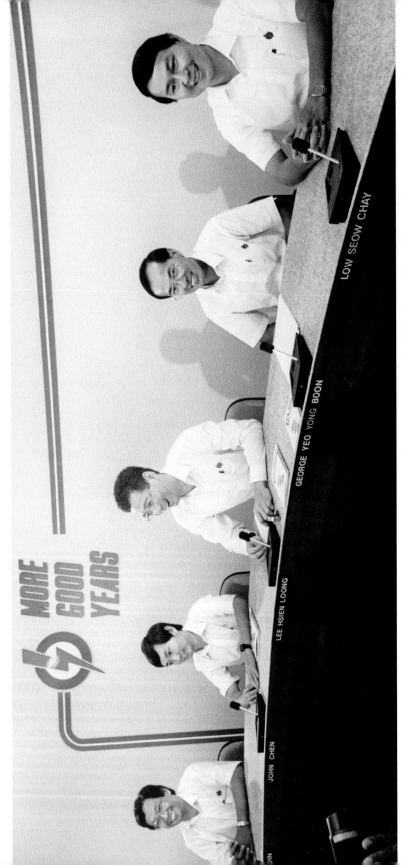


**[Ph38]** Introduced by Lee Hsien Loong as a PAP candidate in August 1988.

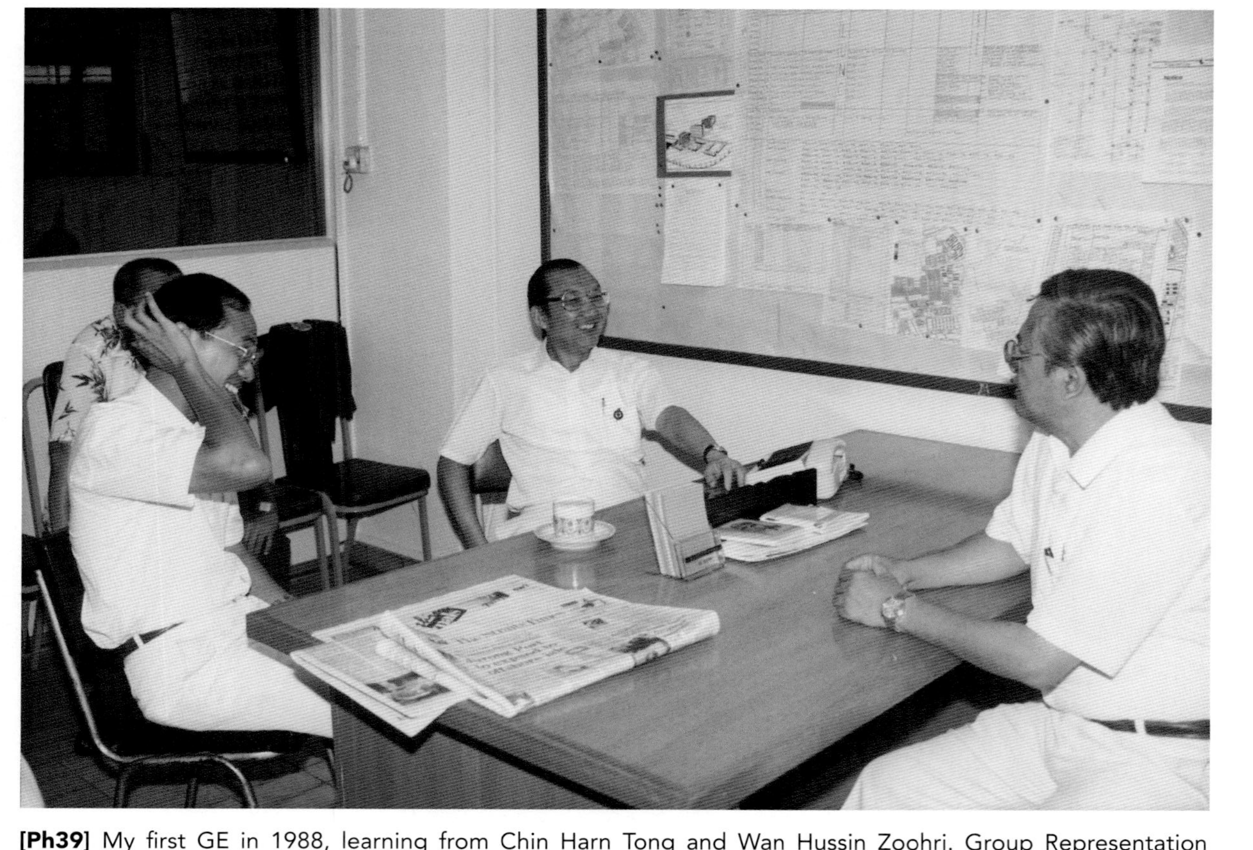

**[Ph39]** My first GE in 1988, learning from Chin Harn Tong and Wan Hussin Zoohri. Group Representation Constituency (GRC) had just been introduced. The three of us made up the Aljunied team.

**[Ph40]** As Minister of State after the 1988 GE in new cabinet under PM Lee Kuan Yew.

**[Ph41]** Opening of Parliament by President Ong Teng Cheong at the Old Parliament House. By chance, I was looking up at the camera from the front bench.

**[Ph42]** I was note-taker for Senior Minister Lee Kuan Yew in his back-to-back private meetings with President George Bush on 4 January 1992 and President Yang Shangkun on 8 January 1992. Bush's note-taker was Brent Scowcroft. Bush asked Lee Kuan Yew to pass a message to Yang. Sino-US relations were still tense at that time. It was a privilege to watch at close range how Lee Kuan Yew interacted with the leaders of US and China.

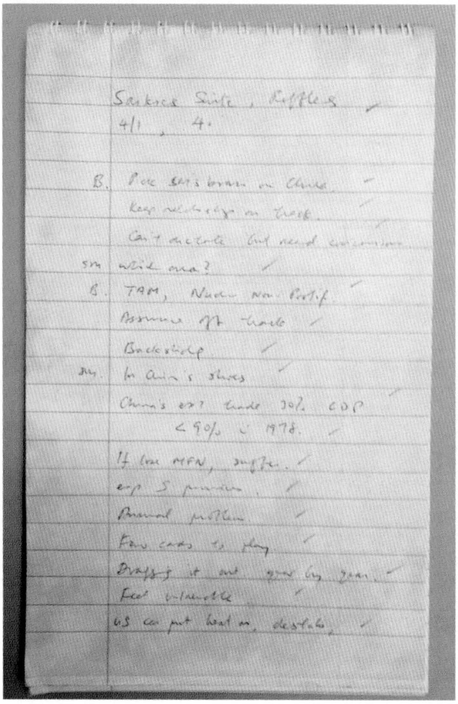

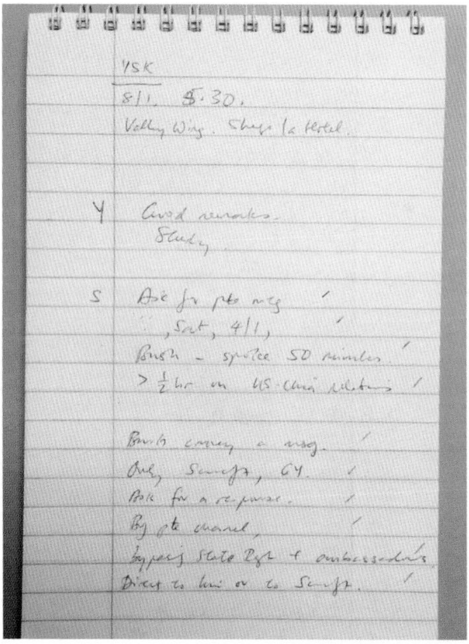

**[Ph43]** My handwritten notes of Lee Kuan Yew's meetings with President Bush on 4 January 1992 and with President Yang Shangkun on 8 January 1992.

**[Ph44]** As President of SAFRA, I launched Swing Singapore at Orchard Road in 1989.

**[Ph45]** Visiting Johns Hopkins University in 1995 when I was Health Minister with a medical delegation led by Permanent Secretary Dr Kwa Soon Bee (on my left) who played a major role in building the excellent healthcare services we enjoy in Singapore today. [Photo source: Annual Report 1995, Ministry of Health, Singapore.]

**[Ph46]** Young PAP's visit to China in 1995. Our host at that time was Chinese Communist Party Youth League Secretary Li Keqiang. On my wife's right are Mohamed Maidin and Matthias Yao — both became office holders. Mohamed Maidin, Yeo Guat Kwang (squatting, fifth from left) and Dr Toh See Kiat (squatting, fourth from right) were fellow Aljunied GRC Members of Parliament in different electoral terms.

**[Ph47]** Young PAP's visit to Salt Lake City in 1996. Meeting with Jon Huntsman who had been the US Ambassador in Singapore. Seated fifth from left is Lee Huay Leng, one of the two editors of this book. Huay Leng was one of the journalists covering the visit.

**[Ph48]** With members of the Young PAP on our visit to Washington, DC in 1996.

**[Ph49]** With David Marshall in Paris when he was Singapore Ambassador to France in the 90s. He always wore an orchid on his lapel. His sight was failing because of macular degeneration. Once, while in a car with him, I told him that his orchid had wilted. With a flourish, he plucked the wilted flower from his lapel and threw it to the side. He was larger than life. After returning to Singapore, he was criticised by *The Straits Times* for some things he said. He complained bitterly to me in a letter with his trademark green signature. I replied that no journalist could possibly subtract from his mountainous reputation but I would, nevertheless, refer his complaint to the editor when I next met him. He wrote to thank me in a most charming way.

**[Ph50]** Calling on Japan PM Tomiichi Murayama in Tokyo. As Minister for Information and the Arts, I commented that his clear apology on 15 August 1995 for Japan's aggression during the Second World War was "symbolically important".

**[Ph51]** When Senator Bill Bradley was preparing for the 2000 US presidential race, a group of us met him regularly at a retreat at Spanish Bay supported by Stanford University. Standing from the left, Dr Han Sung-joo, Sen Bill Bradley, P. Chidambaram, Gareth Evans. On my wife's right are George Shultz, Amnuay Viravan and J. Soedradjad Djiwandono. On my son's left is Shah Mehmood Qureshi. Picture taken in 1996.

**[Ph52]** Witnessing the FTA signed by President George W. Bush and PM Goh Chok Tong in the White House in 2003. PM Goh persuaded President Bill Clinton to launch bilateral negotiations at a midnight golf game in Brunei just before Clinton left office in January 2001. US Trade Representative Charlene Barshefsky and I teed up the ball despite opposition from White House staff. Under George W. Bush, my old friend Robert Zoellick became the new US Trade Representative. The agreement was concluded after an all-night session in Singapore between the two of us. Tempers frayed in the early hours of the morning but all points were resolved before daybreak.

**[Ph53]** With European Trade Commissioner Pascal Lamy in Luang Prabang at an ASEAN meeting discussing closer trade links with the EU in 2003.

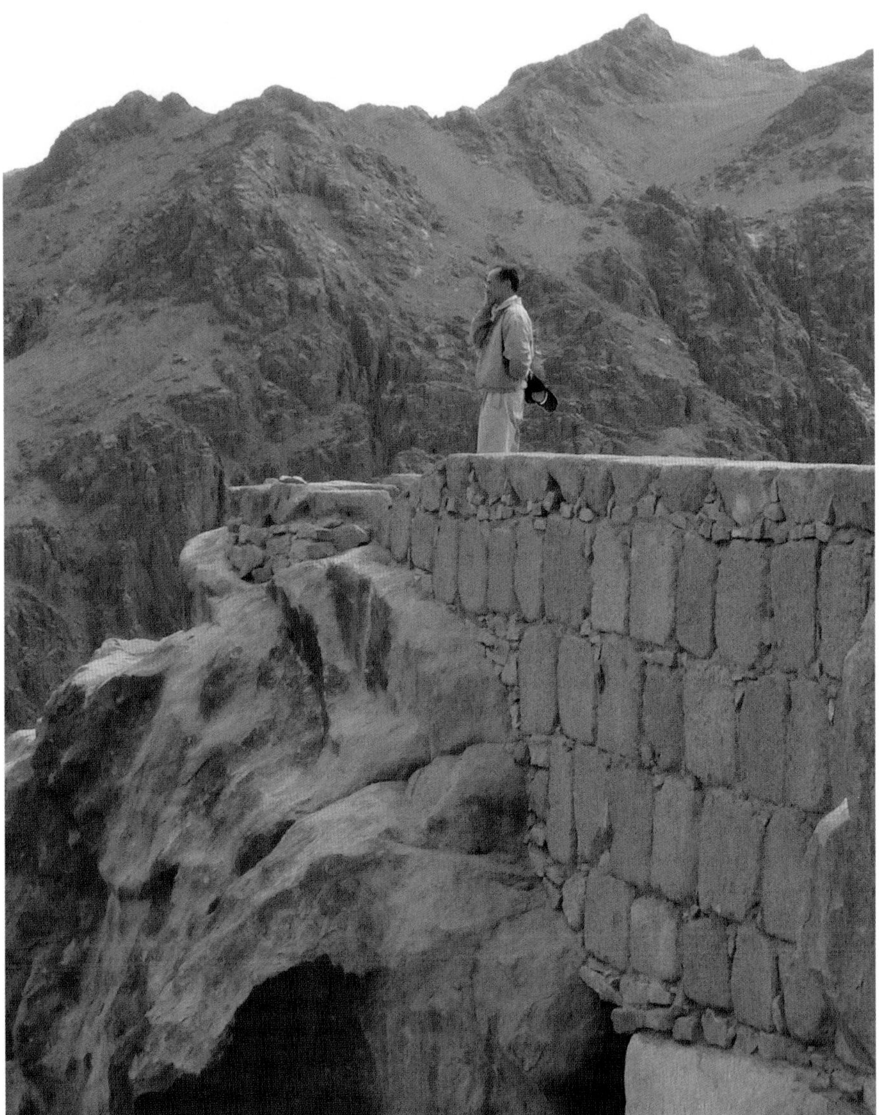

**[Ph54]** Picture of me on the summit of Mount Sinai calling Singapore from my mobile phone on 4 April 2008. I joked to friends that I was downloading the Ten Commandments. It was an auspicious moment. After that, I rushed down the mountain (rather dangerously), had a boxed lunch in the car and barely got back in time to Sharm el-Sheikh for my first meeting with Malaysian Foreign Minister Dr Rais Yatim. He had just taken over the responsibility under PM Abdullah Badawi. At that meeting in the hotel verandah when a warm desert wind blew, we agreed on the principles to settle the issue of Points of Agreement on the Malayan Railways land in Singapore. The final agreement between the two Prime Ministers was made in September 2010. Disagreement over the payability of development charges was settled by international arbitration in London in August 2014. Malaysia won the case. The resolution of the POA opened a new chapter in Malaysia-Singapore relations.

**[Ph55]** Greeting Malaysian Foreign Minister Dr Rais Yatim in 2008. We began negotiations to resolve the railway land problem which had bedeviled bilateral relations for years.

**[Ph56]** With Myanmar PM Thein Sein, UN Secretary-General Ban Ki-moon and ASEAN Secretary-General Dr Surin Pitsuwan in Yangon in May 2008 for the post-Cyclone Nargis ASEAN–UN International Pledging Conference.

**[Ph57]** ASEAN played a major role in laying a bridge between the Myanmar Government and the UN following Cyclone Nargis.

**[Ph58]** Chatting with Indonesian Foreign Minister Dr Hassan Wirayudha in 2008. We worked closely on many regional and international issues. During our time as Foreign Ministers, bilateral relations were in good repair. After leaving office, he kindly agreed to join me on the International Advisory Panel of Nalanda University. Srivijaya had deep links to the old Nalanda.

**[Ph59]** During the ASEAN Regional Forum Retreat in Singapore in 2008, the Foreign Ministers of the Korean Peninsula Six-Party Talks had their first meeting. Unfortunately, there has not been another since then.

**[Ph60]** ASEAN Foreign Ministers at a dinner meeting in the Singapore Botanic Gardens in 2008 to discuss the Preah Vihear dispute between Thailand and Cambodia when Singapore played host.

**[Ph61]** Dinner hosted by Lord Powell in London in 2009. He is an old friend of Singapore. When his father was RAF Air Vice Marshall in Singapore, he lived at Chalet No. 7, Fairy Point, in Changi.

**[Ph62]** Calling on China's Vice President Xi Jinping as Singapore's Foreign Minister in 2009.

**[Ph63]** Breaking a coconut at the front yard of the Nallur Kandaswamy Temple in Jaffna in October 2009. Anxiously watching me was Minister Douglas Devananda whom the LTTE tried to assassinate many times. He had told me that breaking a coconut cast out evil. As I had never done this before, I wondered what would happen if the coconut just bounced off without breaking. I gave it all I got.

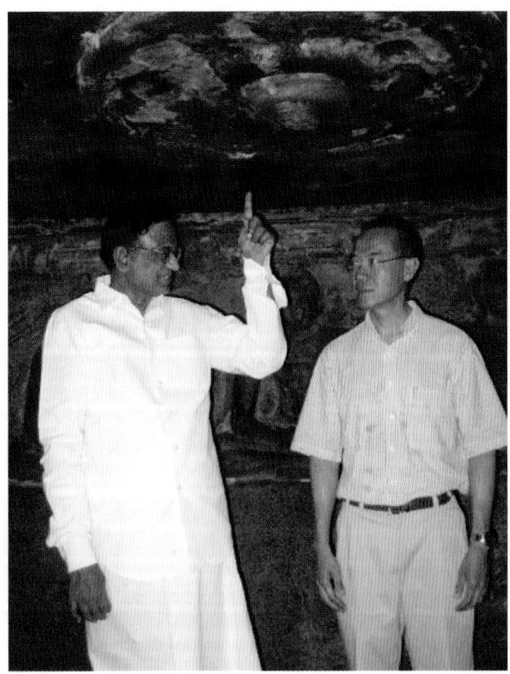

**[Ph64]** With Indian Home Minister P. Chidambaram at a Jain cave in Sittanavasal in Tamil Nadu in 2010. My wife and I were his guests in Chettinad where he was born. The chamber we were in could be reverberated loudly by deep breathing.

**[Ph65]** With Indonesian Foreign Minister Marty Natalegawa on his official visit to Singapore in August 2010.

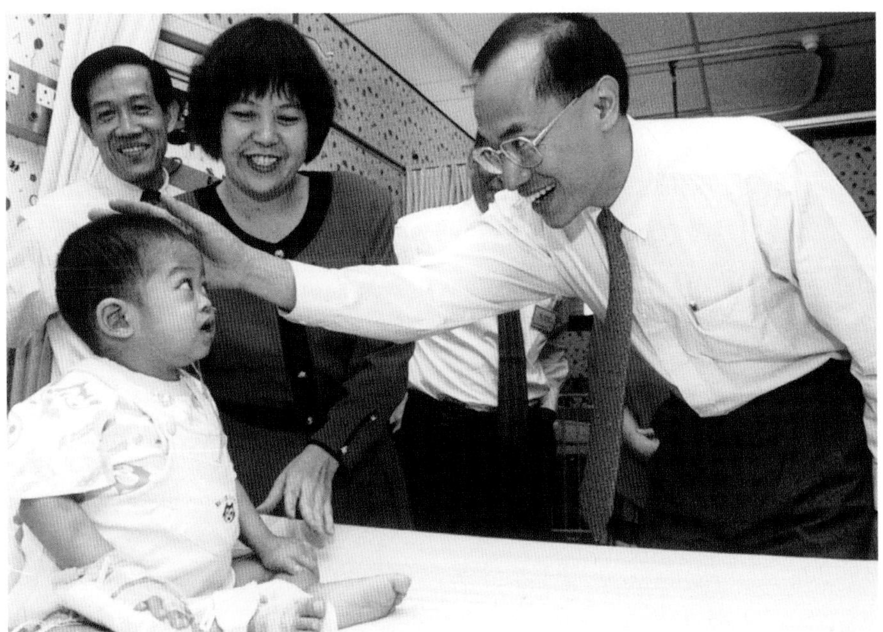

**[Ph66]** Greeting a young child in Meulaboh General Hospital, Aceh, rebuilt by Singapore in 2010 after the 2004 Boxing Day tsunami.

**[Ph67]** With Malaysian Foreign Minister Anifah Aman in his home state Sabah in November 2010. He was my counterpart after Dr Rais Yatim.

**[Ph68]** Greeting Jacques Attali whom I introduced at a seminar organised by the Asia-Europe Foundation in Singapore in early 2011. He is an intellectual soulmate. [Photo credit: Asia-Europe Foundation (ASEF).]

**[Ph69]** My last GE in 2011, with, from right, Zainul Abidin Rasheed, Cynthia Phua, Lim Hwee Hua and Ong Ye Kung.

**[Ph70]** After I lost the elections in May 2011, current and retired MFA colleagues gathered to bid me and Zainul Abidin Rasheed farewell. Before I spoke, I took a picture of them which lifted the mood.

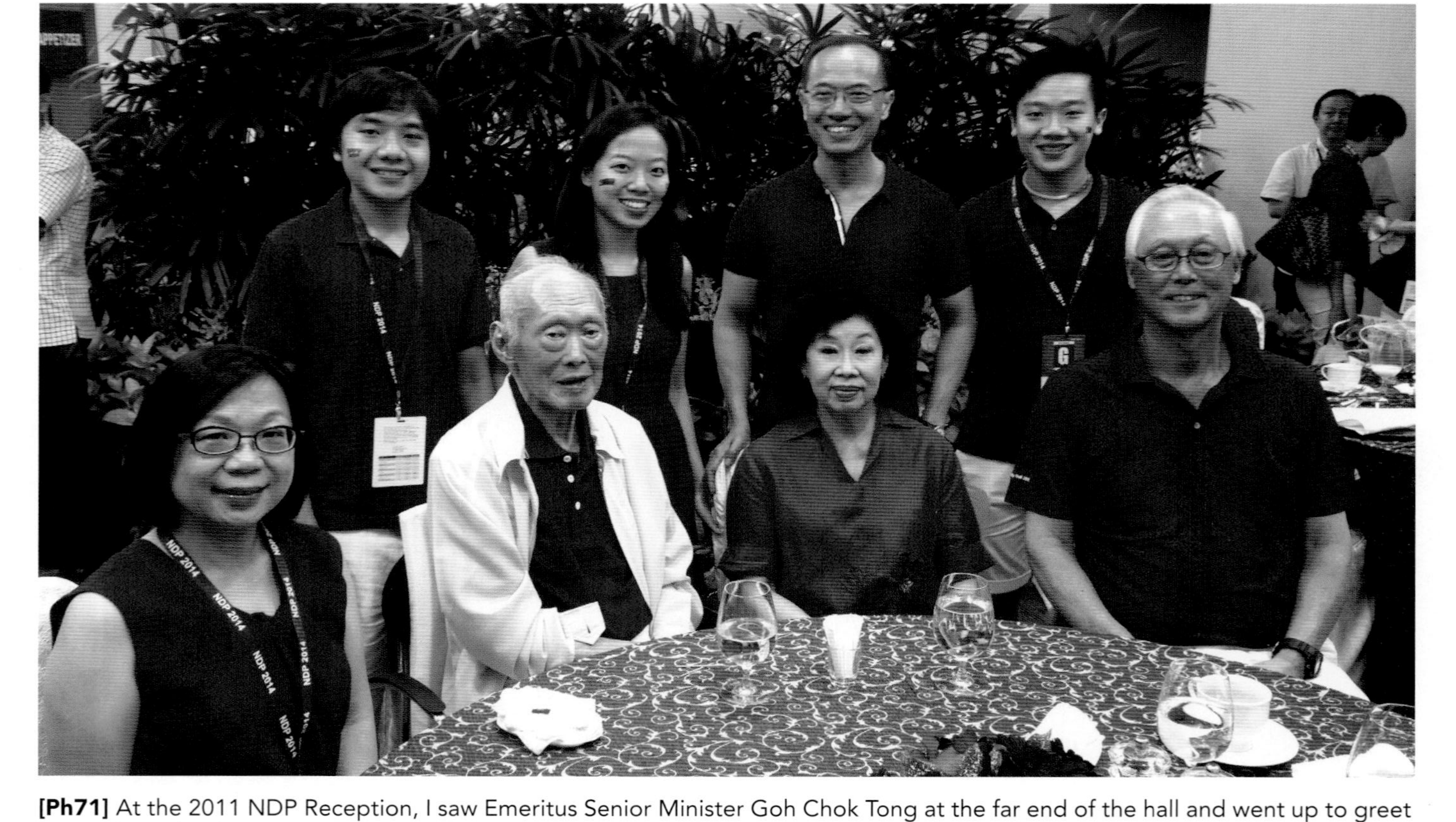


**[Ph71]** At the 2011 NDP Reception, I saw Emeritus Senior Minister Goh Chok Tong at the far end of the hall and went up to greet him with my family. To my pleasant surprise, retired Minister Mentor Lee Kuan Yew was also there seated at a table. My wife, three of our children and I were happy to be able to wish MM Lee a Happy National Day.

**[Ph72]** Dotting the eye of the new Ministry of Information and the Arts logo in 1991. The calligraphy was done by Senior Parliamentary Secretary Ho Kah Leong. I designed the logo as a modified yin-yang symbol, in green (symbolising harmony with nature) and red (symbolising life).

**[Ph73]** When I visit the Esplanade, I always remember DPM Ong Teng Cheong who chaired the Steering Committee until he became President in 1993 after which he continued as Adviser and attended many meetings. In April 1992, I accompanied him on a delegation studying theatre facilities in UK, France and Israel. First picture taken of us at the Barbican in London [photo courtesy of Juliana Lim]. Second picture shows virtual tour of the Esplanade in 1994. I invited Ambassador David Marshall along. Standing beside him is Robert Iau, Director of the Esplanade. The third picture is of the groundbreaking ceremony in 1996 by DPM Tony Tan. The fourth picture is of a visit to the site by President Ong Teng Cheong and Minister Wong Kan Seng in 1998. Unfortunately President Ong did not live to see the opening of the Esplanade in October 2002. The last picture is shot professionally in the Lyric Theatre in 2013 for a souvenir publication by Bryan van der Beek. [Photos courtesy of Esplanade — Theatres on the Bay]

**[Ph74]** Launch of Chinese Heritage Centre in 1995 at the old Nanyang University Administration Building with a grant from the Government. With Chairman of UOB Wee Cho Yaw and Singapore's greatest calligrapher Pan Shou.

**[Ph75]** Unveiling a replica of the old Nanyang University Arch in the Yunnan Garden of Nanyang Technological University in 1995, marking the 40th Anniversary of the founding of Nantah. When I was Minister responsible for heritage, the old arch and the old Nanyang University Administration Building were declared as national monuments. At about the same time, stakeholders agreed to change the shortened form of NTU into Nantah (南大) instead of Lida (理大). Together with many others, I hope that the full name of the old university will one day be restored. NTU has a glorious beginning in the old Nanyang University which was established as the first Chinese-language university outside China with the support of Chinese people in Southeast Asia from all walks of life.

**[Ph76]** Visit by Kuomintang Chairman Lien Chan to the Sun Yat Sen Nanyang Memorial Hall in 2005. From left, Kwek Leng Joo, GY, Lien Chan, Chiang Pin-Kung, Chua Thian Poh, Ker Sin Tze and Foong Choon Han. Establishing the original Memorial Hall in November 2001 was largely the work of Foong who worked on it with passion and love. The building itself was declared a national monument in 1994. [Photo credit: National Heritage Board, Singapore.]

**[Ph77]** Visit by Wang Daohan, President of the Mainland-based Association for Relations Across the Taiwan Straits, to the Sun Yat Sen Nanyang Memorial Hall in October 2008. In 1993, Wang and Taiwan's Straits Exchange Foundation Chairman Koo Chen-fu were in a historic summit in Singapore.

**[Ph78]** With Dr K. K. Phua, Founder of World Scientific (second from left) who arranged for me to meet China's sculptor Wu Weishan (third from left) and Nobel Laureates in Physics, Kenneth Wilson (fourth from left) and C. N. Yang (extreme right), in 2010. I blogged about the session saying that "if like the Italian city-states we are able to attract such brilliant minds to Singapore and make them feel at home here, our future will be very bright".

**[Ph79]** Greeting Kuo Pao Kun in his trademark batik shirt at a fundraising event for Practice Performing Arts Centre organised by The Substation in 1994. Pao Kun's contribution to the development of drama in Singapore is huge.

**[Ph80]** Launch of the SJI International Leadership Council chaired by Philip Yeo (middle) in 2006 to establish SJI International School.

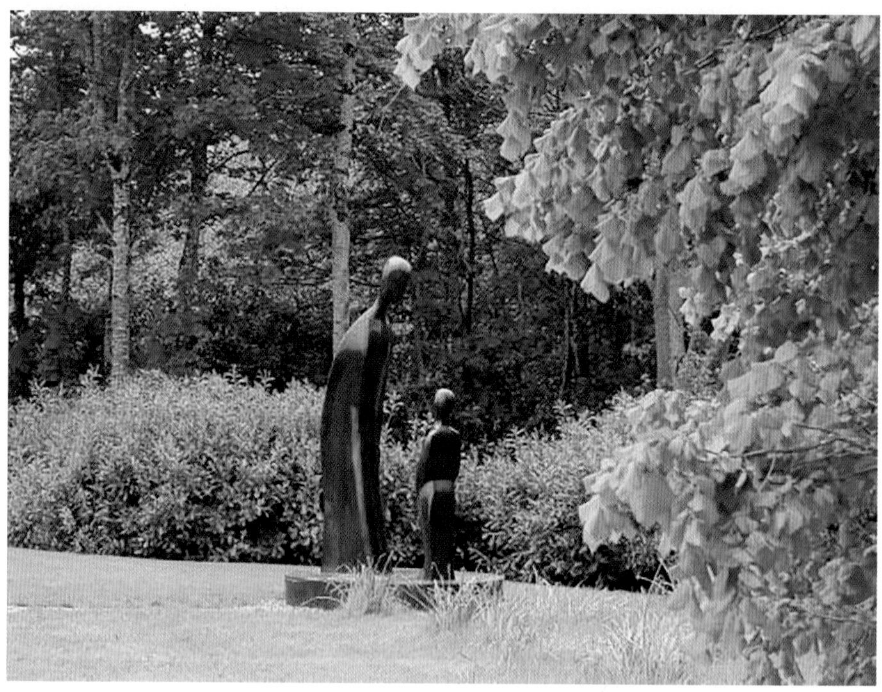

**[Ph81]** Sculpture donated by Singaporeans in 2004 in honour of Bro Joseph McNally at Castlebar, County Mayo, at the Irish National Museum of Country Life, near his birthplace in Ballintubber where St. Patrick preached. It is an enlarged version of "Counsellor II", a sculpture Bro McNally did in Irish yew bogwood.

**[Ph82]** Class reunion with our old principal, Brother Patrick and teachers.

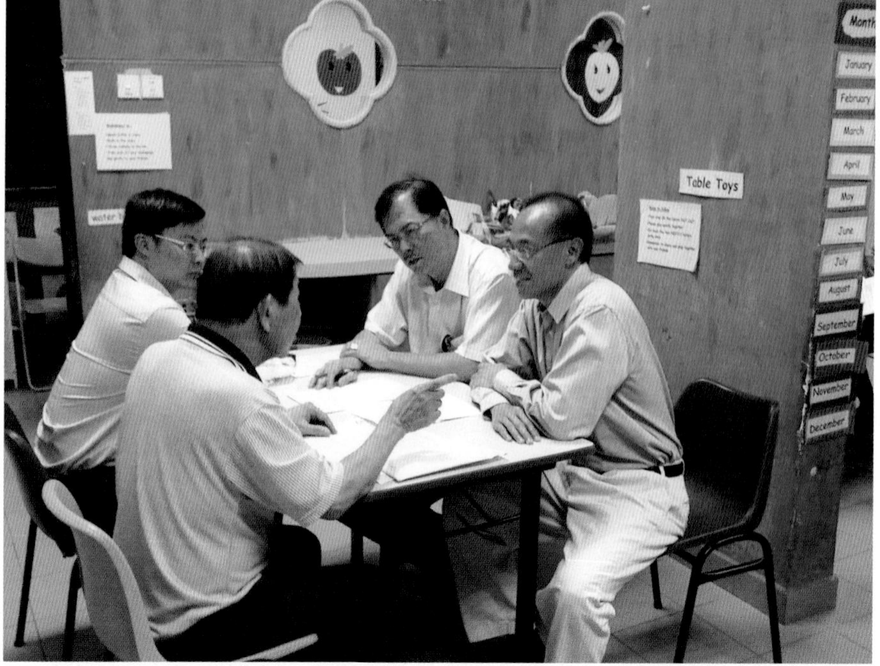


**[Ph83]** Talking to a constituent at a Meet-the-People Session in a PAP Foundation kindergarten classroom. On my right, branch secretary Terry Lim.

**[Ph84]** Unveiling of a segment of the Berlin Wall at Bedok Reservoir in 2009 at the 10th Anniversary of the fall of the Berlin Wall. A group of young friends led by Lien We King (standing fourth from left) organised activities to raise money for the enclosure and surrounding facilities. National Parks Board did a great job. The wall was a loan from an American couple Robert and MeiLi Hefner. After I lost the elections in 2011, they decided to take back the wall despite my appeals. We King introduced me to Facebook and started Mothership.SG.

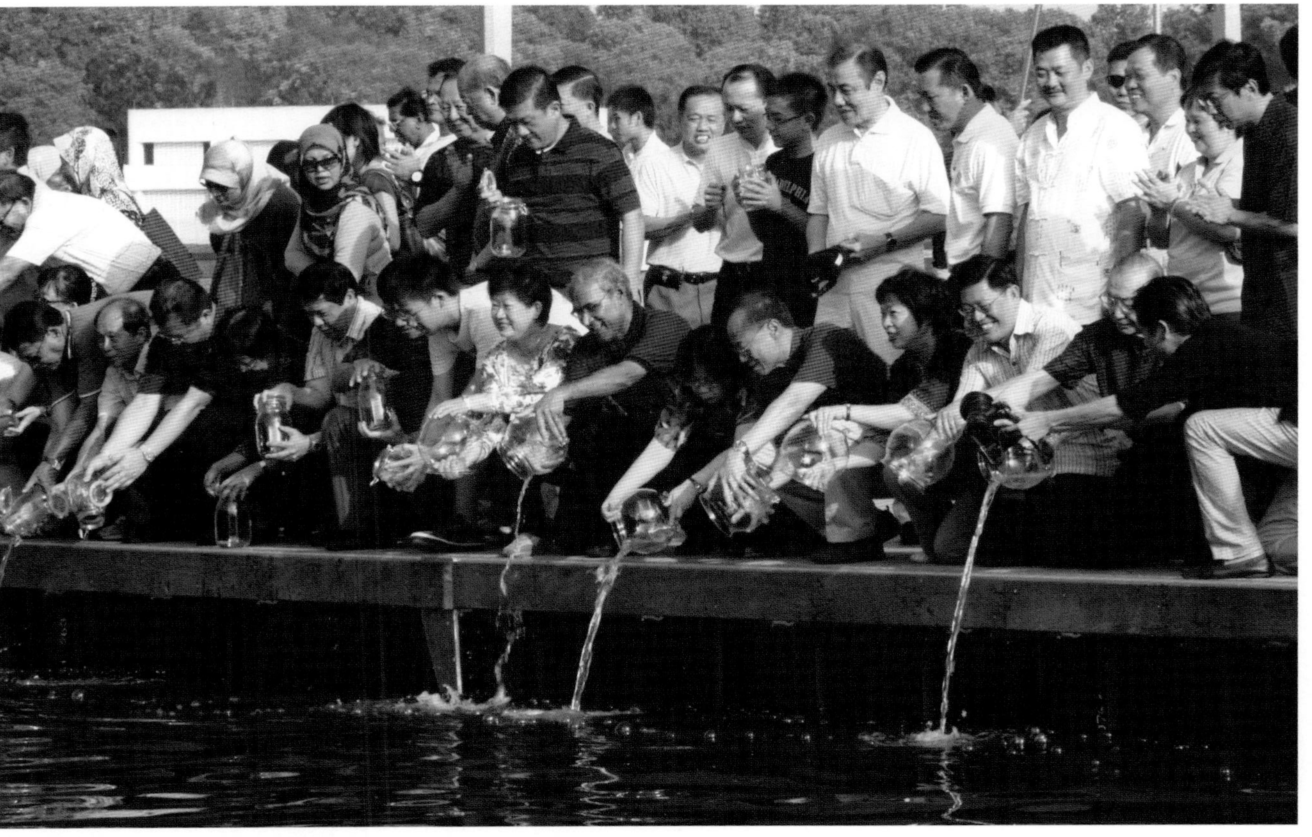

**[Ph85]** Releasing fish at Bedok Reservoir during the Chinese New Year.

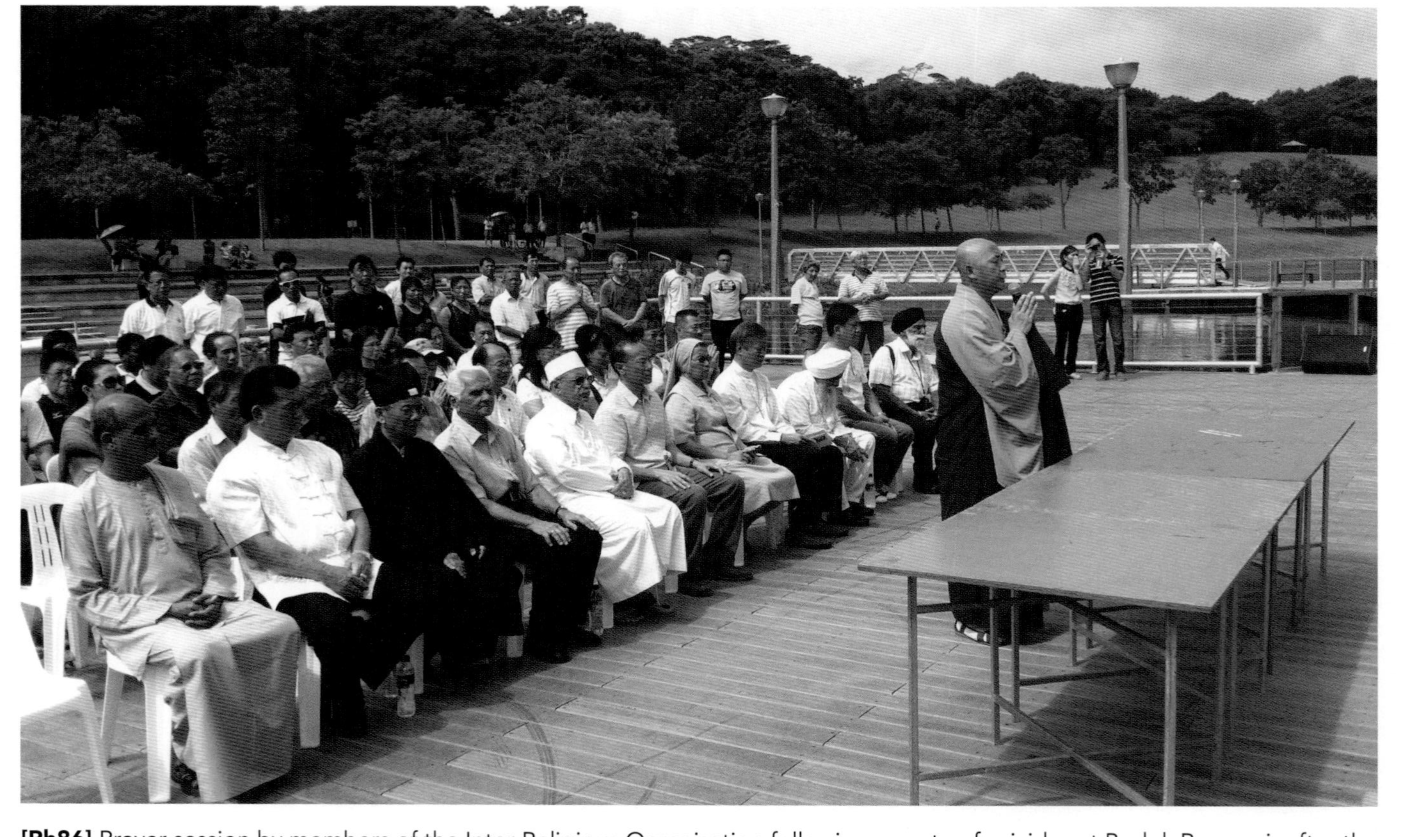

**[Ph86]** Prayer session by members of the Inter-Religious Organisation following a spate of suicides at Bedok Reservoir after the 2011 General Election.

**[Ph87]** A typical picture with grassroots leaders in Bedok Reservoir–Punggol Division of Aljunied GRC. Also present were fellow MPs and retired MPs Sidek Saniff and Chin Harn Tong (second row from front, second from left and second from right, respectively). On the same row, far left Koh Chin Mong and far right, Tan Bee Lan. Chin Mong and Bee Lan were my last two party branch secretaries. We continue to meet regularly.

**[Ph88]** National Day celebration at Bedok Reservoir–Punggol.

**[Ph89]** Makan time! Food is an important part of all grassroots events. With key grassroots leaders, from my left, Andrew Lim (an old faithful), Teo Juay Kiang (who was the PAP Branch Chairman of Kampong Kembangan and like an uncle to me when I entered politics), Ang Yong Guan, Henry Low (who organises my runs around Bedok Reservoir) and Anthony Loh (CCC Chairman of many years). Behind me, in blue shirt, is Gerard Ee, who has always been a great help to me.

**[Ph90]** Celebrating Chinese New Year in the constituency. From my right, retired branch chairman Teo Juay Kiang, old stalwart Jalil Kunimin and retired branch secretary Halim Kader. Jalil and Halim remain dear friends. Juay Kiang passed away some years ago.

**[Ph91]** With key grassroots leaders. From left, Group Constituency Manager Hussein Bapputty, my wife, retired school principal Johari bin Mohamed Rais, Senior Constituency Manager Richard Ang and old friend, Sim Hong Boon.

**[Ph92]** Preview of Resorts World Sentosa's Universal Studios with grassroots leaders. Wearing the tie is my successor as PAP Branch Chairman, Victor Lye.

**[Ph93]** With staff of the People's Association led by Group Constituency Manager Lim Jit Kai and grassroots leaders.

**[Ph94]** With Che Norma of the famous Zion Road Nasi Padang River Valley Restaurant in July 2011 which unfortunately has closed down. Consoling me after my defeat in the elections, she gave me and my friends a treat that day and brought out a special box of tissue paper for us to use.

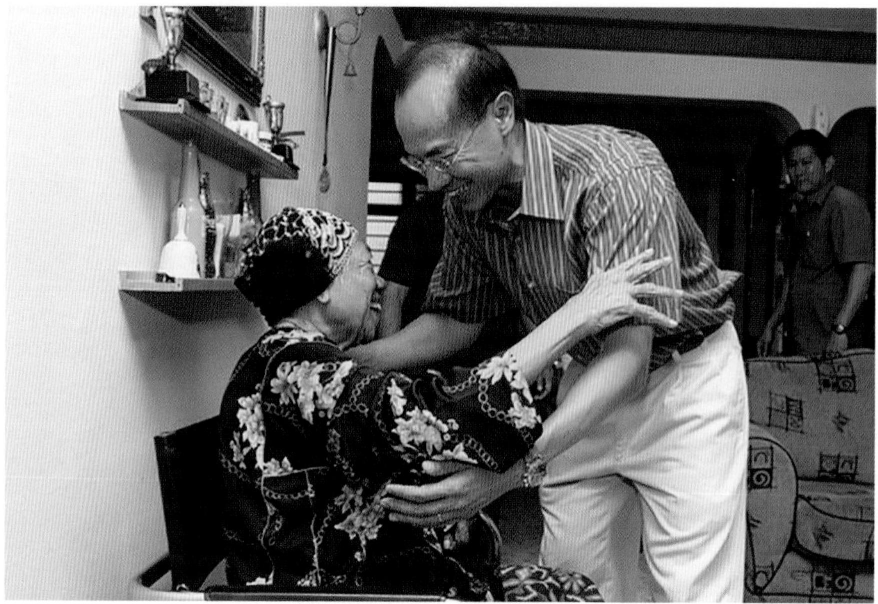

**[Ph95]** Greeting an elderly constituent. Visible signs of demographic aging in all neighbourhoods. Behind me, my security officer of many years, Anthony Tan.

**[Ph96]** Joining Muslim friends at the void deck in my old constituency after a Ramadan prayer session.

**[Ph97]** Hari Raya reception at Habib Hassan's house in 2013. Good relations among religious leaders in Singapore is a great blessing.

**[Ph98]** Nasi padang in Kampong Glam in 2013 with, from left, Johari Mohamed, Mohamed Maidin, Sidek Saniff and Halim Kader.

**[Ph99]** With retired Minister E.W. Barker who, after leaving the Cabinet, asked me to represent the interests of the Eurasian community in the Cabinet. It was a great honour which I accepted in 1992. My association with the Eurasian Association (EA) dates back to the 80s when I knew Col Timothy de Souza from the Air Force. He is also in the picture.

**[Ph100]** Welcoming President S.R. Nathan, a staunch supporter of the Eurasian Association. His house and the Eurasian House are opposite each other at Ceylon Road.

**[Ph101]** With dear friend Joe Conceicao and members of the EA Management Committee.

**[Ph102]** Opening iFly Singapore's indoor skydiving facility in Sentosa after the 2011 General Election. A friend remarked that I was flying away.

**[Ph103]** Dinner with Nobel Laureate Dr Sydney Brenner in 2011. He helped us develop the biomedical sector in Singapore and worked closely with Philip Yeo on the development of the Biopolis. In October 2003, he was made an Honorary Citizen of Singapore, the first time such an honour was bestowed.

**[Ph104]** With Taijigong Master Sim Pooh Ho who is a lineage disciple of Grandmaster Wu Tu Nan.

**[Ph105]** Balancing myself with some difficulty next to Master Sim in Kunming.

**[Ph106]** Simple but tasty lunch after Taijigong practice with Master Sim Pooh Ho on my right at his facility in Kunming. On his right is his son, Master Sim Pern Yiau, who teaches me Taijigong in Singapore.

**[Ph107]** Casual lunch in October 2011 at Mong Hing Teochew Restaurant with Dr Surakiart Sathirathai, former DPM and Foreign Minister of Thailand, and his family. Happily, it was also his father's birthday. Singapore was a strong supporter of Dr Surakiart when he was a candidate for the post of UN Secretary-General, a campaign which was unfortunately torpedoed by the Thai Army coup in September 2006.

**[Ph108]** Calling on Daw Aung San Suu Kyi for the first time in March 2012. I thanked her for seeing me even though I was no longer in Government, remarking that having spent so much of my life talking about her at ASEAN and other meetings, I was happy to be able to meet her finally. Behind her is a beautiful portrait of her father, General Aung San.

**[Ph109]** Chinese New Year dinner with my old bosses, Maj. Gen. Winston Choo and BG Gary Yeo, and Brunei's General Ibnu (left) in February 2011.

**[Ph110]** In June 2011, after leaving Government, I visited Taiwan with my wife and youngest son. In New Taipei, we had dinner with Mayor Eric Chu and his family. After the 2014 elections, Mayor Eric Chu took over the Chairmanship of the Kuomintang without contest.

**[Ph111]** Calling on the Founder of Tzu Chi Foundation Ven Cheng Yen in Hualien, Taiwan in 2011. A bone marrow donation from a Taiwanese man through the Foundation enabled my son to have a successful bone marrow transplant at St. Jude Children's Research Hospital in Memphis, Tennessee. As Foreign Minister, I could not visit Taiwan to thank her. On the night I lost the elections in May 2011, I decided that it would be one of the first things to do after leaving Government.

**[Ph112]** Visiting Chin Harn Tong's birthplace at Shagang in Wenchang, Hainan Island in November 2011 after attending the World Toilet Summit in Haikou.

**[Ph113]** Giving lectures in Peking University as a Visiting Scholar from September – December 2011.

**[Ph114]** When I was in Peking University as a Visiting Scholar, I was invited to give a lecture on China-US Relations from a Singapore Viewpoint at PLA National Defence University in December 2011. I did not realise beforehand that the University is in a protected campus and all students wear uniform. Initially, I felt out of place in my jeans and was pleasantly surprised when my host, Major General Zhu Chenghu, addressed me by my military rank in the SAF. I had a good, positive exchange with the students.

**[Ph115]** With Nicolas Berggruen, founder of the Berggruen Institute of Governance, at a ranch in Cody, Wyoming. Berggruen wrote one of the forewords for this book.

**[Ph116]** At a dinner hosted by Robert Kuok for Captain Ho Weng Toh in 2013. Captain Ho, aged 95, is the oldest surviving Singapore pilot who flew with the Flying Tigers in China. After the war, he became a commercial pilot eventually becoming Chief Pilot of Malaysia-Singapore Airlines when Robert Kuok was its Chairman. Over dinner, Robert Kuok, aged 91, addressed Captain Ho as "Uncle Ho". When he asked why, Robert Kuok replied that it made him feel young. It is a pity that Captain Ho's contribution as a bomber pilot during China's war against Japan is not more known to Singaporeans.

**[Ph117]** Dinner in Hong Kong hosted by Singapore TV producer Robert Chua (extreme right) in 2012. On extreme left, retired Chief Editor of *The Straits Times* Cheong Yip Seng, and old friend and colleague Consul-General Dr Ker Sin Tze.

**[Ph118]** Dinner hosted by my old mentor Toshio Egawa at Industry Club of Japan in Tokyo in 2014.

**[Ph119]** My association with the World Economic Forum goes back to Davos meeting in 1993 when I was nominated a Global Leader of Tomorrow (now renamed Young Global Leader). After I left Government in 2011, Prof Klaus Schwab invited me to become a member of the WEF Foundation Board.

**[Ph120]** Chairing Jusuf Kalla's session at the Singapore Summit in September 2014 before he became Indonesia's Vice President a second time. We were fellow Trade Ministers in 1999 and kept our friendship since then. After leaving Government in 2011, PM Lee Hsien Loong asked me to chair the Singapore Summit co-sponsored by the EDB, MAS, Temasek and GIC.

**[Ph121]** Invitation by former Taiwan Vice President Vincent Siew to dinner with his family in Singapore in November 2012.

**[Ph122]** My wife and son, Freddy, with Dr Ching-Hon Pui of St. Jude Children's Research Hospital and Dr Rupert Handgretinger of Children's University Hospital, Tübingen in June 2014. Ten years before, they helped save Freddy's life with a bone marrow transplant from a Taiwanese donor. In 2006, my wife set up VIVA Foundation for Children with Cancer in Singapore which organises annual conferences to improve cure rates in the region. Under Dr Pui's leadership and with the support of many friends, my wife is setting up a similar foundation for China where the national cure rate is still low, also called VIVA.

**[Ph123]** Having lunch with management trainees at Kerry Logistics staff canteen in Kwai Chung, Hong Kong.

**[Ph124]** With Kerry Logistics Global Executive Committee on day of listing at Hong Kong Stock Exchange.

**[Ph125]** Appearing on CNBC on the day of Kerry Logistics public listing on 19 December 2013. Error by CNBC: IPO price was set at HK$10.20 per share, not $10.80.

**[Ph126]** With fellow members of the Nalanda University Governing Board in Rajgir, Bihar in 2014. From left, Prof Wang Gungwu, Lord Meghnad Desai, Prof Amartya Sen and Prof Sugata Bose. Amartya Sen and Wang Gungwu wrote two of the forewords in this book.

**[Ph127]** Visit by Thai Princess Maha Chakri Sirindhorn to Nalanda in February 2014 as member of the University's International Advisory Panel.

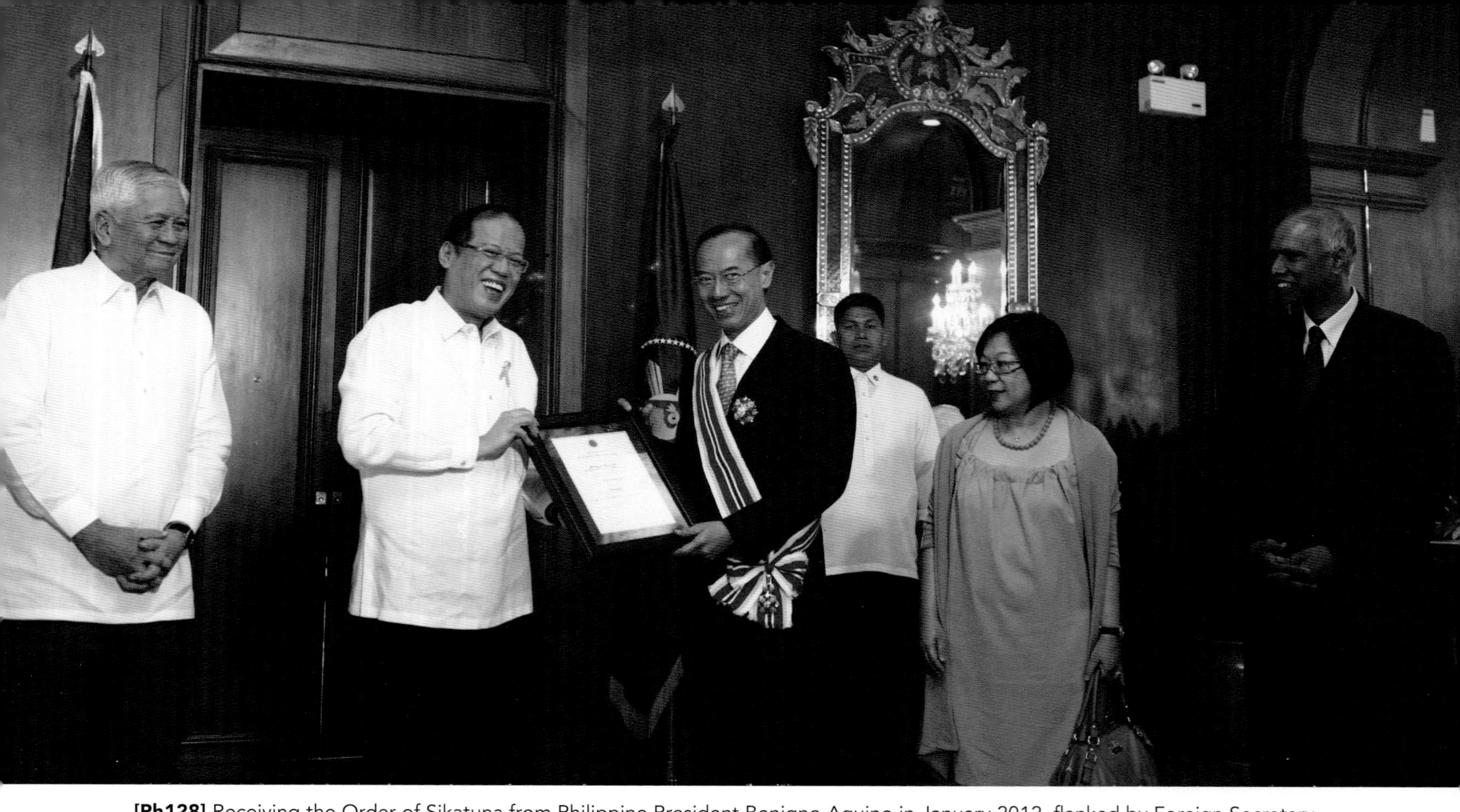

**[Ph128]** Receiving the Order of Sikatuna from Philippine President Benigno Aquino in January 2012, flanked by Foreign Secretary Albert del Rosario and Singapore Ambassador A. Selverajah.

**[Ph129]** Receiving Order of Australia (Honorary) from Foreign Minister Bob Carr in May 2013 at the Australian Parliament in Canberra. On my left, former PM Kevin Rudd and Hon Malcolm Turnbull.

**[Ph130]** Receiving the Padma Bhushan from the President of India in April 2012 at a grand ceremony in the Rashtrapati Bhavan.

**[Ph131]** With a Sikh guard at the Golden Temple in Amritsar, Punjab in January 2007.

**[Ph132]** Laying a wreath at the Yad Vashem Memorial to the victims of the Holocaust on my official visit to Israel in April 2007. Standing on the left is Ambassador Winston Choo who was Chief of General Staff/Defence Forces during my years in the SAF.

**[Ph133]** Calling on Russian Orthodox Church Patriarch Kirill during my official visit to Russia as Foreign Minister in 2009. He indicated his hope for a Russian Orthodox Church to be built in Singapore. I followed up on my return to Singapore and look forward to seeing golden domes rising on the Equator.

**[Ph134]** It is heartbreaking to see pictures of Aleppo today compared to what I saw during my visit there in July 2009. On an official visit to Syria as Foreign Minister, I went to Aleppo as a guest of the Grand Mufti Sheikh Ahmad Badreddin Hassoun, on my right. On his right was his son, the Mufti of Aleppo. On my left was the Bishop of the Armenian Catholic community. After lunch at the Grand Mufti's house with family members and religious leaders of different sects and denominations, I was brought to his mosque for Friday prayers, and invited to speak after him. In the afternoon, he accompanied me to the Armenian Catholic Cathedral for Mass. Since the civil war started in 2011, the country has been ripped apart and Aleppo became a major war zone.

**[Ph135]** Talking to Grand Sheikh Muhammad Sayyid Tantawy of Al-Azhar University in Cairo in April 2008.

**[Ph136]** On my official visit to Iran in November 2010, I called on Grand Ayatollah Sharoudi in Qom. His parting words to me still linger in my mind: May you find what you seek.

**[Ph137]** As Foreign Minister in 2010, I was privileged to be the first foreign official calling on the 11th Panchen Lama Bainqen Erdini Qoigyijabu at the Xihuang Temple in Beijing. He had recently come of age. With me, on my right, Ambassador Chin Siat-Yoon, Member of Parliament Yeo Guat Kwang and Ven Kwang Sheng, Abbot of Singapore Phor Kark See Monastery. Behind Amb Chin is President of Singapore Buddhist Lodge, Lee Bock Guan.

**[Ph138]** Greeting Pope Francis in 2014 as a member of COSEA, an eight-person commission looking into the administrative/financial reform of the Vatican. [Photo © Servizio Fotografico — L'Osservatore Romano]

# Ethnicity and Identity

*It is not possible to deny or to suppress ethnicity because it runs deep in the human psyche.*

Of the different ethnic groups in Singapore, the Eurasian community faces the greatest difficulty identifying itself. Some say it is a miscellaneous category for those who do not fit readily elsewhere. Because of this difficulty, many Eurasians prefer a Singapore where ethnicity is downplayed, better still extinguished altogether.

It is not possible to deny or to suppress ethnicity because it runs deep in the human psyche. Consciously, unconsciously and subconsciously, the cultural genes are passed on from one generation to the next, whether we like it or not. Because Chinese, Malay and Indian Singaporeans feel deeply about their ethnicity, Eurasian Singaporeans are under some pressure to also re-discover their past in order to establish more forcefully their own identity. This is where the problem of self-identification comes in.

We can take one of two approaches. We can be defensive and do it, as it were, under protest. Bertha Henson expressed this feeling in one of her articles in *The Straits Times* about being forced to crawl back into her Eurasian shell. Or we can do it in a more joyous way, not defensively but positively, like Rex Shelley's affectionate treatment of the shrimp people. I know some Eurasians consider the name "*gragok*" pejorative but that should not be the case. After all, it is part of the history of the Portuguese Eurasian community in Malacca.

Speech at the Eurasian Heritage Day, National Museum, 3 November 1991.

Indeed, there is much to be proud of. Prominent Eurasians figure large in the history of Singapore as political leaders, SAF officers, civil servants, academics, professionals, musicians and as priests, brothers and sisters. I grew up in Katong, studied in St. Stephen's and St. Patrick's, helped my father when he was the treasurer of the Pilgrim Virgin Movement and still go to church at Holy Family. In a curious way, I feel close to the Eurasian community and very at ease when I am with Eurasian friends. Even before I entered politics, I encouraged Boris Theseira who took a particular interest in the Eurasian community in Darwin to help organise the community in Singapore. When Timothy de Souza asked me three years ago whether the Eurasian Association should be more active, I said "yes" without hesitation.

There is no denying that at its core, the Eurasian community is Portuguese Catholic, and in this, shares much in common with Eurasians in Malacca, Ambon, East Timor, Macao, Goa, Perth, Darwin and elsewhere. As colonialists, the Portuguese and the Spanish were much more liberal in their attitude to mixed marriages compared to the Dutch and the British, partly because of the Catholic religion and partly because in an earlier period of colonial expansion, it was more difficult to bring the womenfolk along. Because of this cultural heritage, the Eurasian community in Singapore — of all the ethnic communities — is probably the most accepting of others.

There is therefore a willingness to define Eurasianness in a broad way to include the many who are neither Catholic nor of Portuguese origin. This largeness is admirable, idealistic and necessary. Any attempt to exclude or downplay the participation of non-Portuguese Eurasian groups will be counterproductive. Indeed, one major contribution the Eurasian community can make is to encourage all Singaporeans to be tolerant of one another and to remind us that all men are brothers.

This is the first time we are organising a Eurasian Heritage Day. It is an experiment, just as the Eurasian contribution of a folk dance to the 25th anniversary celebrations was an experiment. We should not try too hard to define too quickly what is Eurasian and what is not, but take an approach that is relaxed, generous, interesting and fun. In this way, we celebrate life in Singapore with all its colour and diversity.

I now declare the Eurasian Heritage Day exhibition open.

# EDUCATION, KNOWLEDGE AND VALUES

*We must learn how to be good human beings.*

Let me first thank your Principal, Mr Tee Gee Chai, for inviting me to be your guest-of-honour here today on the occasion of the school's 25th anniversary. Rangoon Secondary School has made steady progress over the last 25 years. It is not one of the top schools like RI or ACS but it is a good school providing a good education to many young Singaporeans.

What is a good education? There are two parts to a good education. The first is knowledge. Every person needs to have a basic knowledge of reading, writing and arithmetic. In addition, it is useful to know science, history, geography and other subjects. In today's fast-moving world, we need a lot of knowledge to get around.

There is no short-cut to acquiring knowledge. As they say, no pain no gain. To learn, we have to work hard and develop the habit of reading books and magazines, learning from those more knowledgeable than us and being curious about the world. Curiosity is very important. A child is always curious; so it is learning all the time. Many adults become bored. They spend a lot of time sitting before the TV set waiting to be entertained. When we are like that we stop learning. That is no good. Our attitude should be to keep on learning even when we grow old. Technology is changing the

---

Speech delivered at Rangoon Secondary School's 25th Anniversary Celebration, Singapore, 31 July 1992.

world so quickly, if we don't keep up, we will be left behind. The thirst for knowledge should therefore be life-long.

Acquiring knowledge is the first part of a good education. The second part of a good education is learning to be a good person. No man lives by himself. Man is a social animal. Every man is a member of the human race, a citizen of a country and a member of a family. From the time he is born, a child learns how to relate to others, first to his mother and father, then to brothers, sisters, grandparents and so on, in an ever-widening circle. Little by little, the child acquires values. He learns how to respect his elders and his teachers. He learns how to relate to his peers in school and in the workplace. He learns how to conduct himself in society.

It is important to have the right values. Without the right values, human society will break down and chaos will result. Thus, all the great religions and all the great philosophies teach us to be honest, to honour our ancestors, to respect each other as spiritual equals and to distinguish right from wrong. With the right values, we will need few laws. Without the right values, all the laws in the world will not be enough.

What it all boils down to is human relationship. We need each other. We are all different but we are all the same. This may sound very strange but it is true. We are all different. Even identical twins are different. Some are smarter than others. Some are stronger than others. Some are richer than others. God made each one of us unique. Everyone is special. What we want is for everyone to achieve the limit of his potential so that he will live a fulfilling life and make a contribution to society. But while we are different, we are also all the same in the sense that every human life is just as precious and just as sacred. It does not matter whom a murderer kills — an old man, a sick baby, a mad person, a cripple — it is still murder. It is this feeling that gives rise to the political idea of one-man-one-vote and the principle of equality before the law. Hence, we say that, within the Four Seas, all men are brothers.

In other words, we have to treat one another as individuals who are different yet equal. Put in another way, we must value human relationships. Friendships should not be made and broken like things. We must feel deeply for each other, for our parents, for our brothers and sisters, for our friends. If we do what is right and refrain from doing what is wrong, it should not be because someone is watching but because it makes us feel good inside. Every one of us must have his own dignity and self-esteem. Yes, we compete very hard in Singapore. We compete to do well in school, to get a place in the poly or JC, for jobs, for status, for money. Competition helps to bring out the best in us. But competition can also bring out the worst in us. There must be limits to competition. Our sense of competition must be tempered by a sense of co-operation and compassion. We must have human feelings. We are not machines. Everyone has a right to be here and to do his own thing. But everyone also has a duty to others. We have one life to live. We must live it well.

To have a good education, it is not enough to acquire knowledge. Knowledge is very important but knowledge is not enough. We must also learn how to be good human beings. We need the right values and we must treasure human relationships. Our parents can scold us. Our teachers can teach us. But in the end it is we ourselves who must learn and do what is right. This is the challenge of life.

By constant learning and doing what is right, we will achieve peace and progress in our society. As the ancient books teach us, cultivate the self, preserve the family, look after the country and all will be harmonious (修身，治国，齐家，平天下).

# Role of Tertiary Institutions in Culture and the Arts

*... cultural development is most rapid when new settlers flow in and when new lands are opened up.*

To prepare for today's occasion, I read the newspaper reports on the Arts vs Arts Seminar organised by Kuo Pao Kun two weekends ago. The discussions were lively and, on the whole, constructive. Some parts were negative but that is to be expected, given the nature of the arts community.

We have made considerable progress over the last few years. A number of foreigners who visit Singapore regularly have mentioned this to me. Expectations have also gone up, which is important, because to shoot far we must aim high. It also means more work for the National Arts Council (NAC) and more criticisms of its work but all that is welcome if we are able to lift cultural standards in Singapore. Of course, we should also be realistic. If we aim too high, the arrow, instead of going further, will fall short.

Let me take this opportunity to address some of the issues raised at the Arts vs Arts Seminar. Some of the participants were worried that the new Arts Centre at Marina Bay will squeeze out existing facilities like The Substation. That will never be. The Arts Centre is only the peak of a pyramid. To support the Arts Centre, we need a wide base of activities and facilities all over Singapore, which the NAC will continue to nurture. Indeed, there can be other pyramids as well. Institutions like People's Association, the National Trades Union

---

Speech at the National University of Singapore's Seminar on Culture and the Arts: The Role of Tertiary Institutions, 25 September 1993.

Congress (NTUC), the universities, polytechnics and junior colleges will also play important roles. This is why we are here today to discuss how the tertiary institutions can play their part.

Another concern raised at the Arts vs Arts Seminar is the inadequacy of our arts education system. We know the difficulties of private art schools in retaining qualified staff, upgrading training facilities and funding. We will continue to help them. The SIA-LaSalle College of the Arts recently moved to a lovely campus at Mountbatten. A few months ago, I opened the new premises of the Singapore Fine Arts Society. The Ministry of Information and the Arts (MITA) and the NAC are jointly helping the National Academy of Fine Arts (NAFA) to get land for a new campus. We are encouraging these schools to work towards affiliation with reputable tertiary institutions. Both NUS and NTU have increased their range of arts courses. More scholarships are now available. It takes time. As demand increases for arts education, supply will increase to meet demand. If we get more and more young people interested and convinced that art is an essential part of life, we will get there.

Censorship was also much discussed at the Arts vs Arts Seminar. It is absurd to ask for complete freedom. There is no such thing in human society. If some of us want full freedom to behave irresponsibly, life for the rest of us will be intolerable. For as long as we live in a community, we must be sensitive to the feelings of others. It is wrong, in the name of creativity, to argue that an artist should not exercise self-censorship. How can that be? Self-censorship is at the heart of all human relationships. Whether we are relating to our parents, or to our brothers and sisters, or to our children, or to our friends, we exercise self-control all the time. Even to our enemies. Robinson Crusoe may be free to do what he likes when he is by himself but, the moment Friday is with him, he exists in a social field and must act within it.

We can argue about how much censorship is necessary and the proper balance between self-censorship and legal or administrative censorship, but we should not take an extreme position that all censorship is bad. At the end of the day, what every community must settle for itself is what balance to strike between the freedom of the individual, including the freedom of the artist, and the interest of the group.

There is also no escaping the reality that he who pays the piper has some say over what tune gets called. No artist can completely disregard the preferences of his benefactor. If the benefactor is the taxpayer, we leave it to the NAC to decide what the preferences should be. At the same time, we must be conscious that a sponsor who overspecifies what he wants defeats himself. Without space, an artist cannot create. Thus, in the history of the arts, benefactors and artists seek each other out. Some relationships are brilliantly successful; others are not. The revocation of the Ministry of Health's sponsorship of the play it had earlier commissioned The Necessary Stage to do is a case in point. We may support one view or the other, but for there to be a successful relationship, both the sponsor and the artist must be happy.

The last point discussed at the Arts vs Arts Seminar which I want to touch on concerns the complaint by some artists that Singaporeans prefer foreign works to local works. There is some justification for this complaint. Partly, it is because Singapore is too small for us to establish our own unique artistic traditions. The instinct is therefore to look for external references. Partly, it is because we lack self-confidence. We suffer a double penalty in being a migrant community, once colonised. First, as Kuo Pao Kun put it, we are "cultural ophans", feeling cut off from the traditions of our forefathers. This gives rise to an occasional inferiority complex *vis-à-vis* the arts in China, India and the rest of Southeast Asia. Second, we also suffer from the residual mentality of a colonised people which sometimes causes us to be in awe of Western norms.

As Singaporeans, we feel in our soul this double anguish, the pain of separation from our ancestral lands and the pain of a love-hate relationship with the West. It is this double anguish which I would like to devote the rest of my speech to.

There is no satisfactory solution within our lifetime. It may be possible after many generations to create a Singaporean identity so distinct and secure that we can fully leave the past behind us. But I doubt, even then, that the double anguish will be completely resolved. Instead of seeking a resolution, we should recognise the tension, manage it, and make it a source of Singapore's creativity. There is no art without pain, no ecstasy without agony.

Before anything else, we must come to terms with our past. Our forefathers came from China, India and elsewhere in Southeast Asia. Now Singapore is our home. While we do not want to cut off our links to our ancestral lands, we are Singaporeans first and our national destiny is in Southeast Asia. From time to time, Singapore's interests will collide with those of China, India, Indonesia and Malaysia. On those occasions, our loyalty must be to Singapore. This is a position which is easier to accept intellectually than emotionally. When Chinese communism was a threat to Singapore in the past, some who were Chinese-educated felt torn emotionally. The tension never disappears. We can go to China or India, Indonesia or Malaysia, and feel a strong sense of kinship but we know we are neither PRC Chinese, Indian Indian, Indonesian nor Malaysian. The challenge is to find our own identity as Singaporeans and for our artists to express this identity in their works. I am not talking about a superficial expression or a plastic representation but something which comes from deep inside. It is not easy but no artist in Singapore can avoid this challenge. It is part of our karma.

The other tension is our love-hate relationship with the West. Because of the long years of Western ascendancy, there is no aspect of our lives untouched by Western influence. Hard though it may be for some of us to admit, the West has had a civilising effect on the East. Without Western science and Western ideas of the individual and society, Eastern societies would still be trapped in the feudal past. Modernisation would not have been possible without a large degree of Westernisation. But that does not make us a Western society. Neither should we allow ourselves to be patronised by the West as if it should be by their standards that we judge ourselves.

In Singapore, we are fortunate in not having to fight a revolution before gaining independence. We never went through an iconoclastic phase. We never felt it necessary to tear down statues and re-name roads and buildings. Empress Place is still there. Raffles is still a hero, and so on. Nevertheless, we do share with the rest of Asia's mixed feelings about the West. We need the West and we must continue to learn from the West but we reject its superior airs and insist on equality in our relationship. The East wind is blowing stronger now.

No Singaporean artist can be unaffected by this continuing dialogue between East and West. We should avoid extreme positions. We should not despise our own heritage and accept Western standards uncritically. But neither should we become chauvinistic about the East and become anti-West.

Out of all these cross-currents, a Singaporean identity will gradually emerge, which accepts our past without becoming a prisoner of it. For many years to come, our artists and our art critics will debate furiously over what is good and what is bad for Singapore and over what is right and what is wrong. We will experiment, we will take wrong turnings, but in the end we will find our own way into the future.

We are not alone in this voyage of discovering ourselves. Other Asian societies have also embarked on this journey. We will learn from each other's experiences and experiments. Collectively, a new Asian identity is emerging, which will draw Chinese, Japanese, Koreans, Southeast Asians and Indians closer together. In historical terms, this new Asian identity and sense of self is the aggregate response of ancient cultures to the centuries of Western domination. It is a response of such magnitude the West itself will be eventually transformed by it.

As we welcome more immigrants to our shores and as we externalise our economy and encourage Singaporeans to work in China, India, Southeast Asia and elsewhere, all kinds of ideas will bubble away in Singapore. In any society, cultural development is most rapid when new settlers flow in and when new lands are opened up. We are at such a phase now. Our arts scene will be in ferment for many years. There will be a Singaporean identity but it will be an identity which is only comprehensible in continental terms and within the context of a new Asia.

I wish you a successful seminar. I do not have to wish you an exciting future in the arts because I know it will be.

# CULTURE AND BUSINESS

*There must be profound reasons why human beings enjoy music and poetry ...*

Over four years ago, Mr Teo Soo Chuan, President of Ngee Ann Kongsi invited me to a dinner he was hosting for Mr Hiroshi Hidaka, President of Takashimaya. They were celebrating the groundbreaking of Ngee Ann City. I had an interesting conversation with Mr Hidaka. He explained to me Takashimaya's corporate philosophy of combining culture with business. I asked him why Takashimaya decided to open a department store in Singapore. His answer stuck in my mind. Mr Hidaka said that Takashimaya did not want to be outflanked by the other Japanese department stores which had already moved here. To maintain its premier position in Japan, Takashimaya had also to expand overseas in order to monitor and keep pace with the competition.

Four years later, I am happy to accept Mr Hidaka's invitation to open Takashimaya's new shopping centre, because of my association with Ngee Ann Kongsi and Takashimaya's support of culture and human resource development. Takashimaya has initiated the Human Resource Development Programme in Singapore, which will eventually be extended to other countries in Southeast Asia. This is a scholarship scheme to train students in Japan in retail management and creative arts. In Singapore, the Economic Development Board is honoured to be Takashimaya's partner through the Takashimaya-EDB Scholarship Fund set up last year.

---

Speech delivered at the grand opening of Takashimaya Shopping Centre, Ngee Ann City, Singapore, 8 October 1993.

The way Takashimaya combines culture with business holds important lessons for us. At one level, it shows that culture and business are not incompatible. But, at a deeper level, it shows that culture and business can strengthen each other in a mutually reinforcing manner.

In fact, culture and business are not separate entities at all. Each influences the other. Some societies are unable to progress because their cultures hold back economic development. In Indonesia, for example, there are primitive cultures which put so much emphasis on conspicuous consumption at weddings and funerals, no economic surplus can be generated and no investment in the future is possible. Such societies stagnate. In the latter days of the Roman Empire, the upper classes indulged so much in food and pleasure, they neglected their responsibilities and became flabby and feeble. This decadence was also the problem of the Chinese Manchu court in the late 19th century.

In contrast, Calvinist values and the Protestant work ethic made possible the rise of capitalism in the West. Many economists now attribute the economic dynamism of East Asia to Confucianist values of education, hard work, thrift and social order.

The arts and culture are therefore not neutral. They can help society to advance or they can impede economic development. Of course, we must never take Mao Zedong's position at Yan'an that all works of art must serve society. That will kill creativity. Thus, Communist propaganda, despite the constant emphasis on socialist reality is, in actual fact, divorced from reality. Far from inspiring, it makes people cynical. While, on the one hand, we are concerned about the effects of the arts and culture on society, we must not, on the other hand, dampen the free spirit without which there can be no real art.

Take Takashimaya as an example. Art is part of the corporate ethos. There is a consistency in the way art is promoted in every aspect of the business. Space is set aside for art exhibitions. Cultural programmes are a regular feature. These things don't come cheap. They cost money. Yet they make good business sense. Too little is not good. Too much is also not good. And the way culture and business are combined is also important. If culture is reduced to propaganda or advertisement, it is counterproductive. Culture must be subtle and indirect.

The same applies to Singapore. Without investment in the arts, we will not achieve our ambition of becoming a developed country in the first world. I do not mean this in a superficial way as if we have to embellish wealth before that wealth becomes legitimate. That would be like a member of the new rich buying an expensive painting to impress neighbours and friends. I am not referring to such behaviour at all.

Our real concern is not with objects but with the mentality of our people. In the new world we are entering, it is important to be good at science and mathematics but it is not enough to be only good in science and mathematics. We must also have artistic sense. With science and mathematics, we can produce accurately and efficiently. But to create high value, we must also produce artistically. Consider Teenage Mutant Ninja Turtle toys. Yes, they must be well-made to meet first world standards of quality and safety. But for such work, workers in China can do under proper supervision. The value of Teenage Mutant Ninja Turtles is not in the physical production but in the concept, in the design and in the marketing. That is not within China's competence for some time yet because the general level of education and culture is still low.

Taichi Sakaiya, in his book, *The Knowledge-Value Revolution, Or, a History of the Future* explains that in the world of the future the subjective aspects of production and consumption become very important. Teenage Mutant Ninja Turtle is a bestseller while Teenage Mutant Ninja Dinosaur may not be, even in Jurassic Park. The reasons are complex. Fashion is as much an art as it is a science. The mind of the consumer is as fickle as the summer breeze. The fact is that goods and services in the world are increasingly bought on the basis of subjective considerations.

For Singaporeans to add value in such a world, and for us to be able to earn much higher salaries than workers in China and India, we must be able to compete on this new basis. Developing the artistic sense of our people becomes critical to our continuing economic development. In this new game, the ability to design well and to respond quickly to changes in the mood of the market is vital. It is no longer enough to produce widgets. We have to be in the business of creating lifestyles and total experiences. Thus, the $2 chicken rice in the coffee shop is not the same product as the $12 chicken rice in a coffee house. Aesthetics has become an inseparable part of production and consumption.

There is an organic relationship between the intellectual and artistic development of man. How this came to be in the course of our biological evolution is still not clear to scientists. It has something to do with our spiritual nature. There must be profound reasons why human beings enjoy music and poetry while the lower animals do not, at least not in the same way. Until we fully understand the hidden appeal of music and poetry to the human mind, we will not be able to make computers which even come close to the human brain. Artificial intelligence has still a long way to go before it can match human intelligence. It may never do so. It may never be possible to reduce our artistic sense to mathematical equations.

Our intellectual development and our artistic development are like the *yin* and *yang* in Chinese thinking. Balance is very important. The scholar-mandarin is a Confucianist in public life but a Taoist in his private life. In the Japanese mind, the philosophy of *zen* cannot be separated from the drive to excel. The more *yang* we want, the more *yin* we must have. Thus, to reach higher levels of economic development, we need higher levels of cultural development.

This is why I mentioned earlier that without investment in the arts we will not be able to become a first world society. Takashimaya's philosophy of combining culture with business should also be Singapore's philosophy.

# English, Indigenous Yet International

*... make English a language of communication among equals rather than a language of domination. Regional and local languages should never be displaced.*

Because of the shared British heritage and the common use of the English language, there is a relaxed quality about Commonwealth gatherings which make them a particular joy to attend. It is a great relief not to have to communicate through interpreters.

The use of English of course goes beyond the Commonwealth and America. For example, English is the language used for international air traffic control. When ministers and officials in ASEAN meet, English is invariably used. And because of the influence of American pop culture, songs in the English language are enjoyed worldwide. Thus, Michael Jackson needs no translation.

From a historical perspective, the popularisation of the English language is the result of, first, the British Empire and, after it, American dominance in economics, politics and culture. How long the English language will be able to maintain its preeminent position in the world, no one knows. Language follows in the wake of an empire and lingers on long after imperial decline. Latin, for example, remained the *lingua franca* of Europe and the Catholic Church for over a thousand years after the fall of Rome.

One thing, however, is certain and that is that, since the tower of Babel, the language map of the world changes ceaselessly. An empire may be needed to first spread the use of a language but, once widespread, the language acquires a life of its own. For instance,

---

Speech at the Commonwealth Writers' Prize Awards Dinner, 4 November 1993.

the Mughals from Central Asia made Farsi their language in India even though Persia was not part of their domain. Farsi was then the language of high civilisation. It is also interesting to recall that the European powers who were allied against Napolean communicated with each other in the French language. Nearer home, in Indonesia, the Malay language, which is the language of a minority, has become the language of Java and as Bahasa Indonesia, is slowly penetrating northern Australia.

Coming back to the English language, it has now got a life of its own beyond Pax Britannica and Pax Americana. The keenness with which Chinese and Vietnamese now learn English as a second language is amazing. Private kindergartens teaching English to Chinese pre-schoolers have sprouted up in China. They are charging exorbitant fees. English is now recognised worldwide as the international language. Those of us who speak English have a vested interest in preserving the present position of the English language.

Two conditions must be met if the position of the English language in the world is to be preserved despite the relative decline of the Anglo-Saxon world. First, its cultural content must be universalised or, to put it in another way, the English language must be indigenised in many parts of the world. If the English language restricts and confines our mental images and emotional references to those of Anglo-Saxon societies, its use elsewhere may be resented and resisted. English may then be seen as a tool of colonial, neo-colonial or post-colonial domination by Anglo-Saxon powers. If this is the case, the fortunes of the English language will flow and ebb with the fortunes of the Anglo-Saxon powers. The Commonwealth can play a big role in universalising the cultural content of the English language and indigenising its use. By encouraging non-Anglo-Saxon writers to write in English about their own societies, the Commonwealth Writers' Prize helps make English a language of communication among equals rather than a language of domination. In this way, the English language will open windows into many cultures, not only Anglo-Saxon culture.

Indeed, the indigenisation of the English language in many non-Anglo-Saxon countries is well underway. There is a growing corpus of literature written in the English language in Commonwealth countries like India, Nigeria, Trinidad and Singapore. Many non-Anglo-Saxon writers, writing in English about their own cultures, have achieved international fame. One thinks of Nobel Prize winners like Wole Soyinka from Africa and Derek Walcott from the Caribbeans. Through high-quality translations, English also serves as a bridge across cultures. For example, we are gradually building up our shared anthology of ASEAN literature by the translation of Thai, Malay, Chinese and Tamil works into English which all can share equally. In ASEAN, English is a language which is unifying and not oppressive.

The English language in the world should be like the Malay language in Indonesia. No Javanese feels threatened by the widespread use of Malay in the archipelago. Conversely, the English language should not be like Hindi in South India or Singhala in Jaffna.

The second condition necessary for the preservation of English as an international language is multi-lingualism. While the English language should cut across cultures, it should not be exclusively used. Regional and local languages should never be displaced. Such indeed was the language policy of the British Raj. Never was there an attempt to extinguish the use of other languages anywhere in the Empire. The same wisdom guided the Romans in an earlier period. Despite having Latin as *lingua franca*, Greek, Aramaic and other languages continued to flourish. By suppressing local languages like Korean, Japanese imperialism early this century engendered a reaction which has effects that are still being felt today. The present problems of Sri Lanka stem directly from the suppression of Tamil in the past. At that time, a prescient Sri Lankan Marxist warned that the choice was between one-nation-two-languages and one-language-two-nations. President Mitterrand expressed much the same sentiment recently at the Fifth Francophone Summit in Mauritius when he said, *apropos* President Clinton's rejection of a cultural exemption clause in the General Agreement on Tariffs and Trade (GATT), that "one cannot, however powerful one is, however much one wants to think and to express oneself, impose a treaty on the rest of the world, and by the power of money, make everyone think with the same words and fix their fate with the same images" (*The Straits Times*, 18 October 1993).

It is always wiser to encourage multilingualism. Even in Anglo-Saxon societies, the lack of familiarity with foreign languages has become a serious handicap. Many of us would have heard the wisecrack that while a person who speaks two languages is called bilingual, and a person who speaks three languages is called trilingual, the person who speaks only one language is called American. It is not a joke. A lot of human knowledge is culture-bound and not easily codified in foreign languages. Societies which operate in many languages gain access to different civilisations. It may seem more convenient to use only one language but in reality those who are familiar with many languages enjoy a great advantage. Commonwealth gatherings are wonderful to attend but they are never at the expense of non-Commonwealth gatherings.

All of us here have a vested interest in keeping English an international language. This can only be done if we succeed in universalising the cultural content of the English language and indigenising its use, and provided we never allow the use of English to become exclusive and at the expense of other languages.

This is the first time the Commonwealth Writers' Prize Awards Ceremony is held in a non-Anglo-Saxon country. We in Singapore feel very honoured to play host to such an important gathering. I take this opportunity to congratulate all prizewinners, those already announced and those yet to be.

# THE SPIRIT OF RAFFLES

*This new world will be made by men like Raffles, men of vision with wide-ranging interests who soldier on in the face of all kinds of difficulties.*

It is a tribute to the greatness of Raffles that, 175 years after his founding of Singapore, we should still find fresh inspiration in his life and works.

The spirit of Raffles is particularly relevant to us today as we struggle to grow a second wing. It was of course the second wing of Great Britain that brought Raffles to Singapore in the first place.

In a curious way, the new world we are entering is similar in many respects to the world which threw up remarkable men like Raffles. At that time, capitalism had developed to a point which made the logic of free trade obvious and irresistible. In politics and business, the frame of reference at that time was not the boundaries of the nation-state but the whole empire and the world. Then, as now, the potential big markets were China and India.

Raffles was a product of that age. He was a visionary who sensed the currents of history and acted in the long-term interest of Great Britain and the British East India Company. Even as the war against Napolean was being fought on the European continent, he saw beyond and sought to displace the Dutch in the East Indies, till then the main impediment to the expansion of British interest in Southeast Asia. Raffles argued forcefully against the return of Java and Malacca

---

Speech at the opening of the exhibition "Raffles Reviewed: Sir Stamford Raffles 175 Years Later", 29 January 1994.

to Holland. Happily for us, Raffles did not have his way as a result of which he founded Singapore instead as a poor alternative.

Raffles was a man of broad interests, a true renaissance man. He was a scholar of the Malay language and many things else besides. He was a naturalist who collected all kinds of botanical and zoological specimens. He started our first Botanic Gardens in Singapore. He had a deep interest in history. While in Java, he studied and documented Javanese art and culture. He was the first to draw the Western world's attention to the Borobudur. Raffles was also an educationist. Raffles Institution which he established continues to be the premier school in Singapore today.

As an individual, Raffles was indefatigable and indomitable. His superiors in the East India Company were often unsupportive and unappreciative of what he did, but he toiled on nonetheless, convinced of his own estimation of the future and of the correctness of his actions. There was never any doubt in his mind that Great Britain needed a base to counter the Dutch in the Riaus and to service the ships which sailed to and from China. And so he persisted, despite the tragic successive deaths of four of his five children. In the way he exploited internecine conflict in the Riaus to establish a factory in Singapore, he showed great entrepreneurial flair (or colonial cunning, from an anti-colonial viewpoint).

We have much to learn from the spirit of Raffles. The post-war era of political nationalism and economic protectionism in Asia is giving way to a new world of porous borders, regionalism and international trade. This new world will be made by men who are like Raffles, men of vision with wide-ranging interests who soldier on in the face of all kinds of difficulties. The one big difference is that while Raffles was an imperialist in an age of rival imperialisms, we live in an age of international competition and cooperation.

It is only natural and fitting that we in Singapore should inherit the spirit of Raffles. Raffles intended Singapore to be larger than its physical size and so it has always been and so it should always be. Singapore should always welcome talent from afar to our island and be a favourite port of call for those travelling between China and India and between the East and West. What Singapore in Southeast

Asia was to the British Empire, Singapore in the new Asia should be to the international trading community. Like the old East India Company, our multinational companies (MNCs) should operate well beyond native shores, loosely associated with the political power and aided by it.

Raffles would have thought the idea of Singapore as an independent nation an absurdity, at least not in the conventional sense of what being a nation meant. It was the same thought which drove our first generation of leaders to seek merger with Malaysia in 1963. It is the same thought which now drives us to grow the second wing. Thus, the compulsion which drove Raffles to found Singapore continues to drive us today. In that sense, *Raffles Reviewed* is the future previewed.

# Chinese Heritage and Cultural Connections

*... long-term peace and stability in the Asia Pacific will partly depend on this clear distinction being made, not just by ethnic Chinese outside China but also by China herself.*

We are here today to open the Chinese Heritage Centre. It is a happy occasion. Our Chinese culture is a precious inheritance that we have received from our forefathers. It is right that we should preserve its positive features and build on them.

There are over 25 million ethnic Chinese living outside China, not counting Hong Kong and Taiwan. Their contribution to the global economy and to international R&D and scholarship is growing year by year. The history of the Chinese people who have left China, some many centuries ago, has been recorded in bits and pieces in different parts of the world. This Heritage Centre will attempt to pool them together so that a more complete story can be told and the right lessons from the past learnt. I hope that Chinese people all over the world will contribute to the work of the Heritage Centre and give it their support.

In conceptualising this Heritage Centre, it is important that we separate the political idea of modern China from the cultural idea of being Chinese. The clearer we make this distinction, the easier and more successful will be our work in the Heritage Centre. This Heritage Centre could not have been established in Mainland China. The reason is obvious. In Mainland China, it has been a persistent tendency by the different dynasties to see all Chinese outside China as being subject to the authority of the Emperor. This is no longer

Speech at the opening of the Chinese Heritage Centre, 17 May 1995.

the policy of the PRC Government. However, I remember 20 years ago as a student in the UK, going to the Chinese Embassy in London to borrow a film about China for the Cambridge University Malaysia-Singapore Association. Seeing that I was an ethnic Chinese, the lady at the counter politely asked me to go over to the Overseas Chinese Section. I was then a young army officer with a certain view of Communist China. Her words left a deep impression on me.

Today, among Chinese people in different parts of the world, there is a revival of interest in our common values and traditions. This is a worldwide phenomenon affecting not just ethnic Chinese, but other ethnic groups as well. But in celebrating our cultural connections, there must not be any attempt to link us back politically to China. Our political loyalty must be to the countries we belong to, whether Singapore, Malaysia, Indonesia, Australia or the US. Professor Wang Gungwu, as the adviser to the Heritage Centre, is an Australian citizen, born in Indonesia, grew up in Malaysia and has worked in Singapore, Australia, Hong Kong and other places. He has a deep understanding of Chinese culture but he is not a Chinese national. In the same way, Lynn Pan, the Centre Director, whose book, *Sons of the Yelllow Emperor*, has rekindled among Chinese all over the world a renewed interest in their own culture and family histories, is a British citizen.

Of course, this does not mean that the Heritage Centre should cut itself off from all contact with Mainland China. This would be absurd. Indeed, the picture cannot be complete without tracing our links back to the various regions of China from which our ancestors had emigrated. But we must always take care to separate our cultural and familial links from our own countries' political relations with China.

Indeed, this separation will become more important in the next century as China becomes a major economic and political power in the world. Ethnic Chinese who invest in China or trade with her or engage in academic exchanges are not her agents. I will go so far as to say that long-term peace and stability in the Asia Pacific will partly depend on this clear distinction being made, not just by ethnic Chinese outside China but also by China herself. Otherwise, a new polarisation can take place in the world along ethnic lines with all the associated racism. The Chinese Heritage Centre must be mindful of this.

It is symbolically appropriate that the Chinese Heritage Centre should be established here in the old Nantah Administration Block. In a sense, the history of Nantah reflects the history of the Chinese people outside China this century. The Nantah spirit is an admirable one because it expressed the determination of a people not to lose its sense of self. Nantah was the result of Chinese in Southeast Asia and elsewhere wanting to preserve their language and culture despite unsympathetic colonial governments. The historical development of Nantah had both a positive and a negative aspect to it. The positive aspect was an indomitable Nantah spirit that would not cower, that persevered despite all kinds of difficulties. Hence, contributions by people from all walks of life, including trishaw riders, to the construction of the University. This Nantah spirit is a deep source of inner strength and deep inspiration to all Singaporeans. It is this spirit which will enable us to survive in adversity and enable us to bounce back even if we are temporarily defeated.

But there is also a negative side of this historical development which we must recognise if we are not to make mistakes in the future. Because many Chinese then did not or could not make a clear distinction between the political and cultural ideas of being Chinese, some Nantah students at that time got caught up with Mainland Chinese nationalism, especially its leftwing manifestation, and instigated student unrests. In a sense, this was historically unavoidable because the idea of Singapore as a separate, independent political entity with its own national culture was still embryonic and unclear. There was no Republic of Singapore in the 1950s and early 1960s. When we honour Lim Bo Seng as a national or proto-national hero, we must not forget that Lim Bo Seng saw himself as a Chinese national fighting for Kuomintang (KMT) China. Indeed, the rank he held as a major-general was conferred on him by the Chongqing Government. It is therefore only natural that the evolution of an independent Singapore should take many decades. Thus, the difficulties experienced by Nantah in the 1960s and 1970s were partly the result of a separate Singapore nationalism struggling to establish itself.

That history is now behind us. Today no Singaporean doubts that whatever our economic and cultural links with China, our political standpoint is solidly based on an independent Singapore in Southeast Asia. We are able to establish this Chinese Heritage Centre now because that position is clear. Twenty years ago, it would not have been possible.

What Chinese people living in the five continents should do is to achieve a position similar to that which the Anglo-Saxon and Irish peoples in the world have established over the last 200 years. The Anglo-Saxon and Irish peoples are today nationals of different countries. They share common cultural attributes but are politically distinct whether they live in the UK, Ireland, Canada, the US, South Africa, Australia or New Zealand. A similar relationship should govern Chinese peoples living in different countries. Of late, we see the same idea also being promoted among peoples from the Indian subcontinent and also among peoples of Malay stock. For example, it is heartwarming to see the interest which Indonesians, Malaysians and Singaporeans have taken in the Malay people of South Africa after the end of apartheid. I myself was thrilled to discover that a mosque I wandered into in Cape Town was the first to have been built in South Africa by Malays from the Dutch East Indies.

I congratulate Mr Wee Cho Yaw and the Singapore Federation of Chinese Clan Association (SFCCA) for establishing this Heritage Centre. I also congratulate Nanyang Technological University (NTU) for giving its support. Indeed, NTU by changing its shortened name in Chinese from *Litah* to *Nantah* has given added significance to the establishment of the Centre. The reconstruction of the old Nanyang University Arch in the *Yunnan Yuan* which we are unveiling today marks the end of one chapter and the beginning of another.

# A ROUNDED EDUCATION

*... good values lay the foundation for a good education.*

This is a very happy occasion. We are here this evening for the blessing and official opening of St. Anthony's Canossian Primary and Secondary Schools. The new facilities are splendid. They are much better than many of us here ever had in primary school, secondary school and pre-university. Without many years of economic prosperity and good government, we could never have afforded such fine school buildings.

But the physical facilities by themselves are not as important as the spirit of the school, the strong sense of mission of the teachers, the motivation of the pupils and the generosity of the benefactors. People are much more important than bricks and mortar. Nice and well-equipped buildings are good to have, but to breathe life into them, we need much more.

Our mission in the St. Anthony's Canossian Schools is to provide a good rounded education for young girls, to help them become upright individuals and good citizens, and to become filial daughters, supportive sisters, loving wives and caring mothers. In all societies, women enjoy a special place because of their role as mothers. This role is both God-given and biological. Last month, I went down to the National University Hospital to meet the mother who had just donated a part of her liver and her son who received this gift of

---

Speech at the official opening of St. Anthony's Canossian Primary and Secondary Schools, 13 July 1996. George Yeo's daughter was then a student in the Primary School.

life from his mother. Both mother and son are doing very well. Before the liver transplant, the son was very ill. Now he is healthy with the promise of leading a normal life. The surgeons told me that there is a difference whether the liver is from the father or mother. If the mother is the donor, her most important concern when she wakes up from general anaesthesia is how well her child is doing. In the case of the father, his first concern when he becomes conscious is usually his own physical condition. This is something very natural. The maternal instinct is very deep and exists in most animal species, particularly human beings. Without strong women and strong mothers, no society can be strong. Fathers also play an important role in raising children but fathers can never replace mothers, certainly not physically, but also emotionally and spiritually.

In Singapore today, we have become a little too materialistic. Sometimes, all of us seem to be caught up in the rat race. But we are not rats. We are human beings and our lives are a gift from God. We have a responsibility to live our lives well, to develop the potential that is in each and everyone of us, and to use our abilities for the good of society. In each of us, there is a tension between selfishness and selflessness. There is no need to teach a child how to be selfish. He is, naturally. But there is also an innate selflessness in the individual that we must draw out and cultivate. For example, the maternal instinct is a selfless instinct. We must harmonise these two instincts in society. If we are all selfish and concerned only with the 5 C's, we will neither be happy nor enjoy peace of mind. Singapore may still be materially rich but we will all be spiritually poor. But, equally, if we do not acknowledge the importance of the self and recognise individual accomplishments, there will also be no growth. We must therefore always try to strike a good balance between these two instincts. They are like the *yin* and *yang* of human existence. In reality, we can only fulfil our lives by fulfilling them in others.

Our education system tries to raise children in a rounded way. Competition is good but only up to a point. We need a healthy spirit of competition to get the best out of every school, every teacher and every pupil. But competition cannot be an excuse for us to trample on others or to act without scruples. At the end of the day, we are all human beings with responsibilities towards each other.

Therefore, an important part of a good education system is the teaching of good values and the right behaviour. In Chinese tradition, filial piety and observance of correct behaviour takes precedence over the 3 R's of reading, writing and arithmetic. *Shou xiao ti, ci jian wen* (首孝悌, 次见闻). In other words, good values lay the foundation for a good education.

It is not only the Chinese who believe in this. The Hindus and the Muslims share similar beliefs. Most Muslim parents send their children to religious classes at a young age. Many Tamil families give a special place to the *thirukkural*. In the Christian tradition, the Bible and the ten commandments are central to a good education.

Of course, in an age of rapid technological development, we must learn science and mathematics and adopt a scientific approach towards solving the problems of the world. But no amount of science or mathematics can give us answers to the deeper questions of human existence. Human wisdom cannot be digitised and reduced to numbers.

The mission tradition of schools like St. Anthony's is therefore very precious. The mission tradition gives a special quality to the education of young girls and boys. We owe a particular gratitude to the religious teachers in our midst, to the Reverend Fathers, Sisters and Brothers who dedicate their entire lives to the education of the young. Their dedication and selflessness are a great inspiration to all of us. Other religious groups also have such teachers and they too should inspire us. By their good work, we become a better people and our lives are enriched.

Our material and spiritual development go hand in hand. We should not pretend that the 5 C's are not important or dismiss them out of hand. That would be hypocritical. But we should not be obsessed with them or think that they are the only important things in the world. They are not. In the same way, while stressing the importance of spiritual development, we should also spur each other on to work hard and to be committed to all that we do in this world. It is through labour that we fulfil ourselves and objectify the goodness of creation. Above all, we must feel for each other, take care of each other, laugh and cry with each other. Before Jesus Christ died on the cross to save us, he took care to instruct the Apostle John, whom he was particularly fond of, to look after his mother Mary. This was a son's filial piety to his mother. It is a poignant reminder to all of us that, however important the work we do, whatever big issues we are involved in, we must have the right values in our hearts, honour our fathers and mothers, and love our neighbours as ourselves.

It is this value system which has established the remarkable reputation of the Canossian Schools. It is the continuation of St. Magdalene's tradition which will give life into our new school buildings. It is a mission which will help to educate successive generations of upright and God-fearing daughters, sisters, wives and mothers for our country.

# Beyond Materialism

*... talk not only about the first 5 C's but also about the additional ones of character, culture, community, courtesy and commitment.*

## A Changing Way of Life

Every week, my children plead with me to bring them to McDonald's. Before I got married, when I was courting my wife, I used to go to McDonald's because I quite like the food there. After I got married, my wife did not want to go because she said she did not really like the food. Now we go because of our children. McDonald's marketing is very effective. Every week, they have a new toy in the "happy meals" which is advertised over TV. The food is not very expensive but it is not that cheap either. In recent years, with the sale of Housing Development Board (HDB) shops, McDonald's has moved to many of our housing estates and opens till very late at night.

McDonald's is only one example. What we are seeing is a changing way of life in Singapore, a different pattern of consumption. Singaporeans work very hard but they also want to spend a little more on better things, especially for their children. This is one reason why, despite many years of good economic growth and rising income, many lower middle-class families still feel squeezed. In actual fact, many things are still rather cheap. An egg costs about 15 to 20 cents today. It has gone up recently because the price of chicken feed has shot up. When I was a school boy, it was 10 to 12 cents. Or take the price of chicken. At many supermarkets, we can buy a small roast chicken for $5 to $6. When I was a small boy, chickens cost

---

Edited transcript of a casual talk on current affairs organised by the PAP, 14 July 1996.

much the same. Of course, other items have gone up many times, like Gardenia bread and Reebok shoes. In the old days, middle-class kids wore Bata shoes and the poor wore cheap rubber shoes from China. Today, a pair of jogging shoes can easily cost $100 or more. I was told that during the Great Singapore Sale, there was a long queue outside Orchard Road's Ferragamo shoe boutique. In a recent Television Corporation of Singapore (TCS) interview, a teenager said that she would only wear Giordano to sleep.

I live near Changi Prison. I go to Changi Village quite often with my family. There, you can still get many cheap items from China which are good value for money. Once, when I had to buy a pair of sneakers to go fishing, I paid $4 for a pair of canvas shoes. My Double Bull singlets still cost $3 to $4. Of course, times have changed and we have to keep up with the times. NTUC Fair Price now sells sushi and Japanese restaurants can now be found all over Singapore. Older Singaporeans do not understand why young people like Japanese raw fish. One evening, I attended a dinner hosted by the Japanese Ambassador. It was a beautiful dinner with lots of delicious food including raw fish items. Among the guests was an elderly Peranakan couple. The old lady whom I sat next to whispered to me that she felt like throwing the raw fish into a *wok* and stir-frying it. The Japanese chef would have committed *harakiri*. Twenty years ago, very few Singaporeans could appreciate Japanese food. Today, it is very trendy among yuppies to eat Japanese food.

## Not by Bread Alone

Nowadays, among educated younger Singaporeans, we keep on hearing about the 5 C's. As you know, the 5 C's refer to career, cash, credit card, car and condominium. Whenever young people meet, they talk about the prices of this and the prices of that. They are very knowledgeable about designer labels. When the ladies take off their shoes, they are very conscious of the brand names. This materialism is the natural result of our economic growth. Singaporeans are better educated now and they deserve better. The issue is no longer whether or not we have jobs or homes or whether our children are educated, or whether we have enough to eat. All those needs have been met. There is not a single squatter left in Singapore. There are no slums. We hardly see destitute people on the streets. Compared to other cities in the world, both in Third World countries and in developed countries, we have done well. Our poor are nothing like the poor in Calcutta or Cairo. Our bottom 10% are better off than the bottom 10% in Hong Kong, London, New York or Tokyo. They are relatively well taken care of. We have become a middle-class society with middle-class concerns. Our concerns today are about the kinds of clothes or shoes we wear, the kinds of homes we live in, the kinds of schools our children go to and the places we travel to for vacation. For most Singaporeans, the problem is no longer one of having enough to eat but eating too much. In the old days, we were taught not to leave food on the table because that was a terrible waste. Our mothers used to tell us that the food could have saved starving people in India and Africa. Today, we are discouraging our children from eating too much. I tell my children — when they eat Hainanese chicken rice — not to eat all the chicken skin, even though it is delicious.

But, have we become happier or wiser? I am not sure, even though we may be wearing shoes with flashing lights, eating in Japanese restaurants and going overseas for holidays. As Singaporeans, we complain a lot. We are very *kiasu*. We want to keep up with our neighbours and not be left behind. Everyone seems to want to own a better home or drive a better car. In Singapore, it is very prestigious to own a Mercedes and many people spend a fortune buying expensive cars. In Germany, 90% of taxis are Mercedes. The Germans do not see cars as a status symbol at all.

If all we do is to keep chasing after material things and status symbols, we will not be happy. Worse, our children will grow up with the wrong values. Already, many are spoilt because parents lavish so much on them. Many working parents are prepared to stinge on themselves in order to splurge on their children. This is partly competition because no mother wants her child to be behind her neighbour's child. Singaporean mothers are anxious to send their children for "this" class and for "that" class. But it is not good if our children grow up knowing only material things. Great men like Tan

Kah Kee, Lee Kong Chian and Chi Owyang took care not to allow wealth to corrupt their children, and to ensure that they have a good education and the right values. When children grow up with too many things around them, they are not likely to grow up strong. Hence, it is said by the Chinese that wealth cannot easily be passed on beyond the third generation. The Japanese say "from slippers to slippers in three generations".

We are human beings, not animals. The material side is only one side of us. Beyond that, we have our intellectual side and our spiritual side. To be fulfilled as human beings, we have to pay attention to all three dimensions. They are like our X, Y and Z axes. Money cannot substitute for a poor education. Intelligence cannot substitute for goodness. All three aspects of ourselves — the material, the intellectual and the spiritual — must be cultivated. And, they are connected. We cannot have material development without intellectual and spiritual development. We cannot be spiritual by ignoring material and intellectual development.

What applies to individuals also applies to our entire society. Our national development must pay attention to all these three aspects of human nature. If we are imbalanced, if we do not have all round development, our society will suffer and our children will suffer. A lot of the development we see in Singapore today is the result of the hard work, thrift and discipline of earlier generations of Singaporeans and their leaders. If we lose these values and become too caught up in material things, we will not be able to sustain the development that we now see. Far from continuing to surge forward, our society will regress. This is precisely the problem in many Western societies today.

Human lives and human fortunes go through cycles. As we sing in the song *"ai bia chia eh yiah, wu si ki wu si lok"* (爱拼才会赢，有时起有时落),* Singapore will also go through cycles. We will not always stay up. At some times, we will be down. When we are down, we will be tested. Whether we are then able to regroup and recover depends on our inner character. The key is internal strength, not external things.

---

*The phrase is in Hokkien, meaning "fight to win, but there are ups and downs".

Mao Zedong once said, in one of his lighter moments, that China has made three great contributions to humanity. The first is Chinese medicine, the second is *Hong Lou Meng* (红楼梦) or *Dream of the Red Chamber*, and the third is *mahjong*. He was only half-joking. In the book *Hong Lou Meng*, we read about the rise and fall of a great family, the Jia family, and about how members of that family became self-absorbed when there was too much wealth. When one of the daughters-in-law died under suspicious circumtances, an extravagant funeral was arranged which the family could not really afford. When one of the daughters who became an imperial concubine came back to visit her family, a magnificent garden was built, called the Da Guan Yuan (大观园). Family members envied each other and plotted against each other. Despite all the material wealth, the core of the family became rotten and almost everyone had a tragic ending. Baoyu himself became a monk. Even though *Hong Lou Meng* described Chinese feudal society, there are lessons to learn from this great romance about the nature of human life.

Always, what is most important is what is inside, and not what is outside. With a strong spirit, human beings can overcome all odds, however poorly equipped. That was how the Vietcong prevailed over the Americans in Vietnam. The Americans had everything — B52 bombers, tanks, sophisticated communications equipment, elaborate logistics. Soldiers in the field were served cakes and ice-cream. In stark contrast, the Vietcong had very little. Before the Tet Offensive was launched in 1968, some of them were shown the boxes which would become their coffins if they were killed in battle. With that kind of spirit, they were prepared to die. In the end, the human spirit triumphed over machines and technology. Mao once said that the contest of strength is not only a contest of military and economic power but also a contest of human power and morale.

Of course, science and technology are important and we must make sure our children master the 3 R's of reading, writing and arithmetic. We must teach them the scientific approach to solving problems. We want our children to be taught computing and the Internet. All this is very good, but all this is not enough. In the classical Chinese tradition, before children learn the 3 R's, they are first taught human relationships and the right values. Only after that, are they encouraged to learn science, arithmetic, philosophy and history — *shou xiao ti, ci jian wen* (首孝悌, 次见闻).

Our children today are very fortunate and they know a lot of things at a young age. But whether we are imparting enough of the right values to them is a question we must ask. Although parents and teachers are primarily responsible, the overall environment of our society affects our ability to maintain and transmit the right values. If the right values are held up in Singapore society, it becomes easier for us to teach them at home and in the schools. It is important that we do not become too obsessive about material things in Singapore. We must take care to nurture the other aspects of life, especially our intellectual and spiritual development.

**Five Other C's**

We should pay attention to 5 other C's — to character, culture, community, courtesy and commitment. We need these additional 5 C's to counter-balance the other 5, so that the *yin* and *yang* in our society are in balance.

Character is very important. If we know only prices but not values, we cannot be called human beings. Even animals look after each other. The first C is therefore about having the right values, about morality, virtue, proper behaviour, wisdom and trust.

By culture, I refer to the totality of our artistic and intellectual development in Singapore. In Asian tradition, if the father has two sons, one educated but poor and the other poorly educated but rich, in his heart, he is always prouder of the educated son. This is a good tradition we should maintain. To hold up education and culture in our society, we must always honour those who are prepared to give up material things in pursuit of intellectual and spiritual matters. We must respect teachers. We should always honour the scholar in our midst. We should also respect ulamas, priests and monks. Without all of them, our society is spiritually poor, however rich we may be materially. We must be rooted to Singapore and in our ancestral civilisations. Our students must learn some history. It is not good that many of our Chinese students, even those from Special Assistance

Plan (SAP) schools, do not know what the major Chinese dynasties are. Many Indian students are not familiar with the stories in the *Ramayana* and the *Mahabharata*. Malay parents worry a lot about the religious education of their children and take care to send them to religious classes when they are young. Because of this, Malay Singaporeans are less culturally endangered than Chinese and Indian Singaporeans.

The third C is community. We must find more time to help each other, especially those who are less well-off. Ironically, it is those who are busy who have the most time for voluntary work. Our party activists and grassroots leaders, for example, are busy people but they are always able to find time to do community work. I am somewhat optimistic. Voluntarism is on the rise in Singapore. More voluntary welfare organisations (VWOs) are being established. In the two Ministries for which I am responsible, MITA and MOH, I see every year, more volunteers coming forward, helping out in cultural activities, looking after the sick and raising money for various causes. Many young people are becoming involved. This is a good sign. The Singapore International Foundation (SIF) has a long list of young volunteers wanting to do good work in less-developed countries. I was chatting with one of Comrade Chin Harn Tong's grassroots leaders the other night — a school teacher, she helps out at his meet-the-people (MPS) sessions. As an SIF volunteer, she spent a year teaching English in Botswana. I asked her about her experience. She was very happy with the year in Africa even though there were many hardships and, to my surprise, she is prepared to go back a second time. This is very heart-warming because it shows that there is a goodness in us which transcends the self, family, race and religion. Confucius taught us not to do to others what we do not want others to do to us. Jesus Christ put it more emphatically by telling us to do for others what we want them to do for us.

The fourth C is courtesy. Last Sunday, Prime Minister Goh Chok Tong launched this year's Courtesy Campaign. He agreed to become the Patron of the Small Kindness Movement. The idea is very simple. Kindness is not a heroic effort which only a few persons among us can do. Kindness can be in small things. Our objective should be to remember doing a kind deed everyday, however small. Before the day is up, we do our exercise, we bathe and brush our teeth. We should consider that the day is not yet done until we also do a little kindness. Kindness should not only be for the Mother Theresas of the world. Kindness can be something we do at home, in school or in the workplace. In this way, we uplift each other's spirit and become a better people. This will also temper our *kiasu* spirit.

The last C is commitment to Singapore, especially in times of crisis. Young Singaporeans today have many choices. We do not even have to work or live in Singapore, and many do not. But our hearts must always remain in Singapore wherever we may be in the world. When there is a crisis, we must be prepared to stand up for our country. During the Michael Fay affair, Singaporeans in Singapore and overseas stood firm. They took precautions but they did not want our government to flinch. Like the Swiss, we should take total defence seriously and always remain committed to Singapore because this is our country.

## Conclusion

We are members of a political party. Our role is not just to convince Singaporeans that they should vote for the People's Action Party (PAP). That is important but that cannot be the only thing we are interested in. Indeed, when we ask someone to vote for the PAP, he will ask why, and we must have good answers. The answer cannot just be that the PAP will give him a better material life. The PAP has already succeeded very well in doing this and, yet, not a few are still unhappy. In fact, the better our economic performance, the greater seems to be the complaint. No, our answer cannot just be to offer Singaporeans more material development. It must also be to offer them a more rounded life in Singapore, one which provides also for intellectual and spiritual development in addition to material development. We should talk not only about the first 5 C's, even though they are important, but also about the additional ones of character, culture, community, courtesy and commitment. Without the second 5 C's, the first 5 C's will turn the Singapore Dream into a nightmare. If we are able to get this point across in a persuasive way and demonstrate it by our own attitudes and behaviour, then we will be convincing. It is not the details of policies which are important. It is what we, as party members, believe deep inside us which will persuade individual Singaporeans, that what we believe in and do, is what they want for themselves and their children.

# HOLISTIC VIEW OF HEALTH

*... what is more important than the prescription is inspiration.*

Over this year's National Heart Weekend, the Singapore National Heart Association is hosting the ASEAN Federation of Heart Foundation Meeting and the Asia-Pacific Heart Network Discussion. We have many participants from the other ASEAN countries, India, Pakistan, Australia, New Zealand, Japan and the United States who honour us by their presence at today's launch. I would like to take this opportunity to welcome them to Singapore and wish them a most pleasant stay here.

It is the custom at the annual launch of the National Heart Weekend for the guest-of-honour to recite a litany of statistics and prescribe a list of do's and don'ts. I propose not to go through this ritual this year because there is already widespread knowledge about the causes of heart diseases and the importance of eating well and living well.

In fact, the difficulty is usually not one of lack of knowledge but one of lack of motivation. When we are inspired, problems are set in perspective and many things are easily done. In any army unit or business corporation, morale can be decisive. High morale creates a conquering spirit, which enables many problems to be overcome. But if morale is low and leaders are dispirited, even simple problems become impossible to solve.

---

Speech at the opening of National Heart Weekend '96, Intercontinental Hotel, 31 August 1996.

All of us know that grief or depression can predispose a person to ill health. All of us know that there is a profound connection between our minds and our bodies. A rudeness encountered in the morning can ruin the whole day. A phone call announcing bad news can drive a person to rage or despair. Conversely, a special act of courtesy or a compliment can lift our spirits, put a spring into our walk and make the whole day seem bright and easy.

Indeed, what doctors or scientists call the placebo effect is not something to be lightly dismissed. The placebo effect only confirms that there is a mind-body connection which we do not fully understand. All pharmaceutical companies know that the placebo effect for pain killers is at least 50%. This means that the right frame of mind can be even more effective in overcoming pain than prescription drugs.

Last Sunday, Prime Minister Goh Chok Tong launched this year's National Healthy Lifestyle Campaign, during which he encouraged Singaporeans to live healthier lifestyles. As always, we have a list of do's and don'ts. But what is more important than the prescription is inspiration. If we get everyone into the right frame of mind, more than half the battle is won.

It is the same with the National Heart Weekend. What we are trying to do is to get Singaporeans into the right frame of mind. A right frame of mind will encourage the individual to seek out the requisite knowledge, deepen his understanding and, from there, to alter and improve his lifestyle.

What we need is a holistic view of health. Western medicine is sometimes not very good at this. It tends to be very scientific. As a result we tend to look at each organ or each system by itself — the heart by itself, the brain by itself, the liver by itself, and so on. In fact, they are all connected and the health of one part of the body has profound effects on the health of other parts. Many of these connections are still not clear to medical science. Long ago, the ancients already knew that the human body had to be viewed in holistic terms. Of course, there was also a lot of superstitions and metaphysics which we should discard. But the idea that life forces must be kept in balance is as relevant today as it was to our ancestors hundreds or thousands of years ago.

All life on earth go through cycles, following the cycles of the day, the moon, the sun, sunspots and other natural phenomena. Over millions of years, through the process of biological evolution, these cycles find their reflections in our bodies. When our body cycles get out of balance, we fall ill. Getting them back into balance is what medical science is all about.

The role of the human mind in moderating and modulating these cycles is very important. Under severe stress, mental strength is critical to physical health. Those who survived the Nazi concentration camps during the Second World War were the ones with the greatest mental strength or spiritual strength. For many medical conditions like cancer, faith in the doctor, faith in the therapy and faith in God are all very important. In fact, deeply religious people often experience better survival chances. All religions can cite examples of miraculous cures and faith healing, which doctors and scientists are often hard put to explain. Here again, the mind-body or the spirit-body connection is at work.

The heart is connected to the mind. The right words or the right feelings calm our hearts. Cutting words, drum rolls or evil odours do the opposite and cause the heart to race. Some individuals raise the heart rate and blood pressure of everyone around them. Other individuals have the opposite effect. We cannot live life without stress but it is dangerous to live life under continuous stress. What we need is to punctuate the stresses of life with laughter, relaxation, love, friendship and idealism. It is not a joke when we say that laughter is the best medicine.

In launching this National Heart Weekend, I would like to encourage a more holistic view of health. I would like to stress, in an unstressful way, the importance of the mind and the spirit in good health. Laughter, love, friendship, relaxation and idealistic pursuits are all antidotes to the stresses of our competitive and materialistic society. This means giving more time to nature and to each other. We feel good when we do good, and that is good for our health. A healthy heart is a good heart. A healthy heart is a big heart.

# Being Chinese

*What we must do is to separate the political idea of being Chinese from the cultural idea of being Chinese.*

We are gathered here today to commemorate the 130th birthday of Dr Sun Yat Sen. More than any one else, Dr Sun Yat Sen symbolises for all Chinese people — both in China and outside China — the 1911 Revolution or the Xin Hai Ge Ming (辛亥革命).

The 1911 Revolution was a very great revolution in human history. It marked the end of over 2,000 years of Chinese feudal society and imperial rule. The modernisation process of Chinese culture in fact started many years earlier. It had its beginnings in the early part of the 19th century. The Opium War of 1841–1842 was a great shock to the Qing Dynasty. Following it, the Taiping Tianguo (太平天国) uprising almost tore China apart. Over 20 million Chinese died and large parts of China were devastated. As the Qing Dynasty weakened, foreign encroachments on China grew. By the time of the Boxer Rebellion, China was in complete disarray. There were many attempts to reform Qing China by men like Zhang Zhidong and Kang Youwei but Imperial China had by then become too ossified to transform itself. It was the 1911 Revolution that did away with imperial rule and created a constitutional government for the first time in China's history.

The revolution of the Chinese mind did not end with the 1911 Revolution. After a year, Dr Sun stepped down as President and Yuan Shikai took over. Yuan wanted to become emperor but died in 1916.

---

Speech to commemorate the 130th birthday of Dr Sun Yat Sen, Sun Yat Sen Nanyang Memorial Hall, 12 November 1996.

On 4 May 1919, Chinese students in Peking University objected to the Treaty of Versailles giving Qingdao to the Japanese. The May 4th Movement gave a strong push to the New Culture Movement. Even so, Chinese society had still to go through many decades of twists and turns before its culture could be fully modernised and equipped for the industrial and post-industrial age. It is a process still ongoing.

From start to end, it would take perhaps 200 years for this historical transformation to be completed. If we count it from the Treaty of Nanjing in 1842 to the return of Hong Kong to China in 1997, the period would be 155 years. But, even today, the rule of law in China is still not well established even though there has been great improvement in recent years. Large parts of China are still culturally backwards.

Singapore's history has been much intertwined with this part of China's history. The reason why many Chinese came from China to Singapore in the last century and in the beginning of this century was because of the breakdown of Chinese society in the Mainland and the lack of opportunities there. In fact, all the great events in China over the last 150 years have created reverberations among the ethnic Chinese in Southeast Asia. Both Kang Youwei and Dr Sun Yat Sen came to Singapore many times. Dr Sun Yat Sen would usually stay here at the Wan Qing Yuan (晚晴园) when he was in Singapore, which is why it is important for us to preserve this estate. When the Tong Meng Hui (同盟会) was formed in Tokyo in August 1905, a branch was formed in Singapore six months later. At the beginning of this century, the Chinese in Singapore were divided between those who supported the Emperor and those who wanted a republic.

When the Kuomintang and the Communists in China fought, their supporters also fought here in Singapore. When they combined to fight the Japanese, the Chinese in Singapore also united to fight the Japanese by partly contributing money, material and personnel. Partly because of this, the Japanese Imperial Army was particularly cruel to Singapore Chinese civilians when it occupied Singapore in 1942. Many Singapore Chinese leaders who supported the anti-Japanese effort in China, including clan leaders, were already marked out for extermination months before the Japanese bombed Pearl Harbour.

After the War, the Chinese in Singapore were again divided between pro-Mao Communists and non-Communists. Right into the 1950s and early 1960s, many Chinese in Singapore identified themselves more with China than with the idea of an independent Singapore with its own destiny.

It is because of this complex history that, for many years, the Wan Qing Yuan was never considered a national monument to be preserved. It was a politically sensitive matter. Now, after 31 years of independence, we can look at that period of our history and our earlier connections with China, in a more objective and dispassionate way. It was only a few years ago that the Preservation of Monuments Board finally included the Wan Qing Yuan on its list. It was only two years ago that we were able to establish a Chinese Heritage Centre at the old Nantah.

What we must do is to separate the political idea of being Chinese from the cultural idea of being Chinese. This is a very important distinction which we must make carefully and deliberately. When we preserve the Wan Qing Yuan and commemorate the 130th birthday of Dr Sun Yat Sen, we are remembering important events which transformed Chinese culture in Singapore. We are not tying ourselves politically to China or Taiwan, both of which still honour Dr Sun Yat Sen as Founder Father or Guofu. Dr Sun Yat Sen is not Singapore's Guofu but what he did and the movement he represented, in which Singapore Chinese also participated, made a great difference to our lives. Without the cultural revolution symbolised by Dr Sun Yat Sen, the Chinese mind would have stagnated and there would not be a modern Singapore today.

The greatest significance of the 1911 Revolution was its transformation of the Chinese mind. The end of feudal relationships, the liberation of women, the baihuawen movement, the Speak Mandarin Campaign, democracy, constitutional government and the rule of law — all this was part of Dr Sun Yat Sen's San Min Zhu Yi (三民主义).

In the 1950s and 1960s, a commemoration such as this today would have been very political. Non-Chinese Singaporeans would view it negatively. Our neighbours would also view it with suspicion. Today, the situation is completely different in all of Asia. In Malaysia,

Chinese education is again on the rise. Many Malays are studying Mandarin. In Thailand, a Chinese language university was recently opened by the Thai King. China itself has changed dramatically. So long as we make a clear distinction between the political idea of being Chinese and the cultural idea of being Chinese, we can be proud of our Chineseness without this causing unnecessary misunderstanding. Our cultural links to China are separate from our political links. Indeed, this is the wish of most Chinese in the world outside China, Taiwan and Hong Kong. When the Huayi Guan (华裔馆) was opened at Nantah two years ago, that distinction was made very clear. Thus, ethnic Chinese Singaporeans are not as excited about the Diaoyu Islands as the Chinese in China, Taiwan and Hong Kong are. This distinction allows us to commemorate Dr Sun Yat Sen's 130th birthday without politicising it, in the same way as Indian Singaporeans are able to remember Mahatma Gandhi without this linking us politically to India.

The conservation of the Wan Qing Yuan is a very important cultural project for Chinese Singaporeans. The 1911 Revolution is a very important part of our cultural history which we must never forget. This building should therefore be preserved as a cultural shrine for all ethnic Chinese Singaporeans. It will also be of great interest to non-Chinese Singaporeans and to others in the world.

# Our Multiracial Reality

*Multiracialism requires a spirit of give and take.*

The Asian economic crisis has put many countries under tremendous political stress. Within a year it caused the resignations of PM Chavalit, President Suharto and PM Hashimoto. In Indonesia, terrible atrocities have been carried out against the Chinese community. Some were organised, others were spontaneous. As companies go bankrupt and unemployment rises in many countries, we do not know what other unhappy consequences will arise out of this severe economic downturn.

We cannot assume that Singapore society is invulnerable to such stresses. Our history is only 33 years. Our multiracialism is both a strength and a weakness. It is a strength because the different ethnic groups link us to different parts of the world. Without this diversity, Singapore cannot be a cosmopolitan entrepôt and an international financial centre. However, our multiracialism also means that we do not always react in the same way to external events and foreign pressures. Take, for example, the way the local newspapers reported on the anti-Chinese rioting in Indonesia. The Chinese press gave it full coverage. The English press took a relatively detached approach. The Malay press, in contrast, was awkward and played down the racial aspects. This is to be expected because ethnic feelings run deep in any society. Similarly, when many Muslims were raped and killed in Bosnia, the Chinese press did not take a strong stand even though

---

Speech at the Sikh Community National Day Dinner, Singapore Khalsa Club, 22 August 1998.

its coverage of the atrocities was extensive. When the new Bharatiya Janata Party (BJP) government in India exploded five nuclear bombs, Hindus and Muslims in Singapore reacted in different ways. When Pakistan then exploded six bombs in response, the emotions of Hindus and Muslims in Singapore were again different. Some Muslims were pleased that a Muslim country had finally produced the bomb. Till today, the storming of the Golden Temple by the Indian Army in 1984 is still remembered with outrage by Sikh communities all over the world, including Sikhs in Singapore.

This is the multiracial reality in Singapore. We cannot escape from it. A few Singaporeans write letters to the press from time to time expressing the hope that the different races in Singapore will one day meld together into a kind of local Singapore Peranakan community. This is unlikely to happen because the races in Singapore have very different historical memories. We have different gods, different patron saints and different heroes. Our religions are not going to fuse into one. The rituals governing birth, marriage and death will always remain different. It is better to be realistic and practical. Of course, in managing the complexities of multiracialism in Singapore, we should try to maximise our strengths and minimise our weaknesses.

So long as we have a good government, and our own Police and Army, whatever racial or religious problems that may arise from time to time can be contained and minimised. When we were part of Malaysia in 1964, the Police and the Army were not under our control. As a result, the racial riots that took place were not immediately squashed. Chinese secret society members tried to right the imbalance and, in the end, there were probably as many Malay casualties as there were Chinese casualties. When the May 13th riots took place in Malaysia in 1969, Chinese secret society members in Singapore tried to take revenge on Singapore Malays on behalf of the Chinese in Malaysia. Fortunately, we were independent in 1969. The Police and Army acted immediately and decisively against these Chinese secret societies, and no riots were allowed to take place in Singapore. National Service is therefore a very important institution in Singapore against both external aggression and internal threats. During this economic crisis, Singaporeans must give even more attention to National Service. Without a credible defence force, we will not be sovereign and our rights will be quickly trampled upon.

National Service in Singapore can only work if all racial and religious groups share a common sense of being Singaporean. An important part of what Singapore stands for is the protection of minority groups. As Zainul Abidin Rasheed once told me, in a curious way, Singapore is a nation of minorities. The Malays, Indians and Eurasians are minorities, but the Chinese too feel that they are a minority in Southeast Asia. Because of this common sense of being members of minority groups, no racial group in Singapore wants trouble. All of us want racial harmony. The desire to protect the rights of all racial groups in Singapore underpins all our institutions, including that of the Police and the Army.

The Sikhs have an instinctive aversion to racial and religious intolerance because of their own painful history. Under the Mughals, the fifth Guru was imprisoned and tortured to death, the ninth Guru was beheaded and the infant sons of the tenth Guru were bricked alive. Only fifty years ago, during the partition of the Indian sub-continent in 1947, millions of Sikhs were displaced and forced to leave their homes and, in some cases, their parents and siblings. There is very little of the Sikh legacy left in Lahore today.

There are only 15,000 Sikhs in Singapore. Although they make up no more than half a percent of our population, all Singaporeans grow up knowing that Sikhs are part of our ethnic and cultural landscape. The Malaysian cartoonist Lat always includes a Sikh every time he depicts a multiracial situation in Malaysia or Singapore. Few Singaporeans think it unusual that there should be two elected Sikh Members of Parliament out of 84.

Provided we maintain this multiracial framework in Singapore, we can rejoice in each other's cultural and religious celebrations. Next year, the Sikh community will celebrate the 300th anniversary of the birth of the Khalsa on 13 April, as pronounced by the tenth Sikh Guru, Guru Gobind Singh Ji. Singaporeans of all races and religions will join the Sikh community in this celebration because of the racial and religious harmony that we enjoy here. We have this harmony only because we work hard to maintain it. We must not allow problems to fester and become worse. We also have laws to act quickly against extremists. Because of this, there is a spirit of mutual tolerance and common celebration. We have come to take this for granted in Singapore.

However, such harmony and respect is not a universal phenomenon. In many parts of the world, racial and religious hatreds are commonplace. In Northern Ireland, the celebration of one community is often an affront to the other. Even in the US, the particular needs of the Sikh community are not commonly recognised. Many years ago, when I was in the Air Force, a problem arose because one of our Sikh pilots was sent to a US Navy airbase for training on the Skyhawk aeroplane. Under US Navy regulations, the pilot cannot wear a beard because, in an oxygen-rich environment, the beard is considered a fire hazard. The US Navy was not prepared to make an exception for this Singapore Sikh pilot. Messages were sent back and forth between Singapore and the US over this issue. In the end, the Republic of Singapore Air Force had to recall the Sikh pilot and train him on a different fighter aeroplane instead.

Multiracialism requires a spirit of give and take. Every racial group should be protected but no racial group should press its claims too hard. This is what we have come to accept in Singapore. Mosques are asked to turn down their loudspeakers and point them inwards. Chinese temples are now prohibited from burning super-large joss sticks. They were getting bigger and bigger, year by year. In every Singapore Armed Forces (SAF) camp, we have two kitchens, a Muslim kitchen serving no pork and a Chinese kitchen serving no beef. Every soldier is free to choose where he eats. In this way, we try to accommodate everyone. Very few military camps in the world have such arrangements. The Singapore multiracial ideal is one worth our defending in the world. In this world, no racial or religious group is in the majority. Out of a total world population of six billion, all groups are minority groups. We have to live together and accommodate each other, or else fight bitter wars till the end of time.

My wife and I are honoured to join the Sikh community's celebration of Singapore's 33rd birthday this evening.

# Speaking Mandarin in the Information Age

*Chinese culture and the Chinese language give us a sense of who we are, where we came from and what we can be.*

## Review of the Past 20 Years

Twenty years ago, Senior Minister Lee Kuan Yew launched the Speak Mandarin Campaign. He explained why Chinese Singaporeans who spoke 12 different dialects would be better off if they encouraged their children to speak Mandarin: Mandarin, not dialect, is what we teach in schools, he said. Very few children could cope with two languages plus a dialect. Mandarin should be the common lingua franca for all Chinese Singaporeans.

Ten years later, Senior Minister reviewed the progress of the campaign. He noted that our bilingual policy had become established and many Chinese Singaporeans now accepted Mandarin as the preferred language at home and for social intercourse. Emotionally this switch from dialects to Mandarin was a painful one. But Singaporeans are a pragmatic people. Once they understood the rationale, they rose to the challenge. It was not always easy but, today, as we look back and see how far we have come, the effort has been worthwhile.

We can take satisfaction in the fact that the basic aims of the campaign have been achieved. Surveys have repeatedly shown that almost all Chinese Singaporeans can speak some Mandarin, though at different levels of fluency (SPH Survey, 1993). A more recent survey

---

Speech at the launch of the 1998 Speak Mandarin Campaign, 12 September 1998.

of 1,000 Chinese Singaporeans by Forbes Research (1997) showed that 81% speak Mandarin daily. Most English-educated Chinese Singaporeans (86%) have no difficulty understanding simple Mandarin. Mandarin is generally used for occasional greetings, to express appreciation and other feelings, and for ordinary conversation.

We have therefore succeeded in the historical task of establishing Mandarin as the high language for Chinese Singaporeans above the use of dialects. As measured by the most frequently spoken language at home for Primary One Chinese pupils, the number of dialect-speaking homes have fallen sharply from 64% in 1980 to 10% in 1988 to 9% this year. I describe this as a historical task because the promotion of Mandarin, called *guoyu* (国语) in Republican China and *putonghua* (普通话) in the People's Republic, was one of the key tasks of the 1911 Chinese Revolution. Chinese schools in Singapore had been promoting the use of Mandarin since the beginning of this century.

Despite our success, there are still some older Chinese Singaporeans who do not understand much Mandarin. Because of the success of the Speak Mandarin Campaign, we have been able in the past few years to allow more use of dialects for news on radio and entertainment programmes on subscription TV. We must do this in a manner that will not compromise our Speak Mandarin policy. We must also not send the wrong signals to our young. The Speak Mandarin campaign and our bilingual policy have established Mandarin solidly as the main language of Chinese Singaporeans. Thus when *Money, No Enough*, largely in Hokkien, succeeded at the box office, we did not worry too much that it would erode our efforts.

## Future Importance of Mandarin

For Chinese Singaporeans at home, the choice today is no longer between Mandarin and dialects, but between Mandarin and English. Because of the common use of English in our schools, in government and for international business, many younger Singaporeans today are much more comfortable in English than in Mandarin. If we look at the most commonly spoken language at home of Primary One Chinese students, the number of Mandarin-speaking homes has increased from 26% in 1980 to 69% in 1988. Mandarin has largely displaced dialects as the Chinese language spoken at home. However, from 1989 onwards, the number of Mandarin-speaking homes started falling from 69% to 56% this year. The drop is by about 1% a year. In a few years' time, English-speaking homes of Primary One Chinese students will outnumber Chinese-speaking homes. We have to watch this trend carefully and manage it. Otherwise, the use of Mandarin in Singapore will decline, both in quantity and in quality. If the majority of Chinese Singaporeans use Chinese, not as the mother tongue but as a second language, not used at home and taught only in school, the nature of our society will change, and it will be for the worse.

Therefore, the objective of the Speak Mandarin Campaign today is not only to establish Mandarin as the preferred language over dialects, but also as a high language for Chinese Singaporeans. We must establish Mandarin as a high language in Singapore on par with the English language. This must be Singapore's commitment to all four official languages.

It is worth recapitulating why promoting Mandarin as a high language for Chinese Singaporeans is necessary. The reasons are both cultural and economic. The use of Mandarin will help us preserve and develop our cultural roots. Chinese Singaporeans are the proud inheritors of 5,000 years of Chinese civilization, the longest continuous civilization in human history. Chinese culture and the Chinese language give us a sense of who we are, where we came from and what we can be. This is crucial as it is easy for the young to be overwhelmed by the culture of Hollywood, so pervasive in the areas of information, education and entertainment today. The culture of a people gives its members their internal strength. Without that internal strength, we will not be able to survive disasters, political turmoil and war. If we use only English, and allow our mother tongue to degenerate into a second language, with Chinese not used at home and taught only in school, we will lose much of our internal strength and become a weak people with shallow roots.

There is also a powerful economic reason to promote Mandarin. The re-emergence of China will have a growing impact on world economics and world politics in the coming decades. Those who speak and write Mandarin, and understand Chinese culture, will enjoy a considerable advantage in the next century. Those who are able to master both Chinese and English at a high level will be much sought after.

### The Necessity for a Broad Base

Unfortunately, not many Chinese Singaporeans will be able to achieve such mastery in both languages. We must accept that for most people one language will be stronger than the other, and what this is depends a lot on the family background of the individual, the schools he attended, his job requirement and his own interests.

To transmit Chinese culture and the Chinese language effectively to successive generations of Chinese Singaporeans, we need a Chinese intellectual and cultural elite. We need political and cultural leaders, intellectuals and scientists, writers and poets, principals and teachers, editors and journalists, and many others who master Chinese at a high level. For some of them, their command of the Chinese language will be stronger than their command of the English language.

We should recruit foreign talents from China, Taiwan, Hong Kong, North America and other countries to help us, but they can only supplement, not replace, our own local talents. Our problem is ensuring a steady supply of local talents who are rooted here and who understand that, although Singapore has a majority Chinese population, we are an independent country with a separate destiny from China. What we need is a new generation of Chinese intellectual and cultural elite workers to replace the present Nantah generation. To create that new peak, we must have a wide base of Chinese speakers, readers and writers among a younger generation of Chinese Singaporeans.

Some trends are worrying. I referred earlier to the declining number of Chinese-speaking households. For news and entertainment, there has been a pronounced shift among younger Chinese Singaporeans to the English media. Among younger Chinese Singaporeans (age 15 to 29), 27% read *Lianhe Zaobao* compared to 41% for older Chinese Singaporeans (age 45 and above). Younger Chinese Singaporeans are bilingual and have a choice between Chinese and English newspapers. This is why it is absolutely important for *Lianhe Zaobao* to make the newspaper more attractive to younger readers.

For television, Channel 8 continues to be more popular than Channel 5 among younger Chinese Singaporeans, but these younger viewers are now able to switch channels freely. If we had not restructured TCS and enabled it to respond to changing market trends, the position would be very different. The sales pattern of Chinese and English radio and TV times reflects this bilingual ability of younger Chinese Singaporeans. Ten years ago, radio and TV times sold 3.5 times more copies in Chinese than in English. Today, *i-Weekly's* circulation is only 1.75 times that of *8 Days*.

We see the same phenomenon in cinema attendance. Since 1993, more tickets have been sold for English films than for Chinese films. This is partly because Hong Kong and Taiwanese films have not been able to match Hollywood in new digital technology. Such a shift, however, can only take place because younger Singaporeans are bilingual and can make the switch easily.

We must monitor the base of younger Chinese Singaporeans who speak, read and write Chinese comfortably. The wider this base, the easier it is for us to create a high peak of Chinese intellectual and cultural elite at the top. But if the base shrinks, we will fail in replacing the Nantah generation, which will be a tragedy for Singapore indeed.

Fortunately, the longer term trends are favourable. The growing economic importance of China will affect the global position of the Chinese language. The Chinese language is already one of the fastest growing foreign languages being learnt in the world. In North America, Australia and Europe, ethnic Chinese are rediscovering their ancestral language and culture. There is growing pride in being Chinese. The worldwide condemnation of what President Habibie described as "barbaric acts" against ethnic Chinese Indonesians reflects this new spirit among ethnic Chinese worldwide. However, we must remember that this international Chinese spirit can also be a threat to non-Chinese if it is imbalanced or excessive. Among many young Chinese parents in Singapore today, there is a strong desire for their children to master more Mandarin than they themselves were able to. This is a good sign and a positive trend.

Thus, we see in recent years, a small but growing pool of younger Chinese Singaporeans who, while being effectively bilingual, love the Chinese language and use it well. They will help to take on the responsibilities now being shouldered by Chinese-educated Singaporeans in government, in the diplomatic corps, in our schools and universities, in the media, and in our civil and cultural institutions. We need many more of them. Then we will succeed in creating a new generation of Chinese intellectual and cultural elite workers who will in turn transmit our language and culture to the next generation. Similarly, we need intellectual and cultural elites in the Malay and Indian languages who can help maintain the standards of these languages and also pass them on to successive generations.

### The New Battlefield

Where do we go from here? It is now time for the Speak Mandarin Campaign to build on the achievements of the last 20 years and help bring Singapore into the Information Age. We must plunge into Chinese Internet. The Internet not only connects the world but has the power to influence people in a way we could never have imagined. The Internet will be a force for both good and evil. The Internet enabled reports of the May riots in Indonesia to be broadcast to the world, but it was also used to misinform and, sometimes, to terrorise.

The Chinese Internet world is expanding very fast in Taiwan, Hong Kong and the Mainland. China hopes to have four million Chinese connected online by the year 2000. *China Economic Times* reported on 13 July 1998 that the number of Internet surfers in China swelled to 1.2 million at the end of June, from half a million at the beginning of this year. Because of the explosive growth of Chinese Internet, a huge market for Chinese online content, information and services will open up. MIT Prof Nicholas Negroponte predicted that, in less than 10 years, Chinese will be the dominant language on the Internet.

The most important development of the Internet in the coming years will be in electronic commerce. By the year 2001, global electronic commerce is likely to exceed US$300 billion. Chinese electronic commerce will be a growing part of world electronic commerce.

Singapore must move into this new world. This new frontier in cyberspace will also help us to achieve the objectives of the Speak Mandarin Campaign. Indeed, cyberspace will be an important new battleground for the Speak Mandarin Campaign.

## Chinese WebTop *Hua Zong Wang*

We are launching today an Internet platform called Chinese WebTop or Hua Zong Wang (华综网). It will provide users an easy and fun one-stop gateway to a rich collection of Internet resources in Chinese. Membership is free to all users who sign up at the website. Members will get a free Chinese starter CD kit comprising a suite of Internet browsers, plug-ins and a Chinese viewer with *hanyu pinyin* input. Users can also purchase very good pen and speech input tools at attractive prices.

Because of our bilingual policy, Singaporeans are in a good position to benefit from the knowledge and opportunities available in both the English and Chinese Internet. Computer penetration and computer literacy are also high in Singapore. We have excellent IT infrastructure. We should exploit all these advantages to establish a strong position in Chinese Internet. In Parliament earlier this year, I announced that MITA has set up a Chinese Internet Steering Committee to look into the promotion and development of the Chinese Internet. The Committee has since adopted the National Chinese Internet Programme which is driven by the Ministry of Information and the Arts (MITA), Singapore Broadcasting Association (SBA), National Computer Board (NCB) and the National Science and Technology Board (NSTB).

Under this Programme, we will establish a comprehensive infrastructure for the Chinese Internet in two years. Examples of specific projects include developing Chinese WebTop as a one-stop directory of local and foreign websites, marketing Chinese Internet kits to end-users at subsidised rates, and encouraging the development of Chinese Internet content by the public and private sectors.

A key area of emphasis is our schools. The Ministry of Education has embarked on several initiatives to promote the Internet, including the Chinese Internet. We have to train our teachers quickly and provide them with information on the Internet resources which are already available. We are also providing one computer for every two students from Primary One upwards. Every school will be connected to the Education Ministry's area network. The National Library Board will supplement these efforts. The next generation of Chinese students should be as comfortable in the Chinese Internet universe as they are in the English Internet universe.

## Conclusion

If we succeed in these efforts, Singapore will be a hub for the international media and for electronic commerce in both English and Chinese. The Speak Mandarin Campaign has come a long way since 1979. While the promotion of Mandarin has achieved certain results, we must now rise to the challenge of information technology. The success of the Speak Mandarin Campaign in cyberspace will consolidate and build on our earlier achievements. If we fail in cyberspace, our earlier achievements will also be affected. The key is the younger generation. For Chinese Singaporeans, Chinese culture and the Chinese language must be an organic part of their lives. To be effective, the next generation of Chinese intellectual and cultural elite workers must be proficient in information technology.

# PREPARING OURSELVES

*When an organisation is perfect, it soon becomes a fossil .... the performance of a creative minority can make an enormous difference to the fortunes of a people.*

## Voyage to a New World

Instead of talking about specific strategies and policies this morning, I thought that we should take a step back and ask ourselves what kind of voyage we are taking into the future. With typical modesty, Alan Greenspan said recently that the future is ultimately unknowable. The technological changes that are taking place make the future a great unknown. No one expected the Asian crisis to break out with such speed and ferocity. No one expected the recovery last year to be so rapid.

In many ways, the process of globalisation has only just started. When we celebrated the arrival of the new millennium 11 days ago, we did so with everyone else on earth. As the world turned, champagne bottles popped like sequential explosions beginning with New Zealand, spreading across Asia, Europe and America and ending with Hawaii. We have become one big inter-connected human family. Y2K marks the threshold to a new era.

Stock markets are at an all time high. Technology stocks have gone through the roof. There is the headiness of a gold rush. Paper is cheap, leading to a rush of mergers and acquisitions. It is fun while it lasts. When just adding dot-com to a company enhances its value by millions of dollars, it is time to worry. We must prepare ourselves

---

Speech at the Economic Development Board Society & Partners Millennium Conference, 11 January 2000.

for an uncertain future. First, we should organise ourselves for rapid change. Second, we should shape Singapore's culture to maximise our chances for the future. And third, we need entrepreneurs in the public, people and private sectors.

## Organising for Rapid Change

First, we must organise for rapid change. Rigid hierarchies are no longer possible. When an organisation is perfect, it soon becomes a fossil. Instead of well-defined lines of authority, we need a certain untidiness to facilitate change. Where we can make use of the market, we should. This means rewarding a person according to his worth and not according to his social position or connection. Whatever we do, we must make sure that we do not allow corruption in Singapore and other opportunities for rent-seeking behaviour.

To improve efficiency in the public sector, we have downsized and outsourced in some areas, corporatised and privatised in others. Finance Ministry and PSC have devolved many responsibilities to the ministries. Government ministries and statutory boards today have more power to deploy people and resources. For sectors like health and education, we cannot leave everything to the private sector. What we try to do instead is to create internal markets so that there is competitive pressure on schools and hospitals to perform. In the arts, the funding of arts groups is based less on patronage and more on audience preference. For example, our students receive money from the Tote Board and Edusave to spend on performances which they are interested in.

We should keep pushing in this direction and encourage organisations in the public and people sectors to be responsive to changing needs. Better to shake the box from time to time than be forced to burn the forest down. But, sometimes, controlled burning is necessary to clear the ground for new growth. For all sectors, while change is not a guarantee of success, not changing is a sure way to failure and extinction. Wherever possible, we should cushion the negative effects of change. The difference between welfare and welfarism is that while one facilitates change, the other obstructs it.

We must keep this distinction clear in our minds and in the policies we formulate.

## Shaping Our Culture

Culture operates at a deeper level than organisation and is more akin to the operating system of computer networks. Culture defines the manner in which human beings in a community — young and old, rich and poor, ordinary and exceptional — interact with one another. All cultural systems are complex and tenacious. When a cultural system is rigid, it is more difficult to bring about organisational change. In feudal China, the Confucianist value system created a fixed social hierarchy of scholars at the top and merchants at the bottom. This prevented China from exploiting the benefits of trade and new technology. The Chinese Revolution, starting with Taiping and ending with the Cultural Revolution, was the greatest revolution in human history. The twists and turns of that Revolution showed how difficult it has been to change the cultural operating system of the Chinese people. Some say that the Revolution is not yet over. The reason for the continuity of Chinese civilisation is its strong culture. Changing it requires a correspondingly extraordinary effort, the death of tens of millions of people, repeated social chaos and the impoverishment of many generations.

Singapore is a city-state. Our culture is an amalgamation of different cultures. Our racial and religious identities are stronger than our common Singapore identity. This is the reality we confront. But our weakness is also our strength. Because we are a young country, we have more control over the way Singapore culture is being shaped. In the same way that a certain amount of organisational untidiness facilitates change, Singapore's cultural untidiness also makes it easier for us to adapt to changing needs.

Singapore culture enables us to move flexibly in different directions depending on what the needs are. When we raise our children at home and in school, we should avoid over-specialisation and over-categorisation. To use a metaphor from biology, we should raise our young as stem cells and not as specialist cells. When a human egg is fertilised, the first cells are completely flexible. They have the potential to become the cell of any organ. In the course of the development of the foetus, specialisation takes place progressively. The faster specialisation takes place, the quicker the human life becomes an adult. Then ageing begins. Early life is characterised by the presence of a large number of stem cells. When surgery is done on the fetus, it leaves no scar.

When we look at the evolution of human culture, similar organic processes are involved. When conditions are uncertain, it is better to have more stem cells than to over-specialise. When conditions have settled down, specialisation becomes an advantage. Looking into the future, conditions are not likely to settle down for a long time because of rapid changes in technology. We should therefore keep our culture young and breed more stem cells in our society.

In practical terms, what it means is that as individuals, we should not bank on a single career path which may lead to a dead end. As parents, we should prepare our children for life and not for particular jobs. As teachers, we should educate our students for a range of possibilities. We should lay them a good foundation and teach them how to learn for themselves. As leaders, we should prepare our people for change both intellectually and emotionally. When we design policies, we should build into them portability and modularity so that we can restructure and reconfigure with less pain and friction. For example, it is important for us to restructure employee medical benefits so that a worker is free to move from one job to another. In many countries, welfare benefits hidebound public and private organisations preventing them from re-creating themselves.

Singapore culture should always rejoice in movement, mixing and diversity especially since the different ethnic and religious groups live cheek-by-jowl here. We should keep cross-cultural and cross-religious relationships soft and easy in Singapore. In this way, we retain our omni-directional capability. If it is in our interest to move closer to China, India or the West, we have the cultural capability to do so because the stem cells are in our body.

Also, without a cosmopolitan culture, we will not be able to bring in foreign talent freely. The Japanese suffer the weakness of their strength. Try as they might, it is very difficult for them to integrate foreigners deep into their midst. Theirs is a tidy culture.

## Entrepreneurship in the Public, People and Private Sectors

In an age of uncertainty, there is particular need for entrepreneurship in the public, people and private sectors. At a time when political correctness was not the fashion, Arnold Toynbee identified the crucial role of creative minorities in the creation of new civilisations. Whether you are building a great wall or a spaceship, most of the men and women involved are ordinary people. They are just doing a job often in a prescribed way. It falls on a tiny few to conceive the Great Wall of China and the Apollo space programme, and to bring about their realisation. For any major undertaking, a few people play a disproportionate role as strategic thinkers, as men of vision, as leaders and as risk-takers. It is not just a matter of IQ or EQ. It is also about vision, passion, courage and faith.

Take the founding of Singapore by Raffles as an example. Singapore was not a historical inevitability. During the Napoleanic War, Raffles was the Governor of Java. When the war was over, he felt strongly that Britain should not give up Java but could not persuade London because the deal had already been made in 1815 at Vienna. He then looked around for an alternative toehold in Southeast Asia. He considered Karimun but decided in favour of Singapore. The history of Singapore could have been very different. In the same way, one wonders whether the Third Reich would have been established in Germany without Adolf Hitler. Would there be Microsoft without Bill Gates?

Let us look at the situation in Singapore today. Whether we like it or not, our future will depend critically on a creative minority making important decisions which will decide our common fate. This creative minority will have to feel passionately for Singapore. They need not be born here but they must want to die here. I call them entrepreneurs because in times of rapid change, we need leaders who can spot new opportunities, mobilise the efforts of ordinary men and women, take risks and get us all to our destination.

We need entrepreneurs as much for the public and people sectors, as we do for the private sector. In this new world, the entrepreneurial skills needed to run GE (General Electrics) are not all that different from the skills needed to run a country, a city or a charitable foundation. How do we throw up the entrepreneurs? It is a question worth pondering over. No system throws up the right people automatically. In stable times, mature societies can afford bad leaders. At critical moments in history, and particularly for young countries, the performance of a creative minority can make an enormous difference to the fortunes of a people. This is a challenge to all of us who care for Singapore. Without a challenge keenly felt, the response may be lacking.

**Taking Bets**

When Chin Nam asked me to speak on the knowledge-based economy at this EDB Millennium Conference, I was reluctant to do so because so many speeches are being made on the same subject. MTI will be conducting its own corporate planning exercise next week and all the statutory boards will be involved. This is the reason I decided on a more reflective perspective. While external factors can be crucial, it is usually the internal factors which are decisive. We cannot predict the future with any accuracy but we can prepare ourselves for uncertainty. It is not difficult to take bets on Singapore for the next 5 to 10 years. Taking bets on Singapore for the next 50 to 100 years is still very much a gamble.

# GLOBAL CITY AND THE ARTS

*We can only be a global city if our environment is conducive for creative intellectual effort and that means an environment in which artists are well-regarded and their works appreciated.*

Having been involved with The Esplanade Project for many years, it is always a pleasure for me to view the progress of its construction every time I pass by. The arts centre has evolved from a concept to a physical structure. It will enrich our lives and help make Singapore a global arts city. Many Singaporeans and foreigners await with eager anticipation the opening of The Esplanade in October next year.

Why are the arts important to us? No one quite knows the reason. But they are an inseparable part of our being. I am told that between the genome of the human being and the genome of the chimpanzee, the difference is very slight, maybe 2% or 3%. In that 2% or 3% is the coding for the arts. The arts set us apart as a species and it should not be surprising that the greater the intellectual achievement of a society is, the greater too is its artistic accomplishment.

## Global City

In the knowledge economy, we need many talented individuals. We need world-class business facilities and an excellent IT infrastructure. But we also need the arts. We can only be a global city if our environment is conducive for creative intellectual effort and that means an environment in which artists are well-regarded and their works appreciated.

---

Speech at The Esplanade Topping-Out Ceremony, 26 February 2001.

In the US, Europe and Japan, cities compete to attract New Economy businesses by providing and marketing their cultural, artistic and theatrical facilities. Mr Dennis Gillings, CEO and Chairman of Quintiles Transnational, who is one of EDB's international advisers, said recently that "one thing Singapore could do to make itself a more attractive place to work and live in is by building a good cultural environment in terms of music, opera, arts, theatre, museums and ballet". Sony's Chairman Norio Ohga, another of our international advisers, has also been making the same point to us. The completion of The Esplanade will therefore be an important milestone in our development as a global city.

Esplanade — Theatres on the Bay will play a role beyond providing a physical facility for the arts. The quality, range and mix of its programmes will be very important. The Esplanade must attract both local and international artists, and interest both local and foreign audiences.

### Enriching Our Lives

Over time, the arts in Singapore will also help us develop our identity as a people. Paradoxically, our identity is defined by our universal character. We readily welcome newcomers into our ranks. We are multi-cultural into our very core, but still bound together by a deep respect for diversity. In Singapore, in everything we do, in every genre of the arts, we celebrate this diversity. Of course, diversity also gives rise to problems and these we have to manage well. For as long as Singapore is Singapore, debate over plays like *Talaq* will never cease. Be it theatre, dance, music, film, literature or the visual arts, our multi-cultural environment is both liberating and disciplining. This tension is part of what makes the arts in Singapore unique and special. It is what makes Singapore a microcosm of the world, a reflection of the universe in our little drop of dew. Thus, The Esplanade is conceived as a centre for all kinds of art forms, both Western and Eastern, and their occasional synthesis.

### A Long Journey

In the 1970s, the idea of an arts centre was first mooted to create a vibrant and a balanced Singapore society. In the masterplan, the best site by the Bay was reserved for it. In the 1980s, a political decision was taken to build the centre. In the 1990s, we started work. Mr Ong Teng Cheong, who was then Deputy Prime Minister, took the lead. By the time it is ready, the whole project would have taken a quarter-century from conception to delivery. Unlike some other cities, we did not rush the construction because we wanted to prepare ourselves for it, so that the software will match the hardware. Now that the structure of The Esplanade has reached its highest point physically, we are close to fulfilling our dream of a generation. But already we are dreaming other dreams for the future. I am honoured to be invited for this topping-out ceremony and would like to congratulate the Board and Management of The Esplanade and the many people who have helped to make this project a reality.

# HEROES

*They are ordinary individuals who, when confronted with difficult moral choices, make the right ones.*

On this Holy Saturday, we bid farewell to Eddie Barker.

When Deborah asked me to say a few words about Eddie Barker at the Service today, I felt both honoured and inadequate. I only joined politics after he had retired from it. Brandon and I were in SJI at about the same time; Eddie Barker was therefore of my father's generation.

Of course, I knew of him. His reputation preceded him and, at Cabinet meetings, Senior Minister Lee Kuan Yew would speak warmly of him, particularly of his role during Separation.

I got to know Eddie Barker through the Eurasian Association. With his consent, the Association had asked me to represent Eurasian interests in the Cabinet after Eddie stepped down, which I was happy to do. I was surpurised how approachable he was, a man totally without airs. He was forthright to the point of being blunt. He had strong views and made sure you knew of them. He enjoyed good company, good music and good food. If the devil's curry was not up to the mark, you will hear from him. Once, as I was sinking my teeth into a piece of sugi cake, he commented that it wasn't moist enough.

He was an ordinary human being, like most of us. But yet he played an extraordinary role in the history of modern Singapore. Asked to serve in 1963, he could not say no. That decision changed

---

Eulogy delivered at the funeral service for the late Eddie Barker, St. Andrew's Cathedral, 14 April 2001.

his life and that of his wife and his children. A voice inside him told him that to opt out then was wrong, maybe cowardly. Gloria went along not because she knew what the full consequences were, but because she loved and trusted him. Heroes are not born. They are ordinary individuals who, when confronted with difficult moral choices, make the right ones. In the language of Star Wars, they choose the bright side. Eddie Barker was one of them. By so doing, he became extraordinary and one of Singapore's Founding Fathers.

We are still too young as a nation to have our founding myths well etched in stone. One day we will, and Eddie Barker's contribution to the creation of modern Singapore will find its proper place. He drafted the Constitution of an independent and multiracial Singapore in August 1965, an act which cannot be repeated. It was fitting that it was not a Chinese or a Malay or an Indian who crafted the words, but a member of our smallest, the Eurasian community.

Tomorrow is Easter Sunday — celebrating the Resurrection of the Lord and the promise of our own resurrection. I can imagine Eddie Barker from up there telling us to cheer up. We remember him fondly.

# Tamils in Singapore

*The more we understand and enjoy diversity, the more we appreciate our common universality.*

When Professor Jayakumar asked if I could officiate at this Conference, I agreed with mixed feelings. I felt honoured to be invited but did not feel qualified to speak on "Tamil in an International Arena". When I learnt that my good friend, Palaniappan Chidambaram, would also be speaking at the same conference, I felt doubly honoured.

The Tamils are an ancient people with a profound sense of their own history, language, culture and architecture. The map of the Indian sub-continent over the centuries show that the empires of the Indo-Gangetic plain and the Deccan rarely extended beyond the Cauvery River, and never to Cape Comorin until the British came. The reason was not geography. There were no natural physical barriers separating Tamil Nadu from the North. What kept out conquerors was the strength of Tamil civilisation which resisted absorption even in the face of superior force.

Why the Tamil race is so talented is for others to explain. The fact that it is can be seen in the persistently disproportionate representation of Tamils in the top universities and the Indian Administrative and Foreign Services. Of the three ethnic Indian Nobel Prize winners in the sciences, two were Tamil. Without Tamil scientists, India might still not be a nuclear power today. I make this last point without value judgement, having read Chidambaram's

---

Opening speech at the International Conference on "Tamil in an International Arena", Centre for the Arts, National University of Singapore, 5 January 2002.

eloquent speech in the Indian Parliament opposing the testing of nuclear weapons by the Bharatiya Janata Party Government.

Despite the idea of one India, which arose out of the British Raj, the distinctiveness of Tamil culture persists. As with any strength, however, this is also a weakness. As a result, Chennai is less cosmopolitan compared to Bangalore and Hyderabad in the IT field. The further Indians are away from India, the more Indian they feel. Sub-group affiliations become less important even though they still exist. Among Tamils, the feeling is stronger. This is because of the strength of Tamil culture.

Thus, in the worldwide Indian diaspora, there exists a Tamil network within the larger network. In an age of economic globalisation, strong tribal networks perform an important economic role by reducing transaction risks. Ethnic business networks become the specialty of Indian groups like the Parsees, Jains, Sindhis and Marwaris, as also Chettiars, themselves a caste group within the Tamil community.

The globalisation of India was first brought about by the British. The Empire scattered Indian seeds in all the five continents, using English as the global language and observing Anglo-Saxon laws and accounting principles in business. In this present age of globalisation, that British inheritance has become a major advantage for Indians all over the world.

Under the British Raj, Singapore was really little more than an extension of India in Southeast Asia. Until 1867, the East India Company ran Singapore from Calcutta. Much of the legal and administrative tradition in Singapore today is derived from British India. Singapore as a city in the British Empire was an important node for the global Indian community operating within the framework of that Empire. Thus, supported by the Japanese, Subhas Chandra Bose established the Indian National Army in Singapore, and the site of his Memorial, which the Japanese built and the British destroyed, is marked across the Padang from the Supreme Court.

The first phase of Indian independence was intensely nationalistic, causing Singapore's links to India to weaken. Unlike India which had a large domestic market, independent Singapore had no choice but to globalise early. When PM Narasimha Rao embarked on the reform and opening up of the Indian economy in the early 1990s, Singapore became again a natural extension of the Indian economy. In 1991, Manmohan Singh as Finance Minister and Chidambaram as Commerce Minister marketed the new India to Singapore. We then decided, as a matter of policy, to position Singapore as India's long-term economic partner, really reclaiming an old role for ourselves. We took the opportunity to attract Indian talent to our shores, re-stocking the pond as it were, thereby strengthening the links between our two countries and Singapore's position as a 21st century Indian hub in the global Indian network.

Culturally, India's influence on Southeast Asia goes back to the earliest days. Much of that influence emanated from South India, the Tamil component being the most important. The ancient Tamil epic — *Manimekalai* — steeped in Hindu-Buddhist-Jain tradition, alluded to the close religious and cultural links between the Tamils of South India and the peoples of Southeast Asia over centuries. The early Sangam literature described the trade links between South India and Kadaaram on the Malay Peninsula, now called Kedah. I-Tsing, a Tang Dynasty Buddhist monk who spent much time studying Buddhism in Sumatra before going to India, reported regular sailings of ships between Kedah and Nagapattinam in Tamil Nadu.

In 1892, Eugen Hultzsch, a European scholar of Dravidian culture, deciphered part of a Tamil inscription found in Sumatra. This established that Tamil was used in Sumatran public documents in the 11th century. The date of the record, AD 1088, corresponded with the reign of the Chola Emperor Kulottunga I, whose long and prosperous rule lasted nearly half a century. Under his reign, the Chola Empire, which encompassed all of South India, extended its influence into large parts of Southeast Asia and conducted trade with Indo-China and China. A Chola fleet defeated Sri Vijaya in Sumatra.

Thus, Singaporeans and other Southeast Asians are more influenced by Tamil Nadu than many of us realise. In Chinese, there is a saying that when you drink water, please remember the source. Unfortunately, when Singaporeans enjoy their fish-head curry, they don't often have time to recall its origin. Happily, economic globalisation is re-establishing the old links and giving it new relevance.

This excellent initiative by the NUS Centre for the Arts under Edwin Thumboo's leadership expresses this new beginning. While it is the new globalisation which is driving all such activities today, economics alone cannot sustain it. We must explore the other dimensions and celebrate them. It is right that Singapore should be an important centre of Indian, and specifically Tamil, economic and cultural activities, because that is a position given to us by history. We are proud of the fact that Tamil is one of our official languages and that it is used on all our coins and banknotes. The more we understand and enjoy diversity, the more we appreciate our common universality. As is written in the *Thirukkural*: To discern the truth in everything, by whomsoever spoken, this is wisdom.

I congratulate the NUS Centre for the Arts and all the Tamil organisations which organised this conference; I thank the speakers for coming here to share their thoughts and insights, especially those who have come from afar; and I wish everyone here an enriching experience.

# TRIBUTE TO BROTHER JOSEPH MCNALLY

*We must give thanks.*

This morning, we unveil one of Brother Joe's own sculptures near where he was born at Ballintubber. We chose this particular piece in Brother's memory because Brother saw himself, first and foremost, as an educator. He educated generations of young men in both Singapore and Malaysia, including many who now hold senior positions in the public and private sectors.

After his retirement in 1982, Brother threw himself to the development of arts education in Singapore. He also found time to create works of art himself. LaSalle-SIA College of the Arts which he founded will be moving into a beautiful city campus in two years' time.

Throughout his life, Brother Joe promoted inter-religious understanding. Singapore and Malaysia are both multiracial and multireligious countries. Among Brother's students were many who were not Catholics. Later in his life, Brother became a leader in Singapore's Inter-Religious Organisation. When he left us two years ago, he was mourned by Singaporeans and Malaysians of all races and religions.

We erect this sculpture to remember an Irishman who contributed so much to our lives in Singapore. He left at the age of 22 to a far-off land and work among a people with whom he had no links. But, like

---

Speech presented at the unveiling of "Counsellor II" in honour of Brother Joseph McNally on 20 September 2004 at the Irish National Museum of Country Life at Castlebar, County Mayo.

so many Irish brothers and sisters, he was doing God's work and, in God's eyes, we are all brothers and sisters.

In expressing our gratitude to Brother Joe, we also thank all the brothers and nuns who dedicated their lives to the education of the young in Singapore. By their lifework, they have helped transform us from a Third World to a First World country.

We thank the Irish people for the gift of these remarkable and wonderful individuals.

Monuments are built for the living, not the dead who have no need for them. For us in Singapore, we undertake this labour of love to remind ourselves of the values which Brother Joe imparted to us, that we should never live only for ourselves, that we share a common humanity, that we must rejoice in the gift of life and in life's gifts, including the arts which are an expression of the Spirit, that we must give thanks, and love.

What Brother has done will nourish the relationship between Ireland and Singapore. He described himself as both an Irishman and a Singaporean. He was always conscious of his Celtic inheritance and proud of the contributions that his race has made to the world. He also became a proud Singaporean and always pushed us to be better than ourselves. He has left behind a legacy and a relationship which will grow and flourish. Just as Brother Joe had made Singapore his home away from home, we hope that many Irish men and women will treat Singapore in the same way, as your outpost in an Asia which is becoming more important economically. As you have us in your hearts, so too we have you in our hearts.

We thank the Department of Foreign Affairs, the Office of Public Works and the Irish National Museum of Country Life for making this undertaking possible.

# Celebrating Our Diversity

*It is only because we are many that we are one.*

## A New Divide

A few weeks ago, a young Muslim lawyer in Singapore told me about a recent experience he had in an East Asian city. Unlike others carrying Singapore passports clearing immigration, he was told to stand aside. When he asked for the reason, the immigration officer muttered that there were too many 'Mohamads' that day. Smiling to himself, the Singaporean waited patiently and peered around wondering how long he had to wait. The officer then warned him in a stern manner to stay still. He suddenly felt a chill running down his spine.

Muslims all over the world are being profiled by security agencies. Since September 11, Muslims travelling to western countries have been subject to all manner of interrogation and searches. Although the profiling is now done more subtly, it continues. What is interesting is that, because of the fear of international terrorism, profiling is increasingly being done in East Asia as well.

It is not realistic to stop security agencies from profiling potential threats. It is their job to narrow the scope of surveillance by concentrating on groups from which the threats are more likely to emerge. However, profiling all Muslims in such a crude way is bound to lead to anger and resentment.

---

Speech presented at the 60th Session of the United Nations General Assembly, New York, 22 September 2005.

When sudden threats appear, however, it is perhaps natural to expect a certain over-reaction from affected communities. After Pearl Harbour, all Japanese living in America became suspect, including those born there. Many were interned. Lives and businesses painstakingly built up over the years were wrecked. By today's standards, this was an affront but, at that time, it was widely felt to be a necessary precaution. Shocked by this reaction, Japanese-American leaders set out to prove their Americanness, for example, by forming the Japanese-American 100th Infantry Battalion which fought heroically in the European theatre. As a result of the Second World War, the Japanese-American community became much more a part of American society. This was only possible because, on the one hand, there was a political will to integrate and, on the other, a willingness by the majority to accept them and, later, to recognise that it had done wrong to that community. Integration does not mean assimilation. Japanese-Americans like other hyphenated Americans remain highly conscious of their ethnic identity in American society.

The travails of the Japanese Americans were not unique. Tribalism is a basic human instinct. We may proclaim that all men are brothers but we reflexively distinguish degrees of closeness. Divisions of race, language, culture and religion run deep in human society and surface under stress. The western ascendancy in the last few centuries created tremendous stresses in non-western communities giving rise to a variety of responses, all of which sought to reconcile each community's own sense of self with the needs of a western-defined modernity. In Asia, for example, the re-emergence of China and India on the global stage has been a prolonged struggle of reconciling transformation with tradition.

This is the broader historical framework against which the relationship between Muslims and non-Muslims in the world must be viewed today. With globalisation and the end of the Cold War, the challenge in this relationship has become more urgent and complex. It will be one of the major global themes of this century. And, whether we like it or not, maintaining a harmonious relationship between Muslims and non-Muslims is an important part of our struggle against international terrorism, a subject which concerns us all deeply in the United Nations.

There are two evolving developments which feed on each other. One is the change within Islam itself; the other is the relationship between Muslims and non-Muslims in different parts of the world. Both require our close attention.

## Within Islam

The response of the Islamic world to the challenge of modernisation will affect the development of the entire world in this century. In some ways, it is comparable to that of the Chinese response to modernisation and would probably take a much longer time. The decline of the Ottoman Empire in the 19th century took place around the same time as the decline of the Qing Dynasty in China. Both collapsed at the beginning of the last century. After many twists and turns, China has finally re-emerged onto the global stage with a bright future ahead of it. In the process, Chinese culture has gone through a profound transformation one of the most important aspects of which is a complete change in the status of women.

There are about as many Muslims in the world as Chinese. In contrast to China, however, the Islamic world is unlikely to re-coalesce in the foreseeable future. Once Ataturk refused the caliphate and, with iron determination, started reforming Turkish institutions on the western model, the Islamic world lost its centre. From then on, different Islamic societies experimented with different approaches and moved in different directions. It has been a mixed story. Turkey today is determined to join the EU. In the Arab world, there is a diversity of political and economic models from monarchies to secular governments. Socialism has been a disappointment while western democracy is viewed with skepticism. In Iran, following the Islamic Revolution in 1979, a system combining theocracy with democracy is still evolving to meet the needs of both the modern economy and the aspirations of a younger generation born after the Revolution. In Southeast Asia, Malaysia and Indonesia offer yet another way into the future. Malaysia's Prime Minister Abdullah Badawi's idea of Islam Hadhari or Civilisational Islam sees the values of Islam as being consistent with the needs of a democratic, knowledge-based, multi-racial and multi-religious society. In Indonesia, President Susilo

Bambang Yudhoyono, the first directly and democratically elected President of the Republic, has reaffirmed his government's commitment to *Pancasila*, the founding philosophy of the republic which gave all religions an equal official status.

The different responses of Muslim societies to the challenge of modernisation are accompanied by a great ideological debate among political and religious leaders. Good governance has become a major issue with calls for greater transparency and more democracy. Widespread corruption has engendered mass revulsion. While Western ideas of women's liberation may never be accepted, the status of women is growing in importance. The end of the Cold War has intensified the debate. While celebrating the collapse of the Soviet Union as a victory against atheism, the triumph of the United States as the world's only superpower was viewed with mixed feelings.

In this debate, it is natural that some groups should look back to a romanticized period when the Islamic world was united and pristine, and seek its re-establishment in the 21st century. Such were the ideas of the Ikhwan Muslimin or the Islamic Brotherhood which emanated from Egypt at the beginning of the 20th century. The ideology of that movement continues to inspire Islamic groups in various parts of the world today. If only Muslims were to abide strictly by the teachings of Islam, there would be no corruption, governments would be just and effective, and Islamic societies would become strong again. In many Islamic countries at various times, these groups have been suppressed for being subversive. Those who funded them were thought to have ulterior motives. The struggle for the soul of Islam is ongoing.

However, it is not a struggle unique to Islam. For two hundred years, Europe was bloodied by religious wars which ended only with the Treaty of Westphalia in 1648 which created the system of modern European states. Even then, there was still religious persecution which led many Europeans to flee to the New World. In the last century, the soul of Europe was torn by communism, fascism and anti-semitism. It was precisely to overcome those divisions that the European Union was established, by stages, creating the longest period of peace on that continent. Even today in the 21st century, we hear echoes of old debates in the western world, now expressed in emotionally fraught arguments over abortion, evolution and gender equality.

How Islamic society evolves in the coming decades is mainly for Muslims to decide. Generally speaking, non-Muslims would have no standing to participate in this debate but for two factors which have become critical and which will have strategic consequences affecting us all.

The first factor is the emergence of the ideology of al-Qaeda and its sister organisations like the Jemaah Islamiyah. This ideology is a malignant mutation of the ideas associated with the Muslim Brotherhood and other groups that argued for a return of Islamic society to an idealised past. It takes those ideas to an extreme and preaches hatred against non-Muslims worldwide justifying violence against innocent bystanders even if they are Muslims. The suicide bomber has become a potent weapon in its armoury. The followers of this ideology will not hesitate to use weapons of mass destruction if they can get their hands on them. We have a duty in the UN to join in the global war against them.

The second factor necessitating the involvement of non-Muslims in the Islamic debate is the growing Muslim diaspora in many non-Islamic countries. As minority communities, Muslims living in countries like France and Germany, for example, have to accept certain limitations in the practice of their religion. With growing religiosity in recent years, issues like the wearing of the headscarf have surfaced. What constitutes a reasonable compromise varies from country to country. For example, Singapore allows aspects of shariah law to apply to Muslims, including Muslim men being allowed four wives, although only under stringent conditions. It would be hard for non-Muslims to accept this in Europe.

The fact is, while some human values are universal, many are not. We have to accept this diversity in the world. A greater tolerance of diversity in the world would create better conditions for peaceful cooperation between Muslims and non-Muslims and influence the debate within Islam itself.

### Muslims vs. Non-Muslims

If non-Muslims tar all Muslims with the brush of terrorism and majority non-Muslim communities treat minority Muslim communities as problem communities, the future will be bleak for all of us. In such a climate, Muslim extremists will gain ascendancy and the terrorists will find fertile ground for recruitment everywhere.

It is ridiculous to argue that terrorism is inherent in Islam. To do so is to play into the hands of the terrorists. That such views are increasingly being expressed in reputable journals and newspapers is troubling. Of course one could find blood-curdling passages in the Koran and the Hadith but these passages must be seen in context. We find similar passages too in the Old Testament. As we would not therefore argue that terrorism is inherent in Judaism and Christianity, so we should not make Islam the problem. That would be a big mistake. There were periods in history when Islamic society was considerably more advanced than Western society.

Equally, it would be a big mistake for Muslim leaders to allow Muslim extremists to make claims on behalf of Muslims worldwide without contest. This causes non-Muslims to suspect that all Muslims are in sympathy with them. To be sure, there are genuine grievances which have to be addressed like Palestine, Chechnya and the future of Iraq, but these are issues which are really more political than religious. The strategy of the extremists is to polarize Muslims and non-Muslims worldwide thereby widening their base of support. Muslim leaders have to counter this strategy. It is also essential for them to reach out to non-Muslim audiences as well. The recent bombings in London unleashed a strong anti-Muslim backlash at the grassroots which threatened the fabric of British society. This put pressure on Muslim leaders in the UK to condemn the terrorists in clear terms. Muslim leaders in Australia took an even stronger position recently. Grand Imam Sheikh Tantawi of Al-Azhar said: "Those responsible for (the) London attacks are criminals who do not represent Islam or even truly understand (its message)". In the end, the fight against the terrorists has to be won within Muslim communities themselves. It is a battle for hearts and minds which require Muslims to work together with non-Muslims against a common enemy.

There is no hierarchy in Islam and no unified position on many issues. Islamic religious leaders are allowed to issue their own *fatwas*. It is not uncommon for *fatwas* to contradict one another. To prevent extremists from exploiting these differences of religious interpretation, Islamic leaders from all the major schools met in Amman in July this year at an International Islamic Conference. It was an important meeting which clarified the mainstream position of the religion. All eight schools of Islam — the four Sunni traditions (Hanbali, Hanafi, Maliki, Shafi'i), the two main branches of the Shi'i (Ja'fari, Zaydi), and the Ibadhis and Thahiris — were represented. Without this clarification, the war against terrorism would be much harder to fight.

With the removal of Saddam Hussein, the relationship between Sunni Islam and Shi'i Islam in the Arab world has entered a new phase. If the Islamic world is sharply divided between Sunni and Shi'i, the political problems of the Middle East would become much harder to solve. A new round of conflict will result with consequences for all of us, starting with civil war in Iraq.

## We Are One Because We Are Many

We have to make a concerted effort to understand each other better. The spotlight today is on the relationship between Islam and the West which has been a difficult one over the centuries. In fact, the historical relationship between Muslims and non-Muslims has been different in different parts of the world. Islam's historical relationships with China, with Hindus in South Asia and with non-Muslims in Southeast Asia have been quite different. We have to learn from each other's experiences. With globalisation making this a much smaller world, and the mass movement of peoples mixing populations to an extent never seen before, all societies have become multi-racial and multi-religious to a greater or lesser degree. The pluralism we hold as an ideal in the UN is not a choice; it is a necessity. And it cannot be based on tolerance alone. It has also to be based on mutual understanding and respect.

At the proposal of Iran, the 53rd UNGA declared in 1998 that 2001 would be the 'United Nations Year of Dialogue among Civilisations'. In 2001 the 56th UNGA adopted a 'Global Agenda for Dialogue among Civilisations', described as a "process between and within civilisations, founded on inclusion, and a collective desire to learn, uncover and examine assumptions, unfold shared meaning and core values and integrate multiple perspectives through dialogue".

This year, the UN sponsored numerous meetings on interfaith dialogues. On 14 July this year, Secretary-General Kofi Annan launched the 'Alliance of Civilisations'. This initiative, sponsored by Turkey and Spain, is intended as a "coalition against extremists in all societies, as a movement to advance mutual respect for religious beliefs and traditions, as well as to reaffirm humankind's increasing interdependence in all aspects of life".

We need to translate these declarations of principle into everyday language and into practice. Are there limits to what politicians can say to win votes? Are religious leaders allowed to preach hatred in places of worship? Do we wish violence on those whom we disagree with? What do we teach our children in school? What does all this mean to the immigration officer in the airport or the waiter in a restaurant?

Singapore as a cosmopolitan city-state with a multi-racial and multi-religious population is particularly vulnerable. We have experienced ugly racial riots before and learnt that racial and religious harmony should never be taken for granted. It has been necessary for the Government to involve itself in many aspects of ordinary life including discouraging Christian missionaries from targeting the conversion of Muslims, stopping mosques from sharply turning up the volume of their loudspeakers when calling the faithful to prayer, limiting the size of joss sticks which Buddhists and Taoists burn for their rituals and arresting those who incite racial and religious hatred. We get criticized by some of our friends for being illiberal but there is no doubt that the overwhelming majority of Singaporeans supports the Government's policy on such matters. What may appear to be a small thing to one community can be a serious provocation to another.

Recently, my wife and I had the great pleasure of hosting an orthodox Jewish couple to a dinner in Singapore. Not knowing the detailed requirements of kashrut, I thought that the safest course of action for me was to serve him a Buddhist vegetarian meal. A Muslim meets his halal requirements when he eats kosher (except alcohol) but not vice versa. Both are safe eating Hindu or Buddhist vegetarian food. But some Buddhist vegetarians would be uncomfortable with the onion and garlic in Hindu vegetarian food. Since not all of us desire to be Buddhist, and Buddhism is probably the least proselytising of all religions, it is just as well that we have different restaurants catering to different religious requirements.

This has become the world we live in. We cannot ignore the diversity around us in our everyday life and the tribalism which is in our nature. We will continue to disagree on many things like the nature of democracy, gender relationships, the death penalty, stem cell research and what we can or cannot eat. The moment we dismiss these differences as unimportant, or lightly condemn those who disagree with us to be in error, the trouble begins.

Therefore, as we strive to achieve the Millennium Goals in the UN — and they are worthy goals — a key task for us is to accept, even celebrate, the differences that divide us in our daily lives. To paraphrase Pope John Paul II, it is only because we are many that we are one, and the UN expresses that ideal.

# Asian Renaissance

*As Asia re-emerges on the world stage in this century Asians will look back to their own past and derive inspiration from it for the future.*

## The Asian Renaissance

Today's symposium is about the past and the future. It is a celebration of the Buddhist heritage that has contributed so much to the cultures of Asia. This is not a symposium about the Buddhist religion as such, but about Buddhist values and philosophy which have become an integral part of East Asian civilisation. Whether consciously or not, Buddhist values and philosophy influence the daily actions of hundreds of millions of East Asians, helping to shape a persistent pattern of social interactions which makes East Asia an identifiable civilisational area.

Let me, for clarity, confine East Asia to the chopsticks people — the Chinese, Japanese, Koreans and Vietnamese. I will talk about the influence of Buddhism on the rest of Southeast Asia later.

Three great value systems undergird East Asian civilisations — Confucianism, Taoism and Mahayana Buddhism. Confucius and Lao Zi lived at about the same time as the Buddha. Both Confucianism and Taoism were adopted very early by Korea and the Taoist *yin-yang* symbol is at the centre of the South Korean state flag. During the Nara and Heian Periods, Confucianism from China took hold

---

Speech at the Nalanda Buddhist Symposium, 13 November 2006. This symposium set the stage for the eventual revival of Nalanda as a modern, secular, postgraduate university near the site of the old. The President of India, Abdul Kalam, participated in the symposium by video-conference.

in Japan and its influence is still evident in Japanese society today. Mahayana Buddhism reached China about 2,000 years ago but did not become widespread until it was thoroughly Sinicised, a process which took many centuries. Buddhism had first to become Chinese in its grammar, invocations and iconography. From China, the different Buddhist sects spread to Korea and Japan with relative ease. Chan Buddhism (禅宗佛教) and Taoism melded in China, and it was that evolved form of Chan that became popular in Japan, giving Japanese Zen Buddhism its present character. Thus one could say that Taoism reached Japan through Chan Buddhism.

I am painting in very broad strokes and you could rightly criticise me on the details. But in the same way as one could identify the origins of Western civilisation in Greece, Rome and Judeo-Christianity, so too one could trace the origins of East Asian civilisation to the influence of Confucianism, Taoism and Mahayana Buddhism.

As Asia re-emerges on the world stage in this century, its civilisational origins will become a subject of intense study and debate. Asians will look back to their own past and derive inspiration from it for the future. This inspiration will cover the entire spectrum including governance, scientific inquiry, architecture and aesthetics. A tremendous burst of creative adaptation is becoming evident across much of Asia. The Western world went through a similar phase as it emerged out of the medieval ages. Hence the word "renaissance" has come to be applied to Asia's re-emergence today. Just as Europe's past was partly retrieved through the Arab vehicle — for it was the Arabs who were fascinated by the civilisation of the ancient Greeks and had its works translated into Arabic when Western Europe was still in the Dark Ages — Asia's past has been partly retrieved through the Western vehicle. Without the massive contribution of Western scholars, our knowledge of our own past in Asia would be much poorer today. I include here Alexander Cunningham's identification of Nalanda from an English translation of Xuan Zang's record of his journey to the West and Joseph Needham's encyclopaedic study of science and civilisation in China. I say this only to remind ourselves that we stand on the shoulders of others.

## The Buddhist Heritage

The recovery and celebration of our Buddhist heritage is an important part of the Asian renaissance. The revival of Mahayana Buddhism in East Asia is a big phenomenon. With the end of ideology, religion has become more important, most recently in China and Vietnam. I don't have the statistics but it is clear to the casual visitor that Buddhist temples are once again flourishing in both these countries and quite a number of young people are becoming monks and nuns.

Buddhist pilgrimages are growing in popularity and proceeding farther and farther afield. The interest in visiting the holy sites in India is bound to see a sharp increase in the coming years. This is a huge opportunity for Indian tourism which calls for the Central and State Governments to put in much more effort. But, much more than tourism, renewed interest in a pan-Asian Buddhist heritage will facilitate the re-encounter of the two great civilisational areas of East and South Asia.

At a seminar on South Asia's contribution to the global community last week, I mentioned that it is much easier to talk about the Buddhist heritage than to discuss the interactions of Judaism, Christianity and Islam. In the case of the religions derived from Abraham, there is too much politics and pain associated with those interactions. In the case of Buddhism, however, after the bloodbath in Kalinga which shocked Ashoka and set him off on a different path, the message is generally one of peace, compassion and acceptance. Buddhism teaches us that nothing is permanent. This reminds us not to be arrogant. Buddhism teaches us that every action has consequences. This reminds us to be good. The deep humanism in Buddhism is a value we need more than ever in a shrinking world where no religion, no ethnic group is in a majority.

## Southeast Asia

In between East and South Asia is Southeast Asia where all the world's great religions and cultures meet and co-exist. If we are not able to live with people who profess different faiths or who are different from us, there can be no peace or development. Over the centuries, there has evolved in Southeast Asian cultures a softness which enables us to co-habitate. That softness has its roots in the Hinduism and Buddhism which came to our shores more than a thousand years ago. Many of the great monks like Fa Xian and Yi Jing who travelled between South and East Asia spent time in Southeast Asia especially in Sriwijaya, Sumatra. Syncretism is a way of life in Southeast Asia. Here in Singapore, it is not uncommon to find mosques, temples and churches operating side by side, cheek by jowl. Are there problems? Yes, of course, every day! But we have learnt how to overcome them, by being fair to one another, by a spirit of give and take, by learning from our mistakes, and by religious and community leaders playing their roles.

Buddhism came to Southeast Asia from different directions. From the earliest days, it travelled over land and along the coast to Myanmar, Thailand and Indo-China. By sea, it crossed the Bay of Bengal to Sumatra, Java and the Malay Peninsula. The first influence was Mahayana Buddhism together with Hinduism. Later, via Sri Lanka, Theravada Buddhism became dominant in Mainland Southeast Asia except Vietnam which received its Buddhism from China, and remains Mahayana to this day, as is also the case with many of the ethnic Chinese who are scattered throughout Southeast Asia. In recent years, with globalisation, other Buddhist groups have established themselves in the region including Soka from Japan and Tantric Buddhism from the Himalayas. We have in Singapore today quite a diverse mix of the different Buddhist schools.

## Islam and the West

In addition to the Buddhist heritage, the Islamic heritage and the Western heritage are also important unifying elements in Asia. Unlike Islam's historical contact with the West which was usually unhappy, Islam's arrival in Southeast Asia was very different. It brought hygiene and a system of trust which facilitated trade. For centuries, the maritime silk route from the Mediterranean to China was dominated by Muslim traders. The Ottoman influence among Muslims in Southeast Asia was profound. The *songkok* which Southeast Asian Muslims wear is a relic of that influence. It was not only from the Middle East and India that Islam came to Southeast Asia. It was also from China. The great fleets from Ming China that sailed to Southeast Asia and the Indian Ocean 600 years ago were commanded by Muslim Admirals, the most famous being, of course, Zheng He. The Islamic heritage is therefore another theme in the Asian renaissance which should one day be taken up. We should not only be preoccupied with the dangers of Jihadist extremism.

The Asian renaissance is also incomprehensible without taking into account the Western influence of the last 500 years. Although the Western dominance has receded, its impact on every aspect of life in Asia is obvious and enduring. Any honest treatment of the Asian revival must acknowledge the many positive contributions of the West including the ideas of democracy, socialism and individual rights. The Christian influence in Asia is pervasive. Without Christian missionaries dedicating their lives to the education of millions of Asians, Asia's modernisation would have taken much longer to happen.

**South Asia and the Meaning of Nalanda**

Whether we are talking about the Hindu, Buddhist, Islamic or Western influence, South Asia played a major role as a source and as a conduit.

The Nalanda project should therefore not be about Buddhism only although Buddhism is a big part of it. For hundreds of years, the great university in Nalanda was a centre of learning for a wide range of subjects including philosophy, science and mathematics. We should develop Nalanda as an icon of the Asian renaissance attracting scholars and students from a much wider region as the ancient university once did. It should be a centre of civilisational dialogue and inter-faith understanding as it once was. In this way, the Nalanda project is not only a celebration of the past but also an inspiration for the future of Asia and the world.

We are very honoured to have joining us at this Symposium by video-conference, the President of India, Shri Abdul Kalam. When I called on him during his official visit to Singapore earlier this year, we discussed Nalanda and I knew then that this is a subject dear to his heart. A Muslim, a nuclear scientist, a great humanist, a devoted teacher, the President of India, with a deep passion in the Nalanda project — we could not have a person more fitting to deliver the keynote address. President Kalam, Sir, we thank you for joining us in our discourse.

# LEGACY OF A SHIPWRECK

*Every salvage should be done carefully because the value is not in the pieces but in the context...*

Dear friends, and I see so many here, ladies and gentlemen

Many Chinese believe that if it is intended that you should own something, then you will eventually own it. But if it is not intended that you should own it, then however hard you try, you will never achieve it. Looking back, maybe it is intended that Singapore should own the Tang cargo. Not as a material possession, but as a responsibility.

**How It All Began**

About eight to nine years ago, a young German salvager Nicolai Baron von Uexkull wrote me a letter. I was at that time the Minister for Trade and Industry. I looked at it; its contents did not seem relevant to me, and it went into the out tray. But my curiosity was pricked and I pulled back the letter to read it again.

He made two arguments that arrested my attention. One, he said that this is a very important wreck, and that it should not be

---

Edited transcript of casual opening remarks at the launch of "Shipwrecked — Tang Treasures and Monsoon Winds" at the Marina Bay Sands ArtScience Museum, 18 February 2011.

*Note*: The *Shipwrecked* exhibition relates the story of an astonishing cargo of some 60,000 objects carried from China by a ninth-century Arab dhow, presenting a dynamic tale of trade between China and West Asia along the maritime silk route. The cargo had lain undisturbed on the ocean floor for more than 1,000 years before its discovery near Indonesia's Belitung Island in 1998.

broken up. And two, Singapore is a natural home for the collection. I thought, well, maybe he's right. At that time we were working on several free trade agreements. I reflected that this Tang cargo is about free trade in an earlier era of globalisation. In fact, it was a glorious era — of the Tang, the Abbasid, Sriwijaya, and Nalanda.

I asked to see Nicolai. He dropped by my office with pictures of the wreck and cargo. I leafed through them and asked "Okay, how much?" He gave me some fantastic number. I said I didn't have the money. Because I was Minister for Information and the Arts for many years, I knew how difficult it was to get money. We never had enough to build museums or galleries, let alone to acquire things. Maybe tourism could provide a peg, because we have got to spend money in order to draw visitors in.

I passed the idea on to Sentosa, which had small reserves, and to the Singapore Tourism Board, which also had some reserves. Sentosa had a maritime museum, but it was not successful. It had to be either closed down or refurbished, and we needed interesting objects. Anyway I left the matter because I knew it was going to be a long shot.

One day, Ong Beng Seng dropped by my office to discuss some matters. When he told me that he invested in wrecks, I asked him if he had heard of this particular wreck. He said no. I showed him the pictures and asked if he could help find me a donor. And he did!

At that time the Khoo family was establishing a foundation and looking for a worthy cause to support. They were prepared to stump up half the money. The Singapore Tourism Board could provide the other half from its reserves, and maybe Sentosa could house the trove temporarily. I did not go to the museums, because I knew they could not bear this burden. Not yet. But they would eventually, because the natural home for this collection is in the museums.

### Where Was the Ship Heading To?

Just researching into the objects, the ship, the construction of the ship, the economy of the day, would take years, even decades of research. Even now, after almost 10 years, we still understand so little.

"Where was the ship headed to?" At that time, Southeast Asia was Buddhist and Hindu, but many of the pieces had Islamic motifs and probably intended for the Middle East.

"From where did the ship originate? And who were the risk takers?" We know that onboard, there were instruments of a Chinese scribe — brushes, ink stones, ink. We also know that at that time, the Abbasids having defeated the Tang army in Talas, had acquired papermaking technology from the Chinese. This led to a renaissance in the Islamic world which eventually seeped into Europe. But that's a story for another exhibition.

## Singapore's Collection

Anyway, one of the last things I did before I left the Ministry of Trade and Industry for the Ministry of Foreign Affairs, was to sign off a little deal that we made with the salvage company. They had run short of cash. They said: "Look, we agree to certain terms and you lend us a million bucks, secured against the core items of the collection." I could not pass this on to my successor, because he would be new to the job. He would have many things to worry about, and this would be right at the bottom of his stack. So I signed and scooted off to the Ministry of Foreign Affairs.

A while later, I was told we got the price down to an amount which was not unreasonable. It is quite a collection and I knew it would be a long time before we could display it adequately.

## The Gift

As chance would have it, I was making a bilateral visit to Oman. In Muscat, the Deputy Foreign Minister who accompanied me pointed out the Sinbad ship that they had built a few years earlier, placed at a road intersection. I said: "You know, we have this Tang cargo. Can you build a replica of the ship for us? The wreck is still intact, in shallow waters. We could do some research, and maybe you could build it for us." I didn't have the money, but I thought there was no harm asking. It was just important file knowledge. And he said: "Yeah, I'm sure we can do it."

A few months later, he wrote to say that Sultan Qaboos would get Oman to build the ship and sail it to Singapore as a gift. I could hardly believe what I read. Building the ship was itself a big story. From the pieces on the seabed, experts reconstructed the design of the ship. DNA testing showed that, except for the teak wood which came from the Malabar coast, the rest of the wood came from Africa. When they studied the stitching pattern, they discovered that it was the same square pattern still used for stitching dhows in Sohar today. "Bingo!", I thought. The dhow must have been built on the Omani coast.

## The Real Value of a Shipwreck

Dhow construction in the Arabian Sea goes back a very long time. The Apostle Thomas went to India as we all know. He went there because there was a Jewish community thriving on the Malabar coast. Around that time, there was in Yemen a great Arab civilization centred on the Marib dam. That dam finally burst in the 6th century opening a new chapter in Arab history. The seaborne traffic which connected the Red Sea and the Persian Gulf to India, Southeast Asia and China has a history of at least two thousand years, probably much more.

Southeast Asia is in between the great civilisations of East Asia and South and West Asia. These civilisations were centred on the great floodplains of China, India, Mesopotamia and Egypt. They had complex division of labour and hierarchies, and were bound by religious rituals. They were also major economies which traded. They traded over land, mostly borne by camels, and also by sea, much more by sea because boats could carry much more than camels. In those days, the sea was the Internet. Once you reached the sea, you could potentially connect to the far shores. That connection by water created a coastal civilisation.

The wreck and its cargo give us a sense of what the world was like more than a thousand years ago. With modern technology, our ability to map the ocean floor improves hugely. Wrecks and their cargos are important research materials for history. They must be respected, researched into, conserved, as if they are like imperial tombs in China, India, the Middle East and Egypt. There should be international laws governing salvage of ancient wrecks. Every salvage should be done carefully because the value is not in the individual pieces but in the context. Through the context, we recover the history of past eras. And understand more about ourselves.

## Singapore: Between Two Oceans

Thus I say Singapore owning the Tang cargo is perhaps not an accident. We are in between the two oceans. We are where the trade winds turn. And all ships from the beginning of time have had to pass through this southern corner of the Eurasian landmass. Here they came, and here they waited till the winds changed direction, before sailing in the other direction. It has always been a dangerous journey in the past.

When the Jewel of Muscat left Muscat in February last year, it had no escort; it had no refrigerators, no electricity. It was a dangerous journey. That morning, when I received news that it had launched off, I suddenly felt a chill down my spine. I thought: "What if that dhow were to sink? And lives were lost?" This would be no small matter. We had taken some precautions, but there were cost constraints. The Indian Navy provided some surveillance for a stretch of the journey, but there was no escort ship.

They arrived safely in Cochin. Then to Sri Lanka where they found the main masts cracked. They had to scurry into the forest to find two tall teak trees, chopped them down and built new masts. And then they sailed across the Bay of Bengal, where they came quite close to a hurricane and almost sank. The crew told me how much they prayed for safety.

When they arrived in Penang, I felt a great flood of relief because down the Straits of Malacca, it ought to be quite safe. And so it arrived, in July. Then I thought, when we had that wonderful celebration at Empress Place; "Why don't we sail the dhow to China?" At which point I was shot down by everybody.

## Links Between the Past and the Future

If you think about it, in those days when a ship launched off, whether it was a Bugis *perahu*, a Chinese ship or an Arab dhow, the chances of it returning were not high. Because of that, the coastal communities which produced the sailors had elaborate rituals for seafarers. They learned to give thanks. When sailors arrived home safely, there was a way to welcome them and to honour them. A little ceremony like that was organised when the Jewel of Muscat arrived in Singapore. We were so happy too, that the captain's own son was flown to Singapore without the father knowing until he arrived. He had such an emotional reunion with his father.

A project like this has linked, or rather relinked Singapore to China, to Indonesia, to India, to Oman and to the Middle East. As we research into the different aspects of the dhow and its cargo, many things will be discovered. Many new links will be created, and what we gain is not just historical knowledge. What we gain is something profoundly useful for the future.

Above all, we learn to celebrate diversity. The ideal cannot be that we should all be the same. In diversity, there is the opportunity for exchange, a source of creativity for new enterprises. In that cargo, sitting side by side, were Buddhist pieces and Islamic pieces. The mirror, which was an ancient mirror from the Han Dynasty, had the Yin-Yang symbol, and the Taoist hexagram, the *bagua*. They were all there. It was an age when different religions and different cultures met, and people rejoiced in trade. Those who invested in it, those who were a part of it, derived great wealth.

So, in a strange way, though the cargo is about the 9th century, it is also about the 21st century. And therefore I commend it to the world.

Thank you.

# The Field of *Qi* Which Affects Our Well-Being

*If the qi field is positive, individuals feel more energised, more positive, more creative and more cooperative.*

Thank you all for honoring me by your presence so early in the morning. I feel very flattered especially to see old colleagues in the audience — Prof Lim Pin, Prof Chew and so many others. Let me take advantage of old friendships to indulge in a subject which in recent years has become of great interest to me and a source of pleasure and insight. When I started *taiji* (太极) a few years ago, it opened my mind to a universe which I did not know existed. Since then exploring that universe has been fascinating.

About three years ago, Indian Finance Minister Chidambaram accompanied me to his home town at Chettinad in Tamil Nadu. He is a Chettiar. While there, he brought me to visit an ancient complex of Jain cave temples at Sittanavasal near the railway town of Pudukkottai. They date back to the first half of the first millennium. Inside one of the cave temples was an inner sanctum measuring maybe two to two-and-a-half square metres. There were three of us in the room. My friend, Chidambaram, asked me to stand in the centre which I did while he stood by the side. The guide went to a corner and suddenly the whole room vibrated with a loud roar. Chidambaram pointed out that the guide himself did not make any sound. I paused for a few seconds and said, "Let me try." I then did my *dan tian* (丹田) breathing, meaning deep breathing from the lower abdomen, and

---

Edited transcript of talk at the NUHS Weekly Grand Rounds, National University Hospital, 18 January 2013.

the room also reverberated, but a few decibels lower. Chidambaram was surprised that I was able to reverberate the space. The wonder was how the ancient Jains knew the resonant frequency of deep breathing such a long time ago.

Let's reflect on this. If we can resonate a room by natural breathing, we must be vibrating each other all the time. When Jains, Hindus and Buddhists chant, they are resonating each other in a synchronised way. This creates a field effect affecting everyone in the group. When individuals in groups chant or pray or sing in unison, there is a resultant effect which is greater than the sum of the parts.

I am increasingly of the view that all living things emanate complex waves of one kind or another and the pattern of these waves can be traced back to our evolutionary past and our embryological beginnings. These waves are essential for life functions. They not only affect our well-being, they also affect our interactions with one another.

Many years ago I visited the research laboratory of Toyota in Nagoya. As part of a project to prevent car collisions, the scientists there studied the behaviour of flocks of birds and schools of fish. While flying or swimming together, the members somehow manage to avoid colliding with one another. When you disturb a flock of birds, individual birds swerve and scatter and then get into pattern again. They never knock into each other. One explanation for this instinct to avoid collision is that when an image suddenly looms large in the mind of a bird, it acts as a strong force pushing the bird away. It may not be just the visual image. It could be a combination of sensory inputs which creates the reaction, and the reaction itself acts like a real force. This is a form of *qi* (气). What is *qi* is hard to define precisely but it is involved in complex coordination in human beings and animals, and in group behaviour. The origin must of course be in the evolution of life itself, both individual life and group life.

I was talking to Ariff Bongso just the other day about his stem cell research at a fund-raising event to bring Tamil and Buddhist youths in Sri Lanka together. I once visited his lab and saw how stem cells did not specialise so long as they were constantly kept separated in small clumps. The moment he stopped separating them when they multiplied, the cells would start to specialise. I offered the view to Ariff that peristaltic-like waves were involved in stem cell coordination, expecting him to laugh at me. To my pleasant surprise, he did not, replying instead that indeed research showed the role of peristalsis in heart muscle movement. Ariff drew my attention to the creation of an artificial jellyfish by a team from Harvard and Caltech last year. The video on the Harvard Gazette website was so wondrous, I posted it on my Facebook. The scientists laid out mouse heart cells on a silicon polymer membrane according to a certain pattern. The membrane was then put into a saline solution and a small electrical charge applied to it. Lo and behold, the membrane moved like a jelly fish. In fact, even before the charge was applied, the silicon membrane twitched. Juxtaposed beside a video of a simple jellyfish swimming, the peristaltic-like movements of the artificial jellyfish and the real one were almost identical. Perhaps that simple directional pulse movement is the basic movement which first enabled cells to be coordinated before nerves appeared. Perhaps complex movements are the result of waves of different types, strengths and frequencies interacting in some kind of a field. In Chinese medicine, meridians and acupuncture points operate in a field called the *qi chang* (气场) or the field of *qi*. When the meridians or acupuncture points are blocked, the *qi* does not flow freely. Over time, the accumulation of poor *qi* flow leads to poor health and illness, *huo yin e ji* (祸因恶积). This applies to all animals, not just to human beings. There ought to be more research on the evolutionary biology of meridians and acupuncture points. Acupuncture is now used to treat animals as well.

The egg, when fertilised, is implanted in the womb and from there it sub-divides and, beyond a critical mass, the stem cells begin to specialise and coordinate. In *qigong* (气功) and *taiji*, the region around the point of implantation which is embryologically the oldest part of the body is roughly the region of the *ming men* (命门) or the gate of life and the *dan tian* which can be said to be the centre of all motion in the body. In the martial arts, this is the master region. If you watch the movement of a child or a teenager, the movements emanate from the *dan tian*. Athletes, gymnasts and dancers all initiate movement from there. As we grow older, that region stiffens. Our *dan tian* stops being supple. Teenagers are gangly. Old people shuffle along. As we age, the movements and the stresses are shifted to the extremities, to the smaller joints, causing problems to the knees, elbows, ankles and wrists. The *dan tian* is a very important part of the qi chang.

In the last few years, my running style has been adjusted to conform to *taiji* principles. I now run with Vibram fivefingers shoes. Running has become a form of *nei gong* (内功) for me. When I run, my mind is turned inwards especially to the *dan tian* as in *taiji*. As a result, my running has improved significantly and at the last StanChart 10-km run, I did my best ever, feeling almost no strain the following day. I'm now 58. Gosh, if I knew all this earlier, I would be much better off today. But, as my *taiji* teacher once said to me, "You are never too old to start learning and you ought to get better with age" — not my running but in *taiji*. I've since become a bit of a missionary talking to relatives and friends about the benefits of *qi gong* and *taiji*.

Increasingly, I suspect that every physiological system in the body has waves associated with it. The brain has a sensory map which enables complex waves to be focused. An eagle stares at a prey a long distance away. That stare enables the eagle to coordinate a bewildering set of movements as it swoops on the prey. How the brain does this, we do not know. Maybe meridian lines and acupuncture points help to define the sensory map which enables an animal to make this coordination. We are all aware how a thought can coordinate complex movements whether one is cracking a whip or executing a golf stroke. In *taiji*, the intention or *yi* (意) must be clear. Then the *qi* flows to effect the action. By combining waves of different amplitudes, frequencies and phases, the force can be focused with pinpoint accuracy. This is how phase-array radars work. Many of us would have seen how a gongfu expert is able to break a particular plank in a stack of planks by mental concentration. What it means is that the fist of the master does not hit the first plank in one impact but with a succession of waves. This is also the way a gongfu master can inflict internal injuries on an opponent. At the point of intention, all the waves come together like in a sonic boom or in a tsunami. LINAC radiosurgery works the same way.

From the individual, let us return to the group. The group exists in a *qi* field which can be positive or negative. The *qi* field affects individual performance in a way which is often not conscious. Take a simple plant as an example. Whatever the plant, where it is placed in a garden or in a house affects how it grows. The philosophy of *fengshui* (风水) is not to be disregarded because good *fengshui* means a good *qi* field which is good for all those living in that field. Sometimes, our conscious thought overrides what we in our primordial self may sense. When looking for a house, it is always good to bring a child or a dog along and watch how they react in a natural way. If they are happy, the house is probably a good house for habitation. The paradox is this: Our intelligence enables us to analyse and to see ourselves. Thus the pre-frontal cortex sets us apart from lower animals giving us a mirror to see the effects of our actions forward in time. In so doing, we curb our natural selves and this enables culture to develop and coordinate the actions of groups in civilised society. Civilisation takes us away from our natural selves, which evolved over millions of years, creating new problems. We cannot return to the natural state by making ourselves less intelligent. We can only return to it by applying our intelligence through wisdom. It is this which *taiji* and *qigong* and the positive management of the *qi* field attempt to do.

To manage the *qi* field, we must first be conscious of it and realise its importance. It affects morale and productivity. If the *qi* field is positive, individuals feel more energised, more positive, more creative and more cooperative. If the *qi* field is negative, everyone is diminished and group effort becomes that much more difficult. *Fengshui* is one aspect of it. Architecture affects the way we interact with one another — the size and shape of spaces, the quality of lighting, colours, ventilation, acoustics, everything which impinges on our senses. There must also be spaces for solitude. Spaces can make us feel good or bad. In lifts or toilets, individuals can feel awkward if they are poorly designed. Small things can improve the *qi* field. A mirror here or a visual barrier there can make a big difference. Not enough attention is given to these aspects of group interaction. From one perspective, it is all about waves and vibrations whether they are electromagnetic, acoustic, olfactory or physical. Waves can be a powerful way to synchronise group effort. In old Chinese cities, there are always the bell tower and the drum tower. Bells and drums generate waves which resonate large numbers of human beings and make them one.

Music can have the same effect. The owner of Zouk, Lincoln Cheng, is a good friend. When I first attended Zoukout on Sentosa beach, I felt out of place and found the music unpleasant. Lincoln encouraged me to relax. Once I relaxed and allowed myself to get into the rhythm of ZoukOut, the experience became pleasant. I chatted with a journalist from Britain who was covering ZoukOut as one of the world's great parties and the performance of the international DJs who were there. What makes a good DJ? It cannot just be knowledge of the music because a machine could do that. A good DJ is one who becomes a part of the *qi* field of the crowd and by varying the quality and volume of the music is able to energise the crowd and bring them to a high. Of course you cannot keep everyone on a high continuously because they soon become numb to it. There must be highs and lows, tension and release. In this way, the DJ is the conductor with the crowd as the orchestra. A good DJ is one who becomes part of the *qi* field and orchestrates it.

The point I am making this morning is that by being conscious of the *qi* field and the way it affects us, we can improve the well-being of a group and its members. Like among a group of musicians, we need some to lead and set the rhythm. It need not be the same person all the time. Everyone can play a part. Of course there must also be good acoustics and the setting must be right. When the overall conditions are positive, the energy level goes up and each of us becomes more creative and productive. In *taiji*, there is a principle that *yi zai jing shen bu zai qi* (意在精神不在气). The key is the spirit; get that right. Once there is a positive spirit, set clear intentions and the rest follows naturally. This applies as much to groups as it does to individuals. It certainly would apply to our environment in NUH. When the spirit is high and the direction is clear, everyone knows what to do and will go about doing it the right way.

# Media and Social Media

# MEDIATING BETWEEN EAST AND WEST

*As Asian societies advance economically, they will become more assertive culturally .... A monologue by the West is not good for the West. We need a dialogue.*

My address to you will be in two parts. I will first talk about the relationship between the Singapore government and the foreign press, after which, I will touch on a more philosophical matter concerning the encounter of Eastern and Western societies.

Let me state very clearly at the outset that the Singapore Government's policy towards the foreign press remains the same. It is not our policy to make it difficult for the foreign press to operate here. Quite the opposite: Our policy is to encourage the foreign press to operate from Singapore and from here to cover Singapore and the region. Our publicly stated objective is to make Singapore an information hub and a media hub.

It is not an objective which is formulated in a whimsical way for presentation purposes. Unless we are an information hub, we will not be able to maintain our position as a hub city for economic activities. Raffles founded Singapore as a trading post and, in a general sense, we remain a trading post, except that when once we switched and added value to spices, opium, rubber and tin, now we switch and add value to manufactured parts, technology, financial instruments and tourism traffic. We can only be an efficient switch if we are constantly lubricated with information. Without the widest access to information, both public and private, our economy will grind to a halt. It is as simple as that.

Luncheon address to the Foreign Correspondents Association members, 18 November 1991.

By being a hub, we are able to enjoy a standard of living higher than what we otherwise deserve. Let me explain what I mean. If you fry *kuay teow* in Jurong or Tampines, you are entitled to a certain standard of living. But if you fry *kuay teow* at Newton Circus, you will earn considerably more because of the location, what the economists call "rent". Because Singapore is at a major crossroad of the world, Singaporeans enjoy a higher standard of living by living here. This is why being an efficient hub is at the heart of our economic strategy. So when I say our policy is to encourage the foreign media to operate here, I do not mean it lightly.

We do have rules. But they should not affect your ability to operate professionally. What we want foreign journalists to do is to refrain from interference in the domestic political process. I noticed that the leader of the opposition, Mr Chiam See Tong, made the same point in his recent address to you. We have local sensitivities which we require you to respect. Whether you work as a foreign journalist in Bangkok or Tokyo, Cairo or London, there are certain areas which you tread lightly on, for example, comments on royalty and religion. We have no royalty in Singapore but we do worry a lot about religion, race and language. These are deep faultlines in our social structure and if we are not careful, our society can break up. When Salman Rushdie's *The Satanic Verses* was published, we knew right away that it had to be banned. I do not think till today many Westerners quite understand what the whole hubbub was about.

If you do not operate in Singapore, then you can of course do what you like and we have no right to tell you what not to do. But if you operate here, and especially if your newspaper circulates here, we do expect integrity and detachment. I assure you that if you act with integrity and detachment, you will find us helpful and courteous.

I am not suggesting for one moment that you must become admirers or apologists of Singapore. That will be self-defeating for us. But integrity must include the right of reply when our honour is impugned. Let me cite the example of *The Wall Street Journal* (*WSJ, Asia Edition*) to illustrate my point.

As you know, the newspaper re-applied to come back in recently. We had frank discussions. *WSJ* knows the rules. On that basis, it is circulating here again. We were not out to score points or to humiliate anybody. In January next year, *WSJ* will be organising a Capital Markets Conference in Singapore. The publisher invited Dr Richard Hu, the Finance Minister, to be the keynote speaker. He was surprised and amused. You remember he was accused in an article in *WSJ* in December 1986 of setting up the Stock Exchange of Singapore Dealing and Automated Quotation (SESDAQ) to palm off dud government companies to an unsuspecting public. How could he grace the occasion when that accusation has never been withdrawn? He was not even given the right of an unedited reply. Naturally Dr Hu said "no" to the invitation. So I offered myself as keynote speaker instead, in order to be friendly to *WSJ*, and because *WSJ* had been fair and balanced in its reporting on Singapore over the last two years. The point I am making is if you act with integrity, we will be helpful and courteous.

What we are asking for is objective reporting and, if we disagree with the points you make, the right of reply. On that basis, I see the relationship between the Singapore Government and the foreign press improving. You might have misunderstood us in the past. I do not think you do now.

Let me now move on to a larger subject, of the encounter between Eastern and Western societies, and the role you can play to help bring about a better future for all of us.

With the collapse of Communism in Eastern Europe and the Soviet Union and the emergence of new democracies in the Third World, there is a growing sense in the West that Western values have triumphed everywhere and forever. All countries seem now to be subject to the test of Western values and are to be judged accordingly. Wittingly and unwittingly, Western journalists are a large part of this phenomenon. I would like to suggest to you that not only is such a point of view arrogant, it is also dangerous.

Manchu China had that kind of a cultural arrogance. After Lord Macartney negotiated a one-knee bow instead of a *kowtow* before the Qianlong Emperor, he was sent back to England with an edict from the Emperor to George III reminding the English King that China had everything and needed nothing from the West.

For that cultural arrogance, China paid a heavy price. Japan in contrast wasted no time after the Meiji Restoration to learn everything it could from the West. The Japanese example in turn had a profound influence on the course of the republican revolution in China. Today, learning from the West is part of the culture of the East. *Liuxue* in Chinese or *ryugaku* in Japanese, meaning to leave home to study abroad, is generally considered a beneficial experience. In the East today, you are only an educated man if you have learnt from the West.

But the reverse does not hold true. There is still no widespread acceptance in the West that before you can be considered fully educated you must also learn from the East. And therein lies the danger for the West and for the world. In a superficial sense, there is some learning from the East, like the interest in Japanese management techniques, but little more than that. If this attitude does not change, Eastern societies will overtake Western societies and the resentment that is engendered in the West will be politically destabilising. If America does not put right her education and her economy, there will be trouble for the whole world. The structure of peace in Europe and Asia will be upset.

When I visited the Juilliard School in New York City last month, I was told that 75% of the freshmen are of Asian origin, counting Americans and non-Americans. I was amazed. A professor told me that at this rate the Western tradition of music will have to be maintained by Asians and Jews in the next century.

Age for age, students in East Asia outperform students in America in science and mathematics. What is happening? Is it all just a problem of methods and techniques?

I fear the problem is much deeper. I fear the problem is in aspects of the Western value system which break up the family, elevate the individual above everything else, carrying the rule of law to illogical limits and reducing all relationships to that of the contract. There is a lot of good in the Western value system, but some elements in it have gone out of balance. Men like Solzhenitsyn and John Paul II see the problem in moral terms.

I hope the West will have the cultural humility to learn from the East. Let me quote Joseph Needham in an essay he wrote in 1955 on "the dialogue of East and West":

> Many people in Western Europe and European America suffer from what may be called spiritual pride. They are firmly convinced that their own form of civilisation is the only universal form. In deep ignorance of the intellectual and social conceptions and traditions of other peoples, they think it quite natural to impose upon them their own ideas and customary practices, whether of law, of democratic society, or of political institutions.

Needham went on:

> An outstanding instance of European spiritual pride concerns law and jurisprudence. ... Roman law has been praised for centuries. The Code of Justinian is ... regarded as a great monument of European culture, and Anglo-Saxons are proud of their structure of case-law and precedent accumulated over the centuries."
>
> "Yet the Chinese had an immense and remarkable legal tradition, and it was based on principles quite different from those which prevailed in Europe. While the West has a penchant for legal fictions, Asians are less deceived by professional sophistry. There was, throughout Chinese history, a resistance to codification, a determination to judge every case on its own merits, a passion for compromise and harmony. There was hardly any rift which put society asunder which Chinese jurisconsults could not join together. Ancient and medieval China knew the rule of law, but consciously preferred the rule of equity.

Of course that also led to corruption and nepotism in China, but Needham ended his section on law by saying:

> . . . Europeans should cease to think that they have nothing to learn from the legal systems of Asia.

Please do not misunderstand me. I am not arguing for one moment that East is all good and West is all bad. Without the leavening influence of the West, not just in science and technology but also in politics and philosophy, there could not have been this remarkable Eastern transformation. Indeed, for the East, it has been a wrenching process over decades because all the old habits and instincts have to be re-evaluated. And for a big country like China, the process is still ongoing.

For the West, learning from the East will be equally wrenching and prolonged because value systems, of all human systems, are the most resistant to change. It is a mistake to think that the only big issue in the world today is that between democracy and totalitarianism, and that once that is resolved all will be well. Because of technology, all societies will have to become broadly democratic when they modernise but the differences between democratic systems will become so great, they should more properly be considered differences of kind rather than differences of degree. Japanese democracy is not the same as American democracy. Pan-European democracy will again be different. All will be in competition. As the dialecticians remind us: thesis, anti-thesis, synthesis, then new thesis and new anti-thesis. One divides into two, endlessly.

As Asian societies advance economically, they will become more assertive culturally. It is not only Japan that can say no. Others will too, increasingly. I hope Western journalists will not disregard such feelings but will instead report on them in a thoughtful way to readers back home. A monologue by the West is not good for the West. We need a dialogue.

In our small house in Singapore, the dialogue of East and West among Singaporeans can sometimes get very heated. As foreign journalists, you are our honoured guests and you should not interfere or take sides. But I hope you will benefit from your experience here and draw whatever lessons you may find useful for your own society. For, in the end, we wish you well because we wish ourselves well.

# IMPACT ON OUR CULTURES OF THE GLOBAL MEDIA SOCIETY

*Cultural differences will not disappear.*

Economic interdependence, the revolution in communication and the global media have put cultures in contact as never before. This encounter of cultures generates heat and light. Heat — in the sense of tension and conflict. Light — in the sense of mutual stimulation and learning.

The involvement of the global media is one aspect of the encounter. The global media is not above the encounter; it is a participant in the encounter. There is no such thing as a media which is culturally neutral. When we report on science, it is possible to be neutral. When we report on human society, however, we can never be. To report on human society is to report on human relationships and that is inevitably coloured and distorted by the values we hold and the lenses we wear. Our cultural assumptions affect what we see. The fracas over Salman Rushdie's *The Satanic Verses* is a case in point. The way the Western media have reported it is not the way the Islamic world sees it. It took a long time for the Vatican to change its judgement on Galileo. It will take at least as long for the Islamic world to change its judgement of Salman Rushdie, if ever.

For the time being, the global media is dominated by the West. I say 'for the time being' because the question is one of cultural power in the world. Cultural power derives from political and

---

Speech delivered at the World Economic Forum, 1993 Annual Meeting, Davos, 2 February 1993.

economic power. When political and economic power shifts, so too will cultural power. When that happens, the global media puts on different lenses.

It is important for us to drop the pretense that all cultures are equal: that is the wrong meaning of multi-culturalism. In polite company, we genuflect before all cultures with equal deference and sometimes with condescension. In private, we take great care to educate our children and marry them off in a certain way. There is no equality; there is only struggle. Cultures are evolving all the time in response to new challenges. European culture changed dramatically from the days of Greece and Rome, through the Dark and Middle Ages, into the Renaissance, Reformation and Counter-Reformation before it emerged into the modern era. The changes were sometimes for good, sometimes for ill. Over time and space, all cultures change for the better and for the worse.

Multi-culturalism in the world should not try to put a stop to the evolutionary process. That is sure to fail. We should not be preserving cultural attitudes not fitted to modern society as if the people who hold these attitudes are interesting anthropological specimens. For example, if we try to preserve tribalism in Africa in the present form, the result must be a colossal human disaster. At the same time, it is not possible to replace Black Africa culture with European culture or East Asian culture.

To cut off a person's past, the way the American slave owners did, cripples him in a terrible way. Without roots, no tree can grow. Black African culture must change if there is to be any hope but it must remain Black African in its essential derivation.

While cultures will converge to some degree because of the way the world is shrinking, cultural differences will not disappear. Religious differences, for one, will not disappear. No amount of Western influence will make Japanese society or Chinese society Western, or vice versa. What we should try to achieve is to make multi-culturalism a part of every culture, in other words, a tolerance of diversity, a philosophical understanding that every culture has its ups and downs, and the acceptance that all human beings are spiritually equal. For the sake of world peace, the global media has a responsibility to promote such multi-culturalism.

East Asia is on the rise. In 25 years, the combined GNP of East Asia will be larger than all of Europe's and twice that of the US. The unfolding East Asian renaissance will challenge and transform all cultures in the world and change the way man looks at himself. The Western domination of the global media will be contested.

This cultural contest — this new encounter of East and West — will generate a lot of heat and light. The hope of all of us must be to reduce the heat and increase the light.

# Localising Television

*The multimedia revolution holds up great possibilities for mankind. But, it also poses new dangers.*

The launch of cable TV by SCV today opens a new chapter in the history of broadcasting in Singapore. The development of cable TV will change the nature of our society in ways expected and unexpected. It is a new challenge which we must respond to in a deliberate and creative way.

Cable TV will strengthen Singapore's position as an international hub city. By wiring up every home, cable TV will help us achieve our national objective of making Singapore an "intelligent island". Through cable TV, Singaporeans and foreigners visiting or living in Singapore will have windows to different parts of the world. Having American, German, French, British, Australian, Japanese, Chinese and Indian channels available in Singapore will greatly reduce the sense of distance and encourage even more multi-nationals to set up their regional headquarters here. Families of foreign executives will then be able to keep in close touch with their home countries. We want Singapore to be, for them, a home away from home. Thus, cable TV will help the globalisation of Singapore's economy.

But in globalising our economy, we should not lose our own sense of living in Singapore and of being Singaporean. Singapore should remain Singapore and should not be no different from Hong Kong, Bombay, London or Los Angeles. That will not be good for Singapore.

---

Speech at the official launch of Singapore Cablevision (SCV), Tampines Central, 23 June 1995.

Although many channels may be similar, cable TV in Singapore must have a different character from cable TV elsewhere. We must preserve our own sense of place, self and community.

Happily, the technology which makes globalisation possible will also be a force for localisation. While multimedia technology enables us to network with the rest of the world in real time, it also enables us to network within Singapore much more intensively. We must therefore exploit the potential at both ends. Put in another way, we have to globalise and localise simultaneously.

In this respect, cable TV is not too different from free-to-air TV and newspapers. All over the world, the experience has been that newspaper and TV markets have strong local characteristics. Truly global media like the *International Herald Tribune* and CNN enjoy small audiences, Invariably, global media companies have to customise their media products for local markets and adapt to regional variations in language, culture, law and taste. Put in another way, while the wholesale market for media products may be global, the retail market is always local. Thus, Dow Jones packages different products for different parts of the world. Even CNN separates its American channel from its international channel. Magazines like *Time* and *Newsweek* produce regional editions.

For cable TV in Singapore to succeed, not only as a business but also as a communal facility for social development, it must be localised. We should think of localisation at different levels. First, there must be a sense of the region we are in, namely, Singapore in Asia and Singapore in Southeast Asia. Then, there must be a strong sense of our being in Singapore. Even within Singapore, we need to have a sense of the neighbourhood we live in, like Tampines Town. And finally, there must be a sense of the home as every Singaporean's own castle.

Our sense of the region on cable TV will be partly achieved by the availability of channels from different parts of Asia like China, Japan and India. We must, however, strengthen ASEAN programming. We already have good links with Malaysia and Indonesia. Malaysian channels are received in Singapore, but we must do more to strengthen our broadcasting links with other ASEAN countries like, for example, making it easier for our channels to be carried in each other's cable TV systems. I will discuss this with my ASEAN counterparts at this year's ASEAN Information Ministers' Meeting which will be held in Singapore in November.

To strengthen our sense of being in Singapore on cable TV, SCV is working on a few channels for education, sports, health, museums, libraries, art performances and other social services. With many channels available, the actual limitations are the availability of good materials and the marketing imagination to package useful products. Channels 5, 8 and 12 will of course be carried on SCV. SCV will also be working on a slew of interactive services including electronic home shopping and electronic home banking.

In addition, SCV will be exploring the development of community channels for different parts of Singapore. They will be like *The Straits Times*' regional weekly supplements. Such community channels will draw in town councils, Citizens' Consultative Committees (CCCs), Residents' Committees (RCs), community centres, schools, libraries and neighbourhood businesses. We should make use of cable TV to strengthen civic and grassroots organisations in Singapore so that there is a strong sense of Singaporeans belonging to local communities.

With cable TV, it is possible to take this a step further and provide channels which monitor goings-on in the immediate neighbourhood. Residents can keep an eye on activities at public parks, neighbourhood centres, carparks, open areas, corridors and even lifts. This can be done on rotation on one or more channels to give those who are home a sense of what is going on around them. This facility will also increase neighbourhood security. SCV will discuss with town councils and management committees on the practical possibilities.

The multimedia revolution holds up great possibilities for mankind but it also poses new dangers. Urban terrorism, for example, may become much more of a problem worldwide because of quick and easy access to information and the ease of travel. One big problem of the Internet is anonymity which tempts individuals to become irresponsible. What we should try to do is to create within our city, smaller communities in which people know each other and care for each other, each with a *kampong* spirit. Of course, we should not become busybodies and invade each other's privacy. But we should also not move to the other extreme and mind only our own business. If we mind only our own business, the city can become an ugly and a dangerous urban jungle.

We must therefore think of ways and means to re-localise our neighbourhoods using the new technologies available. We have to continue insisting on high standards of broadcasting. All channels of SCV will have to be individually approved by the Singapore Broadcasting Authority (SBA) and all programmes, and advertisements must conform to SBA's codes.

But SBA can only do so much to maintain standards. SBA's standards represent overall community standards. They cannot cater to all the specific needs of individual families. As a community, everyone must feel responsible and do his part. As with so many other things, the key is the family. Parental supervision remains the most important. SCV's set-top will allow parents to block off channels they do not like by the use of PIN numbers. In addition, SCV will also provide optional timer controls, like Robomum or TV Guard, which allow parents to set particular viewing slots for their children to watch TV and even set weekly time quotas for them.

Cable TV is an exciting new phase in Singapore's development. The new multimedia technologies will help to make Singapore an international city. We cannot anticipate all the possible side effects but, if we put our minds to it, we should be able to come up with all kinds of interesting solutions which will make us a stronger Singapore in the next century. Cable TV should not only provide us new hotel facilities; it should make us a better home.

On this note, I congratulate SCV on its quick start-up and wish it great success in Singapore and elsewhere.

# EVOLUTION

*In the post-industrial information age, bigness is no longer an advantage. What matters is flexibility. We are moving from the age of dinosaurs to the age of mammals.*

When I was at Business School in the mid-1980s in America, a professor of French origin remarked that China's development path would be unique. China was too big and had too long a history to follow existing models of development. It would create its own model. It was a far-sighted view. Like China, other big countries like India and Indonesia will also create their own models of development. They will not develop as we expect but may instead surprise us by their innovativeness and originality.

We live in an age of intellectual uncertainty. There is no clear path into the future — not for societies in the West, and not for societies in the East either. We are again at a point in history where practice leads theory. We may have to wait many decades before the present theoretical confusion over the political, cultural and economic changes taking place in the world can be clearly explained within a coherent intellectual framework. This is a time of great intellectual ferment which has its reflections in political conflicts around the world.

The underlying cause of this ferment is the technological revolution in information processing, communications and transportation. Social structures of all kinds are being broken up. Jacques Attali describes the process as one of *demassification*. In the post-industrial information age, bigness is no longer an advantage. What matters is flexibility and

---

Speech at the opening of the Asian Newspaper Publishers Convention, Suntec City, 4 December 1995.

the ability to respond to changing threats and opportunities. We are moving from the age of dinosaurs to the age of mammals.

Demassification takes place at many levels. Big countries are under tremendous pressure to devolve and decentralise. The recent referendum on Quebec independence has not solved the problem for Canada. Either Canada becomes a looser confederation or Quebec will eventually secede. What is happening in Canada is a forerunner of what will happen on a larger scale in North America, Europe and Asia. Resentment against the centralisation of power in Washington, Moscow, Beijing, Brussels and New Delhi is building up. The ability of central governments to tax and control the flow of capital and technology is weakening by the day. With knowledge increasingly becoming the basis of all wealth, borders will become even more porous. Governments which try to fight the global market will be defeated by it.

Corporations too come under the same pressure to demassify. AT&T and IBM were dinosaurs which had to be re-constructed, either forcibly or voluntarily. Tightly organised Japanese corporations face similar pressures to loosen up. One reason why ethnic Chinese corporations have become relatively successful in recent years is because they are organised on a smaller scale, being family-centred, and so enjoy a greater flexibility to exploit new markets and political relationships. But their over-reliance on family members is also a major weakness.

More fundamentally, demassification is taking place at the level of human ideas. There are two tendencies which are simultaneously at work. Because technology has made us one world, universal ideas about environmental protection, nuclear non-proliferation and human rights have become part of a new global morality. They are ideas subscribed to in a broad way by urban middle classes and their children in different parts of the world. The sharing of such ideas provides the basis for a common world civilisation.

The second tendency is the fragmentation of political ideas. Socialism and democracy will have to be re-engineered. The socialism practised in the Soviet Union and the Fabian welfare state has been consigned to the rubbish heap of history. Far from promoting brotherhood and common effort, big socialism led to widespread abuse and cynicism. But the idea of socialism itself will never die because it expresses a deep ideal in the human heart. It will be re-expressed at a lower level and on a smaller scale, in communities where human beings feel and care for each other. Japanese society, for example, embodies a strong socialist instinct even though it is not called as such. Friends from China who come to Singapore tell me that Singapore is, in many ways, more socialist than China today.

Big democracy, like big socialism, is also following the way of dinosaurs. Both expressed the necessities of a different age. By big democracy, I am referring to democratic systems in big countries which concentrate political power in relatively small political elites who, in turn, use state power to impose commonality and re-distribute wealth. As the government's power to tax and direct investment weakens, city-regions grow more assertive, sometimes rising in revolt like Quebec. As these city-regions reclaim their power, big democracy gives way to small democracy which was the democracy of Athens and still the ideal in Switzerland today. Further centralisation in the European Union is unlikely. The principle of subsidiarity, of democratic decision-making at the lowest possible level, will become more important. In America, the balance of political power will shift back to the states.

As establishment ideas lose their dominance, political correctness in big countries will gradually dissolve away. When three GIs were alleged to have raped a young Okinawan girl recently, many people wondered whether the GIs were white, black, brown or yellow. The newspapers provided no clue; television pictures gave no indication. In the end, one had to log into the Internet to find out. Increasingly, the Internet and the proliferation of small media will break up the cartel control of ideas by big newspapers and big TV stations. Major newspapers and TV networks in America, China and Russia no longer enjoy the same sway over their audiences.

The process of demassification is transforming all aspects of human society in a profound way. However, countries, corporations and ideas will not break up into isolated fragments. The same technology which breaks them up also enables the fragments to link up with each other. To use John Naisbitt's catchy phrase, the megatrend will be from nation-states to networks. In other words, fragments will still be linked together like neurons in the brain or cells in the body or websites in the Internet, creating new and messier patterns of competition and cooperation. Governments themselves will facilitate such networking across national boundaries. It is a sign of the times that many heads of states nowadays bring along businessmen on their official travels abroad. It is better for governments to add value in this way than to subtract value by inefficiently performing functions which are better left to the private sector.

Newspapers reflect the societies from which they spring forth. There is no such thing as unfiltered reporting. We buy newspapers and watch television precisely because we do not have the time to take in all the information around us. All of us suffer from information overload. Unread documents and magazines pile on our desks everyday, giving us a guilty conscience. Newspapers and television stations add value by subtracting information that we do not want, and presenting what is left to us in an attractive and entertaining way. The process of subtracting, concentrating and packaging information invariably reflects the value norms and cultural assumptions of the society we live in, or segments of it. Let me give an example. When *The New York Times* carried an article reported recently that the Central Intelligence Agency (CIA) had eavesdropped on Japanese Minister Hashimoto during the automobile trade talks, it was not something considered unusual in America. Since Vietnam, it is no longer the responsibility of American newspapers to help keep state secrets. No establishment of Japanese or Chinese newspaper would be party to such a revelation if their own intelligence agencies were involved. It would be considered betrayal. In Singapore, the newspaper would be prosecuted in court for divulging state secrets.

Like all other industries, the newspaper industry is also going through a revolution. The newspaper industry is being submerged into a larger and less structured multimedia industry. The electronic media will increasingly compete with the print media. Broadcasting will give way to narrowcasting. A new pattern of wholesale and retail business in world and local news is emerging. Getting into the wholesale business is becoming very expensive because wholesalers have to operate globally. Only those with very deep pockets can take on CNN, Dow Jones or the big wire services in the wholesale business. CTN, broadcasting in Chinese, avoids a head-on fight by moving into a different segment of the wholesale market.

The retail market, where most of the commercial revenue is, has much lower barriers to entry. In all countries, the retail market for news is local. Every city has its own quirks, its own tastes, its own sense of humour and its own taboos. In Thailand, you cannot show disrespect to the monarchy. In Malaysia, you must be mindful of what Islam disallows. The newspapers and television stations which succeed are those which are closest to local audiences and readers. International media like BBC and the *International Herald Tribune* (IHT) will still cater directly to a sophisticated English-speaking cosmopolitan elite who are a tiny minority in Asia. They will, however, be important wholesalers of international news to local newspapers and cable TV, particularly if they also supply news in local languages.

The growing number of players in the multimedia industry reflects the diversity of local communities and networks. Commercial viability remains the key to success. Rupert Murdoch's far-flung empire is successful because the different parts are able to localise themselves. In Britain, Murdoch owns both the *London Times* and *The Sun*. It may be politically convenient to blame *The Sun* for some of the ills that befall Britain today but *The Sun* is only catering to the proclivities of a large segment of British society. When the Chinese signalled their unhappiness with BBC World Vision, Murdoch took it off Star Television in East Asia. In Hong Kong, as happened in Malaysia and Singapore after independence, media owners are already adjusting to a new political reality after 1997. To expect otherwise is naive. Journalists and cartoonists would like to be independent and portray what they wish, but in the end it is the economic reality which is fundamental. BBC's international marketing of Panorama's riveting interview with Princess Diana, recently telecast live on local stations around the world, is a remarkable example of a new commercialism at work.

We are entering an exciting period of human history and an age of intellectual uncertainty. Much of the drama will take place in Asia where half the world's population is set on a path of organic growth. However, this path will not be smooth. There will be conflicts of all kinds, maybe even wars and revolutions. There will be new prophets and false Dimitris. Mindless acts of terrorism will become more common as the knowledge to make bombs, poison gases and even nastier things becomes more widespread. The period that we are entering harks back to the period of the Greek city-states and the period of the Chinese warring states before the birth of Christ. Although the Greek city-states shared a common Hellenic civilisation, they experimented with a proliferation of political ideas and organisational forms, with Athens and Sparta at two ends of a wide spectrum. In the end, it was a Macedonian who conquered the Western world. In China during the warring states, there was also a common Chinese civilisation but a hundred schools of thought contended for a long time. In the end, it was the legalist Qin Dynasty which created the First Empire, only to be quickly replaced by a Confucianist Han Dynasty. In our own times, it will be many years before it is clear what the future holds in the next century. In the meantime, our Darwinian duty is to survive and to prosper, if we can.

To do that we have to organise ourselves in a flexible way, be alert to international competition, stay close to the changes taking place in local communities and network with others in the world. Human networks which straddle diverse markets and cultural areas are growing in importance. They enable their members to profit from knowledge arbitrage. For example, many ethnic Chinese and Indian businessmen have become rich by arbitraging differences in knowledge levels between the West and less developed economies in Asia. Today, much of the information flow within such networks is informal. Perhaps this is the way to keep valuable knowledge private and confidential. But there are opportunities for media entrepreneurs to meet the information needs of such networks in a more systematic way, the way *Yazhou Zhoukan* is doing for example. In Singapore, the Chinese Chamber of Commerce and Industry is starting a World

Chinese Business Network on the Internet. Only those who think globally but act locally will succeed.

For this reason, this first conference of Asian Newspaper Publishers is timely. No one has a monopoly of knowledge or wisdom. We do well to learn from each other's experiences while taking our own tentative steps forward into the future.

I wish you a good conference and pleasant stay in Singapore.

# THE IT REVOLUTION AND SINGAPORE

*Wealth in the next century will be mostly based on human knowledge. Knowledge assets will not be easily valued on the traditional balance sheets.*

## Unavoidable Changes

The IT revolution will force a reorganisation of human society. Its historical impact will be similar to those of other technological leaps in the past, like the invention of fire, agriculture, writing, the printing press and electricity. Societies which are able to master the new technology and minimise its negative effects will succeed. Those which are unable to make the adjustment will fall far behind.

The explosive growth of the Internet in the last five years after the invention of the World Wide Web has accelerated the pace of the IT revolution. This is speeding up the transformation of institutional structures. In every country, existing economic, political and social structures, both in the private and public sectors, have come under severe stress. The new challenges to human society are huge. The coming years will be a very difficult period of transition, from the industrial world with its defined structures and hierarchies, to a new web-like world based on human knowledge. This period of transition, which may extend over several decades, will be marked by all kinds of discontinuities including political upheavals, economic crises and new social divisions in human society. I would like to talk about three major challenges arising out of this historical change and Singapore's response to them.

---

Speech at the Yomiuri Shimbun Symposium on "Digital Information Society in the New Century", Tokyo, Japan, 12 May 1999.

### Education

The first challenge is the education of the young. It is crucial that the next generation is prepared for the IT world. Like many things in education, children learn best when they are young. This applies as much to information technology as it does to reading, writing, arithmetic and music. Many children who do not learn IT when they are young will be IT handicapped for the rest of their lives. Failure to educate them will result in society having to carry a heavy burden for the rest of their lives. Indeed the social division between those who are IT competent and those who are not will define the politics of many societies in the next century.

In Singapore, we have decided to tackle the problem of IT competence in a systematic and comprehensive way. This policy is especially important for children from families of the lower socio-economic classes. Children of middle-class families are much less of a problem because their parents will ensure that they are taught computers from a young age. Those in the bottom one-third, however, must be specially looked after because, on their own, they may not have the opportunity.

Singapore has an IT education masterplan to create an IT based teaching and learning environment in every school, from the first year onwards. All primary and secondary schools are already equipped with computers connected to the Internet. For secondary schools and junior colleges, the present ratio of students to computer is 5 to 1. For primary schools, it is 7 to 1. Most kindergartens in Singapore already teach computers to young children through play and simple instruction.

The target in the IT education master plan is to increase hands-on use of computers by students to 30% of the curriculum time by the year 2002. To do this, we have to provide one computer for every two pupils. We are making steady progress. By the middle of this year, one in two teachers will be provided with a notebook computer. Every teacher will have his own email account. Every teacher gets a grant of 20% to buy his own computer. He will be expected to use his computer to prepare lessons, to mark homework and to communicate with his pupils.

We have been working overtime to wire up all our schools and put them on the Education Ministry broadband network. We are fortunate that all Singapore students are taught English from kindergarten upwards. This makes it easier for them to access international databases and the Internet. In addition, we encourage Chinese Singapore students to explore the Chinese Internet world which is growing rapidly.

**Entrepreneurship**

The next challenge which we are concerned with in Singapore is entrepreneurship in the global knowledge-based economy. The IT revolution is both a threat and an opportunity. Old patterns are being undermined. The way R&D, manufacturing and distribution is organised is being rapidly transformed by IT and electronic commerce. Some experts believe that the changes which e-commerce and the Internet will bring about in the next 5–10 years will be as great as the changes that have taken place in the last 50–60 years. Increasingly, all businesses are forced to think globally, even when they only operate locally. Those who are slow to change will be outflanked and bypassed. Those who are quick to change and exploit the new opportunities will prosper. As a Japanese businessman remarked to me recently, "in the past, 'big ate small'; in the future, it will be 'fast eat slow'".

Depending on our response, e-commerce and the Internet can either strengthen or weaken Singapore's position as a regional hub for business and financial activities. To remain a hub in the next century, Singapore cannot just be a regional hub. We have to be an international hub in the global web. We are therefore reorganising ourselves in many sectors.

In the public sector, we have carried out the computerisation of all ministries, statutory boards and public agencies, including Parliament and the Judiciary. In the last ten years, we have systematically corporatised and privatised many of our departments to make them more flexible and more responsive to market forces. We make it easier for them to outsource and establish lateral relationships with other public and private agencies.

Despite the economic crisis in Asia, we have pushed the restructuring of our financial sector in order to promote greater transparency and open competition. Singapore can only succeed as a financial hub if it adopts international best practices and serves the whole world.

In 1991, we launched a long-term programme to promote the development of IT and establish Singapore as hub for e-commerce. This involves both hardware and software. The hardware includes the connection of every home, office and school in Singapore to a broadband network called Singapore One. Every home in Singapore already has access to broadband via existing telephone lines using ADSL technology. By the end of the year, every home in Singapore will also be connected by an optical fibre network to the kerbside, and by co-axial cable from the kerbside to the home. But even more important than the physical network is the legal and regulatory structure that we have put in place to facilitate the growth of e-commerce. For e-commerce to flourish, we need certainty in matters like authentication, intellectual property protection, contract definition, dispute resolution and privacy. We need a legal system which is fully equipped to deal with problems arising out of e-commerce.

Singapore is a city-state with a long tradition of trading and entrepreneurship. However, entrepreneurship in the next century will increasingly be of a different kind. The great entrepreneurs of the next century would no longer come from traditional fields like automobiles, shipbuilding, petroleum and real estate, but would come instead from the knowledge industries. The Fortune 500 companies indicate these new trends very clearly. Microsoft alone has a greater capitalisation than all the auto companies in North America put together. In fact, AOL's capitalisation is already greater than GM's and Boeing's combined. Yahoo has a capitalisation bigger than that of the entire Jakarta stock exchange. Of course, one may argue that these Internet companies are overvalued but, however overvalued, the trends are clear. Wealth in the next century will be mostly based on human knowledge. Knowledge assets will not be easily valued on the traditional balance sheets. When a knowledge company is acquired, most of the assets will have to be recorded as intangible goodwill.

The US leads the world in IT. Talented young people from all over the world migrate to the US, especially to Silicon Valley, in the hope of getting rich quickly. Both Europe and Asia are losing many of their best and brightest to the US and this will have profound implications in the years to come.

For Singapore to be in the first league of cities in the next century, we must have our fair share of human talent, especially entrepreneurial talent for the knowledge economy. Either we become a hub for such talent in Asia or we will lose our own talent and become a mediocre city. This is a big challenge for us because of our relatively small size. Singapore's cosmopolitan nature and the widespread use of English are both an advantage and a disadvantage. It is an advantage because foreign talent from other parts of the world find it comfortable and easy to live in Singapore. But this also means the opposite, which is that it is just as easy for Singaporean talent to migrate elsewhere. In order to address this new challenge, the Singapore government has recently launched a high level initiative called the Technopreneurship 21 (T21) Initiative chaired by DPM Dr Tony Tan. The T21 Initiative has three major aspects.

The first aspect is to develop the western part of Singapore near the universities as a Science Hub with world-class facilities which are attractive to international talent working in knowledge industries, especially in high technology. In the coming years, we will turn the Buona Vista area in Singapore into a major Science Hub in Asia.

The second aspect of the T21 Initiative is to change many of our laws, rules and regulations to facilitate entrepreneurship in high tech. For example, our bankruptcy laws must make it easier for entrepreneurs who have failed to try again. In high tech, those who have failed before are more likely to succeed than those who have never failed before. Of course, we should not make bankruptcy too easy for everyone as this will result in moral hazard. But in the high-tech field, we must make major adjustments. The regulations governing the use of apartments for high-tech businesses will also be reviewed to make it easier for budding entrepreneurs to start businesses and to reduce the cost of failure.

The third aspect in the T21 Initiative is to develop the venture capital market in Singapore. Singapore is already an international financial centre. The problem is a lack of expertise in the financing of high-tech projects. This requires a whole new range of expertise which we have to attract from America and elsewhere to Singapore. To promote the growth of this new financial sector, the Singapore government has set aside a US$1 billion venture capital fund to be deployed in the next few years. It is crucial for us to succeed in this area. A lively venture capital market in Singapore will not only serve Singapore, it will serve other countries in the region as well.

**Value System**

With respect to the IT revolution, I have discussed the challenges of education and entrepreneurship. I would now like to talk about the challenge which the IT revolution poses to the value system of human society. This is perhaps the most difficult area to address because it involves the culture and power structure of a country.

The IT revolution subverts the hierarchical relationships which are important to East Asian society. The relationships between the government and the people, between seniors and juniors in a corporation, between parents and children, between teachers and students, and between men and women, are all being transformed. In the initial phase, the Internet has a democratising effect on social systems. It now becomes much easier to break out of traditional relationships and bypass traditional hierarchies. Much more than letters, faxes or telephone calls, e-mail and Internet websites enable individuals anywhere in the world to broadcast their views and to exchange ideas and information. The result is that all organisations become more web-like in their relationships. In fact, organisations which oppose this new tendency are disadvantaged because the people working in such organisations do not have the knowledge and information which their competitors enjoy.

In the family and in school, the ability of parents and teachers to maintain traditional relationships is being weakened everyday by the Internet. Regulating the Internet is now a worldwide problem. Pornography is easily accessible to children and all kinds of groups operate in cyberspace. Some of these groups are evil and can harm children. Therefore, no responsible parent, teacher or government can agree to no regulation of the Internet at all. At the same time, however, regulating the Internet is difficult because of the nature of the technology. When information is reduced to ones and zeros, it is impossible to filter such information completely. Let me explain the way Singapore is attempting to regulate the Internet with a light touch and in a practical manner.

Under the Singapore Broadcasting Act, Internet content providers are automatically licensed and given a clear idea of what their responsibilities are. They have to abide by a Code of Practice. Internet service providers and resellers are required to register with the Singapore Broadcasting Authority (SBA) but they are not required to monitor the Internet or its users. However, they may be required by the broadcasting authority to limit public access to 100–200 sites which the SBA considers to be undesirable. The SBA is only concerned with sites which have mass impact. Sites which have no mass impact are treated as communication sites and left unregulated. Sites which originate from Singapore or do business in Singapore must, however, conform to Singapore laws. The SBA depends a lot on ordinary members of the public — on parents, teachers and concerned adults — to inform it of sites which its attention should be drawn to.

In regulating the Internet, our overriding objective is to promote Internet use in Singapore, especially for education and e-commerce. Singapore is probably the most advanced city in Asia today in terms of Internet use and penetration. However, we have to help parents and teachers protect young children. In the market, many types of filter software are available, like Surf Watch and Cyber Patrol, but it is not easy for parents and teachers to install them. Some children know more about such software than their minders. We have therefore required all Internet service providers in Singapore to offer parents and teachers a filtered Internet service called the Family Access Network. It is for teachers and parents to decide whether or not to subscribe to the Family Access Network. We allow the Internet service providers to use different kinds of filters available in the market so long as they meet SBA's minimum standards. In this way, we allow the market to decide which filters should be popularised. Of course, we recognise that no software filter is 100% effective. Even if it is only 70% effective, that is still better than nothing.

It is no longer possible for any one country to regulate the Internet on its own in an effective way. Increasingly, regulators around the world will have to work together to ensure that the Internet meets certain minimum international standards. For example, there is universal condemnation of the exploitation of children. There are also sites providing information on the making of bombs and poisonous gases which should not be condoned. However, we must recognise that for pornography and hate sites, it is difficult to establish a worldwide consensus on what the minimum standards should be.

Singapore's regulators work closely with other regulators in the world. We support the increasing use of content classification, especially the standard developed by the World Wide Web consortium. This is equivalent to the V-chip in the TV industry.

The Internet challenge to our value system goes beyond the protection of children and the enforcement of minimum standards. In fact, all organisations in the public and private sectors are affected. For example, the Internet is bound to weaken national tax authorities as more and more businesses move into e-commerce.

In the longer term, the IT revolution will create new divisions in human society, between those who master the new technology and those who are unable to. IT will be used for both constructive and destructive purposes. For example, IT warfare will create completely new situations for modern armies. Within each country, political structures will change because of changes in the way wealth is created and income is distributed. Modern political systems arose out of competition between different interest groups in the industrial economy, between those who work on the farms and those who live in cities, between those who own capital and those who earn wages, between the landed and the landless, and between the rich and the poor. In the next century, the pattern will change dramatically. The old trade union structure, for example, will be weakened as work organisation becomes less hierarchical and the division between white-collar and blue-collar work becomes diffused. Political parties will have to re-invent themselves to engage new political constituencies especially among younger voters living in big cities.

One major problem is the inversion of the knowledge pyramid in human society. It used to be that the older one becomes, the more one knows. This may always be true where human wisdom and maturity are involved. But, in many areas — like IT, science, medicine, finance and fashion — younger people often have more updated knowledge than older people. When parents see what their children are able to do with the computer, they feel a tension within themselves. While they are proud of their children, they also feel acutely their own obsolescence. Because of the speed of IT development, every ten years throw up a new generation who are better equipped. Those in their 30s know they are not as good as those in their 20s, and those in their 20s are already behind those in their teens. This has never been the case before in human society. The implications on social value systems are profound. Human cultures will be transformed.

Those organisations which are able to tap the knowledge and creativity of the younger generation will be able to advance more quickly. Those organisations which are unable to do so will be at a competitive disadvantage. What then should be the correct relationship between the old and the young in this new world? What does human wisdom mean in the future? What will happen to those who for one reason or another are unable to cope with the new technology? How should they be accommodated in society? Will some societies or racial groups dominate others? There are no easy answers to these questions and human society may have to go through crisis and revolution before good solutions are found.

In Singapore, we are particularly worried because we are a relatively small, cosmopolitan society. If we do not handle these new tensions well, we will not be able to hold together. We have recently embarked on a nation-wide exercise involving all sectors to prepare our society for the next century. Despite globalisation, we want all Singaporeans in the world to share a common heartbeat. In particular, it is important for us to understand the hopes and fears of younger Singaporeans, and engage them in the process of re-inventing our society. We have launched a Singapore 21 Movement involving Singaporeans of all races and age groups. No one knows all the answers — neither the government nor university professors nor NGOs (non-government organisations) — but we know we face some very serious challenges ahead. The IT revolution will not only create new antagonisms between the old and the young, it will also accentuate antagonisms between racial and religious groups. This is because differences in the value systems of different racial and religious groups will result in different responses and different speeds of response to the IT challenge.

## Conclusion

Whether we like it or not, we are arriving at a turning point in human history. Singapore is like a small boat which is very sensitive to changes in the global tidal flow. Larger boats may take longer to respond to the changing tide but they enjoy the advantage of greater stability. In Singapore, if we are not careful, we can be swept aside. But if we respond early and correctly, we can achieve a good position when the rising tide becomes a full flow. This is the reason why Singapore has responded in a certain way to the challenges of education, entrepreneurship and changing social values.

# TOMORROW

*Ultimately, it is a moral challenge.*

HONG KONG — As a new generation of leadership ascends in the Far East, no one regards the future more deeply — or daringly — than George Yeo, the trade minister of Singapore. Long a port for the movement of money, goods and people, Singapore under Mr. Yeo's leadership is now scrambling to make itself into the Far Eastern hub of Internet commerce. But it must do so within a culture and political structure that many Westerners find constraining.

The 45-year-old Mr. Yeo, a passionate student of history and culture, studied engineering at Cambridge and business at Harvard before beginning an ascent through Singapore's military, eventually becoming brigadier general and air-force chief of staff. A decade ago, he entered politics. As minister of information and the arts, he assumed centre stage in some of the country's well-publicised censorship episodes. But he also moved to make himself a role model for change — conducting Internet chats, hailing the powers of diversity and continually calling on Singaporeans to think boldly about the future.

You may find some of his views unpalatable as well as provocative, but either way you'll benefit from knowing them. Mr. Yeo was interviewed in Hong Kong, where he attended the *Asian Wall Street Journal* Millennium Summit.

— Thomas Petzinger Jr.

---

This interview was for the *Wall Street Journal* Millennium Edition (January 1, 2000) to mark the crossing to a new millennium. 

## Power Devolves

**The Wall Street Journal (WSJ)**: How will technology and globalisation change the face of government?

**George Yeo**: Governments will increasingly come under international competitive pressure to change. Let me put it this way. Human talent is mobile. You don't have to be an American if you don't want to be an American. You can go to Europe. You can come to Singapore. You can return to India. Talent is mobile. Capital is mobile. Knowledge is mobile. So unlike the industrial world where you are trapped within a jurisdiction and at the mercy of a monopoly government, in the coming world, governments will have to compete for that same talent, capital and knowledge.

Big governments can't do this efficiently. Brussels can't do it. Washington can't do it. It has to be done at the state level like California or Guangdong. Or better still, at the city level like Los Angeles, Singapore, Hong Kong and Shanghai. So in all the big countries, there is growing political pressure to devolve power and economic management to provinces, to states, to cities, to the lowest level where good governance decides whether talent flows in or out. This is climatic change.

**WSJ**: So all politics become local. Easy for you to say as the leader of a city-state!

**Mr. Yeo**: In this new age, city-states like Singapore are fleet-footed. Take Singapore's Changi Airport as an example. In many countries, airports are unpleasant experiences. Why? Because they are local monopolies. You have no choice but to use them. Because you must pass through their gates, the gatekeepers are arrogant and they treat you badly.

As a city-state, we have no domestic air travel in Singapore. From the word "go", our airline and airport had to compete globally. So we have always treated travelers well at Changi Airport, which is why large numbers of people choose to use it. They may have only a few hours, but they use Changi because there is a gym there. They get free rides to the city. If you need a hand-phone, we provide one for free. You only pay for what you use. You need a shower? There are clean shower facilities, clean towels. What else do you need? Food? Japanese, Asian, Western, Italian — they're all available. The approach is that of a shopping centre, not that of a monopoly. Come on in!

**WSJ**: This is what government has become? A clearance sale?

**Mr. Yeo**: The pressure on government now is either you compete or you are out. Yes, you still have powers of monopoly, you still have powers of legal violence over your citizens. You can do nasty things to them. You can make life miserable for them. You can hound them for taxes and so on. But eventually the smart ones say, "Why must I put up with all this hassle? I can be just as comfortable in Hong Kong as I am in New York or Sydney." Or at least, the trend is in that direction. Governments are being forced by external competitive pressure to change and reform. But the trouble is, and here I am on politically incorrect grounds ...

**WSJ:** Go ahead. We can take it.

**Mr. Yeo:** The trouble is the one-man, one-vote system. Is it functional or dysfunctional? If it is one-man, one-vote in a city, the approach towards government is level-headed and practical. You have to attract business and talent. You need a good airport, so let's adjust our rules and systems to facilitate its success. But take a big state like California. Between the north, the centre and the south, the interests diverge. You may not agree on a common position. Even worse, if policies and rules are settled in Washington, thousands of miles away, the people there may have no idea what's happening on the ground.

In large polities, the outcome of a one-man, one-vote system can be frustrating and perverse, which is why in many big countries there is growing cynicism toward power centres that are far away — in Beijing, Brussels, Tokyo or Washington. You say, "Hell, these people in the capitals don't know what they are talking about. They are just feathering their own nests." But in a one-man, one-vote system, what do you do? How do you break out of it?

So I see in the next century both democracy and socialism becoming smaller. (You can call "socialism" by a different name in the U.S., but it means the same thing.) They have to be scaled down, to a level where you optimise your domestic consensus and your international competitiveness. If democracy or socialism is over too wide an area, or covers too large a population, the outcome may be fractious domestic politics and a weakening of international competitiveness. Decisions should be taken at the lowest level possible. Competition will force a revolution in the practice of both democracy and socialism, and reshape political thinking in the 21st century. This means a change in the self-identity of human beings. What are you primarily a member of — a city, state, country, region, global tribe, world community?

**WSJ**: I don't understand how that contradicts the idea of one-man, one-vote. I mean, one-man, one-vote is really kind of the ultimate political devolution, isn't it? The ultimate distribution of power?

**Mr. Yeo**: Let me ask you. Would you agree as an American to have one-man, one-vote for a world government? Then your destiny, your taxes, your life would be determined by China, India, Africa and South America, where most people live. Your immediate reaction would be, "I am not joining any world government! That's a stupid idea!"

**WSJ**: That might indeed be my reaction.

**Mr. Yeo**: So within an existing polity there would be subgroups which would also say, "Look, I'm better off on my own. Why should I pool health insurance with people who do not look after their health?" Technology has given us the power to secede.

### Democracy of the Future

**WSJ**: If not "one-man, one-vote", then what?

**Mr. Yeo**: No. The question is, at what level should one-man, one-vote be set up? Is it one-man, one-vote in Athens? Is it one-man, one-vote for the whole of Greece? Is it one-man, one-vote for the whole of

Europe? I think it makes a powerful difference to the outcome. One-man, one-vote in Aceh [a province of Indonesia] may mean Acehnese independence. One-man, one-vote in Indonesia probably means no independence for Aceh.

**WSJ**: So you see the electoral bodies of the future scaling to the city in some cases and the region in others?

**Mr. Yeo**: Yes.

**WSJ**: Which means the boundaries of government become highly fluid.

**Mr. Yeo**: Political structures, instead of being hierarchical, will become more Web-like. And even within the city, is it one-man, one-vote? Or should it be weighted according to property ownership and education? If the propertied and talented are constantly outvoted, why should they remain? They have choices. My feeling is that although these ideas are very politically incorrect to talk about now, adjustments will have to be made eventually. And groups which make the adjustments earlier will surge ahead over those which are trapped in old ideological positions.

**WSJ**: Don't you acknowledge that there may be certain principles that are higher than a municipality's standing in the marketplace? A certain base foundation of human equality, for instance?

**Mr. Yeo**: We are all children of God. So murder is murder whether you murder a rich man or a beggar. We may disagree on whether there should be a death sentence. We may disagree about whether there should be caning. But we do agree there should be no torture and we should not be penalizing parents or children for the crimes of an individual. Because we belong to one global community, we have come to accept that certain common standards should prevail, while allowing plenty of room for individual communities to decide their own affairs. We belong to one world, so there has to be a common base, but upon the common base, there should be plurality. I think that is a fair position.

## Cultural Darwinism

**WSJ**: You're trying to make Singapore into a technology capital, a hub for e-commerce. Yet in your speaking and writing you continually emphasise the importance of culture in society and of liberal arts in education. Why's that?

**Mr. Yeo**: Because the human being is a very strange animal. In evolutionary terms, why do we enjoy music? Why do we need the arts?

**WSJ**: Well, they must have conferred some survival advantage.

**Mr. Yeo**: That's right. They are highly developed and uniquely developed among human beings. *Ipso facto*, they must confer a Darwinian advantage. We have not yet figured out why exactly.

Empirically, we know that to attract scientists, scholars and entrepreneurs to Singapore, we must provide cultural facilities and nurture the arts. They provide brain food. Why have they become brain food? One day we will find out. But provide the food and the brains will come. Starve them of this food and they will leave for somewhere else. It may seem a very utilitarian approach to the arts. But from an evolutionary perspective, it should not be surprising.

Because we brought in tens of thousands of talented foreigners into Singapore in the past 10 years, we're seeing a wonderful cultural efflorescence. It is transforming the social landscape. Cross-fertilisation is an essential part of the creative process.

**WSJ**: So diversity breeds creativity.

**Mr. Yeo**: Yes, when the combination is right. It can also lead to conflict and friction. If you have a culture that enables you to absorb talented individuals and fit them into the community, and allow them to knock against each other in a creative way, then you succeed. If you can't accommodate the tensions, then the diversity is destructive.

**WSJ**: Can a culture like that be designed, or does it develop only through the accumulation of historical accidents?

**Mr. Yeo**: A lot of it is what you have inherited. Then, within what you have inherited, you have some ability to make changes, maybe plus or minus 10%. But you are mostly stuck with what you have inherited. These are deep programs in the cultural system that you might not even be aware of. The Japanese, for example, find it very difficult to integrate foreigners fully into their society, which is both a strength and a weakness.

**WSJ**: I think you've referred to culture as the "operating system" of a people or a land.

**Mr. Yeo**: It is. Many Asians when they go to Silicon Valley feel that they have a fair crack at the system. Silicon Valley has a special culture that is an important part of its success. Asians don't get that same feeling when they go to big U.S. cities. There is always a glass ceiling because you are not white. You are Asian. Yes, you can do the technical work, but ... there is always a "but".

**WSJ**: You can't be a leader.

**Mr. Yeo**: In Silicon Valley it used to be like that. They would always hire a white American CEO. Asians might have provided the financing and do the creative work, but they wanted someone who looked right up front. Now increasingly, Asians are becoming CEOs themselves. California has always represented future tendencies in America. It's very interesting, very exciting, how a new culture is evolving which may eventually engulf the whole of America as it becomes more multiracial and cosmopolitan.

### Censorship and Hypocrisy

**WSJ**: In your role as minister of culture, you had censorship duties. Why should censorship exist when the pendulum swings toward the open and free? Is censorship even possible today?

**Mr. Yeo**: Well, censorship is part of education. We are not trying to prevent young children physically from accessing pornography. They will always be able to find it in college or from their peers. It is on the

Net. You can't stop it. But do you condone it? Do you sanction it? There is always a certain amount of hypocrisy involved in all of this. But then, as they say, hypocrisy is the compliment which vice pays to virtue.

Through symbolic censorship, you establish in young minds that certain standards of right and wrong exist. We will always fall short of those standards, but we must have them. If you access a porn site on the Internet in front of your teacher, you will be rebuked and punished. Now, is that censorship? It is a form of censorship. The teacher is completely aware that when the child is on his own, he is going to access the same site. But not in front of me, please, and not blatantly and not in school and not in the public library. Because if you do it in school or the public library, there will be a negative reaction. In this way, the norms of a culture are established, in the tribe or the community — which is necessary. In the end, you must still have a sense of what is right and wrong.

**WSJ**: You conducted an Internet chat in which, referring to Singapore, you made the comment, "Our management style and governing methods will have to change" for the knowledge era. How will they have to change?

**Mr. Yeo**: It is like the difference between the management of General Motors in the days of assembly lines and the management of a company like Apple or Microsoft, where you require every person to feel committed to his job. You can't police him. He may write a bug into the software that will not be discovered for years, and he may do it to sabotage you. So you jolly well win him over. You can't treat him as if he is a union member to be watched and controlled. If you have a bureaucratic system, there is not going to be very much entrepreneurship or intrapreneurship. The way you relate to your staff is very important. You have to co-opt your employee so that he becomes a part of the larger family.

The kind of culture that is required for cooperative brainwork is like that of an orchestra. Yes, you can play because you have to play. Or you can play with passion. And you must play with deference to the group. If every musician wants to be a soloist, you won't get good music either. The group culture required for classical music is very different from that of rap.

**WSJ**: So what are the implications for national leadership in a country like Singapore?

**Mr. Yeo**: Well, the larger operating system in Singapore is one that accepts change and adaptation as a way of life. We've always adjusted from British days, never overly committed to any product, service or way of doing things. In the 19th century, it was trade in opium and spices. Then during World War One, it became tin. With the auto industry, the rubber industry became very important. Then came manufacturing. Now it is Asian currency units and other financial instruments. In the future, it will be mostly brainwork. We cannot have too strong an emotional attachment to any particular product or service. Whatever is the most interesting game in town, we will learn to play it, and we will make the necessary internal adjustments. The larger culture is always one that is cosmopolitan, adaptable and accepting of foreigners.

**WSJ**: That's a prescription for success in the 21st century for any culture or people or country, right?

**Mr. Yeo**: History is a long time. The pendulum swings one way now; it will swing the other way later. What is now an advantage may become a disadvantage. There may again be a time when the world is divided into political blocs or empires, and strong prejudices are required to unite human beings. Then, as a city-state we would be out on a limb, which was the situation Venice faced when Napoleon arrived. We are not infinitely flexible. History plays tricks with us. I would never say always.

### The Trouble with Trade Regulations

**WSJ**: What's the future of trade regulation in a global economy? Is there any point in it? Is it even possible and sustainable in the long term?

**Mr. Yeo**: I've just come from a meeting of trade ministers in Lausanne, Switzerland. Countries from all the continents were there — rich countries, poor countries, 40 countries with different interests. What is fair for agriculture? Intellectual property? What do you do for poor countries, for countries like Bangladesh? How do you encourage everybody to buy into the [World Trade Organization] ideal? The issues are complicated, but there is a general thrust in favour of globalisation and a more liberal trading regime in the world. Everybody knows from practical experience that trade means wealth. It means greater prosperity and opportunities for the guy down below. We have a responsibility to our own people. Opening the gates to trade is good for everybody.

But it may benefit you more than it benefits me. So the game becomes, "Come on. Let's adjust the rules so that we share a little more fairly the benefits of that surplus." While the powerful motivation is towards a more open trading system, there is inevitably a lot of hard bargaining as well. It is more complicated now because the Cold War is over. During the Cold War, if you were not nice to India, the Soviet Union would be nice to India. That gave India a strong bargaining position. All of us in the Third World had to be treated well. America tolerated dictatorships and all kinds of iniquities in Third World countries because the alternative was worse.

Now the Cold War is over. No big threat. The terms of trade, as it were, have altered for Third World countries. There is a sense among some of them, "Look, you are no longer treating me nice. You used to be nice to me, but now you treat me like dirt." And a few of them have decided that if pushed too far, they will go out of their way to thwart the advanced countries, because the WTO works on consensus. The stakes are high and the actual amounts involved may be in the billions of dollars. But that these hard negotiations are being seriously undertaken shows how important it is to have a more open trading system for everybody.

**WSJ**: Will you name names? Which countries in the developing world play those games now?

**Mr. Yeo**: All countries are involved in this game. Where they are too small to be important, they combine with other countries and they take common positions in order to strengthen their bargaining power. Then they try to play off Japan against the U.S., and the U.S. against Europe and so on. But it is better this way than having armies on the move. China's entry into WTO will make this a safer world.

**WSJ**: So trade is an intellectual game with high stakes. The alternative is a violent game with high stakes.

**Mr. Yeo**: Yes.

### Civilisation's Challenge

**WSJ**: You made your career in the military. Will mankind always have armed conflicts, or is it possible that we are in a secular trend towards a safer world?

**Mr. Yeo**: Many years ago I read an abridged version of [Arnold] Toynbee's encyclopedic *A Study of History*. He had a simple thesis: That civilisation is the response to a challenge. That without a challenge, there would not be creativity and the impulse to change, and it is in response to a challenge — it could be environmental change or an enemy — that elaborate systems are created.

It is the same with the individual. Why did God give us a free will? Why couldn't he have just made us as happy beings in heaven, if he was a good God? Why is the free will an essential part of divinity? Because the choice must be made. You are created, you are challenged, and nobody can respond to that challenge on your behalf. Not your parents, not your teacher, not your brother or your sister. You must take the test yourself. And you either pass it or you fail. If you overcome the challenge, you become a part of God. If you fail, you are rejected. The Greeks understood this.

There can be no happy community that confronts no challenge, which experiences no fear and no danger of failure. So can we somehow create a world community that is challenged in a profound way so that the deepest abilities in our being are brought out? Maybe one day a comet will appear on a collision course with Earth, and then I think we will respond as one. But until that happens, it is more likely that the challenges are by one human group upon another. I don't see this aspect of conflict in human society going away anytime in the near future.

**WSJ**: How will wars be fought in the future? There's a lot of talk about information warfare, but presumably there will always be bullets shot and flesh torn.

**Mr. Yeo**: That will be a very inefficient way of fighting wars in the future. The old Chinese philosopher Sun Zi once said that that the acme of triumph is achieving your objective without having to fight. So perhaps just by paralysing your enemy's systems and causing a rearrangement of facts, your enemy decides that he should surrender. I mean, then you have achieved your objective. Better still, if he surrenders without realising that he has surrendered.

**WSJ**: So how do we obtain those bloodless victories?

**Mr. Yeo**: Warfare will always press every frontier of knowledge known to man. The new frontiers are information technology and biotechnology, and I think warfare will inevitably move into those areas. You can try to bind it with rules, like rules for antipersonnel mines and chemical warfare, but the temptation to exploit new technology is hard to resist. We are not talking about conflict between First World countries and Third World countries. That is an unfair contest. We are talking about conflict between advanced societies, say, between China and the U.S. in the 21st century, with both sides having scientists and Nobel Prize winners. Knowledge economy versus knowledge economy. The New York Stock Exchange may be targeted. Suddenly trillions are wiped out without people knowing what has happened until it is too late. By the time they find out, there will be global horror and confusion among buyers and sellers.

**WSJ**: Trillions of dollars or trillions of bytes?

**Mr. Yeo**: Trillions of dollars. We are so worried about Y2K, but Y2K is an unintended problem. Imagine if the brightest minds are dedicated to creating such problems for each other's complex systems. I am not sure they are not already thinking such dark thoughts. They probably are. And if I were managing a complex system, I'd better assume that such dark thoughts are being thought about, and I'd better think of ways to protect myself. This is an endless game of the sword vs. the shield. There will be spectacular successes and failures. People will learn from these experiences. And then we are on to another spiral of destructive competition.

**WSJ**: Should governments be wary of genetic engineering? Should they regulate it?

**Mr. Yeo**: You can't stop it. You can't ban it. Because you will surely fail. But you can direct it. You can legislate. You can create sanctions, allay public fears and minimise the risks. There are always risks, but you can minimise the risks. Take, say, this whole debate on genetically modified foods.

**WSJ**: Did that come up in your trade meeting?

**Mr. Yeo**: In a peripheral way. It wasn't a major issue. But the fears get overblown. Scientists get shouted down by polemicists. This is just food. One day it will be genetic medicine that may help those with Alzheimer's. Some genetic diseases can be avoided. "Oh, by the way, why don't I also make this correction and your kid will grow up smarter? Would you like me to tinker elsewhere as well?" If you don't, then someone else will, and his kid will be smarter and stronger. Then what about my kid?

**WSJ**: You can't stop it?

**Mr. Yeo**: I don't think so. Ultimately, it's a moral challenge. Without a moral framework, technology will destroy us. The world's major religions must rise to this challenge or strange new religions will proliferate.

**WSJ**: Maybe this is why religion has evolved, to help us deal with the deepest vexations of the time.

**Mr. Yeo**: I think so. The genetic basis of religiosity has been written about.

**WSJ**: Are you frightened or excited about the future?

**Mr. Yeo**: Both. The processing capability is now so immense there is nothing now that you cannot track, no genetic expression you cannot decipher. There will be no anonymity. Although there are six billion human beings, it is theoretically possible to track all their movements and their characteristics right down to the last genetic code. Who does the tracking and who does the controlling? Good men? Evil men? We will be manipulated without our knowing. It is quite a frightening thought. I see the new technology making possible unimaginable evil in the world.

The market today ignores all this. The way dot-coms add value to a company by magic assumes a bright sunny future. I am not that sanguine. We don't know the nature of the beast that lies inside us and the dangers that are ahead.

**WSJ**: You said a moment ago that civilisation demands a challenge.

**Mr. Yeo**: Yes. We can easily feed more than six billion human beings now. Once we genetically modify food in a big way with high yields and pest resistance, we can feed many, many more. Then what challenge is there for us? I think it must be the conquest and colonisation of space. It is in the nature of man to explore the limits, to push the boundaries of his envelope. Popping satellites and vehicles into space is no longer a technical problem. You can create artificial environments. Planet Earth will become the Old World. The New World will be out there — the moon, Mars, Starship Enterprise and, one day, Star Wars. That will be the next phase, if we don't destroy ourselves first.

**WSJ**: We're certainly not making any big moves into space right now.

**Mr. Yeo**: Big moves are made out of fear. During the Cold War, when the Soviets put up the Sputnik, Kennedy launched his space programme. Things moved. The Cold War is over; you humour the Russians with space cooperation. In return, they let you defang some of their nuclear warheads. But one day there will be a huge challenge, and we'll be scrambling again.

# A Global Marketplace for Sensational News

*... there must be no illusion that the media is always impartial.*

## End of the Old Order

Up till the Vietnam War, it used to be in the advanced countries that national newspapers and TV stations reflected the view of national establishments. Thus, *The New York Times*, *The Washington Post* and the major TV networks provided the American view of the world.

In the UK, it was much the same. The London *Times*, *The Daily Telegraph* and the Manchester *Guardian*, together with the BBC, marked out the dominant political space.

The Vietnam War era was a turning point. It destroyed trust in the old institutions. Since then, the Western media has become increasingly an autonomous player in Western society.

Take the continuing criticism of British institutions like the royal family. They are no more imperfect now than they were in the past. Unlike before, there is now no restraint in the media reporting. What sells gets reported. And if readers want sensation, who is to second-guess the market?

Profits have also become more important as media companies are bought and sold like other businesses. Every newspaper proclaims journalistic independence but, in the end, it is the owner who has the final say because he hires and fires the editor. In the UK and the US, Rupert Murdoch upset the old order. As an Australian, he had

---

Speech at the News World Asia Conference, 11 May 2001.

less sympathy for the old arrangements. He is a complete realist. He adjusts to the reality of each market. When the Chinese reacted angrily to BBC World Service TV in 1994 and threatened his interests in China, he pulled BBC out of Star TV's satellite broadcast into China. His son, James Murdoch, raised Western eyebrows recently when he spoke out against the *Falun Gong*.

**Changes in Asia**

The Japanese media is also changing but it is still relatively more conservative than the Western media. Unlike the British media, the Japanese media continues to protect the institution of the monarchy. But below the monarchy, the Japanese establishment is going through a crisis. From the late 1970s, the Japanese media showed greater willingness to report on political corruption. This trend accelerated with the split of the LDP in 1993. Now, the position of the mainline print media is often anti-establishment as more and more Japanese come to the view that the only way to change Japan is to shake up the existing establishment.

Even China is changing. In fact, with the opening up of the economy and the growth of the Internet, the media scene in China is changing dramatically. Externally, Chinese leaders are interacting with the international media in an increasingly self-confident way. Earlier this year, because of the Internet, Premier Zhu Rongji was forced to retract his earlier statement on the cause of an explosion in a Guangxi primary school which led to the death of many schoolchildren. In the recent stand-off over the detention of the US aircrew on Hainan island, the Chinese reacted to American media interviews with families and friends by conducting similar interviews of their own. This would never have been done in the past. In 1976, the year Mao Zedong died, the devastating Tangshan earthquake was hardly reported in the Chinese media and the world found out about the disaster only long afterwards.

While they are changing, the Japanese and Chinese media are not likely to become like the Western media. The cultural values are different. It is not just politics. The O J Simpson trial and the Monica Lewinsky saga were widely reported in Asia, but such dramas are unlikely to be enacted in Confucianist or Muslim Asia. Nor in Europe. The sense of fairness and propriety varies from country to country depending on its culture and traditions.

## The Myth of Impartiality

The polarised reporting of the recent EP-3 incident in the US and China shows that there is no such thing as an impartial media. This has nothing to do with media control or democracy. Understandably, both the American and Chinese media were nationalistic. Chinese chat sites, which provide the freest media space in China, were far more anti-US than the official Chinese media. The BBC was more nuanced in its reporting than CNN but its position was still very much Western. In most Asian countries, the instinct was not to take sides and the Asian media, by and large, took intermediate positions. Even the Taiwanese media was very careful not to be provocative. I found myself sampling different news channels in English and Chinese to get a sense of the overall picture.

We must expect every newspaper and news channel to have its own perspective of an event. Consciously or sub-consciously, political and economic interests often exert their influence. Cultural assumptions can also be quite different. In an age of demassification, particularly in the West, group interests, sometimes assert themselves more strongly than national interests, however defined. Many NGOs now express cross-national group interests.

The battle for hearts and minds is therefore also a battle for power and influence over the media. In economics, there is a marketplace for goods and services, which includes the media. The market does not make value judgements unless these judgements are reducible to dollars and cents. There is no separate marketplace of ideas, which is why when the establishment influence over the national media weakens, sensational reporting can become unbridled. That is where the money is. The marketplace for sensational reporting can be quite irresponsible. When the Monica Lewinsky story broke, the Pope's visit to Cuba was crowded out in the US media.

Each media market segment has its own standard. In France, the sexual peccadillos of political leaders are not usually reported in mainstream newspapers partly because the readers would not reward such reporting.

## A Global Moral Sense

However, with globalisation, there is a growing common moral sense in the world which increasingly unites us all. This is expressed in universal values which, hopefully, will help save us from collective environmental suicide and prevent genocide.

Last year, at the confluence of the Ganga and the Jamuna rivers in India, millions of Hindus converged on the city of Allahabad. Every 12 years, a cosmic river, the Saraswati, also conjoins and last year was particularly auspicious because the planets were in alignment. The whole world watched this religious event, the Maha Kumbh Mela, with fascination. The international media gave it full coverage in all languages. Apart from an excess of interest in naked nagas by some, the overall coverage was much the same.

Last month in Singapore, a pair of Siamese twins named Ganga and Jamuna after the two sacred rivers in India, were successfully separated in Singapore. To the surprise of Singaporeans, the operation attracted worldwide attention because of a universal sense of compassion. The surgery was high risk. I am not sure if the Singapore General Hospital would have agreed to the operation had it known beforehand that there would be so much media coverage.

## Heisenberg's Uncertainty Principle

Media coverage changes the reality it covers. In so doing, there is a Heisenberg's uncertainty principle* at work. The German physicist, Werner Heisenberg, found that observing atomic particles changed the way they behaved. In the same way, the media changes the reality it reports on. Because the media has become a part of the total reality, its control and accountability are issues that will become more important in the future.

---

*Heisenberg's uncertainty principle states that "the more precisely the position of some particle is determined, the less precisely its momentum can be known".

When the next Maha Kumbh Mela is held 12 years from now, commercialisation of some aspects of it is inevitable because of media attention. This will affect its sacredness. The Vatican understands this new media and works with it. John Paul II is the first pope of the new media age. He grants plenary indulgences to those who follow important papal masses on TV.

Unfortunately, the media is also exploited for evil purposes. Terrorists reserve their worst for media coverage to maximise the impact. The Taliban might not have destroyed the Buddha statues in Bamiyan if it was not assured of extensive coverage by the global media.

## Grappling with the New Reality

The competitive nature of the global media has created a set of new dynamics which is increasingly beyond the control of governments. Technically, censorship has become much harder to enforce. Since no government, corporation or organisation can stop the growing cacophony of news reporting, what one must do is to make sure that one's own version of the story also gets through.

In the last few months, tourism in the UK has plummeted because foreigners imagine that the countryside is ravaged by the culling of animals. I was most surprised to learn from the British High Commissioner a few weeks ago that only 1% of animals had been culled so far. Half a million had been killed, which was less than the 600,000 slaughtered in abattoirs every week for meat. Somehow, that perspective never got through the media reports. A graphic picture of dead animals on the front page leaves an indelible imprint on the mind.

Can we improve the regulatory framework to ensure more accurate and balanced reporting? I doubt that very much can be done. Even the Chinese Government has come to that conclusion. In Beijing as in Washington, official media conferences are now directed as much at the domestic audience as it is to the international audience. The media game is now played by everyone. In Singapore, we insist that the domestic media carries the official version accurately. Otherwise, we can't reach out to our own voters.

For the time being, the Anglo-Saxon media is dominant because of their financial strength, their reach and the use of the English language. This will be contested. In Asia, the growth of the middle classes will feed competitors. Even in the English language, non-Anglo-Saxon players will enter the arena. For some years now, NHK's English Service provided some kind of alternative. In recent years, China CCTV's English Service has improved tremendously. Singapore's CNA markets itself as a news channel reporting from an Asian perspective in English and is building up its viewership in the region. Thus, globalisation of the media has also led to fragmentation.

There is no point railing against this new global media that seems sometimes to be out of control. This is all part of the new game. To play it, however, there must be no illusion that the media is always impartial. Instead, we must analyse and understand its nature. The media is always influenced by cultural biases, political interests and the profit motive. In this environment, finding ways to market one's own version of events is very important. Political parties in the West understand this and invest considerable effort in media management and spin control. In Asia, political marketing will also become more important. Willynilly, government departments in many countries are being forced to do more marketing domestically and internationally. They will need considerably more resources than are now being allocated to them by their finance ministries. And for those of us who are at the receiving end of this onslaught of truths, half-truths and lies, the key is to make sure that we choose the right filters. Unfortunately, this also means that we tend to choose the media which share our likes, dislikes and prejudices.

# GEOPOLITICS

# To Wage Peace, Understand War

*...our interest in war must be to wage a better peace whether this be best achieved through fighting a war or fighting to avert it.*

From the records it is hard not to believe that war is a necessary part of human history. War — as civil war, as revolution, as war between nation states — is a discontinuity in the orderly development of human affairs. Whether men are collected in tribes or nations, in social or economic classes, in racial or religious congregations, the contact between groups must be regulated. This is accomplished through institutional arrangements. When existing institutions are no longer able to resolve and to contain the bounds of conflict and disagreement, the result is a rupture, a violent shift from one equilibrium to another, a contested rearrangement of human groups in their relationship with each other. Such has been the course of history and its cycle of war and peace.

Yet war is no more preordained than history is predetermined. Despite the over-plentiful evidence in support, the humanity of man rebels against the suggestion that war is inevitable. Can it be that man with his superior intelligence is unable to rise above the Darwinian law of the jungle, that his cunning cannot design a social framework spacious and elastic enough to accommodate and withstand the stresses of continuous change? Is he so fallen from grace to be forever condemned as either the perpetrator or victim of

This short essay was written in 1979 for *POINTER*, an SAF journal, when George Yeo was a Captain in the SAF. Reprinted with permission from *POINTER*, Vol. 5. No. 3, January 1980.

massive, wanton slaughter? And even if war is in the general sense inevitable, it surely cannot be that all wars are.

Every generation is confronted with this choice of fighting or averting war. For no peace is so perfect that it is beyond improvement. There are occasions when an unfavourable peace is enough justification for war. The blind pursuit of peace is as insane as the lust for war is repugnant. But war once set in motion often develops a force and momentum which rapidly slips it out of control. The passions that are aroused and the violence released cannot be stilled as readily as they are increased. He who pulls the trigger can never be assured that he himself will not be crushed by the ensuing train of events. This uncertainty which the dynamics of war inject into the calculation gives peace its stability, with the latter as a limiting threshold to the slide into war. War may be an instrument of policy but it is an instrument singularly prone to loss of control, an instrument so blunt and ungraduated that its use can never guarantee the intended outcome.

The study of war finds its only justification in peace. From whichever moral standpoint one chooses, there are just and there are unjust wars. Whether our interest in war is professional or historical, the object in every instance must be to wage a better peace whether this be best achieved through fighting a war or fighting to avert it. And not to revel in war like one cocksure of its effects.

# Asian Civilisation in the Pacific Century

*... the encounter of cultures should lead not to the complete absorption by one of the other, but to mutual accommodation and mutual learning.*

## In the Footsteps of Japan

In the 18th and 19th centuries, the Industrial Revolution in Great Britain led to successive waves of industrialisation on the European mainland and in North America. In the same way, the successful economic transformation of Japan is setting off successive waves of change in the Asia-Pacific region. In the wake of Japan are the newly industralised economies (NIEs), followed by the ASEAN countries (with the temporary exception of the Philippines) and, behind them, China, Indo-China, Burma (or Myanmar) and eventually North Korea as well (as part of a re-united Korea). These are historic changes on a continental scale. There is every possibility that East and Southeast Asia will lead the world economy in the next century. It is the turn of Asians to take their place on the world stage again.

## Asian Settlement of The Rim

The economic, social and political transformation of East and Southeast Asia is accompanied by the migration of Asians to North America and Australasia. This migration is a large, long-term phenomenon caused by high population densities in Asia and relative low population densities in the US, Canada, Australia and New Zealand.

---

Keynote speech at the World Chinese Entrepreneurs Convention's Plenary Session on Cultural and Social Issues, Mandarin Hotel, 12 August 1991.

We are talking about a complex, multi-faceted phenomenon. We can trace it back to the decline of Qing China in the 19th century when large numbers of Chinese migrated to Southeast Asia, North America and Australia in search of a more tolerable life. After the Second World War, the threat of Communism sent waves of migrants from China, Taiwan, Hong Kong, Korea and Vietnam to the US and Canada. More recently, the uncertainty over the reversion of Hong Kong back to the PRC in 1997 has prompted countries like Canada and Australia to encourage capital transfer and to actively source for human talent. The flow of peoples is now not only from East Asia but also from Southeast Asia and the Indian sub-continent.

As a result, what we are witnessing is a growing settlement of cities on the Pacific Rim by Asians. Let me cite some statistics to illustrate my point. Using the latest US census results, the Asian population in the San Francisco-Oakland metropolitan statistical area (MSA) has increased from 10% in 1980 to 16% in 1990, in the Los Angeles-Long Beach area from 6% to 10% and in the Seattle-Everett area from 4% to 7%. If we zero in on Silicon Valley, we discover that the Asian population in San Jose has shot up from 8% in 1980 to 17% in 1990. Of the 70,000 or so engineers in the Valley, 10,000 to 15,000 are ethnically Chinese. About 5,500 engineers, managers and other professionals are from India.

If we look at British Columbia, the increase is equally dramatic. Ethnic Chinese are already 27% of Vancouver City's population of 560,000 and 15% of the 1.5 million population of Metropolitan Vancouver. Some demographers predict that the core city will reach 40% ethnic Chinese before the turn of the century which will make Vancouver the most Asian city in North America.

In Australia and New Zealand, the trends are not as startling but they point in the same direction. I do not have the latest figures for Australian and New Zealand cities, but from 1981 to 1986, over a short 5-year period, the Asian population in Perth increased from 3.4% to 4.3%, in Darwin from 4.9% to 6.2%, in Sydney from 2.8% to 4.7%, in Melbourne from 2.4% to 3.9%, in Auckland City from 2.3% to 2.9% and in Wellington City from 3.8% to 4.7%.

The migration of Asians to North America and Australasia is likely to continue well into the next century. The reason is simple. It will take that long for the Chinese and Indian heartlands to achieve the complete transformation of their societies. In the meantime, many of their more talented individuals will emigrate to secure better lives for themselves and their relatives. In short, the push factor will continue to operate. The pull factor will also continue to operate because the white peoples of the US, Canada, Australia and New Zealand are in relative decline. They are hardly reproducing themselves. Asians are needed to top up the numbers and also to revitalise their economies. Here, we must expect public policy to change from time to time because large scale Asian immigration creates social problems in the host communities. Unlike European immigrants, Asian immigrants are less likely to melt fully into the pot. While the economic advantages are self-evident, there will inevitably be cultural clashes because these Asian migrants will not want to lose their Asian identity completely. To begin with, the skin colour cannot change. Depending on the political considerations of the day, immigration policies in North America and Australasia can be tighter or looser, but the general trend will remain one of continuing Asian immigration.

The benefits to states like California, British Columbia, Western Australia and New South Wales are obvious. This Asian settlement of the Pacific Rim is becoming an important part of the drama of the Pacific Century. At the individual level, many of us here today would have relatives in all four corners of the Pacific, often siblings or first cousins. Contact is easy because of the advances in communications and transportation. You can be in Sydney today, Singapore tomorrow and Vancouver the day after. These family links weave a network of relationships which help bring Pacific communities closer together.

This pattern of Asian settlement in the Pacific is not unlike that of the Greek colonisation of the shorelines and islands of the Mediterranean and the Black Sea more than 2,500 years ago. Then, because of overpopulation on the Greek mainland, Greeks migrated from their city-states to found sister colonies in North Africa, Asia Minor, Italy and elsewhere. Before Alexander the Great, there was no single power. The city-states were all part of a larger Hellenic civilisation. They co-operated, competed and were in communication with one another, and met regularly for the Olympic games. In the same way, Asian communities all round the Pacific are in cooperation, competition and communication with one another, and we meet sometimes in conventions such as this.

In the 19th century and the early part of the 20th century, the European peoples spun the same kind of web across the Atlantic, connecting Europe to the Americas. The demographics were then quite different. At that time, the white peoples were growing in numbers and Europe exported people to populate entire continents. In 1900, about a third of the world's population lived in Europe. Today it is only about a tenth.

What happened across the Atlantic is now happening across the Pacific. We are part of this unfolding drama and we should try to be clear of our roles. While we ought to be proud of Asian achievements, we should, however, not overleap ourselves and become cultural chauvinists. I would like instead to argue that what is taking place is an interesting dialogue between Eastern and Western cultures which will lead to the general improvement of both.

## Dialogue of East and West

When the West was expanding, Western intellectuals selectively absorbed the best of Eastern science, art and ideas. Great men like Napoleon and Clausewitz, for example, found inspiration in Sun Zi's Art of War. The process was called "Orientalism". I use the term "Orientalism" in a serious, non-pejorative sense and not in the way Edward Said described it. I am referring to the kind of "Orientalism" that sought to absorb the best from the East. There is now a reverse process of "Occidentalism" at work, of Asians selectively absorbing the best of Western science, art and ideas. "Occidentalism" as the obverse of "Orientalism" describes the process better than the word "Westernisation" because "Westernisation" suggests that we have lost our Asian character while "Occidentalism" describes selective change within our Asian character without giving up the essence of that Asian character.

Japan was the first to occidentalise. While China was sure it had nothing to learn from the West, which was what Qian Long told George III, Meiji Japan wasted no time in overhauling every aspect of Japanese society.

In the case of Taiwan, South Korea, Hong Kong and Thailand, tens of thousands left to study and work in North America in the 1950s and 1960s. Many have since come back in return waves to help modernise their homelands, often using Western ideas and methods. Without their contribution, the NIEs would not have been able to make such rapid progress. Thailand and Malaysia are now benefiting from their returnees. Vietnam will one day also benefit from returning occidentalised Vietnamese.

China too needs occidentalised Chinese to help it modernise. The growth of the last 10 years would not have been possible without the role played by Hong Kong and Taiwanese businessmen who are familiar with Western ideas and methods. One day, part of the PRC diaspora now in North America, Japan, Europe and Australia will also go back to help transform Chinese society. Because of the immensity of China, this historic transformation will take many more decades. It has already taken China well over a century if we date the start of the process back to the humiliation of the Opium War, so we can afford to wait a few more decades.

We should draw a distinction between China as a political entity and Chinese civilisation. For a large part of its history, China was divided. Even when the Empire was united, there was always a penumbra of countries which were wholly or partly under Chinese cultural influence but not owing political allegiance to the Emperor. In other words, Chinese civilisation has always been much larger than China itself and the interaction of the centre with the periphery is a fascinating theme in the history of Chinese civilisation. It is the periphery which first absorbs outside influences and which then transmits these influences into the centre, and vice versa. Japan, Korea and Vietnam are examples of states at the periphery. The remarkable success of Chinese communities outside China means that these communities must also be considered part of the periphery.

At this stage in the history of Chinese or East Asian civilisation, the occidentalised periphery is more advanced than the centre. The centre, which is China, needs the periphery to help it achieve its great transformation. Even within China itself, it is the coastal regions which have made the most progress.

What all this means is that we have today many communities which are part of and contributing to a larger East Asian civilisation. I use the term East Asian civilisation rather than Chinese civilisation to avoid any suggestion that the centre should be intrinsically more important than the periphery. Take the Chinese community in Singapore as an example. Chinese Singaporeans are not Chinese nationals and have no wish to be. We are Singaporean; we are Southeast Asian. But Chinese Singaporeans are part of a larger East Asian civilisation, not just in terms of our cultural inheritance from the past, but also in terms of our continuing contribution, however minor, to that civilisation. In the same way, Chinese communities in Sydney, Vancouver and San Francisco are integral parts of that same larger civilisation, drawing from and adding to it. It has become in effect a civilisation with many poles and with much local variation.

The evolution of Confucianist thinking provides an interesting illustration of this multi-polarity. Confucianism as a broad stream no longer belongs exclusively to China. Indeed, up to the mid-1970s, Communist China renounced and denounced the teachings of the ancient philosopher. Only recently is he being rehabilitated. Confucianism in Korea and Japan developed in different directions centuries ago, giving rise to different patterns of social organisation. Qing China, Yi Korea and Tokugawa Japan were all Confucianist states but different. Till today, the pattern of business organisation reflects this divergence. While the Japanese established *zaibutsus* and the Koreans *chaebols*, Chinese businessmen have always found it difficult to break out of family control. It does not matter whether we are talking about Taiwan, Hong Kong or Southeast Asia; this Chinese pattern is resistant to change, except possibly in Singapore, where state involvement has created a group of government, government-linked and privatised government companies which reject family relationship as a factor in human resource management.

But, otherwise, succession is a recurrent problem among Chinese businessmen worldwide. This particular aspect of our Confucianist heritage is a weakness which has to be overcome. From opposite shores of the Pacific, we are all now taking a fresh look at Confucianism and its role in the modern world. China has no monopoly of wisdom here. This is a debate which encompasses all of East Asian civilisation.

Thus when we meet to discuss Chinese entrepreneurship, the unifying idea is not political but civilisational. Logically, we should also meet to discuss other subjects like the arts, letters, sociology or education.

Education is a big problem for Asians, especially in North America and Australasia. Among Asian migrants, there is always a fear that the next generation will lose their Asianness. If they speak only English, half the battle is lost. Whether we are talking about Los Angeles, Singapore or Sydney, the apprehensions are the same. The determination to remain Asian is strong. As individuals, we can do little beyond what the family can provide. But if we are organised, much more can be done to promote the teaching of Asian languages in schools in California, British Columbia and Australia, not just Chinese but also Japanese, Korean, Vietnamese, Thai, Malay and Tagalog. In addition to education, we should also promote Asian culture. I refer to culture here in a broad sense and not just to calligraphy or music.

I recommend the formation of a Pacific Foundation to help promote Asian education and culture all round the Pacific Rim. Existing efforts are not enough. The Foundation should support the teaching of Asian languages and Asian subjects in schools and colleges. It should also promote the development of Asian culture by organising seminars, sponsoring exhibitions, offering scholarships, honouring the successful and awarding prizes. It should not be difficult to raise the funds needed to launch such a Foundation. Asian businessmen are well-known for their philanthropy, especially in the field of education and culture. What we need is a little organisation and a lot of vision.

But will all this lead to conflict? Let me put it this way. White Americans, white Canadians and white Australians will of course prefer Asian migrants to be meek and to be as white in their values as possible. Then they can be absorbed like European migrants. But I doubt if this will happen. Yes, Asian migrants will want to blend in as much as they can, and they will indigenise, but they will not want to lose their Asian identity completely. In fact, the more successful they are as a group, the prouder will they be of their Asianness. To put it in another way, if these Asian migrants were to become white in everything but skin colour, their dynamism will surely be affected.

In other words, the encounter of cultures should lead not to the complete absorption by one of the other, but to mutual accommodation and mutual learning. It is in the interest of Western societies to accommodate the cultural differences of Asian migrants and to learn from them. Western societies need a new Orientalism to reinvigorate themselves. The discovery of Japan from quality control circles to sumo wrestling is the start of this new Orientalism. It will widen to include Korea, Taiwan and Southeast Asia. Australian society is a case in point. At the top, there is considerable intellectual consensus that the future of Australia lies not in Europe but in Asia. But there is still no widespread emotional acceptance of what it means to be part of Asia in a cultural sense. Without a much greater orientalisation of Australian society, Australia will not be able to fully become a part of Asia. In that regard, British Columbia and California, with higher proportions of Asians, are much more orientalised than Australia is.

Therefore, in answer to my earlier question on the possibility of conflict, there will be tension, and the tension is inevitable, but it can lead to good. Many years ago, Joseph Needham talked about the dialogue of East and West. It is a continuing dialogue and for the dialogue to be fruitful, the East should speak a little louder.

## Conclusion

While we should not be immodest, we must have a sense of the historical current sweeping us and make our contribution to its flow. Japan was the first in Asia to succeed in transforming its feudal structures. Many others are now following and it is by no means clear who will lead two, three or four decades from now. Great Britain led the Western pack for many years but America, Germany and

France eventually overtook her. How long Japan will continue to lead the rest of Asia is, however, not the important question. What is important is the fact of the larger Asian transformation in the next century which will draw into its sphere of influence the western states of North America, the whole of Australasia and possibly parts of Latin America as well. We are talking about an Asian civilisation which, while it may share many points in common with Western civilisation, will remain different and distinct. That we should be inspired to come from across the four seas to attend this Convention is proof that we feel for this Asian civilisation. I hope we will be able to build upon our sense of identity and help promote the development and the spread of our common heritage.

# Global Restructuring and the Prospects for Southeast Asia

*So long as political conflicts among the major powers are kept within bounds, large parts of Asia and Europe are poised for rapid economic development.*

Empires wax and wane. One superpower has crumbled with astonishing speed. The other is in decline. New power centres have emerged in Europe and in Asia. In all cases, the driving force is economic. Marx is right. When the institutional structure impedes economic development, the result is political upheaval. Global politics is still catching up with global economics. What we are witnessing is *perestroika* on a global scale.

In Asia, the three power centres are Japan, China and India. Their perspectives of global restructuring are quite different from those usually presented by the Western media which tend to take the perspectives of North America and Western Europe. In Southeast Asia, we have to take into account these different perspectives because they affect the condition of our existence.

## The Japanese Perspective

The Japanese perspective is dominated by Japan's profound sense of insecurity. After Meiji, Japan was determined to become a part of Western civilisation. Now it knows that is not possible. The more Japan succeeds economically and technologically, the more it is resented in North America and Western Europe. The reason is partly cultural. It is also partly racial.

---

Keynote address at the *Asia Wall Street Journal* Capital Markets Conference, Hyatt Regency Hotel, 16 January 1992.

But it is necessary for Japan to play a major role in international politics. Political power must follow economic power. The Americans do want Japan to play a bigger role but in a way prescribed by America. This will get more difficult as Japan becomes more assertive. It will not be content just writing the cheques. The Japanese know of course that they must not re-arm.If there is another war, they are more likely to lose than to win. They know that their strategic alliance with the United States is of central importance.

Notwithstanding this alliance, Japan's relationship with the United States (US) will come under increasing stress because of the relative decline of the US economy. There is only so much the Japanese can do to buy up US bonds and treasury bills and to help restore American competitiveness. The solution to America's economic problems must lie in America itself, not elsewhere. Unfortunately, there is no solution in sight. The tendency is still to blame everyone else for America's problems. Therefore, these problems will have to get worse before they can get better. The inescapable reality is that Americans will have to accept a lower standard of living and work harder. On the way there, American domestic politics will turn nasty. At some time in the future, a new president, a new administration, a new congress, will ask why America should continue to look after the world peace. Why not squeeze Japan to pay even more? Some Japanese politicians already consider the US forces in Japan as mercenaries. If you are not careful, mercenaries can extort money from you.

Insecure as they are, the Japanese must explore long-term alternatives to this complete dependence on the US for security. The alternatives are all in Asia. The long-term interest of Japan in the next century requires it to become more Asian. Culturally, the Japanese are of course Asian even if, in some respects, they are the most Westernised of Asians. What will change is their subjective perception of themselves. After Meiji, the Japanese desire was to be fully Westernised in the process of which they came to look down on other Asians. This attitude will change as the world's economic centre of gravity shifts to the Western Pacific. The Japanese will have to come to terms with the Chinese and the Koreans, much like the way the Germans had to come to terms with the French and the British.

When that happens, the Japan-US alliance will become less absolute. This does not mean that Japan will become less international. Quite the opposite: a Japan that is firmly rooted in Asia will find it easier to play an international role.

A new Greater East Asian co-prosperity sphere is already emerging. Other Asian economies are following in the wake of Japan's progress, first the newly industrialised economies (NIEs), now the ASEAN economies and the coastal regions of China, and eventually, the whole of East Asia. Japan will not be the imperial overlord of East Asia, but Japan will for many years be the leading economic player in the region.

The re-Asianisation of Japan will also help solve one of its most vexing internal problems, namely, the ageing of its population. Unlike America and Singapore, the Japanese are reluctant and unable to use immigration as a solution. An ageing population must inevitably affect the dynamism of the Japanese economy. The creation of a larger East Asian economic area will greatly ameliorate this problem. For example, the potential for cooperation between Japan and China is limitless. Thus, in their relations with China, the Japanese refuse to follow American policy blindly. They may make perfunctory statements about human rights in China but their actions reflect much deeper strategic considerations.

All this does not mean that a Pacific community which includes North America will not come about. It will come about and no line can be drawn down the middle of the Pacific Ocean. What it means is that the political centre of gravity in the Pacific will shift westwards with the economic centre of gravity.

## The Chinese Perspective

The Chinese perspective of global restructuring is dominated by the need for domestic political stability and the problem of Islamic and Russian Central Asia.

The collapse of the Soviet Union has confirmed to Chinese leaders their belief that economic reform must precede political reform. Without political stability, there can be no economic development. This has been the historical experience of the Chinese people throughout the ages. It is also the ideological justification for the present monopolisation of political power by the Chinese Communist Party (CCP). Any attempt by outsiders to interfere with the domestic politics of China is bound to meet with the stiffest resistance. If the American support for human rights in China goes beyond words, we can expect China to find ways to exert countervailing pressure on American interests in the most inconvenient places, especially in West Asia. For the same reason it will be foolhardy for the people of Hong Kong to interfere in the politics of the Mainland after 1997. "One country, two systems" will be tolerated for only as long as the second system does not attempt to subvert the first.

This does not mean that there will not be political change in China itself. Major change there will be. The more developed China's economy becomes — and its progress has been remarkable by any measure — the looser must political control be. In fact, political control today is much looser than it was ten years ago and must become much looser still ten years from now. When and how the CCP gives up its monopoly of power is the major political challenge confronting China in the next phase of its historical development. The example of the Kuomintang (KMT) in Taiwan is instructive. Defeated by the CCP on the Mainland, the KMT adopted the same Leninist organisation as the CCP, in order to better fight the CCP. Now, the KMT is a democratic party. The manner in which the KMT has successfully democratised itself in Taiwan will in turn be studied closely by the CCP. It is ironical how the compliment is returned. One day, democracy with Chinese characteristics will also appear on the Mainland.

For the rest of us in East Asia, from Japan and Korea in the Northeast to Indo-China and ASEAN in the Southeast, we wish China well in her effort to maintain domestic stability and promote economic growth. We wish China well in our own self-interest. A China divided and rent by civil war will destabilise the whole of Asia. But what is more important than our wish is the fact that China will also be increasingly preoccupied with the problem of Islamic and Russian Central Asia and will want to stabilise all other fronts on her long border.

With the disintegration of the Soviet Empire, Central Asia is entering a prolonged period of instability. The Commonwealth of Independent States is not likely to last long and cannot hope to contain the enormous stresses that will build up between and within the independent republics. Russia itself may have to go through a Bonapartist phase. In the same way as the Mongolians, having cast off Marxism-Leninism, now cling on to the atavistic symbol of Genghis Khan, the Muslim peoples of Central Asia are likely to revert back to Islam. China is exposed to all this upheaval in Russia and the Muslim republics over thousands of kilometres in the North and West. These borderlands are also where China's own minority populations are most concentrated.

The problem of Central Asia is a recurrent theme in the history of the Chinese Empire. Time and again, for every major Chinese dynasty, it becomes the central, most important strategic question confronting the Empire, although never in exactly the same way. One of the great achievements of the late Qing, not often recognised by Chinese historians themselves, was its success in keeping the greater part of the Chinese empire in Central Asia intact. The Qing Government, despite its parlous condition in the 19th century, accomplished this by a combination of skillful diplomacy and ruthless suppression of local revolts. Although large swaths of territory in Central Asia were lost to Imperial Russia, including what is now Alma Ata, the present capital of Kazakhstan, the vast expanse of Tibet, Qinghai and Xinjiang was held. Central Asia was then of far greater strategic importance to the empire than the coastal regions of China. Treaty ports and extra-territorial concession on the China coast were, in comparison, of minor significance. The coastal plains are part of the Chinese heartlands. They can never be conquered for very long. It is the conquerors who get absorbed like the Mongols and the Manchus. But Central Asia is another matter. Once lost, it can be lost for centuries. Republican China inherited all of Qing Central Asia except Outer Mongolia and it is interesting that, till today, Taiwan considers Outer Mongolia part of China and China officially recognises Genghis Khan as Chinese. With the collapse of the Soviet Union, Central Asia will once again loom large in China's strategic consciousness. In the 1960s and 1970s, the threat in the North and West came from a militarily powerful Soviet Union. That threat subsided in the 1980s. The new threat is of a different nature, less significant in the strategic military sense, but more troublesome politically.

For China, the need for domestic stability and the problem of Central Asia are bound together. It is part of the dynastic cycle that when the empire is strong, it absorbs the borderlands and loses them when it is weak. When there is economic prosperity in China, the borderlands will compete to court Chinese favour for trade and other exchanges. These two preoccupations of domestic stability and Central Asia will encourage China to stabilise all the other fronts from the Korean peninsula to Taiwan, to Hong Kong to the South China Sea, to Indo-China to the Himalayan border with India.

In the early part of the 15th century, many decades before the Portuguese and the Spanish set sail on their oceanic voyages, Ming China sent seven expeditions of enormous size to the Indian Ocean, going as far as the Red Sea and the East Coast of Africa. As many as 28,000 men participated in each expedition. They sailed in huge ships each capable of carrying up to 500 men. After 1433, all contacts with the Southern lands were stopped. Why? Because the resources of the empire were stretched and the Mongolian threat in the North was growing. In 1421, the capital was shifted from Nanjing to Beijing. The strategic preoccupation had once again shifted from the South to the North.

The point I am making is that the collapse of the Soviet Union and China's twin preoccupations make it easier for us to solve the major problems in East Asia and greatly improve the prospect of an East Asian economic area consolidating.

### The Southeast Asian Perspective

Let me now turn to the perspective from Southeast Asia. Historically speaking, Southeast Asia is the area of overlap in between the two great cultural spheres of China and India, hence the geographical names like Indo-China and Indonesia. The name "Singapore" is of Sanskrit origin even though the city-state is 77% ethnic Chinese. Although Southeast Asia lies astride the trading routes between

China and India, it was never of such strategic importance to either as to merit their sustained military attention.

It is part of the historical instinct of Southeast Asians to avoid being fully absorbed, politically and culturally, by either China or India. Vietnam, for example, will want to be part of Southeast Asia to counterbalance China. In the same way, Myanmar will want to join ASEAN, not the South Asian Association for Regional Cooperation (SAARC). ASEAN reflects the political desire of Southeast Asians to live in a zone of peace, freedom and neutrality. Neutrality does not mean the exclusion of major powers. That is neither possible nor realistic. Neutrality means balancing the influence of the major powers so that none is dominant. By major powers, I mean the US, Japan, China, India and, until recently, the Soviet Union.

Let me talk a little about India because India is a factor which Southeast Asians can never ignore in the longer term. With the end of the Cold War and under increasing domestic pressure to de-regulate its economy, India is now set on a new course. India can no longer depend on the Soviet Union for the supply of sophisticated weapons and as a market for shoddy products. India needs the West and Japan for her economic development. And like China, India will also be concerned with instability in Central Asia and the world of Islam.

Through the centuries, the threat to the sub-continent has traditionally come from Iran, Afghanistan and Central Asia, through the mountain passes of the Hindu Kush, from Aryan invaders and Alexander the Great to the Mughals. In the late 19th and early 20th centuries, British policy in Iran, Afghanistan and Central Asia was very much dictated by the security considerations of British India.

India's longstanding conflict with Pakistan has to be seen in this light. With the emergence of new Muslim republics in Central Asia, the instinct of Pakistan is to seek out allies among them. The instinct of India must be to counter such a pattern of alliance. For India, Islam is a complicating factor made more complicated by the large number of Muslims in India itself.

The world of Islam — that large belt stretching from the Atlantic coast of the Maghrib to the deserts of Chinese Central Asia, with a branch running down to Southeast Asia — is still going through a very difficult historical transition. Modernisation is sometimes accepted as necessary and at other times seen as a new crusade by Christendom to be resisted. No one can predict the progress of this historical evolution. The Turkish state offers one model, Egypt another, Saddam's Iraq a third, revolutionary Iran a fourth and Southeast Asia a fifth. Which model Algeria will follow is still too early to tell. All Muslims believe in the religious brotherhood of the *ummah*. Even India, with 850 million inhabitants, can do little to influence this process of change in the Islamic world.

The long-term hope of India must be to create an Indian Ocean economic area which extends in an arc from South Africa on one side to Southeast Asia and Australia on the other. Despite endless domestic conflicts, India's national institutions are on the whole stable, in particular, its Civil Service and the Army. Its middle class is thickening and there is no shortage of human talent. To make good progress, India must minimise strategic distraction in the Islamic Northwest and open up her over-regulated and over-protected economy. Because India's present concerns run parallel to China's, neither sees the other any longer as a natural enemy. Like China, India will seek cooperation with Japan and the countries of Southeast Asia. On the other side of the equation, it is in the long-term interest of Japan and Southeast Asia to have India as a long-term counterweight to China.

Thus, for the foreseeable future, the major external factors appear favourable to Southeast Asia. Japan will pay increasing attention to the region and become its most important investor and trading partner. The influence of both China and India is likely to be benign for many years to come.

The US is the big question mark. If the relative economic decline of the US continues unarrested and American domestic opinion turns sour, a sharp pull-back of US military forces from Asia can conceivably be decided in the year 1996, 2000 or 2004. All our hopes for East and Southeast Asia may then come crashing down. Japan will be forced to re-arm. China and Korea will oppose Japan and a whole chain reaction of destabilisation will be triggered off in the region. To forestall such an eventuality, we need a structure of peace and economic cooperation in the Asia-Pacific region which brings the

US in as an insider and which keeps the US in even if its economy continues to decline in relative terms. It is possible to imagine a Europe without the North Atlantic Treaty Organization (NATO) in five to ten years. It is frightening to conceive of an Asia without the US military presence for the next 20 years.

However, a complete withdrawal of US forces is not likely because East Asia has become even more important to the US than Europe. The economies of the US and Japan are inextricably bound together and add up to 40% of the world's GNP. With increasing number of Asians settling on the West Coast of North America, the links across the Pacific are also cultural. Furthermore, Japan needs the US for her Asian policy and as a counterweight to China. For all these reasons, the US is more likely to stay than not. In fact, the US, Japan and China are in a triangular relationship. The political challenge in the years to come is to create an institutional structure across the Pacific which will hold this strategic triangle in place.

Whatever the scenario, it is in the common interest of Southeast Asians to bunch together, the better to bargain with the big powers. ASEAN's decision to form a free trade area (FTA) in 15 years is a major milestone in the history of Southeast Asia. The process of political and economic cooperation in ASEAN is gathering momentum. With the end of the long war in Indo-China, Vietnam, Cambodia and Laos will eventually be brought in, and Myanmar as well. The alternative to a strong ASEAN is a balkanised Southeast Asia and that is neither in the interest of Southeast Asians nor in the interest of the major powers.

## Laying the Infrastructure for the Pacific Century

On balance, we can be optimistic about the continued economic development of East and Southeast Asia and the promise of the Pacific Century. There is no greater demonstration of this optimism than the enormous commitment to infrastructural development, both public and private, in all the countries of the region. Trillions of dollars will be spent on ports, airports, roads, rail, tunnels and public utilities. In Japan, some three trillion dollars will be spent over the next ten years. Huge projects are planned for the Kansai and Tokyo regions.

In South Korea, there are bottlenecks everywhere crying out to be cleared. When Korea is re-unified, the North will have to be rebuilt. Taiwan has budgetted $300 billion for infrastructure over the next six years. The first phase of Hong Kong's port/airport development scheme (PADS) alone will cost at least $19 billion. China's infrastructural needs are immense. For trunk roads alone, the plan calls for 50,000 kilometres to be built over the next five years. Expressway construction is only just starting. In ASEAN, the story is much the same all the way from Thailand to Indonesia, with infrastructural investments for the next five years estimated at US$160 billion. Indo-China will need billions of dollars for re-construction. What is important is not the fact that there are all these needs, but that all over East and Southeast Asia, infrastructural investments are likely to yield quick paybacks. A large part of the infrastructure will therefore be privately financed on the basis of build-operate-transfer (BOT). What we are seeing is the laying of infrastructure on a continental scale for the Pacific Century.

## Conclusion

But nothing is inevitable in history. Over the next few years, we may not be able to avoid a global recession as part of the price of global restructuring. American consumption will have to be brought down and it may take a while before rising investment and consumption in Asia and Europe can fully take up the slack in global aggregate demand. In the meantime, trade disputes will intensify and the US may lose the will to lead. It is truly an irony of history that the final victory over the Soviet Union should be accompanied by such domestic gloom in the US itself. Japan, Germany and others will have to cheer America on and help prop up its economy until new structures are in place to take some of the burden off America's shoulders.

There are dangers but the longer term prospects are good. So long as political conflicts among the major powers are kept within bounds, large parts of Asia and Europe are poised for rapid economic development. The bets are still on East and Southeast Asia leading the world economy in the first half of the next century. And if we succeed in keeping the US engaged in the region, the odds become that much more favourable.

# A Common East Asian Future

*A common East Asian consciousness is re-emerging. A new political configuration is taking shape in the region.*

It is common to hear Western scholars, politicians and journalists argue that East Asia is fragmented, with countries like China and Korea deeply distrustful of a resurgent Japan. America is therefore needed as a moderator without whom East Asians will fight one another.

This is certainly true for the next 10 to 20 years. A precipitate American withdrawal from the Western Pacific will destabilise the entire region from Northeast Asia to Southeast Asia. How long America can play this role is, however, unclear. As we enter the next century, the balance of economic and political power is likely to shift in favour of East Asia. And while America can be a political moderator in East Asia, it cannot be a cultural moderator.

## A Common Civilisational Area

We are entering an era of "soft" nationalism. It will not be a borderless world but borders will become increasingly porous. In such a world, cultural links become very important. In East Asia, the cultural relationship between China, Japan and Korea will be a critical factor in the political and economic development of the whole region. The more Chinese, Japanese and Koreans feel that they are part of a common civilisational area, the greater the chances of continuing peace and prosperity even if the American military presence is much reduced.

---

Speech at Jiji Press TOP Seminar, 18 June 1992.

Historically speaking, Chinese, Japanese, Koreans and Vietnamese are part of a common civilisational area — the "chopstick" area. The basis of this common civilisation is as deep as that of Western civilisation. For Westerners, "from Vancouver to Vladivostok" is a sentiment which has its roots in Rome, Greece and Judeo-Christianity. Frenchmen, Germans and white Americans may have fought bloody wars with one another but they do share a sense of a common cultural inheritance. In an era of "soft" nationalism, this shared emotion facilitates political and economic cooperation.

The basis of East Asian civilisation is the common inheritance of not only Confucianism but also Taoism and Mahayana Buddhism. As Greek and Latin are to Western civilisation, so classical Chinese is to East Asian civilisation. It is not caprice that leads Japan to go back to the ancient Chinese classics for the characters of the new Heisei emperor. It is not by accident that the national flag of South Korea has on it the Taoist yin-yang symbol. *Zen* in Japanese or *chan* in Chinese is a sect of Mahayana Buddhism heavily influenced by Taoist philosophy.

When I visited Vietnam for the first time recently, I was struck by the cultural similarity between Vietnam and South China. The same religious festivals are observed like the Lunar New Year, the annual sweeping of the ancestral graves, the Dragon Boat Festival, mid-Autumn and so on. The same gods are worshipped, except that in Vietnam they have added on to the pantheon their national heroes who have fought the Chinese. Of course, Vietnam and China were mortal enemies for a decade during the Cold War and repeatedly over the last thousand years. But the relationship between the two countries has since been normalised and the Vietnamese are now consciously adopting the Chinese model of economic development.

### Japanese Imperialism and the Cold War

A common East Asian consciousness is re-emerging. For much of the 20th century, this consciousness was submerged by two major events — Japanese imperialism and the Cold War.

Japanese imperialism was defeated at the end of the Second World War but its effects linger on. Painful memories of the period of Japanese imperialism and the atrocities committed continue to affect the relationship between China and Japan and between Korea and Japan. Considerable efforts have been made to improve these relationships, but without a full catharsis involving the people of China, Korea and Japan, suspicions of Japan will remain.

It is necessary for Japan to face up squarely to the past. It took the Kuomintang over 40 years before it was able to recognise and accept full responsibility for the events of 28 February 1947. A generation of leaders had to pass away first. The catharsis having taken place, the healing can now begin. The result will be a stronger and a more united Taiwan.

In a small way, the Japanese living in Singapore show the way forward. The largest Japanese school outside Japan is in Singapore. The textbooks used in the Singapore school now carry a full account of the period of Japanese imperialism, including the atrocities committed here. When Singaporeans commemorated the 50th Anniversary of the Fall of Singapore earlier this year, the Japanese Ambassador publicly expressed remorse and contrition, not once, but on a few occasions. This has not gone unnoticed. Has Japan lowered itself in the process? I do not think so. On the contrary, it has made for a more open relationship between Japan and Singapore. No country has a monopoly of vice or virtue.

Japan's reconciliation with China and Korea is politically very important not just for these three countries, but for all of East Asia. I believe that the process is underway although it will take time, because of domestic politics in Japan and the depth of feelings in China and Korea.

The other factor which held back the re-emergence of a common East Asian consciousness was the Cold War. With the collapse of the Soviet Union, the Cold War has ended and with it, the normalisation of relations between Vietnam and China and the prospective reunification of Korea. A new political configuration is taking shape in the region.

### Demystification of Japanese Culture

It is in Japan's interest to help shape this new configuration. There might have been a time when Japanese leaders thought it better to be de-Asianised and to join the West. For deep cultural reasons this is obviously not possible. In fact, Japan must now re-Asianise itself to strengthen its position in the world.

As part of this process of re-Asianisation, Japanese culture has to be demystified to the outside world. For many years, particularly in the West, Japanese culture has been presented as something so unique and exotic only very few could understand it. In fact, this has no basis in history. The mystification of Japanese *haiku*, *chado* and *zen* in America has been a source of puzzlement to other East Asians who share much in common with Japan. For Japan to play a world role, Japanese culture must be seen as part of a larger East Asian culture and indeed as part of a larger world culture, from which Japan has borrowed and will continue to borrow, and to which Japan has contributed and will continue to contribute.

### China and East Asia

Some Chinese believe and some Japanese fear that such a presentation of Japanese culture would make Japan little more than a subsidiary civilisation of China. This is absurd. Although China may once have been the mother of East Asian civilisation, China is today only one part of it and still struggling to take its place in that larger civilisation. Over a thousand years ago, the influence of Tang China radiated into all of East Asia. It was a multi-national empire. Among the officials, generals and monks were many who were of Korean, Japanese and Vietnamese origins. The inheritor of Tang China will not be the People's Republic but a 21st century East Asian community. Within that larger community, China, Japan, Korea, Vietnam and the other nations of Southeast Asia will find their places. In a hundred years, China may once again carry a preponderant weight but that is a long time away and it will be a very different China.

Southeast Asia is a mixed civilisational area. The ethnic Chinese in Southeast Asia play a very important role in the economic development of the region. Although they identify themselves culturally with the other Confucianist cultures, they know that their political destiny is in Southeast Asia where they constitute only a small minority. The Chinese in Southeast Asia are completely comfortable being part of an East Asian community. They will not want to be a part of a "Greater China".

In other words, whether we are from Northeast Asia or Southeast Asia, we share a common interest in bringing about a common East Asian consciousness.

## Japan's World Role

For the next 10 to 20 years at the least, Japan will continue to grow stronger in economic terms. While it is right that Japan should not re-arm, it is also necessary for Japan's legitimate security interests to be safeguarded. No one knows for how long America can continue to provide the security umbrella for Japan. Increasingly, the responsibility for world peace and order must shift to the United Nations. While East Asia will find it very hard to accept a militarily powerful Japan, East Asia can more readily accept a politically influential Japan within the framework of the United Nations. In this regard, whether Japan can become a permanent member of the Security Council will depend a great deal on Japan's being accepted as a trusted member of a larger East Asian community. Japan has to practise a softer form of nationalism to help bring this about.

## East Asia and America

It should not be an East Asian community which keeps out America. America is a country which contains within it all the contradictions of the world, not just the doubts of Europe but also the despair of Africa, the uncertainties of Latin America and the hopes of Asia. It is in the interest of East Asia to help East Asians living in America succeed, not only to help themselves but also to help uplift American society as a whole. The recent riots in Los Angeles and other American cities show how sharp the contradictions are in America and how

East Asians can become the target of the mob for no other reason than the fact of their economic success. If this great experiment in cultural integration fails in America, we all fail and the world will be a much poorer place. That is why we in East Asia have a large stake in the success of America and why we must try to bring the two sides of the Pacific closer together even as we forge closer links among ourselves.

# A World of Cities

*If we turn inwards and remain in the shallows, we will be finished. The challenge for us ... is in overcoming our fears and in having the courage to sail with the rising tide.*

## Our Basic Attitudes

We often say we are a cosmopolitan people. Our economy is completely open with trade many times our GDP. Every year, we receive millions of visitors and we make over a million overseas trips. In some ways, we are indeed a cosmopolitan people. But, in other ways, we remain a parochial people. For example, while many of us have visited London or Tokyo or New York, our knowledge of these cities often do not extend much beyond the tourist sights, the souvenir shops and the usual complaints about the traffic or the food being bad.

When I was studying at the Harvard Business School, my American classmates had to decide not just whom to work for when they graduated but where they wanted to live. Between New York or Chicago, Los Angeles or San Francisco, they had to weigh many considerations — climate, cost of living, education for the children, crime, and so on. The average American student is familiar with conditions in many American cities. So too the average Japanese student. He knows the relative advantages of Tokyo, Osaka, Nagoya and other Japanese cities. In Europe, with the emergence of a Single European Market, the average European student today has the whole European Community as his oyster. For example, compared to ten years ago, many more Britishers now work on the Continent. Even

Address at the National University of Singapore Political Association Forum, 20 August 1992.

in China, with the economy fast opening up to the outside world, there are growing opportunities for the fresh graduate. Why not go South, for example, to Shenzhen perchance to make a fortune? The advantage of living in a big country is the sense of greater choice. The mind automatically carries a larger map.

In Singapore, most of us do not carry such a large map in our minds. If we ask the average Singaporean undergraduate to sketch the city layout of Jakarta or Bangkok or Hong Kong, I believe he will be hard put to do so. What for? What is the need? The trouble is we are too comfortable in Singapore. Everything is available here, hence our parochial outlook.

Despite our parochial outlook, we have been able to maintain a cosmopolitan economic life. This has mainly been the work of government agencies and the multinational corporations (MNCs). The MNCs establish a large part of our international business connections. Without the MNCs, it would have taken Singapore much longer to get to where we are now. Unlike Taiwan and Hong Kong, we did not receive a large inflow of entrepreneurs who fled Communism in China. What talent we had in Singapore had to be concentrated in building up our national institutions. For business, we needed the MNCs. We still need them and should continue to attract them to Singapore. Even if some of their operations have to be distributed out of Singapore because of the labour shortage here, we should encourage their headquarters to be based in Singapore.

But we should not be wholly dependent on the MNCs. We should also strike out on our own. To be able to strike out, we have to shed some of our parochial attitudes. The basic problem is in the mind. If the mind is closed, no amount of money or organisation will help. A million excuses will be found — children's education, food, safety and so on. But if the mind is open, the solutions to all these problems will be found.

This year the world celebrates the 500th anniversary of the discovery of the Americas by Christopher Columbus. Five hundred years ago, the Spanish and the Portuguese people, then numbering only a few million, set out to conquer the world for the three G's — for gold, for glory and for the Catholic God. By 1511, the Portuguese took Malacca. By 1570, Manila was founded by the Spanish from Mexico. The famous galleon trade from Acapulco to Manila was then established, which brought the Mexican silver dollar to our part of the world. These vast enterprises were possible only because throughout Spain and Portugal, from the King to the villager, from the Cardinal to the parish priest, from the conquistador to the galley cook, the same attitudes were held, that it was honorable to venture out and risk life and limb, for wealth, honour and religion. Priests, teachers and parents passed these attitudes on to successive generations.

In Southern Sulawesi, for centuries, the Bugis people lived on trade and piracy. Every year, the womenfolk, the old men and the children would send the young men out on long voyages in their perahus. Many would never return. Those who did brought back wealth and honour to their families. In the few months they were home, they married and fathered children, after which, following the monsoons, they were out sailing again. For the Bugis boy growing up, he had but one dream, which was to follow in his father's footsteps. The entire social and political order supported these remarkable voyages which eventually brought Johore-Riau and Selangor under Buginese sway. In contrast, there were tribes living in the mountains of Sulawesi, like the Torajas, which never even saw the sea.

Our basic attitudes as a people must be consistent with the kind of society we live in and the kind of economy we operate. If our basic attitudes are parochial, we will remain dependent on the MNCs for most of our international connections, and this, in the long run, is not good for us. We become their servants instead of their partners. We must create more of these international connections ourselves and have our own MNCs operating alongside foreign MNCs, like the Swiss have succeeded in doing with Swiss MNCs like Nestlé, Oerlikon-Buehrle and Ciba-Geigy. To achieve this, our basic outlook must change.

### Perpetual Insecurity

As the PM reminded us at the National Day Rally, our basic need is to stay competitive in the world environment. It is not enough to stay competitive within the Singapore environment. As a city, we are competing with other cities for business, for investments and for human talent. Our frame of reference must be an international one.

A foreign ambassador paid a farewell call on me a few weeks ago. He gave me his views of Singapore which are mostly favourable but he ended by saying that other cities like Kuala Lumpur and Bangkok are catching up. They too are building up their ports, airports and telecommunication facilities. Whatever advantage we have is transient. Furthermore, Singapore's base is small. I listened carefully to what he said because he had no axe to grind. Of course he is right. Our position is never secure. When I met the Mayor of Zhuhai City three months ago, he asked me how long it would take for Zhuhai to catch up with Singapore. I was not sure how to answer him. Zhuhai is growing at 30% to 40% every year. At that rate Zhuhai will catch up with Singapore in no time. In the end, I told him in a diplomatic way that while Zhuhai can catch up with Singapore very quickly, we will try very hard to stay ahead. But it is worrying, isn't it? How can we be sure that we will always be able to stay ahead?

We must always look outwards. Whatever we do in Singapore must pass the test of international competition. What matters in the end is whether we are able to win medals in the world's economic Olympics. Take the question of academic pressure. During the Cultural Revolution, Mao abolished examinations because examinations treated students like enemies. Students should study at their own pace. The result was a disaster, the effects of which are still felt today. I am not saying that all academic pressure is good but it is not possible to do well without effort. No pain, no gain. In the West, under the influence of a generation of liberal educationists, many teachers and students have gone lazy. In the US and Canada today, Asians consistently outperform non-Asians. We hear of white students avoiding courses which Asian students enrol in because they fear the competition. The end result is a less competitive US economy. In Singapore, we should work smarter but we can never avoid the competition. We cannot, for example, stop others from listing the NUS degree on an international exchange rate table in comparison with degrees from London University, Todai and Stanford.

The objective of NUS cannot be to debase the coinage of the NUS degree but to upgrade it as much as possible.

Like it or not, we live in a state of perpetual insecurity. That is our *karma*. Of course we dislike the insecurity but if we manage our insecurity well, we can convert it into a positive force.

The Singapore Armed Forces (SAF) is a good example. One of the first things we did when we became independent 27 years ago was to build up the SAF. As we all know, training areas are very limited in Singapore — land, sea and air. We could not train in a big way in Malaysia or Indonesia. Two things happened. First, we learnt very quickly to maximise what little areas we have in Singapore. Today, our camps and training areas are intensively developed. Second, we learnt to upstake entire units and train overseas — in Thailand, the Philippines, Brunei, Australia, Taiwan and the US. The SAF now has a sophisticated logistical support system that can operate over hundreds and thousands of miles. More importantly, we have a large number of officers and non-commissioned officers (NCOs) — in the active and reserves — who think nothing of operating over such long distances. Not only must they be competent professionals, they must also be good diplomats in the countries they train. Today, at the press of a button, we can field an SAF of over a quarter million men, fully armed and equipped. From day one, basic attitudes in the SAF have not been parochial but outward-looking. There was no choice. MNCs could not help us build the SAF. We had to do it ourselves. Sometimes it is better to have no choice. Paradoxically, if Singapore were bigger, the SAF would be weaker today.

In a larger sense, we have no choice but to internationalise our basic attitudes. In the world unfolding before us, the international competition is relentless. Either we are winning or we are losing. There is no middle, static position. It is a race we cannot opt out of. Increasingly, the competition is between cities rather than between nations. In this new game, we do enjoy some advantages as a city-state.

### A World of Cities

Human history goes through long cycles when the most important political entity is either the city-state, the nation-state or the multi-national empire. Depending on the state of technology and other factors, what Marx called the productive forces, size can either be an advantage or a disadvantage. When size is an advantage, empires form as in the period of European colonial expansion in the 17th, 18th and 19th centuries. When size is a disadvantage, empires collapse as in this century, the latest being the dissolution of the Soviet Union. And there are signs that even the nation-state has become too big and unwieldy.

The most important agent of change today is information technology and the knowledge revolution. The essence of a nation or an empire is its ability to maintain a barrier to entry, and with it, the power to incarcerate, the right to tax and the ability to control resources and information. All this has become more difficult for the nation-state to enforce. More and more, the basis of wealth is knowledge which is impossible to restrict within national boundaries. Capital and labour have become mobile as never before, constantly moving in response to competing legal and tax conditions. Even the knowledge to destroy has become so widespread that mutual deterrence has confined its use to regional conflicts. This is the borderless world which Kenichi Ohmae envisions.

In such a world, cities become very important because cities are where knowledge is produced. The production of knowledge is a creative process which requires human brains to be stimulated and to be in communication with one another. While the essence of a nation or an empire is its ability to restrict entry, the essence of a city is its open character. If the national authority restricts entry into a city or over-taxes a city, that city will not flourish. This has been the fate of Shanghai until recently. In all nations, political power is now shifting back from the national authority to the city. This trend will change the course of history. In China, the dynamism of cities in the South is posing a new challenge to central government. In Europe, the growing power of cities is weakening the nation-state at one level and creating the European Community at another because a larger framework of peace and stability is needed to promote trade between cities. The same process is happening in the US where the economic decline has affected some but not all cities. Even when we study the Malaysian or Indonesian economy, it is becoming more helpful to look at city and regional, rather than national, economies.

Each city radiates its influence into a larger metropolitan area which may extend into another country. Our Singapore-Johore-Riau growth triangle is only one of many examples in the world. In North America, Vancouver, Seattle and Tacoma are cities in a larger economic area. The Los Angeles area spreads into Mexico. In Europe, the Baltic is becoming one large economic region, so too the Mediterranean Riviera which extends from Spain to Italy. In Asia, many economic regions are forming, linking the cities of Japan, Korea, Taiwan and Hong Kong to cities on the Chinese Mainland.

To use the metaphor of the brain, every city becomes a node with synaptic connections to other city-nodes in a neural network which envelops the whole world. What all this means in historical terms is still unclear. We are entering a new era where city-states like Singapore may play quite important roles, where our smallness may well become an advantage.

**The City-State of Singapore**

We are all aware of the disadvantages of being a small nation. This puts us in a position of perpetual insecurity. But being a city-state gives us advantages over cities which are not sovereign.

The most important advantage is that we are able to keep out the slums. Because we are a city-state, we control whom we allow into Singapore. Cities like Cairo, Bombay or Sao Paulo cannot. All over the world, there is a tremendous movement of peoples from the countryside into the cities. Rapid urbanisation is one of the mega-trends of the next century. This inflow into the cities makes it extremely difficult to control crime, pollution and traffic. Infrastructural development cannot keep pace with population increase. Even the cities in the developed countries will be affected, in Europe by the migration of people from North Africa, Turkey, Eastern Europe and the former Soviet Union, and in North America by the migration of people from Mexico and the rest of Latin America. Because we control access into Singapore, we are able to keep our roads uncongested, our parks free of crime and our air clean.

As a city-state, we also avoid having to subsidise the countryside. In many countries, the cities are taxed to subsidise the rural areas. Farm prices have to be supported. Roads have to be built and telephone lines laid even when few people are served. National authorities do this either to win votes or to slow down the drift of the rural underemployed into the cities. We do not face this problem at all. Unlike Tokyo, we do not have to pay off rice farmers. Unlike Air India, Singapore Airlines (SIA) need not fly unprofitable domestic routes.

Yet another advantage of being a city-state is the constant pressure on us to be financially prudent. A big country with gold mines, oil fields and vast agricultural areas is always tempted to mortgage off its inheritance. This is the story of Canada and Australia. The greater the number of people feeding off a common buffet table, the greater the tendency to irresponsibility and waste. If a city is profligate and raises taxes, those who are wealthy and talented will leave, along with their businesses. New York city is a classic example. We have always been frugal in Singapore because we know, as our forefathers knew, that there is no free lunch anywhere on earth. Someone has to pay. The national reserves we have accumulated are nothing compared to the patrimony of large countries like Brazil and Mexico. There, they thought they could borrow against the income of future generations without limit. What was a blessing became a curse. I was talking to a Mexican diplomat on National Day. He congratulated us on our remarkable economic performance. When I told him we practised a simple, common-sensical form of economics, he remarked that I did not know how difficult it is to be so simple and common-sensical. When we have no gold mines or oil fields to distract us, economic life is a simple matter of earning a living and stashing some away for a rainy day. The real wealth is not in the ground but in the instincts of the people. We must not let our modest national reserves become a distraction.

Our approach to life in Singapore is a practical one. Whether it is to house the people, to educate the young, to provide citizens with amenities or to attract investment's, we concentrate on the basics and always insist on the individual being responsible for his actions. Morally, this is the right thing to do. No one shirks responsibility.

Of late, our success in solving the problems of a city-state has attracted the attention of others. Others have been studying our experiences more than what many of us are aware of. I was surprised travelling around South China how much the city and provincial leaders know about Singapore — our housing programme, Urban Redevelopment Authority (URA), Central Provident Fund (CPF) and so on. In December 1990, Taiwanese Prime Minister Hau Pei-tsun held Singapore up as a model. This year, Chinese leader Deng Xiaoping also held Singapore up as a model. Imagine that — a little city-state of three million held up as a model for a continental nation of over a billion people! Even in the West, Singapore's experiments have been favourably cited on many occasions over the last few years.

Of course we must never be boastful or let the compliments get to our head. The more we are praised, the more worried we should be. While we are flattered that others want to learn from us, we should also learn from them. For example, before we built our Mass Rapid Transit (MRT), we studied the Hong Kong system and we were determined to build a better one. Now the Hong Kong airport authorities are studying Changi Airport and they are just as determined to build a better airport. This is how it is. Cities compete with one another and stimulate one another. When our performing arts centre is built, I hope it will be better than the one in Hong Kong. We should never be self-satisfied and stop learning from others. At the same time, we should be aware of the political and cultural influence that we have in the region and think of ways to use that influence to strengthen Singapore's position in the world.

This is where I come back to where I started. We have concentrated on building up our national institutions and left the MNCs to make our major international business connections. The basic attitudes of our people are still parochial. In our minds, we have not yet caught up with our position as an international city of influence in the region. This is not good. For as long as we are dependent on the MNCs for our major international business connections, the economic benefits of our political and cultural influence as a city-state will accrue more to the MNCs than to Singapore. Indeed, if we are not careful, others will soon catch up with us and surpass us. When that happens, it may well be in the interest of some of these MNCs to relocate to other cities.

There is a great difference between a foreign MNC which recruits Singaporeans and a Singaporean MNC which recruits foreigners. Both employ a mix of Singaporeans and foreigners. For the foreign MNC, Singapore is one of many possible locations to site the regional headquarters or a factory. If Singapore ceases to be competitive, some other city will be chosen. No hard feelings. If the MNC is Singaporean, however, whatever happens, the interest of Singapore will always be taken into account. Without SIA, Singaporeans will still be able to find jobs with United Airlines or Cathay Pacific as pilots, cabin crew or ground staff. But it makes a big difference for us to have our own SIA. We need many more SIAs. We rather others work for us than we to work for others.

### A Different Worldview

What we need is a different mental orientation — a different worldview — so that from an early age, the Singaporean looks beyond Singapore for fame and fortune. He will then view other cities not merely as tourist destinations but also with an eye for business and other opportunities. A good idea developed in another city should be quickly adopted in Singapore. A good idea homegrown in Singapore should be rapidly transplanted elsewhere at a profit. If we are slow to react, others will leave us behind. This competitive logic applies as much to the cultural field as it does to business. To make it big in Singapore, an artist or a musician must also have a market beyond Singapore. He will not succeed if he is only known in the Singapore market. Looking beyond Singapore applies as much to Dick Lee as it does to Ong Beng Seng. If this worldview is inculcated at home, in school, in the university and in the workplace, then we will succeed. We must have some knowledge of world history and geography. Without such attitudes, neither the Spanish nor the Portuguese nor the Bugis people would have been able to fan out the way they once did.

An outward-looking people will also set municipal problems in perspective. On the whole, we are very well run as a city. But

Singaporeans are a demanding people and we are always expecting things to be better than what they are. So we complain a lot. That is all well and good so long as we do not lose our instinct to act together in the face of external threats and opportunities. As a city-state, our politics are relatively straightforward. We have no complicated farm lobbies to worry about or tensions between the federal and state governments to resolve. Our competitive advantage is our ability to react quickly to changed conditions. The more outward-oriented we are as a people, the easier it will be for us to forge a common response to an external challenge.

To be able to compete as a city-state, we must attract human talent from all over the world in large numbers and encourage them to make Singapore their home, and if not their first home, then at least their second or their third home. Great cities are constantly rejuvenated by fresh talents and new ideas from outside. As Mr Lee Kuan Yew once reminded us, the great majority of ministers in his first Cabinet were not born in Singapore. We must always strengthen our Singapore team. The stronger our side, the better will we be able to compete with other cities. In 1492, Ferdinand and Isabella of Spain made use of Christopher Columbus who was not Spanish but Italian. In the 21st century, the basis of competition will be knowledge and the more brainpower we have on our side, the better. If our basic attitudes discourage foreign talent from settling here and instead encourage our own local talent to leave, we will be in deep trouble. We will then have no hope of ever developing our own MNCs, indeed of having any influence beyond the shores of Singapore. We will end up a backwater.

Is there a danger that internationalisation will cause us to lose our sense of self? Our sense of being Singaporean? I do not think so. The Spanish, the Portuguese and the Bugis never lost their sense of self. Neither did the merchants of Venice nor the officers of the British East India Company. Nor the Japanese businessmen who now romp all over the world. As Professor Chan Heng Chee argued in a recent talk she gave, we must and we can stay centred in Singapore. Even as we internationalise, we must work hard to strengthen our own sense of identity. Indeed, the more we succeed internationally, the prouder we become as Singaporeans.

All over the Pacific, a tide is rising. Along the entire Pacific Rim, a ring of cities is being sustained by this rising tide from Los Angeles, San Francisco and Vancouver on the Eastern Pacific to Tokyo, Seoul, Beijing-Tianjin, Shanghai, Taipei, Hong Kong-Guangzhou, Ho Chi Minh City, Bangkok, Kuala Lumpur, Singapore, Jakarta, all the way to Sydney on the Western Pacific. It is a league of cities not unlike the Hanseatic League which once linked the trading cities of the North Sea and the Baltic in an earlier period of European history. The cities of the Pacific League will compete and cooperate with one another. They will not all flourish equally. Some will succeed more grandly than others. How Singapore fares in the 21st century will depend on how well we rise to the challenge of a new age. If we turn inwards and remain in the shallows, we will be finished. The challenge for us — the challenge for you whose good fortune it is to be entering full adulthood at this exciting moment in world history — is in overcoming our fears and in having the courage to sail with the rising tide. In a modest way, we must have our own sense of destiny.

# Partners in Progress

*... as regions and metropolitan areas become more autonomous, coordination among them becomes more necessary.*

## End of the Cold War and Rise of East Asia

In the last two years, bilateral relations between India and Singapore have improved considerably. During the Cold War, India and Singapore often took opposing sides on major international issues. At the UN and other international forums, our diplomats had to defend different positions. India had close ties with the Soviet Union. India's economy was heavily protected and regulated. In contrast, Singapore together with the rest of ASEAN opposed the Soviet Union over its sponsorship of Vietnam in Cambodia. Singapore's economy is also far more export-oriented. In 1990, Singapore, with a population of less than 3 million, exported much more than the whole of India — US$53 billion[1] as against US$18 billion for India.

With the collapse of the Soviet Union and the end of the Cold War, every country in the world is forced to take stock and re-align its interests. In the new world now emerging, cooperation between India and Singapore will grow. Politically, there are many areas for us to work together in the international arena. For example, India and Singapore worked closely to achieve consensus at the Paris Conference on Cambodia. India is now a sectoral dialogue partner of ASEAN. Philosophically, we are both secular democracies committed

---

Speech made at the National Economic and Political Forum held in Mumbai on 19 February 1993, during a two-week visit by a Singaporean delegation led by George Yeo to study India's new policies under PM Narasimha Rao.

[1] Reported in *The Economist*, 28 November 1992.

to the ideals of multi-culturalism. Economically, Singapore could be of use to India as it reorientates its economy, and India could provide Singapore with new opportunities for trade, tourism and investment.

As we enter the 21st century, India will increasingly look eastwards. The rise of East Asia is a development of historic importance. Barring a major disaster, there is every likelihood that the centre of the world economy will shift some time in the next century from North America to East Asia. The economies of the West Coast of North America, Australia and New Zealand will become increasingly Asianised. According to a Japanese MITI report, in about 25 years, the combined GNP of East Asia will be bigger than all of Europe's and twice that of the US.

For the next 20 years, Japan will play the key role in bringing about this amazing East Asian transformation. Economic development has spread from Japan, first, to the newly industralised economies (NIEs), then to the ASEAN countries and, now, to China and Vietnam.

China's growth is the most dramatic. Over the last 14 years, China's annual growth rate has averaged 9%.[2] In 1992 it was 12%.[3] For the rest of the decade, China's annual growth rate is expected to be between 7.5% to 8.5%.[4] China's present per capita GNP is officially estimated to be US$370, compared to US$350 for India. However, China's figure is grossly underestimated. According to the survey of China in *The Economist* of 28 November 1992, China's GNP is possibly 4 to 5 times larger. China's total exports is now US$85 billion,[5] already exceeding Taiwan's. In 10 years, China's GNP may overtake Japan's.[6] According to Lawrence Summers, the World Bank chief economist, China's per capita GNP can reach that of Taiwan today at US$10,000 in the year 2020. When that happens, China's economy will be easily the largest in the world with an output equal to 80% of the OECD's output at that time.[7]

These are rough projections and may be overstated. Many things can go wrong in China. Historical development is never smooth. But the underlying trends in East Asia are clear. The development

---

[2–5] IMF Direction of Trade Statistics, Yearbook 1992.
[6] *The Economist*, 28 November 1992.
[7] World Bank, *China: Country Economic Memorandum Reform and the Role of the Plan in the 1990s*. World Bank Report, June 1992.

of the US economy in the 19th century was rudely interrupted by a devastating Civil War from 1861 to 1865, but this did not stop the US from moving on to become the world's greatest economy at the turn of the century.

We can expect all kinds of political problems to accompany the rise of East Asia. For 300 to 400 years, the West has been dominant — militarily, economically, politically and culturally. This dominance, in all its aspects, will be challenged in the next century, first by East Asia, later by South Asia as well. There is bound to be conflict of one kind or another. One only hopes that there will not be a major war.

It is vitally important for the US to maintain its military presence in East Asia for as long as possible. This will make it unnecessary for Japan to become a nuclear power. A rearmed Japan will cause China and Korea to react in a violent way and destabilise the entire region for decades to come. For the US to remain militarily engaged, however, there must be strategic and economic advantage for the US. This inclusion of the US as a full partner in the economic development of East Asia is therefore of strategic importance. This is what the Asia-Pacific Economic Conference (APEC) tries to achieve.

As India integrates its economy into East Asia, India can also help stabilise the region by counterbalancing the other political heavyweights. Because the fear of China will grow with the growth of the Chinese economy, Japan and ASEAN will always value the strategic presence of India. For India to look East is nothing new. Long before the interruption of Western colonial rule, India has been linked by the overland and maritime silk routes to East and Southeast Asia. From India, Buddhism in its various vehicles converted all of China, Korea, Japan and Southeast Asia. It was via India that Islam later spread into Malaysia and Indonesia. Sooner or later, India will re-assert its economic, political and intellectual presence in the East.

### From Nation-States to City-States

It will, however, be a big mistake to see power only in national and military terms. Technology and the integration of the world economy has made power much more diffused. In this day and age, battles can be won but wars are seldom won. Whether it is Israel in Lebanon, the Soviet Union in Afghanistan or Vietnam in Cambodia, military might alone cannot decide the outcome. We have become interdependent as never before.

In some ways, we are going back to the period of history before nation-states became dominant. All over the world, power is flowing downwards. The devolution of power from national authorities to regional and metropolitan authorities is one of the most important factors driving world history today. It is changing the nature of world politics.

Take China for example. The kind of autonomy provinces and cities like Guangdong and Shanghai now enjoy will require another Chinese revolution to take away. The different regions and cities compete fiercely with one another. They find their own foreign partners. Thus, the Southern province of Guangdong looks to Hong Kong, Fujian province looks to Taiwan, Shandong province to South Korea and the Chinese Northeast to Japan, Korea and Russia.

It is the same elsewhere in the world. Brute force could no longer hold the Soviet Union together and so it broke up. In the US, the Northwest and British Columbia form one economic region, the Los Angeles metropolitan area and the Mexican Northwest another, and so on. In Europe, it is the same. All are in competition for investments and human talent.

But, as regions and metropolitan areas become more autonomous, coordination among them becomes more necessary. Thus, we see all kinds of supra-national organisations forming to perform this task of coordination like the European Community (EC) in Europe, North American Free Trade Agreement (NAFTA) in North America, Association of South East Asian Nations (ASEAN) in Southeast-Asia, Asia-Pacific Economic Cooperation (APEC) for the Pacific basin, and many smaller ones like the Growth Triangle which links Singapore to the adjoining parts of Malaysia and Indonesia. They are like the old Hanseatic League which linked the cities of the Baltic and the North Sea in an earlier era. Ties of race, language and religion become important. They straddle national boundaries.

The structure of nation-states in the world is giving way to a more complex organic reality of regions and cities linked to one another in a web of economic and cultural relationships. Nation-states will still be important but in a much less forceful way. How all this will affect international politics is still not clear.

What is clear is that the pressure of competition is relentless, causing governments to de-regulate, and creating new combinations which enhance the competitive position of member regions and cities. Indonesia, for example, used to be highly regulated and protectionist. The justifications were the standard ones — self-sufficiency, nurturing indigenous enterprises, preventing foreign exploitation, socialism and nation-building. The resulting inefficiencies were financed by the revenue from oil and gas. In the early 1980s, energy prices plummeted forcing the Indonesian government to alter course. The strategy is now one of decentralised development with maximum reliance on market forces. Even so, Indonesia is losing out on foreign investments to China putting pressure on Indonesia to deregulate even further. In the process, Indonesia has found greater use of Singapore as a switch for goods and services. Singapore lowers the cost to Indonesia of importing and exporting.

What has happened to Indonesia is now happening to India and the rest of the sub-continent. The sub-continent cannot be insulated from the changes sweeping the world. India too will be forced to devolve some power to its cities and regions. The future will be bright if the sub-continent can overcome the divisions of ethnicity, caste, language and religion. But it will take time. Within and beyond India, there is also the difficult transformation which the world of Islam has to go through to meet the challenge of modernisation. As a regional grouping, the South Asian Association for Regional Cooperation (SAARC) is not quite like ASEAN in its spirit of cooperation. One learns to accept that while things are never quite as good as they look in India, they are also never quite as bad. India has the resilience of an ancient civilisation. There is such an amount of human talent available that India has for years been an exporter of brainpower to the rest of the world. It is not at all surprising that, of all ethnic groups in the US, the one-million-strong Indian community is the best educated and the most well-paid. Indian scientists and engineers are prominent in California's Silicon Valley. One day, many of those who left will come back to help India develop with their wealth, knowledge and connections. This has been the experience of the NIEs. In a recent *Asia Wall Street Journal* article, Joel Kotkin predicted that "like the overseas Chinese now transforming the (Chinese) mainland, the roughly 20 million expatriate Indians, up from a mere 5 million three decades ago, constitute a powerful force for the shift of their homeland from a socialist backwater to a strong, rapidly growing economy". Kotkin added that "these overseas Indians have performed well in commerce, technology and the professions in virtually every country which they have settled, even in xenophobic Japan". Kotkin's "20 million" includes those Indians who live in Southeast Asia.

India's links with Southeast Asia go back at least 2,000 years. The languages and the cultures of Southeast Asia have been heavily influenced by the region's long contact with the sub-continent. Place-names like Indo-China and Indonesia make this obvious. The influence of Hinduism is everywhere. The Ramayana is as well-known in Bangkok as it is in Bali. No Indian needs to be told what Singapore means. It was the British East India Company in Calcutta which sent Raffles to found the free port of Singapore in 1819. Until 1867, Singapore was ruled from India. It was British India which supplied Singapore its Indian population and much of our legal jurisprudence. The common British inheritance of India and Singapore makes us familiar to each other. I remember visiting the Indian National Defence Academy at Khadakvasla in 1988. I was in the Army then. We were going to build our own military college in Singapore and wanted to learn from India's experience. Visiting the laboratories, I was surprised to find exactly the same kind of equipment I used as a schoolboy — the same copper calorimeters and the same potentiometers.

That we enjoy such a high degree of comfort with each other is to our mutual advantage. Like Indonesia, India will find Singapore useful to its economic development. Singapore can help India source more cheaply and sell more dearly. Let me give an Indonesian example of the role Singapore can play. Indonesia's biggest conglomerate grows orchids for the Japanese market on a small Indonesian island near Singapore. The botanists and supplies come from Singapore. After the orchids are cut, they are barged to Singapore and flown to Tokyo where they arrive cheaper and fresher than orchids from Thailand which is now the world's largest exporter of cut orchids. Indonesia has every intention of overtaking Thailand in the orchid business and will do this by exploiting the facilities available in Singapore.

I am told that it is often cheaper to ship containers from Calcutta and Bombay to Europe through Singapore despite the additional distance. This is probably because the facilities at Calcutta and Bombay are still not good enough. The big container ships prefer to call at as few ports as possible because of the high cost of demurrage. As the Indian economy opens up, the cost structures will change. Some things done through Singapore will no longer be worth doing. Other activities become profitable. Singapore can be India's most convenient point to plug into the economy of East Asia. In addition to trade, Singapore can help Indian businessmen invest in Southeast Asia and China. Singapore can also help draw investment into India. Singapore will become an important switch for the Indian economy, for trade, finance, investments and knowledge.

The purpose of my delegation's visit to India is to strengthen the links between our two countries. We are here to increase cooperation in three areas: economic, human resources and cultural.

First: economic cooperation. Key indicators show that PM Rao's reforms are showing good results. World Bank reports are optimistic. As the Indian economy opens up, there will be many more opportunities for two-way trade, tourism and investments. India, or to be more precise, the different regions and cities of India, will face increasing pressure to match conditions available elsewhere in Asia. Just as Indonesia is being forced to match investment conditions in China, India will have to compete against countries like China, Indonesia, Vietnam and Pakistan for the same finite pool of investment funds available worldwide. India and Singapore can strengthen each other's international competitive position. We should build on the existing economic links between Bombay and Singapore, and exploit established networks whether this be Marwari, Parsee, Sindhi, Khoja,

Bhora or whatever. We will also be studying closely the proposal to establish a Madras-Singapore Industrial Corridor.

Second: human resources. We would like to increase the number of Indian professionals and skilled workers working in Singapore. We will be very happy if some of them decide to make Singapore their second or their third home. Many Indian nationals are employed in our corporations and universities. We hope there will be more. Some will join Singaporeans to work in third countries. When PM Narasimha Rao met Singapore PM Goh Chok Tong in Jakarta a few months ago, PM Rao said that it is better for India to export its talent to Singapore than to the West. Even though Singapore's absorptive capacity is limited, we are very honoured by his gracious offer.

The third area my delegation is looking at is increased cultural cooperation. There is a lot of India in Singapore, which makes Singapore very different from a city like Hong Kong. We want to enhance this Indian facet of Singapore by strengthening the cultural links between our two countries. I have just signed a Memorandum of Understanding with Mr Arjun Singh in New Delhi. Next year, we will be presenting at Singapore's National Museum a major exhibition of Indian rare arts as the first in a series. We will also arrange for more Indian cultural groups to visit Singapore. Singapore is located in between two oceans — the Pacific and the Indian — in both the geographical and the cultural sense. Singapore should provide a window into the civilisation of India as it does into China.

The new course on which India is set is irreversible. There will be twists and turns along the way but the chances are good that India will eventually succeed. We would like to be your partner in progress.

# Cities as Information Hubs

*The challenge for cities is the creation of internal systems which preserve them as warm and wholesome human habitats.*

## The Challenge

Two big forces will shape the Asia Pacific in the next century. The first is information technology which will change the pattern of power concentration and social organisation in the region. Political and economic power will become more decentralised. What was far can become near and what was once near can become relatively far. Thus, we see new patterns of international trade and global manufacturing.

The other big driving force is urbanisation. With the reopening of Asia and its rapid industrialisation, hundreds of millions of peasant folks will become urbanised in China, India and Southeast Asia. This urbanisation process will have earth-shaking consequences. Just take China alone as a multiplier of trends. If all Chinese were to eat meat like Americans, there will not be enough agricultural land in the world. Or if all Chinese were to eat fish the way Japanese do, there will not be enough fish in the oceans. Whether it is carbon dioxide in the atmosphere, energy consumption or food production, the industrialisation of China, India and Southeast Asia will alter the course of human civilisation.

Information technology and urbanisation will change the politics of Asia. It does not matter whether we are talking about democratic or authoritarian systems. In every country, the ability of

---

Speech at the Yomiuri Shimbun International Forum on Multi-Media, Tokyo, Japan, 25 May 1995.

national governments to tax and control resources is weakening. Factors of production have never been more mobile. Because of this, the devolution of political power is inexorable. Thus, we see the phenomenon of weak central governments in big countries which, in turn, gives rise to problems of currency fluctuation.

All over Asia, managing the aspirations of large urban populations will become critical. Many of the major political parties in Asia today evolved their characters in response to the needs of strong agricultural constituencies. Thus, Japan's Liberal Democratic Party (LDP), China's Communist Party, Taiwan's Kuomintang (KMT), Vietnam's Communist Party and Indonesia's Golkar all have strong party machines in the countryside. In contrast, their political bases in the cities are often weak. Cities like Tokyo, Osaka, Taipei, Bangkok and Jakarta have a tendency to be less supportive of national governments.

As more and more people enter the cities, those political parties which are better able to solve urban problems will succeed. This is the fundamental change driving political development throughout Asia today.

The problems of the city are those of housing, crime, traffic, drugs, prostitution, pollution, terrorism, and so on. All these problems are likely to become worse in the coming decades in many parts of Asia. Modern technology makes possible a concentration of population never seen before. But it also results in urban problems of terrifying magnitude.

Take urban terrorism as an example. It is bound to become more prevalent because of the flow of knowledge and the movement of peoples. The expertise to make bombs and other weapons of mass destruction is easily available, whether from Northern Ireland, the Middle East, the former Soviet Union or elsewhere. The knowledge is available in the Internet. It is also easy to stay anonymous in large cities and be lost in the crowd, especially in places like airports, city centres and train stations.

Unless cities as organic entities develop immune systems to protect their own life functions, urbanisation can lead to misery and self-destruction. Thus, the challenge for cities in the next century is the creation of internal systems which preserve them as warm and wholesome human habitats, despite the large number of human beings living and working in close proximity.

## The Wealth of Cities

In the next century, the most relevant unit of economic production, social organisation and knowledge generation will be the city or city-region. Nation-states will still exist but an increasing number of policy issues will have to be settled at the city level. This will create new patterns of competition and cooperation in the world, a little like the situation in Europe before the era of nation-states.

In this competition among cities, those which are better at acquiring, processing and making use of knowledge will prevail over those that are less able to. Thus, more and more, cities will become information hubs. Information efficiency will become a key factor determining the success of a city.

Cities also need to cooperate with one another. Thus, regionalism will be another trend in the next century. The creation of regional free trade areas is one aspect of it. The growth of ASEAN, the re-Asianisation of Japan, and American and Chinese interest in APEC all express regional imperatives in different ways. Regionalism is in reality a sharing of markets and, at a deeper level, a sharing of knowledge and destiny.

When we talk about knowledge, we must make a clear conceptual distinction between public knowledge and private knowledge. In a competitive situation, it is important to have access to knowledge already available in the public domain, or else one will be at a disadvantage compared to one's competitors. But the key to competitive advantage is private knowledge which one's competitors do not possess. In a competitive situation, the basis of profit is private knowledge. Of course, once private knowledge is used to achieve an advantage, it becomes available to others. So there is an incentive all the time to generate new knowledge and keep it private for as long as possible.

In thinking about public and private knowledge, there are two aspects to consider. One is the physical infrastructure — telecommunication systems, satellites, computers, switches, multimedia facilities and so on. This ensures the rapid movement of information. In the financial markets, even a fraction of a second can make a big difference.

The second aspect is what I call the culture of a city, by which I include civic society, the quality of administration, the legal framework, the immune systems to fight infections of all kinds, and the ability to protect private knowledge. Japanese society has many strengths in these areas.

In discussing information technology, we must not ignore the role of the cultural environment. Indeed, the cultural environment may well be more important than the physical infrastructure. Satellites, optic fibres and computers are commodities which can be easily bought and sold and therefore available to all players. What is decisive is the cultural environment which determines how efficiently and effectively knowledge is created, communicated and applied.

Take, for example, the quality of the city as a human habitat. Without a favourable environment, talented people from all over the world will not come and even homegrown talent will leave. In reality, all cities are in the game of attracting brains. The cities which will succeed the most are those which are best able to attract the most number of interesting and creative minds to work there.

This means good housing, excellent education, safety, smooth traffic, clean air, trees and flowers, music and opera, and an environment which is both wholesome for the family and interesting to individuals. Such an environment must be of human scale at the local level, however big the city. It must not be impersonal and there must be a civic sense of human beings caring for each other.

Cities are complex systems and the word "culture" is but a convenient way to describe this complexity. Urban politics and urban culture are both parts of one organic whole. That organic whole includes the immune systems which identify problems when they are still minute and react to them. Thus, the difference in response between the population of Kobe and the population of Los Angeles to a major earthquake reflects the profound difference in the character of two complex systems. In one, there was quiet grief and social discipline. In the other, there was widespread looting.

The physical structures of a city can be repaired and rebuilt. The cultural system of a city, in contrast, is unique and not transferable.

Different cultural systems will gradually create their own analogues in cyberspace. The widespread use of English will eventually be contested in cyberspace and the Internet itself will become multi-cultural.

## Singapore's IT 2000 Strategy

Singapore's response to the twin challenge of information technology and urbanisation is therefore two-pronged. On one prong, we are building up the physical infrastructure for information technology. On the other, we are doing all we can to build up a complementary cultural infrastructure.

Because we are a small island of 640 $km^2$, it is relatively easy to build up the physical infrastructure. Singapore's telecommunication system will be totally digital within a few years. We are laying the information highway to every household. By the end of the decade, every household in Singapore will be wired up via broadband co-axial cables linked to an optical fibre trunk and branch network. We are laying this network as city infrastructure. Every real-estate developer will soon be required to provide every new house or apartment with a broadband cable in the same way as he is required by law to provide the lines for water, gas, electricity and telephone. We are also encouraging the use of existing telephone lines for interactive multi-media services.

Since the early 1980s, we have taken measures to computerise the public and private sectors in Singapore. Large numbers of IT personnel have been trained. In 1981, we had 850 IT personnel. Today, we have 10,000. All government departments are now more or less computerised. For example, Singapore Port has become entirely paperless. Ship manifests, customs declarations and immigration clearance are completely online.

We are now taking computerisation a step further by promoting the use of the Internet across all sectors. 30% of Singaporean households already own personal computers. As a city-state, Singapore now has its own homepage on the Internet's World Wide

Web called Singapore InfoMap. It is spearheaded by the public sector. All government departments and statutory boards are getting onto it. We are encouraging the private sector in Singapore to jump in too. We are also promoting the use of the Internet in our universities, polytechnics, junior colleges and secondary schools. In this way, anyone anywhere in the world can gain ready access to any part of Singapore via cyberspace. We are convinced that an important dimension of competition and cooperation in the next century will be in cyberspace.

However, we are also aware that what physical infrastructure we have, other cities can also introduce in a short period of time. The physical infrastructure alone is not an enduring competitive advantage.

What is much more enduring is the urban culture. We refuse to accept that the free flow of information means allowing an environment for crime and sleaze to flourish. We continue to censor our films, books, magazines and television programmes, not because censorship can ever be one hundred percent effective, but because the act of censorship is itself symbolic and an affirmation to the young and old of the values we hold as a community. Whatever technology may bring forth, the world will remain multi-cultural. On this issue, I share completely the sentiments expressed by Mdm Edith Cresson. The Darwinian process of mutation, competition and selection in the evolution of human values is endless. The world will not all turn Anglo-Saxon. New urban cultures will evolve in response to the challenges of the next century.

For Singapore, urban culture has to be built both bottom-up and top-down. By bottom-up, I mean keeping the family strong and not undermining its integrity by misguided social policies. Family ties and education must remain paramount. By top-down, I am referring to urban government and politics, the way we achieve social consensus and effective administration. Thus, we have strict laws and regulations governing crime and other forms of anti-social behaviour, traffic control, environmental protection and so on. Singapore's ruling party, the People's Action Party (PAP), is fortunate in that it has always been an urban political party. We have never had to worry about farmers or an agricultural constituency. From the beginning, the strength of the PAP rested on its ability to build apartments, create jobs, provide good education and a safe, wholesome environment.

Singapore's multi-cultural makeup, which is a legacy of British colonial rule, is both an advantage and a disadvantage. It is an advantage because it gives us cultural access to different parts of the world. For example, Singaporean Chinese businessmen are comfortable operating in China, the way many Europeans can never be. Equally, our Indians and Malays gain us privileged access to other parts of Asia. Our widespread use of English as a common language is also an advantage in the access it gives us to North America, Europe and Australasia. A lot of human knowledge is in fact coded in cultural practices and not reducible to bits and bytes. Japanese culture is unusually well-coded in this regard, which is both a strength and a weakness. In Singapore, our simultaneous access to different cultures helps us to be knowledge arbitrageurs between East and West, and between the Southeast Asian region and the world.

However, our multi-cultural society also makes it harder for us to cohere the way, for example, the Japanese are able to. It makes our urban politics much more complicated. Books like *The Satanic Verses* and movies like *Bombay* have to be banned.

Singapore's status as a city-state is also an advantage and a disadvantage. It is an advantage because it gives us powers of self-determination. We are able to control the inflow of peoples, without which we could not solve problems of over-crowding, crime, traffic congestion and urban pollution. We are able to bring in talented people without having also to bring in slums. During the Indian bubonic plague scare last year, we were able to effect border controls immediately in a way which other cities without their own borders would have found harder to do.

But being small is also a great disadvantage because we have very little control over the external environment. We do not know whether the next century will be a peaceful century or a violent one. Information technology and urbanisation will create new tensions and new forms of conflict. Terrorism and small-scale wars may well become more common. No one can predict the future. As a small city-state, we have to take the world as it is and make the most out of a given situation. We console ourselves with the fact that other cities which we compete against will also have to do the same.

# OVERCOMING THE VULNERABILITIES OF A SMALL NATION

*Human bonding does not take place at room temperature.*

## Smallness Not Always a Disadvantage

Being small opens us to many vulnerabilities which larger nations do not face. One obvious vulnerability in our case is the need to import even the most basic necessities, including food and water. Our air and sea lanes are also subject to interdiction in the event of war in the region.

But smallness also confers us certain benefits which we should not discount. Because we are a city-state and not one city in a large nation state, we are able to solve urban problems which many cities in the world are not able to. A city-state has its own borders. This is its great advantage. It is able to control and regulate the inflow of people. Because of this, Singapore has been able to clear its old slums and prevent new slums from forming. We have better control over our own environment. This is the key reason why we have been able to overcome problems of traffic, pollution, prostitution, drugs, crime, education, housing, healthcare and so on. In many Third World cities, like Rio de Janeiro, Mexico City, Manila, Bombay and Shanghai, the more the city is able to improve its facilities, the greater the number of people it sucks in from the countryside. This swells the population of the city, making large parts of it unattractive. What we do in Singapore to fight crime, control traffic, reduce pollution and

---

Speech to SAF officers at the Temasek Seminar, 7 November 1996.

provide urban amenities is not a secret to anyone. The reason why other cities find it very hard to implement the same measures with the same effectiveness is because they cannot control the inflow of people. This is one major advantage we have as a city-state.

The fact that we do not have an agricultural sector is also a big plus. In many countries, the cities subsidise the countryside. Farmers form important political lobbies in North America, Europe and Japan. In many Asian countries, farmers provide the main political base for the ruling political party, like the Communist Party in China and Golkar in Indonesia. The agricultural constituency complicates immensely the politics of many countries. We are very fortunate not to have this complication in our domestic politics. For us, the issues are relatively straightforward.

Because we do not have an agricultural sector to subsidise, it is also easier for us to balance our budget and even generate a surplus. We do not have to provide electricity, water and roads over long distances to villages and small towns. This partly explains why many of our public utilities in Singapore have been able to operate without subsidies while keeping prices low.

## The Waxing and Waning of States

Small states can, however, be very vulnerable in the areas of economics and security. All societies, whether gathered in tribes, city-states, nation-states or empires, must solve the twin problem of economics and security. In other words, we must first be able to make a living, and earn enough to clothe ourselves, educate the young, look after the sick and so on. This is the economic problem. Then we must also be able to defend ourselves. Otherwise, what we have will be taken away from us. We would be eaten up. This is the security problem. No human society can avoid this twin problem. Indeed, no living thing can avoid this twin problem. Whether you are an ant or a dinosaur, you must solve both the economic problem and the security problem in order to survive and reproduce.

When international conditions are peaceful and trade is free, smallness can be advantageous. Those who are small can respond more quickly. They carry less dead-weight. However, under conditions of armed conflict or economic warfare, smallness can be a decisive disadvantage. Under certain conditions, big animals like dinosaurs flourish. Under other conditions, dinosaurs go extinct while little mammals prosper.

Human history go through long cycles, the causes of which are not always clear. Sometimes, the competitive dynamics favour empires. At other times empires turn unwieldy and nation-states become important. There are also times when city-states flourish in profusion, like the Greek city-states before the empire of Alexander the Great and China's warring states before the empire of Qin Shihuang.

In the *Romance of the Three Kingdoms*, the first sentence of the first paragraph of the first chapter talks about the waxing and waning of empires. The three kingdoms arose after 400 years of the Han dynasty when the forces of disunity in China became too strong for anyone including Zhuge Liang to overcome. The question we must ask ourselves is: What is the kind of world we are living in? And what stage of the historical cycle are we entering in the next century?

Technological change plays a big part in the shaping of the historical cycle. One reason why both Europe and China were unified more or less in the same historical period was the growing importance of metals, especially iron, in warfare. This, coupled with new forms of political, economic and military organisation, enabled Alexander the Great to conquer first the Greek city-states and then large parts of West Asia. Greece in turn gave way to Rome. At the other end of the Eurasian landmass, a corresponding process took place when Qin Shi Huang unified a large landmass and started China on its 2,000 years of dynastic rule. Over time, new technologies came into play transforming both the economic and security spheres. The balance of political power then changes, either causing empires to form or causing them to collapse. The cross-bow, for example, gave the Han army a great advantage over the nomadic tribes of Central Asia. Genghis Khan's mounted archer was for many decades irresistible. When Napoleon fielded artillery, he overran much of Europe including city-states like Venice which had existed for hundreds of years. When gunboats appeared on the historical stage, maritime empires were created. Thus, European gunboats operating in Southeast and East Asia were able to force kings and emperors to their knees.

With the modern revolution in transportation, communication and information technology, the historical pendulum is swinging back. There are clear signs that the world is breaking up once again. Empires are no longer in fashion. The collapse of the Soviet Union provided us with a recent dramatic example, for it was the last of the great empires. Even big nation-states are finding that bigness can cripple. Countries like China, the United States, India, Russia and Brazil are often unable to reform their institutions because of inertia. In all of them, political and economic power are flowing down to city-regions.

## Into the Next Century

Alvin Toffler was in Singapore recently. Many of you would be familiar with his books and his thesis of the third wave. Kenichi Ohmae talks about the world becoming borderless. In many parts of the world, we see secessionist tendencies. Quebec almost became independent last year. In Belgium, there is a growing debate whether the people would be better off divided into two halves, the way the Czechs and Slovaks are happier living in separate nation-states. But secessionists create other problems. In the Balkans, the logic of secession is war and ethnic cleansing. In many parts of the former Soviet Union, the forces of secession are growing. The proliferation of Mafia organisations is symptomatic of a weakened centre.

In the next century, smallness may therefore not be such a terrible disadvantage after all. But a world reorganised into smaller units will create all kinds of new dangers for us. It is not possible for us to foretell how the future will unfold but it will be, for sure, a messier world. Regional conflicts can become more common. Domestic and international terrorism is likely to grow. Nation-states will still be important but national boundaries will matter much less. The international political environment will not be clear-cut like it was during the Cold War. Instead, nation-states and cities will be competing and cooperating at the same time. City-region and city-states will be where the action is. In some ways, the world in the next century will be like the Greek city-states, or the Chinese warring states, or the Hanseatic trading towns in earlier periods of human history. In such a world, human loyalties will become more complex. Old fashion patriotism will be diluted by other loyalties, including tribal and religious loyalties. The phenomenon of business families straddling national boundaries, already the case with many business families in Asia today, will become more common. Religious fervour may also grow in the next century. New forms of religion or sects will appear.

Thus, with the end of the Cold War, old threats have receded but new problems appear. In the coming decades, the world will enter a new period of order and disorder. No one knows how long this period will last. But, eventually, new technologies will emerge and push the historical pendulum back again.

## The Idea of Singapore

Many Singaporeans today think that the present peaceful situation in our region will continue for a long time to come, that peace is the norm and continued prosperity is a given. This flies in the face of man's historical experience. Looking back at history, no empire, nation-state or city-state existed in the same form forever. At the most, they survived a few hundred years. The mighty Tang Dynasty collapsed after 300 years. The British empire on which the sun never set fell within a period of 200 to 300 years. For city-states, the outstanding example was Venice, but even it could not withstand Napoleon's onslaught. It was subsequently absorbed into a united Italy. But one day Venice may rise again because the Venetian spirit still lives on among its people. The point to remember is that there has been no century without war and revolution.

For Singapore, our instinct must be to prepare for all weather conditions. The weather will always change. It may be sunny now but it will rain. We may be in the middle of a storm but sunshine will follow. What we must mentally prepare ourselves for is to survive both sunny weather and stormy weather, even a typhoon.

The most important factor is our internal strength, our national life-force. What we must have is a sense of ourselves and of our own separateness and identity. This is not a question of economics or politics or technology. It is a moral question and a spiritual question. To put it in another way, deep inside the heart of every Singaporean, what is he or she? If the sense of being Singaporean is in our very soul, then we will survive even if we are temporarily conquered and occupied, and if we are dispersed the way the Kuwaitis were after the Iraqi army walked into Kuwait in August 1990. We will continue to live on as an idea and that idea will enable us to gather together again on this island. The Jews never lost the idea of Israel since defeat and dispersal by the Romans 2,000 years ago. For a long time, they said to each other, "next year in Jerusalem." They finally succeeded when the State of Israel was established in 1948. But the Jewish state confronts an opposing idea in Palestine, which is another potent force seeking expression in a physical reality. Until the idea of Israel and the idea of Palestine can co-exist in some way, there will be no enduring peace in the Middle East.

Many years ago, the Israeli Air Force Commander Major-General David Ivry gave a speech to the Temasek Society. I was in the audience. He was like me today, talking about the challenges which small states face. He used a metaphor which I will always remember. He said that if you uncork a bottle of whisky and throw it into a swimming pool, the whisky will gradually mix with the water, and what is inside and what is outside will eventually become one and the same. When that happens, the whisky might have changed the taste of the water in the pool but the whisky has lost its identity and therefore its usefulness. The challenge was to keep what is inside the bottle different from what is in the pool.

We can easily achieve this if we do not uncork the bottle. Then providing the bottle does not break, the whisky will remain whisky. But if the bottle is tightly sealed, it has no effect on the pool. It then has no value to the world outside. It has value only by being open to the world.

The real challenge is how to allow contact between the whisky and the water in the swimming pool without allowing the whisky in the bottle to be completely diluted. What we really need is a little distillery inside the bottle which produces new whisky to overcome the effects of dilution. For Singapore to remain Singapore — despite the regionalisation of our economy, despite many Singaporeans' working and living overseas, despite the inflow of new migrants, despite the large number of employment pass holders, work permit holders and domestic maids working here — we must have within our society distilleries which produce our Singaporean essence and enable us to remain different and separate from the world outside. These distilleries are our institutions — our family traditions; our schools, polytechnics, and universities; the SAF; mosques, temples and churches; clan associations and cultural organisations; and Parliament.

The key, therefore, is not economic growth or military strength or technology, but our sense of identity as Singaporeans. Whatever may be our race, language or religion, provided we have deep within us a sense of being Singaporean, we will survive. It is that spirit which will sustain us and which will turn moral strength into physical strength.

For as long as we unite around the idea of being Singapore, we will be able to do all the other things that are necessary to sustain ourselves from both the economic and security standpoint. From the economic standpoint, we must always be of value to others. We make a living by offering a superior service to our neighbours and to others in the world. To do this well, we must be completely rational in the way we formulate policies and carry them out. We must educate our young and re-educate our adults. We must have the necessary infrastructure. It is important to give emphasis to science, mathematics, R&D and so on. We must also be able to attract foreign talent into Singapore to supplement our own.

From the security standpoint, keeping our identity as Singaporeans means picking up the gun, mastering it and having the will to use it when there is no choice. In peace time we often take our independence for granted. It is only when we become prisoners or refugees that we realise how sweet it is to be free. We cannot be free if we are not able to defend ourselves. Others may help us but there is no substitute for our collective will to stand firm.

How then do we arm ourselves morally and spiritually as Singaporeans? How do we encourage young and old, men and women of all races and religions to work together and to feel for one another? After all, for over 100 years under British rule, the different racial and religious groups worked and lived in Singapore without really feeling for each other. Our first common experience was the Second World War and Japanese Occupation. That trauma convinced an earlier generation of Singaporeans that Singapore is not a British colonial hotel but a home that we have to fight for, protect and cherish. Singapore's path to independence from 1945 to 1965 went through many twists and turns. Out of war, revolution and civil strife emerged an independent Singapore spirit which now binds us together. It is still not a very strong bond. We will have to be further tested and forged in future crises. Each time we succeed, we become stronger. Human bonding does not take place at room temperature. It occurs under conditions of crisis. Every crisis is a test. If we fail, we fail and the game may be over. But if we succeed, the next round will be easier.

Old nation-states like France and Japan are in no danger of extinction. Even if they are conquered and occupied, they will re-emerge. There is much less assurance for city-states. The key factor in each generation is leadership. There is nothing inevitable in human history. At critical moments, when the currents of history are at the watershed and can turn either way, leaders play a decisive role — political leaders, military leaders and spiritual leaders. When leaders fail at such critical moments, they fail their whole people.

At the Singapore Armed Forces Training Institute (SAFTI), we grow our new generation of leaders. You are the best and brightest in your generation. It is upon you to rise to the challenge of leadership if history decides that the test should come in your generation.

# Reinterpreting Confucianism in a Confused Age

*In a confused age, where no existing ideology provides satisfactory answers to many current day problems, Confucianism may offer new insights.*

## Decline and Revival

The great Cambridge scientist and historian Joseph Needham, on the occasion of the 2,500th birthday of Confucius in 1951, spoke of the renewed importance of Chinese thought to the West. Needham said:

> "Confucianism was a deeply humanitarian paternalistic ethic cast in the mould of the feudal society in which it was born. It was passionately devoted to social justice, in so far as that could be conceived in feudal, and later in feudal-bureaucratic, society. It embodied a sceptical rationalism which had echoes throughout Chinese history, and which would have been very favourable to the development of modern science if its effect had not been overweighted by the intensive concentration of Confucian interest on human society and human society alone. If bureaucratism, in suppressing the rise of the merchants as a group to a position of power in the body politic, sterilised that very social class which was in European history so closely bound up with the rise of modern science and technology, that was not the fault of Confucianism as a philosophy. But Confucianism mirrored in the world of the mind the actual conditions of

---

Speech made at the opening ceremony of the International Conference on Confucianism and World Civilisation, 16 June 1997.

> Chinese medieval social life, in which all intermediate feudal lords had disappeared, and the imperial house collected its taxes by means of a bureaucracy of scholars so gigantic and so influential as to have no counterpart in European history."*

In that one paragraph Needham summarised the great strength and weakness of Confucianism as it evolved over 2,500 years.

In fact, the conservatism of Confucianist China in the 18th and 19th centuries was so deep set, it led to the greatest revolution the world had ever seen. The Chinese Revolution did not start and end in 1911. The Chinese Revolution had its first beginnings in the Opium War of 1840–1842 and, in its many twists and turns, encompassed the Taiping Revolution, the Boxer Rebellion, the 1911 Revolution, the new Culture Movement, May 4th, the split between the Kuomintang and the Communist, the Anti-Japanese War, the second civil war between the Kuomintang and the Communist, the Great Leap Forward and the Great Proletarian Cultural Revolution. This period of 155 years, from the Treaty of Nanjing in 1842 ceding Hong Kong to the British, to the return of Hong Kong to the motherland on 1 July, recorded the trials and tribulations of the Chinese Revolution and the tens of millions of lives sacrificed to it. The Chinese Revolution was also a revolution in the mind of every individual Chinese and how he saw himself and the world. Thus, a very important dimension of the Chinese Revolution was its struggle with the weight of the Confucianist tradition. The Taiping Revolution, Western democracy and Marxist-Leninism, which were all strange ideas to the traditional Chinese mind, represented different attempts by the Chinese people to shake themselves off from the past and find their way into the future. Herculean efforts were made to debunk and reject Confucianist thoughts and institutions. After some 150 years, this process of creative destruction is largely complete. It had its final paroxysm in the early 1970s when the Gang of Four launched the *Pi Lin Pi Kong* (批林批孔) Movement and compared Zhou Enlai to Zhou Gong. The fact that Confucianism is a subject of serious and

---

* "The 2,500th Birthday of Confucius" by Joseph Needham, in *Within the Four Seas*, George Allen & Unwin Ltd, London, 1969.

sympathetic study in China today marks the end of a long historical cycle and the beginning of a new one.

East Asia is now entering a very creative phase in its historical development. This is reflected not only in economic progress but also in the cultural and spiritual development of hundreds of millions of people. What we are witnessing is the beginning of an Asian renaissance which will transform Asia and the world. In many ways, this Asian renaissance will be like the European renaissance of the 15th and 16th centuries — growing commerce, rapid economic development, rediscovery of the past, developments in science and technology, human travel, the growth of cities and, most importantly, the proliferation of knowledge. What the printing press did to diffuse knowledge in Europe in that earlier period, mass education, information technology and the Internet will now do for Asians in the coming century. The European Renaissance also transformed the moral framework of European society. It was accompanied by the Reformation and the Counter-Reformation, which reshaped the European mind and prepared it for the scientific and industrial revolution of the 18th and 19th centuries. In the same way, East Asian societies will be re-established on new moral foundations in the coming decades, an important part of which will be a new Confucianism freshly re-interpreted to meet the challenges of a new age.

Throughout its history, Confucianism, as a living philosophy, often adapted to changing needs and situations. Confucianism as it evolved in Korea, Japan and Vietnam also showed great creativity. But during the period of Western expansionism in the last 300 to 400 years, Confucianism as an organising principle of human society stagnated and kept much of East Asia backwards. It is at long last reviving. Renewed interest in Confucianism is growing all over the world, especially in Asia. Its wisdom in ordering human society is being recognised again. In a confused age, where no existing ideology provides satisfactory answers to many current day problems, Confucianism may offer new insights. That Confucianism should play a major role in the East Asian revival is not surprising. Indeed, it was the genius of Confucianism that enabled East Asian civilisation to survive unbroken for so long, despite war, famine and dispersal. However, in this revival, Confucianism itself will be transformed. In the next century, Confucianism must make three great accommodations if it is to provide a moral foundation for the Asian renaissance. These are:

(a) Confucianism and Marxism-Leninism;
(b) Confucianism and democracy; and
(c) Confucianism and the equality of nations in inter-state relations.

## Confucianism and Marxism-Leninism

Some Western intellectuals think that Marxism-Leninism will wither and die in China. A few even say that China is no longer communist. These are simplistic notions. If China were to reject its Marxist-Leninist past, the way Russia did, the country would be thrown into turmoil once again. Overnight, the legitimacy of every institution would be questioned. Marxism-Leninism cannot be cast aside if there is to be stability in China. Instead, Marxism-Leninism would have to be re-interpreted afresh beyond the thoughts of Mao Zedong and Deng Xiaoping and be reconciled with a new Chinese Confucianism. This is not as difficult as it seems. The ideas of Marxism-Leninism were never completely alien to the Chinese mind in the first place. The Chinese mind had no difficulty accepting historical materialism because of its own historiographic tradition beginning with Sima Qian's *Shi Ji* (史记). In fact, Karl Marx's thesis of the relationship between the economic base and the political superstructure is today widely accepted by economists and political scientists all over the world. The dialectic was also an idea which fitted in easily with Taoist philosophy. Both understood the unity of opposites. In some ways, Taoist philosophy can be said to be broader and deeper than the dialectic propounded by Hegel. Marxism-Leninism's contribution in all the countries it took over was the promotion of science and mass education. This made possible China's rapid economic development in the last 18 years. But Marxism-Leninism as expressed in Lenin's idea of the state and a highly-centralised communist party bureaucracy proved incapable of running a modern diversified economy. In fact, Leninist bureacratism took root easily in China because of the Confucianist tradition. This is a huge problem urgently in need of a solution in China and Vietnam today.

In the last decade, Confucianism has been gradually creeping back into official Chinese society. At Mao Zedong's birthplace in Shaoshan, his museum is located alongside the ancestral temple of the Mao clan. Recently, the graves of Mao's ancestors have all been marked and prettified. Thus, despite the official atheism of Marxism-Leninism, the Confucianist tradition of venerating ancestors continues to be practised today because that practice springs from the very soil of China itself. Confucius would not have been surprised by Mao's mausoleum in Beijing. Mao has entered the Chinese pantheon, as will Deng Xiaoping.

In Hanoi, the Confucianist temple established a thousand years ago is accorded great importance as a historical site because many of the heroes and scholars of Vietnam were associated with that temple. Thus, we see Confucianism and Marxism-Leninism gradually accommodating each other. Socialism with Chinese characteristics will be softened and humanised by Confucianism. The secular morality of Confucianism will provide a much stronger foundation for Chinese and Vietnamese society in the next century than class struggle and the dictatorship of the proletariat.

## Confucianism and Democracy

Confucianism must also accommodate the ideas of democracy. Historically, Western democratic ideals helped to shatter the feudal fetters which encased the Asian mind for centuries. There is no doubt that Western democracy has been a progressive force in modern Asian history, especially in the task of creatively destroying old feudal institutions. However, in the task of re-construction, without the creative adaptation of Western democratic ideals to Asian culture and tradition, democracy may not work well at all. Even in the West, many thoughtful intellectuals now question whether democracy as practised in its present form has not become an impediment to social change and further economic development. For example, while one-man-one-vote recognises the spiritual equality of all human beings, it disregards the fact that human beings are not born equal, that some contribute more than others and that the views of a minority may matter much more than the views of the majority. Furthermore, there is a tendency in any democracy for the majority to vote in favour of the redistribution of wealth to itself, whatever harm this may do to the economy. The problems of the welfare state and socialism are a direct consequence of one-man-one-vote taken to its extreme. Deficit financing, for example, borrows from the future to pay for the present. Because the young and the not-yet-born do not have the vote, they are unable to protect their own interest. It is doubtful whether human society can be held together solely on the basis of one-man-one-vote democracy and the market, without an underlying moral framework which encourages the voter to calculate not only in his self-interest but also that of the larger community. Without a moral sense, democracy can lead to its own self-destruction especially in a large state. It is easier for democracy to work well in a smaller community, or in a city-state, where the citizens feel for each other, like in Athens. Indeed, the word "citizen" has its original meaning in membership of a city.

Confucianism can give Asian democracy a humanism which the old socialism has been unable to provide. While recognising that all men are brothers, Confucianism also devotes attention to the fact that human beings are different and perform different roles in society. A good democratic system is one which recognises the differences in ability among human beings while at the same time honouring the spiritual equality of man.

Another aspect of democracy which Confucianism must incorporate is the rule of law. In the Confucianist mind, the rule of law is to be tempered by the rule of man. In the ideal Confucianist world, *li* (礼) is more important than *fa* (法). China never lacked legal codification in its history. But China never accepted the ideal of Roman law that even the emperor himself is subject to the law. The Chinese never delighted in legal fictions the way Western Europeans and Americans do. In the Confucianist mind, it is fairness and natural justice which is paramount, not intricate legal arguments. Take for example Ms Paula Jones' legal suit against President Clinton, or the saga of O. J. Simpson. While some of us in Asia may follow these cases, it is quite inconceivable that similar cases in East Asia would be dealt with in the same way. The Asian mind has a different construction from the Western mind. The Western mind is a unique creation of Western society with its roots in Greece and Rome, and the separation of church from state in Western Europe. From there the idea spread to North America and Australasia. In Asia, our roots are profoundly different but we should still learn from the good points of Western civilisation including the rule of law adapted to Asian conditions. Indeed, without the assault of Western civilisation on our shores and without the permeation of Western influence into every aspect of life in Asia, we will not be talking about the Asian renaissance today. Reconciliation of Confucianism with Western democracy is therefore a key task before us. If we do this well, Asia may in the next century provide ideas to the world on how democracy and one-man-one-vote can be better adapted to meet the needs of a fast-changing, unequal world. In other words, there must be a re-evaluation of Confucianism, especially of Confucianism in an urban setting, just as there must be a re-evaluation of Western democracy. The role of women in the Confucianist universe, for example, must be changed. But however it is changed, it is unlikely that Asian society will ever accept the more radical feminist ideas current in the West today.

## Confucianism and the Equality of Nations

The third accommodation which Confucianism must make is with the realities of inter-state relations and the equality of nations. For most of East Asian history, China was the dominant power. It was not for nothing that China called itself the Middle Kingdom. In that world, China dealt with other powers as a superior to inferiors. Thus countries seeking economic relations with China were expected to pay tribute to it. This idea was so ingrained that when Lord Macartney refused to kowtow to the Qianlong Emperor in 1793, the Chinese court was shocked. Not surprisingly, that mission was a failure. Qianlong's reply to George the Third was that China needed nothing from England. China's arrogance became its undoing. It had no response to Western gunboats a few decades later.

China will probably become a very big political and economic power again in the next century. If China insists on the old Confucianist method of dealing with foreign powers, the result must again be war because other countries will not accept peacefully the idea that they should pay tribute to China. The world in the next century will be multi-polar and the equality of nations is essential to world peace. This is not to pretend that all countries carry the same political or economic weight. They do not. But the relationship between nations must recognise the independence of nations and their sovereignty. The nominal equality of nations is perhaps one of Europe's greatest contribution to human civilisation. It is an idea that is alien to Asian Confucianism, but one absolutely necessary for continuing peace and economic co-operation in our region. When President Clinton hosted the APEC Summit meeting at Blake Island in 1993, the setting was an informal one, so typical of the American view of itself and the world. Whether the leader was from a big country or a small country, everyone dressed casually and sat around in a circle. Implicit in the seating was the recognition that all nations, big and small, enjoy a kind of equality. Without the American presence in East Asia and its influence on East Asia diplomatic protocol, formal summit meetings in East Asia will always be characterised by high ritual and careful ranking of participants. No seating arrangement will be left to chance. No official photograph will be taken which did not put the most important players in the middle. If the revival of Confucianism means the revival of China as imperial overlord, it will be resisted everywhere especially by Japan, Korea, Vietnam and other Southeast Asian countries. What is needed instead is a Confucianism which incorporates the many positive aspects of the West and which extols the equality of nations.

## World Peace

Among the chopstick peoples of East Asia, three major philosophical traditions have defined their characters over long centuries. They are Confucianism, Taoism and Mahayana Buddhism. All three will experience huge revivals in the next century and become important aspects of the Asian renaissance. But they must be updated and take into account ideas from Western and other traditions. Buddhism, of course, originated from India. It was the influence of Taoism on Mahayana Buddhism which gave Zen or Chan Buddhism its particular East Asian character. Of the three, the one which will have the strongest impact on social, economic and political development will be Confucianism. By its emphasis on education and scholarship, Confucianism will advance the development of science and information technology. A key reason for the high performance of East Asian students in science, mathematics and classical music is the Confucianist drive for educational excellence. In the way it keeps religions at arm's length, Confucianism also provides a secular moral framework which allows disciples of different religious persuasions to work and live together in harmony. Confucian secularism was usually able to keep religion out of politics, while preserving the moral aspect of politics. It was a different kind of secularism from the modern secularism of the West which was the result of political contests between church and state. Thus China never had the kinds of religious wars which Europe experienced so often in its history. In this world, no religious group is in the majority. All are minority groups — Christians, Buddhists, Muslims and Hindus. We have no choice but to live together in a globalised economy. Confucianism will help to create such a world.

But before Confucianism can play such a role in the next century, it must be reconciled with Marxism-Leninism, democracy and the equality of nations in inter-state relations. Let me end by again citing Joseph Needham who said on the same occasion of Confucius' birthday: "In the 18th century, the Encylopaedists, who carefully studied the Latin translation of the Chinese classics made by the Jesuits, discovered that for centuries Confucianism had inculcated a morality without supernaturalism, and that the Pelagian doctrine of the intrinsic goodness of human nature (essential for any progressive social philosophy) had been orthodox, not heretical, in China. Such discoveries prepared the way for the French revolution. Is it not possible, therefore, that, given time, the philosophical background of so vast a population and so deep-rooted a culture, may exert similar stimulating effects upon the development of collectivist thought, and even do something towards drawing the two halves of the world together?"

In other words, our re-interpretation of Confucianism must be done in a way which brings all of humanity together in the next century and not divide it once again. If, instead of a universal humanistic re-interpretation, Confucianism becomes a way to confront and combat the West, then the outcome will be an unhappy one and certainly one which will not do justice to the memory of Confucius.

# Looking at East Asia from Within

*We are not … outsiders. We are East Asians rediscovering ourselves and collectively facing the challenges of rapid, massive change.*

The establishment of the East Asian Institute is part of Singapore's overall efforts to deepen knowledge of our own region. This may seem surprising but, in fact, in many areas, we know more about the Western world than about countries in Asia. This reflects our colonial background.

When I was a young boy studying at St Patrick's Primary School, before the sea there was reclaimed, one of my teachers once pointed out to us the Riau islands on the horizon. He said that they were Indonesian islands, which at that time seemed a world away. The geography books which we used in those days invariably showed Singapore with Peninsular Malaysia and never with the Riau islands. They reflected the colonial perspective. Singapore and Malaysia were part of the British Empire in the Far East which, of course, was only "far" because we took London's perspective. The Riaus were part of the Dutch East Indies with their own links to the Netherlands.

After Soekarno's Confrontation against Malaysia ended, a new chapter opened in the history of independent Southeast Asia. ASEAN was formed in August 1967 even though, and partly because, Indo-China was still at war. We needed deep knowledge of Indonesia. As part of this endeavour, the Institute of Southeast Asian Studies was

---

Speech made at the official opening of the East Asian Institute (EAI), 22 July 1997. George Yeo was involved in establishing the EAI as a successor to the Institute of East Asian Political Economy (IEAPE).

established in 1968. Slowly but steadily, Singaporeans rediscovered Indonesia. I remember the first joint air exercise between the Air Forces of Singapore and Indonesia in 1980. It was held over southern Sumatra. We knew very little about the Indonesian Air Force at that time and our pilots were briefed to be particularly careful not to cause offence. Even so, one of them caused a sonic boom by diving his Hunter aircraft over Palembang. Today, the Singapore and Indonesian Armed Forces are very close to each other. Today, Singaporeans think nothing of hopping over to Batam and Bintan for a weekend outing.

Because of the success of ASEAN, Southeast Asians have restored the interconnections which existed before the Western colonial powers came and divided the region up. ASEAN is today a prospering regional organisation with bright prospects for the future.

It is now timely for us to broaden and deepen our knowledge of the whole of East Asia. This is the part of the world which will affect all our lives most profoundly in the coming decades. The countries of East Asia, including the countries of Southeast Asia, have a combined population of about two billion people, which is over one-third of mankind. The economies of the countries of East Asia are developing so rapidly that we can expect the East Asian region to account for some 40–50% of the world's GNP some time in the middle of the next century. East Asia is therefore an enormous reality for all of us in Singapore. It is crucial that our political, intellectual, cultural and emotional perspectives take into account the economic trends transforming Asia and the world.

The reason many young Singaporeans today know more about Nova Scotia than they do about Kamchatka, or Lake Tahoe more than Lake Baikal, is because of our history and the importance of the West to us. All this will change dramatically in the coming decades. The next generation of Asians will be skiing in Tibet.

The establishment of the East Asian Institute is to help Singaporeans prepare for this new world. Our efforts to build up knowledge on East Asia started many years ago even before China embarked on Deng Xiaoping's policy of reform and opening up. It was clear even then that China would once again play a very important political and economic role in Asia. Thus, the Singapore government made the critical decisions to promote the use of Mandarin and the simplified Chinese script. The Institute of East Asian Philosophy was established by Dr Goh Keng Swee in 1982. It was given a different orientation and renamed the Institute of East Asian Political Economy in 1992. Earlier this year, the Institute of East Asian Political Economy was wound up as a private company and has now been reincarnated as an independent institute of the National University of Singapore.

The dominant emphasis has been on China. This is because of the disproportionate weight China carries in East Asia, both in terms of its geographical size and its population size. Over many dynasties stretching back over 2,000 years, China's political and cultural influence on East Asia has been extensive and persistent. And so it will again be in the next century. Thus, a major focus of the East Asian Institute will be contemporary developments in China. What happens in China will affect all of us in a major way. As China industrialises in the coming decades, it will be transformed from a predominantly agricultural to an increasingly urbanised society. This will set new patterns unprecedented in China's long history. The urbanisation of China, which is on a scale and at a speed unseen anywhere in the world, will put every Chinese institution under severe stress, from the Communist Party and the People's Liberation Army to the Chinese clan and the extended family. It is not realistic to expect that such a huge transformation of Chinese society can be accomplished without periodic social upheavals. The test of one-country-two-systems does not only apply to Hong Kong, it will apply to all of China because the fast-growing urban areas will have to be governed differently from the countryside which provided the traditional political base of Chinese dynasties and the Chinese Communist Party.

While we are in no position in Singapore to affect the course of Chinese history, we must be alert to the changes taking place and understand the forces driving Chinese society into the next century. It is not only Singaporeans who have to make this analysis. Every country and every city in the world should make this analysis because the developments in China will have a big impact on them. The work of the East Asian Institute will therefore be helpful not only to

Singaporeans and Singapore organisations, but also to others in the world.

Unlike similar institutes in North America and Europe, however, Singapore's East Asian Institute will take an insider perspective of developments in East Asia. We are not Westerners rooted in different philosophical traditions looking into East Asia as outsiders. We are East Asians rediscovering ourselves and collectively facing the challenges of rapid, massive change. The East Asian Institute should not only collaborate with institutes in the West, it should also work closely with individuals and organisations in China, Japan, Korea and Southeast Asia, especially with practitioners in the public and private sectors. We live in a period of human history when practice races ahead of theory. We are insiders in East Asia but at a sufficient distance from China to have a good perspective of the unfolding drama.

We are very fortunate to have Prof Wang Gungwu as the first director of the Institute. His accomplishments are well-known to us. At this point in time, he is better known than the new institute he heads. We hope that, under his leadership, the Institute will eventually enjoy the reputation that he himself enjoys. In many ways, Prof Wang Gungwu's own life history anticipated the changes now taking place in East Asia.

It gives me great pleasure to declare open, officially, the East Asian Institute.

# CRISIS AND CONFIDENCE: BUILDING A NEW ASIA

*If there is one thing good coming out of this crisis, it is the renewed awareness of the importance of global leadership.*

## Tectonic Shifts

We meet in the midst of an economic crisis that is sweeping through the region. From 2 July last year, a day after the return of Hong Kong to China, the crisis started with the collapse of the Thai baht and spread quickly from one country to another. The crisis unfolded with incredible speed and on a scale which no one could have foreseen. Nobody can be sure how much longer the crisis will last, nor how much worse it must get before the outlook improves. Its effects on North America and Europe can already be felt and there is a risk that the Asian economic crisis could lead eventually to a world economic crisis.

Many explanations have been advanced to explain what led to the crisis but no explanation has been entirely satisfactory, which is why it has been so difficult to predict the course of the crisis. It may be many years before economists are able to agree on the causes but, by that time, it will be history. Till today, the causes of the Great Depression in the early 1930s are still a subject of dispute among scholars. What we know is that a major historical process is underway affecting all of Asia. This is not a normal cycle which will lead us back to more or less where we were before. When night becomes day again, it will be a different world. It will not be business as usual in Asia. In some countries, the economic crisis has become a political

Speech at the Business Week Asia Leadership Forum, CHIJMES Chapel, 23 June 1998.

crisis. In the case of Indonesia, the political situation is still unsettled despite Suharto's resignation. All over Asia, economic and political structures have come under great stress. Historically speaking, this is the most important event reshaping the whole of Asia since the Second World War.

Trying to predict the course of this crisis is like trying to predict the occurrence of earthquakes. In reality, complex forces are at work giving rise to chaotic outcomes. What we are seeing is akin to tectonic shifts on the earth's crust.

With the end of the Cold War, old certitudes are gone. The world is in transition from one equilibrium to another in the next century whose shape is still unclear. However, the major forces driving historical change can be identified. If we understand these tectonic shifts, we can do some things to prepare ourselves better for further earthquakes and their aftershocks.

### US-Japan Relationship

A key driving force is the evolving US-Japan relationship. The regional havoc wreaked by the volatility in the dollar-yen exchange rate is the result of underlying tensions in this relationship. The shocks reverberate throughout Asia. In mid-1995, US$1 was worth about 80 yen. Today, US$1 is worth over 135 yen. In just three years, the yen has dropped by about 40%. This reflects the relative weakness of the Japanese economy and Japanese institutions, and the relative strength of the US economy. Even a highly sophisticated system will find it difficult to adjust smoothly to such a drastic change in the value of currency. This is like the effect of sudden climatic change on biological species.

If we go back to an earlier period, as dramatic a shift in the opposite direction led to an era of prosperity in Southeast Asia. The Plaza Accord in September 1985 revalued the yen from about 240 yen to US$1 to about 130 yen to US$1 in 1988. The result of the revalued yen led to a massive outflow of investments from Japan to Southeast Asia. It was accompanied by parallel outflows from Hong Kong, Taiwan, South Korea and Singapore. This led to a long period of boom in Malaysia, Thailand and Indonesia. After 1990, ethnic

Chinese capital in turn fuelled rapid economic development in the coastal regions of Chinese mainland.

Unfortunately, the rapid rise of the yen also created an asset bubble in Japan. In the heady atmosphere of the late 1980s, one can still remember it being said that if the land in Tokyo on which stood the imperial palace were sold, it could have bought the whole state of California. The asset bubble burst in Japan hit the stock market in 1990 and the property market in 1991. Japanese financial institutions were severely damaged by this asset implosion, the ramifications of which still plague Japan today. At its peak, the Nikkei almost reached 39,000. In yen terms, prime property prices in Tokyo today are still less than one-third of what they fetched in 1991.

The Plaza Accord was forced on Japan. In hindsight, it might have been overdone. The underlying tension was Japan's high savings rate relative to the US. It led to persistently large current account surpluses which resulted in US mercantile pressure on Japan. Since the US occupation of Japan after the Second World War, Japan was basically subordinate to the US and prospered under that regime until the breakdown of the fixed exchange rate system in 1971. Japan is not a normal power. In some ways, because of the terrible experiences of the last war, it does not want to be a normal power, preferring instead to rely on the US as its big brother and for its security umbrella.

While politically weak, Japan is economically powerful. The Japanese economy is two-thirds of the Asian economy. Japan accounts for one-third of the world's total savings. With its enormous savings of about $20 trillion, Japan has the economic wherewithal to stabilise Asia in this economic crisis, but is unable to do so because of its economic and political structure. In recent years, the post-Second World War consensus in Japan has broken down. Institutions which were once held in high esteem are being called into question, like the Liberal Democratic Party (LDP), the Finance Ministry and Tokyo University. If Japan were a normal power with strong financial institutions, it would have been the biggest winner in this Asian crisis. All the countries in trouble would have sought Japan's assistance and Japan would have been able to reshape much of maritime

Asia according to its worldview. Fortunately or unfortunately, this is not the case. The size of the Japanese economy, instead of being an important part of the solution, has become a major part of the problem.

It will take some time, maybe many years, before a new consensus re-emerges in Japan. The breakdown in the old consensus has led to the current recession. It is in the nature of Japanese society that, while slow to change, when it does change, it does so suddenly, decisively and comprehensively. When that change is made, the might of the Japanese economy will reassert itself throughout the region, not just economically but also politically. No one knows how Japanese society will evolve and change, but an important determinant is the evolving US-Japan relationship.

With the end of the Cold War, the US is the only superpower left in the world. Since the Second World War, the peace in non-communist East Asia was largely an American peace, with Japan closely allied to the US position. In the next century, however, the strategic picture in Asia will become more complicated. It will be a multi-polar world in which US power will be contested. China and Japan will play bigger roles. The recent nuclear tests in India and Pakistan demonstrated clearly the limits of US dominance in world affairs. The economic crisis now raging through Asia can also lead to an anti-US backlash of one kind or another.

Although the US economy is the largest in the world, it is an economy increasingly based on debt. The problem is a persistently low savings rate. Since the 1980s the US has depended on large inflows of foreign capital to keep its economy going. The US today is by far the world's largest debtor nation. Although the Federal budget will soon be in surplus because of unexpectedly strong growth in revenues, the US economy on the whole is heavily dependent on domestic and foreign debt. The deficit in the current accounts was US$166 billion last year and is expected to grow significantly this year. In other words, to keep the US economy going, it has to suck in some half a billion dollars a day. Wall Street has boomed not only because of productivity growth but also because of low interest rates. Low interest rates are only possible because of the inflow of foreign funds. Of the US$1.3 trillion in outstanding Treasury securities, about one-quarter are held by Japanese institutions. Together, Japan, Taiwan, China, Hong Kong and Singapore hold over one-third of US Treasuries.

We thus have a situation where the greatest power on earth is also the world's largest debtor nation, while the world's greatest creditor nation is, for historical reasons, unable to lead. This creates a dangerous faultline in world politics and economics. If Japan were part of the US, that faultline would disappear and a major economic problem in the world would be solved. The Asian financial crisis would never have been allowed to spread. But Japan is not the 51st state, and the tension between Japan and the US is reflected in the volatility of the dollar-yen exchange rate and a lack of decisive response to the Asian contagion.

There is no substitute for US leadership in the foreseeable future. The US remains the most creative society on earth and continues to attract some of the best and brightest from Asia to its shores. Without the continuing strategic engagement of the US in East Asia, the future will be troublesome.

## China

Another major tectonic shift is the emergence of the Chinese behemoth. Barring a major catastrophe, it is a fair bet that, some time in the first half of the next century, China would become the world's largest economy, as it was for most of human history. When we talk about China, it is important to remember its relative homogeneity and population size. With 1.2 billion people, China's population is almost four times that of the European Union and almost twice that of the rest of East Asia combined.

It is not possible for the incorporation of China into the global economy to be smooth or easy because of its sheer size. In the last hundred-plus years, the emergence of Germany in Europe from the time of Bismarck, and of Japan in Asia since the Meiji Reformation, created great tensions in the world. The emergence of China is on a much larger scale and will have a correspondingly huge impact on world economics and politics. This complex historical process of incorporating China will take place over many decades and will be punctuated by upheavals in the global system. The cycles of China's history have always spread tidal waves throughout the region. In one such cycle, modern Singapore was created as millions of Chinese sought a better life in Southeast Asia. All it took was for the Governor of China's Central Bank to hint elliptically that the renminbi might have to be devalued for financial markets throughout the region to tumble. This is in 1998 when the Chinese economy is only one-tenth that of Japan. China's decision not to devalue the renminbi despite the loss of export competitiveness has helped to stabilise the economic situation in Asia. China is willing to pay the price for this decision because of its concern for Hong Kong and its sense of regional responsibility. An expensive renminbi makes it more difficult for China to restructure its state-owned enterprises and bureaucracy, and to create jobs for a growing number of urban unemployed. It is a game of high stakes.

The triangular relationship between the US, Japan and China will be of decisive importance to peace and prosperity in the region. The Asian crisis today is partly the result of tensions in that relationship. The European Union will also play an important role in the region. The euro will become an alternative reserve currency to the US dollar in the next century. Together with the European Union, the US and Japan will have to manage carefully and strategically China's incorporation into the global system. The alternative is global conflict. President Clinton's present China policy recognises this necessity. An early entry of China into the WTO is good for the whole world. It is also important for China to be gradually brought into the G8 or G9. China's economic role in the world cannot be less than that of Russia.

## Disintermediation

Another tectonic shift in the world is the disintermediation brought about by the IT revolution. The IT revolution has undermined traditional hierarchies and weakened government monopolies all over the world. Disintermediation of old financial structures are well known. It has forced the restructuring of the international financial system. International financial markets are now beyond the control of any particular national authority. It started with the growth of the euro dollar market in the 1960s in response to attempts by the US government to restrict movements of the US dollar. The growth of the Asian Currency Unit (ACU) market in Singapore continued that process in Asia. Today, national governments which try to fight the international financial markets cannot win.

The disintermediation goes beyond financial institutions. Economic and political structures are also being disintermediated. Inefficient state-owned enterprises like those in China and huge government-supported enterprises like the *chaebols* in Korea can no longer rely on cheap financing. Everywhere in Asia, these privileged entities are in crisis. Political structures are also being disintermediated. The ability of national governments to tax, to divert investments and redistribute incomes is weakening everywhere. Rapid urbanisation in East Asia is shifting political power from the countryside to the major cities. Urban dwellers resent the heavy subsidy of the agricultural sector which provides the political base for many ruling parties. In Southeast Asia, the ability of national governments to tax and confine ethnic Chinese capital has also been undermined. Old economic and political institutions are breaking down before new institutions are in place. The present Asian crisis is very much an institutional crisis.

## Responses

The evolving US-Japan relationship, the emergence of China and the disintermediation of economic and political structures by IT are tectonic shifts which will cause earthquakes throughout the region for many years to come. These are faultlines which cannot be wished away. Our strategy for survival must take them into account at three different levels.

For individuals and corporations, we must go back to the basics. In a sense, we have always understood this in Singapore because of our precarious circumstances. There is no free lunch in the world. If you don't work, you don't eat, that is all. The most important asset is the human being and the culture which enables human beings to work together for common purposes. There is no substitute for good education and hard work. This crisis has reminded us that too much greed destroys itself and to be suspicious of shortcuts. Old-fashioned values like thrift, honesty and strong families should never be given up. Far from being weakened, these aspects of Asian values are being reinforced by the present crisis.

In these uncertain times, leadership and a good government are particularly important. Until old economic and political institutions are reconstructed, it is difficult for some Asian economies to recover. This is a huge challenge which affects as much the present government in Indonesia as it does the LDP in Japan and the Communist Party in China. While there will be a plurality of political systems in Asia, building on the history, culture and traditions of different Asian societies, all of them must meet the test of good leadership, good government and wider political participation. Democracy can help to bring about a good government, but is no guarantee of it. One way or another, the problem of corruption and lack of transparency must be tackled head on. We are likely to see a new generation of Asian leaders emerging in the coming years, either by smooth succession or by revolt. Their worldviews, including their attitudes towards the West, are being forged in the heat of the present crisis.

The third response is the most difficult to achieve. This concerns the problem of world governance. During the Cold War, world governance was broadly achieved in the non-communist world by the US and by international institutions created after the Second World War, like the UN, the IMF and the World Bank. Right up to the mid-1950s, the US economy was some 40% of the world economy. Today it is about 25%. In the next century, the US economy will still be dominant but not as much as in the past. Furthermore, the international institutions created at the end of Second World War are becoming less relevant to new situations. New power centres in the world have to be accommodated. We are entering a different era. IT has unleashed forces in the world which are beyond anybody's control. The international financial markets, which are capable of unsettling the world like an El Nino, must somehow be tamed. No one knows how this can be achieved but there is a growing view that something must be done to create greater stability. When exchange rates fluctuate wildly, the real economy cannot operate properly. Volatile exchange rates can debase the meaning of hard work for ordinary human beings.

We are entering a dangerous period in world history. Federal Reserves Chairman Alan Greenspan has said that there is a small but not insignificant chance that the Asian crisis will reach America. If it does, the whole world can plunge into recession. A prolonged recession in the world will in turn unleash dark forces of reaction against globalisation and the free market. The last Great Depression led to the rise of fascism, anti-semitism and the Second World War. Another world depression will take humanity down a different path from the one which we have all been looking forward to. It took the calamity of the Second World War to create the UN, the IMF and the World Bank. We should not wait for another such calamity before rising to the challenge of world governance.

At a time like this, we need points of stability in the world. Singapore can be one small point of relative stability in the region. We have no external debt. Our banks and financial institutions are among the strongest in Asia. However, we are exposed to the regional crisis. Preliminary figures from the second quarter show that growth momentum continues to slow down. The expected growth rate for this year will have to be revised downwards, although it is still not likely to be negative. Next Monday, on 29 June, the Finance Minister will announce in Parliament a package of off-budget measures to ameliorate the economic slowdown. The focus will be to reduce business costs and help businesses to cope with this difficult period, rather than to pump-prime the economy or stimulate consumption. But whatever the government does, Singapore cannot be fully insulated from the regional crisis. Unlike 1985–1986, the causes of this economic downturn are largely external to us and beyond our control.

What we hope for are leaders in the world who can see far. Too many national leaders today are preoccupied by domestic concerns. Without the US, Japan and China acting decisively, the Asian crisis can get much worse. If there is one thing good coming out of this crisis, it is the renewed awareness of the importance of global leadership. The success of President Clinton's visit to China in the next two weeks is very important for this reason.

Like all crises, this Asian crisis will either strengthen or weaken us. If there is sufficient global leadership, the promise of the Pacific century will eventually be realised. If not, Asia will still emerge, but it will be a troubled world.

# Dialogue between Asians and Europeans on Human Rights

*... for completely selfish reasons, it is in our interest to evolve a common set of human values...*

There are mixed motives behind the advocacy of universal human rights. The altruistic motives express a desire to see human societies everywhere in the world become better and more civilised. However, there are also selfish motives which should be recognised. Human rights are also used to further political and economic objectives. In an earlier age, Catholic missionaries in the New World not only spread the Gospel, they also made conquest and colonisation easier. Thus, while from our present moral standpoint, it was right to stop the human sacrifices of the Aztecs, it was also politically expedient at that time to christianise the native population. Latin America today is by no means the most perfect of continents but it is certainly the least racist in its culture, and that is to be extolled.

It is important for us to recognise both altruistic and selfish motives when we push for the greater observance of human rights in the world. From a social Darwinian viewpoint, the selfish motives are probably more important than the altruistic motives. To succeed as a historical movement, the human rights movement must help societies become stronger and more productive. If particular aspects of human rights weaken human society, they are not likely to take root. One recalls the contest between Athens and Sparta during the Peloponnesian Wars.

Speech at the Colloquium on Human Rights and Human Responsibilities, Hamburg, Germany, 20 November 1998.

We are now standing on the threshold of a new millenium and, within limits, the future is for us to grasp and to shape. If we look back on the 20th century, it has been a century of astonishing human progress. But it has also been a century of unspeakable evil. The technologies which made possible the economic development of this century were also the technologies applied to warfare and which made possible the industrial slaughter of tens of millions of human beings. And, still, the technological revolution continues unabated. Information technology (IT) is causing great upheavals to our lives. The present financial turmoil sweeping like an El Nino around the world is only one manifestation of it. Behind this IT tidal wave is the biotechnology tidal wave which will enable us to tinker with the very essence of life itself. The moral challenges are immense. The capacity to do good is only matched by the capacity to do evil.

Therefore, for completely selfish reasons, it is in our interest to evolve a common set of human values which enables us to exploit technological development while minimising its ill effects. We need values which bind us as human beings on this fragile planet even as we compete fiercely. Even if there has to be armed conflict, we need limits beyond which no one is allowed to trespass whatever the circumstances. Our consensus of what universal human rights and responsibilities are should not end with declarations on paper. Declarations on paper should only be the start of a worldwide mass education effort to inculcate certain values in the young. Unless they grow up with common human values hardwired in their minds and in their hearts, we may repeat in the next century the mistakes of this century. The key is consensus at a high level leading to education at all levels. Without effective follow-through, debates on human rights and responsibilities are of little consequence to the issues of war and peace.

What we must work hard to find is common ground. Human cultures are complex and tenacious, and the search for common ground is not easy. The quicker we get away from slogans, the better. There must also be a certain honesty and humility in the way our dialogue is conducted. It is not possible to have a dialogue if we are only talking at each other and no one is interested to listen.

For example, it is absurd to talk about human rights independent of the overall economic development of a society. Let us look at the issue of human rights in China. Many Singaporeans are the descendants of migrants who left a China in revolution, war and chaos. My own mother left China in 1937 at the age of 18, a month after she married my father who was from Singapore. The Japanese had just invaded China and my parents were rushing back to what they thought was a more secure Southeast Asia. For over 40 years, my mother was cut off from her parents and relatives in China, who after expropriation by the Communists, lived in terrible poverty during the dark days of the Great Leap Forward and the Cultural Revolution. Singaporeans packed meat and lard into kerosene tins, then sealed and sent them to China to help keep relatives there alive. When Deng Xiaoping took over the leadership from Mao Zedong and started the process of opening China up to the world in 1978, the situation in China changed dramatically. I accompanied my parents back to China after that on many occasions. Year by year, we could see the improvement in the lives of so many people.

In 20 years, as a result of political stability and the right economic policies, over 200 million Chinese have been lifted out of grinding poverty. It is therefore very difficult for me to sympathise with my Western friends who criticise China for the lack of human rights, while at the same time, choosing to ignore what the present Chinese government has done for a large number of its people. At an interview preceding Hong Kong's return to China last year, I suggested that China should be given a Nobel Prize for human rights. I said this not facetiously but from a heartfelt awareness of the improvement in the daily lives of millions of human beings. This is not to say that China has not got a long way to go or that one should not criticise the Chinese government for not putting enough emphasis on human rights. It is common knowledge that, in many parts of China, local authorities still behave in a corrupt, cruel and arbitrary manner. However, we cannot talk about human rights in China out of the historical context.

It is difficult for a Singaporean like me to be as understanding of human conditions in Africa or Latin America because these are continents far away. Together with everyone else in the world,

Singaporeans condemn genocide in the region of the African great lakes in the strongest terms but we do not understand in any depth the actual situation on the ground or the historical relationship between the Hutus and Tutsis. What we do know is that when ancient patterns of tribal relationships are suddenly upset, the result is often war and chaos, which is probably the situation in Zaire today. Those of us who seek to prescribe remedies are under a moral obligation to study first the nature of these societies and what the underlying pathologies are. A doctor who prescribes medicine must first diagnose the illness and he cannot do this without acquainting himself with the medical history of the individual he is treating. To be more keen to prescribe medicine than to understand the illness is not only unprofessional, it is criminal negligence. For example, it is easy for Asians to criticise Europeans on their Balkan policy but are Asians really familiar with the political complexities of the Balkans?

The point I am making is that to find common ground in human rights and responsibilities, we must have deep knowledge of each other's culture and value system. The Jesuits understood this when they attempted to christianise China during the Ming and Qing dynasties. Matteo Ricci was one of the most brilliant minds in European history. After he arrived in China in 1582, he immersed himself in the study of the language and the culture. He became the first person to translate the *Four Books** into Latin. Chinese emperors welcomed the presence of Jesuits in the courts because of the knowledge that they had in mathematics, astronomy and geography. One major contribution which the Jesuits made to Chinese civilisation was the correction of the Chinese calendar. The Chinese calendar is a complex calendar incorporating both the solar and lunar cycles. It is in fact a solar calendar with the lunar cycles built in. Thus, Chinese New Year is always celebrated on a new moon while the mid-autumn festival always takes place under a full moon. One can tell from the calendar when the tide is ebbing or flowing. However, to synchronise the solar and lunar cycles, intercalary months and days have to be inserted at

---

*The *Four Books* are Chinese classic texts that illustrate the core value and belief systems in Confucianism.

different points in different years. The calculations were fiendishly difficult and Chinese astronomers did not have enough knowledge to do a good job. The Jesuits corrected the Chinese calendar which is still widely used in East Asia today for secular and religious purposes. However, very few Chinese realise how much Catholic priests had contributed to something which they now take for granted.

The Jesuits had only one goal which was to convert the Chinese emperor to the faith so that all China would be christianised. They understood the enormity of the challenge and how crucial it was to understand China's history and culture, and to change the Chinese mind from within. They tried to reconcile ancestor worship with Catholic teaching which led to the bitter rites controversy with the Dominicans and Franciscans. In the end, China proved resistant to attempts at conversion. But, in a larger sense, Judeo-Christian values have succeeded in transforming China and laying the basis for China's resurgence in the world.

Take the position of women in China as an example. The liberation of women is one of the most important achievements of the Chinese Revolution in this century. For a few thousand years, women had been put in such a subordinate position that sons outranked their mothers. The binding of women's feet for the sexual gratification of Chinese men was a mutilation so gross and grotesque, it would constitute a high crime today. Yet it was an unquestioned practice for centuries. Little girls begged to have their foot arches broken so that they would become eligible wives. Without the unwelcome intrusion of the West, the practice would have gone on much longer. There are many other such Judeo-Christian influences like monogamy. Monogamy is a relatively recent development in Asia and, even today, Muslims reject monogamy as un-Koranic. But we do not know what the effects of monogamy would be in the long term. For the Chinese, it was the practice for a long time that those who were successful had more wives and more offsprings, thereby propagating themselves.

One must also not forget that Marxism-Leninism in China is a Western idea with Judeo-Christian roots. China did not adopt Western ideas by choice but by necessity. Without the absorption of Western ideas, China could not modernise itself and prevent its colonisation by Western powers or by a Westernised Japan. Western values took root in Asia not by persuasion but by force of Western economic and military prowess. Historians have no difficulty understanding this. Western ideas embedded in universal human rights have gained ascendancy in the world precisely because of the success of Western societies. But this does not mean that Asian societies, however Westernised, will cease to be Asian. In many ways, the ideas of Marx have been sinicised beyond recognition in China. We must expect resurgent Asian societies to assert gradually their own viewpoints of what is right and what is wrong in the world. That is only natural. In the process, what is considered common and universal between East and West will be struck at a different balance point. In this dialogue about human rights and responsibilities, we must avoid the temptation to be triumphalist.

In the last year and a half, incipient Asian triumphalism has taken a severe knock because of the Asian economic crisis. Among some quarters in the West, there was a corresponding *schadenfreude*. Now that the economic crisis threatens to engulf the whole world, the discussions have become more sober and circumspect. Europe's search for a third way into the future reflects a new age of uncertainty. It is still not clear whether the present economic crisis will lead to a global recession. If it does, we must beware of the re-emergence of forces of reaction. The last great depression led to the rise of fascism in Europe and militarism in Japan, and drew the whole world into the Second World War. A new great depression will reverse the globalisation process in the world, encourage neo-fascism and accentuate tribal feelings in many countries.

We must take heed of the warning lights and do everything in our power to prevent the beginning of the next century's becoming a tragic replay of the beginning of the 20th century. On the issue of human rights and responsibilities, a sincere, honest approach based on a deep understanding of each other's history and culture is of paramount importance. Our dialogue would be unproductive if it becomes a polemical debate about political systems. It would be wrong to equate universal human rights and responsibilities with

Western democratic values. If the starting point is that Western democratic systems are morally superior embodiments of human rights, our dialogue would not go very far. The Catholic Church is not a democratic organisation. Yet no one questions its commitment to human rights and responsibilities. When Hong Kong was a British colony without any democracy, it was a haven for human rights. This is not to say that political systems are unimportant but we must go beyond political systems and look at the everyday lives of ordinary human beings. Cultural differences and the issue of development cannot be simply swept aside.

But, if we succeed in our task, a certain convergence of political systems will take place in the world. China's recent repeated expressions of concern for the plight of the ethnic Chinese in Indonesia, many of whom are not Chinese nationals but Indonesian nationals, show a shift in the Chinese position. This is inevitable because globalisation has made us all members of the same club and, being members of the same club, we have to observe certain common norms and values. But convergence is only up to a point. We will still be a diverse and a pluralistic world. On issues like abortion there is not likely to be consensus. Between Western and Islamic societies, profound differences of view on many issues will persist for a long time to come. We must at least agree to disagree and concentrate on what is common. All men are brothers, whatever the race or religion we belong to, and that is a good starting point.

# Chinese Culture and Politics

*The Chinese revolution which overthrew imperial rule is still ongoing.*

## "Artificial Stability"

Throughout Chinese history, a profound tension exists between stability and instability. Chinese civilisation is the longest continuous civilisation on earth, going back more than 5,000 years. This shows the tenacity of the culture and its deep stability. However, Chinese society is also highly fragmented. The father of modern China, Sun Zhongshan, once described Chinese society as a tray of loose sand. Outside the extended family, Chinese people tend to be lacking in public spirit. In their minds, a clear distinction is made between what is within the family and what is outside the family. Within the extended family, mutual trust and assistance is taken for granted. Beyond the extended family, liberties are often taken unless there is a threat of punishment.

Without a strong state to hold Chinese society together, it can dissolve quickly into internal dispute and civil war. In physics, there is a phenomenon called "artificial stability". This describes a situation when stability is achieved by external control over what would otherwise be unstable. For example, a fighter aircraft, whether it is a Sopwith Camel, a Spitfire or an F-16, is designed to be unstable so that the aeroplane can manoeuvre freely in a dogfight. The control system or the pilot has to maintain stability all the time. Once the

---

Special lecture at the Golden Jubilee Anniversary of New Asia College, Hong Kong, 29 October 1999.

control is withdrawn, the aeroplane quickly turns left or right, up or down. In the same way, a bicycle is more stable when additional load is placed at the back but this makes it less manoeuvreable. When the load is placed in front, the bicycle is more unstable, but the rider finds it easier to steer the bicycle. Chinese society is "artificially stable". Without a good control system externally imposed, it becomes chaotic.

Many years ago, I had an interesting discussion with a Suzhou official. He told me that the Jiangsu Provincial Government was reluctant to develop the parts of Jiangsu adjacent to Shanghai because Shanghai might one day take over those areas as the city grew. When there were floods in the lower Yangtze Delta, decisions had to be taken whether to sacrifice large areas of farmland in Jiangsu or to allow Shanghai to be affected. Furious arguments would take place and Beijing would have to step in to arbitrate and decide. Without a strong centre in China, the different provinces could quickly go to war with one another as had frequently happened in the long history of China. No wonder the *Romance of the Three Kingdoms* began with the famous saying that "long disunity leads to unity and long unity leads to disunity".

This tendency of Chinese society to be chaotic is both a strength and a weakness. The frequent disorderliness is also a source of creativity and dynamism. While China today remains an authoritarian state, there is intense competition at the provincial and city levels. It is a situation of controlled chaos.

### The Idea of One China

Cycles of growth and decline are common in human history. What is unique and extraordinary about Chinese history is the ability of Chinese society to re-gather itself into a single polity again and again. The Han Dynasty was roughly contemporaneous with the Roman Empire. Both broke up at about the same time. The areas under the control of the Roman Empire never succeeded in reuniting themselves. Attempts were made by Charlemagne, Napolean, Hitler and others, but they never came close to achieving the dominance of Rome. Even the European Union today is a loose confederation of tribal groups. In contrast, China was able to reunify itself many times since the fall of the Han Dynasty. This is because the idea of One China is deeply embedded in the minds of all Chinese people.

For centuries, Chinese children, before they could read or write, were taught to recite the *San Zi Jing* (三字经) through which the Confucianist idea of society being one big happy family is programmed into young minds. The three-character phrases are like strands of cultural DNA which are passed on from generation to generation. Thus, the political idea of one China is also a cultural idea. This distinguishes Chinese culture from other ancient cultures. For example, Jewish culture is as tenacious as Chinese culture but it does not put the same emphasis on political unity. Hindu culture is also an ancient culture. While Hindu culture encompasses political ideals, it does not programme into all Hindus the idea of one India the way Chinese culture does. For this reason, the idea of Taiwanese independence is emotionally unacceptable to many Chinese people because it goes against a long-held cultural ideal.

**Stability of the Chinese Family**

However, like Jewish and Hindu cultures, Chinese culture places great emphasis on the family. This is the basic building block of Chinese society and is almost indestructible. Despite wars and revolutions, floods and famines, the Chinese family has held together. In this century, despite family members being separated by hundreds or thousands of miles over long years, the Chinese family held together in a remarkable way. Strong Chinese families explain the strength of Chinese diaspora culture. Diaspora Chinese culture is much more tenacious than diaspora Japanese culture.

However, the strength of the Chinese family also means that, outside the circle of relatives and friends, Chinese people tend to be less public-spirited. The difference between the public spirit of Japanese people and Chinese people is well-known. I remember once visiting the Meiji Shrine in June when the blue irises were in bloom. Because the Meiji emperor planted blue irises which the empress loved, Japanese women romanticise this particular iris. On the day when I visited the shrine, there was a long procession of Japanese women lining up to view the blue irises. There was no rush. When it was their turn to take photographs, they took them quickly so as not to hold others back. When they saw litter on the ground, they picked them up. It is hard to imagine Chinese people ever behaving in this way. If there were a similar event in Singapore, we will need many workers the following day to clean up the park.

### Weakness of Independent Chinese Civil Society

In the Confucianist classic *The Great Learning*, we learn to cultivate the self, establish the family and govern the state, thereby bringing harmony to human society. At one end, we have the individual and the family; at the other we have the state as one big happy family. In reality, between the Chinese family and the Chinese state, there is a big disconnection. In Western society, the space in between the family and the state is usually occupied by relatively independent civil society. This civil society makes possible Western democracy. In Chinese society, civil society is more problematic. When civil society is independent, the state takes a negative view of it because it dilutes central power. When central authority is strong, Chinese civil groups instinctively look to it for support and patronage. Without firm leadership, Chinese civil groups often suffer from internal conflict as individuals and groups jostle for control and official favour. This is a phenomenon which affects Chinese civil groups all over the world, including Singapore. In the journal *Foreign Affairs*, Francis Fukuyama described the same phenomenon from a different perspective. He traced it to the lack of "social capital" in Chinese society.

What is the reason for weak Chinese civil society? This is an important question because without a strong civil society, Western-style democracy cannot take root. The weakness of the Chinese civil society is a direct result of the strength of the family on the one hand and the centralised state on the other. Independent groups are hard to organise because of the lack of public spirit outside the family and state structure. These tendencies are deeply coded in Chinese culture and not easily changed. They are in the cultural DNA and shape the political institutions governing Chinese society. One way or another, democracy in Chinese society must take these tendencies into account. How democracy with Chinese characteristics will evolve in the next century is an important question in global history. I doubt very much that Western democratic systems will take root in China because the history and tradition are so different. Some scholars recommend a federal system for China, but that is not likely to succeed because of the idea of one China.

## Genius of Chinese Statecraft

The genius of Chinese society is in statecraft. Without this genius, China could not have re-constituted itself again and again. I would like to highlight some key aspects of Chinese statecraft.

The first aspect is the separation of religion from politics. In many countries, religion remains an important part of politics, making governance more difficult. In South Asia today, we have in India a self-conscious Hindu government, and in Pakistan an army that has become more Islamic over the years now in control. In Western Europe, religious wars decimated entire populations right up to the 17th century. In Eastern Europe, religion is still an important factor in politics, no more so than in the Balkans. In contrast, the Chinese state has been secular for most of China's history. Communist atheism took easy root in China partly because it conformed to Chinese political culture. Confucius advised that the state should keep religion at arm's length.

Another important aspect of Chinese statecraft is recruitment of officials on the basis of examinations. When the civil service was invented in China, it was a revolutionary idea in the world. It was only 200 to 300 years ago that this idea found its way to the West. Now it is universally accepted around the world. But nowhere in the world, except in China, is this elitist system extended over such a wide geographical area and to such a degree. In the Chinese mind, that the provincial governor could be from another province is culturally acceptable. One cannot imagine in Europe today, despite the European Union, that a German could become the mayor of Paris, much less, the president of France. In China, this cross-posting from one end of the empire to the other has been done for over 2,000 years. During the Tang Dynasty, a few prime ministers were of non-Han origin. A Korean general led the Tang army across the Tianshan mountains into Central Asia where it was defeated by the Arabs. A Japanese governed Vietnam, then a part of the Chinese empire.

Chinese statecraft always recognised the problem of corruption and nepotism. By various means, the Chinese state set up systems to limit this problem. But it could never be got rid of completely because of the strength of family ties. During the Ming and Qing dynasties and in China today, high officials are not posted to the districts they come from, not within a distance of 500 *li*. By this rule, no Singaporean could be a minister in Singapore, and no Hong Konger should be governing Hong Kong. This point is worth reflecting on. In China, a high official working in his native district would face unbearable pressure to favour relatives and friends. Therefore, it is always better to bring in an outsider who can be objective. But this outsider is not a foreigner. He is still Chinese and therefore legitimate. Such an outsider would not be acceptable as a high official in a European country or in Singapore. In Hong Kong, under one-country-two-systems, Hong Kongers are supposed to govern themselves. This is only possible because the public institutions of Hong Kong are derived from the British, which is also the case in Singapore.

A system which enables high officials to be posted from one corner of the empire to another can only be achieved if power is concentrated at the centre. This has long been an essential aspect of Chinese statecraft. The Leninist method of organisation was in line with that political tradition which explains why it was easily transplanted onto Chinese soil. In fact, both the Communist Party and the Kuomingtang adapted Leninist party organisation. The People's Action Party in Singapore also developed the same method of organisation because it had to fight the Communist Party of Malaya. Certain cultural characteristics are persistent.

In the next century, China will have to move towards more democratic organisation, the rule of law and constitutional governance. It will evolve its own system, taking ideas from the West and adapting them to Chinese conditions. The technological revolution sweeping the world also requires the Chinese state to devolve more power downwards and to empower as many individuals as possible.

These changes are unavoidable if China is to be economically strong. Without economic strength, the Chinese state will be weak. Once the Chinese state declines, it will eventually break up and society will be in chaos again.

### Confucianism — Past, Present and Future

In making this adaptation to the challenges of technology and the modern world, Confucianist ideas will have to be interpreted afresh. Confucianism will not be discarded because it is an inseparable part of Chinese culture. To remain close to the people, Chinese communism must gradually accommodate Confucianism. A reverse takeover is likely to happen. China will eventually digest the ideas of Marx and Lenin so completely that they become Chinese. Chinese civilisation will transform and absorb Communism the way it transformed and absorbed Buddhism from India.

When I visited Mao Zedong's birthplace in Shaoshan three years ago, it was interesting to see how Chinese culture is incorporating Mao, the man and his ideas. The Mao ancestral temple where joss sticks are burnt is next to the Mao Zedong memorial hall. The grave sites of Mao Zedong's parents and grandparents have been cleaned up. Mao Zedong has entered the Chinese pantheon as another deity to be worshipped. His good deeds are remembered; the evil deeds are blamed on others. This is nothing new in Chinese history.

The same digestion and absorption of Western democratic ideas will also take place. In theory, all Chinese accept the ideas of democracy whether they live on the Mainland, Hong Kong or Taiwan. But the practice of democracy is quite another matter. Even in Taiwan, the evolution of democratic institutions has still to go through many twists and turns. Political corruption in Taiwan and the involvement of secret societies in local politics are serious problems. For Hong Kong, it will also be a long road which must eventually lead back to the Motherland. For Singapore, democracy with Singapore characteristics will continue to evolve in response to the challenges of the knowledge economy, globalisation and racial politics in Southeast Asia.

Internationally, a China, however strong, will have to contend with other big powers which are neither tributary states nor barbarians. While no country can ignore China in the next century, China cannot expect to be the middle kingdom in the world. In official policy pronouncements, China is very humble and recognises the equality of all nations. But, deep down, Chinese people feel culturally superior with a sense of their own destiny. If they did not feel so, Chinese culture could not have survived for so long. This sense of superiority can give rise to big problems if it becomes excessive. The idea of the Chinese race will have to be moderated in this new world. A Hong Kong Chinese has become the Governor-General of Canada. Another Hong Kong Chinese is the Governor of the State of Washington in the US. In Southeast Asia, many ethnic Chinese hold important political positions. They can only do this by not allowing their sense of race to become excessive. This is a challenge for China in the next century. The Confucianism of the 21st century cannot place China at the centre of the universe.

So long as we recognise this to be a problem, it can be managed. We face the problem of inter-racial relations everyday in Singapore. When the Chinese Foreign Ministry, in response to the outrage expressed by Chinese people inside and outside China, took a strong position against the violence done to Chinese Indonesians in May 1998, eyebrows were raised in Southeast Asia. When President Jiang Zemin asked to visit the Chinatown in Bangkok last month, eyebrows were raised in Thailand. The Li Wenhe case in Los Alamos has racial undertones which we must recognise.

I have touched on some aspects of Chinese culture which influence the development of Chinese politics without giving clear answers to many of the problems that exist. There can be no clear answers. The Chinese revolution which overthrew imperial rule is still ongoing. It is the greatest revolution the world has ever seen, starting with the Taiping Revolution, 1911, May 4th, the anti-Japanese war, 1949, the Cultural Revolution and Deng Xiaoping's final push to reform and open up China. The destiny of Hong Kong is bound up with the progress of this revolution. But how much better is it to be a young Chinese today than it was to be a young Chinese 50 years ago,

100 years ago or 150 years ago? Whatever the current problems, there is a cultural self-confidence that they can be overcome and the future secured. This is also a story about the past, present and future of Confucianism and its pervasive influence on the continuing evolution of Chinese culture and politics.

# A Leap Forward

*Better to have furious arguments in the WTO than to deploy ships and fire missiles.*

China's entry into the World Trade Organization (WTO) will make this a safer world. This is not only about commercial pluses against minuses; the WTO is an international agreement that will transform Chinese society and affect China's long-term political relationship with the United States.

As China reforms its economy, it is strongly in its interest to have normal relations with the United States. The United States is by far the largest market for China's manufacturing exports, and after Hong Kong and Taiwan, it also is the most important investor in China. China's leaders know how important China's ties to the United States are to the modernization of their country's economy. They maintained extraordinary strategic discipline in keeping relations with the United States last year despite the rebuff of Zhu Rongji by the White House, the Cox Report and the bombing of the Chinese embassy in Belgrade.

Joining the WTO has become a cornerstone of China's economic strategy. The reform of China's state-owned sector has reached a critical point, and Chinese leaders hope that the external pressure generated by international competition will help reform its banks and state-owned enterprises. Once in the WTO, trade disputes would be resolved according to international rules overriding what were previously considered sovereign prerogatives.

---

First published in *The Washington Post*, 29 February 2000. George Yeo was invited to write this op-ed after engaging senior journalists of the *Post* on Sino-US relations.

In taking this leap, the Chinese Communist Party undermines its own monopoly of power. In 1978 Deng Xiaoping made the fateful decision to reform and open China's economy. The easy reforms have been made; now comes the hard part. Once Chinese banks and state-owned enterprises come under the disciplines of the global market, the ability of Chinese leaders to allocate (or misallocate) resources and direct the lives of individuals will be weakened. China's leaders have concluded that this is a risk that they must take because the alternative is worse; still, it is a gamble for the Communist Party.

The United States should encourage China's participation in the global economy. Once China is linked at a million points to the global economy, it will become difficult to break these links. Better to have furious arguments in the WTO than to deploy ships and fire missiles.

To be sure, China might one day become a competitor to the United States for power and influence in the Pacific and beyond. If it were possible to prevent China from growing, a policy of containment and harassment may be in United States' interest. But it has never been the political instinct of the American people to behave in this way.

China has approached a fork in the road. Either it joins the world and observes the rules of international trade and diplomacy, which means that the nature of Chinese communism eventually will change beyond recognition. Or China strikes out on its own and persuades others to join it. The latter course would one day lead to war, which would affect all of maritime Asia.

Beyond commercial considerations, the debate in Congress about permanent Normal Trade Relations (NTR) for China is about strategic choices. In signing the WTO deal with the United States, China's leaders have made their choice. We should help them stick to it. It is a choice with momentous consequences for all of us.

When Zhu Rongji was humiliated in April, the mood in China turned sour and shifted in favour of the hardliners. When China reached agreement with the United States in November, the internationalists were vindicated, and the mood changed to one of hope and optimism. This is a time for Congress to weigh in on the right side.

# Between North and South, Between East and West

*We are too small to change the world but we can change ourselves, within limits. Our best strategy is to accept the diversity of the world for what it is and adapt to it.*

## Political Change in Southeast Asia

Last month, we opened a new naval base in Changi large enough for a US Navy aircraft carrier to come alongside. It has a berth the length of four football fields. We built it at our own expense to facilitate the deployment of the US 7th Fleet in Southeast Asian waters. At a time when the region is going through dramatic political change, the presence of these ships has a stabilising effect, notwithstanding the recent mid-air collision between a US EP-3 spy plane and a Chinese F-8 fighter.

Indonesia is going through a difficult political transition from Suharto's New Order to a looser, decentralised democracy. It will be many years before the situation there settles into a new equilibrium. The role of the Indonesian Armed Forces has to be redefined. While it was part of the problem in the past, it has to be part of the solution for the future. Without the Indonesian Armed Forces playing a positive role in holding the Indonesian nation together, ethnic and religious tensions can easily get out of control as we have seen in the Malukus and Kalimantan.

The devolution of power to the provinces and regencies is also a tricky process which needs careful management. The issue is not only one of legislating new laws. Trained manpower is needed and a new

---

Speech at the Singapore General Hospital Lecture, 29 April 2001. Former Malaysian Prime Minister Dr Mahathir Mohamed attended this lecture.

balance between Jakarta and the regions has to be established. This will take time. I could see for myself the new dynamics between ministers and governors, and between governors and *bupatis*, in my last visit to Indonesia in January. In the old days, once a presidential decree was issued, it was executed like a military order. This is no longer the case.

What happens in Indonesia in the coming months and years will affect us profoundly. If Indonesia dissolves into chaos, we will all be very busy. The investment climate in Southeast Asia will darken. But if Indonesia recovers, there will be many areas for us to work together on. There is no city outside Indonesia which follows events there as closely as Singapore.

Whatever eventuates, we must strengthen our links to the provinces around us. When I called on the Governor of South Sumatra in Palembang and the Governor of Riau in Pekan Baru, both expressed a strong wish for better links with Singapore, not only for trade and investment, but also to send their people here for training and exposure.

Malaysia is also going through a period of transition. DPM Abdullah Badawi made a very successful visit to Singapore in February. He brought with him many up-and-coming cabinet ministers and state chief ministers. Whatever bilateral problems we may have from time to time, the futures of Malaysia and Singapore are bound together. We are really one people divided into two countries. When Dr Mahathir attends medical class reunions here or in Malaysia, there is little consciousness of who is Malaysian and who is Singaporean. Among younger Malaysians and Singaporeans, there is more distance, but I do not think we will continue to diverge. With globalisation, the Malaysian and Singapore economies have become more integrated. Last year, Malaysia became our No. 1 trading partner again, overtaking the United States. It is no longer rubber and tin. Now it is mostly electronics, with components and parts going back and forth before final export to the US, Japan and Europe. We have become an integrated economic space for global manufacturing.

At the human level, intermarriage between Malaysians and Singaporeans has increased sharply in the last 10 years. In other words, the ties of blood and culture will continue into future generations.

Some commentators think that political Islam may become a problem in the future. PAS has captured more political ground in recent years and its leaders have been wooing Chinese voters. But many of us would have read Dr Mahathir warning Chinese Malaysians that this is just a trick for PAS to win power. We have to follow events in Malaysia closely because what happens there will affect us directly. The next few years will be critical ones.

Both Indonesia and Malaysia were severely affected by the last financial crisis. So too Thailand and the Philippines. In both Thailand and the Philippines, new leaders have taken over but they face severe economic problems. It will take at least another three to five years before Southeast Asia as a whole returns to the pre-crisis path of steady growth. For Indonesia, it will take longer. This time, however, the external environment will be more challenging. The present global economic downturn will have a dampening effect on the entire region. Many of us are very dependent on electronic exports which are declining sharply. Longer term, we face the challenge of a China that is becoming stronger and more competitive by the day.

## Emergence of China

The emergence of China as a political, economic and cultural power will affect our lives in a thousand ways. Many of us have been to China and seen the astonishing economic transformation of the country. Because of the depth and size of its domestic market, the Chinese economy is less dependent on exports even though China has already become one of the world's great trading nations. While the current global economic downturn will affect China, it will affect China less than Southeast Asia. Premier Zhu Rongji in his recent report to the National People's Congress forecast an annual growth rate of 7% for the next five years at the end of which China will have a considerable middle class. We are already feeling the purchasing power of that growing middle class. Right through the last financial crisis, when overall tourist arrival into Singapore was falling sharply, Chinese tourists continued to increase by double-digits. In another 10 years, China will be the No. 1 or No. 2 source of foreign tourists for many countries in the Asia Pacific.

In direct and indirect ways, the rise of China will affect many decisions we make. For example, many Chinese Singaporean parents want their children to speak and write better Chinese than they do because they have all come to the conclusion that China will become more important in their lives. When I was Health Minister some years ago, I started a section at Ministry HQ to look into Traditional Chinese Medicine (TCM) and led a delegation to study TCM institutions in China. Since then, there has been a major change in the attitude of the Western medical community worldwide to TCM. With better regulation, standards will be better maintained and patients will benefit. If China were still mired in war and revolution, I doubt this change would have come about.

Historically, a prosperous China brought prosperity to Southeast Asia. Sri Vijaya prospered from the maritime trade of the Tang and Sung dynasties. Majapahit benefited from the international routes opened up by the Mongol Yuan. In Ming times, Admiral Zhenghe came to these waters and fostered the growth of Malacca. It was the lure of the China market during the Qing Dynasty that brought the European powers to Southeast Asia in more recent times.

China's growth in this century will have an equally positive effect. However, until a new equilibrium settles down, China will suck in a disproportionate share of the investments in Asia. It used to be that China took 20% of the total foreign direct investment coming into East Asia (excluding Japan), while ASEAN had 50%. Now, it is the opposite. For a long time, Singapore's most important investment destination was Malaysia because of our common historical links but, from 1997, China overtook Malaysia to be our No. 1 investment destination in cumulative terms.

This is the reason why we are the strongest proponent of ASEAN economic integration. Unless the countries of ASEAN combine their markets into a free trade and investment area of 500 million people, we will lose many investment projects to China. There is no time to lose because foreign investors will not wait for us. Even though Singapore has not done badly by itself, we cannot be a manufacturing hub in the longer term if we are not integrated with the economies around us which have lower cost structures. We hope that the free trade agreements we are negotiating with the US, Japan and Australia will spur our neighbours on towards more rapid trade and investment liberalisation.

Singapore's economy has both a regional and an international dimension. While we cannot confine ourselves to the region, we also cannot ignore the region. We cannot be an international hub without also being a regional hub. Without our links to the US, Japan and Europe, we could not have gotten here. But we must also strengthen our links in the region because, as a region, we compete with other regions in the world.

Southeast Asia is our immediate neighbourhood. Beyond that, there is a wider region which includes China, India and Australia. They are all within a seven-hour flying distance. Within that radius, there is a middle class outside Japan already numbering in the tens of millions which will grow to hundreds of millions. Doctors in our hospitals tell me that they are now seeing more patients from Bangladesh and Vietnam. With the development of the biomedical sciences in Singapore, we can become a Mayo Clinic serving a huge hinterland.

## India Stirring

Although not as fast as China, India is also stirring. In certain sectors, especially in IT, India is making dramatic progress. In the last 10 years, India's export of software grew at an astonishing growth rate of 45% a year. Last year, India exported over US$10 billion in computer and software services. This will continue to grow for many years to come. In 8 to 10 years' time, the Indian software industry may be worth US$50 billion in annual exports despite the crash of NASDAQ.

In cities like Bangalore, Chennai and Hyderabad, the campuses where software development is concentrated are provided with amenities comparable to those in the US and Europe. The Indian immigrant community in the US, which is the most successful immigrant community there, has become a huge asset for India. Bill Gates wanted the Microsoft Software Centre in Hyderabad to grow as fast as possible. A whole team of Non-Resident Indians (NRIs) went back to India from Seattle to start it off.

India has long been held back by its encrusted old economy. It will be the new economy in India which will drag the old economy kicking and screaming along. So we see telecommunications opening up which immediately drew in hundreds of millions of dollars of Singapore investment. As each sector opens up, foreign investment will move in. India's share of global foreign direct investment is still minuscule totalling only US$2.6 billion last year.

We have positioned Singapore as a long-term economic partner of India. We cannot hold our breath waiting for policies to change there, but when there is change, we should be prepared to respond. Our links to India are natural ones. During the British Raj, India was the jewel in the crown while we were a small semi-precious stone on the side. Because of the common British heritage, we speak the same language, not just the English language, but also the common language of Anglo-Saxon law, accounting and medicine. Culturally, Singaporeans of all races get along easily with Indians from the sub-continent. In recent years, the reputation of Singapore in India has grown and our companies are sought after for joint ventures. Even the Indian Administrative Service, with its high tradition, takes an occasional interest in Singapore's administrative methods which surprised me when it first happened.

Both India and China have become important sources of talent for us because of their reservoir of talent. I remember talking to the Chairman and Founder of Infosys, Narayana Murthy, last November. Infosys is one of the top software companies in India. He apologised that his wife could not join me and my wife for dinner at the Infosys campus in Bangalore. Their son was sittting for the Indian Institute of Technology (IIT) entrance examinations the following day and she wanted to be with him at home. Some of you may know that the IIT produce some of the best scientists in the world. Many end up working in the United States. The brightest students in Computer Science go to the IIT at Kanpur. The father was not sure whether his son could make it there and, just in case, asked him to apply to MIT and Stanford in the event that he could not get into Kanpur. That is the kind of standard we are talking about.

## Cultural Broadband

Our links to the region — to Indonesia, Malaysia, China and India — are very precious. Without them, we will be of less value to the US, Japan and Europe. It was precisely our position as the headquarters of the British empire in the Far East that made Singapore a key strategic objective of the Japanese Imperial Army during the Second World War. The Japanese encouraged Subhas Chandra Bose to set up the Indian National Army using Singapore as the base.

Several years ago when I was in the SAF, I attended an American intelligence briefing on China. The presentation was very impressive and I was amazed by the technical intelligence that the Americans had on the Chinese. But when it came to interpreting the Chinese mind, I was rather disappointed by the lack of cultural understanding without which the technical intelligence was of limited use. What is obvious to us with our Chinese background is not at all obvious to others. And because our background is Chinese, Malay, Indian and Anglo-Saxon, we enjoy an important advantage in many situations. Of course we do make mistakes from time to time, but we learn from them. For example, by owning two-thirds of the Suzhou project initially, the locals there thought we were short-changing them and played games with us. Once we restructured it to give the Chinese two-thirds of the project, it progressed very smoothly. Later this year, the management of the project will be formally handed over to the Chinese side. Suzhou is an accomplishment we can feel very proud of because it has become one of the best industrial townships in China and incorporates many positive aspects of our experience in Singapore. On our side, we have acquired valuable knowledge about operating in China.

So, too, India. Doing business in India can be an incredible hassle but once we understand how the locks work, some doors can be opened. Others are permanently shut and it is important to know which these are. Some of our projects in India have done well like the IT Park in Bangalore. A few have been disappointing.

We are too small to change the world but we can change ourselves, within limits. Our best strategy is to accept the diversity of the world for what it is and adapt to it.

In human affairs, the most difficult thing to change is human culture. Whether we like it or not, one day we will be able to clone human beings. But the clone will not be a twin because acculturating the individual takes easily 20 years. It takes at least that long to fit that clone into society, into a network of human relationships. Human culture is the operating system which enables individuals to work together in society. It is a complex operating system which cannot be changed at will. Software engineers call this "system legacy". Compared to the physical body, it is much more difficult to clone the human mind.

Some years ago in Australia, the Government tried to pole-vault the aborigines into the 20th century by taking children away from their families and bringing them up in modern environments. The result was an absolute disaster. Even when tribal peoples are modernised, it is often superficial because, deep down, they still hear the echoes of their ancestors. Thus, when the Dyaks get very angry, they revert to ancient practices.

When the Talibans destroyed the Buddha statues in Bamiyan recently, both Muslims and non-Muslims all over the world were shocked and revulsed. What is it in the human mind which drives it to do these things? Of course, historically speaking, there is nothing new. Oliver Cromwell also destroyed statues. During the Cultural Revolution in China, people went mad. But that madness must itself be explained. The fact is that human culture is complex and multi-layered. The sub-conscious and unconscious layers are much thicker than the conscious ones.

If Singapore were not at a major cultural crossroad of the world, we would not have the multi-cultural facility we enjoy here. Physical structures can be replicated. Individuals can be enticed to come. But culture is deep and difficult to transplant. When we talk about links to the region, at the most fundamental level, we are talking about our cultural links. Without these cultural links, the political and economic links are weak and superficial.

The Chinese in Singapore share similarities with the Chinese in China but we are different in important ways. Similarly, the Malays in Singapore are becoming more different from the Malays in

Malaysia, and even more different from the *pribumis* in Indonesia. So, too, the Indians here. There is, in every individual Singaporean, a deep multiracial coding which is programmed from early childhood. In kindergarten and school, the Singaporean child learns to be sensitive. When mistakes are made, the consequences are severe. When a Chinese boy invites a Malay friend home, the parents make sure the family dog is leashed, and so on. New immigrants lack such sensitivity but they learn quickly provided there is already that larger social environment of tolerance and respect. Indian brahmins who migrate here adapt quickly to an environment which can never be as "pure" as what they are used to in India.

The Singapore cultural environment is therefore unusually broadband. It is this which gives us our cosmopolitan character. Many of you would have read A. T. Kearney's recent ranking of Singapore as the most global city in the world. For many Americans, Japanese, Chinese, Europeans and Australians, we are their favourite city in Asia outside their own country. It is not a superficial cosmopolitanism to be found only in expensive hotels, theatres and restaurants, but one which extends deep into our hawker centres and housing estates. We are a cosmopolitan city because even our heartlanders share cosmopolitan instincts.

Promoting cultural integration in Singapore is different from promoting cultural assimilation. A policy of assimilation will never work because no one wants to be forcibly integrated into another person's culture. We have no policy to encourage mixed-race marriages but we do not discourage them either. In fact, if we are too assimilated, we will lose our broadband facility. If few Chinese Singaporeans speak Chinese at a high level, we will lose some of our advantages in China. If the majority of our Sindhis marry outside the tribe, they will be cut off from the international Sindhi network. This is the dynamic balance that keeps Singapore vital.

Our Anglo-Saxon overlay is also an important part of what we are as Singaporeans. Hong Kong has it too but Hong Kong will lose some of it as it gets re-absorbed into China. Of course, we are not Anglo-Saxon the way the Australians and New Zealanders are, but our British heritage is a crucial part of our success. In the

19th century, the British were ascendant in the world. That was when Raffles founded Singapore as a trading post of the East India Company. In the 20th century, the Americans became top dog, after fighting two World Wars and one Cold War. In the 21st century, the Anglo-Saxon dominance will be contested but it will continue for at least several decades to come. Our facility in the English language is a great advantage not only in commerce but also on the Internet. Take the biomedical sciences which we are giving emphasis to as an example. So much of the scientific literature is in English which we can access directly without the need for translation.

## Big Singapore vs Small Singapore

It is important to understand why we are what we are because, if we do not understand how we got here, we will not know how to move forward. From time to time, there are expressions of angst in Singapore about racial integration and the lack of a national identity. In reality, these tensions we experience are the result of our essential make-up. Is the Chinese in Singapore too Chinese or not Chinese enough? Are new Indians resensitising caste divisions among old Indians? What happens if the Malay community in Singapore becomes more Islamic in thought and practice? Are our young getting too Americanised? And so on.

Without these tensions, we cannot maintain our broadband capability and our links to the world. The tensions cannot be wished away. However, they must be well-managed, and managing them well requires political sensitivity and absolute impartiality. Since we are running into election season, let me say here that without the PAP government constantly staying on top of the situation, racial and religious differences in Singapore can easily get out of control. Yesterday, it might have been Tang Liang Hong. Today, it may be the AMP. Tomorrow, it will be something else. The position is never static because the environment around us is changing all the time.

Managed well, we can be much larger than what we are geographically. Already, Singapore plays a role in the region and in the world out of proportion to its size. We are entering a creative phase of our history. While we do not offer ourselves as a model to anyone, many cities in Asia view us as an interesting experiment in social and economic management. They avoid our mistakes and try to emulate our successes. We have no intellectual property rights on many of the things that we do here, and if foreign friends ask to be briefed about port operations or industrial park management, we have to oblige them. But we know that the most important aspects of Singapore, which are the cultural aspects, cannot be easily copied. For example, however many briefings we give to the Chinese, the Anglo-Saxon rule of law can never be fully implemented there because of China's very different political tradition.

However, we are limited by our numbers. If we can bring in the foreign talent and absorb them, we can do much more in Singapore and out of Singapore. We can't simply buy the talent; it never works well that way. We have to woo talent. This is especially true for the knowledge economy. Brainworkers cannot be forced to produce. We have to provide the right cultural and intellectual environment. And that right environment is ultimately made up of individual Singaporeans relating to foreigners in a generous way. Charm is important.

This brings me to the main point of my lecture today, which is the importance of creating the mentality of a Big Singapore. The Singaporean can be Chinese, Malay, Indian or Eurasian, but he must have a big mind and a big heart, and he should think of Singapore not only in terms of our island geography, but also against the backdrop of our Asian and Anglo-Saxon history and connections. Consider the Chinese or Indian migrant who takes up Singapore citizenship. Yes, the Singapore passport may open more doors than a Chinese or an Indian passport. But that is relatively minor. The key is: when that new Singaporean is in London, New York or Tokyo, is he enlarged or diminished by being a Singaporean? That is not an easy question to answer. The answer may depend on whether the individual is a businessman, a professor, a politician, a journalist, a doctor or a general.

I come back to the Sindhi example. If the price of being a Singaporean is the loss of his Sindhi identity, that is a tough choice. In the same way, we must not force the Chinese or the Indian migrant to give up his Chinese or Indian identity. And we can only say that convincingly if our own Chinese and Indians have not lost their ethnic identities. In other words, becoming Singaporean should open more doors for the individual and not the opposite. Then, many will queue up to join our ranks.

This means that our sense of nationalism cannot be strident and exclusivist. We should be patriotic without being jingoistic. That is the way we should see our past and our future. Take for example the conversion of the old Sun Yat Sen Villa into a Memorial Hall by the Singapore Chinese Chamber of Commerce and Industry. For a long time, we refused to gazette it as a national monument because we thought it had nothing to do with independent Singapore. Now we approach it differently. Singaporeans played a significant role in the Chinese Revolution of 1911 which was not only a political revolution but also a cultural revolution which changed the way Chinese all over the world saw themselves. That altered the course of world history and we should be proud of the contribution of our forefathers. Following in their footsteps, some of our top doctors are helping to establish medical centres in China today. This does not make them any less Singaporean.

Another project with a larger-than-Singapore conception is the cultural restoration of Kampong Glam. Historically, Malay-Muslims from all over the region gathered there around the old Istana. Till today, the Sultan Mosque has a Board of Trustees which requires Arabs, North Indians, Tamils, Buginese, Malays and Javanese to be represented. That is the rich and diverse heritage of the Malay-Muslim community in Singapore. Although our Malay-Muslim community is small, it sees itself against that larger canvas.

We must educate all our children with that larger mental compass. That is the difference between the mentality of a Small Singapore and that of a Big Singapore. A Small Singapore mentality finds the region with all its problems uncomfortable and our diversity a constant source of friction and irritation. A Big Singapore mentality engages the region, celebrates our diversity and uses it to access economic and cultural spaces all over the world. And by bringing our children up in this way, the entire world becomes their oyster, and others in the world will then want to join them and be like them.

Thus, in a paradoxical way, our particularity is our universality. The visit of the USS Kitty Hawk last month was not just a news event. It reflected our worldview.

# New Singapore in a New Asia

*Our culture must become more cosmopolitan while staying uniquely Singaporean.*

## A Strong Tide Flowing

I visited the four countries of Mercosur recently after an APEC meeting in Chile. Mercosur consists of Brazil, Argentina, Uruguay and Paraguay. Of the four, Brazil is by far the most important to us because of the size of its economy. In the last few years, our bilateral account with Brazil has grown significantly. Both Keppel FELS and Jurong have established shipyards in Rio de Janeiro which now employ more than 10,000 workers. They are involved in converting old supertankers into highly sophisticated offshore platforms called FPSOs (floating, production, storage and offloading units) for Petrobras oil operations in the South Atlantic. Each is a floating oil refinery. Today, the FPSOs built by our shipyards are responsible for 60% of Brazil's offshore oil production. Keppel FELS and Jurong have recently secured another US$2.5 billion worth of contracts for the coming years. Three years ago, I opened the two shipyards. Each shipyard has a small team of Singaporeans there to train Brazilian workers and supervise the work. I was worried for them then. They were far from home, spoke no Portuguese and knew little of the local culture. This time round when I met them, they were at home. Many prattled away in Portuguese and had Brazilian friends.

The global tide is changing dramatically. President Lula made a very successful visit to China recently with a large delegation of

---

Speech at the Economic Society of Singapore Dinner, Grand Copthorne Waterfront Hotel, 28 June 2004.

businessmen. Brazil and China are embarking on major economic projects together. One Brazilian diplomat told me that there are one million square kilometres of arable land in Brazil in the Mato Grosso and elsewhere which can be opened up for cultivation. China is looking to secure long-term food supplies and is willing to help build rail links from Brazil to the Pacific coast. The Brazilian Foreign Minister Celso Amorim thought that the integration of North America from coast to coast by rail in the 19th century would finally happen in South America in this century. China and, to a lesser extent India, are major factors in the new South American calculation. The Mercosur countries are hoping that the prosperity which food exports to Europe in an early period brought them will now be repeated by food and other exports to Asia. President Batlle of Uruguay reminded me that Columbus was looking for Asia when he discovered America.

The re-entry of China and India into the global marketplace is altering global trade flows fundamentally. What we are seeing today is just the beginning. The tides are changing and inexorably gathering force. No continent is unaffected. We have to be very alert to the trends and remember the words of Shakespeare[1] that reading and riding a rising tide well will lead to great fortune but misreading or missing it will land us in the rocky shallows.

### Half the World

Singapore is well-placed to catch this new tide. The combined population of Northeast Asia, Southeast Asia and India is over 3 billion, about half the world's population. Their combined GDP is about a quarter of the global GDP today. In PPP terms, it is about a third. Few economists doubt that in the coming decades, Asia's share in the global GDP will match that of its population. Looking

---

[1] "There is a tide in the affairs of men.
Which, taken at the flood, leads on to fortune;
Omitted, all the voyage of their life
Is bound in shallows and in miseries.
On such a full sea are we now afloat;
And we must take the current when it serves,
Or lose our ventures."

— William Shakespeare, *Julius Caesar*

at it historically, this should perhaps not be surprising because for most of human history, China and India were the largest economies in the world. Up to the early 19th century, the Chinese and Indian markets brought much wealth to Europe and America.

The implications are huge not only for countries, but also for companies and individuals. Like the emergence of new poles in a magnetic field, new configurations will emerge, from the biggest things to the smallest. Who could have imagined even five years ago that Chinese New Year would be a public holiday in Indonesia or that Brazilian chicken wings should now dominate our fresh food market?

The key factor in China's and India's growth is not cheap labour, although labour is still very cheap in these countries, but the huge reservoirs of human talent which are spilling onto the global marketplace. China alone produces about 460,000 engineers a year[2] and India another 150,000[3]. Today, only a small fraction of each age cohort in these two countries get into university. In the coming years, many more will and these two countries will become major suppliers of human talent to the global economy across a wide spectrum from engineers and programmers to musicians and sportsmen. The competition we are now feeling is only from the early flow. That flow will become a flood.

### Singapore's Response

When the waters are rising, what we need is a good boat, a good crew and a good map. We have all three, which is why I believe that Singapore will benefit powerfully from the growth of China and India provided we make adjustments to both our external and internal policies, remaking Singapore into a New Singapore in a New Asia.

### Strengthening Our Links to the Advanced Countries

I will discuss our policies on China and India later but let me emphasise at the outset that the OECD countries are still our most important economic partners. They will remain the major players on the global

---

[2] Source: *China Statistical Yearbook*, 2003.

[3] 151,000 in 1997 [latest figures available]. *Source*: Ministry of Human Resource Development, Technical Education, India.

scene for a long time to come because of their economic strength. It is helpful to remember the numbers: the EU of 25 and the US each has a GDP of US$11 trillion; Japan's is US$4.3 trillion. In comparison, China's GDP today is US$1.4 trillion, India is US$560 billion and ASEAN combined is US$700 billion.

We must therefore continue to strengthen our links to the advanced countries. They account for most of the inbound investments brought in by the Economic Development Board (EDB) in knowledge-intensive industries. Throughout the Asian financial crisis and the global economic downturn, and despite growing competition from China and India, EDB was able to achieve annual Fixed Asset Investments of about S$8–9 billion a year. We have core strengths which are not easy for others to copy: good public administration, high system efficiency, strong protection of intellectual property, our tripartite cooperation and a cosmopolitan outlook that goes into our heartlands. Together they enable Singaporeans to earn a significant premium in the international labour market.

Our free trade agreements with the US, Japan, Australia, New-Zealand and the countries of the European Free Trade Association (Switzerland, Norway, Liechtenstein and Iceland) strengthen our links to the advanced countries. We are in negotiation with Canada and South Korea. We are also proposing a new-generation European Union-Singapore Partnership to establish stronger rules and harmonise standards for the facilitation of trade and investment.

It is our extensive links to the advanced countries which enable us to be a major hub for the flow of goods, services, people and money between the First World and the New Asia. The greater the role we want to play in this New Asia, the more must we strengthen our links to the advanced countries.

Let me now turn to our relationship with China, India, the Middle East and the rest of ASEAN.

### China

Singapore's relationship with China is growing from strength to strength. China has become a big account for us with non-oil domestic exports growing by 40% in 2002 and 34% last year. Since two years ago, our trade with Greater China (China, Hong Kong and Taiwan combined) overtook our trade with the US. China is now by far the most important recipient of our foreign direct investment with cumulative contractual investments reaching US$45 billion last year.

DPM Lee Hsien Loong and Chinese Vice Premier Wu Yi co-chaired the first meeting of the Joint Council for Bilateral Cooperation last month. We are stepping up our cooperation in China's West and Northeast, in science and technology, in human resource development and in the internationalisation of China's companies. SM Lee Kuan Yew, China's Vice Premier Wu Yi and retired Vice Premier Li Lanqing have just officiated at the celebration of the 10th Anniversary of the Suzhou Industrial Park which the Chinese want to build up as the most advanced industrial township in China. We are now thinking of establishing a Singapore Centre in Suzhou to help Singapore companies get into the Chinese market. We are also working on the establishment in Singapore of a China Centre and centres for Chinese media and culture, and Traditional Chinese Medicine.

As China's presence in Southeast Asia grows, Singapore will be an important base for Chinese companies. Over 1,000 Chinese companies are already based here. Last year, 15 Chinese companies launched their IPOs in Singapore. This year, we already have 12 new listings from China. Last November, Zhejiang established a provincial centre in Singapore. A few other provinces such as Shandong and Liaoning are also thinking of following suit. Recently, Xi'an also announced its interest to establish a centre here.

This November, Singapore and China will launch negotiations for a comprehensive bilateral FTA. Our bilateral FTA with China will help to create favourable conditions for a full-fledged FTA between China and ASEAN by the year 2010. The China-ASEAN FTA will have a big political impact and help secure peace and prosperity in the wider region. Japan, India and Korea are also keen to have FTAs with ASEAN. All this is good for ASEAN.

### India

Singapore's negotiations with India for a Comprehensive Economic Cooperation Agreement (CECA) are now in the final stages. The change of government in Delhi may cause a slight delay but will otherwise not affect the conclusion of negotiations. This is because India's economic liberalisation and "Look East" policy have broad multi-party support. We have good links with the new Indian government as we had with the last. After all, it was the Congress government under PM Narasimha Rao which started the policy of opening up the Indian economy in 1991. That year, Manmohan Singh as Finance Minister and Palaniappan Chidambaram as Commerce Minister visited Singapore and gave a seminar here.

We have deliberately positioned Singapore as a partner for India's development since then. Despite episodic political changes at both the federal and state levels, we have maintained this policy. Political leaders, civil servants and entrepreneurs on both sides enjoy a high degree of comfort with each other. Singapore investments in India have grown in areas like telecommunications, ports, industrial parks, logistics, the healthcare industry, the financial industry and township development. Changi Airport is interested in bidding for the privatisation of Delhi and Mumbai airports.

It should not be surprising that, as India looks eastwards, Singapore should be regarded as a useful facility. After all, Singapore was founded by the British East India Company for the China trade of an earlier era. From 1819 to 1867, Singapore was directly governed from Calcutta. Our legal and administrative systems are very much derived from the Raj in India. Our re-engagement of India is reviving all those earlier links. In recent years, we have also received large numbers of new and highly talented Indian nationals who have invigorated Indian culture and cuisine in Singapore. Over 1,400 Indian companies are now based in Singapore including the top 20 IT companies. The numbers will grow in the future. The recent Bollywood (International Indian Film Academy) Awards Ceremony held in Singapore was one of the most successful ever.

Singapore has also played a major role in fostering stronger links between India and ASEAN as a whole. India's trade numbers with Singapore, with ASEAN and with China are all growing. In the same way as Singapore is becoming a major hub for China in Southeast

Asia, Singapore will also be a major hub for India in the years to come. CECA will facilitate this growth.

We are expanding our links beyond India to the whole South Asian region. PM's current visit to Pakistan, Bangladesh and Sri Lanka are part of this effort. We will soon launch FTA negotiations with Pakistan and Sri Lanka. To build up knowledge in Singapore of all these countries, a South Asia Institute is being established in NUS.

**The Middle East**

We have also stepped up our ties with the Middle East to build up our links with the countries there. September 11 necessitated visa restrictions on some countries in the Middle East. Although security considerations are still important, we will be more selective in our approach so that legitimate visitors can travel here more easily. To do this, we have to build up our knowledge of the Middle East.

Not many Singaporeans are aware that Singapore is held up as a model of development all over the Middle East, especially in the Gulf region. Harvard Business School cases on Singapore are carefully studied. Dubai and Abu Dhabi recruit Singaporeans consciously. Emirates Airlines has become a serious competitor to SIA. We enjoy a reservoir of goodwill in the Middle East which we have hardly tapped. This will change in the coming years.

After all, the Middle East represents a sizeable market of 400 million people, with a combined GDP of more than US$1 trillion. 9/11 and the war in Iraq have also fundamentally changed the geo-political and economic landscape in the Middle East. The countries in the region are adopting a "Look East" policy, seeking new partners and markets.

We have concluded an FTA with Jordan and will soon launch negotiations with Bahrain. We are also talking to Egypt, Qatar and Oman about the possibility of launching negotiations. We are strengthening our links to the UAE and Kuwait as well. All this will encourage more Middle Easterners to come to Singapore for their holidays, for healthcare and for financial service. The Monetary Authority of Singapore (MAS) is keen to promote a conducive environment for the development of Islamic financial services in Singapore.

In addition to the smaller countries, we are also reaching out to other Arab countries like Saudi Arabia. I was pleasantly surprised to hear from the Governor of the Saudi Arabian General Investment Authority that he saw EDB as a model. He has proposed that our officials meet to discuss areas for closer cooperation.

We are also giving more attention to Iran. In April this year, I visited Iran to build better economic relations. The Iranians gave me a warm welcome and the businessmen in my delegation were optimistic about prospects there. Although Iran's nuclear programme continues to be an issue with the US and the EU, the Iranian government has decided that this should not stop it from liberalising its economy to trade and foreign investment.

It is interesting to see how the wheel of history has turned one full circle. Singapore's ethnic make-up reflects our ancestry in China, India, the Middle East and Southeast Asia. With the end of the colonial period and the end of the Cold War, globalisation is re-establishing our ancestral links to these different parts of Asia.

## ASEAN

The rapid growth of China and India is giving a strong push to the economic and political integration of ASEAN. Singapore is actively involved in this effort. Economically, we are a funnel for investments, trade and knowledge into the region. As the most advanced economy in Southeast Asia, what we do here is closely observed by our neighbours. We are like a nearby experiment for them. They benefit by avoiding the mistakes we have made and copying some of our successes.

With the competitive challenge from China and India, the countries of ASEAN have come to the conclusion that each of us is more competitive if ASEAN as a whole becomes a common economic space. When the leaders met in Bali last year, they issued a historic document called the Bali Concord II which envisioned the creation of an ASEAN Economic Community by the year 2020. Eleven priority areas for fast-track integration were identified and are being worked on.

Singapore has important trade links with all the other nine ASEAN countries. We are a major investor in every one of them. Under Prime Minister Abdullah Badawi, Singapore's relationship with Malaysia has taken a turn for the better. Singapore's investments in Malaysia are now more welcome there. Recently, Minister Rafidah and I agreed to launch an expanded fund to help our companies work jointly in third countries. Our two exchanges linking up is another sign of greater trust between the two sides. Once the Presidential elections are over, we should try to raise our economic relationship with Indonesia to a new level. The economies of Singapore and Indonesia are highly complementary. There is much more that we can do together for the mutual benefit of our peoples. With the devolution of power in Indonesia, many Indonesian provinces now want closer economic links with Singapore. With Thailand, we have struck up a strategic partnership. Our relationship with Vietnam has also been raised to a new level in the last one year.

Political and security cooperation in ASEAN is growing in tandem with economic cooperation. In the fight against terrorism, our security agencies are working much more closely together. Terrorism is a long-term problem which can only be countered if we watch out for each other, share information and act in concert.

## New Singapore

All these efforts we are making to strengthen ASEAN and build links to China, India and the Middle East will position Singapore well for the new tide flowing in Asia. Good positioning is critical. If we sail where the current is flowing strongest, we will be carried along even if we do not do everything right. If we are badly positioned, however, the most strenuous efforts may still get us nowhere.

To get into a better position, we have to do many things in Singapore including restructuring our economy. They were mainly addressed by the Economic Review Committee and the Remaking Singapore Committee in the last two years. Last year, we took advantage of the strong sense of solidarity fostered by the challenge of SARS to restructure our Central Provident Fund (CPF). We must remake Singapore in many areas from the shortening of National Service and the establishment of a private university to the idea of allowing a casino here. Central to everything is our ability to make Singapore a talent capital — both keeping our own talent and attracting others to join our ranks. Without a large pool of international talent and a host community which welcomes them, all our dreams will remain dreams. Our culture must become more cosmopolitan while staying uniquely Singaporean. Indeed, our Singaporean-ness will be partly defined by our cosmopolitan view of life. Paradoxically, it is big countries which can afford to be inward-looking and narrowly nationalistic. City-states like Singapore have to be outward-oriented and open in our attitudes. Provided we stay well-centred in Singapore, the growth of our external economy will give a boost to economic growth in Singapore itself. In the coming years, more Singapore companies will be venturing overseas. Many more Singaporeans will seek fame and fortune in foreign lands as far away as South America, leveraging off Singapore's reputation, and doing things which their parents could never imagine.

This is an exhilarating voyage, full of promise but not without danger. If Sino-US relations floundered on the rocks of Taiwan, our boat will be immediately put at risk. If we let our guards down on terrorism, we can be suddenly knocked off-course. If we lose our sense of solidarity, we may be forced to slow down and miss the current. But we can be cautiously optimistic. China and the US are likely to calculate rationally and not go to war. Singaporeans are a sensible people and will rally around the Government in times of crisis. Provided nothing cataclysmic happens, Singapore will be able to ride this new tide in a rapidly-growing Asia and sail towards a brighter future, one which will afford younger Singaporeans many new opportunities.

# Diversity in Unity

*What we need profoundly is a respect for plurality in the world, one that is built on a common substrate …*

I congratulate His Excellency Mr Jean Ping, Minister for Foreign Affairs, Cooperation and La Francophonie of the Gabonese Republic, on his election as the new President of the General Assembly. Singapore is delighted that for the third consecutive year, a fellow member of the Forum of Small States holds this high office. Mr President, you can count on our whole-hearted cooperation. I would also like to congratulate the Foreign Minister of Saint Lucia, His Excellency Mr Julian Hunte, for his able leadership during the 58th session of the General Assembly.

We meet in New York under conditions of high security. All over the world, governments, corporations and individuals are allocating vast amounts of resources to combat terrorism — for intelligence-gathering, surveillance, defensive and offensive measures. The Beslan massacre last month and the Jakarta bombing two weeks ago remind us once again that this war against terrorism is a long struggle requiring the mobilisation of entire communities from the top all the way down to the grassroots. Fighting it requires us to cooperate worldwide. It is also important for us to understand more deeply why

---

Statement to the 59th Session of the United Nations General Assembly (UNGA), 24 September 2004. This was George Yeo's first address to the UNGA after becoming Foreign Minister in August 2004. Relations with China had taken a dip following then DPM Lee Hsien Loong's visit to Taiwan. George Yeo reiterated Singapore's one-China policy in his address which evoked a strong response from Taipei. While in New York, George Yeo had a confidential meeting with China Foreign Minister Li Zhaoxing to begin a process of restoring good bilateral relations.

terrorists are prepared to sacrifice their own lives to take the lives of others, including those of innocent children.

The human condition has not changed. There is in human beings a restless, competitive spirit that strives to get ahead, make discoveries and order or re-order the world according to our values and worldview. It is this spirit which drives us to achieve the 3 G's of gold, glory and God, a compulsion which can lead to great good or great evil.

The greatest evil is committed out of a sense of self-righteousness. This has been the case throughout history. Al Qaeda carries out its actions in the name of Islam which is a gross perversion. Religious wars are the most cruel because human beings are maimed and killed in the name of the divine. Ethnic and ideological conflicts sometimes turn genocidal when one side believes that right is completely on its side. Not a long time ago, the Khmer Rouge turned against fellow Cambodians with unbelievable ferocity in an absurd attempt to recreate human society. Ordinary people can be brutalised after long years of conflict, which was the case in Indo-China. More bombs were dropped on Laos alone than on all of Europe during the Second World War.

Untrammelled economic competition can also lead to grave injustice. Without rules, ruthless economic competition will return us to the jungle. Without the WTO, globalisation can become a means through which the strong dominate the weak around the world. In an earlier period, this resulted in entire continents being carved up by imperial powers.

Global organisations like the UN and the WTO give us hope that this century can be better than previous ones. We need rules which put limits on our competitiveness in the political and economic arenas. Like the Olympic Games, clear rules and the rigorous policing of the rules enable individuals to compete fiercely and triumph within a framework of sportsmanship and fairness. The rules are not there to dampen our competitive spirit, which is in the nature of man, but to channel it towards positive achievement.

The rules have to be determined by common consensus. Their legitimacy is derived from shared values which bind participants together. The rules have evolved over the years along with our collective sense of what is fair and proper. They cannot be imposed. If they are imposed, what we have will not be the Olympics but the gladiatorial pits of the Roman Colosseum.

At the most fundamental level, discussions and debates in the UN and the WTO are really about the values which bind us together as human beings.

As the world grows smaller, our sense of inter-dependence grows. As we interact more, we discover that we are more similar than we think. So many problems like global warming, epidemics and terrorism can only be overcome if we work together. So many opportunities made possible by new scientific discoveries can only be fully exploited if we combine our efforts.

Yes, we have become closer. We celebrated together when for the first time the entire human genome was mapped a few years ago. We grieved as one when September 11 happened. The slaughter of children at Beslan outraged us all. But will we ever become the same? That is not possible. It is neither in our biological nature nor in the nature of the historical process for human societies to converge and become identical. Even the same society changes over time in response to changing conditions.

There is in each and everyone of us a deep desire to be free, to experiment and to do better than others around us. Like all forms of energy, human energy must be channelled so that it is constructive and not destructive. This is the challenge of governance at all levels, from the village to global institutions. With the world becoming a village because of the ease of travel and instant communication, the design of global institutions is very important. They help us solve problems which each of us cannot solve by ourselves and set limits on unacceptable behaviour.

The problem of Palestine, for example, cannot be solved without the participation of the larger global community. All of us are aware of the rights and wrongs, and sometimes particular issues are right or wrong depending on the perspective we take. However, we should never lose hope. We should always look for new and creative ways to break old deadlocks. After all, it was only a few years ago that the prospects for peace seemed so much brighter. I remember meeting the Israeli Trade Minister as Singapore's Trade Minister at Davos in the year 2000. He said that he would like to visit me in Singapore with his Palestinian counterpart and, together with me, take a boat to the Singapore industrial park on a nearby Indonesian island where he hoped we could all be received by the Indonesian Trade Minister. I worked on this project of understanding and goodwill with my Indonesian counterpart immediately. Unfortunately, within half a year, the Intifada started and the cycle of violence got steadily worse, with each side blaming the other. However, we must not give up. With goodwill and statesmanship on both sides, and the support of the international community, it is possible to re-establish trust and start again.

The international community should also not allow the deteriorating relationship across the Taiwan Strait to get out of control. The push towards independence by certain groups in Taiwan is most dangerous because it will lead to war with Mainland China and drag in other countries. At stake is the stability of the entire Asia-Pacific region. The relationship between the Mainland and Taiwan was much better in the not-too-distant past. In 1991, APEC, which is a grouping of economies around the Pacific Ocean, admitted China, Taiwan and Hong Kong based on certain agreed principles. In 1992, I remember chatting with the trade ministers from China, Taiwan and Hong Kong over an informal lunch in Bangkok. Later in 1993, representatives from China and Taiwan met in Singapore for informal talks with both sides acknowledging 'one China, to each its own interpretation'. All problems seemed soluble then. But, in 1994, Taiwan President Lee Teng-hui gave a shocking interview to a Japanese magazine describing himself as Moses leading his people out of Egypt. From then on, cross-strait relations went from bad to worse as pro-independence forces in Taiwan became increasingly adventurous. Like in the Middle East, the international community has a strong vested interest in supporting a peaceful resolution of cross-strait conflict, based on the 'One-China' position adopted and settled by the UN in 1971.

Even when the UN has no legal authority to enforce its wishes, its views carry moral weight. This legitimacy of the UN is derived from its wide membership, its transparent processes and the active participation of member states. It is important that the Security Council, which has the power to pass resolutions binding on all UN member states, be reformed and enlarged to reflect the reality of the current international environment, not that of 60 years ago.

We need rules which enable us to make decisions and express our collective judgement of right and wrong. These rules must evolve according to our collective moral sense. If any party believes that it has a monopoly of truth or wisdom, that is the beginning of evil. While there is much we share in common as human beings wherever we live, there will never be a unanimity of views on all matters. Human society is changing all the time. New scientific discoveries throw up new challenges to which different societies must respond differently. On matters of religious belief, for example, no one should expect convergence. Our disagreements over issues like the death penalty, abortion, the nature of democracy, gay rights, animal rights and therapeutic cloning are in a sense inevitable and necessary.

What we need profoundly is a respect for plurality in the world, one that is built on a common substrate which defines us as civilised human beings in the 21st century. In the 19th century, slavery was abolished. In the 20th century, gender equality became the norm. In this century, we must add more layers to what we share in common. Upon this shared substrate, however, we must not only accept diversity, we should encourage it. Indeed, like biological diversity, it is essential for human progress that there should be cultural and political diversity in the world. Without diversity, our ability to respond to new challenges will be weakened.

For all their imperfections, the UN and the WTO represent this diversity in unity. The idea of subsidiarity in the European Union acknowledges the diverse origins of the European peoples. In my own region of Southeast Asia, ten countries with different histories, speaking different languages and practising different religions, are also embarked on a similar journey of moving closer together while respecting each other's differences. At the WTO, however complicated and arduous the process of multilateral trade negotiations, this is still a more civilised method of resolving conflicts and harmonising national differences than erecting protectionist walls and fighting trade wars.

Respecting plurality does not mean that we stop recognising strengths and weaknesses. That would be hypocrisy. Some cultural values are more suited to modern times than others. Some economic systems are more productive. Some political systems are better able to mobilise the creative energies of their people. We must be honest enough to recognise that others can be superior to us in this or that area, and that it is therefore in our interest to learn from them. But no one should force his views on others. We should never impose a particular political or economic system on societies with different histories and traditions. What we need instead is an environment which encourages mutual learning and healthy competition. For this, we need to respect one another.

Recognising the need for diversity, the UN's Millennium Development Goals make no policy prescriptions on how countries should achieve those goals. Each country is free to choose its own path to the future. There is no one-size-fits-all solution to the challenge of human development.

When Singapore became independent in 1965, there was no ready solution which fitted us. We had to seek our own way forward. Many countries helped us with aid and advice for which we remain grateful to them. The UN Development Programme provided valuable assistance. With no natural resources, we had to organise ourselves in a practical way, add value and be of service to others. Little by little, we worked out pragmatic solutions to specific problems like job creation, ethnic differences, social security, education, housing and healthcare. Good governance was a precondition to all our efforts. We were tough on corruption and crime. When we saw attempts by international drug dealers to target young Singaporeans in the 1970s, we passed draconian laws. We were criticised for some of our actions by the Western media but we persisted with the support of the majority of Singaporeans, always acting with their consent and in their interest. Having now reached a reasonable standard of economic development, other developing countries have approached us for assistance. Of course we feel honoured to be asked. But we prefer them to see Singapore more as an experiment to be studied than a model to follow. Every country is different and each must customise its own solutions.

Small countries like Singapore need a stable external environment. We are ardent supporters of international organisations like the UN and the WTO because they give us a say, together with other countries, in global governance. A world in which countries big and small can resolve disputes according to commonly-agreed rules is infinitely preferable to one in which might is right.

Over four centuries ago, a wise man from the West* visited the East. The Italian Jesuit, Matteo Ricci, went to China with the goal to convert China to Catholicism. He had a deep respect for the civilisation which he wanted to Christianise. Realising that the only way to impress the Chinese was to interact with them on their own terms, he proceeded to study the Chinese language, master the Chinese classics and employ Chinese philosophical concepts in his discourses on Christianity. Instead of talking at them, he talked to them in conceptual terms they could relate to. The Lord's Prayer, for example, was rendered as if Jesus was preaching in a Chinese environment. Although Matteo Ricci did not succeed in converting the Chinese, he left behind a lasting legacy. When he died, the Chinese Emperor consented to his burial in China and his tomb, inscribed with his Chinese name of *Li Ma Dou*, is to be found today in the compound of the Party School of the Beijing Municipal Committee.

History is unending. We need wise men like Matteo Ricci from the West and the East, and from the South and the North, to help us prevent the clash of civilisations through debate and dialogue. Respecting diversity should never reduce us to cultural relativism as if all points of view are equally valid. We should never stop trying to influence one another, and here in the UN we are always trying to, but we must always be prepared to see the same issues from the perspectives of others. Here in the UN, we have an institution which can help us create this better world.

---

*Vincent Cronin, *The Wise Man from the West: Matteo Ricci and His Mission to China*, Harvill Press, 1955.

# Singapore and the Xinhai Revolution

*Singapore will do its utmost to maintain peace in Asia. For without peace, there can be no development.*

His Excellency Dr Lien Chan,
Dr Lily Sun,
Director General Xiong Changliang,
Mr Zhuang Yanlin,
Distinguished Guests

We are greatly honoured by the presence of Honorary Chairman Lien Chan, an old friend. We are delighted by the presence of Mdm Lily Sun, granddaughter of Dr Sun Zhongshan, and of so many distinguished visitors from the Mainland, Taiwan and other countries.

The Xinhai Revolution (辛亥革命) of 1911 was an epochal event in human history. It overthrew a system of over 2,000 years of imperial rule in China, making China a constitutional republic. When the Chinese Communist Party celebrated the 80th Anniversary of its founding in 2001, it traced its political origins 80 years before its founding in 1921 to major events like the Opium War, the Tai Ping Revolution, the Boxer Rebellion and, of course, the 1911 Revolution which created the Republic of China.

The Chinese Revolution was itself part of a larger drama of Asian peoples responding to long years of Western imperial domination.

---

Speech at the 100th Anniversary Celebration of Tong Meng Hui (同盟会), Sun Yat Sen Nanyang Memorial Hall, 12 June 2006.

The Japanese led the way with the Meiji Restoration in 1868. Japan's early modernisation was an inspiration to the rest of Asia. Many Western ideas and methods of organisation entered the Asian mainland through Japan. However, Japan quickly became an imperial power itself, joining the Western imperial powers in their exploitation of other Asians.

Human civilisations learn from one another. To achieve independence, Asians assimilated ideas and methods from the West to fight the West. The Western ideas of democracy and separation of powers became important. In drawing up the Constitution of the Republic of China, the Kuomintang (KMT) under Sun Zhongshan's leadership, adopted the Western structure of the Executive, the Legislative and the Judiciary and added to them the Examination Yuan and the Control Yuan from the old imperial system. The Chinese Communist Party adopted the Western ideas of Marxism and Leninism in its theory and practice. But whether it was the Kuomintang or the Chinese Communist Party, all these Western ideas had to be modified and adapted to fit Asian conditions. China has a long history of which the period of Western influence is only one of many layers.

After many years of experimentation, Asian countries are now making rapid political, economic and cultural progress. Among the Asian countries, the progress of China will have the greatest impact on world history. The 21st century holds much promise for China and for all of Asia. All this is only possible because of the heroic efforts of individuals like Sun Zhongshan and his early supporters a hundred years ago. They risked their lives to change the destiny of the Chinese people.

In 1905, Sun Zhongshan established the Tong Meng Hui in Tokyo. It was of course illegal in Qing China and any member of the Tong Meng Hui would have been immediately executed on the Mainland. In 1906, the Southeast Asian headquarters of the Tong Meng Hui was established in Singapore at Wan Qing Yuan (晚晴园). Singapore was then a British colony. At that time, both the Japanese and British governments did not oppose the Chinese republican movement because they too saw advantage in seeing the Qing government overthrown. But the Qing Consulate-General officials in

Singapore tried to intimidate the supporters. For example, Chinese businessmen who kept their shops open when the Guangxu Emperor died in 1908 were stoned.

Singapore was a major centre of the Chinese republican movement in Southeast Asia. Sun Zhongshan visited Singapore eight times to meet his supporters here and raise money for the revolution. Overseas Chinese also went back to China to take part in various uprisings. When KMT Chairman Ma Ying-jeou visited Wan Qing Yuan last month, he remarked that four individuals from Singapore went to take part in the Huanghuagang Uprising. All four of them died. There were two who went from Taiwan. They survived.

In the first half of the 20th century, every major event in China had its reflection in Singapore. Whether it was the Kuomintang or the Chinese Communist Party, both had their supporters here. When they fought each other in China, their supporters fought each other here. When they united in China, their supporters were united here. During the anti-Japanese struggle, the Chinese in Singapore and other parts of Southeast Asia raised money and sent volunteers to China. When the artist Xu Beihong visited Singapore eight times between 1919 and 1942 and held several exhibitions in Singapore to raise money for the anti-Japanese struggle, the local support was overwhelming. All this was carefully noted by the military government in Japan. Before the invasion of Southeast Asia on 8 December 1941, Japanese Military Intelligence in Taipei had already drawn up a list of many Chinese leaders to be exterminated in Singapore. The invasion of Malaya and Singapore was planned in Taiwan and rehearsed on Hainan Island. After the British surrender on 15 Feburary 1942, a terrible massacre was carried out in Singapore called the *Sook Ching* (肃清), probably the worst during the Second World War after Nanjing.

After the Second World War, a multiracial nationalist spirit arose in Singapore which enabled us to gain independence in 1965. While we share close cultural links with Chinese people all over the world, we are a sovereign state and have our independent political destiny. With Japan, we now have warm relations. We will long cherish the visit of the Japanese Emperor and Empress last week. While we cannot forget the mistakes and tragedies of the past, we decided to accept Japan's apology and move on to a new chapter of mutual cooperation.

From the very beginning, we have had a one-China policy which reflected the historical feelings of the Singapore people and the role they played in the Chinese revolution. We treasure our close friendship with the people of Mainland China and Taiwan. It will pain us to see the two sides coming to blows, hence our close watch over cross-strait developments. We welcome the close interactions between Mainland China and Taiwan. This 100th anniversary of the establishment of the Tongmenghui in Singapore reminds us of our historical and ethnic ties with the Mainland, Taiwan and the large Chinese diaspora across the globe. More importantly, it reminds us of an era of great change and turbulence in Asia which brought so much suffering to the peoples of this region. Singapore will do its utmost, on our own and in concert with other powers, to maintain peace in Asia. For without peace, there can be no development.

# South Asia in the Global Community

*It is the part South Asia plays in the re-emergence of Asia that tells the most interesting story.*

In a strange way, we seem to be returning to the past. Take Singapore as an example. Strand by strand, we have been recovering all the old links which created modern Singapore — our links to the rest of Southeast Asia, to China, to India and, now, to the Middle East. As a city-state, it is natural that we should experience first what larger polities would eventually also pick up.

In Southeast Asia, we are rediscovering the connections which made the region an intelligible area of cultural and historical study before the Western powers carved it up. Like pre-colonial Southeast Asia, ASEAN remains a diverse collection of big and small countries alternately influenced by China and India, benefiting from the East-West trade.

South Asia was completely dominated by the British Raj for some 200 years. In many ways, the Raj was an inheritor of the Mughal empire. The British influence in India was so deep and profound, one could even argue that the British Raj was Indian, and that today's South Asia is but a collection of its successor states. When Singapore was negotiating the Comprehensive Economic Cooperation Agreement with India, I remarked half in jest to my Indian friends, but half seriously, that we were only restoring the position of the Raj when trade and investment between the subcontinent and Singapore flowed freely according to the same laws and standards. China is fast

---

Speech at the Institute of South Asian Studies Conference, 8 November 2006.

becoming India's biggest trading partner which was of course the position in the 19th century. The China trade was of the greatest strategic importance to the East India Company and, after it was wound up, to the British Indian government directly. Singapore grew on that trade and became the headquarters of the British empire in Southeast Asia, safeguarding the Straits of Malacca and Singapore.

Unlike South Asia and Southeast Asia, Northeast Asia consisting of China, Korea and Japan was much less thoroughly colonised. The Western powers dominated China but their presence was concentrated in the concession areas, mostly along the coast. Japan, after Meiji, tried to be like a Western power but failed. The transformation of Northeast Asia began at the periphery, Japan first, then the newly industrialising economies of South Korea, Taiwan, Hong Kong and Singapore, before spreading inland. The four Special Economic Zones which Deng Xiaoping started in 1980 were all at or near port cities which experienced a strong Western presence. Not long afterwards, Shanghai resumed its old position as the dragon's head. Now the growth in China is spreading back to its ancient heartland around the cities of China's great plains and river basins.

In examining the role of South Asia in the global community of the 21st century, we need this perspective of time and space. Although history never repeats itself in the same way, the deep tendencies are persistent. The geography has not changed; the climate, maybe a little. Cultural characteristics do change but slowly. The populations are an order of magnitude bigger today but the relative sizes have not changed that very much. What has changed dramatically is technology, but the ability of a society to acquire new knowledge and apply it to production and security has its roots in that society's past.

Against this backdrop, let me now talk about South Asia in the global community at three levels. First, the dynamics within South Asia itself. Second, South Asia vis-à-vis the West. And, third, South Asia in larger Asia, which will be an important theme in this century.

Within South Asia, it is likely that the fragmentation which began with the end of British Empire has reached its limit — Partition in 1947, the establishment of Bangladesh in 1971, the Tamil separatist movement in Sri Lanka and other relatively minor ones elsewhere. Now technology and globalisation are re-connecting the parts. As one South Asian diplomat remarked to me recently, if China could find creative solutions for Hong Kong, Macao and Taiwan so that economic activities could carry on, why can't India and Pakistan find a creative solution for Kashmir? Indo-Pakistan trade which is reaching $1 billion can easily become $10 billion which will still be quite small. The sad fact is that South Asian cooperation is held hostage to India-Pakistan relations. However, despite all kinds of difficulties, trade in South Asia will become freer year by year. As with China, change is flowing in from outside. The influence of Indians who studied, worked or lived overseas has been a great help. The non-resident Indians (NRIs) who return home create bubbles of India's future, in the IT companies and campuses, in the industry and trade associations, in the new suburbs. Now India has become a pace-setter for all of South Asia in a positive way. What India does, Pakistan watches carefully and follows. I remember many years ago the Pakistan finance minister telling me in Lahore that he listened to the Budget Speech made by the Indian finance minister live on radio. An India that is economically strong must be a challenge to its neighbours. Just as Southeast Asian countries are galvanised by China's rapid strides, India's strides will energise all the other countries of South Asia. This competitive development is good for the world.

However, there is a counter-trend which, if mismanaged, can create a lot of problems. I am of course referring to Jihadist extremism. If the madness in the Middle East gets worse, Pakistan, India and Bangladesh will all be affected. If the Sunni-Shi'ite divide widens, both Pakistan and India will feel the shocks. We are fortunate that President Musharraf has been steadfast in the fight against Jihadist extremism after September 11. As for India, there is a wisdom in the civilisation which enables it to digest extreme tendencies and dilute their poison. On the whole, therefore, except for the borderlands between Pakistan and Afghanistan, I am not pessimistic about the ability of South Asia to contain the problem of Jihadist extremism. As has repeatedly been the case in history, Iran will play a significant role in maintaining the peace in the lands beyond the Khyber.

Let me now move to South Asia's relationship with the West. Because India is not viewed as a competive challenge to the West the way China is, India's strategic relationship with the US, EU and Russia will not be as complicated as China's. This is a great advantage. The fact that India is a democracy is also a plus. The large NRI communities in the US and Europe (principally the UK) are a major asset. As a major successor state to the British Empire, India enjoys a special position in the English-speaking world. India's companies can internationalise easily. Many ethnic Indians hold senior positions in Western MNCs. Outside South Asia, Indians, Pakistanis, Bangladeshis and Sri Lankans feel close to one another, attesting to their common cultural heritage. In Singapore, all are considered Indians because their ancestors came here before British India was divided. India's relationship with the old Soviet Union continues with Russia. This is not surprising because it was a relationship based not on ideological considerations but for geostrategic reasons. While India is happy to strengthen its links with the US and Europe, it will never want to be too dependent on them especially for military technology. Looking ahead, India will be able to maintain good relations with all the major Western powers. This, in turn, will provide a better environment for peace and development in the subcontinent.

It is the part South Asia plays in the re-emergence of Asia that tells the most interesting story. Asia is more than half the world. Its strong growth is changing the face of the whole world. In this drama, the resumption of India and China as two major poles is re-drawing the global political and economic map. Both are continental nations having by far the largest populations on earth with enormous reservoirs of human talent. Historically, separated by high mountains and vast deserts, the two civilisations interacted sparingly and only with difficulty. Except for 1962, there was never a major war between them from the beginning of time. Except for the Buddhist heritage, there are few common reference points in their relationship. Where India and China met in a significant way, it was in Southeast Asia which became a separate civilisational area buffering the two. In more recent times, India and China met again under a Western ascendancy, first British, later American. Today the common terms of interaction are Anglo-Saxon — contract laws, accounting standards, corporate structures, the common jargon of business schools and the English language.

The common Buddhist heritage will be revived in the coming years, if nothing else, because millions of Buddhists from Northeast and Southeast Asia will want to visit the holy sites in South Asia and the economic gains from religious tourism will bring great benefits to local people in all the countries of South Asia. The influence of Buddhism on human civilisation is largely benign and beneficient. It is an easy subject to talk about unlike discussions about the interactions of Christianity, Judaism and Islam. Next week, a seminar on the relevance of the Buddhist heritage to 21st century Asia will be held here in Singapore. President Abdul Kalam of India, for whom this subject is a passion, will be taking part live by video-conference.

The improving relationship between India and China will be a hugely positive factor in the development of Asia, second in importance only to the relationship between the US and China. The current border talks, the reopening of the Nathu La Pass, the rapidly expanding trade account, the explosive increase in bilateral exchanges — all this are but a prelude to a major re-encounter of two civilisations on their own terms. It is only natural that Southeast Asia will be an important venue for this re-encounter. To be sure, it will not all be smooth as no encounter of such a scale can be. Along the way, there will be disappointments, distrust and recriminations. All this we must expect when large forces are in play. There will always be an element of strategic rivalry between them which the smaller countries around them will carefully analyse and which the other major powers will try to turn to their advantage. The East Asia Summit is a way of encouraging the development of India-China relations in a direction beneficial to everyone.

However, as of now, and for many years to come, it is Japan and Korea which will be able to benefit South Asia more in terms of technology, marketing and industrial management. Cities like Singapore and Hong Kong will offer models of municipal management. It is no longer fantastical to envision an Asia well connected by road, rail, air and electronic links permitting the easy movement of goods and people across its length and breadth. The roads and railways which China and India want to connect to Southeast Asia will in the end link them both.

One can therefore be very optimistic about the coming cooperation and collaboration between South Asia and East Asia. Let me now complete the picture for Asia by talking briefly about South Asia's links with West Asia and Central Asia. Here again, there is nothing new. We return to the arena of the Great Game. Kissinger has always argued that the foreign policy of the British empire was often dominated by the strategic needs of British India. As India's economic power grows, so too will its political influence and strategic weight. India should not unnecessarily entangle itself in the horribly complex politics of the Middle East, for there is no profit in that. But India can always be a force for peace and stability. India's relationship with Iran will always be important. The millions of South Asians working in the Middle East have become indispensable to the booming economies there. At a serious conference like this, I should not talk about the influence of Bollywood but it is pervasive. As for Central Asia after the collapse of the Soviet Empire, India is gradually becoming a player, a role China, which moved first, has come to accept.

Let me end by going back to the internal politics of South Asia. This is critical. South Asia can only play a major role in global politics if the sub-continent itself is not embroiled in its own conflicts and there are any number to choose from if one is looking for them. In recent years, the picture looks a little more hopeful. The South Asian Association for Regional Cooperation (SAARC) can play a more important role if some of the basic distrust in the sub-continent can be reduced. Realistically, this will take time. India has perforce to take the lead although it would be unfair to put the entire burden on India.

All said, if the past is a guide to the future, we can be fairly optimistic about the contribution of South Asia to the global community on many dimensions.

# UNDERSTANDING CHINA

*... once we have a sense of China's past, it is easier to anticipate its moves and be less surprised by its actions.*

Thank you, Kishore, for your kind words. Dear friends, ladies and gentlemen.

I was in India two weeks ago. While in Calcutta, after calling on the Chief Minister, I attended mass at Mother Theresa's house. There I met a Singapore nun — Sister Maria Tony. She had been in Calcutta for over ten years. I wondered why someone from Singapore would want to dedicate her life to do what she did — picking up the dead and caring for the dying in the back alleys of Calcutta. There were many nuns there who were in their ninth year. They take their first vow in the fifth year, renewable every year. In the 10th year they have to decide whether or not to take the final vows which are for eternity. So if you are not sure, please, there's a way out now; if you are sure, then you're in the room to make the commitment. The priest gave a very tough sermon. While he was talking, I could hear the incessant din of traffic outside. Then suddenly, I heard the call of the muezzin. Remembering that Calcutta is mostly Hindu, I marvelled at the diversity of India and its ability to internalise such disparate elements and the way Indians find it unremarkable that a tiny woman from Albania should come into their midst, become one of them, and have her life celebrated as an Indian, already beatified on the way to canonisation.

---

Edited transcript of George Yeo's off-the-cuff speech at a dinner held by the Lee Kuan Yew School of Public Policy (LKYSPP), The Ritz-Carlton Millenia Hotel, 5 February 2007.

## India is India and China is China

Superficially there are similarities between China and India, as there are between China and the US, and China and Europe. But once we plumb deep, we discover that China is very different. When we talk about China's future — China in the 21st century, how China will behave in the world community, China's attitudes towards democracy, towards law, towards social justice — it is important first to study China against its long history. Naturally we should not be deterministic because there is nothing inevitable in human history, but once we have a sense of China's past, it is easier to anticipate its moves and be less surprised by its actions.

A few years ago, the Chinese government embarked on a major project to write the official history of the Qing Dynasty which lasted from 1644 to 1911. Ever since the Han Dynasty, which was roughly contemporaneous with the Roman empire, the Chinese developed a historiographic tradition of each dynasty writing the history of the previous dynasty. Sima Qian of the later Han wrote the first official history, which covered the earlier Han and the entire period before that. Jin wrote up the Three Kingdoms; Ming wrote up the Yuan. Yuan, which was Mongol in its origins, wrote up the Sung. Sung wrote up the Tang which was the Classical Period. The last dynasty, the Qing, collapsed with the Republican Revolution of 1911. This is now 2007. I think it was in 2003 when the Chinese embarked on this project to write the official history of the Qing Dynasty. When former Vice Premier Li Lanqing visited Singapore recently, I asked him about its progress. He said he told the scholars not to rush to conclusion. The effort would take many years, easily ten, he emphasised. The raw material has largely been assembled, both internal and external sources, including material from Europe and Christian missions. This would be China's 25th official history.

## China's Sense of Itself

Mao Zedong was a great revolutionary. While he overturned everything that existed before, he knew his history of China. He read all 24 official histories. Not only did he read them, he annotated them carefully. But he wrote with a terrible, illegible scrawl, which scholars had to decipher after he died. Then they wrote commentaries on his commentaries and now they're all published and available in the bookshops. It is very difficult for the Chinese to depart from their own history because the drama is periodically re-enacted on the same great plains, the same high mountains, with more or less the same neighbours. While there are always variations, some patterns recur. During the Ming Dynasty, the Romance of The Three Kingdoms known to all Chinese was written. It is not an official history but a popular version of it with heroes and villains sharply etched.

The first line reads: "Below heaven, there are great movements, great currents; long disunity leads to unity and long unity leads to disunity." The Chinese internalise this wisdom. They know there are cycles in their civilisation, that there are always ups and downs.

In recent years, the Chinese are feeling their own re-emergence. It's a bit scary. In the initial years, they lacked confidence; they asked many questions; but now they know that there is an organic vitality to their growth, that it is deep and will continue for some time. It is like an adolescent who becomes conscious of his own development, and feel growing strength. I say "scary" because for those of us who live on the periphery of that empire, what happens there will radiate its influence to us and, eventually, to a greater or lesser degree, envelop us.

In analysing China, it's important, from an intellectual viewpoint, not to transpose our own experiences onto China, because it will develop according to its own logic, according to its own DNA. It is growing now and it will continue to grow, but it will develop its own contradictions and one day those contradictions, many years from now, will lead to decline. Studying their own history, the Chinese know that at the beginning of a dynasty the taxes are light but the treasury is full and, at the end of a dynasty, the taxes are crushing but the treasury is empty.

Because the size of the country and the depth of its culture, some things are deeply resistant to change. How could it be otherwise when the civilisation has lasted so long unbroken? Take Confucius as an example. Every time they overturned a dynasty, they had first to overturn Confucius or at least some aspects of his teachings, because Confucius justified the status quo. Throughout the 19th century, whether it was the Taiping Revolution, the Communist movement or Sun Yat Sen, huge efforts were made to debunk Confucius. It reached its final moment when they criticised Lin Biao together with Confucius. That was the last paroxysm. Today, Hu Jintao promotes hexie shehui (和谐社会) or "harmonious society". Suddenly we hear the resonance of Confucius coming back. And all over the world, on the pattern of Alliance Francaise, the Goethe Institute and the United States Information Agency (USIA), the Chinese government has established Confucius Institutes. The learning of the Confucianist classics is resurging in China, not yet officially. Parents want to teach their children Confucianist values and individual Chinese are rediscovering their intellectual and philosophical inheritance. Ditties like the *San Zi Jing* (三字经) are once again taught to young kids who recite the rhymes without understanding but who, when they grow up, will appreciate the wisdom in the words. With the revolution over, Confucius is once again needed.

Confucianism is now digesting Marx. From Mao to Deng to Jiang Zemin, at every stage, the Chinese have had to re-interpret Marx. They are comfortable with the young Marx, the idea of the superstructure resting on the economic base, the idea that politics is concentrated economics, the dialectic — all this they like because there are analogues in Chinese thinking. Deng downplayed the class struggle. Jiang propounded the "Three Represents" which represent the new progressive forces. Now Hu Jintao stresses "harmonious society" and "China's peaceful re-emergence". China is sinicizing Marx and Lenin the way it sinicised Buddhism.

Over the centuries, the Chinese mind has developed a certain approach towards law, democracy, religion and foreign policy. I would like to deal with each in turn.

## Law

Many years ago, Joseph Needham, who wrote the great encyclopaedic work *Science and Civilisation in China*, corrected the view that China had a weak legal tradition. By his estimation, the Chinese had a greater corpus of legal codification than the West. A greater corpus of legal codification than the West! But with a fundamental difference. The idea that the law is above the emperor is completely alien to their thinking. Where did that idea come from? In the West, you could trace it back to Hammurabi and Moses, to Greece, to Rome and to Justinian. That is the evolutionary history of the western DNA on law. The Chinese had a different evolutionary starting point. After Qin Shihuang, what mattered most to the cohesion of Chinese society was not law or *fa* (法), but *li* (礼), which can be loosely translated as proper conduct among human beings. It is a Confucianist idea. Historically, the Chinese saw law as only a means to an end, which can be justice or equity. When the outcome of a law is perverse, then that law must be overridden, because justice, proper conduct, the proper relationship among human beings must take precedence. From time to time when we hear of big corruption cases being prosecuted, they are never about law alone; other factors are also in play. This will not be the New York state prosecutor pursuing legal cases to their logical limits. In China, they will ask themselves — what do we want to achieve, what is the desired end point?

The individuals who have done wrong have to be punished and an example made of them, but the larger system has also to be protected. You do not want to upset the order of the universe because that causes chaos and hardship to many. Thus the Chinese approach is a very different one. Yes, there is growing legislation on a wide range of subjects. But when it comes to ultimate power, that must remain with the Emperor or, in the case today, with the Chinese Communist Party. The top leaders cannot be subject to law in a mechanical way. In the PRC Constitution, judges and prosecutors work under the leadership of the Communist Party. They are expected to be members of the Communist Party and be imbued with its ideas and ideals.

Will this change? I doubt it. Why would it not change? Because these are ideas which have served China well for centuries. Suddenly to say that all that has been practised in previous dynasties, all that earlier histories have pronounced to be good, are now all wrong and that China should instead adopt alternative ideas with origins in Western Europe and the Middle East, to the Chinese, all that is absurd. Adaptation to modern conditions, yes. Changing axioms, that is much harder. For the Chinese, laws are akin to regulations. They are means to a larger end.

### Democracy

The Chinese attitude towards democracy follows a parallel pattern. Democracy is also not seen as an end in itself. Democracy is a means and the Chinese are quite happy to make use of democratic methods to achieve better government. They accept that at lower levels, democracy is good because it puts pressure on local leaders to perform. Thus, in towns and villages, there is democracy with universal franchise. Once a slate of candidates is approved, elections are held and they can be very competitive, but without the involvement of political parties. Those who are incompetent or arrogant or despotic get chucked out. But for cities and provinces, the government takes a more cautious approach and there is no direct democracy. Why not? Because they do not believe that that is the way to produce good government any more than the Catholic Church believes that the Pope should be elected by universal franchise. For the Catholic Church, parishioners do not decide who should be the parish priest. Election of lay members to the Parish Council? Maybe, that's ok. But electing parish priests? Bishops? Universal franchise? That's against God's laws. The Chinese internalise a similar instinct. This is not communist; it is just Chinese. And they know that too much democracy invariably leads to "localitis", with leaders coming under pressure to favour local communities at the expense of the larger good. There is also the persistent problem of officials favouring relatives and friends, which arises out of Confucianist values.

The resilience of Chinese society is largely due to very strong family and extended family ties. Yet officials are expected to behave impartially towards all citizens. Democratic arrangements have to take this contradiction into account. In an "ideal democracy" the bonds of citizenship should be primary. In a Chinese society, the bonds of family are much stronger. For this reason, most Chinese companies rely on family members and relatives in key positions to maintain ultimate control because they are the most trusted, regardless of what western management schools may preach.

Precisely for this reason, during the Ming and Qing dynasties, no senior official could serve within 400 miles of where he was born. This means that if Singapore is part of China, no Singaporean can be involved in governing Singapore at a high level. Today there's almost no province in China where the provincial leader grew up in that province. Let's transpose this onto Europe; it's as if, routinely, the President of France is not French and the Chancellor of Germany is not German. Englishmen can't be trusted in London, nor Italians in Rome. Can you imagine how absurd such a notion is to Europeans and Americans?

What is remarkable is that this system is widely accepted as legitimate in China. It is not considered outrageous or oppressive that the Guangdong Provincial Party Secretary is not Cantonese. This has always been the way China is governed and, in fact, you are more likely to have an impartial governor that way than if a local boy is in charge, because he is under constant pressure to favour relatives and friends of relatives.

So when we talk about democracy in China, it must be against this cultural and historical backdrop. The regulations against locals serving in leadership positions have been further tightened in recent years. There are also rules against staying in a ministry or a department for too long. Despite these rules, scandals still occur from time to time and the Centre must have the will to act. For as long as the central leadership is virtuous, the system can be maintained. But one day the centre itself may become corrupt, as has happened in previous dynasties, and a downward spiral begins.

India is not a country that can sustain a nationwide revolution, because its deep structure, which is fragmented, would not allow for it. In contrast, China is a country which can only be renewed through periodic revolutions. Over dinner, Kishore [Mahbubani] asked me when? I replied, well, maybe in two to three hundred years' time because China has long cycles. The official history of the People's Republic will not be written by the People's Republic. It will be written by the next dynasty. Of course, we shouldn't call the PRC a dynasty. It is a republic and there is no emperor. But whatever the term we use, we have to wait a long time for the official history of the PRC to be written.

## Religion

Let me now talk about China's attitude towards religion. Being a Roman Catholic I follow closely the ups and downs in China's relationship with the Vatican. It is a fascinating history. The Jesuits, when they went to China during the Ming Dynasty, had hoped to convert the Emperor so that all of China would become Catholic and a great mission would be achieved.

They never succeeded. Some of the brightest minds from Europe like Matteo Ricci went on this mission to China. Ricci corrected the Chinese calendar and repaired the clocks in the palace. He saw the throne but never got to meet the emperor. Ricci died in China. His tomb is in the compound of the Beijing Party School today. And the church which he founded is still there today. Li Madou, that's what he called himself, applied for permission to be buried in China, which was granted. But the Catholic Church made little progress. When the Manchus swept southwards, establishing the Qing in 1644, the missionaries thought, perhaps, there was now a chance. The Manchus had seemed more sympathetic to Christianity.

The despatches of the missionaries during that period, which the Jesuits called the Tartar War, were full of hope. But not a chance. They appealed to the second emperor, Kangxi. "Can we send more missionaries? Can we have them all reporting to a papal legate in Beijing?" Kangxi's reply was that "you can send as many priests as you want to China but they must die in China" and there would be no papal legate to whom they would report. The Chinese see in the Catholic Church an organisation too much like their own, with similar moral claims on its members. Mind you, neither China nor the Catholic Church tries to control everything; they just control the big things — dogma, doctrine, party line. After that you are left on your own and you are to a large extent financially independent. But the loyalties are to the centre. Beijing appoints ministers and provincial secretaries. Rome appoints bishops. The Chinese empire and the Catholic Church, each with about the same population in the world, share strange similarities which is why their interaction is a complex and difficult one. Over the appointment of Chinese bishops, both seek ultimate authority. Eventually they have got to compromise so that each stays within his own theology or ideology.

I can anticipate the Vatican arguing that "we are not of this realm, we are of the other realm, so please, we are not in conflict". As for the Chinese leaders, their attitude towards religion from the earliest days is to keep religion at arm's length, following the advice of Confucius. Those who govern the empire are expected to be a-religious in public life. They can have private religious beliefs but in public life, they are Confucianists.

The early Jesuits in China were surprised that it was possible to create a moral order based not on religion but on ethical principles. They wrote about it and influenced European thinkers like Voltaire. According to Needham, that helped inspire the French revolution. You could get rid of the Church and maintain moral order in society without religion.

**Foreign Policy**

I've talked about China and law, China and democracy, China and religion. Now let me talk about China and foreign policy, which is perhaps your greatest interest, and about which I can only talk generally because you are the experts in this field.

It's very difficult for the Chinese to depart from the view that they are *Zhong Guo* (中国), the Middle Kingdom. China is at the centre; at the penumbra, there are the other chopsticks peoples who are considered semi-Sinic. I think the Chinese consider Singapore semi-Sinic too. Then there are those who are beyond, who are what the Greeks would have called barbarians. Now all that politically-incorrect jargon is of course not in use today. In foreign affairs, the Chinese are formal and correct. They observe protocol punctiliously and welcome you with great hospitality, proclaiming the equality of all nations, big and small. They ply guests with lavish dinners and courteous words, offering you the best of everything in the house.

It reminded me of the way my mother used to teach us at home. She grew up in southern China and was of that tradition. We were a big family and guests had always to be treated well. The guest has to be treated well because you are afraid of him. It is common for guests to be treated better than family members because the guest can be capricious; he can cause problems, so it is better to confine him within the bounds of hospitality. Those in the tradition know exactly what's going on. I can therefore understand why Koreans, Japanese and Vietnamese, and to some extent, Singaporeans as well, feel somewhat uneasy when they see old patterns recurring.

Will the Chinese approach to foreign policy change? It has to, because never in their earlier history have they to be in such close contact with competing centres of power. China cannot use old methods to deal with the US and Europe. With India, China was separated by high mountains and both are ancient peoples. Today, we are all connected and adjustments have to be made.

It will be interesting to watch how the Chinese handle the coming Olympics in Beijing. If the Olympics becomes an exercise in Chinese nationalism, international reaction will be negative. But I think the Chinese will be sophisticated. I expect they will organise cheer teams for the Americans, Japanese and others, and great courtesy will be shown to foreigners. They are very careful to ensure that their words fit the conditions of today.

Let me say in China's defence that many of the methods they use arise out of fear, not out of a desire to dominate. If you analyse the old tributary system, those who sent tributes got much more in return. Japanese merchants competed to get trade tokens because the China trade was very lucrative. The Chinese are fearful of foreigners. They are fearful of the Russians to the North, Muslims to the West and Americans across the Pacific. Their strategy is to keep a low profile, stay out of the local politics of other countries, and concentrate on economic development.

Internally, will they make preparations for war? I have no doubt, because they have a legitimate fear that other powers do not want them to succeed. Is their intention to dominate, to conquer, the way the European powers did in the past? I don't think so. I don't think there is any desire to colonise or to turn non-Chinese into Chinese. As they become stronger, while their old nature will re-assert itself, the Chinese will also be reacting to the rest of the world. If they are threatened, they will develop their own responses in self-defence.

Quite early in the day, they had a policy to neutralise ASEAN through economic integration. Historically, Southeast Asia was never a threat to China. They do not want this to change. But of course they worry about the sea lanes which pass through Southeast Asia.

A few years ago, China made a dramatic move. When Premier Zhu Rongji was in Singapore for the ASEAN-China summit, he proposed that the common future of China and ASEAN be strengthened by a free trade agreement. The leaders of ASEAN did not know how to react and almost fell off their chairs. At that time, we in ASEAN were still reeling from the Asian financial crisis. Some saw China as an economic threat. It took ASEAN almost a year to digest the implications of Premier Zhu's proposal and to respond positively to it. Negotiations were phased, with China assuring us that we would benefit more in each phase.

When the Framework Agreement was signed in 2002 in Phnom Penh, Premier Zhu made two remarkable statements. He said that, if after ten years, the agreement benefits China more than it benefits Southeast Asia, it should be renegotiated in ASEAN's favour. I can never imagine the United States Trade Representative or the European Trade Commissioner ever talking the same way. For them, a deal is a deal; it's settled for eternity. Then Premier Zhu added: "China does not seek for itself an exclusive position in Southeast Asia." He acknowledged that we in ASEAN are not just going to date one girl. We fully intended to be promiscuous. That showed great wisdom on China's part.

Towards Northeast Asia, China's foreign policy is not as easy to manage because there is so much history and legacy. Towards Central Asia and Russia, they harbour deep historical fears. As for America, the two countries are now bound together at so many points, a serious rupture is almost unthinkable. But it is going to be a very difficult relationship; it will be the single most important relationship for both countries in this century. If it's badly managed there could be war; if it's properly managed there will be another generation of peace and hundreds of millions of people in the world will be raised out of the depths of poverty. In this area, you are the experts.

It's not easy for a country so vast as China, with such a sense of itself, to depart too much from its deep nature. From that perspective, we can be optimistic for the future.

# THE GREAT REPRICING

*Human civilisations learn from one another more than we realise.*

Madam Pro-Vice Chancellor, Kate Pretty, my old tutor, Professor Navaratnam, dear friends, ladies and gentlemen

**What the Current Crisis Represents**

It may seem inauspicious that Cambridge should be celebrating its 800th Anniversary at a time when the world is heading into a deep recession the likes of which have not been seen for a long time. From the perspective of Cambridge's long history, however, this sharp economic downturn is but another discontinuity in the affairs of man of which the University has seen many and participated in not a few. Whether this crisis marks a major break in world history we don't know yet. Turning points are only seen for what they are in hindsight.

What is becoming clearer is the severity of the crisis. No one is sure where the bottom is or how long this crisis will last. In the meantime, at least tens of thousands of companies will go bankrupt and tens of millions of people will lose their jobs. What started as a financial crisis has become a full-blown economic crisis. For many countries, worsening economic conditions will lead to political crisis. In some, governments acting hastily in response to short-term political pressure will do further harm to the economy.

---

Distinguished lecture at the University of Cambridge in conjunction with the University of Cambridge's 800th Anniversary, 27 March 2009.

In an editorial last December, *The Financial Times* commented that the US Federal Reserve was flying blind. But, in fact, all governments are flying with poor vision. Markets are volatile precisely because no one knows for sure which policy responses will work.

I remember an old family doctor once explaining how every disease must run its course. In treating an illness, he said, one works with its progression. Attempting to short-cut the process may worsen the underlying condition. While emergency action may be needed and symptoms can be ameliorated, the body must be healed from within after which its immunological status changes.

The Austrian economist Joseph Schumpeter understood the importance of creative destruction. The end of an economic cycle does not return the economy to where it was at the beginning. During the downturn, firms go bankrupt, people lose jobs, institutions are revamped, governments may be changed. And in the process, resources are reallocated and the old gives way to the new.

Charles Darwin, whose 200th birth anniversary we mark this year, understood all that. Life is a struggle with old forms giving way to new forms. And human society is part of this struggle.

The question we ask ourselves is, what is the new reality that is struggling to emerge from the old? History is not pre-determined. There is, at any point in time, a number of possible futures, each, as it were, a state of partial equilibrium. And every crisis is a discontinuity from one partial equilibrium state to another within what scenario analysts call a cone of possibilities.

Well, whatever trajectory history takes within that cone of possibilities in the coming years, there will be a great repricing of assets, of factors of production, of countries, and of ideas.

### Economic Repricing

Let me first talk about economic repricing. Many bubbles have burst in the current crisis starting with sub-prime properties in the US. All over the world, asset prices are plummeting. In the last one year, tens of trillions of dollars have been wiped out. How much further this painful process will continue, no one can be sure. Many months ago,

Alan Greenspan, in his usual measured way, peering into the hole said he saw a bottom forming in the fall of asset prices; it turned out to be the darkness of an abyss very few knew existed. That bottom is only reached when assets are sufficiently repriced downwards. Public policies can help or hinder this process. Unfortunately, many stimulus packages being proposed will make the adjustment more difficult. For example, bailing out inefficient automobile companies may end up prolonging the pain of restructuring at tremendous public expense.

The repricing of human beings will be even more traumatic. With globalisation, we have in effect one marketplace for human labour in the world. Directly or indirectly, the wages and salaries of Americans, Europeans and Japanese are being held down by billions of Asians and Africans who are prepared to work for much less. China and India alone are graduating more scientists and engineers every year than all the developed countries combined. Now, while it is true that trade is a positive sum game, the benefits of trade are never equally distributed. We can therefore expect protectionist pressures to grow in many countries.

Governments will try to protect jobs often at long-term cost to their economies. It is wrong to think that we can spend our way out of a recession. Beyond a point, the stress will be taken on exchange rates. If governments try to prevent the repricing of assets and human beings, international markets will force the adjustment on us. A country that is over-leveraged, living beyond its means, will itself be repriced through its currency. Its currency will be devalued, forcing lower living standards on all its citizens.

The world is in profound imbalance today. All the G7 countries are in recession. The West is consuming too much and saving too little while the East is saving too much and consuming too little. China, India and others need to consume much more of what they produce but they are unable to take up the present slack in global demand because their GDPs are still too small. In 10–20 years, they may be able to, but certainly not in the next few years. In the meantime, the global economy may suffer a prolonged recession, a global Keynesian paradox of thrift.

## Political Repricing

When this crisis is finally over, which may take some years, out of it will emerge a multi-polar world with clearer contours. Although the US will remain the pre-eminent pole for a long time to come, it will no longer be the hyperpower. Power will have to be shared. The Western-dominated developed world will have to share significant power with China, India, Russia, Brazil and other countries. Thus, accompanying the economic repricing will be political repricing.

Following the spectacular opening of the Olympic Games in Beijing, Tony Blair wrote in the *Wall Street Journal* of 26 August last year: "This is a historic moment of change. Fast forward 10 years and everyone will know it. For centuries, the power has resided in the West, with various European powers including the British Empire and then, in the 20th century, the US. Now we will have to come to terms with a world in which the power is shared with the Far East. I wonder if we quite understand what that means, we whose culture (not just our politics and economies) has dominated for so long. It will be a rather strange, possibly unnerving experience."

Those words were said by Tony Blair in August last year before the financial meltdown. How much more they ring true today. Sharing power is, however, easier said than done. But without a major restructuring of international institutions, including the Bretton Woods institutions, many problems in global governance cannot be properly managed. The meeting of G20 leaders started by President George Bush in November last year is a necessary new beginning. But it is a process. Prime Minister Gordon Brown is hoping that the next meeting on 2 April in London will sketch out the main elements of a global bargain. To be sure, the reform of global institutions is a process that will take years to achieve. During the transition, many things can go wrong. In his analysis of the Great Depression in the last century, the economic historian Charles Kindleberger identified a major cause in the absence of global leadership during a critical period when power was shifting across the Atlantic. Great Britain could not exercise leadership while the US would not. In between, the global economy fell.

In the coming decades, the key relationship in the world will be that between the US and China. Putting it starkly, the US is China's most important export market while China is the most important buyer of US Treasuries. The core challenge is the peaceful incorporation of China into the global system of governance, which in turn will change the global system itself. This was probably what led Secretary Hillary Clinton to make her first overseas visit to East Asia.

## Three Points About China

The transformation of China is the most important development in the world today. Much has been written about it, the re-emergence of China. But I would like to touch on three points.

### *China's sense of itself*

The first point is China's sense of itself which was written about by Joseph Needham many years ago. Over the centuries, it has been the historical duty of every Chinese dynasty to write the history of the previous one. Twenty-four have been written, the first a hundred years before Christ by Sima Qian in the famous book, *Shi Ji* (史记). The last dynasty, the Qing Dynasty, lasted from 1644 to the Republican revolution of 1911. Its official history is only now being written after almost a century. When I visited the Catholic Society of Foreign Missions of Paris in January this year, I was told, by a Mandarin-speaking French priest who served many years in China and in Singapore, that out of the 90 volumes envisaged for the official history of the Qing Dynasty, 5 volumes would be on the Christian missions in China. At the Society, I met a Chinese scholar researching into the history of missionary activities in Sichuan province. No other country or civilisation has this sense of its own continuity. For the official history of the People's Republic, I suppose we would have to wait a couple of hundred years. It was Needham's profound insight into China's sense of itself that led to his remarkable study of science and civilisation in China. Ironically, China's sense of itself was mostly about its social and moral achievements within the classical realm. It was Needham who informed the Chinese of their own amazing scientific and technological contributions to the world.

However, China's sense of itself is both a strength and a weakness. It is a strength because it gives Chinese civilisation its self-confidence and its tenacity. Chinese leaders often say that while China should learn from the rest of the world, China would have to find its own way to the future. But it is also a conceit, and this conceit makes it difficult for Chinese ideas and institutions to become global in a diverse world. To be sure, the Chinese have no wish to convert non-Chinese into Chinese-ness. In contrast, the US as a young country, believing its own conception to be novel and exceptional, wants everyone to be American. The software of globalisation today, including standards and pop culture, is basically American. And therein lies a profound difference between China and the US. The software of globalisation today, including standards and pop culture, is basically American. If you look at cultures as human operating systems, it is US culture which has hyper-linked all these different cultures together, in a kind of higher HTML or XML language. And even though that software needs some fixing today, it will remain essentially American. I doubt that Chinese software will ever be able to unify the world (in place of American software) because of its unique characteristics, even when China becomes the biggest economy in the world as it almost certainly will within a few decades.

### *Cities of the 21st century*

The second point I wish to highlight today about China is the astonishing urban experimentation taking place today. China is urbanising at a speed and on a scale never seen before in human history. Chinese planners know that they do not have the land to build sprawling suburbia like America's. China has less arable land than India. Although China already has a greater length of highways than the whole of the US, the Chinese are keenly aware that if they were to drive cars on a per capita basis like Americans, the whole world would boil. Recognising the need to conserve land and energy, the Chinese are now embarked on a stupendous effort to build mega-cities, each accommodating tens of millions of people, each the population size of a major country. And these will not be urban conurbations like Mexico City or Lagos growing higgledy-piggledy, but city clusters designed to accommodate such enormous populations. This means planned urban infrastructure with high-speed intra-city and inter-city rail, huge airports like Beijing's, forests of skyscrapers, and high-tech parks containing universities, research institutes, start-ups and ancillary facilities. In March last year, McKinsey Global Institute recommended 15 "super cities" with average populations of 25 million or 11 "city-clusters" each with combined populations of more than 60 million. Unlike most countries, China is able to mount massive redevelopment projects because of the communist re-concentration of land in the hands of the state. If you think about it, the great Chinese revolution was fundamentally about the ownership of land. This is the biggest difference between China and India. In India and most other parts of the world, land acquisition for large-scale projects is a very difficult and laborious process.

As we looked to the US for new patterns of urban development in the 20th century with its very rational grid patterns, we will have to look to China for the cities of the 21st century. Urbanisation on such a colossal scale is reshaping Chinese culture, politics and institutions. The Chinese Communist Party which had its origins in Mao's countryside faces a huge challenge in the management of urban politics. From an urban population of 20% in Mao's days, China is 40% urban today and, like all developed countries, will become 80–90% urban in a few decades' time. Already, China has more mobile phones than anybody else and more Internet users than the US.

### *China's political culture*

My third point is about China's political culture. Over the centuries, China has evolved a political culture that enables a continental-size nation to be governed through a bureaucratic elite. In the People's Republic, the bureaucratic elite is the Communist Party. When working properly, the mandarinate is meritocratic and imbued with a deep sense of responsibility for the whole country.

During the Ming and Qing Dynasties, there was a rule that no high official could serve within 400 miles of his birthplace so that he did not come under pressure to favour local interests. This would mean that for a place like Singapore, it would never be governed by Singaporeans. A few years ago, that rule was re-introduced to the People's Republic, and indeed, in almost all cases, the leader of a Chinese province is not from that province — neither the Party Secretary nor the Governor, unless it is an autonomous region, in which case the number two job goes to a local, but never the number one job. It is as if on a routine basis, the British PM cannot be British, the French President cannot be French and the German Chancellor cannot be German.

Although politics in China will change radically as the country urbanises in the coming decades, the core principle of a bureaucratic elite holding the entire country together is not likely to change. Too many state functions affecting the well-being of the country as a whole require central coordination. In its historical memory, a China divided always meant chaos, and chaos could last a long time.

To be sure, China is experimenting with democracy at the lower levels of government because it acts as a useful check against abuse of power. However, at the level of cities and provinces, leaders are chosen from above after carefully canvassing the views of peers and subordinates. As with socialism, China will evolve a form of "democracy with Chinese characteristics" quite different from Western liberal democracy. The current world crisis will convince the Chinese even more that they are right not to give up state control of the commanding heights of the economy.

With the world in turmoil, many developing countries are studying the Chinese system wondering whether it might offer them lessons on good governance. For the first time in a long time, the Western model has a serious competitor.

I make these three points about China to illustrate how complex the process of incorporating China into a new multi-polar global system will be. The challenge is not only economic, it is also political and cultural. Yet, it must be met and the result will be a world quite different from what we are used to. Developing countries will no longer look only to the West for inspiration; they will also turn to China and, maybe, to India as well.

### The Nalanda Revival

The simultaneous re-emergence of India and China, together making up 40% of the world's population, is endlessly fascinating. Two countries cannot be more different. One is Confucianist and strait-laced, the other is democratic and rambunctious. Or to use Amartya Sen's words: "The Indian is argumentative." Yet, in both countries, we can feel an organic vitality changing the lives of huge numbers of people. The re-encounter of these two ancient civilisations is itself another drama. Separated by high mountains and vast deserts, their historical contact over the centuries was sporadic and largely peaceful. In recent years, trade between them has grown hugely, making China India's biggest trading partner today. But of course, we must remember that during the Raj, China was also British India's biggest trading partner. But they are suspicious of each other. India remains scarred by its defeat by China in 1962 during the border war, a point which Chinese leaders seem not to understand fully. We in Southeast Asia have a strong vested interest in these two great nations who are our immediate neighbours having peaceful, cooperative relations. Let me talk briefly about a project which may help bring South, Southeast and East Asia together again. This is the revival of the old Nalanda University in the Indian state of Bihar.

Through Chinese historical records, the world is aware of the existence of an ancient Buddhist university in India which for centuries drew students from all over Asia. At its peak, Nalanda accommodated ten thousand students, mostly monks. It had a magnificent campus with a nine-storey library and towers reaching into the clouds, according to the extravagant but remarkably accurate account of the 7th century Tang Dynasty Buddhist monk Xuan Zang. Xuan Zang's journey to India to bring back Buddhist sutras was such an odyssey, it has long been mythologised in Chinese folklore — the *Journey to the West*. He spent a number of years in Nalanda. Unfortunately, Nalanda was destroyed by Afghan invaders at about the time Oxford and Cambridge were established 800 years ago. The Indian Government has recently decided to revive this ancient university as a secular university, offering it for international collaboration.

A 500-acre site not far from the ruins of the old has already been acquired. Like the old, it will be multi-disciplinary, drawing on the Buddhist philosophy of man living in harmony with man, man living in harmony with nature, and man living as part of nature. A mentor group chaired by Amartya Sen has been appointed by the Indian Government to conceptualise its establishment, of which I am privileged to be a member. I hope the new Nalanda University will help usher in a new era of peace and understanding in Asia. I also hope it will have strong links to Cambridge.

### Cultural Repricing

A multi-polar world is a messy world. It means that no particular value system will hold complete sway over others. The current crisis has already caused many people to question the nature of capitalism, socialism and democracy. Chemically-pure capitalism, to use a phrase coined by former French Premier Lionel Jospin, has become a dirty word. In contrast, John Maynard Keynes seems to have been repriced upwards again. Many of us have been dusting off old copies of *General Theory.* A recent *Newsweek* cover proclaimed that "we are all socialists now". Even Karl Marx is being re-read. Ideas, cultural norms are all being repriced as countries search for ways out of the crisis. If high unemployment persists for many more years, dangerous ideas and ideologies may reappear as they did in the 1930s.

Without American leadership, multi-polarity can easily lead to global instability. And there is much expectation of what a new Obama Administration, sensitive to cultural nuances, can do to restore order and growth in the world. Unfortunately, there are no quick or easy solutions. We should expect instead a fairly long period of untidiness and confusion. Most importantly, we should be sceptical of absolute or ultimate solutions for these are often the most dangerous.

### The Inspiration of Darwin and Needham

In responding to the current crisis, let us be inspired by two Cambridge men, Darwin and Needham. Darwin's publication of *The Origin of Species* 150 years ago represented one of the greatest intellectual leaps by mankind. At the British Museum of Natural History, they call it "The Big Idea". It was a very big idea. Natural selection has an obvious analogue in man's intellectual and social development. Like biological species, human ideas and systems are also subject to selection through wars, revolutions, elections, economic crises, academic debates and market competition. Those which survive and flourish should, we hope, raise civilisation to a higher level.

Needham understood China like few other men did. As Simon Winchester wrote in his recent book on Needham, *The Man Who Loved China*, Needham might not be surprised to see the huge transformation of China today.

Both Darwin and Needham were drawn from our university tradition of being sceptical without losing our moral sense. Only by being sceptical can we be objective, can we see ourselves critically and learn from others. Only with a moral sense will we be motivated to work for a larger social good. It was China's corruption and inability to learn from others in an earlier period that led to its long decline. The Qian Long Emperor told George III during Lord Macartney's mission in 1793 that China had nothing to learn from the West. That marked the beginning of China's long decline.

Human civilisations learn from one another more than they realise, more than we realise. In a collection of essays published by Needham on the historic dialogue of East and West in 1969, he chose for his title *Within the Four Seas*. That title was from *The Analects* of *Confucius*, who said: "Within the Four Seas, all men are brothers". In the heyday of Third World solidarity in the 1950s, the Indians had a saying "Hindi-Chini, bhai bhai" — Indians and Chinese are brothers. In these confused times, we need to learn from one another on the basis of a deep respect for each other as human beings.

# May 4th Is Part of Singapore's Rich Inheritance

*That spirit lives on ...*

The May 4th Movement played a major role in the modernisation of China. Reacting against the refusal of the European powers to return German territories and rights in Shangdong back to China after the First World War, the students of China took to the streets in protest. Starting in Beijing, the protests spread all over the country drawing in much of its intelligentsia.

At one level, the outrage was directed against the imperial powers. China had joined the Allied powers in 1917, contributed over 100,000 Chinese labourers in the fight against Germany, on condition that all German concessions in China would be restored to China upon victory. Instead, the Treaty of Versailles in April 1919 gave the German concessions in Shandong to Japan, including Qingdao, completely ignoring the earlier promise to China.

At a deeper level, the outrage of China's intelligentsia was directed at the weakness of its own culture, in frustration at the inability of the Chinese people to shake itself off the past and modernise the way Japan was able to. Despite the Republican Revolution of 1911, China remained in complete disarray. The contempt showed by the imperial powers was the inevitable result of China's own decay. The May 4th Movement forged a collective determination to create a new Chinese culture ridding itself of

---

This piece is a short reflection on the 90th anniversary of May 4th Movement, 1919. Also published (in Chinese) in *Lianhe Zaobao*.

feudal mindsets, promoting gender equality, opposing yellow culture, emphasizing mass education and extolling science and technology. This spirit infused both the Kuomintang (KMT) and the Chinese Communist Party (CCP) which was founded a few years after May 4th. Business leaders and newspaper owners weighed in with their support. Many newspapers began introducing regular supplements on a new culture in ferment, a tradition which continues in *Lianhe Zaobao* today.

The May 4th Movement had a profound impact on Singapore's own development. Indeed, without reference to May 4th, it is impossible to understand the origin and evolution of Singapore's own nationalism. In the early stages, the influence of May 4th swept all Chinese organisations in Singapore along — business and clan associations, newspapers, schools and student groups, cultural organisations. It was natural to be of the left then because without a certain revolutionary fervour, this cultural renewal could not have been accomplished. Every major event in China had its resonance in Singapore. Both the KMT and the CCP had their supporters in Singapore. When they fought in China, they fought in Singapore. When they united to fight the Japanese in China, they united in support here. It was for this reason that the Japanese militarists saw Singapore as an extension of the war in China which led tragically to *Sook Ching* (肃清).

After the Second World War, Singapore's own nationalism struggled to separate itself from the political drama on the Chinese mainland. For as long as the local Communist movement was largely based on the Chinese population of Malaya and Singapore, it could not succeed. Nationalism in Singapore had to be founded on the multiracial character of our society and take into account our colonial history and the regional reality. After twists and turns, the PAP eventually prevailed over the Communist left that it was initially in alliance with, leading Singapore to self-government in 1959 and full independence in 1965.

After 90 years, the legacy of May 4th in Singapore can be seen in the cultural renewal of the ethnic Chinese who make up three-quarters of Singapore's population. The vitality and dynamism it gave to the 'Chinese ground' in colonial times frightened the British and contributed immensely to Singapore's self-government and independence. That spirit lives on in Singapore's Chinese business and clan associations, in Nantah and the SAP schools, in the Chinese newspapers, and in many of our cultural organisations. May 4th is part of Singapore's rich inheritance.

# TIBET IN THE 21ST CENTURY

*Tibet is part of a much larger Asian drama that is changing the world.*

The encounter of China and India in this century will change the world. For thousands of years, the two civilisations were separated by the high mountains of Tibet. Except for a brief war in 1962, there were no major conflicts between them in their long histories. However, they knew of each other through traders and monks. Going around Tibet, the old silk routes were long and difficult, passing overland through Central Asia and by sea through the peninsulas and archipelagos of Southeast Asia. During the Great Game of the 19th century, both Britain and Russia saw it in their own interest to keep Tibet as part of Qing China, providing a buffer between them. When Chinese and Indians meet, they recognise each other as an ancient people. In his laconic way, India's Prime Minister Manmohan Singh observed that each is too big to be contained by the other and that the world is big enough to accommodate both. Chinese leaders doff their hats in return.

Together, China and India make up more than a third of the world's population and will supply much of the talent for global development in this century. The concentration of Chinese and Indian talent in Silicon Valley foreshadows what is coming. How China and India relate to each other in the coming decades will affect everyone. If peaceful, this will be a golden age for Asia.

---

Essay on Tibet was written after George Yeo visited Tibet as Singapore's Foreign Minister in September 2009, the first Foreign Minister to do so after the disturbances in the run-up to the 2008 Beijing Olympics.

Tibet is changing from being a barrier to a region linking China and India together. Tibet was so inaccessible even in the recent past, neither Mao Zedong, Zhou Enlai nor Deng Xiaoping ever visited it. Today, there are good roads connecting Tibet to Xinjiang, Qinghai, Sichuan and Yunnan. Three years ago, an amazing thousand-kilometre railroad from Golmud in Qinghai to Lhasa in Tibet was opened. 80% of it is over 4,000 metres in altitude; 50% on permafrost. Oxygen is pumped into the carriages to help passengers adjust to the thin air. This railroad is the fulfilment of a 100-year-old dream. When first proposed, many foreign engineers said that it could not be built. From Lhasa, the railroad will be extended to Shigatse, Tibet's second largest city, taking it very close to the Indian and Nepali borders.

Economically, there is much to be gained by improving road and rail links between Tibet and South Asia. The distance from Lhasa to Calcutta is less than a thousand kilometres. Indeed, the Chinese have suggested that they be linked by rail as well. The Indian government is understandably apprehensive about moving too quickly. Scars of the 1962 war are still raw in India. When the Indian Army moved to liberate Bangladesh in December 1971, an important factor it considered was winter snow preventing the Chinese Army from interfering through the mountain passes. Thus, the reopening of the 4,400 metre-high Nathu La Pass in July 2006 was politically significant. As part of it, China recognised India's ownership of Sikkim. Hundreds of kilometres of fibre optic cables have been laid in the past year from Yadong in Tibet to Siliguri in West Bengal with an initial capacity of 20 gigabytes per second.

Trade between China and India has grown rapidly in the last ten years. China has already become India's biggest trading partner. And this is only the beginning. Perhaps this should not be thought remarkable since Qing China was British India's biggest trading partner in the 19th century. Common economic interests are driving the two countries into closer political cooperation both bilaterally and internationally.

Culturally, there are growing areas of contact as well. The most important rivers of South Asia have their sources in the Tibetan highlands, including the Ganges and the Brahmaputra. Mount Kailash is sacred for many religions. Hindus believe it to be the Abode of Shiva. A trickle of Indian pilgrims trek over the border to visit. Others fly to Kathmandu and travel overland. To serve this region of Tibet, a new airport will soon be opened with an extra long runway because of the high altitude. The trickle is becoming a flow.

Buddhism has long linked China to India. Ironically, there are many more Buddhists in China today than there are in India. As physical infrastructure improves in India, the flow of pilgrims from East Asia to the Buddhist holy land in Bihar and Uttar Pradesh will become a flood in the coming years. Riding this tide, the Indian government is reviving Nalanda University as a secular, international university. Nalanda was a great university in the first millennium. At its peak, it had 10,000 students. Many came from East, Southeast and Central Asia, including the famous Tang monk Xuan Zang. Indeed, the most important accounts of Nalanda came from the Chinese records. Nalanda was sacked by Afghan invaders in the 12th century at about the time Oxford was founded. Two years ago, a committee of mentors headed by Nobel laureate Amartya Sen was formed by the Indian government to spearhead the re-establishment of the university. It is a project which China fully supports.

As China and India move closer together, Tibet is both an opportunity and an issue. The economic opportunity is obvious, but rapid development has brought about great stress to the Tibetan way of life. This complicates bilateral relations between China and India.

Over long years, Tibetan culture and Tibetan Buddhism evolved in response to the challenges of extreme physical conditions at high altitudes, developing in the process a deep spirituality. However, old Tibet should not be romanticised. It was not Shangri-La. The political economy was based on the feudal domination of monasteries over rural serfs. Like the endless turns of the prayer wheel, it was an internally consistent way of life which could have gone on and on for as long as Tibet stayed isolated from the outside world. In 1951, Mao Zedong's Government negotiated the "peaceful liberation" of Tibet with the local Tibetan government, guaranteeing that Beijing would not force changes to the feudal political economy of Tibet.

But the Chinese revolution had its own internal dynamic. By the mid-1950s, land reforms had begun in Tibetan-inhabited areas outside Tibet in Qinghai, Sichuan, Gansu and Yunnan. Monastic lands were seized and redistributed to peasants. Nomads were settled and their children sent to school. These contributed to the Tibetan rebellion of 1959. While the Dalai Lama fled to India where Tibetan exiles were settled in Dharamsala, the Panchen Lama remained in China and worked within the system, but not always effectively. In 1962, he sent a letter to Beijing expressing Tibetan grievances. During the Cultural Revolution, Tibetan youths, following Chinese youths in other parts of the country, engaged in an orgy of destruction. Since then, as in the rest of China, monasteries and temples have been restored or rebuilt, often to a state better than what they were before, although some precious artifacts were lost forever. Without land and serfs, these places can only be sustained with the patronage of the Chinese state.

The marriage of Tang Princess Wencheng to Tibetan King Songtsen Gampo in the 7th century began a complex relationship between Tibet and imperial China which ebbed and flowed with the rise and fall of Chinese dynasties. The links between Tibet and Mongolia reached high points during the Mongol Yuan and Manchu Qing dynasties. Mongol princes during the late Ming and early Qing Dynasty intervened on behalf of the Yellow Hat Gelugpa (the order of the Dalai Lama and the Panchen Lama), making it the dominant sect in Tibet. Because religious and political leadership was fused from the time of the 5th Dalai Lama, the appointment of high lamas often required the approval of the Emperor. This was certainly so during the Qing Dynasty. It was a practice carried into Republican and Communist China. Chiang Kai-shek's Kuomintang government approved the appointment of the 14th (present) Dalai Lama in 1940 and the 10th Panchen Lama in 1949. At the Forbidden City in Beijing today, the old buildings still carry inscriptions in the four main languages of the Qing Dynasty — Han, Manchu, Mongolian and Tibetan.

Unlike the encounter of Spanish conquistadores and the Andean Incas in the 16th century, which saw one side extinguishing the other in a short span of time, the encounter of these four nationalities with one another took place over many centuries. The Incas, like the Tibetans, had developed values and institutions adapted to high altitudes.

In the last 50 years, China devoted huge resources to the development of Tibet because of its strategic importance. Economic growth has been in the double digits in the last 15 years. Social indicators like average life spans have shown remarkable improvement. But, relative to Han Chinese, Tibetans lag behind especially in economic performance. This should not be surprising because an entrenched way of life cannot change quickly within a few decades. As in Singapore, the tensions which naturally arise when different ethnic and religious groups living side by side respond at different speeds to globalisation cannot be wished away; they simply have to be recognised and managed. Affirmative action, however, creates its own problems.

Education is clearly the key to the future. Although it would make sense to set a minimum age for young boys wanting to become monks so that they could have a strong educational foundation first, this is still deemed too sensitive. At Tibet University which has a beautiful new campus, the faculty is two-thirds Tibetan. The need for affirmative action limits the university's faculty size and expansion. Instead, Tibetan students are offered places in middle schools and universities elsewhere in China, which is probably what Beijing wants as well.

As part of the recent stimulus package, satellite dishes were given to farmers enabling them to receive dozens of Chinese TV channels. Pole-vaulting a medieval society to the 21st century is however never easy. At the Norbulinka Palace, the summer residence of the Dalai Lama, devotees still prostrate themselves before objects once used by him, like his bed and sofa.

The 14th Dalai Lama is now 74 years old. In a recent TV interview, he said that he was born to accomplish certain tasks and as those tasks were not completed, it was "logical" that he would be reincarnated outside China. Many believe that "outside China" means Tawang in Arunachal Pradesh where the 6th Dalai Lama came from, a Tibetan area controlled by India but claimed by China. This would greatly complicate the border demarcation between China and India. Beijing of course insists on the old rule that the appointment of high lamas must have its approval.

The 11th Panchen Lama is coming of age. When chosen as the reincarnation of the 10th Panchen Lama, Beijing gave its approval but not the Dalai Lama. Six months ago, at the Second World Buddhist Forum in Wuxi, he surprised many people by giving his speech in English.

It may seem strange that the reincarnation of high lamas should be a subject of such intense interest today. That perhaps is a reflection of the past in the present and the importance of the China-India relationship. Looking ahead, however, Buddhism in Tibet will have to adjust to change as it has in other parts of Asia where it is enjoying a huge revival in many countries. Tibet is part of a much larger Asian drama that is changing the world.

# China in a Multipolar World

*... China which is re-emerging powerfully, an India which is also growing but which will be a pole unto itself and an America which is not only a reality, but also a necessity.*

In the last two days, we have discussed much about China's internal developments and its external relations. For my presentation today, I thought we take a step back and set China's growth in historical perspective. There are many people in the world who fear the rise of China, who wonder whether in this re-emergence of China on the global stage, they will see a China that is aggressive and domineering. In official speeches, fine words are used but in inner councils and in dark rooms, real concerns are expressed and sometimes the fears are acted upon. That is in the nature of human society.

Churchill once said that to see far into the future, we must look far back into the past. To read China's re-emergence in this century, it is important to recall China in its earlier incarnations. For us in Southeast Asia, China is deep in our historical memory. Just last week, a replica of an ancient dhow sailed from Oman to Singapore. The original dhow from Tang Dynasty days, carrying 65,000 pieces of pottery, sank 500 miles south of Singapore. The pieces were from different kilns in China. Many had Buddhist and Islamic motifs. That was also the age of Nalanda and the Abbasids. Even then, more than a thousand years ago, the China trade was a huge trade which brought great prosperity to the region. During the Sung Dynasty, when China was a large part of the global economy, the kingdoms of

Edited transcript of talk given at the FutureChina Global Forum, The Ritz-Carlton Millenia Hotel, 13 July 2010.

Southeast Asia and Southern India competed and fought each other over the China trade. In one of those wars, a fleet from South India, the Cholas, defeated Srivijaya.

So when I say re-emergence, there is a particular meaning. Unusual for any other country, China has been able, over a wide geographical expanse, to reconstitute itself again and again. To my European friends, I tell them that it is like the Roman Empire after it was destroyed and broken up, reconstituting itself again and again till modern times. Of course, that never happened in Europe. Till today the nations of Europe have deep tribal loyalties. We see it during the World Cup. It is expressed in their languages, food and wines and in their passions. China is unusual in that over 90% of its population consists of Han Chinese who believe that they belong to a common race. The Americans, because of the exceptional nature of their conception, believe that it is good for everybody in the world to become American. It is good for you to be American and share American values. Then you would be better off and the world will be a better place. There is a natural missionary spirit among Americans, which is expressed from time to time in American foreign policy. For the Han Chinese, there is no such wish. The Han Chinese are a little like the Jews. If you are not born one, there is no need for you to become one. By all means, learn the language, understand the habits, enjoy the food, observe the niceties; but if one day a non-Chinese were to say, "Look, I will become Chinese," everyone will feel a little awkward because if you are not born one, how can you be one? It is like those who convert to Judaism and proclaim themselves Jewish. In formal terms, they may be accepted but in deep emotional terms, that is a different story. And because of this, the Chinese attitude towards "empire", which is really a Western term, is very different from those of empires created by Europe in the age of imperialism. For China, it is the domestic world inside which is decisive. If it coheres, if the waterways and irrigation canals are in good repair, if grain can be easily transported, once the country is well-governed, its economy becomes very productive and prosperous because of the size of the internal market. All this requires central authority and a central bureaucracy. But when the system breaks down, all hell breaks loose and the chaos can go on for decades or centuries, and millions of people die when that happens.

For this reason, those who govern China are always preoccupied by its internal development. Its foreign policy is often geared towards creating an environment which enables the country to be well-governed and its domestic economy to grow. I do not think that China is naturally aggressive. Of course, if you are Korean, Mongolian, Central Asian or Vietnamese, you may have a different view because at various periods in history, they were part of or subordinate to China. From China's perspective, these are border regions which may have to be secured for defensive reasons. Perhaps nothing expresses this mentality more than the repeated reconstruction of the Great Wall of China which has a history going back to the Warring States over 2,000 years ago.

That China should seek to influence developments in the border regions is to be expected. Today, the border regions include all of Southeast Asia. What is important for us to remember is that China's strategic objective is not *lebensraum* or a wish to turn us into subject populations but defensive. Understanding China's defensive concerns, which includes its fear of the U.S., helps us manage our relations with China and benefit from its growth while preserving our own independence and freedom of action.

China's dominant concern is internal because it is a vast country with a huge population. It can only be well-governed if there is central authority. Over centuries, a political culture has evolved which facilitates central rule. High officials owe their loyalty to the centre, not to the localities they come from. With minor variations, regulations bar high officials from holding office within 400 or 500 miles from their place of birth. In China today, provincial leaders, particularly the Party Secretary and the Governor, are generally not from the province itself, and the people accept it. I tell my European friends that it is as if, by practice or regulation, the Chancellor of Germany cannot be German and the President of France cannot be French.

Looking ahead, is China's growth likely to be smooth? Will it grow uninterrupted until it becomes the greatest power on earth? It will not be so simple because the challenges confronting China today are enormous. Keeping so many moving parts in balance is a huge task and an unending task.

The biggest issue in China today is urbanisation — urbanisation on a scale and at a speed never seen before in Chinese history. This is something new. It had always been a rural society in the past, and governing the country was really about making sure that the countryside was productive. Today China is 40% urban. During Mao, it was 20% urban. One day it will be like Taiwan and Korea, becoming 80–90% urban. Urbanisation is creating a whole new set of challenges requiring a whole new set of skills. The Chinese Communist Party achieved power when Mao Zedong broke from the Bolsheviks by capturing power first in the countryside, not through the urban proletariat. All the skills and instincts of the Communist Party are based on control of the countryside, of the peasantry. But now the cities are growing rapidly, creating a new situation: small families, very often one-child, the anonymity of city environments, everyone with a handphone, instant messaging and the Internet. China already has more Internet users than any other country on earth. Urbanization is a challenge not only to the Communist Party but to Confucianism itself. Confucianism, which is what held Chinese society together from the time of the Han dynasty, requires hierarchical social relationships which are dissolving in the modern world. Hierarchies are giving way to complicated networks. Singapore is a city-state and three-quarters Chinese. The stresses we feel here China will experience on a much larger scale in the years to come. Somehow, traditional Confucianism has to be replaced by what I call 'urban Confucianism'. China's Communist Party has to re-invent itself to take into account these dramatic changes in Chinese society. If it succeeds in doing this, China will become the greatest country on earth. But it is not going to be easy because there is no precedent. In fact, no one in the world has a clear solution to the challenge of network society. Everybody is grappling; we are grappling.

In Asia, all the traditional political parties are running into difficulty including the LDP in Japan and the KMT in Taiwan. In Korea, the pattern has not quite settled. In Thailand, the tension between

Bangkok and the rest of the country is serious. In Malaysia, UMNO which was rural-based is still trying to win over city inhabitants. In Indonesia, the Golkar has lost its dominant position. In India, the Congress Party is struggling. All are now confronting urban populations which are disaffected with traditional government. Partly for this reason, the Chinese Government in recent years has taken a deep interest in the Singapore experiment.

Compared to China, Singapore is like a bonsai; it is too small to be of general relevance but it has some genetic similarities. From time to time, researchers and social scientists in China study Singapore and say: "Oh well, if it can work in Singapore, maybe it can work in China." We found in our interaction with China over the years that their interest in the Singapore experiment is episodic. From time to time when it confronts issues and scours the world for solutions, it looks at what Singapore does. Sometimes it likes what it sees, sometimes it does not like what it sees. And then it draws lessons for itself, good and bad. This of course puts Singapore in a rather interesting position *vis-à-vis* China.

When people say China is going to dominate the world, they worry that China is not only going to become very strong economically, but that it will also seek to subjugate others and force them to behave like Chinese. I do not think that will happen because that goes against the grain of Chinese history and Chinese civilisation. Chinese statecraft over the years, mostly defensive in its fundamental objectives, has always been to treat foreigners as foreigners, making a clear distinction between what is within and what is outside, between *nei* (内) and *wai* (外). Elaborate methods are used to handle what is outside so that it is not a threat to what is inside. We see this again and again expressed in modern terms in China's policies. So when it comes to WTO trade liberalisation, trade yes, this yes, that yes, but when it impinges upon core structures — the commanding heights of the state economy, cultural issues — I do not think China, whoever governs China, will ever allow the world outside to determine how the country is governed within. Take, for example, the recent quarrel with Google over how it should operate in China. The Chinese did not want it to become a big problem but Google on its own wanted to politicise it. Of course once you politicise it, then China has no choice but to stick to its fundamental principles. Google has since stepped down, and decided, let's handle this in a pragmatic way, and China is prepared to handle it in a pragmatic way. Insofar as an issue does not impinge upon its core interests, they can be flexible. But if it does, well, that is a separate matter.

In the 19th century, after the Opium War, China lost control of its financial system. Some years ago, a senior LDP politician told me that by 1860 or so, Japanese ships landing on the Asian mainland would be inspected not by Asians but by Europeans. Japan knew that unless it quickly recreated itself, it too would suffer the fate of China. But unfortunately Japan thought the solution was to become a competing imperialism and that led to grief. For this reason, while China will benefit from the international financial system, while it will allow its own financial industry to be opened up, when it comes to core structures, it will never allow itself to lose its sense of autonomy. Policies governing finance, media, culture, strategic state industries cannot depart from this imperative.

China's uniqueness is linked to the nature of the Chinese language itself especially the use of ideographs. As a child, it's easier to read Chinese characters than alphabetic words because Chinese characters are pictures. Little children of two to three years old can recognise Chinese words before they can read alphabetic words. As an adult, alphabetic words are more convenient. Chinese is a language which is difficult to access as an adult. But if you are born into it, then it becomes a part of you naturally. Some scholars have described the Chinese character system as a digital system because it is not phonetic, so it does not alter over time. The same characters can be read today as they were 1,000 years ago, 2,000 years ago. For alphabetic languages, that cannot be done because the written word changes with the sound.

Looking ahead, if China succeeds in becoming strong and powerful, with its influence radiating into a much wider region, what will the world be like? However strong China becomes, I do not think that the world will ever come under a *Pax Sinica*. To begin with, the world is too big for that. Also, China will always be too internally preoccupied to have aspirations for global dominance. China is not interested in making the Myanmar people democratic, or in making Muslims Confucianist. China is quite prepared to accept the world as it is with all its diversity, so long as "you" do not threaten "me" (China). But there has to be a certain structural stability, for that it is in the nature of political power. And it will be a multi-polar world. In our part of the world, in Asia, there will be three major poles — China, the US and India. It is this triangle and how the poles interact with one another which will decide the big issues of war and peace in this century. Sino-US relations have already been discussed. I believe Minister Mentor (MM) Lee talked about it last night. US Ambassador Jon Huntsman also addressed you. So I think there is no need for me to go over ground which is already familiar to you, and which some of you know more about than I do.

But I would like to talk a little about India because India, in terms of size and depth of civilisation, is comparable to China. The two countries, really two civilisations, have never fought each other except for a border war in 1962. This is because China and India are separated by the high Himalayas and the great deserts of Central Asia. There was some contact through traders. Monks did carry ideas and knowledge between them. China and India also interacted through Southeast Asia which has always served as a buffer. There is deep respect for each other as an ancient people. The Chinese traditionally see India as a source of wisdom including Buddhism and gongfu (功夫) and a source of knowledge including mathematics and astronomy. The Indians on their side of the Himalayas have always known that there is a great realm beyond ruled by an emperor who commanded the resources of a vast economy. China was the No. 1 trading partner of British India in the 19th century. China has become India's No. 1 trading partner again, and bilateral trade continues to grow strongly.

A few years ago, the Nathu La Pass between the Siliguri corridor of India and Tibet was reopened. When I visited Tibet last August, a local official told me that the gaoyuan tielu (高原铁路, high railroad) from Xining to Lhasa would soon be extended to Shigatse. He told me that it would pass near the Nathu La Pass. If the Indian government agrees, the Chinese rail system could be connected to the Indian rail system. It would only be a short connection. Calcutta is less than a thousand kilometers from Lhasa. Such a link would give that part of China much easier access to the sea. When I mention this to my Indian friends, they have mixed feelings because the 1962 War is still deeply etched in their memory, a scar not completely healed. In contrast, most Chinese are not even aware of the war. But I believe that India and China will gradually draw closer because there is no natural antipathy between them. It will take time to resolve the border disputes of course. But the benefits of trade and economic cooperation are overwhelming. Each can benefit the other hugely.

For this reason, I and some others have been involved in a project to revive the ancient university of Nalanda which existed from the 5th to the 12th century. It was arguably the world's first university. At its peak, it had 10,000 students from all over Asia. It was the university which the great Tang monk Xuanzang (玄奘) went to. He was there for many years. Yijing (义净) went there after him, by sea through Sumatra. It was from the record of Xuanzang, *Da Tang Xiyu Ji* (大唐西域记) written more than a thousand years ago that India rediscovered a large chunk of its history. Yijing also left an interesting account. We are hoping that by reviving Nalanda as a modern international university, we can bring scholars from all over Asia, indeed from all over the world, together and help create better conditions for a peaceful 21st century. Nalanda is a project financed by the Indian government supported by all the leaders of the East Asian Summit.

There are people who think that they can use India to counterbalance China. To me, that is much too simplistic. Yes, India is the world's biggest democracy and that is often trotted out as an explanation why India and America are natural partners. For certain issues, yes, America and India are natural partners. For other issues like climate change, India and China are natural partners. I believe each will, in the end, calculate according to its own interests. India is too old, too wise, too spiritual, too worldly, to be anything but itself. Democracy is one layer, but there are many layers in India's long history, going down many kilometres.

I think it is mentioned in the Upanishads that the Hindu pantheon has 33 crore gods — that is, 330 million gods and goddesses! Which is quite mind-boggling. Of course, the Indians also believe in one spiritual essence. Over the centuries, there is no aspect of the human condition which the Indians have not experienced or thought about or tried to explain. India will always be India. It is not going to be made use of by anyone. It will act in its own self-interest. There are therefore three independent poles — China, the US and India — and each has its own deep nature.

I do not believe that America is in decline as some people like to think. America is the new world. It created a new political culture, a new social culture, based upon free individuals joining it. It is a little like the Internet protocol, TCP/IP. If you accept the protocol, you can join America. You can be Chinese or Jewish or Arabic — once you take the pledge and accept the laws, you are part of America. Because the culture is open-ended, it seeks to extend its reach to the rest of the world. From another perspective, the globalisation that we see today is an American globalisation. It is American culture, American norms, American standards which are hyperlinking Chinese, Indians, Europeans and others in the world today, enabling us all to be part of a common economic system.

China cannot provide that globalisation software because China will always be internally preoccupied and to the extent that it is interested in the world outside, it is so that its internal management can be improved, and always in self-defence. China is not interested to create a *Pax Sinica*, or to have its own version of the TCP/IP. Yes, it has Confucius Institutes; it encourages you to learn Chinese and so on, but like the Jews, if you are not born one, thank you very much. Whereas with America, it is different. What will link China and India together? Not Chinese software, not Hindu software; it will be American software through American universities, through the English language, through Anglo-Saxon rules of trade and international finance. This is an interesting multipolar world we are entering; a China which is re-emerging powerfully, an India which is also growing but which will be a pole unto itself and an America which is not only a reality, but also a necessity.

Thank you.

**Transcript of Q&A Session**

**Moderator MP Josephine Teo**: Minister, I would like to ask you about our ASEAN neighbours. In your interactions with them, what do you sense as their attitude towards China? And what is it that consumes the minds of the leaders in ASEAN when they think of the re-emergent China?

**Minister George Yeo**: Even when China was down, when it was economically inconsequential, all the countries of Southeast Asia bar none had a certain deep respect for China because they remember the China of the Qing Dynasty, they remember the voyages of Zheng He. All over Southeast Asia, there are Chinese communities which, by their performance and their abilities, are a reminder to them of what China can become again. For this reason the re-emergence of China is not completely unexpected among the countries in Southeast Asia and as the realities impinge upon them, in trade numbers, in visits and so on, the responses, which have historical antecedence, all come back. They do not want to be dominated by China but they want China's friendship. They are careful about impinging on China's core interests but at the same time, instinctively, they want diversification. Take the example of Myanmar. Myanmar, because of the Western embargo, has had to depend a lot on China. China has a lot of influence in Myanmar. But Myanmar does not want to be part of the Chinese realm. It prefers to remain in ASEAN even though it gets criticised every time we meet. But it is prepared to bear with all that because ASEAN gives it some room to play. India, which is also a neighbouring country to Myanmar, doesn't want China to have exclusive influence so it also keeps its border with Myanmar open. I was quite surprised to read a recent report that, between India and Myanmar, they have decided to reopen the old Stilwell Road from Arunachal Pradesh into northern Myanmar. We know part of Arunachal Pradesh is claimed by China but I think that the Myanmar government has decided that it would act in its own self-interest and open up the border region because it would help its own development. I would say that you find countries of Southeast Asia respectful of China, wanting China's friendship and at that same time wanting diversification and wanting to have friends in all directions.

**Question**: Good afternoon, sir. My name is Chan Zhixing and I'm a third year law student from the Singapore Management University (SMU). You mentioned about elements of *nei* (internal) and *wai* (external). My question is: What are some of the guiding principles which determine what is *nei* and what is *wai* from a Chinese perspective? Do we know what is considered important to them, what is their core interest, but what is the guiding principle for them in deciding whether something is internal or external?

**Minister**: You know, it's hard to reduce this into rules. I think those of us who are raised as Chinese instinctively feel the distinction, and learn to apply it as a core principle — learning as a young child how to deal with people who are not like you. And one important way to treat those who are not like you is to be extra nice to them. You always treat strangers better than your own people because you are afraid of strangers. So the best food, the best items are reserved for strangers. [Laughter] Among yourselves you get the second best, but when a foreigner comes, try to win him over by generosity because you are afraid of him. How do you define that? Is it genetic? It is not genetic because Han people are genetically very diverse. Is it a fixed set of cultural norms? But the norms in the Northeast are very different from the norms in Gansu which are very different from the norms in the South. Even the Chinese outside China often make this clear distinction between *nei* and *wai.* If you talk to Indonesian Chinese, or Malaysian Chinese, they also make that distinction. Even among Chinese who are more assimilated in the Philippines and Thailand, you often find the same instinct expressed. But I am hard put to say, look, these are the hundred rules by which you distinguish inside from outside.

**Moderator**: Well, even our grandparents think of us as *nei sun* (paternal grandson) or *wai sun* (maternal grandson). When we visit China as *wai bin* (foreign visitor) we have to pay higher entrance fees. So sometimes if we can get away with it, it's ok to pretend to be *nei bin* (domestic visitor). [Laughter]. But Minister, I have another question that I would like to pose to you. You said very briefly earlier that there are episodic levels of interest in Singapore from the Chinese and sometimes they like what they see in Singapore, sometimes they don't like what they see — that got me very interested. In your interactions, what have you uncovered as likeable aspects and not-so-likeable aspects, as far as the Chinese are concerned?

**Minister**: You mean, what they like of us and what they don't like of us?

**Moderator**: That's right.

**Minister**: Well, I think because Singapore is so small and has a different history, there are limits to what the Singapore model can hold to the Chinese. At the same time, the leaders on the Mainland know that there are deep historical and cultural connections between Singapore and China going back to the Qing Dynasty. Wan Qing Yuan provides a good example. It was the house which Sun Zhongshan lived in when he was in Singapore. He was there eight times, he lived in the house six times with his mistress. I think three or four of the uprisings in China were organised in Singapore and the money was collected in Singapore. Six months after the Tong Meng Hui, the precursor of the Kuomintang, was established in Tokyo, the Southeast Asian branch was established in Singapore. The KMT flag, which is the flag of Taiwan today, was chosen from four designs shortlisted in a competition held in Singapore. Based on the design finally chosen, the wife of the owner of the bungalow Teo Eng Hock, who was our Defence Minister's great granduncle, sewed together the flag and that original flag today is in the KMT Museum in Taipei. Then during the anti-Japanese struggle in China, Singapore was a major base for the raising of funds to help China. Singapore was the headquarters. Many discussions were held in the Ee Hoe Hean Club which was the main Chinese businessman club. It still exists today, recently refurbished. The Japanese Army, when it drew up plans in Taiwan for the invasion of Malaya and Singapore, also prepared a list of thousands of Chinese community leaders in Singapore to be neutralised. So it was not an accident that after Nanjing, the place where the greatest slaughter took place was in Singapore. And then after that, the great twists and turns in China all had their reflections here in Singapore. A scholar recently attributed the decline of the left wing in Singapore, including the Barisan Socialis, to the aping of Cultural Revolution policies and tactics which were out of line with the reality of Singapore. Under Mao, the contacts were minimal, but after Mao, when China began opening up, when Deng Xiaoping was trying to find a new way forward for China, Singapore became an inspiration to China because of the cultural and historical connections. If Singapore could succeed, why can't China succeed? China has more people, cleverer people, a prouder tradition. When the special economic zones were established, the Chinese appointed Dr Goh Keng Swee as Adviser to State Councillor Gu Mu. Whether it was special economic zones or industrial townships, Singapore provided China with a ready model to abstract lessons from. The Chinese learn fast. Once they think they know, they move on and Singapore ceases to be of interest. However, I notice in recent years a new interest in Singapore's management of urban politics. The PAP is probably the most successful urban political party in Asia, and the Chinese want to know what is the secret. Every year, many Chinese delegations visit our constituencies and observe how our Members of Parliament conduct their Meet-the-People sessions. Well, if we can play a helpful role to China, we should. It costs us nothing, and a strong China, a wealthy China, is good for Singapore. We hope also that it is not just China learning from our mistakes and failures; I think we should also have the good sense and wisdom, the humility, to learn from China's experiences, and in the process, also improve ourselves and keeping the relevance of our own model.

**Moderator**: On that note Minister, I have a question about the role of Singapore. Is it a farfetched idea to think of Singapore as a bridge between China and the world? If there is one thing we can do to strengthen ourselves...?

**Minister**: No, Singapore cannot be a bridge. A bridge suggests a certain exclusive channel of communication. We are in a networked world, there are numerous, almost infinite number of bypasses. What Singapore can do...

**Moderator**: So *a* bridge rather than *the* bridge.

**Minister**: It can be a node. If we are creative, if we are far-seeing, we can enlarge this node and increase its connectivity to other nodes. But if we become self-satisfied or inward-looking, then we will shrink and become less relevant to others. But it is becoming a networked world, and everybody has bypasses. No one is indispensable.

**Moderator**: And the one thing we can do to strengthen ourselves as that node?

**Minister**: It is a little paradoxical, that the more we want to strengthen our links with China, the more we must strengthen our links to other parts of the world. Because if you look at it like a node in the brain with many synaptic connections, the more connected we are to India, to Southeast Asia, to Europe, to Japan, to Africa, the more valuable are our links to China. The key to Singapore's good relations with China is in our ability to grow synaptic connections to other parts of the world, in particular the parts of the world which in an earlier age of globalisation created Singapore. It was the age of the British Empire which brought Indians, which brought Jews from Baghdad through Calcutta to Singapore, which brought Indonesians and Malaysians, Thais and Vietnamese, Australians and Japanese, here. All those links which created us in the 19th century we should now revive, because these are now the links which will supply us our life nutrients in this century to grow and to prosper.

**Moderator**: Well ladies and gentlemen, although we invited Minister George Yeo to speak to us on China, but you can see from the breadth of his knowledge and his interest in history, and also his keen observation of everything that's going around in the world, you do not get just China, you will get synapses, you will get TCP/IP, you will get everything else that is related to this in the most interesting, stimulating and engaging way. May I just ask all of us to just show our appreciation to Mr George Yeo for sharing with us so generously. Thank you so much!

# The Tree and the Bush: Re-emergence of China and India on the Global Stage

*Each doffs its hat to the other as an ancient civilisation.*

## Introduction

China and India are old civilisations. When the Portuguese and the Spanish braved the oceans at the end of the 15th century, it was to find alternative routes to the east — to India, the Spice Islands and China. One was often confused for the other. Hence native Americans were called 'Indians' by Columbus. For the Middle East and Southeast Asia, however, China and Indian reside deep in the historical memory, going back to the mist of early times.

The current rise of China and India is therefore but a re-emergence of ancient peoples on the global stage. In recent centuries, both came to be dominated by western powers. India was fully colonised; China partially so. Each responded in a different way according to its own nature and circumstances. As they become major powers again, the western domination of the world will recede. In its place, a multipolar reality will define this century, as was indeed the case for much of human history. Provided human beings do not go mad again, which one can never say for sure, the prospects for continuing peace and development in the coming decades are good.

---

7th Tsai Lecture delivered at Harvard University Asia Center, 7 March 2012 when George Yeo was an Ezra Vogel Distinguished Visitor.

## China's History and Response to the West

Emperor Qianlong's arrogant response to Lord McCartney's mission in 1793 was part of Qing China's long, painful decline. Even after the Opium War, the western intrusion was seen not as a fundamental challenge but as a secondary problem. Suppressing the Taiping Rebellion was far more important. Non-Manchu Han commanders like Zeng Guofan and Zuo Zongtang played major roles. Because the Communists in the 20th century viewed Taiping rebels as proto-revolutionaries, Zeng Guofan was vilified in the official accounts until recently. In the case of Zuo Zongtang, however, the Communists honoured him for defeating a Uighur rebellion in Xinjiang in a brilliant but brutal campaign which was sustained by a carefully-prepared supply line stretching thousands of kilometres. Though corrupt, the statecraft of Qing China remained strategic and sophisticated. Without that grand strategy, the China inherited by Republican China and the People's Republic would have been shorn not only of Mongolia but of Xinjiang and Tibet as well.

Japan's aggression was closely linked to western aggression. Not long after the Opium War, all Japanese ships arriving on mainland Asia were inspected by western officials. It was only a matter of time before Japan suffered the same fate as China and India. This led to the Meiji Restoration and a fierce determination to identify Japan with the west. Out of necessity and ambition, Japan became a competing imperial power. Proximity meant that the most dangerous competitor to Japan for supremacy on the Asian mainland was Russia which it overcame after sinking the Russian fleet in the Battle of Tsushima in 1905.

The problem for China in the 19th century and much of the 20th century was not statecraft but internal decay that rendered it progressively vulnerable to external threats. After many failed attempts, the 1911 Revolution led by Sun Yat-sen established China as a republic. But that only opened a new chapter in the internal struggle. For Chiang Kai-shek, the Japanese invasion was a distraction from the fight against the Communists. For Mao Zedong, it was an opportunity to gain the support of the Chinese people.

Even after the People's Republic was established in 1949, the struggle continued for the mind and soul of the Chinese people. It was only after Mao died and Deng Xiaoping took over in 1978 that China's astonishing development began. Without the creative destruction of over a hundred years, in the Schumpeterian sense, that explosive growth could not have happened. Such is the long cycle of Chinese history and its continuity. As it were, China had to retreat deep into itself first before reopening to the world outside. After a hundred years, the People's Republic is finally carrying out its duty of compiling the official history of the Qing Dynasty, the 25th official history since Sima Qian. For the official history of the People's Republic, we might have to wait a few more centuries.

Because the past is so deeply embedded in the present, China is not likely to become an imperial power in the pattern of the west. That it should become more self-confident and assertive is to be expected, even militarily. But it would go against the grain for China to seek colonisation and the conversion of others to Chineseness. Unlike Americans and Muslims, it is not in the nature of the Chinese to be missionary. In this regard, Chineseness is like Jewishness. If you are not born one, there is no need for you to become one. Converts are tolerated but not really welcome. Sinicisation when it does take place along China's borderlands is osmotic and over decades and centuries, rarely if ever imposed by force.

Against this historical backdrop, it is unlikely that China and the US will go to war despite inevitable conflict of interest. While trials of strength there will be episodically, China will not be encroaching on distant countries the way the western powers and Japan encroached on China in the past. (China's relationship with neighbours on the border like Korea, Mongolia, Central Asia and Vietnam is a different matter. Depending on the cycles of Chinese dynasties, they were either a part of the empire, its enemies or in its penumbra.) China will fight to defend its interests but it is unlikely to be aggressive like the European powers during the age of colonialism. From this perspective, the way Chinese Vice President Xi Jinping conducted his recent visit to the US was in keeping with an old pattern of behaviour.

### India's Differences from China and Its Response to the West

Both China and India have been described as civilisational states. But while historical China has often been a strong state, historical India was frequently not, and certainly never over the entire sub-continent until the British arrived. For example, the idea of Taiwan being independent of China is something emotionally unacceptable to the Chinese mind, even among ethnic Chinese in the diaspora. But the idea of Pakistan and Bangladesh being independent, while it may be matter of regret to some Indians, is not as keenly felt.

India's internal divisions facilitated its colonisation by the British. By the time the British were expanding in Bengal, the Mughals were already in decline. The lack of a single legitimate historical model also made it much easier for Indians to adopt Anglo-Saxon institutions as their own after independence. The fact that India did not have to gain independence through armed struggle helped. Gandhi, Nehru, Jinnah and Bose were all much more westernised than their Chinese equivalents. Because China was only semi-colonised, its westernisation was correspondingly shallower even before the Communists took over in 1949, and mainly confined to the concession areas. Communism itself was a western idea but Chinese Communism under Mao and his successors is strongly marked by Chinese characteristics.

India's heterogeneity stands in sharp contrast to China's homogeneity where Han people make up over 90% of the population. In India, it is inconceivable that the chief executive of a state should not be from that state. In China, it is the rule from the Ming Dynasty that the chief executive of a province cannot be from that province, an arrangement which is by and large accepted by ordinary Chinese. Since independence, more and more states in India have been created to better reflect the diverse makeup of the country. In China, provincial lines have historically been drawn to prevent sub-groups from becoming too powerful.

India's politics therefore has a different rhythm from China's. India is always in ferment which is probably why it will never have a revolution. There is no central order to overthrow and replace. Instead, to paraphrase Amartya Sen, the Indian is endlessly argumentative. It is relatively easy to remember the main outline of China's history because the core empire breaks up and reunites ever so often. Indian history in contrast is fractured with details.

China's dynastic cycles are persistent. At the beginning of each dynasty in China, the taxes are light but the state coffers are full. At the end of the dynasty, the taxes are crushing while the treasury is empty. Property rights are fairly distributed at the beginning and highly concentrated at the end. If one looks at the Chinese revolution from 1911 all the way to the Cultural Revolution, it was one gigantic effort to re-gather property rights into the hands of the collective. I remember once talking to my maternal grandfather in my mother's ancestral home in Chaozhou not long after Deng opened up the country. He recalled how documents kept in the attic were burnt during the Cultural Revolution. This happened all over China. No one wanted to be accused of harbouring ambitions to reclaim old properties. That was the final clearing of the land before reconstruction on a continental scale could begin. China could embark on gargantuan public projects today because property rights are largely collective.

Acquiring land for development in India is a different matter and often subject to protracted litigation. Because of this, urban growth is higgledy-piggledy. Despite all the difficulties, however, the growth is widespread and organic. Infrastructure is improving year by year and city amenities are getting better, although nothing like in China.

However, India has one critical long-term advantage over China which is its demographic profile. China's population will reach a maximum of about 1.5 or 1.6 billion after which its population will decline like Japan's. Although the Chinese Government is relaxing population control, the declining birth rate is hard to reverse. Ethnic Chinese populations all over the world face this problem regardless of public policy. Declining fecundity has its roots in the republican revolution. Once women are liberated and educated, many do not want more than one or two children if they marry at all, unless the menfolk are prepared to take on a different role in the family. India faces this problem but to a significantly lesser degree. Its population will overtake China's in about 20 years and with a healthier age profile.

In terms of organic growth, China is like a magnificent Californian redwood adding height each year. India, in contrast, is more akin to a big bush, growing all over the place. While the tree will stop growing and one day will collapse with a big bang, the bush shoots off in new directions even as some parts are dying. In terms of biomass, the weight of the bush is considerable and may eventually be comparable to that of the tree.

What keeps the bush coherent are its roots in Indian civilisation. It is hard to define what that civilisation consists of when it is so diverse and divided. But, in the same way as one might trace the coherence of western civilisation to its beginnings in Greece, Rome and Judeo-Christianity, there is in Indian civilisation a deep common Hindu-Jain-Buddhist substrate with relatively recent Mughal-British overlays. In the Hindu pantheon, there are three hundred million deities. Whether gods make us in their image or we make gods in our image, that number says something about the Indian mind and its acceptance of diversity. My good friend Indian Home Minister Chidambaram once explained to me how the many regional stories of Shiva show no contradiction with one another. Visiting an air-conditioned sanctum for Shiva at the Sri Meenakshi Temple in India's deep south, a priest whispered to me that where Shiva came from in Kailash, it is cold and some air-conditioning in Madurai is appropriate.

Because of what India is, the US does not feel threatened by India at all. There is no equivalent legacy of the Korean and Vietnam wars. At one level, because of the English language and Anglo-Saxon institutions, India seems much more like the west than China. India is also said to be the world's largest democracy although that is often put across in a patronising way. In the English-speaking world, Indians hold high positions in the corporate world, in international organisations and in academia. And they are entering politics in growing numbers. The NRI (non-resident Indian) network is a huge asset for India.

However, despite being closer to the US than China, India will not be used by the US against China unless this is in its own interest. Particularly on issues vital to it like world trade, climate change, Iran,

Afghanistan and Myanmar, India is often prepared to take positions opposed to the US. In a number of areas, India will cooperate with China for mutual benefit. For example, in climate talks, India finds common cause with China. Both are part of the BRIC (Brazil, Russia, India, China) grouping which holds regular summits. In return for China supporting India as an observer in SCO (Shanghai Cooperation Organisation), India supports China as an observer in SAARC (South Asia Association for Regional Cooperation).

**Past, Present and Future Relationship between China and India**

Apart from the 1962 War, there has been no major conflict between China and India in their long history of contact as neighbouring civilisations. This was mainly because of geography. The high Himalayas separated them. In Central and Southeast Asia, smaller states in between provide a wide buffer.

The Buddhist connection is well-known. Monks do not travel on their own. It was along the overland and maritime silk routes that they were transported on animals or by ship. Over the centuries, through these silk routes, the two civilisations learnt from each other in many fields of human knowledge from philosophy, mathematics and astronomy to practical subjects like meditative practices, ship design and sugar-making. Recently, as part of PM Wen Jiabao's visit to India, both sides agreed to compile an encyclopedia of their contact in different fields from the earliest times. Properly done, this work should be carried out like Joseph Needham's monumental study of *Science and Civilization in China* which continues after his death. Even with what we know today, it is clear that each built upon the contribution of the other.

The 1962 War was an aberration which left a deep scar in the Indian psyche. It arose from border disputes which ought not to be an insuperable obstacle to better relations. India's claims are based on the McMahon Line, an agreement between the British and the local Tibetan government at a time when the Raj recognised Qing China as suzerain over Tibet. Curiously, the British Foreign Secretary, when specifically asked, equated suzerainty to sovereignty a few years ago. From the 50s to the 80s, China was quite prepared to settle on the line of control, which means China keeping Aksai Chin in return for India keeping Arunachal Pradesh. And, when China delineated its border with Myanmar in 1960, it accepted the McMahon Line as the basis of negotiation. But India was not prepared to accept that exchange with China for a long time. When India came round to it in the 90s, it was China which became difficult especially over Tawang where the 6th Dalai Lama was born. When the present Dalai Lama indicated that he might reincarnate outside Tibet, the natural supposition was that it could be in Tawang. China naturally views this as a provocation. The border disputes between China and India have therefore become hostage to the Tibetan question.

The political relationship between China and India lags behind the economic relationship which has been growing strongly. China is already India's biggest trading partner. Bilateral trade exceeded US$70b last year and is expected to hit US$100b in 2015. China has greatly improved road, rail, air and electronic connections to the Tibetan plateau and wants to link them to Indian networks through the mountain passes. With Myanmar opening up, Southeast Asia will again become a major connector between China and India. Chinese cities like Chongqing and Kunming are eager for political obstacles to be removed because of their geographical positions. Kolkata will benefit hugely too as it is less than a thousand kilometres by road from Lhasa and a little over 2 hours by air from Kunming. When Japan controlled the Chinese coast, it was from Bengal and Bihar through Burma and over the Hump that Kuomintang China was kept supplied.

India's fear of Pakistan complicates the bilateral relationship between China and India. During the Cold War, India and Pakistan belonged to opposite camps. Supported by the Americans, Pakistan facilitated the establishment of radical Islamic bases on its side of the border to support the mujahideen in Afghanistan against the Soviet Union. That Frankenstein has come to haunt both the US and Pakistan. From worrying *about* Pakistan, India now worries *for* Pakistan. This is a profound change in India's attitude. While bilateral relations between India and Pakistan are far from normal, they have improved considerably. China in turn maintains a careful balance between historical friendship with Pakistan and growing economic and political relationship with India. If this positive trend continues, Tibet will gradually become less of an issue and serious border negotiations can then take place. Even if negotiations are slow to conclude, the overall relationship between China and India is more likely to improve than not.

Looking ahead to the second half of the century, the Sino-Indian relationship may become as important as the Sino-US relationship in global affairs. Together China and India make up 40% of the world's population and will probably supply more than half its brainpower. In every field of human endeavor, how Chinese and Indians work together will matter a great deal. Their current role in Silicon Valley presages the world that is to come.

Over the long run, it is the cultural relationship between China and India that will matter most. Today, they frequently stereotype each other. Coming from Singapore where the mandalas of China and India overlap, to use Wang Gungwu's elegant phrase, there is clearly considerable prejudice and misunderstanding between them. At the same time, each doffs its hat to the other as an ancient civilisation. Every Chinese knows that Buddhism came from India. One Indian ambassador in Beijing told me how he was frequently received like a papal nuncio when visiting Buddhist temples in China.

If China and India can maintain stable relations in the coming decades, there is great hope for the future. It is not too optimistic to envisage an Asia-Pacific region stretching across the Pacific to India with over 60% of the world's population living in relative peace and enjoying economic development for years to come. Of course minor conflicts there will be from time to time. If instead China and India are locked in confrontation, the future will be troubled. We must expect some third parties to sow seeds of discord between them.

Working for good long-term relations between China and India is therefore a worthwhile cause. There is no danger that they will get too close to each other and give the rest of us problems. China and India as connected but separate poles will make a multipolar world more stable. In such a dispensation, smaller countries will enjoy greater autonomy of action.

It is partly to make a modest contribution to better long-term Sino-Indian relations that Amartya Sen, Sugata Bose, myself and others have been promoting the revival of Nalanda University. For centuries it was a centre of learning which brought learned people, mostly Buddhist monks, from all parts of Asia together. This project has been blessed by leaders of the East Asian Summit which now includes the US. An Asia in peace and playing a bigger role in world affairs will also help untangle the knotted problems in the Middle East.

### Middle East and Islam

Instability in the Middle East poses a serious challenge not only to the west but to Russia, China, India and Africa as well because of Muslim extremism and possible disruption of energy supply. But perspectives of the Middle East from different parts of the world differ. While the west often views Islam as threatening because of their long history of conflict, for China, Islam is only a problem to the extent that it encourages rebellion among Muslim minority groups. There is no deep historical antipathy between Islam and China. For India, the picture is mixed. Some Indians view Islam in the same way as the west. But many do not, and there are enough historical examples to support a range of views.

Iran is a case in point. For the west, Iran is a feared opponent after the Islamic revolution. For Israel, Iran is an existential threat. For China, Iran or Persia has been a friend for most of its history. For India, Persia is associated with high civilisation and culture.

The influence of China and India in the Middle East is bound to grow. While this weakens the position of the west in the nearer term, the rise of Asia will relax many of the tensions in the longer term, which is good for the west. Iranians, Arabs, Ayatollahs, Sheikhs and Muslim Brothers will all feel less trapped in what is often now seen as a Manichean conflict with the west. The view of China and India from the Middle East is very different from the view of the US and Europe. Perhaps to make the point, the first countries Saudi King Abdullah visited when he became king were China and India, with Malaysia as the third.

It was not very long ago that the Raj in Delhi controlled the Gulf and the Indian rupee was common currency. Bollywood movies and Hindi music are part of popular culture. India not only supplies a part of the manpower needed in the Gulf, it provides much of the brainpower deployed to run systems and services in the private and public sectors. Because of history and proximity, India's role in shaping the future of the Middle East will be greater that of China. China's advantage is its veto power on the UN Security Council.

### Changing Tides

The simultaneous re-emergence of China and India on the global stage is lifting not only Asia and the rest of the developing world as well. The contribution of growing Asian middle classes to global investment and consumption is increasing year by year. With their favourable resource-to-population ratio, Latin America and Africa are bound to benefit more and more.

For those living in developed countries, the rise of Asia is both a threat and an opportunity. Many individuals face increased competition. They have to work harder and maybe for less pay. Existing government benefits cannot be sustained. In contrast, those with knowledge, capital and networks profit from cheaper access to land and labor overseas, and selling to growth markets. As income distribution worsens, the politics in many developed countries sour and forging a common response to new challenges becomes harder.

The tides are changing regardless of whom the winners and losers are. Whether as countries, corporations, congregations, tribes, families or individuals, how we reposition ourselves for the ebbs and flows will affect our chances of success decisively. Of course nothing is inevitable in human affairs. For example, we do not know what new eruption may occur in the Middle East. The Iranian nuclear program is an obvious source of concern. There also the unknown unknowns. The biggest mistake is clinging to old positions in the hope that what is happening is transient and will blow away. It will not because what we are witnessing is a sea change.

# ASEAN IN THE NEW GLOBAL ECONOMY

*...we in ASEAN are not a great power, but we are not unimportant. If we play our role, we can create a better Asia, and that better Asia will usher in a better world.*

His Excellency, distinguished guests, friends, ladies and gentleman

Looking ahead, there are two possible choices for ASEAN: either we become more integrated and our citizens feel a greater sense of ASEAN citizenship in addition to national citizenship, or we begin to disintegrate.

**South China Sea Dispute**

I would like to spend a little bit of time talking about the failure of the recent foreign ministers' meeting in Cambodia to issue a joint communique because of disagreement over the South China Sea. That failure should sound a loud alarm to us to put things right because if we do not put things right, things can go badly wrong. It is natural for the foreign ministry of each claimant country to say that its claim is incontrovertible, but the claims do overlap. When incontrovertible claims overlap, the claims cannot all be incontrovertible. And unless there is recognition that there are different points of view, it is not possible to sit down, have a discussion, and try to work out win-win outcomes.

Many problems in life cannot be solved immediately, they can only be managed; and we must leave the future to solve some of

Edited transcript of George Yeo's keynote speech at the ASEAN Business Club Dinner, Bangkok, Thailand, 14 August 2012.

our problems. China's nine-dash claim in the South China Sea seems to many in Southeast Asia to be excessive, almost turning the South China Sea into a Chinese lake. But in fact, China's claim is not without a certain historical basis. To begin with, it is not a new claim. It was an old claim from the Republic of China under Chiang Kai-shek. And when China drew that map, the predecessor powers of Southeast Asia — the Americans, the British, the French, the Dutch — did not object. Well, maybe they thought China was in such a mess at that time, they could ignore what China claimed.

But China was involved as a big power in some of the most important discussions that shaped the post Second World War world. When the Japanese invaded China in 1937, they were at war with China but not yet at war with the European powers or America. And as part of that war they occupied coastal China and the South China Sea islands, and incorporated them into their maps. So in a court of law, the Chinese claim is not to be immediately dismissed. But, at the same time, the idea that "China's waters stretch all the way to my front yard", that troubles, even outrages, Vietnamese, Filipinos and others.

The claims of the four ASEAN states — Malaysia, Brunei, the Philippines, Vietnam — are mostly based on the United Nations Convention on the Law of the Sea (UNCLOS). When China acceded to UNCLOS, China registered its reservations based on this nine-dash map. So you cannot use UNCLOS as an argument against China.

I was asked about the South China Sea in Manila when I addressed the students of De La Salle University earlier this year. I could sense the grievance and anger. So I went through these arguments with them. I fully understand their feelings as Filipinos. I could empathise with their point of view. But there are other points of view and each government is constrained by its own population not to concede any claim in a negotiation.

Take the Preah Vihear[1] dispute between Thailand and Cambodia as an example. For both sides, it is a highly charged issue. We have to recognise this. The emotion is part of the political reality. In the

[1] The Cambodian–Thai border dispute is an ongoing border dispute between Bangkok and Phnom Penh. It involves claims to 2.4 $km^2$ of land that surrounds the Preah Vihear temple.

case of the Philippines claim to the South China Sea, there is a further complication because the claim is written into their Constitution. If the Philippine Government agreed to joint development, of economic resources, that can be interpreted to be against the Constitution. Of course Sabah[2] is also in the Philippine Constitution, but somehow ways have been found around that.

With Vietnam, it is much more complicated because during the war years, Vietnam conceded China's claims but it then subsequently said it acted under duress. Vietnam's relationship with China goes way back into history, and is rather fraught.

Between Malaysia and China, between Brunei and China, the parties take a more practical approach and so there is no big fuss. And between Malaysia and Brunei, they have settled their own claims between themselves for mutual benefit.

The Americans, sensing unhappiness in certain quarters in ASEAN, thought they should give support but their support is calibrated. I used to tell my American friends when I was in office: "Do come closer, within radar range, but over the horizon please. Because if you come too close, everybody feels very awkward. In any case, you yourself say that your only interest is freedom of navigation and peace in the region, that you don't take sides on the claims." All of us share a common interest in freedom of navigation and peace.

But of course the Chinese are not happy that American aircraft, ships and submarines patrol just outside China's territorial waters with radars and other sensors. In 2001, we had the Hainan spy plane incident which caused bilateral relations to become rather tense and which were only fully repaired after September 11. I remember it well because I was at the APEC meetings in China and witnessed some of the tension that existed between the two sides.

Indonesia, which must always take the leadership role in ASEAN, was very worried by the recent outcome in Cambodia. I was told the President instructed Foreign Minister Marty to visit all

[2]This refers to the North Borneo territorial dispute between the Philippines and Malaysia. The Philippine Constitution stipulates that the territory belongs to the Philippines.

ASEAN capitals and help repair the damage. Pak Marty succeeded in getting ASEAN countries to agree on key points.

### Businesses Rely on a Stable and United ASEAN

We cannot afford a repeat at the Summit. If so, our future will be troubled. We in business have to state our views and speak up if necessary. We have a strong interest in peace and stability. If there is a big fight over the South China Sea and ASEAN itself is divided, we will have no credibility in the eyes of the world. There is no guarantee that ASEAN will always cohere.

During the Cold War we were divided. During a meeting in Luang Prabang some years ago, I climbed a hill one free afternoon and saw rusting anti-aircraft guns pointing in the direction of Thailand. It was not long ago when the Mekong was the line across which two great powers confronted each other. And when Vietnamese divisions crossed the Mekong, between Thailand, Singapore, and Malaysia, we huddled together in the trenches to resist them.

After Vietnam finally settled with China and joined ASEAN, I remember a visit by Nguyen Van Linh[3] to Singapore where he met Lee Kuan Yew at the Istana. After dinner, he held Lee Kuan Yew's hand tightly and asked him to be Vietnam's advisor. Lee Kuan Yew could not believe his ears because for years we were fighting Vietnam at every forum, hammer and tongs, tooth and nail. We were then determined not to allow Vietnam to lay claim over all of French Indo-China because that must mean their overlordship of Southeast Asia.

### Fears Bind ASEAN Together

Time has elapsed and today we have an ASEAN that has come a long way. Year by year, progress can be frustratingly slow. But if we take five-year snapshots, it has not been bad at all. And today, in every ASEAN foreign mission, our national flags fly side by side with the ASEAN flag. That's something that would have been unimaginable even a few years ago.

---

[3] Nguyen Van Linh was the general secretary of the Communist Party of Vietnam.

The reason why ASEAN works is not because we have a natural affection for each other. That does not endure. It is because we share common fears. It is fear that binds, not affection which can be fickle. And the fear is that if we are divided, Southeast Asia will be Balkanised. We will become dispensable pieces on the chessboard of the big powers. We will lose our sovereignty and be much worse off.

Yes, we have differences, and these differences persist. But if we do not come together, we cannot negotiate with China, Japan, US or India on any basis of equality. Each of them will be in a position to bully us individually. For this reason, Vietnam wants to ASEAN-ise the South China Sea issue. China is naturally against it. And this was one of the underlying tensions in the recent meeting in Cambodia. If there is only one big power with us in the room, then of course we have to recognise certain limitations in our negotiating position. But if there are a few big guys in the room when we're negotiating, it is a bit more comfortable. For this reason, it is critical for ASEAN and China to agree on a Code of Conduct in the South China Sea.

## China's Relationship with Smaller Countries and with ASEAN

This is not to say that China is unreasonable when it deals with small countries bilaterally. The fact is, if you look at China's history of borders negotiations, they were often marked by Chinese concessions. I remember once crossing the Yalu River to Dandong in China after visiting North Korea. The Chinese told me that all those little islands in the river near the Chinese side belonged to North Korea. I asked: "How come?" Well, they were given to North Korean on one condition: that the entire river would be open to navigation by both sides. On that basis, China was prepared to be nice to North Korea which was a close ally.

Many years ago, I discussed with Myanmar ministers about how the border between Myanmar and China was delineated in 1960. They told me it was mostly resolved along the McMahon line. The McMahon line was the boundary the British settled with the local Tibetan government at a time when Great Britain recognised China as "suzerain" over Tibet. Qing China never recognised the McMahon

Line. Nevertheless, China under Mao and Deng was prepared to take a practical approach and negotiate with India around the actual line of control. When China negotiated with Myanmar, China was quite happy to settle around the McMahon line.

The point I am making is that it is not in China's interest to bully ASEAN countries because China knows that if ASEAN countries feel bullied, we will invite others into the room and this would give them complications.

And it is for this reason, that in the year 2000, when Premier Zhu Rongji was attending a regional meeting in Singapore — at a time when we in ASEAN were reeling from the Asian financial crisis while China was streaking ahead — he offered a Free Trade Agreement (FTA) between ASEAN and China. At that time the ASEAN leaders did not know how to respond. They thought that China would eat us up if there was an FTA. I remember trade ministers discussing this in Hanoi. It was September 11, 2001. Our handphones were all buzzing because of what was happening in New York. That night, we agreed that we should negotiate the FTA because China wanted it politically but only provided we could get something for it. This led to the early harvest idea which benefited ASEAN countries disproportionately. The following year in Phnom Penh, China and ASEAN leaders signed a framework agreement. At that ceremony, Premier Zhu Rongji said China did not seek for itself an exclusive position in ASEAN.

In other words, China knows that ASEAN will never want to have China as its only friend. ASEAN prefers to be promiscuous, to have many friends. China knows that, we know that, and this creates a more comfortable situation for all of us. In my view, those who argue that China was out to wreck ASEAN at the recent Cambodia meeting are wrong. It is not in China's interest. China of course has territorial interests to defend and does not want those issues to be ASEAN-ised. A divided ASEAN is not in China's interest because the Americans, Indians and others will be sucked in. China needs a peaceful Straits of Malacca because 80% of the oil it imports goes through it.

### Major Powers Want a United ASEAN

Is it in the US interest to divide ASEAN? I also do not think so.

The U.S. knows that if ASEAN is divided, China will be able to pick off ASEAN countries one by one. Can the US match China in this game? Maybe the Philippines would remain with the US but even that I'm not so sure because looking at the trade accounts, China matters more and more to the Philippines. Over the years, the U.S. has decided it is better to go along with ASEAN. The Indians and the Japanese have also come to the same conclusion. In other words, all the major powers want us to be united.

The key is that we ourselves must be united and not allow internal differences to divide us. The big powers are happy to have ASEAN in the lead because we are non-threatening. We have no ICBMs[4], no nuclear submarines, no cruise missiles to threaten anyone, so everybody trusts us to be in the driver's seat. Recently, after the Cambodian meeting, China again affirmed ASEAN's leadership.

### Business Influencing Politics

I applaud Dato' Sri Nazir Razak and your other nine conferees on the creation of the ASEAN Business Club. ASEAN business interests have to work together and make a stronger case for a stronger ASEAN. At critical moments, the voice of business can tip the balance in favour of a more integrated ASEAN.

I told the students at De La Salle University in Manila that there are two ways to look at the South China Sea. One is to see it as a dividing line between China and Southeast Asia. But has that been the South China Sea historically? On the contrary, the South China Sea has always connected China and Southeast Asia. It is through the South China Sea that trade flowed benefiting all parties. That is the history of the maritime silk route. In Malays, we call the islands and peninsulas of Southeast Asia *tanah di bawah angin*, the land below the monsoons. Ships sailing the South China Sea and the Straits of Malacca carried goods and ideas, mixing blood.

---

[4] Inter-continental ballistic missile.

All over Southeast Asia, we find Chinese artefacts going back to the earliest dynasties. If we do genetic testing of Southern Chinese, we will find a lot of Southeast Asian blood and vice versa. Thus, we can either see the South China Sea as a dividing line or as a bridge which links us together.

Between the two futures, between conflict and cooperation, there is much more to be gained from good relations and cooperation. The value of all the oil and gas that lie below is small compared to the value that can be gained through working together. When we set things in perspective, the original unhappiness is actually small. I was involved in negotiating a settlement of railway land between Singapore and Malaysia. In the end, the numbers were puny compared to the stakes involved. And today, between Malaysia and Singapore, we have opened a new chapter in bilateral cooperation.

### ASEAN Needs to Link Up

What we need to do in ASEAN is to link up and improve connectivity, within and between countries, by land, sea, air and the Internet. The moment you throw a bridge, or pave a road, or establish an Internet connection, you create opportunities for arbitrage, for trade, to do new things and grow new businesses. After a while, new vested interests grow, altering the political equation.

You look today — Bangkok Bank, CIMB, and many here in the room including companies in my own group like Shangri-La and Wilmar — what flag do you attach to each of them? It's not easy; you have to attach multiple flags. Increasingly, more and more companies in ASEAN know that if they do not go regional or international, they do not stand a chance. You can hide behind barriers, but that is only good for a few years. You only weaken yourself and, when the protection is removed, you are in danger. Better to create within the ASEAN economic space conditions for the growth of regional companies. I am not being idealistic; there are always nationalist pressures. Within each country there are those who favour liberalisation and those who want protection. There is little point preaching to another country. Within each country, those of us who subscribe to this vision of the future should weigh in so that, at critical moments, governments will make the right decisions.

Today, connectivity is a big, big agenda item for ASEAN. Here, if we are skillful, like a *taiji* exponent, we can borrow energy from the environment around us. China of course wants to build links into Southeast Asia. From Nanning and Kunming to Hanoi, through Laos, through two separate routes to Myanmar, and from there into Thailand. From Kunming, China is building pipelines to Kyaukphyu[5] in Myanmar on the Bay of Bengal.

China wants a fast speed rail, Kunming to Vientiane — agreement already signed, still not moving yet but I think it is going to move — and from there to Bangkok. China's big objective is Bangkok not Vientiene. From Bangkok, it is a short distance to Dawei on the Andaman coast in Myanmar which will enable China to bypass the Malacca Straits.

I went through this exercise with Kerry Logistics. The signs are clear. China wants to come down to Bangkok via Laos. With Vietnam, it is always more complicated. China knows that Vietnam will be more amenable to opening up its northern border if it knows that China has alternative routes into Southeast Asia. The link between Ho Chi Minh City and Bangkok through Cambodia is also improving. Thus, with each year, internal and external borders in ASEAN become more porous facilitating the economic integration of ASEAN with larger Asia.

## Opening of Myanmar Completes the Jigsaw Puzzle

What is absolutely critical is the opening of Myanmar because it has been the missing piece in the entire jigsaw. Myanmar has long borders with both China and India. The opening of that country makes our collective future much brighter. Therefore, we must help Myanmar, in our own interest. We know it is politically complicated. The future depends on the relationship between Aung San Suu Kyi, the Tatmadaw and the ethnic groups.

But there is no way they can go back to the past. The dam has broken. You cannot put the water back. How the water flows into the sea, well, that depends on how the players interact with one another, and how we who are Myanmar's friends are able to influence good

[5] Special Economic Zone of Myanmar.

behaviour by all parties. I am very pleased to hear that Asean Business Club (ABC) is thinking of inviting Aung San Suu Kyi to Jakarta. She has only visited Bangkok during the World Economic Forum and has yet to visit other parts of Asia. Indonesia would be a good place for her to visit.

Once Myanmar is politically, economically, physically and culturally linked to the rest of Southeast Asia, both our North-South links and our East-West links will open up. ASEAN will then link China and India. I remember two road trips I did with other ASEAN foreign ministers. One, from Mukdahan to Savannakhet to Quang Tri, then to Hue and Danang. It went through what was the most heavily bombed piece of real estate on Earth during the Indo-China War. Today, we have peace, villages have become towns, signs of growth everywhere. The following year, we travelled by road from Chiang Rai, crossed the Mekong to Laos and from there to Jinghong in Yunnan. In time to come, we will lose count of the number of bridges crossing the Mekong River. We need better links to Myanmar, to Bangladesh, to India. Of course it will take time and there will be twists and turns. We have to be skillful and create competitive pressures so that those who are slow come under pressure to move faster.

### China-India Relations and Its Impact on ASEAN

Today, the single most important relationship in the world is the Sino-US relationship, but further down the century, China-India relationship will also become very important. Together, China and India account for 40% of the world's population. In terms of brain power, I think they are more like 60% of the world.

So imagine this. We have on one side China, and on the other, India. We are in between and everything that we are, our food, our culture, our habits, our blood, are a mixture of both. Surely, we must have the ability and instinct to benefit from this simultaneous rise of China and India. Between them, there is a cultural gap. You watch them when they interact, whether in the UN or in business circles or in America; it is not so easy between Indians and Chinese because of civilisational differences.

But for us in Southeast Asia, perhaps not all of us, but certainly for many of us, we are multi-channel. We are able to switch from one frequency to another. If there are Chinese in the room, we switch; when there are Indians in the room, we re-tune our amplifiers and receptors; if there are Americans or Japanese in the room, we adjust again. We do this often without thinking because this instinct is in our blood.

Sometimes we are criticised for being soft, that we are not Cartesian enough, that we do not always make clear decisions. All that may be true, but for many things, being soft, being indirect and being ambiguous can help us overcome difficulties. To take a hard position when we are in between the two tectonic plates of China and India is unwise. It is better for ASEAN's external policy to be like Thailand's. Over the years, Thailand has been able to keep its independence by subtle sensing and reaction to external forces. Try pushing or pulling a *taiji* master. You will not succeed because he is always adjusting and turning the force against you; Thailand has that skill. This should be ASEAN's skill. So if anybody pushes us too hard, we will make slight adjustments so that other forces come into play. In this way nobody can push us too hard and our future will be all right.

Therefore, it is crucial that the South China Sea problem is not mismanaged. We should keep pushing for economic integration, within ASEAN, and between ASEAN and its neighbours. In national councils, we in the business community should be a force for opening up so that the ASEAN economic space is real and not just a plan on paper. We want the younger generation to feel that the whole of ASEAN is their region. This is the region that I belong to. If we can do this, we will be the bridge between India and China. Provided if they cooperate and do not fight we will stand to benefit greatly.

If they clash, our lives will be very different. But will they clash? Some people say that it is inevitable, but that is a Western view of the world. You know the argument — new powers rise, there must be contest leading to war and revolution. However, in the long history of contact between China and India, which goes back to the mist of early history, they have only fought once in 1962. It was a border war which, on the scale of things, was minor, still a scar in the Indian psyche but largely forgotten in China except by a few.

### Significance of Nalanda University

In the last few years, I was privileged to be involved in a wonderful project that I commend to all of you, which is the rebuilding, as a secular university, of an ancient Buddhist university called Nalanda.

Nalanda, for those of you who are not familiar with the history, was probably the world's first university. It existed from the 5th to the 12th century. At its peak, it had over 10,000 students from Southeast Asia, China, Japan, Korea, Central Asia, Persia and elsewhere. In the 12th century it was destroyed by Afghan invaders, about the time when Oxford was established, but before Cambridge. Many subjects, not just Buddhism, were taught. When the British were in India, no one knew what the ruins were until the British Army engineer, Alexander Cunningham, chanced upon the English translation of an ancient text written by a Chinese monk, Xuanzang or Tripitaka, the monk from the *Journey to the West* which is also the story of the monkey god. That monk, whom every Chinese kid is familiar with, went to India and lived in Nalanda for many years. He left China without permission, under the Tang Emperor Taizong, which was of course a very serious crime.

After many years, he brought *sutras* back to China. But first, he had to ask for permission to re-enter China which he did from Hetian or Khotan along the southern Silk Road. By that time, his reputation had spread back to China. The Emperor sent an imperial guard to escort him back to Chang'an (present day Xi'an). There, he translated the *sutras* into Chinese. He also wrote a very important book, *Records of the Great Tang Western Regions*. It was that book written in the 7th century, which Alexander Cunningham read in the 19th century in English. When he read it, his eyes must have dropped out. Xuan Zang's record was like a tour guide not only of Nalanda, but of many historical places in the Indo-Gangetic Plain. It was through China that India recovered a significant part of its history. As a result of that rediscovery, many Indians took on Buddhist names.

For a long time, there was a hope, a longing that somehow the university would be re-established. And finally we succeeded in getting the East Asian Summit leaders, which consist of the 10 ASEAN countries, India, China, Japan, Korea, Australia and New Zealand, to support the revival of Nalanda as an international project. Upon this support, the Indian Parliament, enacted a special law to establish Nalanda as an international university two years ago. It is located in the Indian state of Bihar near the old ruins. The Chief Minister has acquired 450 acres of land flanked by the Rajgir Hills. National authorities are making sure that the national infrastructure development, including airport, highways, and railroad, will support Nalanda. Faculty for the first two schools will be recruited next year and students will be enrolled for the year after. The buildings will take longer to build.

I have been involved in the project from the beginning under the leadership of Amartya Sen, the Nobel Laureate Harvard professor, who is now the first Chancellor of Nalanda University. As chairman of the International Advisory Panel, I was so delighted, so honoured when Princess Sirindhorn agreed to join us as a member. When I came to Bangkok to invite Her Royal Highness a few months ago, she had me to her palace for dinner and I was amazed by her knowledge. Her Royal Highness had been to Nalanda before and was completely familiar with its history. At dinner, there were professors from Chulalongkorn University who were interested in cooperating with Nalanda University. I proposed the establishment of a Nalanda-Suvharnabhumi Centre in Chulalongkorn University as Suvharnabhumi encompasses Myanmar, Thailand and Indo-China. In Singapore, we have established a Nalanda-Sriwijaya Centre. Sriwijaya encompasses Indonesia, Malaysia, Singapore and Southern Thailand. It is good for us to go beyond national definitions.

## Man Living in Harmony with Man, with Nature, as Part of Nature

All of us, in our own different ways, can promote the Nalanda ideal, Buddhist in inspiration, of man living in harmony with man, man living in harmony with nature, and man living as part of nature. This should be the philosophy which underlies competition and cooperation in Asia. If we can achieve this for India, China and ASEAN — that is half of the world — we will help change the world for the better. That is something worth doing.

Yes, we in ASEAN are not a great power; we do not get many medals in the Olympic Games; Thailand has a few, Indonesia has a few, but not many, but we are not unimportant. If we play our role, we can create a better Asia, and that better Asia will usher in a better world. If each of us does a little bit, if each business leader does a little bit, including ABC and others, collectively, we can affect national decisions, and make the region safer and more attractive. Small actions can position ASEAN in a way which enables larger forces to push us and everyone else in a favourable direction.

Thank you.

# Handling It with Military Precision

*Be in the flow.*

The city's stock investors may know George Yeo only as the new chairman of Kerry Logistics, a unit of Hong Kong-listed Kerry Properties.

But a simple Google search would turn up photographs of Yeo with political dignitaries such as Foreign Minister Yang Jiechi, former US secretary of state Condoleezza Rice, Thai Prime Minister Yingluck Shinawatra and Myanmar's opposition leader Aung San Suu Kyi.

Yeo, also a vice-chairman of Kerry Group, which publishes the *South China Morning Post*, was in politics for most of his life before he joined the private sector. He is a former Singapore Member of Parliament and Minister for Foreign Affairs but retired from politics after he lost his seat in the general election last year.

Prior to entering parliament, Yeo, who studied at Cambridge University and Harvard, was a brigadier-general in the Republic of Singapore Air Force (RSAF). He served as the chief of staff of the RSAF from 1985 to 1986 and as the director of joint operations and planning at the Ministry of Defence from 1986 to 1988.

That experience has stood him in good stead in his new role at the head of a logistics firm. In January this year, he accepted Kerry Group chairman Robert Kuok's invitation to join the company as vice-chairman and took up the chairmanship of Kerry Logistics on 1 August.

---

This article by Peggy Sito first appeared in the *South China Morning Post*, 13 October 2012. 

Yeo feels he has long been connected, indirectly, with the logistics industry. In his youth, he helped his father take care of a rubber godown. Later, he was involved in logistics planning and operations during his time in the air force. While he was trade minister and foreign minister of Singapore, he kept an eye on the logistics industry in member countries of the Association of Southeast Asian Nations [ASEAN] from a policy perspective.

But Yeo, 58, has a more personal reason to appreciate the services provided by the industry. Once, the global logistics firm FedEx, based in Memphis, Tennessee, helped saved his son's life by delivering bone marrow to a hospital for a critical operation.

**What made you become a businessman?**
I was in politics for 23 years until I lost in the last election. The opposition leader who beat me, when he was interviewed, said: "We won not because my opponents [meaning me and my team] did not do a good job, but because people wanted us in Parliament." I thought if there was not something that I could change, because it was not something about me, maybe it was time to open a new chapter of my life.

**Do you know the logistics industry well?**
I cannot claim to know it very well at all. But I do have some knowledge of logistics. When I was a teenager, I helped my father, who was a rubber godown stockkeeper: Sometimes I looked after his godown, sometimes I helped him deliver goods. Then in the army, I was involved in air force logistics. When I was in politics, I was in the trade ministry. Free-trade negotiations were a very big part of our portfolio. As Foreign Minister, I was involved in ASEAN activities, both between ASEAN and China and ASEAN and India; that is the backdrop of what we are talking about.

One of my most memorable (brushes with logistics) is when my younger son had leukaemia and needed a bone marrow transplant at St Jude [Children's Research] Hospital in Memphis. I got FedEx to help me.

There is a direct flight from Taiwan to Memphis every day, but the doctor could not be on the flight. So he flew Singapore Airlines to Los Angeles. FedEx put him on a corporate jet [with the bone marrow] from LA to Memphis for me. After that, my wife has been very loyal to FedEx.

**What do you see as the outlook for Kerry Logistics amid the global economic slowdown?**

We are staying true to our strategic position, which is to be Asian specialists and to focus on China. Europe will go through a prolonged period of difficulties. The US economy is still at an uncertain stage. But Asia is still growing, and intra-Asian links have become more interesting. We are well positioned for this pan-Asian role.

The slowdown in economic growth affects the industry at one level, but you also see the opportunities. Because companies come under stress, they have to look at cost cutting. They've got to be more creative to provide new products and services. Whether they cut costs or move to new areas, logistics organisations become very important. We are very good at providing customised services to companies.

We [now] also have more acquisition opportunities. We will continue to grow despite the downturn. The challenges for us are digesting our acquisitions so that the internal systems are efficient and maintaining strong local presences.

**How do you describe your management style?**

Cope with people. First you must respect them and understand their perspectives. Very often, when you respect somebody and there is trust, you will find ways to work together. If you do not respect each other, you will see no possibility of finding solutions that are win-win.

And you must always be part of the larger flow. If you want to fight the flow, you will be very tired. It is always important to know where the big flows are and to move to the big flows, then you can do a lot of things.

In all my responsibilities from a young age, I always tried to know what was the flow and be in the flow, rather than trying to fight the flow. If you ask me now for Kerry Logistics what the big flow is, the big flow is the growth of Asia. Within Asia itself, three major flows are Greater China, India and Southeast Asia.

**Which role do you prefer: businessman or politician?**

I am still as busy [as before], which is a bit surprising. In addition to [heading] a ministry, I was also a Member of Parliament. In politics, you deal with all kinds of everyday concerns of citizens.

One day, I was travelling in Europe on some mission; one of my constituents called me, saying: "My neighbour's dog is barking all night, driving me mad. Can you do something about that?"

As a Member of Parliament, you cannot say: "I am too busy for you." You are representing them, and you have got to look after your constituents. It is a big part of your time.

In the private sector, you are more focused on doing things that are more connected with business.

Objectives are more focused. In terms of intellectual [content], they are actually the same, as you are dealing with the same reality — you are working with people.

# The Spirit of the Young

*Human communities will increasingly be defined not by geography but by networks.*

Chairman Yang, President Tong, guests and friends

I am deeply honoured by this award from The Hong Kong Polytechnic University and would like to dedicate it to the young people of Hong Kong and Singapore.

I dedicate it to the young because they have to rebuild a world that is corroding.

Technology and globalisation have altered the power relationship among human beings, enabling old lines of authority to be bypassed. With the ease of travel and communication, individuals enjoy choices and freedoms which never existed before.

Everywhere, old hierarchies are breaking down. The relationships between parents and children, teachers and students, doctors and patients, priests and flock, government leaders and citizens, are changing dramatically. The social media has become unstoppable.

However, what all this will lead to is not chaos but the emergence of new patterns in the organisation of human society.

Human communities will increasingly be defined not by geography but by networks. Each of us has multiple loyalties and we do not want to have to choose from among them.

---

Response speech at the Hong Kong Polytechnic University Convocation, 27 October 2012 after conferment of Honorary Doctorate.

Human society will have to be rebuilt from the bottom up, strand by strand, network by network, on the basis of trust and respect for diversity.

In times of great transition, it is natural that the burden of leadership should shift to younger members of society. Communities and organisations trying to prevent this will be left behind.

Hong Kong and Singapore are two cities most alive to the changes taking place in the world. Because we are so connected, our citizens are among the first to feel the stresses of change. But we can also be among the first to adapt to them, helping to create new patterns for the future. In this exciting journey, the spirit of the young will be decisive.

# THE SPIRIT OF NALANDA

*Without a moral sense, not only do we harm man's relationship with man, we imperil his relationship with Nature.*

In early 2009, over dinner in Patna in the midst of the global financial crisis, I asked Bihar's Chief Minister Nitish Kumar how the state economy was being affected. He looked at me, somewhat puzzled, and replied: "Not at all ... we are continuing to grow at over 10% a year." I should not have been surprised. Bihar's economy was of course at a low base with limited links to the global economy. But the growth had become organic and internally driven. Like an adolescent, it would take much more than a global financial crisis to stop Bihar from growing.

I first visited Bihar in early 2004 to attend the dedication of the Mahabodhi Mahavihara in Bodh Gaya as a UNESCO World Heritage Site. When DPM Advani visited Singapore a year earlier, we discussed Buddhist tourism from East and Southeast Asia. At that time, I was Singapore's Minister for Trade and Industry. He then put me in touch with Tourism Minister Jagmohan who invited me to the ceremony. Economic conditions in the vicinity of Bodh Gaya and Sarnath, which we also visited, were dreadful. My accompanying Singapore security officer asked me why the people living there were so poor. Since then, I have been back to Bihar three times in connection with the establishment of Nalanda University. Each time, I saw clear improvements. Each time, the

---

Originally published in *The New Bihar: Rekindling Governance and Development*, eds. N.K. Singh and Nicholas Stern, India: HarperCollins Publishers, 2013, pp. 373–377.

roads were better paved, the saris brighter, the shops better stocked with goods. Even the animals looked healthier.

My involvement in Nalanda sprang from a lunch I hosted for the Deputy Chairman of India's Planning Commission Montek Singh Ahluwalia along the Singapore River in 2006. By that time, I was Foreign Minister. Having been inspired by Sun Shuyun's account of the remarkable journey of the great Tang Dynasty monk Xuanzang (Hsuan-tsang) to India in the 7th century (*Ten Thousand Miles Without a Cloud*), I suggested the revival of Nalanda University as an international university. It should be an expression of peace and sharing in 21st century Asia, an icon of the Asian renaissance. Montek was enthusiastic and asked if I could write him a short paper. This I happily did within a week. He then linked me up with the Deputy Chairman of the Bihar Planning Commission N K Singh who informed me that the Bihar government under Nitish Kumar had just drafted legislation for the revival of Nalanda as a state university. He agreed with me that we should work with the Bihar government to make it an international university instead.

Many streams were flowing into the river. PM Manmohan Singh invited Prof Amartya Sen to chair the Nalanda Mentor Group. For Amartya, having dreamt of the revival of the university since his youth, this became a labour of love even though he knew it would be difficult. Sitting next to him in the coach on our way to Nalanda, he recalled his school days when he and his mates hiked in the Rajgir hills. When Former President Abdul Kalam visited Singapore in 2008, his entire conversation with me was about Nalanda. In his capacious mind, he had already reconstructed the university as a modern institution. When the Indian Ministry of External Affairs formally proposed the new Nalanda as an international university to East Asia Summit leaders at the end of 2009, it received unanimous support. Upon this endorsement, the Indian Parliament enacted the law establishing Nalanda University in August 2010, with Members from both Houses competing in the acclamation.

To some, it must seem fantastical to believe that such an idealistic project could thrive in the poor soil of Bihar. Was there even the precondition of law and order? While it is true that local governance has improved remarkably in the last few years, one is justified to worry about the future on the basis of the past. Looking further back to the past, however, there is reason for hope. For the old Nalanda University to have flourished over so many centuries, there must have been a vibrant regional economy. To sustain an academic community of over 10,000 in Nalanda, the land must have generated a considerable surplus. Indeed Patna or Pataliputra could not have been a capital city for over a thousand years if the earth were infertile or the inhabitants indolent. In fact, the earth is fertile and the water table is not far beneath the surface, especially north of the Ganges. With organisation, infrastructure and knowledge, Bihar will prosper again. India's sister civilisation, China, provides a parallel. Patna (or Pataliputra) is to Bihar what Xi'an (or Chang'an) is to Shaanxi. Like Patna, Xi'an was the capital city for several Chinese dynasties. Like Bihar, Shaanxi was a cradle of civilisation. As Bihar is today, Shaanxi was also very poor, until recently. And, like Shaanxi, Bihar too will reclaim its past. It is not an abstract comparison; Bihar and Shaanxi were in contact with each other for hundreds of years. As an illustration, it was from Bihar that Xuan Zang returned to Shaanxi bearing the sutras. With relations between China and India resurging, the old links are reviving.

The revival of Nalanda and Bihar is part of a much larger story — the re-emergence of India and China on the world stage. After a long period, the historical pendulum is swinging back to Asia. However, while the future of Asia is full of hope and possibilities, there are dangers we have to worry about. Three deserve particular attention — growing global imbalances, Sino-Indian relations and man's pride. To all three, Nalanda is an inspiration.

Unless we find within ourselves the will to cooperate and compromise, the inevitable result of growing imbalances in the world is conflict. The consequences of a major war in this day and age are so horrendous, we really have no choice but to work together to overcome the challenges of economic development, financial instability, environmental destruction, global warming, pandemics and transnational terrorism. International and regional efforts can only produce positive results if, despite our differences, we interact with one another as spiritual human beings. Acting on self-interest alone is often not enough to achieve international agreement because many problems are not positive-sum in the short and medium term. Man's peaceful relationship with his fellow man requires a common spirituality which goes beyond self-interest. Without a moral philosophy, the market economy is not sustainable and the effectiveness of international diplomacy is limited. That moral philosophy was what Nalanda stood for.

In the world today, the Sino-US relationship is the most critical and will remain so for decades to come as the Chinese economy overtakes the US economy in size. However, looking further down the 21st century, the Sino-Indian relationship could become as important a factor in world affairs. China and India make up 40% of the world's population and will together supply the greater part of its brainpower. How these two civilisations relate to each other will have portentous consequences for the future of humanity. Over the centuries, vast deserts, high mountains, tempestuous seas and malarial swamps have kept them largely separate. Through traders and monks, they exchanged goods, knowledge and ideas. It was for the most part a peaceful relationship. While the scar of the 1962 war is still raw in India, against the sweep of history, that war was a minor event. Now, however, China and India are encountering each other massively, in all fields, by land, sea, air and electronically. There are mutual suspicions but there is also a deep mutual respect. Each recognises the other as an ancient people. After 2,000 years, Buddhism has become so well-ingested in China, it is viewed everywhere in China as a local religion unlike Islam or Christianity. All Chinese know that Buddhism originated from India. Beneath the prejudices and stereotypes, there is a widespread sense in China that India is a source of high knowledge and wisdom.

How Buddhism penetrated China and became indigenised is itself a long story which cannot be told without recalling the role of Nalanda. For centuries, Nalanda was a beacon which drew scholars from all over Asia and a symbol of peaceful intra-Asia interaction. It was a model for libraries in East Asia, including the great libraries of Chang'an which contributed immensely to Tang China's classical tradition. The descriptions of ancient Nalanda found mostly in Chinese sources enabled India to recover a large part of its Buddhist history in recent times. This is a favour which China has returned to India.

In the new encounter between China and India, the legacies of Buddhism and Nalanda are precious. When India proposed the revival of Nalanda as an international university, it received fulsome support from China. Both grasped immediately its significance and saw the project as, in the words of a senior Chinese official, "a good thing" for bilateral relations. Needless to say, any platform that brings China and India together will also draw other Asians to it. With growing incomes among the middle classes of East and Southeast Asia, millions will visit the holy Buddhist sites in Bihar and the surrounding regions. The ruins of the old Nalanda and the campus of the new Nalanda will become important destinations. The new university will be a shining example of Asian collaboration and a venue for international meetings.

The third danger is perhaps the greatest of all — man's pride in his own intelligence. With the rapid advancement of technology, nothing seems beyond eventual reach of the human mind, from inner earth to outer space, from sub-atomic particles to artificial life. The IT revolution has changed our lives from top to bottom. The biotech revolution will change it from outside to inside. From the beginning of civilisation, every new technology that appeared has been two-edged, a force for both good and evil. Without a moral sense, not only do we harm man's relationship with man, we imperil his relationship with Nature. Indeed, man exists only as a part of Nature. Many challenges in the world today can only be overcome if we internalise this truth that we are part of Nature, not separated from it. Looking into the telescope from the other end, the solution to many big problems has first to be found within ourselves.

A few years ago, I had a fascinating conversation with a Grand Ayatollah in Qom. His parting words to me were: "May you find what you seek." The words lingered in my mind as I pondered over the meaning. Recently, Google's Tan Chade-Meng published a book which supplied me the answer: Search inside yourself. The inner self is the key to most things and therefore a subject that deserves emphasis and study. That understanding was the foundation of the old Nalanda and must be the foundation of the new. In this regard, the new Nalanda can only succeed if Bihar, which is its host, also succeeds upon the same foundation.

The emphasis put on education in Bihar today is the single most important reason for hope in the state. Bihar's unqualified support for the re-establishment of Nalanda as an international university is not a chance event. It reflects a deep desire to raise the level of education in the state and reconnecting it to the world. The goal is not only the teaching of knowledge but also the imparting of values.

The Nalanda lamp has been re-lit in the State of Bihar. May that lamp light other lamps and inspire us all to be better than what we are.

# Moral Leadership

*Society cannot be organised purely on the basis of law and the operation of the market. Without moral values, society breaks down.*

On 14 March 2013, both China and the Catholic Church announced their new leaders to the world — Xi Jinping in Beijing and Francis in the Vatican. In a different period, their accessions would have been described as coronations. But not in today's circumstances. Each has responsibility for about a fifth of humanity. China and the Catholic Church are similar in many ways. Both are ancient. Both are run by Mandarins.

In the case of the Catholic Church, according to historian Arnold Toynbee, it was the clergy which inherited the legacy of the Roman Equestrian Order. Both China and the Church make moral claims to leadership. Each sees in the other a natural competitor.

Neither Xi nor Francis was elected by the entire citizenry or congregation. In both China and the Catholic Church, the idea of direct election to the top leadership would have been thought absurd. However, for both polities, there is deep commitment to democratic centralism (a Leninist term which Catholics might object to in name, but should not in substance).

In China, despite centralised bureaucratic governance, there is much regional and local diversity. Post-Mao China has seen considerable democratisation. With urbanisation and the social media, this process of democratisation will evolve further.

---

This piece was published in *The Globalist* (1 August 2013) before George Yeo was appointed by Pope Francis in August 2013 to a commission tasked to look at the reform of the Vatican's administrative/economic structure. Reprinted with permission from *The Globalist*, www.theglobalist.com.

But many aspects of China's governance will have to remain centralised if the country is not to break up. The ideal of a united Chinese state is in the DNA. Within this unified framework, however, Chinese society is often factious.

Similarly, the Catholic Church is both highly centralised and decentralised. In matters of doctrine and Canon Law (derived from Roman Law), the Vatican holds very firm. Dogmas like Apostolic succession are not up for debate. Otherwise, the Church is largely devolved with a high degree of local initiative. A Jesuit father who pioneered US-style community colleges in India told me that the country's transgender community approached him to set up a college for them — so that they would not be trapped in prostitution. There are many such heartwarming examples.

With the social media revolution, the hierarchical structure of leadership in China and the Catholic Church is under attack. Leaders once protected by ritual and distance and sometimes also by hypocrisy and ignorance are now seen as quite human after all. Corruption and sexual misbehavior have been widely reported, not necessarily because they have become more common — but because they are harder to hide or cover up. Both President Xi and Pope Francis recognise the seriousness of the challenge. After assuming their respective posts, they have taken actions to set a new tone and in highly symbolic ways.

By coming down hard on public extravagance, President Xi sent a strong signal to all China. When Pope Francis washed the feet of young prisoners on *Maundy Thursday*, he reminded all Catholics of the humility of Christ. By meeting and praying with refugees from Africa and the poor in Rio's *favelas*, he led by example.

Whether the two men succeed or not will depend on their persistence in following through, but an important start has been made. There are no perfect leaders and those who appear so are fakes. In today's circumstances, it is crucial to be authentic and close to ordinary people.

For China and the Catholic Church, moral leadership is an inseparable part of all leadership. The world needs more of it. Society cannot be organised purely on the basis of law and the operation of the market. Without moral values, society breaks down. What these common moral values should be in the world we live in today, however, has to be discussed and debated. It is certainly not enough to be amoral.

For both Chinese and Catholics, the cultivation of individual virtues and the sanctity of the family are fundamental. It is unfortunate that China and the Catholic Church are still estranged from each other. If the two are reconciled, the entire world will benefit. And it is not as if the differences are irreconcilable.

Give to Caesar what is Caesar's and to God what is God's — that surely can be a basis for cooperative co-existence. The appointment of bishops in China is not an insurmountable problem from the viewpoint of Communist and Catholic dogma. In the 16th century, the great Jesuit Matteo Ricci researched deep into Chinese philosophy before deciding on the proper translation for "God". For the Chinese, all existence is thought of as what is under Heaven. The emperor was the Son of Heaven, reigning over all human affairs. Ricci decided that God should therefore be properly translated as the "Lord of Heaven", in a sphere which posed no political threat to anybody.

It may be the calling of the first Jesuit Pope to propose an equally profound yet artful answer to a new Chinese President.

# America Might Be a Friend but China Cannot Be an Enemy

*The common objective must be the "normalisation" of Japan on all dimensions.*

## Changing Dynamics in US–China–Japan Relations

As tensions rise between the US and China over China's islands dispute with Japan, American strategists have been thinking about how to accommodate China while at the same time standing behind their Japanese ally.

It may be helpful to look at the situation also from an Asian perspective. Historically, in East and Southeast Asia — until the Western arrival — there has only been one major power rising and ebbing: China. When it rises, it is best to accord it some respect in return for which one derives considerable economic advantage.

Over the centuries, a rich China invariably brought prosperity to all of East and Southeast Asia. Therefore, while Asian countries might value the US as a friend, no one wants China as an enemy. There is a spot that is sweet for everyone. If the US moves closer to China and to other countries of Asia, all will benefit. If the US, in response to China's rise, moves too close to some as a move against others, everyone is caught in a lose-lose situation. Finding the limits of that sweet spot is part of statecraft and diplomacy.

Japan is the first Asian country to meet the Western challenge by becoming an imperial power itself. After its defeat, it effectively became an adjunct power of the US In a curious way, both China and the US may be happy to keep Japan in that "abnormal" position for

---

First published in the *WorldPost*, 20 August 2014. Reprinted with permission.

as long as possible. Prime Minister Abe and other Japanese leaders want Japan to become a "normal" country. For the US, such a Japan may help counterbalance a rising China.

### The Re-Asianisation of Japan

For China, such a Japan is only acceptable if it acknowledges history. This re-Asianisation of Japan is a complex process that will take another generation to achieve. The Diaoyu/Senkaku issue is only one manifestation of it. The re-Asianisation or "normalisation" of Japan need not lead to war. Domestic and international pressure on the Japanese elite to recognize history is not only right and doable, it will also relax tension in the Pacific and lead to a better future for everyone, including Japan. But it also requires China and the US to do their part. The common objective must be the "normalisation" of Japan on all dimensions.

### The Missionary Superpower

The US is, by self-identification, a missionary superpower. It judges others by its own standards and tries to shape them in the US' own image — by hard and soft power. If China is also a missionary power, like the Soviet Union, perhaps a titanic struggle will again be inevitable. However, China is, by self-proclamation, not a missionary power. For China, a cardinal principle of statecraft, not just the PRC but also its earlier incarnations, is non-interference in the internal affairs of others unless those affairs affect China's core interests.

In fact, this is now a western criticism of China — that it is "amoral" in the way it deals with countries in Africa and the Middle East. But it is precisely the fact that China is unlike the US in missionary zeal that there is hope for the future.

# APPENDIX

# ARTICLES IN CUMSA* NEWSLETTER

*During his undergraduate days in Cambridge from 1973–76, George Yeo was active in student politics. In his second year, he was elected the Secretary of the Cambridge University Malaysia-Singapore Association (CUMSA). In his third and final year, he was elected President. In 1974, the Singapore Government arrested a number of Singaporeans under the Internal Security Act. Many Singapore and Malaysia student activists in the UK protested and a demonstration against the Singapore Government was held in London with a march from Hyde Park to the Singapore High Commission. He and another Singapore student leader who was not on scholarship encouraged other Singapore students in Cambridge, many of whom were on scholarship, to take part. They failed and they were the only two representing CUMSA at the London demonstration. The following two pieces were written by George Yeo for the CUMSA newsletter. The first was a report on the London event; the second reflected on the effect it had on the Singapore students in Cambridge.*

## Protest March by FUEMSSO in Support of the People's Struggles at Home

On Friday 13 December, FUEMSSO† held an open meeting in

* CUMSA — Cambridge University Malaysia-Singapore Association.

† FUEMSSO — Federation of United Kingdom and Eire, Malaysian, and Singaporean Student Organisations.

London. The first two weeks of December had seen tens of thousands of M'sian peasants going on hunger marches and thousands of students battling with troops on M'sian campuses. A telegram from the Australian Union of Students' President had just arrived, carrying the news of the deportation of M'sian student leaders in the Singapore University, and the press blackout on Tan Wah Piow's trial. With events happening so quickly, it was felt that students in England must come together just as quickly in a demonstration of strength and unity in support of the struggles at home.

Present at the meeting were about 90 representatives from various places in U.K.; Hull, Manchester, Oxford, and other various colleges in London. After a brief summary of events, the FUEMSSO President said a demonstration will be held on the 16th of December. It would be a peaceful demonstration with placards, chants, songs, and handouts. Police permission had been obtained for the planned route. Everyone present was enthusiastic about the protest march.

In the ensuing discussion, the constituent unions exchanged information about what they had done so far concerning the events back home. The Hull union had been very active seeking to pressurise the Govt. through the local Labour M.P.s of the Socialist International. Many unions had started discussion groups so that they could understand the issues better. Nearly all the unions had sent home letters and telegrams of protests to the Home Affairs Ministers, and of support to the student unions. FUEMSSO itself had been able to rally the support of the NUS-UK National Union of Students which had also sent back statements of support to the Prime Ministers of M'sia and S'pore.

It was clear that a great deal of support was necessary for the protest march to be an effective demonstration of solidarity. We were glad to learn that many sympathetic student unions (the Palestinian students, the African students, NUS, etc.) would be giving us their support. Spirits rose as we found out that although Sheffield was not present at the open meeting they would be sending about 15 supporters. We then returned to our constituent unions to gather support.

In Cambridge, an Emergency CUMSA meeting was held the following night. About 40 members attended despite the short notice given. They were informed of the recent happenings in M'sia and S'pore, and of the proposed demonstration. Most of the members present were concerned with what had happened and twelve of us agreed to participate in the demonstration on the following Monday.

Noon on Monday 16 Dec at Speakers' Corner, Hyde Park, was wet, cold and windy. Cool and collected policemen could be seen in little groups. Cheers welcomed new arrivals joining the throng of people already gathered beneath the FUEMSSO banner.

## Reflections

October 1973 saw a great change in Cambridge with a sudden increase in the number of Singapore students. Our seniors, both Malaysians and Singaporeans, had read what we were supposed to have said in *The Pioneer*, *Singapore Bulletin* and *The Mirror*. They thought we were a bunch of cocky, smug, self-satisfied and elitist snobs. Not surprisingly then, the relationship between the first and third years did not start off well.

As happens so often, each fresh misunderstanding only served to further strengthen initial misconceptions. Some of the seniors felt confirmed in their views and labelled us 'apolitical', 'proud', etc. Equally we in the first years felt we were wronged, that THEY were aloof and unfriendly. It took over a term to sort things out eventually, thanks to the tireless effort of juniors such as Jacob, Chun Wei and Kai Yeng.

There was a period of intense soul-searching after eight of us attended the FUEMSSO Annual Delegates Conference at Hull. Students from all over Britain had come together for the Conference to discuss matters relating to Malaysia and Singapore. When we came back to Cambridge we resolved to endeavour not to allow prejudices and preconceptions sour up interpersonal relationships in Cambridge.

We examined our relationships with the nurses — how we used to invite them to our discos and parties, adding and subtracting to balance the men with the ladies. Once it was embarrassing to discover that we had 'too many girls'. It was even more painful to become aware that we treated them as so many dancing partners to do arithmetic with.

Some were criticised for their 'mightier than thou' attitude towards our friends from the Tech. It was true that at times we did feel over-pleased with ourselves — after all we WERE in Cambridge. Vis-à-vis the Malay students there was a danger of mutual suspicion becoming self-fulfilling.

The year ended well. There were many late nights of serious and heated discussion, ranging from the more immediate problems in Cambridge to race, culture, religion and politics. Many of us felt that precisely because we understood better why things happen, we should be able to achieve in CUMSA a lively atmosphere where we would feel at ease with each other.

Sheer zeal alone enabled us to make Herculean efforts the following year to integrate one and all. In our first CUMSA Squash and our first CUMSA Dinner for 74–75, we brought everyone together physically. We did not reckon with the social forces at work. Events slid along the line of least resistance. We attempted too much too quickly. Instead of making sustained efforts and clearing one obstacle at a time, we had hoped, in vain, to move heaven and earth with one stroke.

The situation was further complicated when in November and December, students in both Malaysia and Singapore struggled to have a say in the social process. When Wah Piow was arrested, Juliet Chin wrote to us appealing for support. In Malaysia over a thousand were hauled in for voicing the plight of starving peasants in Baling. Many of us in the second and third years, felt we had to do something to help. When FUEMSSO (parent organisation of Malaysian and Singaporean societies in the U.K. and Eire) called for a demonstration in London to give support and show solidarity to people back home, we hurriedly gathered everyone in Cambridge, from the University and the Tech., together for an emergency meeting. During the meeting those who had doubts or reservations were steamrolled over. The issue was forced to everyone without regard to personal sensitivities.

In the event, ten of us took part in the London demonstration. We carried a banner proclaiming 'Cambridge Malaysian and

Singaporean Students Fully Support the People's and Students' Struggle for Justice at Home'. The damage was done — what should have been a useful lesson for one and all became a source of division. It was at least fortunate that the Committee saw this quickly enough. It was time to rebuild trust and understanding. By the end of the last academic year, the wounds were healed although the scars would take longer to disappear. The most important thing is to learn from mistakes.

CUMSA necessarily means differently to different people. Ultimately our conception of what the Association should be must depend on what we see as the role and responsibilities of students in society.

The atmosphere in Cambridge has become, willy-nilly, increasingly local. This need not be bad. We come abroad with a mentality no wider than a keyhole. It is no wonder that our confidence becomes readily shaken. We were, when we were in Malaysia and Singapore, tremendously self-assured. Precisely these three years provide us with the splendid opportunity to rid our minds of stereotypes, to think things afresh, to forge new values if need be.

Of course times have changed. Ours is not the red hot crucible of intellectual ferment and the spirit of rebellion that distinguished the immediate post-war era and provided the education of such ardent nationalists as Lee, Razak, Goh and others. We are a great deal more comfortable today but living in a world no less in flux. Whether it is in religion that we find fulfilment, or in the liberal values of the West that we discover the ideal, or whether the answer lies in politics or philosophy or whatever, the process of searching and learning, alone and in fellowship with others, is exciting.

# Diary of First Visit to Ancestral Village in Chaozhou

*In 1983, I accompanied my parents to their ancestral village in Anbu (庵埠), a town under the city of Chaozhou (潮州). It was my first visit to China at the age of 28. At that time, young Singaporeans were forbidden to visit China without permission and I had to make a special application. I was then a Lieutenant Colonel in the SAF. ISD called me up for a one-hour interview to find out why I wanted to visit China. It was a pleasant interview at the end of which the two officers talking to me requested that I contact them upon my return to Singapore so that they could debrief me. As it did not seem urgent, I thought I wait a few days. Before I contacted them, they contacted me. The debrief also lasted an hour. The officers explained that the Government was reviewing its policy governing visits by young Singaporeans to China and said my impressions of China were useful to them.*

*It was the first and last time in my life I kept a detailed diary. We began our journey in HK from where we took an overnight boat ride to Shantou (汕头) or Swatow in my Teochew dialect. After about a week with my relatives, we flew to Guangzhou and then to Guilin. On the second day in Guilin, I got very sick with a bad flu. I was unable to enjoy the scenic boat ride down the Li River to Yangshuo. It was only after I felt better on the flight back to Hongkong that I filled in the missing days in my diary.*

*Dr K.K. Phua, who knew I had the diary, suggested I include it in the book. I was unsure. When I re-read what I had written more than half a lifetime ago, it brought back happy memories. Since that first visit, I have returned to the ancestral village many times, first with my new wife, then later with all my children. It pleased my relatives in China greatly that all my three sons also visited on their own when they were studying in Beijing.*

*My old secretary Lilian deciphered the scrawls in my handwritten diary as best she could before I went through them. Some words still do not make sense to me.*

**Saturday 28/5/1983**

S'pore–HK

Ocean Park
Sung Dynasty Village
Tram up Victoria Peak

**Sunday 29/5/1983**

HK–Macao–HK

**Monday 30/5/1983**

HK–Swatow

A foretaste of China.

Morning spent trying to contact relatives in Shenzhen and Swatow. First by telephone which required that a special arrangement be made with the telephone operator. Lines were either engaged or out of order. All to no success. Dad flustered, decided to cable, which necessitated a trip to Ocean Terminal, and my having to fill in the cablegram in Chinese.

How can there be business with such poor communications?

In the afternoon, to the terminal for China. A different crowd from that one sees in downtown UK and Kowloon. Elderly. Crippled. Poor. Worried. Anxious. An old lady, hair all white and brushed back, dressed in black samfoo, pushed in a wheelchair. The look of dread and hollow death on her face. Why the trip to Swatow? Like a salmon on a compulsive tryst with the ancestral homeland?

A blind man, cane in hand, or what was left of hands gnarled up like metal melted away. Sat opposite us in the hot, congested hell-hole which was the 3rd class cabin we were in. Dad was scared to death that he was leprous. Couldn't stop worrying about it until we managed to remove our belongings to Mrs Heng's cabin, a haven, no, a paradise, in comparison. Wondered whether the boat ride was better than the coach ride from Shenzhen which everyone claimed was a trial.

Still settling in now. Dinner was poor. Rice was not the fluffy, white, whole grains we were familiar with, but broken, coloured and lumpy. Vegetables and fishballs were crunchy like as if there were pieces of grit in them. Maybe they were good for the soul.

We looked everywhere for a niche to lodge in. Where we thought we found a suitable spot, we soon found out why it was still empty when we got there. Usually, because it was blasted by hot air from the engine room or whatever.

Disorganisation reigns, or so it appears to us who associate boat rides with cruises on the Love Boat. An association as appropriate as that between Shangri-La and the Black Hole of Calcutta.

Could not get coins to slot into the coke machine. They were not available. Mum wanted 开水 [water] which was supposed to be both upstairs and downstairs but nowhere to be obtained. Drank San Miguel beer instead as there was no other way to quench the thirst.

The Ting Hu (鼎湖轮), an old, solid, German ship with fairly nice first class and deluxe cabins, nicer no doubt because we weren't occupying them.

Trying to transcend all this BS is an effort in Taoist acceptance of things. Maybe we'll lodge in Swatow where there is running water and proper WCs, not the horrid public cesspools I've been told so much about. I've good excuses — a sprained ankle which prevents me from squatting for long durations, piles which require tender nursing, and a host of other hyperchondrial problems.

**Tuesday 31/5/1983**

Arrive Swatow 0700.

Cleared immigration and customs at 1030.

Woke up at 0600 hrs beholding the sight of the Chinese mainland. An emotional refreshment that was quickly overtaken by the humdrum of queuing up to leave the ship. Health clearance was a routine which raised the question of whether it was in fact at all needed. Collecting the baggage was utter confusion in the warehouse. Still we found our belongings and trundled out to clear customs which was far easier than we expected, than our worst expectations after having heard so much about the toothcomb searches of Chinese petty officials.

Bureaucratic courtesy was infinitely better than the grasping greed of the leeches we soon came to expect as being a part of the ecology, but which we could never get accustomed to.

The telegram had not arrived in time, we were not met, anxiety surrounded us; beggars were importunate; parasites abounded. We did not know there were 2 currencies; the foreign exchange and the local. 1:1 officially but 1:1.3 or so on the black market. By motor tricycle to the Overseas Chinese Hotel to make telephone calls. With tempers fraying at the edges, we found ourselves undecided between going straight to the village, staying first at Swatow, calling on relatives, etc.

Then we located Keng Hwee whom we came to rely on for many things; an early Party member; now the head of the *lao dong ju*; surrounded by tragic circumstances — an insane father, a wife losing her sight to glaucoma and afflicted by a heart problem; a son also with a heart problem, and himself hypertensive to an alarming degree.

Contacts made, we had lunch — a good lunch, reunion with mum's brother and sister and others, then to the village.

The countryside was a pretty sight, bright green padi fields, cut across by irrigation canals, dappled by myriad ponds, populated by people, geese, chicken, ducks, pigs and water buffaloes. But a very bad road described in the tourist blurb as a highway. What a highway. Pockmarked by craters. A lunar landscape. An incredible number of cyclists.

Into Ang Po [Anbu], to the ancestral house. Met first, grandfather, then grandmother. A remarkable pair.

Grandfather, 92, wonderfully alert and alive, puckish, diplomatic, raising his voice only at children. Was very proud of the $300 (that my brother) Jim wanted to donate to his medical centre, took it rather well when the family decided against it for good reasons.

Grandma. Bedridden. Irritable. Deaf. A pair to behold. Fighting against her condition, hating herself for it. 不应该的 [should not have happened]. A needless fall, not an illness brought abt by advancing age. Sat her up. Grandad chided her for being lazy and ill-tempered.

Photographs were taken. Eggs in a sweet soup were served. Dinner. Mosquitos. Well water. Damp floors. Primitive facilities I would not have been used to, save perhaps the experience of field camps in the Army.

**Wednesday 1/6/1983 (Children's Day)**

Ang Po.

Tour centre, Yeo house, lunch at overseas facility, back.
Yeo house, Yang Song's wife, poverty-stricken, emotional, recriminative.
Saw mum's and dad's bridal room.
Tua Tee Pek's sister came over.

2 sisters brought me around the village.
Saw mum's primary school, temple, punt boats, dragon boats.

**Thursday, 2/6/1983**

Teochew [Chaozhou] city.
0700 — Left home. — Managed to shit in the horrid toilet after 3 days.

0730 — Bus.

0900 — Arrive.

0900–1100 — West Lake.

1100–1200 — Lunch.

1200–1600 — East gate.
— Xingzi Bridge.
— Water Buffalo.
— Phoenix Pagoda — up the stairs, thanked God that my ankle was OK.
— Hang Si, Pavilion for viewing the Han River (Guang Han Lou).
— Kaiyuan temple.
— Bus stop.

1645–1750 — To Ang Po.

Teochew a pleasant tour with innumerable back alleys.
Familiar dialect. Proud trishaw riders.
Hang Si and Kaiyuan reconstruction and restoration of the damage of the Cultural Revolution.
Jee Ee's and mum's first visit. How remarkable! No wonder towns only a few 10s of kms apart have such different sounding of dialects. Chaoyang, Dinghai, etc.

Conversation with Chay Huay's daughter about Chai Deng's problems, unemployment, birth control, bad government, etc.

**Friday, 3/6/1983**

Ang Po–Swatow

0830 — Yeo Village.
— Tua Tee Pek's 2 brothers & sister.
— Lovely new house. 2 storeys. 10 rooms. Possible only after the reform after the Gang of 4's downfall.
— From where their wealth?

1130 — Swatow — Hong Tat's house.
— Keng Hwee — flight arrangement.
— 中山园 [Zhongshan Park].
— Overnight at Keng Hwee's new home.
— Met Keng Hwee's wife (glaucoma).
Son (Keng Seng), daughter.

**Saturday 4/6/1983**

Swatow.

Pleasant outing to Kak Cheok by boat from Swatow. Ballad beggars on board, shabbily dressed, pathetic. Mum and dad easily exhausted, age catching up. Dad seemed particularly fatigued. Commented that his health has greatly [been] deteriorating over last 6 months.

Back at 2.40 pm. While waiting for van, stood observing a riverside story-teller captivating an all-male audience, young and old, sitting on mats in the shade of a tree.

To the bank, friendshop shop, before a most bumpy ride back to Ang Po.

**Sunday 5/6/1983**

0900 — Visit to Grandad's medical centre.

1100 — Sok Leng's hospital. Amazed at how everyone wanted to be photographed. Hospital was crowded but organised. Rather shabby. On the way back, pursued by beggars. Kian Heng almost got into a fight with them. We were torn between disgust and pity, between being hard and soft. Dad, as usual, wanted to pay them off, which greatly annoyed Heng and the 2 little girls.

Lunch — 5 tables
Cuisine —
sweet white fungus, lotus seeds
Boiled chicken
Turtle soup
Seo Bee
Prawns
Snails
Sotong ball soup
Frog legs
Crabs
Liver sausage roll
Kailan veg.

Mushroom soup

Tsingtao Peking beer
白酒

Crowd of relatives, far and near. Most unfamiliar to me. Keng Nan's younger brother was most interesting. Dad had a long chat with him, was rather forthright, probably correct in being frank about why Sar Ee and Teor didn't want to visit China. Keng Nan's bro was obviously doing well, making plaster. An example of the great freedom over the last few years. More wealth now. Differentiation between rich and poor. New houses being built. Interminable photograph-taking. Everyone wanted to be in film, colour film especially. Good thing I got 3 more rolls of film – one from Sok Leng, 2 from Keng Hwee. I can afford to take scenery now.

Later in the afternoon, visited Lau Sim's daughter's new home. Didn't know whether purpose of invitation was to be photographed. But one must not be cynical. Motives are always complex.

Dinner
At night, had a chat with grandad. An amazing man, greatly concerned with the propriety of social conduct, explaining the importance of 'liang' (pride), of treating both high and low well. Greater for the poor to offer a gift of a small fish than for the rich a large one.

*Confucianist propriety*

Presentation of gifts.
Mutuality of obligations.
Correctness of address.
Hierarchical order of social relationships.
Importance of having the right connections.

Am reminded of Dr Goh's comment that the [Chinese] system was loaded against success, defect was 'built into the system'.

Hong Tat said that in addition to Keng Hwee's recommendation for the flat, he had to bribe officials to the tune of 2300 RMB.

*Return to Capitalism?*

General outcome of Cultural Revolution.
Significant improvement of economy over the last 4 yrs.
More colour, life.
Rediscovery of the market and the price mechanism.
Labour can be hired but land can't be bought and sold.
Currency speculation rife because of controls and restrictions.
3 types of currencies — 外汇 [Forex], overseas Chinese vouchers, ordinary RMB.
外汇 may be phased out in the near future.
Yugoslav model?

*The Genetic Pool*

Suddenly, familiar faces.
Mum's side, dad's side.
Not only features, but character traits and defects.
Madness on mum's side?
Species diversity the only strategy for survival in an ever-changing environment.
Strengths and weaknesses are relative.
Randomness is necessary but produces more failures than successes.
Defects have to be carried.

*A Haj*

An emotional indulgence. Not an ordinary tour. Village offers nothing by way of sights and tastes.
Quite the opposite.
But I'm proud to be able to make this pilgrimage, almost enjoying the deprivations, a perverse indulgence.

*Impressions*

Incredible backwardness.
Toilet facilities which obsessed dad.
Electricity.
News about the world outside.

Eyeing the tin of coffee, both for the way it was wound open and the content.
The tape recorder.
Towel.
Roads and vehicles.
General poverty. Income between S$30 to S$70–80.
28 grades for 干部 [cadres], 8 grades for 工人 [workers].
Polaroid photo-taking was a constant draw, a sure list with everyone.
Drabness & filth. Equal misery removes the patronage of art and architecture. Little man-made beauty.

Overseas Chinese an exalted class. Especially Swatow and Teochew.
Rich relatives with huge amounts of money to spend.
The proportions are embarrassing.

**Monday 6/6/1983**

0830–1430 To Sok Leng's hospital. Dad had his urine & BP taken. All OK which was comforting. Dad rewarded himself with breakfast in town, kway teow [noodles], cheng teng [a Chinese dessert], a hearty lunch with a sweet thrown in.

Walked to the bank of the Hanjiang. A pleasant respite under the spreading branches of a flame tree. Some workers came by, took their pictures, promised to send them prints when they were developed.

1600 Walked to the Hanjiang again near the village. A breezy afternoon at the dyke. On the way back, learnt that the coffin shop was called 长年店 [a shop for many years], a nice way of presenting an awkward merchandise. Dinner and the anticipation of separation the morning after.

I thought I saw tears flowing from grandma's eyes this afternoon. Sought grandad's permission to take a picture of them conversing with mum and 二 Ee [二姨 or mum's second sister) by the bed. Kiat skipped in after school, greeted them chirpily, one a life budding, another a mature flower withering. This is life, its cycle of beginning and ending. A depressing comparison. For we must all travel the same path. Still, it was touching to see grandad bending over grandma to talk into her right ear, poking fun at her; pinching her nose with great affection. "She calls me lau ah pek [old man]; I call her lau ah erm [old woman]."

Grandad, always concerned about the propriety of things. A minor dispute over the gifts presented at lunch the day before illustrated the complexity of the Chinese, Confucianist family tradition, the web of obligations which surrounded, even entrapped, the individual. Yesterday, Hoon Tat, suitably intoxicated by alcohol, was uncommonly frank about how he was unable to move farther afield because of the obligations. The young are caught. Kiang is more individualistic, less prepared to be tied down, more assertive.

I'm glad to have come. I shall be both sad and glad to leave. Maybe, I'll come back. I'm sure conditions in China will improve. This was the subject of conversation tonight with Kiang, Heng and Sok Leng. All complaining about the backwardness, the rigidity of things. Complaints which lacked understanding of causes and effects, which were without historical perspective. The local newspaper, Yang Cheng, is a 4–6-page exhortative piece of government propaganda. A number of articles on how the economy should, would, be stimulated by greater freedom and enterprise. One on the 农市场 [farmers' market] at Changsha and how Guangdong could learn from it. Hardly any world news.

A short write-up on the decision of the Singapore Govt to renovate the home of Dr Sun Yat Sen, the great founder of the Republic.

**Tuesday 7/6/1983**

Swatow–Kwongchow

| | |
|---|---|
| AM | Confusion over transportation to Swatow was a comedy of errors. The problem at the bottom of it all was the poverty of communications, the same which made it impossible for us to book a flight from Kwongchow to Guilin from Swatow. |
| | Looked for scroll paintings in various shops and found few of interest. Bought some as gifts for friends back home. |
| Lunch | At Ek Seng's restaurant. The same Teochew repertoire — quails, tortoise, frogs, lotus seeds, etc. Enjoyed it all the same. Teochew cuisine emphasises greatly seafood (水货). |
| PM | To the airport to the East of Swatow. New building, quite empty, catering to 2 to 3 flights (x2) a day. Keng Hwee was always an asset to have around. Exuding power with unfailing courtesy. A man with vast powers of patronage. |
| | Took off in a Russian Antonov after waving off relatives. For many of them, it was their first visit to the airport, probably their first close look at an aircraft. I left behind a world quite different from that I've been used to in Singapore. Felt a strange sadness. That morning, farewell to grandparents was hard, not least for mum. Maybe their last meeting. Who knows? At 92, anything can happen. |

*Kwongchow*

Flight on CAAC was Spartan but reasonable. Ice cream, sweets, little gifts, a fan.

Aircraft turned landwards, crossed the Lian Hua Mt, the delta of the Zhujiang to land.

Kwongchow a large city, suddenly reminding us of civilisation; of home, roads, cars, whites. Arrived at Overseas Chinese Hotel (华侨大厦) in an air-conditioned Toyota Crown.

Mum was exhausted. After dinner, all retired early.

**Wednesday 8/6/1983**

AM Trishaw to the China Bank, bought air tickets to Guilin, sent mum to the clinic for indigestion, arranged afternoon programme. A great deal of hassle one is spared from by going on tour.

Lunch

PM Taxi to the Zoo, saw the pandas. Dad's sight was poor. Had great difficulty trying to make out the 3 lumbering animals in the dark cage. It caused him [to be] upset. It made me think. Both he and mum tired easily.

From the Zoo to Yuexiu Park which involved much walking. I left them at a hilltop and went off on my own to see the Zhenhai 5-storey tower, and the 5-stone rams. A tremendous rush. I returned, sweating, thoroughly fagged out. Dad was irritated by the wait in the hot afternoon sun. Back to the hotel.

Dinner The same frustrating queue for a table, for food to arrive, for service.

After dinner, took a walk by the Pearl River for ½ hr, retired to the room to prepare for the early morning flight to Guilin. Hope hotel rooms there will not be hard to find.

**Thursday 9/6/1983**

*Arrive Guilin*

Woke up at 4.30, packed, had a light breakfast, was transported to the airport, checked in, first in line, flew in a 737, landed at Guilin at abt 8.10. Arrangements were quickly made for a 3-day tour from pm 9/6 to am 12/6. 丹桂 [Osmanthus] hotel was a great improvement over the 华桥大厦 at 广洲 [Kwongchow].

Had lunch at a restaurant opposite the road. Took an eternity for the dishes we ordered to arrive. Saw the cooks preparing a rodent which looked like a rat. Spoilt our appetite. Found out soon enough that game meat was popular in 广西 [Guangxi], snakes, frogs, turtles, mountain rats and pigs, beavers, pangolins, etc. I even saw a cat in a cage.

Afternoon itinerary consisted of tour to the Lu Di Cave and the Du Xiu Peak. Dad was tired, ill with a cold. Jaded, nothing impressed him. Climbed Du Xiu Peak, a steep ascent, found the scenery from the top rather disappointing; hills around looked more impressive from the bottom than from the top.

Accompanied dad to see the doctor who on the advice of our driver gave an injection. Driver was a voluble fellow who did not hesitate to charge ¥6 外汇 for the ride.

After a poor dinner — 广西 food was unfamiliar and unpalatable. Got tired of the hoojoo flavour in the dishes — mum and dad tucked in.

I went to the Tourist Centre to book train tickets, which was a hassle. Walked back along the busy main road. Saw a shop with a signboard which read 'State-Run Ice Restaurant'.

**Friday 10/6/1983**

*Guilin*

AM A bad breakfast. Or rather an unfamiliar one. Service was slow. Dad was irritable.

At Diecai Hill, we ascended the peak. Easier and nicer climb than yesterday. Mum and dad managed well. Photograph-taking at the Elephant Hill. Lunch was slow and hot. The mid-day was very hot and still. We were all tired. Got worried about dad at the 7-Star Park. Coming to realise that he has aged tremendously. Took ages to empty his bladder. Spilled tea all over at lunch. Couldn't walk far. The 1-km tour of the 7-Star cave was filled with anxiety, mum & I for dad, I for both. Could not help comparing both to the younger set who were with us, who skipped and climbed and laughed and still seemed fresh and vigorous. I was depressed by this cycle we must all go through. Well, one should live life to the full, and climb mountains when one can.

Dinner at the hotel.
Left for the Tourist Centre to collect tour tickets. Trishaw rider brought me to an Art Shop; Bought a scroll painting for ¥60. A good buy. Look forward to the cruise on the Lijiang tomorrow.

**13/6/1983 — 广州火车站 [Guangzhou Railway Station]**

10.07 — Waiting for direct train to HK to pull off. Catching breath after clearing customs and immigration. The usual hassle made worse by the tax on the camera we left behind and the transfer of money to the home village, RMB we could not take out. Feeling more alert now to jot down notes of events of the last few days. Was too sick to write. And feared that had I written the account of the last 2 days at Guilin would not have been fair.

**Saturday, 11/6/1983**

Woke up with a sore throat which rapidly worsened to a full blown attack of flu.

Trip down Lijiang was pleasant. Weather was reasonable but at this time of the year, warm. Autumn would have been a better time to visit Guilin.

The usual sights of limestone hills, steep sides, fantastically shaped, left to each imagination of what each represented.

6 hrs — 0830 to 1430 — was too long. Most reached saturation after the first 2–3 hours.
We were on the top deck. It was nice but I was sick.
Couldn't eat lunch.

Towards Yangshuo, the karst landscape was even more pronounced. Yangshuo nestled amidst towering hills which looked like so many stalagmites extending from the floor. That is a strange isomorphism in the external erosion and the internal erosion, the hills and river reflecting the hills, outside, and the stalactites and stalagmites reflecting each other in the caves.

At Yangshuo, walked around a bit, saw the Ancient Banyan Tree, then rode back on the coach. Became nauseated. Flu was raging. Couldn't eat a morsel at dinner time. Felt utterly miserable. Bought a packet of Luohanguo essence. Didn't help.

**Sunday, 12/6/1983**

Skipped the morning tour of Guilin. We were refunded 350 RMB each, quite unexpectedly. Ate a little, slept after that, packed up, went to the airport. Got quite tired of Guilin. Landscape didn't seem to enthrall any longer. 广西 food seemed nauseating, particularly the fermented bean and taste and smell that I seemed to sense everywhere. Probably psychological but even now (14/6) the thought of it still nauseates. Quick flight to 广 州 by the same 737 we arrived in. The usual paper fan, packet orange juice, sweets. Air hostesses were quite petite. They served on the ground as well, as it were, processing the passengers right through. Simply but gracefully dressed.

Arrived at Guangzhou, were met at the airport by the ubiquitous China Travel Service, got despatched to 华侨大厦, checked in, went for dinner, queued up for a table, waited for the food which arrived at long intervals, all of us got upset, what disorganisation! Slept well. Woke up for breakfast, went upstair instead where the service was better, got sent to the train station in an extremely packed mini-van. Principle in China is to seize the initiative. Don't wait for your turn for your turn may never come. Harsh conditions such as these do not conduce civility.

**Monday, 13/6, 广州 [Guangzhou] to HK**

Train ride was pleasant. Coach was spacious, air-conditioned. An air of gaiety and cleanliness pervaded the atmosphere. In 2 hours or less, reached Shenzhen, saw the construction activity. Crossed the bridge to the New Territories. Stretched across the hills was the barbed wire fence, bent China-wards, leaving no doubt as to the purpose of the fence. But not too imposing a bamboo curtain as one might have expected.

Mum had a boxed lunch, ate it heartily. Dad bought me a bowl of white fungus soup with egg which I consumed. Had not been eating much.

HK, what a change from China. Bustling, modern, intense, intimidating, decadent, cosmopolitan. Alive. For us, more predictable. Mum was glad to leave. I was glad to be going home. The flu still gripped me.

Now, winging home in an SIA jet, I jot down these notes. I return from the Haj. I had laughed at myself for spontaneously referring to the trip to China as a trip 'back' to China. When I met the CIS/SDE group at the HK airport lounge, they too used the words 'going back'. So it's not only me. It's a tradition, a great tradition. And I shall have stories to tell everyone. Must persuade Sar Ee to go back. They fear now, yes, but they will not find it all that difficult. They owe it to themselves. We are salmon with a homing instinct. I noted it in dad, now in his autumn years, wanting to recollect his early days.

Went to Wanchai yesterday evening to see the Oriental Theatre which has been demolished and Hennessy Road. He saw nothing of what he knew over 50 years ago. He remembered that the beef kway teow was good. So at the restaurant at Wanchai, he ordered beef kway teow.

1632, 14/6/83<br>Between HK and S'pore

# Entering Politics

In the eyes of George Yeo Yong Boon, one of the problems Singapore will face in the long term, and which he is keen to tackle, is how to develop a sense of nationalism that does not become narrow and small-minded.

On the one hand, Singapore is an open economy which must continue to be worldly and look outwards if it is to prosper.

On the other, exposure and travel to other countries sometimes bring dissatisfaction, and there will be Singaporeans who do not want to return home after going abroad.

"So we have to create a sense of belonging to Singapore. So we have to be nationalistic, we sing songs and celebrate together," Brigadier-General (Res) Yeo said.

"But we must balance it against losing too much of our cosmopolitan outlook because, I think, a narrow nationalism is dangerous for Singapore," he added.

"In the end, I think what we want is for Singaporeans to be worldly, to travel, to be everywhere but to leave your hearts behind. To come back, come back to enjoy the food, come to make your

---

Interview with George Yeo after he announced his intention to take part in the 1988 General Elections. Published in *The Straits Times*, 20 August 1988. 

contributions, come back occasionally to be an MP. Whatever. But though we may be small, our minds must not be confined."

BG Yeo, who is widely expected to be given a ministerial post if successful in the elections, candidly admitted that he had some misgivings when first approached to enter politics.

He said this was because of the personal sacrifices it would involve, the difficulties of the job and because "the style of Government sometimes does not settle very well with younger people".

But he was persuaded, by First Deputy Prime Minister Goh Chok Tong and Trade and Industry Minister Lee Hsien Loong, that he had "a duty to represent those in his generation, their hopes and fears".

He added: "Among the young Singaporeans, particularly the more educated ones, I think there are some who are still cynical about the Government. I think this is an unhealthy development because in the end, the young people will inherit Singapore ... I think part of the challenge for me and for my younger colleagues is how to reattach these younger ones, to get these people back to the Government."

Asked how he thought younger MPs could win the confidence of young Singaporeans, he said they could best achieve this by "being true to ourselves". When they become MPs, they should continue to do what they normally did and liked to do, be it wearing colourful clothes, jogging or partying at discos, he said.

Under questioning, he said he thought the reason behind the young's cynicism could be due to the style of the Government, how it packaged and presented its policies, rather than the substance of those policies.

A Roman Catholic, he cited the Government's arrest last year of Catholic Church worker Vincent Cheng for involvement in a Marxist conspiracy as an example of how some people could be alienated.

He said that although the arrest was clearly not a case of the Government taking on the Church, and this was recognised by the Vatican, that was how it was perceived by many people in the church he attended.

Speaking of his own qualifications for politics, BG Yeo disarmingly declared that he was depending on the prestige of the PAP to win. He had no grassroots experience.

He added, however, that the SAF was a good place to learn to understand Singaporeans and human beings in general.

It was also a good place to understand what enabled a Government to survive, as army officers were always planning for emergencies and contingencies, he said.

BG Yeo, who had to forgo $80,000 in pension money and pay $60,000 in liquidated damages for breaking his bond to the SAF in order to enter politics, refused to say what his role after the elections might be.

But Brigadier-General (Res) Lee [Hsien Loong] gave a slight hint: "We have decided that he will be able to make a much greater contribution outside of the SAF than inside, and it is with that in mind that we have asked him."

# INTERNATIONAL RELIEF FOR MYANMAR IN THE AFTERMATH OF CYCLONE NARGIS

The official statement from the Chairman of the Conference which I will now read out will be released to the media. Allow me first just to say a few words.

On behalf of Myanmar and on behalf of all of us in ASEAN, first, I would like to thank all of you for the good work you have done, for your pledges of support and most importantly, for your affection and goodwill to the people of Myanmar.

We know that there is still a lot of work to be done. There have been calls for greater access to information, for roadblocks to be cleared. I hope this will be done step by step in the coming days, weeks and months. I think all of us have agreed that the immediate priority must be on the relief efforts in the coming months before we talk about full reconstruction. And there is assurance of better damage assessment and greater access.

Many countries have stated that they will give more. It is for lack of information that not more has been given at this particular point in time. The problem is not one of generosity but of establishing greater trust between Myanmar and the world community.

Mr Secretary-General Ban Ki-moon, you came here to Myanmar with a message of hope for the people here. And indeed, when we

---

Transcript of Minister for Foreign Affairs George Yeo's preliminary remarks at the closing of the ASEAN-UN International Pledging Conference on Cyclone Nargis in Yangon, Myanmar, 25 May 2008.

saw pictures of you having a two-hour meeting with Senior General Than Shwe and visiting the refugee camps, our hearts leapt because we felt yes, we are at a turning point. We thank you for your tireless efforts and for saying that you will come again. And indeed, we want a good claim on your time, attention and energy even though we know that a hundred priorities and duties await you at the UN. Thank you, Secretary-General Ban.

Prime Minister Thein Sein, when the ASEAN Foreign Ministers met in Singapore on Monday, we did not know whether we would be able to come to any agreement and I must report to you that when we did finally achieve agreement after Foreign Minister Nyan Win called from Naypyidaw, there was a wave of relief that ASEAN could play a role in helping to bridge the gap between the world and Myanmar, for it was that psychological gap which we have to bridge for the aid to be able to flow in.

Prime Minister Thein Sein, we thank you for opening your heart to us, for opening your country to us and we assure you that we will match your welcome. Indeed, I believe many countries here will more than match your welcome with aid, assistance and expertise, for all of us mean you well.

Let me, by way of closing, talk about the role of ASEAN. At the Foreign Ministers' Meeting on Monday, there was a moment where we asked ourselves what Myanmar meant to ASEAN and what ASEAN meant to Myanmar. At that moment, suddenly all minds were clarified and it was clear that there was no other way but this way. And because ASEAN has its own credibility both with Myanmar and with the rest of the world, so ASEAN is able to play this particular role. We can never hope to match the resources, the abilities, capabilities of the UN and its organisations, or the many international organisations and NGOs who have been so ready to come forth with assistance, but before there can be a matching of demand to supply, there has to be trust and a mechanism. And that trust and mechanism, ASEAN will work hard to provide. It is still a long road forward and one which has many obstacles in front of us, and if we persist with goodwill and understanding, I believe we can clear these obstacles one at a time. It is true I heard what the Spanish Ambassador said — we are late but better late than never.

At least now, we are on the right road and if we keep to that road and clear the obstacles one at a time, that road will lead to a better future for the people of Myanmar. So, I thank all of you for making this journey here at such short notice. I thank Secretary-General Ban Ki-moon for your good offices. I thank Prime Minister Thein Sein, Senior General Than Shwe, the government and people of Myanmar, for welcoming us all here to be your partners in recovery and progress.

Thank you.

# Ravi Velloor* on George Yeo

### Standfirst

In early February 1993, as the South Asia bureau chief for ASIAWEEK magazine, I drifted into a press conference at New Delhi's Shastri Bhawan, addressed by a young minister from Singapore whose unlikely title, Brigadier-General (Res), tickled my curiosity even further about the man and his nation. Not yet 40, BG Yeo, as the Singapore delegation seemed to call him, was then the island republic's Minister for Information and the Arts, as well as Second Foreign Minister.

As much as his youth, which contrasted so severely with the old-boy herd in New Delhi — the prime minister, Narasimha Rao, was pushing 72 and his finance minister, Manmohan Singh, was past 60 — I was intrigued by the candour of this young politician from Singapore. Just two months earlier, Hindu militants had razed a historic mosque in Uttar Pradesh state, leading to riots and the question was put to BG Yeo. Rather than duck and say he would not like to comment on an internal matter, Mr Yeo took it full on. His response, if I recall correctly, was that such events did not help India's image overseas.

In the two decades that have passed since that first encounter I have tried to keep up with this peripatetic intellectual pilgrim, reading his speeches with great interest, and following his career.

---

* Ravi Velloor is currently Associate Editor (Global Affairs) of *The Straits Times*.

As a correspondent and editor of Bloomberg News and The Straits Times I've had the privilege of observing him not only in Singapore but around the world. I've seen him mingle easily with his Asean counterparts at trade meetings in Bali, Indonesia, at ease among the great and the good who gather annually at the World Economic Forum in Davos, Switzerland, and not break a sweat in the dusty outback of India's Bihar state as he inspected the future site of Nalanda University. If Singapore today is a welcoming home for people from around it is in no small part to leaders like George Yeo and their capacity to understand and assimilate alien cultures, even as they remain firmly rooted in their own identities.

The piece below was a blog[†] I penned on George Yeo in November 2009, after travelling with him in Sri Lanka shortly after the end of a quarter-century's civil war on the island.

* * *

"Happy Deepavali."

At 6:30 a.m. as I waited in the lobby of the Cinnamon Grand Hotel in Colombo recently, that was the call from the man striding by.

At first it didn't quite register. Then I awoke from my reverie:

"Happy Deepavali to you, Minister!"

Perhaps it was fitting that the first person to wish me that day was George Yeo, Singapore's foreign minister. For Mr Yeo is an uncommon personality. Among all the global personalities I have encountered in a three decades-long career, I have met no one with such an interest in other cultures. I have watched him on an early winter morning, finishing up his breakfast, changing into chinos and a leather jacket to visit the historic Mughal-built Sunday Mosque in Delhi's old quarter, only his bodyguards in tow. I have watched him in the dusty outback of India's Bihar state, standing amidst the ruins of the ancient university of Nalanda, fittingly in the company of some of the world's best known intellectual luminaries. He was there to participate in a Singapore-backed dream to revive that ancient Buddhist seat of learning for a new generation of Asians. Last month in Hua Hin, Thailand, the East Asia Summit endorsed that effort.

---

[†]Published in *The Straits Times*, 4 November 2009. © 2009 Singapore Press Holdings Ltd.

I am not a big fan of blogsites, but one I unfailingly check every few weeks is Mr Yeo's blog, if nothing else to catch up on some speech of his I may have missed.

On this Deepavali day, we would travel in a quiet land where there was little celebration despite the area being home to large numbers of Hindus. We would move by helicopter to Mannar in the northwest of Sri Lanka, then to Jaffna in the north and on to Trincomalee in the northeast. We would be briefed by military commanders and civilian administrators. We would visit irrigation projects and the Prima factory in Trincomalee, that iconic Singapore investment in Sri Lanka whose products have been consumed by every citizen of that nation. We would visit the historic Jaffna library and the famous Nallur Kandasamy temple in that town.

"Did you see the look on his face when he broke that coconut as an offering at the temple?" a Tamil Singaporean who was part of Mr Yeo's delegation told me later. "The reverence was real."

At the end of the day, having dined with a local industrialist and before embarking for Singapore, Mr Yeo sat down for a media wrap-up. There, he unerringly pronounced correctly the names of every town we had visited and every person he met. I was taken aback.

I must have been to Sri Lanka more than a dozen times, sometimes for more than two weeks at a time, but I will not lay claim to have the same facility. Yet, this was only Mr Yeo's second visit to the island and the first was many years ago, when he holidayed there with his wife.

Does all that make him less Chinese, or less interested in the culture of his own forefathers?

Not at all.

In Trincomalee I watched a retired Sri Lankan admiral, now governor of the Eastern Province, brief Mr Yeo. The admiral mentioned an area called China Bay. Immediately, Mr Yeo's ears pricked up. He asked how the area got that name, then went on to answer his own question by discussing various possibilities, including a port call by the Chinese seafarer Zheng He.

Foreign ministers come in all sizes of intellect. Around the world there must be a few who can match Mr Yeo's intellect. But what probably sets him apart is his genuine interest in alien cultures and this surely must be of use in what probably is the world's most globalised island-state.

Mr Yeo gives the impression of a man overawed by the splendour of the universe even as he marks his own place in it.

That thought struck me after seeing the transcript of a door-stop interview he gave Colombo journalists after bilateral talks with his Sri Lankan counterpart, Rohitha Bogollogama.

Dwelling on the talented Sri Lankan diaspora and how it could be harnessed for the country's post-war development, he had this to say: "All my four children were delivered by Sri Lankan doctors."

As a lifelong journalist my only regret about Mr Yeo is that he did not choose to join my profession. Certainly, he had the opportunity.

My former editor-in-chief, Mr Cheong Yip Seng, once told me he had talent-spotted a young George Yeo just as he had entered government service as a bureaucrat. They were in Indonesia together, accompanying some heavyweight on an official trip.

Sadly, Mr Yeo declined Mr Cheong's offer of employment, choosing to stay on in government.

Too bad. *The Straits Times* newsroom could have used his skills to teach how to convey the most complex and beautiful thoughts in the simplest language.

And on that subject here is my favourite George Yeo line.

Turning up at an inter-religious meeting a couple of years ago in Singapore, Mr Yeo had this to say about the Parsis. This is the tiny community of Zoroastrians who migrated to India from Persia a thousand years ago and have been successful in business while being great philanthropists.

"The Parsis," said Mr Yeo at that meeting, "have always sweetened the milk that is their host."

# Timeline of George Yeo

| | |
|---|---|
| 1916 | Birth of my father, Yeo Eng Song, in Johore, registered in Singapore. |
| 1919 | Birth of my mother, Kan Lee Hoon, in Anbu, Chao'an, Guangdong. |
| 1937 | Passing of my paternal grandfather, marriage of my parents in Anbu. |
| 1937 | August, a month after Marco Polo Bridge Incident which began Japan's invasion of China, my parents returned to Singapore. |
| 1941 | December–1945 August, World War II in the Pacific. Second brother died during the war; third brother died after the war, baptized by my father before he passed away; my mother and elder siblings became Catholic. My father had been baptized when he was a student at St. Joseph's Institution. |
| 1954 | September 13 — I was born. |
| 1961–1964 | St. Patrick's School which still had primary classes at that time. |
| 1963–1965 | Malaysian years. In anticipation of this, my mother had me take Malay as second language in Primary One. |
| 1965–1966 | St. Stephen's School. |
| 1967 | Secondary One in St. Patrick's School. |
| 1968–1972 | St. Joseph's Institution. |

| | |
|---|---|
| 1973 | Basic Military Training at 1SIR; Officer Cadet School in SAFTI, awarded SAF Scholarship and President's Scholarship. |
| 1973–1976 | Read Engineering at Christ's College, Cambridge. |
| 1974 | Platoon Commander of a Hokkien Basic Military Training Platoon at School of Artillery during my summer vacation. |
| 1976 | July–September, became a Signals Officer after attending US Army Communications & Electronics Basic Officers Course at Ft Gordon, Augusta, Georgia. |
| 1976 | 6 SIR Battalion Signals Officer. |
| 1977 | Officer Commanding, Signal Support Company at 3 Signal Battalion of Third Infantry Division. |
| 1979 | Singapore Command and Staff College, 9th Batch. |
| 1979–1983 | Posted to Air Force, Head of Air Weapons Branch, then Head of Air Plans Department. |
| 1983–1985 | Harvard Business School, Section E. Public Service Commission frowned on my doing the MBA instead of the MPA at Harvard. Had to resign from the Administrative Service (Dual Track). Took a one-year scholarship from the SAF with second year on no-pay leave. |
| 1984 | June 17 — Married Jennifer at St. Paul Church, Cambridge, Massachusetts; small wedding dinner at Boston Chinatown. |
| 1985 | Returned to the SAF, became Chief-of-Staff of Air Staff and Director of Joint Operations and Planning in the Defence Ministry. |
| 1988 | August, broke bond, resigned from the SAF to stand for elections. |
| 1988 | August, my first general elections (GE), elected MP for Aljunied GRC with Chin Harn Tong and Wan Hussein Zoohri. |
| 1988 | September, appointed Minister of State for Finance and for Foreign Affairs under PM Lee Kuan Yew. |
| 1989 | May, arrival of my daughter, Edwina. |

| | |
|---|---|
| 1990 | Chaired Committee to recommend measures recognizing contribution of reservists to Total Defence (RECORD). |
| 1990 | April, arrival of my eldest son, Edward. |
| 1990 | November, appointed Acting Minister of the new Ministry of Information and the Arts and Senior Minister of State for Foreign Affairs under PM Goh Chok Tong. |
| 1991 | Chaired the committee to make recommendations for Singapore's Next Lap. |
| 1991 | May, arrival of my second son, William. |
| 1991 | July, Minister for Information and the Arts and Second Foreign Minister. |
| 1991 | August, mother passed away. |
| 1991 | September, my second GE, uncontested. |
| 1991–2000 | Chairman of Young PAP. |
| 1992–2001 | Represented the Eurasian community in Cabinet at their request. |
| 1992 | January, notetaker for Senior Minister Lee Kuan Yew's back to back meetings with US President George Bush and China President Yang Shangkun. |
| 1992 | December, PAP Campaign Manager for Marine Parade GRC by-election. |
| 1994 | January, arrival of my youngest son, Frederick. |
| 1994–1997 | Concurrently Minister for Health, dropped Foreign Affairs. |
| 1996 | November, my father passed away. |
| 1997 | January, my third GE, contested by Singapore Democratic Party, Aljunied GRC grew from 3 to 4 Members of Parliament, boundaries expanded to include Eunos and Bedok Reservoir. Halfway during the campaign, I came down with measles and was very ill. My wife overheard one doctor telling another, as they were looking at my worsening chest X-ray, "let's not panic". |
| 1997 | Frederick diagnosed to have leukaemia, underwent chemotherapy for two and a half years. |

| | |
|---|---|
| 1997 | Dropped Health portfolio to become Second Minister for Trade and Industry, while concurrently Minister for Information and the Arts. |
| 1998–2004 | Harvard University Board of Visitors to the Business School. Made use of the annual meetings to visit Washington and lobby Congressional leader for the US–Singapore Free Trade Agreement after negotiations were launched in December 2000. |
| 1999–2004 | Minister for Trade and Industry, relinquishing Ministry for Information and the Arts after nine years. Launched and concluded bilateral free trade agreements with New Zealand, Australia, Japan, European Free Trade Association, US, Jordan and Panama. Began negotiations for the Trans-Pacific Partnership and free trade agreements with Korea, India and Gulf Cooperation Council which were concluded after my watch. |
| 1999 | November–December, chaired agricultural group at failed Seattle WTO meeting. I did this three times. They were some of the most stressful moments of my life. |
| 2001 | November, my fourth GE, walkover because WP filled forms wrongly. Aljunied GRC boundaries changed to encompass Cheng San, dropping the old Kembangan. |
| 2001 | November, chaired agricultural group at Doha WTO meeting which launched the Doha Development Agenda ("Doha Round"). Coming shortly after September 11, there were serious security concerns. A small security contingent accompanied me with chemical suits complete with atropine injectors in the event of nerve gas attack from Saddam Hussein's Iraq. |
| 2002 | Frederick had relapse of his leukaemia, underwent two more years of chemotherapy. |
| 2003 | September, chaired agricultural group at failed Cancun WTO meeting. |
| 2004 | July, Frederick had second relapse of his leukaemia, went to St. Jude Children Research Hospital for a bone marrow transplant, accompanied by my wife, all |

his siblings and his grandmother. They were away in Memphis, Tennessee, for 9 months. During that period, I visited them 7 times.

2004 August, became Foreign Minister under PM Lee Hsien Loong.

2006 May, my fifth GE, contested by The Workers' Party.

2007–2008 Chaired ASEAN Ministerial Meeting. It was an eventful year which saw ASEAN taking a strong stand against the shooting of monks in Yangon and ASEAN building a bridge between ASEAN and the UN to help victims of Cyclone Nargis in Myanmar.

2007 Appointed by Government of India to Nalanda University Mentors Group (later, Governing Board) chaired by Amartya Sen.

2008–2010 Negotiated with Malaysia on resolution of railway land dispute culminating in the Joint Statement of May 2010 by the two PMs.

2009 Elected Honorary Fellow of Christ's College, Cambridge.

2011 May, my sixth and final GE, losing to The Workers' Party. Announced my decision to leave parliamentary politics.

2011 June, became a disciple of Taijigong Grandmaster Sim Pooh Ho.

2011 August, became a Visiting Scholar at the LKY School of Public Policy. Also joined WEF Foundation Board.

2011 September–December, Visiting Scholar at Peking University.

2012 January, joined Kuok Group as Vice-Chairman.

2012 January, conferred Order of Sikatuna by Philippine President Benigno Aquino III.

2012 April, conferred Padma Bhushan by Government of India.

2012 July, appointed Chairman of International Advisory Panel of Nalanda University.

2012 August, took over as Chairman of Kerry Logistics Network.

| | |
|---|---|
| 2013 | January, appointed by Hong Kong Chief Executive as member of Economic Development Commission. |
| 2013 | May, conferred Honorary Member of the Order of Australia. |
| 2013 | August–2014 May, appointed by Pope Francis on Pontifical Commission for Reference on the Organisation of the Economic-Administrative Structure of the Holy See. |
| 2013 | December, listed Kerry Logistics Network on Hong Kong Stock Exchange. |
| 2014 | May, appointed by Pope Francis as Member of the Vatican Council of the Economy for 5-year term. Also, from September, member of Vatican Media Committee. |

# INDEX

*Note*: Page numbers in **boldface** refer to photos and text in the photo captions.